**Running Head** tells you the part and section you are in

**Page number**

**Section number and title**

# 6

## SENTENCE FRAGMENT

The usual sentence contains a subject and a verb and at least one independent clause. In writing, we indicate sentences by capitalizing the first word and placing appropriate end punctuation, usually a period, after the last. Any group of words that is set off as a sentence but that lacks a subject, a verb, or an independent clause is a **sentence fragment.**

Such fragments are common in speech, and they are sometimes used for certain special purposes in writing. But in most writing, the subject-verb sentence is what readers expect, and they will want some special effectiveness if that expectation is not met.

**Tab,** including subsection number and letter, tells you what section you are in

**6a**

*frag*

**Correction symbol** tells you what topic is being discussed on this page

**Subsection number and letter**

**6a** Do not punctuate phrases, dependent clauses, and other fragments as sentences.

**Basic rule,** printed in blue

A fragment is usually an improperly punctuated phrase or dependent clause that is part of the sentence that precedes or follows it. Thus the fragment can almost always be revised by joining it to that sentence, although other revisions may be possible and sometimes desirable. The most common types of fragments, together with revisions, are illustrated on the following pages.

**Explanation,** printed in black

**Incorrect example,** labeled in black

**Correct example,** labeled in green

FRAGMENT    For as long as there have been cities, there have been parks. *For the enjoyment of city dwellers.*

REVISED    For as long as there have been cities, there have been parks *for the enjoyment of city dwellers.*

FRAGMENT    Initially parks were for the people in the houses surrounding them . *Not for the city or town as a whole.*

REVISED    Initially parks were for the people in the houses surrounding them, *not for the city or town as a whole.*

Initially parks were for the people in the houses surrounding them—*not for the city or town as a whole.* [Here both revisions join the prepositional phrase introduced by *for* with the main statement, to which it clearly belongs. The dash gives greater emphasis to the phrase. See **23b**. ].

**Cross-reference** refers to another place in the handbook where information about this topic can be found

# Prentice Hall
# HANDBOOK
# FOR WRITERS

ELEVENTH EDITION

GLENN LEGGETT
*President Emeritus, Grinnell College*

C. DAVID MEAD
*Michigan State University*

MELINDA G. KRAMER
*Prince George's Community College*

PRENTICE HALL, Englewood Cliffs, New Jersey 07632

*Library of Congress Cataloging-in-Publication Data*

Leggett, Glenn H.
    Prentice Hall handbook for writers / Glenn Leggett, C. David Mead,
Melinda G. Kramer.—11th ed.
        p.     cm.
    Includes index.
    ISBN 0-13-716093-3
    1. English language—Rhetoric.  2. English language—
—Grammar—1950–   I. Mead, C. David (Carl David).
II. Kramer, Melinda G.   III. Title.   IV. Title: Handbook
for writers.
PE1408.L39   1991
808'.042—dc20                                          90-46905
                                                        CIP

Cover art: Mark Rothko, *Untitled*, 1961. Private Collection.
© 1991 Kate Rothko-Prizel and Christopher Rothko/ARS, N.Y. /Art Resource

Development editor: Kate Morgan
Editorial/production supervision: Patricia V. Amoroso
Interior design: Anne T. Bonanno
Prepress buyer: Herb Klein
Manufacturing buyer: David Dickey
Page layout: Maria Piper

Acknowledgments for quoted works appear on pages XX–XXI

 © 1991 by Prentice-Hall, Inc.
A Paramount Communications Company
Englewood Cliffs, New Jersey 07632

Printed in the United States of America

10  9  8  7  6  5  4  3  2

ISBN 0-13-716093-3

Prentice-Hall International (UK) Limited, *London*
Prentice-Hall of Australia Pty. Limited, *Sydney*
Prentice-Hall Canada Inc., *Toronto*
Prentice-Hall Hispanoamericana, S.A., *Mexico*
Prentice-Hall of India Private Limited, *New Delhi*
Prentice-Hall of Japan, Inc., *Tokyo*
Simon & Schuster Asia Pte. Ltd., *Singapore*
Editora Prentice-Hall do Brasil, Ltda., *Rio de Janeiro*

This edition of the *Prentice Hall Handbook for Writers* is dedicated to the memory of Richard S. Beal, 1916–1989, late Emeritus Professor of English, Boston University.

# CONTENTS

## Sections 40–43

# THE WRITING PROCESS  345

Sections 44–46

## RESEARCHED WRITING 459

# Preface

This eleventh edition of the *Prentice Hall Handbook for Writers* would please Richard Beal, to whose memory it is dedicated. Though unacknowledged on the title page, Dick Beal really became one of the authors of the *Prentice Hall Handbook* in 1963, with the preparation of its fourth edition, published in 1965. His work as an editor and reviser was crucial to the success of that edition as well as with the fifth through the tenth editions, when his illness made it impossible for him to go on as an active author—though not before his sturdy and perceptive mind had persuaded the rest of us what kinds of revisions would have to go into the eleventh edition. Dick had the competence and commitment to manage successfully for many years a composition and communication program in a large metropolitan university. But he also had the ability to translate that experience into textbooks helpful to teachers and students everywhere. He was an endearing man, extraordinarily personable and congenial. In the course of his long career as a teacher, writer, and roving editor, he became a figure of affection and respect for dozens of teachers and editors. For us three, for whom he was an especially stalwart colleague, he had a unique, and delightful, mixture of hard good sense and sweetness and light.

He would be pleased by this edition of the *Handbook*, because it meets the high standard he set for the text. The eleventh edition preserves what our users have told us they value most in a handbook: clear explanations, numerous, interdisciplinary examples drawn from the work of both student and professional writers, emphasis on the writing process, ample illustrations of revisions in progress, thorough but succinct coverage of the problem areas many writers encounter—all in a color-keyed format that lends itself to ready and easy reference. Basic rules are printed in blue, as are section subheadings dealing with specific applications or special cases. Examples of acceptable usage are labelled in green, with other examples labelled in black. Exercise headings are printed in red, so that practice sentences and paragraphs will be easy to find.

To increase its usability, the eleventh edition maintains the same order of presentation as the tenth, but divides the writing process sections into "Preparing to Write" and "Drafting and Revising." A section called "Critical Thinking and Argument" emphasizes the connection between persuasive writing and analytical thought. The sections devoted to research and the research paper have been reorganized and reworked to point up their process orientation. A new research paper, dealing with the social implications of an aging American population, is relevant for the English composition students of any age This edition of the *Prentice Hall Handbook* also includes an entirely new section, "Writing About Literature." Fresh, new exercises have been added throughout the text, the majority of them containing extended discourse.

The positive response we received to the "Writers Revising" feature introduced in the tenth edition encouraged us to expand it in the eleventh. Not only are there now more of these case studies in the *Handbook*, but they have been rearranged so that the case situation and first draft appear at the opening of a section, with a final revision and explanatory analysis appearing at the end. That way students can revise the draft as they progress through a section and compare it to the case revision at its conclusion. As before, the "Writers Revising" cases are cross-curricular, drawing upon writing situations found in a variety of college courses as well as on the job.

We believe that all writers are colleagues, sharing many of the same problems and facing many of the same choices. So, too, believed Dick Beal. Thus, mindful of his stewardship and guidance of the *Prentice Hall Handbook for Writers* over 27 years, we have again worked to create a text that is at once comprehensive, concise, reliable, thoughtful, and humane.

MELINDA KRAMER
GLENN LEGGETT
DAVID MEAD
1990

THE NEW YORK TIMES and PRENTICE HALL are sponsoring A CONTEMPORARY VIEW, a program designed to enhance student access to current information of relevance in the classroom

Through this program, the core subject matter provided in the text is supplemented by a collection of time-sensitive articles from one of the world's most distinguished newspapers, THE NEW YORK TIMES. These articles demonstrate the vital, ongoing connection between what is learned in the classroom and what is happening in the world around us.

So that students can enjoy the wealth of information of THE NEW YORK TIMES daily, a reduced subscription rate is available. For information, call toll-free: 1-800-631-1222.

PRENTICE HALL and THE NEW YORK TIMES are proud to co-sponsor A CONTEMPORARY VIEW. We hope it will make the reading of both textbooks and newspapers a more dynamic, involving process.

# Acknowledgments

The *Prentice Hall Handbook for Writers* has benefitted from the thoughtful comments of many colleagues who reviewed the tenth edition: Robinson Blann, Trevecca Nazarene College; Suzanne Clepper, Tarrant County Junior College; Joseph Davis, Memphis State University; Robert Funk, Eastern Illinois University; L. M. Grow, Droward Community College; Geneva Moore, Bergen Community College; Marie Nigro, Lincoln University; Jill Owens, Louisiana State University; Hugh Pascal, Hillsborough Community College; Leigh Ryan, University of Maryland; Ronald Smith, University of North Alabama; Annie Stevens, Trevecca Nazarene College; John Taylor, South Dakota State University; and Mel Wininger, Clemson University.

Special thanks go to Mamie Atkins, University of Maryland Overseas Program, who created new exercises for Sections 1–39 that both teach and delight. Dorothy Bankston of Louisiana State University also receives our heartfelt gratitude for contributing new exercises to the second half of the text as well as for supplying new "Writers Revising" cases and for preparing the Annotated Instructor's Edition.

Josephine Koster Tarvers, Rutgers University, prepared Section 50, "Writing About Literature," impressing us with her ability to present a complex subject so lucidly in such a short space.

As it is being written, many students, colleagues, friends, and family members come to have a hand in a text such as this. Their contributions range from apt (or suitably outrageous) examples and insightful and timely comments to words of encouragement at just the right moment. A by-no-means-exhaustive list of such supporters includes John Leland, Tammy Gibson, Dan Lupo, Bonnie Blake, Ulla Connor, and Judy Hatcher of Purdue University; Joe Buchman, University of Tennessee at Knoxville; Brad Buehler, University of Michigan; Robert Failey, Kent State University; Lincoln Turner, Carolyn Russ, and Claire Rigodanzo, Hewlett-Packard Company; and Steven Ruppel, NCR Corporation. Devona Gamble, Winter Haven, Florida, provided the inspiration for the research paper as well as helpful comments along the way.

The library staff of Purdue University also deserve special mention for their unfailing helpfulness, as does that educational librarian *par excellence*, Evan Farber of Earlham College.

Thanks to Gary Kramer's technical and emotional support, the eleventh edition could be completed on time, in spite of major life

moves and changes. Every author should enjoy such in-house expertise.

Prentice Hall marshals a team of outstanding publishing professionals to bring the *Handbook* to market: Philip Miller, the Editor-in-
Chief for Humanities who steered the project with a sure hand as
always; Kate Morgan, our development editor, whose cheerfulness
and knowledgeable guidance we could not have done without; Pattie
Amoroso, our able and organized production editor; Ann Knitel, our
supplements editor, who masterfully orchestrated the parts of the
*Prentice Hall Handbook* supplements package. These people, and others
at Prentice Hall, have been crucial to the success of our endeavors. We
thank them all.

Throughout the *Handbook* we have quoted from copyrighted
material, and we are grateful to the copyright holders acknowledged
below for their permission.

John M.. Allswang, Macintosh: *The Definitive Users Guide*. Bowie: Brady Communications Company, Inc.
A Prentice-Hall Publishing Comany, 1985.

Maya Angelou, *I Know Why the Caged Bird Sings*. New York: Random House, Inc., 1969. By permission
of Random House, Inc.

W. H. Auden, *Tales of Grimm and Andersen*. Copyright © 1952 by Random House, Inc.

Jacques Barzun, *Simple & Direct*. New York: Harper & Row, 1975.

Jacques Barzun, *Teacher in America*. By permission of Little, Brown and Company, in association with the
Atlantic Monthly Press.

Isaiah Berlin, *Mr. Churchill in 1940*. By permission of the author and John Murray (Publishers) Ltd.

Newman and Genevieve Birk, *Understanding and Using English*. By permission of the Odyssey Press, Inc.

Alan S. Blinder, "Abolishing the Penny Makes Good Sense," *Bussiness Week*, 12 January 1987. Reprinted
by permission of the author.

Lawrence Block, "Fiction: Huffing and Puffing," *Writer's Digest*, August 1982, p. 11.

Paul Brodeur, "Radiation Alert," in *Family Circle*, November 7, 1989.

James V. Catano, "Computer-Based Writing: Navigating the Fluid Text," *College Composition and Communication*, 36 (Oct. 1985), 311.

Peter Davis, "The Game," from *Hometown*. Copyright © 1982 by Peter Davis. Reprinted by permission of
Simon & Schuster, Inc.

Joan Didion, excerpt from "On Keeping a Notebook," from *Slouching Towards Bethlehem*. Copyright ©
1966, 1968 by Joan Didion. Reprinted by permission of Farrar, Straus & Giroux, Inc. and Andre
Deutsch Ltd.

Maureen Dowd, "Rape: The Sexual Weapon," copyright © 1983 Time Inc. All rights reserved. Reprinted
by permission from *Time*.

Peter Drucker, "How to Be an Employee," *Fortune*, May 1952. Copyright © 1952 by Time, Inc.

Kent Durden, *Flight to Freedom*. Reprinted by permission of Simon & Schuster, Inc.

Loren Eiseley, excerpts from "Big Eyes and Small Eyes" and "Instruments of Darkness," in *The Night
Country*. Copyright © 1972 Loren Eiseley. Reprinted with permission of Charles Scribner's Sons.

John Erskine, "A Note on the Writer's Craft," in *Twentieth-Century English*. Ed. William Skinkle Knicker-
bocker. New York: Philosophical Library, 1946.

Charles Fenyvesi, "Why a Tree," in *Organic Gardening*, November 1989.

H. W. Fowler, *Modern English Usage*. Rev. Ernest Gowers, New York: Oxford UP, 1965.

S. I. Hayakawa, from *Language in Thought and Action*, Fourth Edition. Copyright © 1978 by Harcourt
Brace Jovanovich, Inc. Reprinted by permission of the publisher.

William A. Henry III, "Only 2,500 Miles from Broadway," *Time*, August 4, 1986.

From the book *How Children Fail* by John Holt. Copyright © 1964 by Pitman Publishing Corporation.
Reprinted with permission of Fearon-Pitman Publishers, Inc.

Jane Howard, *Families*. Copyright 1978 by Jane Howard. By permission of Simon and Schuster, Inc.
Reprinted by permission of A. D. Peters & Co. Ltd.

Robert Huges, "Tarted up Till The Eye Cries Uncle," *Time*, May 1, 1989, p. 80.

Elaine Kendall, "An Open Letter to the Corner Grocer," *Harper's* Magazine, December 1960. Reprinted
by permission.

Tracy Kidder, *The Soul of a New Machine*. Copyright © 1980 by John Tracy Kidder. By permission of
Little, Brown and Company in associated with the Atlantic Monthly Press.

Stephen Koepp, excerpt from "Pul-eeze! Will Somebody Help Me?" Copyright 1987 Time Inc. All rights
reserved. Reprinted by permission from *Time*.

George Laycock, "Games Otters Play," from *Audubon*, January, 1981. By permission of the National
Audubon Society.

Barry Lopez, *Arctic Dreams*. New York: Bantam, 1987.

William H. MacLeish, "The Year of the Coast," from *Smithsonian*, Sept. 1980.

Beryl Markham, *West with the Night*, San Francisco: North Point Press, edition reprinted by arrangement with the author and Houghton Mifflin Co.

Robert K. Massie, *Peter the Great: His Life and World*. New York: Knopf, 1980.

Joan Mills, excerpted wth permission from "The One, the Only . . . *Joanie!*" by Joan Mills, *Reader's Digest*, July 1983. Copyright © 1983 by The Reader's Digest Assn., Inc.

Lance Morrow, excerpt from "A Dying Art: The Classy Exit Line." Copyright 1984 Times Inc. All rights reserved. Reprinted by permission from *Time*.

Robert Pattison, from *On Literacy: The Politics of the Word from Homer to the Age of Rock*. Copyright © 1982 by Oxford University Press, Inc. Reprinted by permission.

S. J. Perelman, *Keep It Crisp*. By permission of Random House, Inc.

"Resorts seeking to expand . . ." from *Skiing*, February, 1987.

James Harvey Robinson, *The Mind in the Making*. By permission of Harper & Brothers.

Kenneth Roman and Joel Raphaelson, *Writing That Works*. Copyright © 1981 by Kenneth Roman and Joel Raphaelson. Reprinted by permission of Harper & Row, Publishers, Inc.

William Ruckelshaus, "Lapel Shaking," from *Chemical & Engineering News*, October 8, 1984.

William Safire, from *What's the Good Word?* © 1982 by William Safire. Reprinted by permission of Times Books/The New York Times Book Co. Inc.

Carl Sagan, *Cosmos*. New York: Random House, 1980.

Herbert H. Sanders, *How to Make Pottery*. Copyright © 1974 by Watson Guptill Publishers. Reprinted by permission.

May Sarton, *Plant Dreaming Deep*. New York: W. W. Norton & Co., Inc., 1968. By permission of W. W. Norton & Co., Inc.

Paul Scott, *The Raj Quartet*. New York: William Morrow, 1976.

Mina P. Shaughnessy, *Errors and Expectations: A Guide for the Teacher of Basic Writing*. Copyright © 1977 by Mina P. Shaughnessy. Reprinted by permission of Oxford University Press, Inc.

Carla J. Stoffle, "The Library's Role in Facilitating Quality Teaching." *New Directions for Teaching and Learning*, 5, 1981, pp. 67–68.

James Taylor, "Nothin' I'd druther do than chase these hogs," *Smithsonian*, September 1989, p. 124.

Barbara Tuchman. *A Distant Mirror*, New York: Alfred H. Knopf, 1978. By permission of Alfred H. Knopf.

"The Venture Communists Setting Up Shop in China," from *Business Week*, July 7, 1986.

G. Michael Vose, "The Tandy 1000," *Byte: The Small Systems Journal*, December, 1984.

Eudora Welty, *One Writer's Beginnings*. Cambridge: Harvard UP, 1983, 1984.

E. B. White, Introduction to *The Elements of Style*. From *Essays of E. B White* (Harper & Row). © 1957 E. B. White. Originally in *The New Yorker*.

A. N. Whitehead, *Science and the Modern World*, copyright 1925. By permission of The Macmillan Company.

John Yount, *Hardcastle*. New York: St. Martin's Press, 1980.

William K. Zinsser, from *Writing with a Word Processor*, © 1983 by William K. Zinsser. Reprinted by permission of the author.

# BASIC
# GRAMMAR

*gr*

*Writing always presents problems, dilemmas, some of which beset all writers, even great ones; but there is no need to be baffled by all the difficulties every time you write. The effort to which you are being invited is to learn the usual pitfalls and how they are avoided, while also learning the devices—tricks of the trade—by which writing can be both improved and made easier than it seems to most people. . . . By the same effort, you may also learn to be clear and to afford pleasure to those who read what you write.*

JACQUES BARZUN, Simple & Direct

**W**e use grammar whenever we speak or write. As a subject, grammar is a way of *describing* what happens to language when you use it. In this sense, grammar is in the same class as physics. Both are concerned with systems that operate according to principles. Physics describes how light, sound, and other kinds of energy and matter work. Grammar describes how language works. The following pages explain the details of English grammar in terminology that is widely used to describe the way our language functions. Any language is composed of individual words and grammatical devices for putting them together meaningfully. English has several devices for putting words into meaningful combinations. The three most important are **word order, function words,** and **inflections.**

In English, grammatical meaning is largely determined by **word order.** *Blue sky* and *sky blue* mean different things: in the first, *blue* describes *sky;* in the second, *sky* describes *blue.* Here is the principle in action:

> The thief called the lawyer a liar.
> The lawyer called the thief a liar.
> The liar called the lawyer a thief.

> Our new neighbors bought an old house.
> Our old neighbors bought a new house.

Word order can be extremely important to meaning, as the following example shows: *The shoes on the steps with the run-down heels are mine.* Word order indicates that *with the run-down heels* describes *steps,* but common sense tells us that steps don't have heels. However, until our common sense overrides the meaning created by word order, we are momentarily confused.

**Function words,** sometimes called **grammatical words,** are words such as *the, and, but, in, to, because, while, ought,* and *must.* The main use of function words is to express relationships among other words. Compare the following:

> I am lonely *at* dark.         The cook prepared *a* rich feast.
> I am lonely *in the* dark.     The cook prepared *the* rich *a* feast.

**Inflections** are changes in the form of words; these changes indicate differences in grammatical relationship. Inflections account for the differences in meaning in the following sentences:

The rivers flow slowly.        Stop bothering me.
The river flows slowly.        Stops bother me.

Readers depend on your using these grammatical devices—word order, function words, and inflections—to signal what you mean.

A distinction is sometimes made between grammar and *usage.* Grammar is concerned with generally applicable principles about language. **Usage,** in contrast, is concerned with choices, particularly with differences between *formal* (less conversational) and *informal* (more conversational) English and between *standard English* (well established and widely recognized as acceptable) and *nonstandard English* (generally considered unacceptable by educated speakers and writers of English) (see Section **36**).

The differences between *tile floor* and *floor tile, he walks* and *he walked, she was biting the dog* and *the dog was biting her* are grammatical differences of word order and inflection. The differences between *I saw* and *I seen, she doesn't* and *she don't,* and *let me do it* and *leave me do it* are differences in usage. These statements may identify the persons who use them as speakers of standard or nonstandard dialects, but they do not mean different things. Because this book is concerned with writing standard English, it is concerned with both grammar and usage.

# 1

## *SENTENCE SENSE*

Research regarding how people receive and process language indicates that we are capable of holding between five and nine separate chunks of information in our short-term memories at a time. If this is true, how is it that we can learn complex tasks, express complex ideas, and think even more complex thoughts? Researchers think that by "superchunking" information—by combining individual chunks into condensed, meaningful units—the short-term memory is able to continue receiving new information. If we apply this theory to the words *age, buggy, the, and, horse,* we see that the phrase *the horse-and-buggy age* results in one meaningful superchunk instead of five separate chunks of information. Although we do not yet fully understand how the brain works to create and process language, we are able to describe how language works when we use it.

To describe the way a language works, grammarians assign words to categories according to their function and also classify them by type, assigning terms for each type. These terms, or grammatical function labels, are traditionally referred to as **parts of speech.** The major types of words in English and the functions they usually perform are as follows:

**1a**

*SS*

| *Function* | *Type* | *Example* |
|---|---|---|
| Naming | Nouns and pronouns | *corn, summer, it* |
| Predicating (stating | Verbs | *grows, was* |
| or asserting) | | |
| Modifying | Adjectives and | *tall, quickly* |
| | adverbs | |
| Connecting | Prepositions and | *in, and* |
| | conjunctions | |

Nouns and verbs, the naming and stating words, are the basic elements. Working together, these chunks of meaning make our simplest sentences: *Corn grows.* Other types of words and word groups expand and refine those simple sentences: *The tall corn grows quickly in the summer.*

---

## WRITERS REVISING: COMPLETE SENTENCES

While brainstorming about a question on his mid-term exam, Robert made the notes reproduced below. Turn these phrases and clauses—isolated chunks of information—into complete sentences. As you work through Section 1, organize the sentences into a paragraph that answers the question "What were the economic effects of the plague—the Black Death—in fourteenth-century Europe?" Then compare the decisions you made to Robert's, whose version appears at the end of Section 1.

Notes on Black Death

```
Killed about 50-75 percent of population

that many dead by end of century

little planting and harvesting of crops

land returned to wilderness

no laborers-shortages

diminished food supply    villages disappeared

goods scarce    rise in prices
```

This *Writers Revising* continues on page 22.

---

**1a**   Recognizing sentences, their basic parts, and patterns

A **sentence** is a group of related words that expresses a complete thought. It is an independent construction; that is, it does not depend on any other word group to complete its meaning. *She is studying* and *What is she studying* are sentences. But *although she is studying* is not a sentence because the connecting word *although* makes the whole word group depend upon something else for completion, as in the statement *Although she is still studying, she will be finished soon.* Grammatically, a sentence also must contain a subject and a predicate to be complete.

**1. Subjects and predicates.** All complete sentences have two main parts, a subject and a predicate. The **subject** names the person, thing, or concept that the sentence is about. The **predicate** makes a statement or asks a question about the subject:

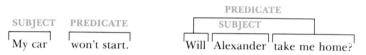

**2. Nouns.** Nouns typically serve as the subjects *(The wind blew; Sally arrived; Honesty pays)* and the objects of verbs and prepositions *(I sent John to the store).* (See Sections 1a4; 1a5; 1b2.) **Nouns** name or classify persons, places, things, activities, conditions, and concepts: *girl, home, dog, hat, studio, committee, athletics, courage, wealth.* **Proper nouns** name particular people, places, or things *(Dorothy, Kansas, Toto).* Nouns have the following characteristics of form:

a. Nouns naming things that can be counted (sometimes called **"count nouns"**) add *-s* or *-es* to make the plural form which indicates more than one: *chair, chairs; car, cars; church, churches; bush, bushes.* A few nouns have irregular plurals: *woman, women; foot, feet; sheep, sheep.* **Mass nouns,** which name things not usually counted *(gravel, milk, courage, honesty),* do not ordinarily have plural forms. **Collective nouns** have a singular form but name a group of persons or things as a single unit: *team, flock, class.* (See Sections **8a, 8b.**)

b. Many nouns have characteristic endings such as *-ance, -ence, -ism, -ity, -ment, -ness, -tion,* and *-ship,* as in *relevance, excellence, realism, activity, argument, darkness, adoption, citizenship.*

**3. Pronouns.** Pronouns are words that can substitute for nouns. Thus, pronouns can be subjects or objects of verbs or prepositions. Pronouns are classified according to type: **personal, relative, interrogative, demonstrative, indefinite, reciprocal, intensive,** and **reflexive.** See "Pronoun" in Section **51** for a list and examples.

The noun for which a pronoun substitutes is called its **antecedent.** In the sentence *Clara Barton is the woman who founded the American Red Cross,* the pronoun *who* refers to its antecedent, *woman.* Usually antecedents are expressed, as is *woman* in the previous sentence. Sometimes, however, antecedents are implied and must be deduced from the context. In the sentence *Those who need assistance in boarding the aircraft should come to the gate now,* the meaning of *those* is implied by the context itself; that is, *those* refers to any passengers needing help in boarding. Implied antecedents can cause confusion for readers; in the sentence *Whichever you choose will be acceptable,* it is impossible to know what *whichever* means without the larger context of surrounding sentences that may reveal what *whichever* refers to. **Indefinite pronouns,** words like *anybody, everyone,* and *somebody,* require no antecedent.

The **personal pronouns** *I, we, he, she,* and *they,* and the pronoun *who,* which is used either to relate one group of words to another or to ask a question, change form in the subjective, possessive, and objective cases; for example, *I, my/mine, me. You* and *it* change form as possessives only: *you/your, it/its.* (See Section **2.**)

**4. Verbs.** The predicate of a sentence *always* contains a **verb,** a word that makes an assertion about the subject. A sentence cannot exist without a verb. Verbs indicate action, occurrence, being, possession, or the presence of a condition. Examples of verbs are *ask, eat, give, describe, own, am, have, criticize, seem, appear, become, throw.*

In the simplest English sentences, a verb may stand alone as the predicate: *Lions hunt.* Or it may be followed by a word called its **object,** which indicates who or what receives the action of the verb: *Lions hunt prey.*

Verbs have the following characteristics of form:

a.   When verbs indicate present time, they usually add *-s* or *-es* to the **infinitive form** (the form listed in the dictionary) when their subjects are *he, she,* or *it* or a word for which *he, she,* or *it* can be substituted: *the boys run,* but *the boy* [he] *runs; the logs burn,* but *the log* [it] *burns; the lions hunt,* but *the lion* [it] *hunts.*

b.   Almost all verbs have a separate form to indicate past tense. Most add *-d* or *-ed* to the form listed in the dictionary: *hunt, hunted; walk, walked; repeat, repeated.* A few indicate past time in irregular ways: *eat, ate; go, went; run, ran; sleep, slept.* A few verbs do not have a separate form: *cut, put, hit, hurt.*

c.   The infinitive form of verbs can always be preceded by any one of the following words: *can, could; may, might; will, would; shall, should;* and *must,* as in *can hunt, may go, would leave, should pay,* or *must read.* These words are called **auxiliaries** or **helping verbs** and are used to convey special shades of meaning. Other forms of the verb can combine with other auxiliaries to form verb phrases that express various time relationships as well as other shades of meaning such as *have been hunting, will be finished, could have been working.* (For a full discussion of auxiliaries, see Section **4.**)

d.   Many verbs have typical endings, called **suffixes,** such as

*-ate*, *-en*, *-fy*, and *-ize*, as in *implicate, operate, widen, hasten, liquefy, simplify, recognize, modernize*.

**la**

**SS**

**5. Basic sentence patterns.** All English sentences are built on a limited number of patterns. No matter how long or complex, all sentences can be reduced to one of these patterns. The five most basic patterns are illustrated and explained below. In all of them the subject remains a simple noun or pronoun. Differences among the patterns lie in the predicate part of the sentence—the verb and what follows it.

### PATTERN 1: S + V

| Subject | Verb |
|---|---|
| Red | fades. |
| The woman | arrived. |
| The snow | fell. |

The simplest of all English sentence patterns consists of a subject and its verb. Sentences as simple as these are relatively rare in mature writing, yet simple sentences (subject-verb) are the core of all sentences.

### PATTERN 2: S + V + DO

| Subject | Verb | Direct Object |
|---|---|---|
| Dogs | eat | bones. |
| The carpenter | repaired | the roof. |
| John | likes | the movies. |
| Someone | insulted | her. |

The verbs in the second pattern are always action words that can pass their action on to another word called an object, or more exactly, a **direct object.** The direct object is always a noun, a pronoun, or a group of words serving as a noun that receives the action of the verb; it answers the question "what?" or "whom?" after the verb. Verbs that can take objects are called **transitive** verbs (See Section **4.**)

### PATTERN 3: S + V + DO + OC

| Subject | Verb | Direct Object | Object Complement |
|---|---|---|---|
| The press | called | him | a star. |
| They | appointed | Shirley | chairperson. |
| We | made | the clerk | angry. |
| The jury | found | her | innocent. |

With a few verbs, such as *appoint, believe, consider, judge, make,* and *name,* the direct object may be followed by another noun or a modifying word that renames or describes the direct object. These are called **object complements,** and they distinguish the third sentence pattern.

**1a**

**SS**

### PATTERN 4: S + V + IO + DO

| Subject | Verb | Indirect Object | Direct Object |
|---|---|---|---|
| My friend | lent | me | his car. |
| The college | awarded | her | a scholarship. |
| Wellington | brought | England | victory. |
| Mark | got | us | tickets. |

The fourth pattern includes the indirect object. After such action verbs as *ask, give, send, tell,* and *teach,* the direct object is often preceded by an **indirect object** that names the receiver of the message, gift, or whatever, and always comes before the direct object.

The same meaning can usually be expressed by a phrase that begins with *to* or *for* and is positioned after the direct object: *Wellington brought victory to England; The college awarded a scholarship to her.*

### PATTERN 5: S + LV + SC (PN or PA)

| Subject | Linking Verb | Subject Complement Predicate Noun | Predicate Adjective |
|---|---|---|---|
| Napoleon | was | a Frenchman. | |
| My brother | remains | an artist. | |
| Natalie | may become | president. | |
| The traffic | seemed | | heavy. |
| Water | was | | scarce. |
| The knife | felt | | sharp. |

The fifth pattern occurs only with a special kind of verb, called a **linking verb.** (See Section **4.**) The most common linking verb is *be* in its various forms: *is, are, was, were, has been, might be,* etc. Other common linking verbs include *appear, become, seem* and in some contexts such verbs as *feel, grow, act, look, taste, smell,* and *sound.* Linking verbs are followed by a **subject complement,** which may be either a predicate noun or a predicate adjective. A subject complement following a linking verb, in contrast to an object after a transitive verb, identifies or describes the subject of the sentence. **Predicate nouns** rename the subject; **predicate adjectives** modify the subject. It may be helpful to think of a linking verb as an equal sign. The verb "equates" the subject and the complement: *My brother = an artist.*

**6. Other sentence patterns.** Other kinds of sentences may be thought of either as additional patterns or as changes in the basic patterns, called *transformations* by some grammarians. For example:

QUESTIONS

*Inversion of Subject and Verb*
*Will* they run in the first race?

**1a**

**SS**

*Function Word Placed Before Basic Subject-Verb Pattern*
*Do* they run in the first race?

COMMANDS

*Omission of Subject*
[*You*]   Open the door.
[*You*]   Know thyself.
[*You*]   Keep calm.

Two variations on basic patterns are especially important because they create special effects by changing either the usual actor-action relation of subject and verb or the usual order of subject and verb. These variations are the **passive sentence** and the **expletive** construction.

In a **passive sentence** the subject no longer names the performer of the action described by the verb, as it does in active patterns. Rather, the subject names the receiver of the action. The original active subject may be either omitted or expressed in a phrase usually beginning with *by*. The verb in passive sentences consists of some form of the auxiliary, or helping, verb *be* and the past participle (see Section **4**).

ACTIVE
The carpenter *repaired* the roof.
Someone *complimented* her.
The doctor *called* my recovery a miracle.
Wellington *brought* England victory.

PASSIVE

| Subject | Passive Verb | (Original Subject) |
|---|---|---|
| The roof | *was repaired* | (by the carpenter). |
| She | *was complimented* | (by someone). |
| My recovery | *was called* a miracle | (by the doctor). |
| Victory | *was brought* to England | (by Wellington). |

Because the subject in a passive sentence names the receiver of action, this pattern is especially useful when we do not know who performs an action. Thus we normally say *He was killed in action* rather than *Someone killed him in action*. (See "Voice," in Section **5**.)

An **expletive** construction involves a change in word order. By beginning a sentence with the expletive *there*, or *it*, we can postpone the subject until after the verb.

| Expletive | Verb | Complement | Subject |
|---|---|---|---|
| It | is | certain | that they will arrive. |
| There | was | | no reply. |
| There | are | | five letters. |
| It | will be | hot | early next week. |

Because they postpone the subject, expletive constructions slow the pace of a sentence and can be useful for gaining the reader's attention. They announce "Get ready. Something is coming. Don't miss it." Expletives can provide effective sentence variety, but they can also create unnecessary clutter in a sentence and so should be used thoughtfully. (See "Roundabout Constructions" in Section **38a**.)

---

EXERCISE 1a

In the following sentences and paragraph, identify the subjects (S), verbs (V), direct objects (DO), indirect objects (IO), and complements—i.e., object complement (OC), predicate noun (PN), predicate adjective (PA). Remember that some sentences, such as those using passive voice or the expletive construction, vary from the five basic sentence patterns; indicate any variations you find in the following sentences. Then use each sentence as a model for writing a sentence of your own, using subjects, verbs, direct objects, indirect objects, and complements as in the model.

**SENTENCE PRACTICE**
1. Many readers like science fiction.
2. Science fiction got its name in 1926.
3. In that year Hugo Greenback called his all-male technological adventure stories science fiction.
4. There are many types of science fiction.
5. A common setting for science fiction stories is outer space.

**PARAGRAPH PRACTICE**
     Mary Shelley's novel *Frankenstein* is an early example of science fiction. In the novel, Mary Shelley gave readers the story of Victor Frankenstein and his monster. Victor Frankenstein collects bones, constructs the monster, and gives it life. The novel was written in Switzerland. The author was only nineteen years old at the time.

---

## 1b   Recognizing modifiers, connecting words, and verbals

    In English, we use modifiers, connecting words, and verbals to expand basic sentences with detail and to combine basic sentences in ways that show the relationships among chunks of information. Our writing gains variety, complexity, and—at the same time—clarity and efficiency when we use these words and word groups. Compare the sentences that follow:

    Men wear toupees. Others have hair transplants.
    Some balding men wear toupees, but others have hair transplants because they think transplants look more natural.

When modifying and connecting words are added to the first two sentences, they not only become more precise (telling us exactly which men), but also deliver much more information. Furthermore, the connecting word *but* clearly establishes the contrasting relationship between the ideas in the two sentences.

**1. Modifying words: adjectives and adverbs.** **Modifiers** are words or word groups that identify, limit, qualify, or make more exact the other words or word groups to which they are attached. Adjectives and adverbs are the principal single-word modifiers in English.

**Adjectives** modify nouns or pronouns. Typical adjectives are the underlined words in the following: *brown dog, Victorian dignity, yellow hair, one football, reasonable price, sleek boat, good work.* Adjectives have distinctive forms in the **positive, comparative,** and **superlative:** *happy, happier, happiest; beautiful, more beautiful, most beautiful; good, better, best.*

**Adverbs** modify verbs, adjectives, or other adverbs, although they may modify whole sentences. Typical adverbs are the underlined words in the following: *stayed outside, walked slowly, horribly angry, worked well, fortunately the accident was not fatal.*

For a discussion of the special forms by which adjectives and adverbs show comparison, and of certain distinctions between the two, see Section **3.**

**2. Connecting words: prepositions and conjunctions.** Connecting words enable us to link one word or word group with another and to combine them in ways that allow us to express our ideas more concisely and to express the relationships between those ideas more clearly. For example, we don't need to say *We had coffee. We had toast.* Rather, we can say *We had coffee and toast* or *We had coffee with toast.* We don't need to say *We talked. We played cards. We went home.* Rather, we can say *After we talked and played cards, we went home,* or *After talking and playing cards, we went home.* The kinds of words that enable us to make these connections and combinations are prepositions and conjunctions.

A **preposition** links a noun or pronoun (called its **object**) with some other word in the sentence and shows the relationship between the object and the other word. The preposition, together with its object, almost always modifies the other word to which it is linked.

> Skaters glide *over* the ice. [*Over* links *ice* to the verb *glide; over the ice* modifies *glide.*]
> The distance *between* us is short. [*Between* links *us* to the noun *distance; between us* identifies *distance.*]

Although a preposition usually comes before its object, in a few constructions it can follow its object.

> *In what town* do you live?        *To whom* do I send the check?
> *What town* do you live *in?*        *Whom* do I send the check *to?*

**1b**

**ss**

The most common prepositions are listed below:

| | | | |
|---|---|---|---|
| about | below | into | through |
| above | beside | near | to |
| across | by | next | toward |
| after | down | of | under |
| among | during | off | until |
| around | except | on | up |
| as | for | out | upon |
| at | from | over | with |
| before | in | past | within |
| behind | inside | since | without |

Many single-word prepositions combine with other words to form phrasal prepositions, such as *at the point of, by means of, down from, from above, in addition to, without regard to, such as.*

Note that some words, such as *below, down, in, out,* and *up,* occur both as prepositions and as adverbs. Used as adverbs, they never have objects. Compare *He went below* with *He went below the deck.*

Note too that *after, as, before, since,* and *until* also function as subordinating conjunctions. (See below.)

A **conjunction** joins words, phrases, or clauses. Conjunctions show the relationship between the sentence elements that they connect. The following are types of conjunctions.

**Coordinating conjunctions**—*and, but, or, nor, for, so, yet*—join words, phrases, or clauses of **equal** grammatical rank. (See **1c** and **1d,** "Recognizing Phrases" and "Recognizing Clauses.")

| | |
|---|---|
| WORDS JOINED | We ate ham *and* eggs. |
| PHRASES JOINED | Look in the closet *or* under the bed. |
| CLAUSES JOINED | We wanted to go, *but* we were too busy. |

**Correlative conjunctions** are coordinating words that work in pairs to join words, phrases, clauses, or whole sentences. The most common correlative pairs are *both . . . and, either . . . or, neither . . . nor, not . . . but,* and *not only . . . but also.*

> *both* courageous *and* loyal
> *either* before you go *or* after you get back
> *neither* circuses *nor* sideshows
> *not only* as a child *but also* as an adult

**Subordinating conjunctions** join clauses that are not equal in rank. A clause introduced by a subordinating conjunction is called a *dependent* or *subordinate* clause (see **1d**) and cannot stand by itself as a sentence; it must be joined to a main, or independent, clause.

We left the party early *because we were tired.*
*If the roads are icy,* we will have to drive carefully.
*Whether we like it or not,* all things must end.

The following are the most common subordinating conjunctions:

| | | | |
|---|---|---|---|
| after | even if | so that | when |
| although | even though | than | whenever |
| as | if | that | where |
| as if | in order that | though | wherever |
| as though | rather than | unless | whether |
| because | since | until | while |
| before | | | |

**3. Verbals.** Verbals are special verb forms that have some of the characteristics and abilities of verbs but cannot function as predicates by themselves. Verbs make an assertion. Verbals do not; they function as nouns and modifiers. There are three kinds of verbals: infinitives, participles, and gerunds.

**Infinitives** are usually marked by a *to* before the actual verb *(to eat, to describe).* They are used as nouns, adjectives, or adverbs.

> *To see* is *to believe.* [Both used as nouns]
> It was time *to leave.* [Used as adjective]
> I was ready *to go.* [Used as adverb]

**Participles** may be either present or past. The present form ends in *-ing (eating, running, describing).* The past form usually ends in *-ed (described).* But note that some end in *-en (eaten),* and a few make an internal change *(begun, flown).* Participles are typically used as adjectives.

> *Screaming,* I jumped out of bed. [Present participle]
> *Delighted,* we accepted his invitation. [Past participle]

**Gerunds** have the same *-ing* form as the present participle. The distinctive name *gerund* is given to *-ing* forms only when they function as nouns.

> *Writing* requires effort. [Subject of *requires*]
> You should try *swimming.* [Object of *try*]

Although verbals can never function by themselves as predicates, they can, like verbs, take objects and complements, and like verbs, they are characteristically modified by adverbs. Note the following:

I prefer *to believe him.* [*Him* is the object of *to believe.*]

It was time *to leave the house.* [*House* is the object of *to leave.*]

*Screaming loudly,* I jumped out of bed. [The adverb *loudly* modifies the participle *screaming.*]

*Swimming in the Atlantic* is refreshing. [The prepositional phrase *in the Atlantic* here functions as an adverb to modify the gerund *swimming.*]

---

## EXERCISE 1b(1)

In the following sentences and paragraph, identify the adjectives (ADJ), adverbs (ADV), prepositions (P), coordinating conjunctions (CC), and subordinating conjunctions (SC). Then use each sentence as a model for writing a sentence of your own that uses adjectives, adverbs, prepositions, and conjunctions as they are used in the model. Also, go back to Exercise 1a and identify the adjectives, adverbs, prepositions, and conjunctions in those sentences.

### SENTENCE PRACTICE

1. Pirates are common figures in literature for children, but pirates who actually lived are also fascinating figures in history.
2. One of the most famous pirates is William Kidd, although he is more familiar as Captain Kidd.
3. In 1695 the British government employed Captain Kidd to guard English ships in the Red Sea and the Indian Ocean.
4. Although he had been hired to protect the ships, Kidd soon became a pirate himself and was eventually tried for piracy and murder.
5. Kidd still remains an intriguing figure to modern readers, for he is said to have left various hoards of buried treasure.

### PARAGRAPH PRACTICE

When Robert Louis Stevenson wrote *Treasure Island,* he created a classic pirate in Long John Silver. In fact, this courageous and ingenious pirate is often seen as the real hero of the novel. In *Peter Pan,* J. M. Barrie invented Captain Hook, another famous literary pirate. The wicked Hook hunts ruthlessly for Peter Pan and his Lost Boys, but the pirate is also dreadfully afraid of the hungry crocodile that bit off his right hand. Before the crocodile devours him near the end of the story, Captain Hook tries unsuccessfully to poison Peter Pan; imprisons Wendy, her brothers, and all the Lost Boys; and almost manages to kill Tinker Bell.

---

## EXERCISE 1b(2)

Expand each of the following sentences, using adjectives, adverbs, prepositions, conjunctions, and verbals to add information. After expanding the sentences, go back and label the adjectives, adverbs, prepositions, conjunctions, and verbals.

1. People read for relaxation.
2. The children's father read to them.
3. I went to the library.

4. Choosing a book can be difficult.
5. She bought a magazine at the newsstand.

## 1c Recognizing phrases

A **phrase** is a group of related words that has no subject or predicate and is used as a single part of speech. As we process language, we recognize phrases as chunks of information that expand a basic sentence, adding to its meaning, but we also recognize that phrases cannot express complete thoughts by themselves. *I fell on the sidewalk* is a complete thought; *on the sidewalk* is not.

Typical phrases are composed of a preposition and its object *(I fell on the sidewalk )* or a verbal and its object *(I wanted to see the parade)*. Phrases are usually classified as prepositional, infinitive, participial, or gerund phrases.

**1. Prepositional phrases.** Prepositional phrases consist of a preposition (see **1b**), its object, and any modifiers of the object *(under the ground, without thinking, in the blue Ford)*. Prepositional phrases function as adjectives or adverbs and occasionally as nouns.

He is a man *of action.* [Adjective modifying *man*]
The plane arrived *on time.* [Adverb modifying *arrived*]
She came early *in the morning.* [Adverb modifying *early*]
*Before breakfast* is too early. [Noun, subject of *is*]

**2. Infinitive phrases.** Infinitive phrases consist of an infinitive (See **1b**), its modifiers, and/or its object *(to see the world, to answer briefly, to earn money quickly)*. Infinitive phrases function as nouns, adjectives, or adverbs.

I wanted *to buy the house.* [Noun, object of verb]
It is time *to go to bed.* [Adjective modifying *time*]
We were impatient *to start the game.* [Adverb modifying *impatient*]

**3. Participial phrases.** Participial phrases consist of a present or past participle (see **1b**), its modifiers, and/or its object *(lying on the beach, found in the street, eating a large dinner)*. Note that a prepositional phrase may function as a modifier in a verbal phrase, as in *found in the street*. Participial phrases always function as adjectives describing either nouns or pronouns.

The dog *running in the yard* belongs to my mother.
The man *walking his dog* is my father.
*Covered with ice,* the road was dangerous.
*Beaten into stiff peaks,* the egg whites were prepared for meringue.

**1c**

*ss*

**4. Gerund phrases.** Gerund phrases consist of a gerund (see **1b**), its modifiers, and/or its object *(telling the truth, knowing the rules, acting bravely).* Gerund phrases always function as nouns, as subjects or objects.

> *Running in the yard* keeps the dog fit. [Subject]
> She earned extra money by *working overtime.* [Object of preposition]
> He hated *living alone.* [Object of verb]
> *Walking his dog* is my father's only exercise. [Subject]

Note that since both the gerund and the present participle end in *-ing,* they can be distinguished only by their separate functions as nouns or adjectives.

**5. Absolute phrases.** Absolute phrases are made up of a noun or pronoun and a participle. Unlike participial phrases, absolute phrases do not modify particular words in the sentence to which they are attached. Rather, they modify the whole sentence.

> The whole family sat silent, *their eyes glued to the TV screen.*
> *Mortgage rates having risen drastically,* Isabel gave up searching for a new house.
> The old man lay sprawled on the sofa, *eyes closed, arms folded across his chest, his loud snores almost rousing the dog sleeping near him.*

In absolute phrases with the participle *being* followed by an adjective, *being* is often omitted so that the phrase itself consists simply of a noun followed by an adjective and any other modifiers.

> *Final examinations over,* Linda returned to work.
> The den was thoroughly inviting, *the lights low, the long sofa and over-stuffed chairs luxuriously comfortable, the logs burning brightly in the fire-place,* and *our host open and friendly.*

---

### EXERCISE 1c

In the following sentences and paragraph, underline the verbal phrases once and put the prepositional phrases in parentheses. Note that a prepositional phrase may sometimes be part of a verbal phrase or vice versa, as in the verbal phrase *lying on the beach,* or the prepositional phrase *after going to bed.* After marking the sentences, write five sentences of your own, using these sentences as models for the use of verbal and prepositional phrases.

**SENTENCE PRACTICE**

1. The beverage known as coffee comes from the berries of the coffee tree.
2. Standing about six feet high, coffee trees have shiny evergreen leaves covering slender, vertical branches.

3. Before A.D. 1000, Ethiopians used the fruit of the coffee tree for food and to make wine.
4. Drinking coffee had become a pastime for Europeans by the mid-seventeenth century.
5. To grow well, coffee plants need to have a hot, moist climate and rich soil.

**1d**

*ss*

### PARAGRAPH PRACTICE

Caffeine, a stimulant contained in coffee, can create problems for you. After drinking lots of coffee, you may find yourself getting restless or irritable. Going to sleep may be difficult, for caffeine also contributes to insomnia. Other beverages containing caffeine include tea and cola, so you should be careful to avoid these drinks before going to bed. You may find that drinking hot cocoa before bedtime keeps you awake also, for in drinking cocoa, you are also ingesting caffeine.

## 1d  Recognizing clauses

A **clause** is a group of words containing a subject and a predicate. The relation of a clause to the rest of the sentence is shown by the position of the clause or by a conjunction. There are two kinds of clauses: (1) main, or independent, clauses and (2) subordinate, or dependent, clauses.

**1. Main clauses.** A main clause has both subject and verb, but it is not introduced by a subordinating word. A main clause makes an independent statement; by itself, it can stand as a simple sentence. It is not used as a noun or as a modifier.

Eagles are beautiful.

**2. Subordinate clauses.** Subordinate clauses are usually introduced by a subordinating conjunction (*as, since, because,* etc.) or by a relative pronoun (*who, which, that*). A **relative pronoun** is a connecting word that refers to a noun or pronoun in the main clause. Subordinate clauses function as adjectives, adverbs, or nouns. They cannot stand alone but must be attached to a main clause. They express ideas that are intended to be subordinate to or dependent on the idea expressed in the main clause. The exact relationship between the two ideas is indicated by the subordinating conjunction or relative pronoun that joins the subordinate and the main clause.

MAIN CLAUSE              SUBORDINATE CLAUSE

Eagles are beautiful *when* they soar high above the cliffs.

**1d**

**ss**

MAIN CLAUSE

SUBORDINATE CLAUSE

Will the person   *who* has the winning ticket   please come forward?

**a.** *An* **adjective clause** *modifies a noun or pronoun. It usually begins with a relative pronoun that serves as the clause's subject or object.*

This is the jet *that broke the speed record.* [The subordinate clause modifies the noun *jet.*]

Anyone *who is tired* may leave. [The subordinate clause modifies the pronoun *anyone.*]

Basketball is the sport *he plays best.* [The subordinate clause modifies the noun *sport,* with the relative pronoun *that* understood.]

**b.** *An* **adverb clause** *modifies a verb, adjective, another adverb, or a whole main clause. It explains when, where, why, how, or with what result.*

The child cried *when the dentist appeared.* [The subordinate clause modifies the verb *cried.*]

My head feels sore *where I bumped it.* [The subordinate clause modifies the predicate adjective *sore.*]

She thinks more quickly *than you do.* [The subordinate clause modifies the adverb *quickly.*]

We can leave for home *unless you are too tired to drive.* [The subordinate clause modifies the entire main clause.]

**c.** *A* **noun clause** *functions as a noun. It may serve as subject, predicate noun, object of a verb, or object of a preposition.*

*What you need* is a vacation. [The subordinate clause is the subject of the verb *is.*]

This is *where we came in.* [The subordinate clause is a predicate noun.]

Please tell them *I will be late.* [The subordinate clause is the object of the verb *tell,* with the relative pronoun *that* understood.]

I have no interest in *what I am reading.* [The subordinate clause is the object of the preposition *in.*]

---

EXERCISE 1d(1)

Underline the subordinate clauses twice in the following sentences, and identify each as an adjective, adverb, or noun clause. Then use each sentence as a model for writing a sentence of your own, using adjective, adverb, and noun clauses in similar ways.

1. The American folk-hero Buffalo Bill, whose real name was William F. Cody, was a frontier scout during the Civil War, a rider for the Pony Express, and a buffalo hunter.
2. Cody became famous as Buffalo Bill when Edmund Zane Carroll Judson, who was a dime novelist, gave him that name and began to write stories of Cody's adventures.
3. Judson also wrote a play about Buffalo Bill, and that play is what helped make Cody famous throughout the United States.
4. After he toured in the play, Cody created Buffalo Bill's Wild West Show, which played to enthusiastic audiences in the United States and Europe.
5. When Cody died in 1917, he had created an image of the wild west hero that would live on in western movies and novels.

**1d**

**ss**

### EXERCISE 1d(2)

In the following sentences and paragraph, underline each main clause once and each subordinate clause twice. Indicate the function of each subordinate clause as adjective, adverb, or noun. Then use each sentence as a model for writing a sentence of your own, with similar structure.

#### SENTENCE PRACTICE

1. Santa Fe, which is the capital of New Mexico, was founded in 1609 by the Spanish, who used the city as a center of trade with the southwestern Indians.
2. Although Santa Fe was officially founded in 1609, the Pueblo Indians had already used the site as a living place where they stayed for part of the year.
3. Because Santa Fe has served as a center of government since its founding by the Spanish, it is considered the oldest capital city in the country, even though the city didn't become part of the U.S. until 1846.
4. Whenever tourists visit modern Santa Fe, they often go first to the Plaza, a tree-shaded area that has been the heart of the city since 1610.
5. If they walk a block east of the Plaza, visitors can see the St. Francis Cathedral, which was begun in 1869 by Jean Baptiste Lamy, who was Santa Fe's first archbishop.

#### PARAGRAPH PRACTICE

The American painter Georgia O'Keeffe, who spent much of her life in New Mexico, often used elements of southwestern landscape in her works. Although she spent most of the later part of her life in the Southwest, O'Keeffe was born in Sun Prairie, Wisconsin, in 1887; in 1924 she married photographer Alfred Steiglitz. Steiglitz owned the gallery where O'Keeffe's work was first exhibited. Many of Georgia O'Keeffe's paintings are of abstract forms, but what sets them apart from other abstract works is their vivid coloring. Whenever people think of O'Keeffe's work, they often recall her flower paintings, which have become well-known after the works were exhibited throughout the United States.

**3. Sentence classification by clausal structure.** The number of main or subordinate clauses in a sentence determines its classification: simple, compound, complex, or compound-complex.

A **simple sentence** has a single main clause.

The wind blew.

Note that a sentence remains a simple sentence even though the subject, the verb, or both are compounded and modifying words and phrases are added.

The cat and the dog fought.
The dog barked and growled.
With its back arched, the cat jumped to the top of the bookcase and hissed nastily at the dog.

A **compound sentence** has two or more main clauses.

The wind blew, and the leaves fell.

A **complex sentence** has one main clause and one or more subordinate clauses.

When the wind blew, the leaves fell.

A **compound-complex sentence** contains two or more main clauses and one or more subordinate clauses.

When the sky darkened, the wind blew, and the leaves fell.

See Section **34** for a discussion of how sentence structure and length can be varied to create emphasis and accentuate meaning.

---

EXERCISE 1d(3)
In the following sentences and paragraph, underline each main clause once and each subordinate clause twice. Then indicate whether the sentence is simple, compound, complex, or compound-complex. Revise the simple sentences and the compound sentences, adding the necessary clauses to make them complex or compound-complex.

SENTENCE PRACTICE
1. J. R. R. Tolkien, who is best-known for his fantasy novels *The Hobbit* and *The Lord of the Rings,* was a professor of Anglo-Saxon literature at Oxford University.
2. *The Hobbit* was originally written for children, but adults also love the story of Bilbo Baggins, the hobbit who left his comfortable home to set off on a dangerous adventure.

3. The characters in *The Hobbit* include dwarfs, trolls, goblins, a wizard, and a huge dragon.
4. Bilbo Baggins, Tolkien's main character, doesn't look like a hero, yet he manages to overcome incredible obstacles in the novel.
5. *The Hobbit* was the first of a series of books that eventually brought Tolkien a vast audience of readers around the world.

**1d**

**ss**

#### PARAGRAPH PRACTICE
C. S. Lewis, Tolkien's colleague at Oxford, also wrote fantasy literature for children. Tolkien and Lewis were close friends, and they often met to talk and to listen to each other's work. Although Lewis had no children of his own, his Narnia books appeal vividly to children's imaginations. The Narnia series consists of seven books, which are set in the imaginary land of Narnia; in the first book, the children get to Narnia by traveling through a wardrobe. In addition to children's books, Lewis also wrote science fiction, religious works, and works of literary scholarship.

### EXERCISE 1d(4)
Using coordinating and subordinating conjunctions, combine the following sets of simple sentences in two ways. First, combine each set into a single compound sentence. Second, combine each set into a single complex or compound-complex sentence, changing wording and compounding and subordinating sentence parts as necessary.

#### SENTENCE PRACTICE
1. Standing in line can be boring. It can also waste a lot of time.
2. Some people get frustrated while standing in line. They complain to others near them. They sometimes give up and leave the line.
3. People have to stand in line at banks. They have to stand in line at automatic teller machines. They have to wait in long lines at the supermarket. Drivers have to wait in line at gas stations. People even have to wait in line to relax at restaurants. They have to wait in line to have fun at movie theaters and amusement parks.

In the following paragraph, use coordinating and subordinating conjunctions to combine the simple sentences into either compound, complex, or compound-complex sentences.

#### PARAGRAPH PRACTICE
People can avoid waiting in lines. They can also make the waiting time less tedious. Some people shop early in the day. Some shop late at night. Long lines are less common early in the morning. Shoppers encounter shorter lines late in the evening. Sometimes people can't avoid waiting in a long line. Taking along a book to read makes the wait seem less tedious. Some people balance their checkbook while waiting in line. Others write postcards to friends. Some use earphones to listen to music. Some people even learn a foreign language by listening to tapes while waiting in line.

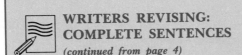

## WRITERS REVISING:
## COMPLETE SENTENCES
*(continued from page 4)*

### Robert's Response

| | |
|---|---|
| R1 | By the end of the century, the Black Death |
| R2 | had killed about 50 to 75 percent of the          1c |
| R3 | population. Because there were not enough laborers |
| R4 | for planting and harvesting crops, cleared land |
| R5 | returned to wilderness. Whole villages          1d |
| R6 | disappeared. Labor shortages also meant a |
| R7 | diminished food supply and scarce goods, resulting   1c |
| R8 | in a rise in prices. |

### Analysis

Notice how the writer has combined chunks of information from his notes into both simple and complex sentences. Notice particularly how he puts details in subordinate clauses and phrases, emphasizing the conclusions he wishes to draw by putting those in main clauses (sentences 1, 2, 4). See how the shortest simple sentence in the paragraph (sentence 3) receives extra emphasis because its length contrasts with the other sentences.

# 2
## CASE

**Case** shows the function of nouns and pronouns in a sentence. By means of its distinctive forms, case can indicate whether a noun or pronoun is being used as a subject **(subjective case),** an object **(objective case),** or is functioning as a possessive **(possessive case).**

SUBJECTIVE  OBJECTIVE  POSSESSIVE

*He* gave  *me* a *week's* vacation.

Nouns have only two case forms: the possessive form and the common form, which serves all other functions. Pronouns typically have three case forms: the subjective, possessive, and objective. These forms are shown below. Note that the personal pronouns *you* and *it* have distinctive possessive forms.

### NOUNS

| *Singular* | COMMON | POSSESSIVE |
|---|---|---|
| student | student | student's |
| *Plural* | | |
| students | students | students' |

### PERSONAL PRONOUNS

| *Singular* | SUBJECTIVE | POSSESSIVE | OBJECTIVE |
|---|---|---|---|
| FIRST PERSON | I | my, mine | me |
| SECOND PERSON | you | your, yours | you |
| THIRD PERSON | he, she, it | his, her, hers, its | him, her, it |
| *Plural* | | | |
| FIRST PERSON | we | our, ours | us |
| SECOND PERSON | you | your, yours | you |
| THIRD PERSON | they | their, theirs | them |

### RELATIVE OR INTERROGATIVE PRONOUN

| | SUBJECTIVE | POSSESSIVE | OBJECTIVE |
|---|---|---|---|
| *Singular* | who | whose | whom |
| *Plural* | who | whose | whom |

### WRITERS REVISING: CASE AND MODIFICATION

While revising a draft of her article for the student newspaper about a campus appearance of civil rights leader Jesse Jackson, Tracy corrected some errors in noun and pronoun case endings as well as in adjective and adverb usage. She also changed some case forms and adjectives and adverbs to make her writing more concise, as newspaper stories need to be. As you work through Sections **2** and **3**, see if you can spot and correct the errors in her first draft. Then compare your revision with hers, which appears at the end of Section **3**.

**Draft**

D 1    The highlight of the evening was the speech by the

D 2    Reverend Jesse Jackson. Jackson, whom had been the black

D 3    contender for the nomination for President in 1984 and

D 4   1988, said if a black candidate can succeed in being

D 5   nominated it could be him. In his speech, Jackson called

D 6   on minority groups to get solid behind whomever might

D 7   better represent their interests. Many observers feel

D 8   real strong that of the two blacks who have tried for

D 9   the Presidency, Jackson has been the most viable

D10   challenger.

This *Writers Revising* continues on page 38.

## 2a  Subjective case

We use the subjective form for the pronoun subjects of all verbs and for all pronouns after all forms of the verb *be* (such as *is, are, were*, or *have been*). *They won the game, but in terms of sportsmanship the real victors were we.* Speakers of English are unlikely to say or write "Us are happy" or "Him is going away." But compound subjects and some constructions in which the subject is not easily recognized may cause problems.

**1. Use the subjective pronoun form in all parts of a compound subject.**

*He* and *I* went shopping for a doll for my mother.
My father and *she* collect dolls, so my brother and *I* wanted to buy one for her birthday.

If you are unsure about the pronoun form in a compound subject, you can test for the correct case by separating the compound and saying each pronoun against the verb separately. For example, *My father collect(s) dolls / she collects dolls,* so *my brother wanted to buy one / I wanted to buy one* for her birthday.

**2. After the conjunctions *than* and *as,* use the subjective form of the pronoun if it is the subject of an understood verb.**

My brother is better at choosing collectible dolls than *I.* [*I* is the subject of *am at choosing them,* which is understood by the reader.]
I am not as expert at judging value as *he* [is].

**3. Use the subjective form of a pronoun in an appositive describing a subject or a subject complement.** An **appositive** is a word or phrase set beside a noun or pronoun that identifies or explains it by renaming it. When an appositive renames a subject or subject complement, it is grammatically equivalent to the subject or complement and thus takes the same case.

> We two, *Sam and I*, went to an antique shop. [*Sam and I* is an appositive renaming the subject *We two*.]
>
> *We children* had seen a doll there that our mother might like. [Not *Us children*. *Children* is an appositive defining the pronoun *We*.]

**4. Use the subjective case forms of the relative pronouns *who* and *whoever* when they serve as subjects of a clause.**

> The person *who* thinks dolls are inexpensive should price antique dolls. [*Who* is the subject of the verb *thinks* in the clause *who thinks dolls are inexpensive*.]
>
> *Whoever* is familiar with antiques knows they can be costly. [*Whoever* is the subject of the verb *is* in the clause *Whoever is familiar with antiques*.]

The form of the pronoun is always determined by its function in its own clause. If it serves as the subject of its own clause, use the subjective form even though the whole clause may be the object of a verb or preposition.

> Antique dealers can tell *who* is educated about price and value. [*Who* is the subject of the verb *is educated* in the subordinate clause. The subordinate clause *who is educated about price and value* is the object of the main clause's verb *can tell*.]
>
> They will usually negotiate a fair price for *whoever* knows an object's true worth. [The *whoever . . . worth* clause is the object of the preposition *for*. *Whoever* is the subject of the clause.]

Note that the form of the pronoun used as subject does not change when such expressions as *I think* and *he says* come between the subject and its verb.

> We chose a dealer *who* we knew was reputable. [*Who* is the subject of *was*.]
>
> She was a businesswoman *who* the owner of the antique shop on Grand Street said had a fine collection of dolls for sale. [*Who* is the subject of *had*.]
>
> *Who* do you think stakes reputation on quality? [*Who* is the subject of *stakes*.]

If you are not sure which form to use in sentences such as these, try testing by temporarily omitting the interrupting words.

**2a**

**ca**

> She was a businesswoman (who, whom) had a fine collection of dolls
> for sale.
> (Who, Whom) stakes reputation on quality?

The test will help you determine in each case whether the pronoun
*who* is the subject of the verb in the subordinate clause.

**5. In writing, use the subjective case of the personal pronoun
after forms of the verb *be*, except when you are writing dialogue.**

In spoken English in all but the most formal situations, *it's me*,
using the objective form of the pronoun, is common, and *it's him, her,
us, them* is becoming increasingly common. In your writing, however,
you should follow the conventions of standard written English, choosing the subjective case for pronouns following forms of *be: It's I.*

> It was *he*, my brother, who first noticed the antique Japanese doll,
> not *I*.
> It was *we*, however, who had to pay for it.

When you are writing dialogue, choose between the formal subjective case or the conversational objective case depending on the
character whose speech you are quoting.

> It was *he* who said, "Since this is a gift for Mom's birthday, it's *her*
> we should be trying to please, not our bank accounts." I replied,
> "Since it's *she*, and since this Japanese doll is very unusual, you're
> right. Let's buy it."

**6. In writing, use the subjective case for a pronoun following
the infinitive *to be* when the infinitive has no expressed subject.**

Spoken English commonly uses the objective case of the pronoun in this construction. (See **2c(5)** for the case of the pronoun after
the infinitive when the subject is expressed.)

> WRITTEN    I would like to be *she* when she opens the package. [The
>            infinitive *to be* has no expressed subject.]
>
> SPOKEN     I would like to be *her* when she opens the package.

---

## EXERCISE 2a

In the following sentences and paragraph, correct any errors of case
in accordance with formal written usage. Be ready to explain your
reasons.

**SENTENCE PRACTICE**

1. Anyone whom wants to take a long bicycle trip should begin training
   six to eight weeks before the starting date of the trip.
2. We two, Maria and me, plan to take a long bicycle trip along the

California coast, so we asked an experienced bike rider whom we know if she would help us set up a training plan.
3. Us weekend riders need to begin training slowly and then gradually increase mileage and time.
4. I've ridden long distances in one day, but I'm sure that cyclists whom ride long distances every day for two or three weeks must be in much better condition than me.
5. After Maria and me started our daily training rides, her and I noticed that we no longer huff and puff so much when we go up a hill.

**PARAGRAPH PRACTICE**

The bicycle rider whom wants to buy a new bicycle should do some research before investing in expensive new equipment. The owner of the local bike shop told me that him and his assistants enjoy showing customers the two major categories of bicycles: road bikes and mountain bikes. Whomever wants an all-terrain bike designed for rough trails as well as for pavement should get a mountain bike. When my friend and me talked with the bike shop owner, we also learned that the road bike category includes touring bikes, racing bikes, and recreational bikes. After looking at all the types of bicycles available, I decided that us bike riders have to know exactly what we plan to do with a bicycle before we make a purchase.

---

## 2b Possessive case

**1. Generally, use the *s*-possessive *(anyone's, boy's, Jane's)* with indefinite pronouns and with nouns naming living things.** The possessive case of such words usually is formed by adding an apostrophe (') and the letter *s*. (See **29a.**) With nouns naming inanimate things, the *of*-phrase *(the point of the pen)* is sometimes preferred, but the *s*-form occurs very often.

ANIMATE    Jane's hair; the cat's meow; a friend's car
INANIMATE  the point of the joke, the wing of the airplane; the words of the title; the city's newsstands; the article's tone

The *s*-possessive is commonly used in expressions that indicate time *(moment's notice, year's labor)* and in many familiar phrases *(life's blood, fool's gold)*. Choice of possessive form may also depend on sound or rhythm: the *s*-possessive is more terse than the longer, more sonorous *of*-phrase (the President's signature, the signature of the President). *The title's words,* however, seems more awkward and less pleasing than *the words of the title.*

Note that the possessive form of personal and interrogative or relative pronouns is *not* formed with *'s* (see p. 23).

**2c**

*ca*

   **2.** In formal English, use the possessive case for a noun or pronoun preceding a gerund. In informal English, however, the objective case (pronoun) or common form (noun) before a gerund is typical. A **gerund** is a verb with the suffix *-ing (skiing, reading, driving)* that functions as a noun.

> FORMAL    What was the reason for *my* studying Japanese?
> INFORMAL   What was the reason for *me* studying Japanese?
>
> FORMAL    You know about *Japan's* dominating the world marketplace.
> INFORMAL   You know about *Japan* dominating the world marketplace.

Even in formal English the common form is frequently used with plural nouns.

> I understand *people* wanting to learn about another culture.

Your choice of case may sometimes depend on the meaning you want to convey.

> Imagine *my* traveling to Japan. [The act of traveling is emphasized.]
> Imagine *me* traveling to Japan. [The emphasis is on *me*. *Traveling* is used here as a participle modifying *me*.]

   **3.** Use the possessive form *whose* to refer to impersonal antecedents when the phrase *of which* would be awkward.

> There were two empty seats, one *of which* was by the window.
> We bought two tickets for a flight *whose* destination was Tokyo. [Compare *We bought two tickets for a flight the destination of which was Tokyo.*]
> Japanese companies *whose* products sell well internationally have captured a large market share. [Compare *Japanese companies the products of which sell well internationally have captured a large market share.*]

**2c**   Objective case

   Objective pronoun forms are used for the objects of all verbs, verbals, and prepositions.

> OBJECT OF VERB    Did you see *him* yesterday?
>                   Our friends visited *us*.
>
> OBJECT OF VERBAL   Visiting *them* was pleasant. [Object of gerund *visiting*]
>
> OBJECT OF VERBAL   I wanted to invite *her* to lunch. [Object of infinitive *to invite*]

OBJECT OF PREPOSITION  Give the check to *me*.

We will split the total between *us*.

**2c**

**ca**

Problems with objective pronoun forms usually occur in the same kinds of constructions that cause problems with subjective pronoun forms. (See **2a.**)

**1. Use the objective pronoun forms in all parts of a compound object.**

We discovered the cat and *him* under the bed. [Not *the cat and he; him* is a part of the compound object of the verb *discovered*.]

They were afraid of you and *me*. [Not *of you and I; me* is a part of the compound object of the preposition *of*.]

If you have trouble deciding whether a singular pronoun form is in the correct case, sometimes it helps to say the sentence aloud, changing the pronoun to the plural as a test for proper case. For example, it may be easier for you to hear the correct form in "They were afraid of *us*." *Us*, the objective form, is equivalent to *me*, the corresponding singular pronoun form.

**2. After the conjunctions *than* and *as*, use the objective form for a pronoun that is the object of an understood verb.**

He fears the Great Dane more than [he fears] *me*.

The cat dislikes the Great Dane as much as [it dislikes] *us*.

In these examples, an error in pronoun case would change the meaning of the sentences. The subjective pronoun, used instead of the objective pronoun, would indicate a different understood verb and, hence, a different meaning.

He fears the Great Dane more than *I*. [fear the Great Dane.]

The cat dislikes the Great Dane as much as *we*. [dislike the Great Dane.]

**3. Use the objective form of a pronoun in an appositive describing or renaming an object of a verb or a preposition.**

The two of them stared at us—*me* and the dog—and refused to come out from under the bed. [*Me and the dog* is an appositive renaming *us*.]

**4. Standard written English requires *whom* for all objects, even though *who* is common in conversation unless it immediately follows a preposition.**

2c

ca

In subordinate clauses, use *whom* and *whomever* for all objects. Remember that the case of the relative pronoun in a subordinate clause depends upon its function in the clause and not upon the function of the whole clause.

The visitors *whom* we had expected did not come. [*Whom* is the object of the verb *had expected*. The clause *whom we had expected* modifies *visitors*.]

*Whomever* you like best is the person you should invite. [*Whomever* is the object of the verb *like* in the subordinate clause *whomever you like best*. The entire clause is the subject of the sentence.]

A helpful test is to put the words in the clause in subject-verb-object order *(you like whomever best)*. That way you will be able to tell more easily which case form of the pronoun is appropriate.

**5. Use the objective case for a pronoun that is the object of a verb, even if the pronoun also functions as the expressed subject of an infinitive.**

We wanted *him* to take the part. [*Him* is the subject of the infinitive *to take*, but is the object of the verb *wanted*.]

Tim believed *her* to be me. [*Her* is the subject of the infinitive *to be*, but is the object of the verb *believed*.]

The voters selected *them* to be the state senators.

---

### EXERCISE 2b–c

In the following sentences and paragraph, revise the errors of case in accordance with formal written usage. Be prepared to explain your answers.

SENTENCE PRACTICE

1. Our art instructor gave my friend and I tickets to a modern photography exhibit at the local art museum.
2. Many of we viewers at the exhibit were particularly interested in documentary photography of the Great Depression and World War II.
3. During these periods, documentary photographers such as Margaret Bourke–White and Dorothea Lange contributed photographs to popular picture magazines like *Life;* when I saw their work, I admired them having the skill to get such images on film.
4. In some of the photographs taken during the Great Depression, the people who the photographer captured on film seem to have a look of despair on their faces.

5. Looking at these photographic images of the Great Depression was an unsettling experience for us—my friend and I—because we had not realized the kinds of hardships the people who we were gazing at had faced.

**PARAGRAPH PRACTICE**

My friend liked the contemporary photograph section of the exhibit more than me. In that section of photographs, we saw lots of innovative photographic techniques such as collage and multiple images; when I saw the work of these photographers, I thought they to be very skillful at their art. I wondered, however, who do you think would want to pose for a photograph of a face broken into thousands of tiny images? My friend likes the work of these artists and believes that them trying out new techniques will lead to even more unusual uses of photography.

EXERCISE 2a–c

In the following paragraph, revise the errors in case forms in accordance with formal written usage. Be prepared to explain your answers.

Since we enjoy eating at Italian restaurants, my friend and me decided to enroll in a three-day Italian cooking class. The other people in the class, many of who had more experience in cooking than us, seemed to know what to do when the chef explained how to make pasta. The chef, whom was from Bologna, was amazing. He asked another student and I to measure the flour for the pasta while he chopped lots of garlic and onions for the sauce. Whomever wants to learn Italian cooking should not mind getting messy, for some of we students ended up with flour and eggs all over us by the time we had finished the pasta dough. You could certainly see whom had worked on the pasta! After the chef and us had prepared the food, we all decided that us having taken the course was a good idea. The chef was right, for it was him who had said that our hard work would pay off in a great meal. Now that I've finished the course, I think that whomever wants to learn Italian cooking should enroll right away.

# 3
## ADJECTIVES AND ADVERBS

Adjectives and adverbs are modifying words; that is, they are words that limit or qualify the meaning of other words, thus adding information to a sentence. **Adjectives** modify nouns and pronouns; they are usually placed either immediately before or immediately after the word they modify. Adjectives qualify meaning by indicating *what kind of* about the words they modify.

Our *local* doctor told me I probably needed *new* glasses; *blurred* vision was giving me headaches too *severe* to treat with aspirin *alone*.

**Adverbs** normally modify verbs, adjectives, and other adverbs, although they may sometimes modify whole sentences. When they modify adjectives or other adverbs, they are adjacent to the words they modify. When they modify verbs, they are frequently, but not always, adjacent to the verbs.

Adverbs qualify the meaning of the words they modify by indicating such things as *when, where, how, why, in what order,* or *how often*.

> The office closed *yesterday*. [*Yesterday* indicates when.]
> Deliver all mail *here*. [*Here* indicates where.]
> She replied *quickly* and *angrily*. [*Quickly* and *angrily* describe how she replied.]
> *Consequently*, I left. [*Consequently* describes why.]
> He *seldom* did any work. [*Seldom* indicates how often.]

Most adverbs are distinguished from their corresponding adjectives by the ending *-ly: strong—strongly, happy—happily, doubtful—doubtfully, hasty—hastily, wonderful—wonderfully*. But the *-ly* ending is not always a dependable adverbial indicator, since some adverbs have two forms *(quick, quickly; slow, slowly);* others have the same form as adjectives *(fast, much, late, well);* and some adjectives also end in *-ly (lovely, lonely)*. (See Section **35**, "Vocabulary," for a discussion of the ways adjectives are formed from nouns.) Nevertheless, where there is a choice between a form with *-ly* and a form without it, formal English prefers the *-ly* form for the adverb—*runs quickly* rather than *runs quick, eats slowly* rather than *eats slow*—even though the shorter forms are widely used in informal English, particularly in such commands as *Drive slow*.

**3a**   Use an adverb, not an adjective, to modify a verb.

> INCORRECT   He writes *careless*.
> CORRECT   He writes *carelessly*. [The adverb *carelessly* is needed to modify the verb *writes*.]

> INCORRECT   We worked *diligent*.
> CORRECT   We worked *diligently*. [The adverb is needed to modify the verb.]

Note that *badly* always functions as an adverb; *bad* always functions as an adjective. Use *badly* to modify a verb. Similarly, *good* always functions as an adjective. Choose the adverbial form *well* to modify a verb.

| INCORRECT | The chorus sang *bad* from the first song to the last. |
|---|---|
| CORRECT | The chorus sang *badly* from the first song to the last. [*Badly* modifies the verb *sang*, telling *how* they sang.] |

| INCORRECT | He plays the saxophone *good*, doesn't he? |
|---|---|
| CORRECT | He plays that saxophone *well*, doesn't he? [*Well* modifies the verb *plays*, telling *how* he plays.] |

Remember, *good* and *bad* as adverbs are nonstandard. The sentence *She talks good but writes bad* is nonstandard. Standard English requires the use of the adverbs *well* and *badly: She talks well but writes badly.*

**3b**  Use an adverb, not an adjective, to modify another adverb or an adjective.

| INCORRECT | I am *terrible* nearsighted. |
|---|---|
| CORRECT | I am *terribly* nearsighted. [The adverb *terribly* is needed to modify the adjective *nearsighted*.] |

| INCORRECT | Contact lenses cost *considerable* more than glasses do. |
|---|---|
| CORRECT | Contact lenses cost *considerably* more than glasses do. [The adverb *considerably* is needed to modify the other adverb *more*.] |

The use of adjectives in place of adverbs is more common in conversation than in writing. The use of the adjective *real* as a substitute for *really* or as an emphatic *very* to modify adjectives and adverbs is heard at all levels of speech. Similarly, the adverb form *surely* should replace *sure* in formal speech and writing.

| FORMAL | My flight was *really* late. |
|---|---|
| COLLOQUIAL* | My flight was *real* late. |

| FORMAL | You will hear from me *very* soon. |
|---|---|
| COLLOQUIAL | You will hear from me *real* soon. |

| FORMAL | I will *surely* be glad to get home. |
|---|---|
| INFORMAL | I will *sure* be glad to get home. |

**3c**  After a linking verb, use an adjective to modify the subject.

The common **linking verbs** are *be, become, appear, seem,* and the verbs pertaining to the senses: *look, smell, taste, sound, feel.* Predicate adjectives after such verbs refer to the subject and should be in adjective form. In each of the following sentences, for example, the predicate adjective modifies the subject. The verb simply links the two.

*Colloquial* means characteristic of or appropriate to conversation but not to formal writing.

You look *tired* tonight. [*Tired* modifies *you*.]
The milk smells *sour*. [*Sour* modifies *milk*.]

One of the most frequent errors in this construction is *I feel badly* in place of the correct subject–linking-verb–predicate-adjective form *I feel bad*. Though *badly* is common even in educated speech, *bad*, an adjective, correctly modifies the subject *I*.

| | |
|---|---|
| FORMAL | He feels *bad* [ill]. |
| COLLOQUIAL | He feels *badly*. |
| | |
| FORMAL | He felt *bad* about it. |
| COLLOQUIAL | He felt *badly* about it. |

**3d**  Use an adverb after the verb to describe the manner of the action of the verb.

The cat looked *slyly at the canary*. [The adverb *slyly* modifies the verb *looked*. Contrast *The cat looked sly to the canary*.]
*The church bells sounded mournfully*, announcing the king's death. [The adverb *mournfully* modifies the verb *sounded*. Contrast *The queen thought the church bells sounded mournful*.]

In these examples the verbs *look* and *sound* express action, and must be modified by adverbs. But in constructions like *She looks tired* or *He sounds happy*, the verbs serve not as words of action, but as links between the subject and the predicate adjective. The choice of adjective or adverb depends on the meaning and function of the verb— that is, on whether the verb is being used as a linking verb. In making the choice, ask yourself whether you want to modify the subject or the verb.

---

EXERCISE 3a-d
In the following sentences and paragraph, revise in accordance with formal written usage any errors in the use of adjectives and adverbs.

**SENTENCE PRACTICE**
1. In recent years, car sound systems have gotten increasing elaborate and expensive.
2. Advanced technology has allowed car owners to install auto sound systems that sound as well as those in their living rooms.
3. In the mid-1970s, car owners began replacing their eight-track tape decks with cassette tape players, whose steady sound seemed ideal suited to the inside of a car; now cassettes are routine installed in new cars.
4. Although cassettes are still the most popular auto sound system, the rapid growing use of compact disk players indicates what car owners will be buying in the future.

5. Now, car owners can install compact disk changers that allow them to play music continuous from a selection of six to twelve disks.

**3e**

**ad**

**PARAGRAPH PRACTICE**
   The new advanced sound systems are perfect suited for those who like the sound of the concert hall or rock concert in their car. However, some drivers, who forget that not everyone enjoys loud music, play their stereos at a real high volume and bother other drivers stopped near them in traffic. In addition, loud music coming from cars cruising through residential areas at night sure does disturb people's sleep. As a result, many city councils have acted real quick to pass ordinances to ticket drivers who thoughtless disturb others by playing their car stereos loud at night.

---

**3e**  Use the comparative form of adjectives and adverbs when expressing a greater degree of quality or quantity. Use the superlative form when expressing the greatest degree of quality or quantity.

Adjectives and adverbs show degrees of quality or quantity by means of their **positive, comparative,** and **superlative** forms.

| *Positive Form* | *Comparative Form* | *Superlative Form* |
|---|---|---|
| no comparison | greater degree, or compares two persons/things | greatest degree, or compares three or more persons/things |
| quick | quick*er* | quick*est* |
| rich | rich*er* | rich*est* |
| delicious | *more* delicious | *most* delicious |
| inflamed | *more* inflamed | *most* inflamed |
| good | better | best |
| bad, badly | worse | worst |

   Most one-syllable adjectives and a few one-syllable adverbs form the comparative and superlative with *-er* and *-est*. Adjectives of two syllables often have two possible forms (*fancier, more fancy; laziest, most lazy*). Where there is a choice, use the form that sounds better or is better suited to the rhythm of the sentence. Adjectives and adverbs of three or more syllables always take *more* and *most* (*more beautiful; most regrettably*). Some common adjectives and adverbs, such as *good* and *bad*, have irregular forms. If you are unsure about the appropriate form, consult a dictionary.

   Some adjectives and adverbs, such as *unique, empty, dead, favorite, perfect, round*, are considered "absolute" in their meaning and thus cannot be logically compared. Logically, a room is either *empty* or *not empty*, a person is either *dead* or *alive*. Nevertheless, phrases such as "emptier than," "more perfect than," and "more dead than alive" are common in speech and very informal writing.

**3f**

*ad*

| | |
|---|---|
| FORMAL | His diving form is *more nearly perfect* than mine. |
| INFORMAL | His diving form is *more perfect* than mine. |
| FORMAL | The new stadium is *more nearly circular* than the old one. |
| INFORMAL | The new stadium is *more circular* than the old one. |

Also, check your writing for "redundant" or "double" comparatives and superlatives. Standard usage does not recognize such expressions as *You are more luckier than I* or *That was the most craziest thing I've ever seen.*

**3f**  In formal usage, use the comparative to refer only to one of two objects; use the superlative to refer only to one of three or more objects.

| | |
|---|---|
| COMPARATIVE | This car is *cheaper* than that one. |
| SUPERLATIVE | This car is the *cheapest* subcompact on the market. |
| COMPARATIVE | Ruth is the *more* attractive but the *less* good-natured of the twins. |
| SUPERLATIVE | Ruth is the *most* attractive but the *least* good-natured of his three daughters. |

---

**EXERCISE 3e–f**
In the following sentences and paragraph, revise in accordance with formal written usage any errors in the use of the comparative and superlative forms of adjectives and adverbs. Then use each revised adjective and adverb form in a sentence of your own.

SENTENCE PRACTICE
1. The sun is perhaps the reliablest source of energy available to humans.
2. When compared with other stars, the sun is an average star, but to humans, who depend upon it for energy, the sun is the more important star in the sky.
3. The sun is approximately 865,000 miles in diameter, making it 333,000 times more large than the earth.
4. The sun consists mainly of two gases, hydrogen and helium; hydrogen, which makes up 72% of the sun, is the most common of the two.
5. The temperature at the sun's core is 27 million degrees F, making the core much more hot than the surface, where the temperature is only 10,000 degrees F.

PARAGRAPH PRACTICE
Although humans depend on the sun for energy, they are becoming cautiouser about exposing themselves to its powerful rays. Overexposure to the sun can cause painful sunburn, can bring on premature wrinkling of the skin, and more worse of all, can cause

skin cancer. Sunscreens can help reduce the risks of exposure to the sun, but people should be sure to use a sunscreen with a skin protection factor more high than 14; sunscreens with protection factors of least than 15 don't screen out enough damaging ultraviolet rays. Because the sun is hotter between the hours of 10 A.M. and 3 P.M., midday is not the better time to work outside.

**3g**    Avoid the excessive use of nouns to modify other nouns.

The use of nouns to modify other nouns in expressions such as *rock garden, steel mill, silver mine,* and *telephone booth* is very common in English. (See Section **37**.) When there is no appropriate adjectival form and when the modifying nouns are short, such constructions are usually clear and concise. But when nouns are used to replace appropriate adjectives or when the series of nouns modifying other nouns is long, such expressions are awkward at best, confusing at worst.

**1. Choose an adjective instead of a noun modifier whenever possible.**

AWKWARD    a comedy performance at a Paris theater
IMPROVED    a comedic performance at a Parisian theater

**2. Avoid long series of nouns modifying other nouns.**

CONFUSING    office management personnel report [A report about the management of office personnel? A report by personnel who are managing an office? Something else?]
CLEAR    a report about the management personnel in this office

CONFUSING    teacher education program analysis [An analysis of a program for educating teachers? An analysis by teachers of an educational program? Something else?]
CLEAR    teachers' analysis of an educational program

EXERCISE 3a–g
In the following sentences and paragraph, revise in accordance with formal written usage any errors in the use of adjectives and adverbs. Then use the revised forms in sentences of your own.

SENTENCE PRACTICE
1. Modern zoo planners are doing away with cages and bars in order to provide a naturaler environment for the animals.
2. Although traditional zoo practices still exist, these practices are rapid disappearing as zoo designers construct habitats that realistic re-create the animals' natural environment.
3. To create these natural environments, zoo designers often have to

duplicate exotic landscapes such as a Brazil rain forest or an Alaska ice field.

4.  Visitors observing these environments frequent have to watch patient, for the animals often hide in the underbrush or in the foliage of the trees.

5.  Fortunate, the wait is worthwhile, since visitors to these zoos feel that they have entered a faraway world where they see the animals behaving natural in conditions much like their native environment.

**PARAGRAPH PRACTICE**

Many zoos in the United States exemplify the changes current taking place in zoo planning and design. For example, the Bronx Zoo, the country's larger urban zoo, has a new area called Himalayan Highlands where visitors can see rare Tibetan snow leopards chasing each other playful in a mountain setting. The Brookfield Zoo, west of downtown Chicago, was one of the first zoos in the country to have no bars enclosing its animals; today this zoo has a glass-covered jungle habitat that accurate depicts Asia, Africa, and South America rain forests. Another real popular exhibit at the Brookfield Zoo is the Seven Sea Panorama, a recent expanded marine habitat that includes an indoor dolphin pool and an outdoor Pacific Coast seascape. In Tucson, Arizona, the Arizona-Sonora Desert Museum is a very unique combination of natural history museum, botanical garden, and regional zoo; the desert display is spectacular colored in March and April when the desert plants bloom.

---

## WRITERS REVISING: CASE AND MODIFICATION *(continued from page 23)*

Notice in the revision how Tracy revised for conciseness. Once ideas have been fully developed, revising the language for conciseness is an important step for any kind of writing, not just newspaper articles. (The code numbers in the right margin refer to section numbers in this textbook.)

**Tracy's Revision**

R 1    The highlight *evening's* of the evening was the

R 2    speech by the Reverend Jesse Jackson, *speech*

R 3    Jackson, *who* whom had been the black                    **2a(4)**

R 4    contender for the *Presidential* nomination for

R 5    President in 1984 *and 1988* said if a black

R 6    candidate can succeed in being nominated

R 7    it could be h̶i̶m̶. In his speech,    2a(5)
*he*

R 8    Jackson called on minority groups to get    3a

R 9    solid behind w̶h̶o̶m̶e̶v̶e̶r̶ might b̶e̶t̶t̶e̶r̶    2a(4), 3f
*ly*        *whoever*        *best*

R10    represent their interests. Many observers    3b

R11    feel r̶e̶a̶l̶ ̶s̶t̶r̶o̶n̶g̶ that of the two blacks    3b
*really strongly*

R12    who have tried for the Presidency,    3

R13    Jackson has been the m̶o̶s̶t̶ viable    3f
*more*

R14    challenger.

## Analysis

R3, R7, and R9 show errors in case form. The subjective case of the relative pronouns *who* in R3 and *whoever* in R9 are appropriate because they are subjects of the verbs in the subordinate clauses. The subjective case *he* is the appropriate form in R7 since it follows the verb *to be*. R8–9 and R11 call for adverb forms of words to modify verbs or adverbs. *Solidly* modifies *to get* in R8 and *really strongly* modifies *feel* in R11. The writing is made more concise by substituting one-word modifiers for prepositional phrases. In R1 and R2 the possessive case of the nouns, *evening's* and *Jackson's* saves four words. The adjectival form of *president, presidential,* saves two words in R4.

# 4

## VERB FORMS

Verbs are the most complex parts of speech in English. This section covers various forms and kinds of verbs, their function, and some common usage problems. Section **5** covers the forms, use, and problems of tense, voice, and mood in verbs.

### WRITERS REVISING: VERB FORMS

Robin has just finished a draft of her paper for her sophomore literature class. See if you can discover errors in her use of verbs in the excerpt from her paper that follows, and then compare your revisions with hers at the end of Section **4.**

**4**

*vb*

> **Robin's Draft**
>
> D1    The illness that ultimately kill Ivan Ilych force
>
> D2    him to start thinking about his life. As he lays
>
> D3    in his bed, he start to ask why he was put on this
>
> D4    earth. He start to ask why he must suffer this
>
> D6    pain and why he have to die. He pondering his
>
> D7    reasons for doing what he has done in his life. At
>
> D8    this point, he has sank in pain and just want
>
> D9    Gerasim to set by his bed.
>
> This *Writers Revising* continues on page 50.

## FORMS OF VERBS

All verbs except *be,* which we will discuss separately, have five forms. The first three forms—the **plain form,** the **past tense,** and the **past participle**—are called the **principal parts** of the verb. The five forms of two verbs are illustrated below:

|  |  | Regular Verb | Irregular Verb |
|---|---|---|---|
| PRINCIPAL PARTS | Plain form | I *work* | the games *begin* |
|  | Past tense | I *worked* | the games *began* |
|  | Past participle | I have *worked* | the games had *begun* |
|  | -*s* form (present tense) | he *works* | someone *begins* |
|  |  | she is *working* | the games are *beginning* |
|  | Present participle |  |  |

**1. Plain form or infinitive.** Verbs are listed in the dictionary by their plain form, sometimes called the *base form.* We use the plain form with all plural nouns and the pronouns *I, we, you,* and *they* to indicate present time or habitual action: *rivers flow to the sea; I owe you money; they work downtown.* We also use the plain form with helping verbs, such as *will, can, must, should* (except forms of *be* and *have*): *the river will flow; birds can fly.* The infinitive forms of most verbs are created by adding *to* to the plain form: *he likes to work downtown; I used to owe you money.*

**2. Past tense form.** The past tense form shows that the action or state of being indicated by the verb occurred at some time in the past. (*Tense* means the time of the verb's action.) In most verbs the past tense is **regular,** formed by adding *-d* or *-ed* to the plain form (sometimes doubling the final consonant—see Section **39e[4]** for an explanation of this spelling rule): *smoked, worked, planned.* But in about two hundred verbs the past tense is formed in some **irregular** way, usually by a vowel change: *grow, grew; swim, swam; drive, drove; begin, began.* (See **4b**).

**3. Past participle.** The past participle combined with *has, have,* or *had* forms the perfect tense, indicating that the action is finished before a given point in time: *has worked, have grown, had driven.* (See Section **5.**) When combined with forms of *be,* the past participle forms the **passive voice:** *is defeated, was being driven, were discovered.* (See Section **5.**) In the past tense and the past participle, most verbs have the same form: *played, have played; found, has found; slept, had slept.* But about forty-five verbs are irregular in the past participle: *did, has done; grew, had grown; spoke, have spoken; wrote, has written.*

**4. -s form.** Used with the pronouns *he, she,* and *it,* with all singular nouns, and with certain indefinite pronouns such as *each* or *someone,* the *-s* form indicates present time or habitual action by adding *-s* to the plain form: *she asks, the dog wags its tail, someone always wins.* Note that the *-s* forms for the verbs *be* and *have* are *is* and *has.*

**5. Present participle.** Used after *am, is, are, was,* or *were,* the present participle indicates progressive tense—action continuing at the time indicated: *I am working, he is playing, they are working, the car was stopping.* For all verbs, this form is made by adding *-ing* to the plain form (sometimes doubling the final consonant). (For a discussion of the present participle in phrases that function as adjectives, see Section **1c.**)

**6. The verb *be.*** Rather than the five forms of other English verbs, the verb *be* has eight forms, as follows:

| | |
|---|---|
| Plain form | Jokes can *be* funny. |
| Present tense, singular, first person | I *am* funny. |
| Present tense, singular, -s form | It *is* funny. |
| Present tense, plural | Jokes *are* funny. |
| Past tense, singular | The joke *was* funny. |
| Past tense, plural | The jokes *were* funny. |
| Past participle | The joke had *been* funny. |
| Present participle | I was *being* funny. |

# KINDS OF VERBS

**1. Regular and irregular verbs.** A verb is either regular or irregular, depending on the form of its past tense and/or past participle.

**Regular verbs** form the past tense and past participle by adding *-d* or *-ed* to the plain form, occasionally doubling the final consonant (see Section **39e[4]** for the applicable spelling rule): *complete, completed, completed; plan, planned, planned.*

**Irregular verbs** form the past tense and/or past participle in some other way, usually by changing an internal vowel. In some cases, the verb form may be the same in both past tense and past participle *(strike, struck, struck; spin, spun, spun)*, or—in the case of about forty-five verbs—the form may change in all three principal parts *(give, gave, given; freeze, froze, frozen)*. About twenty irregular verbs stay the same for all three principal parts: *cut, cut, cut; hit, hit, hit.* English has about two hundred irregular verbs. See Section **4b** for a list of the most common ones.

**2. Main and auxiliary verbs.** In a verb phrase such as *is going, had been winning,* or *must have been found,* the last verb form is called the **main verb** because it indicates the principal meaning. The other verb forms in the phrase indicate special shades of meaning, such as time, obligation, and possibility, and are called **auxiliary verbs** or helping verbs.

Auxiliary verbs make up a small group of function words that may be divided into subgroups according to the kinds of functions they perform. With the exception of *be, have,* and *do,* all auxiliary verbs have only one form.

a.    The forms of *be (am, is, are, was, were, been,* and *being)* and of *have (has, have, had, having)* combine with main verbs to indicate tense and voice (see Section **5**) as in *have worked, were studying, is planned, had been defeated.* The auxiliaries *will* and *shall* are used to indicate future time, as in *will go.*

b.    The auxiliaries *can, could, may, might, must, ought (to), should,* and *would,* sometimes called **modal auxiliaries,** combine with main verbs to indicate ability, obligation, permission, possibility, etc.: *can go, could have gone, must go.*

c.    The auxiliary *do* is used to form questions and negative statements and to give emphasis, as in *Does she work; She did not work yesterday; She does work hard.*

**3. Transitive, intransitive, and linking verbs.** Verbs may be grouped as intransitive, transitive, or linking according to whether they do or do not pass their action to another word, called their object, or whether they are followed by a word which refers to the subject, called a subject complement. (See also Section **1**.)

**Intransitive verbs** are those that are not followed by any object or complement. They do not pass their action to a "receiver."

The church bells rang.
The book lay on the table.

**Transitive verbs** are those that are followed by one or more objects, words that receive the action of the verb. In other words, transitive verbs *transfer* action from the subject to the object.

> The hurricane *struck* the coast.
>
> Rescue workers *gave* the storm victims aid. [*Victims* is an indirect object, *aid* a direct object.]
>
> The storm *made* the roads impassable. [*Roads* is a direct object, *impassable* an object complement modifying *roads*.]

**Linking verbs** are those that are followed by a subject complement, a word that renames or describes the subject. Linking verbs do not transfer action; rather, they join the subject and the complement. Common linking verbs are forms of *be (is, are, was, were,* etc.), *appear, become, seem,* and, in certain contexts, verbs such as *smell, taste, feel, sound, look, act, grow.* (See also Section **3a**.)

> Mata Hari *was* a German spy. [*Spy* renames *Mata Hari.*]
>
> Her life *appears* glamorous to us now. [*Glamorous* describes *life.*]
>
> Undoubtedly it *seemed* very dangerous to her. [*Dangerous* describes *it.*]

Many verbs may be used as either intransitive or transitive according to the sentence in which they are used.

> Would you please *walk* the dog? [Transitive]
>
> Don't *walk* so fast. [Intransitive]
>
> The storm *broke* the power lines. [Transitive]
>
> The storm *broke* violently. [Intransitive]

**4. Finite and nonfinite verbs.** A **finite verb** can stand alone as the main verb in a sentence or clause. It can function as a main verb without an auxiliary, and it changes form to show person and number: *the bus stops here; the buses stop here.* **Nonfinite verb** forms (infinitives, participles, gerunds) cannot stand alone as main verbs, do not indicate person or number, and cannot by themselves make an assertion about the subject: *the bus stopping here.* They must be accompanied by auxiliaries to form sentences or clauses: *the bus is stopping here.* Unaccompanied nonfinite verbs usually appear in phrases: *This bus goes to Monroe Street after stopping here.*

Compare the finite and nonfinite verbs in the following lists. Note particularly that all the word groups containing a finite verb are complete sentences but that none of those containing only nonfinite verbs are. Note also that the nonfinite verb forms remain unchanged.

| FINITE | NONFINITE |
|---|---|
| The man plans his meals. | The man planning his meals. . . |
| The men plan their meals. | The men planning their meals. . . |
| The dog has slept. | The dog having slept. . . |
| The dogs have slept. | The dogs having slept. . . |
| She defeats her opponents. | The opponent to defeat. . . |
| They defeat their opponents. | The opponents to defeat. . . |

## DIFFERENT VERB FORMS

**4a** **Use the -s and -ed forms of the verb when required.**

Whenever the subject is (1) *he, she,* or *it,* (2) a singular noun, or (3) an indefinite pronoun such as *someone* or *anybody,* standard written English requires the *-s* ending on present-tense verbs: *she likes potato chips; he skips lunch; it rains occasionally; the dog wants to go out; everybody sits down.* Similarly, standard written English requires the *-ed* ending on the past tense and the past participle of all regular verbs used with these types of noun and pronoun subjects: *he skipped lunch; the dog wanted to go out.*

---

EXERCISE 4a
In the blanks in the following sentences and paragraph, supply the correct present tense form of the verbs given in parentheses. Then use each of the sentences as a model to construct a similar sentence of your own.

SENTENCE PRACTICE
1. My roommate always (disagree) _____ with me about what movies we should see; she (like) _____ horror films, but I hate scary movies.
2. Each week she (search) _____ the movie listings and then (ask) _____ me to go with her to see the latest gruesome film.
3. If someone (mention) _____ to my roommate that Stephen King has written a new novel, she then (wait) _____ eagerly for the novel to be made into a movie.
4. Whenever anyone (ask) _____ me to go to a horror movie, I try to say no, but my roommate always (insist) _____ on dragging me to see the latest movie.
5. As a result, I (go) _____ with her, but I (sit) _____ next to her and (keep) _____ my eyes closed while she (sit) _____ there and (enjoy) _____ every horrible minute.

PARAGRAPH PRACTICE

Every weekend during baseball season, my brother (go) _____ to the ballpark. During the winter he (watch) _____ old baseball movies. He (rent) _____ the movies at his local video store and (take) _____ them home. On Friday and Saturday nights, he (make) _____ popcorn and watches movies like *The Babe Ruth Story* and *The Pride of the Yankees,* which (be) _____ the story of Lou Gehrig. Another of his favorite baseball movies is *The Jackie Robinson Story,* which (star) _____ Jackie Robinson as himself.

**4b**   Select the correct principal part when using irregular verbs.

Because they form their past tense and past participle in an irregular way—a way other than the addition of regular verbs' -*d* or -*ed*—irregular verbs merit extra attention. (See Section **4,** "Kinds of Verbs," for further discussion of irregular verb forms.) Standard English requires the use of the correct irregular verb forms.

When in doubt about a verb form, check your dictionary. If at the verb's entry the dictionary lists only the plain form, the verb is regular and forms both its past tense and past participle by adding -*d* or -*ed*. If it lists only the plain form and one other form (*bend, bent,* for example), the verb is irregular and the second form is both the past tense and the past participle. If an irregular verb changes form in all three principal parts, the dictionary will list all three at the entry (for example, *begin, began, begun*).

The principal parts of many commonly used irregular verbs are listed below. When two forms are listed, both are acceptable, although the first form listed is preferred according to most dictionaries. Add to the list any other irregular verbs that you find troublesome.

| Present Infinitive (Plain Form) | Past Tense | Past Participle |
| --- | --- | --- |
| beat | beat | beaten |
| become | became | become |
| begin | began | begun |
| bet | bet | bet |
| bite | bit | bitten |
| blow | blew | blown |
| break | broke | broken |
| bring | brought | brought |
| burst | burst | burst |
| buy | bought | bought |
| catch | caught | caught |
| choose | chose | chosen |
| come | came | come |
| cut | cut | cut |
| dive | dived, dove | dived |

(*cont.*)

| | | |
|---|---|---|
| do | did | done |
| draw | drew | drawn |
| drink | drank | drunk |
| drive | drove | driven |
| eat | ate | eaten |
| fall | fell | fallen |
| feel | felt | felt |
| find | found | found |
| fly | flew | flown |
| forget | forgot | forgot, forgotten |
| forgive | forgave | forgiven |
| freeze | froze | frozen |
| get | got | got, gotten |
| give | gave | given |
| go | went | gone |
| grow | grew | grown |
| hang (suspend) | hung | hung |
| hang (execute) | hanged | hanged |
| hide | hid | hidden |
| hit | hit | hit |
| hurt | hurt | hurt |
| keep | kept | kept |
| know | knew | known |
| lead | led | led |
| leave | left | left |
| let | let | let |
| lose | lost | lost |
| make | made | made |
| mean | meant | meant |
| read | read | read |
| ride | rode | ridden |
| ring | rang | rung |
| rise | rose | risen |
| run | ran | run |
| see | saw | seen |
| shake | shook | shaken |
| shine (emit light) | shone | shone |
| shine (polish) | shined | shined |
| sink | sank, sunk | sunk |
| speak | spoke | spoken |
| spin | spun | spun |
| spring | sprang, sprung | sprung |
| stand | stood | stood |
| steal | stole | stolen |
| stink | stank | stunk |
| strike | struck | struck |
| swear | swore | sworn |
| swim | swam | swum |
| swing | swung | swung |
| take | took | taken |
| teach | taught | taught |

*(cont.)*

| tear | tore | torn |
| tell | told | told |
| think | thought | thought |
| throw | threw | thrown |
| wear | wore | worn |
| weave | wove, weaved | woven, weaved |
| weep | wept | wept |
| win | won | won |
| wind | wound | wound |
| write | wrote | written |

**4c**
*vb*

## EXERCISE 4b
In the blanks in the following sentences and paragraph, supply the correct forms of the verbs given in parentheses.

### SENTENCE PRACTICE
1. Last night the telephone (ring) _____ just as I was finishing my sociology paper.
2. I had (write) _____ everything but the conclusion when my friend called to ask if I'd like to get a pizza.
3. I should have (know) _____ that after I had (eat) _____ the pizza and (drink) _____ a beer, I wouldn't want to get back to work.
4. As a result, I (get) _____ up early this morning to finish the paper.
5. Getting up was hard, though, for I (feel) _____ as though I had not (get) _____ much sleep.

### PARAGRAPH PRACTICE
Earlier in the term, my sociology professor (give) _____ us some hints about doing research. She (draw) _____ a timetable on the board and suggested that we start our research early. I (forget) _____ that advice, so I had to work at the library all weekend, but now I have (catch) _____ up on my work at last. I just wish I hadn't (forget) _____ my professor's advice, for I (lose) _____ a lot of valuable research time. I wonder if I'm the only person in the class who (leave) _____ so much work until the last minute.

## 4c  Distinguish between *lie* and *lay*, *sit* and *set*.

These two pairs of irregular verbs are often bothersome. *Lie* and *sit* are always intransitive, which means that they cannot pass action to objects or occur in the passive voice. *Lay* and *set* are always transitive and therefore always must either have objects to receive their action or be in the passive. Although not always carefully observed in speech, the distinction between the verbs in the two pairs continues in written English and is important to communicating meaning precisely.

The principal parts of *lie*, meaning "recline," are *lie, lay, lain.* The principal parts of *lay*, meaning "place," are *lay, laid, laid.*

### LIE (INTRANSITIVE)

| | |
|---|---|
| PRESENT | *Lie* down for a while and you will feel better. |
| PAST | The cat *lay* in the shade and watched the dog carefully. |
| PRESENT PARTICIPLE | My keys were *lying* on the table where I dropped them. |
| PAST PARTICIPLE | After I *had lain* down for a while, I felt better. |

### LAY (TRANSITIVE)

| | |
|---|---|
| PRESENT | *Lay* the book on the table and leave. |
| PAST | He *laid* the book on the table and walked out the door. |
| PRESENT PARTICIPLE | *Laying* the book on the table, he walked out the door. |
| PAST PARTICIPLE | *Having laid* the book on the table, he walked out the door. |

The principal parts of *sit* (meaning "occupy a seat") are *sit, sat, sat;* the principal parts of *set* (meaning "put in place") are *set, set, set.*

### SIT (INTRANSITIVE)

| | |
|---|---|
| PRESENT | *Sit* down and keep quiet. |
| PAST | I *sat* in the corner for half an hour. |
| PRESENT PARTICIPLE | *Sitting* down angrily, I glared at my teacher. |
| PAST PARTICIPLE | *Having sat* in the corner for half an hour, I was subdued. |

### SET (TRANSITIVE)

| | |
|---|---|
| PRESENT | *Set* the basket on the table and close the door. |
| PAST | Yesterday he *set* the grocery cartons on the kitchen table; today he *set* them on the porch. |
| PRESENT PARTICIPLE | *Setting* her glasses on the table, she rubbed her tired eyes. |
| PAST PARTICIPLE | *Having set* his skis in the corner, he stooped to take off his boots. |

---

EXERCISE 4c
In sentences 1, 2, and 3, supply the correct form of *lie* or *lay* in the blanks. In sentences 4, 5, and 6, supply the correct form of *sit* or

*set*. Then write four sentences of your own, one each using a correct form of *sit, set, lie,* and *lay*.

**4d**

*vb*

1. The day was so hot that all I wanted to do was _____ in a hammock, drink lemonade, and read a book.
2. I had _____ my clippers on the grass when I _____ down.
3. If my neighbors had seen me _____ there, they would have thought I was lazy, so I _____ down my book and got up.
4. As I got up, I _____ my lemonade glass on the table and reached for the clippers.
5. When I looked around and saw my dog _____ in the shade, I felt jealous, for I would rather _____ under a cool tree than go back to my clipping and mowing.
6. I decided I needed to _____ down and think about what to do, so I _____ the clippers on the table and _____ and thought for the rest of the afternoon.

**4d**   The main verb in every sentence should be a finite verb.

Remember that only finite verbs or verb phrases can make assertions and serve as the main verbs of sentences. Nonfinite verb forms—infinitives *(to steal)*, present participles *(stealing)*, and past participles *(stolen)*—cannot serve as the main verbs of sentences unless they are accompanied by a helping verb. A group of words that has only a nonfinite verb will always be a sentence fragment. (See Section **6** for a full discussion of sentence fragments: see Section **4,** "Finite and Nonfinite Verbs," p. 43, for definitions.)

INCORRECT   When the pitcher wasn't looking, the runner stole third base. The crowd cheering wildly.

CORRECT   When the pitcher wasn't looking, the runner stole third base. The crowd cheered wildly.

EXERCISE 4a–c
In the blanks in the following sentences and paragraph, supply the correct form of the verb or verbs given in parentheses. Then use each of the sentences to construct a similar sentence of your own.

SENTENCE PRACTICE
1. Christopher Columbus (become) _____ the first European to (sit or set) _____ foot on Cuba when he discovered the island in 1492.
2. During the 1600s and 1700s, the number of people on the island (rise) _____ when immigrants from Spain (come) _____ to the island.

**4d**

**vb**

3. Cuba, which (lie or lay) _____ 90 miles south of Florida, (consist) _____ of the large island of Cuba as well as many small nearby islands.
4. Sugarcane, which (be) _____ Cuba's major crop today, has been (grow) _____ on the island for hundreds of years.
5. Today, Cuba's population (consist) _____ of people of Spanish, African, and Spanish-African descent, most of whom (speak) _____ Spanish.

**PARAGRAPH PRACTICE**

In the harbor of Havana, Cuba's capital, (lie or lay) _____ the U.S. battleship Maine; the ship (explode) _____ and (sink) _____ on February 15, 1898. Although experts never (determine) _____ the cause of the explosion, some American journalists (write) _____ stories blaming the Spanish. After the sinking of the Maine, the U.S. (ask) _____ the Spanish to withdraw from Cuba, but on April 24 Spain (declare) _____ war on the U.S. During the Spanish-American War, Theodore Roosevelt and his Rough Riders (win) _____ fame when they (ride) _____ up San Juan Hill. American troops captured the city of Santiago de Cuba on July 17, an event which (lead) _____ to the end of the war a month later.

## WRITERS REVISING: VERB FORMS

*(continued from page 39)*

Robin knows her main weakness in writing gramatically correct prose is verb form. She has to be vigilant about the third person singular verb, certain intransitive forms, and occasionally irregular forms. Armed with this knowledge, she revises her work carefully.

**Robin's Revision**

| | | |
|---|---|---|
| R 1 | The illness that ultimately ~~kill~~ *kills* Ivan Ilych | 4a |
| R 2 | ~~force~~ *forces* him to start thinking about his life. As | 4a |
| R 3 | he ~~lays~~ *lies* in his bed, he starts to ask why he was | 4c |
| R 4 | put on this earth. He ~~start~~ *starts* to ask why he must | 4a |
| R 5 | suffer this pain and why he ~~have~~ *has* to die. He | 4a |
| R 6 | ~~pondering~~ *ponders* his reasons for doing what he has | 4d |
| R 7 | done in his life. At this point, he has ~~sank~~ *sunk* in | 4b |
| R 8 | pain and just ~~want~~ *wants* Gerasim to ~~set~~ *sit* by his bed. | 4a, 4c |

> **Analysis**
>
>
> Robin recognized that the singular noun subject *illness* requires the *-s* form of the verb *forces* (line R2). Likewise, *kills* (R1) must agree with the singular subject because the subject of its clause, *that*, has *illness* as its antecedent. In line R3, Robin changed *lays* to *lies* when she realized that the verb is intransitive, having no object and meaning "to recline" in this sentence. *Start* in line R4 requires the *-s* form to make it agree with the third-person singular pronoun *he;* similarly, *has,* the *-s* form of the verb *have,* is needed to match *he* in line R5. Robin saw that she had written the participle *pondering,* a nonfinite verb form, instead of the finite form, *ponders,* in line R6. The final sentence of the revision needs the correct form of the past participle for the irregular verb *has sunk* and the addition of the *-s* form *wants* to agree with the third-person pronoun subject *he.* Finally, Robin changed *set* to *sit* (R8) to reflect her meaning, "to occupy a seat."

# 5

## *VERBS: TENSE, VOICE, AND MOOD*

The form of a verb or verb phrase tells us three things about the action or state it names. It tells what time the action occurs (tense); whether the subject is performing the action or receiving it (voice); and what the attitude of the speaker or writer is (mood).

> ### WRITERS REVISING: VERB TENSE, VOICE, MOOD
>
> Phil wrote the following rough draft as he was doing library research for a short paper on the etymology (history) of a common word. He knew the draft had a number of errors in verb usage and more verbs in the passive voice than necessary, but at the time he was primarily interested in recording information. As you work through this section, revise the verb usage, and then compare your version to Phil's version at the end of Section 5.
>
> **Draft**
>
> D 1    Although Americans are making blue jeans an
>
> D 2    international fashion, they were not the first on the

D 3    "blue jean scene." Centuries ago, heavy cotton

D 4    cloth called <u>genes</u> was wove in Genoa, Italy.

D 5    Henry VIII buys a large shipment of the cloth for

D 6    his royal household. <u>Genes</u> is French for Genoa,

D 7    and French immigrants bring the cloth to America.

D 8        The word <u>dungarees</u> comes from Dhunga, India,

D 9    where during the fifteenth century work pants were

D10    made from cloth that was wove in Nimes, France.

D11    About the same time, the cloth is imported by the

D12    English and the name <u>serge de Nimes</u> (cloth of

D13    Nimes) is shortened to <u>denim</u>.

This *Writers Revising* continues on page 61.

# TENSE

**Tense** is the time of the action or state expressed by the verb. Almost all verbs show the difference between **present** and **past** time by a change in the verb form. All verbs show **future** time by using *shall* or *will* before the infinitive, or plain form, of the verb.

| Tense | Regular Verb | Irregular Verb |
|---|---|---|
| PRESENT | She walks today. | The sun rises today. |
| PAST | She walked yesterday. | The sun rose yesterday. |
| FUTURE | She will walk tomorrow. | The sun will rise tomorrow. |

A few verbs have only one form for both present and past time: *set, burst, cast, hurt, split.* By themselves these verbs cannot show time; to do so, they must depend entirely on modifying words (*I split wood yesterday*) or auxiliary verbs (*I was splitting the wood*).

In addition to past, present, and future tenses that indicate the natural divisions of time, all verbs have three **perfect tenses:** present perfect, past perfect, and future perfect. The perfect tenses indicate that action is completed or finished before a given point in time. They are formed by using the forms of the auxiliary *have* before the past participle of the main verb: *He <u>had eaten</u> before his sister came home.*

The six tenses, together with the way each is formed, are summarized in the following table:

| Tense | How Formed | Example |
|---|---|---|
| PRESENT | Plain form of verb with *I, we, you, they,* and all plural nouns; -s forms of verbs with *he, she, it,* and all singular nouns | I, we, you, they, the men *eat*<br><br>he, she, it, the man *eats* |
| PAST | Plain form plus -*ed* in regular verbs; internal change in irregular verbs | she, they *talked*<br><br>she, they *ate* |
| FUTURE | *Shall* or *will* before plain form of verb | he, they *will talk/shall eat* |
| PRESENT PERFECT | *Have* before past participle; *has* with *he, she, it,* and singular nouns | we, you, they, the men *have talked/have eaten*<br>he, she, it, the man *has talked/has eaten* |
| PAST PERFECT | *Had* before past participle | she, they *had talked/had eaten* |
| FUTURE PERFECT | *Shall/will have* before past participle | he, they *will have talked/will have eaten* |

All six tenses can have **progressive tense** forms. These progressive forms indicate that the action named is continuing (in progress) at the time indicated. They are made by using the forms of the auxiliary verb *be* with the -*ing* form of the main verb *(is giving, was winning, have been going).*

The most common uses of the tenses of the active verb forms are as follows:

| Tense | Use | Example |
|---|---|---|
| PRESENT | Expressing a present or habitual action | He *is talking* to the students now. He *talks* to the students at least once every year. |
| PAST | Expressing an action that was completed in the past | He *talked* to the students yesterday. |
| FUTURE | Expressing an action yet to come | He *will talk* to the students tomorrow. |
| PRESENT PERFECT | Usually expressing an action carried out before the present and completed at the present; sometimes expressing an action begun in the past and continuing in the present | He *has talked* to the students before. [Action carried out before the present and now completed]<br><br>He *has* always *talked* to the students. [Action begun in the past and continuing in the present] |

| PAST PERFECT | Expressing a past action completed before some other past action | This morning I saw the speaker who *had talked* to the students last month. |
| FUTURE PERFECT | Expressing an action that will be completed before some future time | He *will have talked* to the students before next Thursday. |

For a full synopsis of a regular and an irregular verb, see *conjugation* in the Glossary of Grammatical Terms, p. 600.

## WORKING WITH TENSE

In spite of the relatively complicated tense system, writers whose native language is English ordinarily have few problems with its use. The main problems that occur involve either special uses of the present tense or the choice of the appropriate tense in the subordinate clauses of some complex sentences.

**5a**  Use the present tense to express general truths or accepted facts and to indicate habitual action. Use the present tense in critical writing about literature, arts, and sciences.

| GENERAL TRUTHS | All that glitters *is* not gold. |
| | Corn *grows* rapidly in warm, humid weather. |
| HABITUAL ACTION | The old man *exercises* daily. |
| | The bank *closes* at four o'clock. |
| CRITICAL WRITING | In Dickens' novel, David's harsh stepfather *sends* him to London, where every day David *works* in a warehouse pasting labels on bottles. |
| | Jonas Salk's discovery of a polio vaccine *is* one of the great discoveries of the twentieth century. |

Note that the present tense is also often used in sentences that express future action, as in *Our trip begins tomorrow.*

**5b**  Place the tenses of verbs in appropriate sequence.

The term **tense sequence** refers to the relation of the times expressed by the verbs in main and subordinate clauses in a complex sentence. When the verb in the main clause of a complex sentence is in any tense except the past or past perfect (*had talked*), the verb in the subordinate clause will be in whatever tense the meaning requires.

The weather service *predicts* that it *will be* hot again tomorrow. [The prediction occurs in the present but refers to the future.]

Our friends *will* not *know* that we *were* here unless we *leave* them a note. [Future, past, present]

If the verb in a main clause is in the past or past perfect tense, the verb in a subordinate clause following it will usually be in the past or past perfect tense, unless the subordinate clause states a general truth.

You *said* that you *wanted* [not *want*] to live in an apartment.
I *thought* that I *had left* my coat in the car.
The owners *discovered* later that the fire *had destroyed* their house. [The destruction of the house occurred at a time before the owner's discovery of it.]

BUT   The child *discovered* painfully that fire *burns*. [Here *fire burns* states a general truth. Thus the verb is in the present even though the child's discovery occurred in the past.]

---

EXERCISE 5a–b
In the following sentences and paragraph, choose the verb form in parentheses that is in appropriate tense sequence. Be prepared to explain your choices. Do any of the sentences have more than one possible answer?

### SENTENCE PRACTICE
1. Tropical rain forests (affect, affected) our lives in many ways.
2. Tropical rain forests (contain, contained) 40 to 50 percent of all species of life on earth, even though these rain forests (cover, covered) only 6 to 7 percent of the earth's surface.
3. The author of a recent article about ecology (states, stated) that if we (act, acted) now, we can preserve these valuable rain forests.
4. When I went to the drugstore to have a prescription filled, my pharmacist (tells, told) me that tropical rain forests (supply, supplied) the sources for many medicines.
5. Tropical rain forests (play, played) a part in climate control, and they (are, were) also sources of food and timber.

### PARAGRAPH PRACTICE
I recently learned that my community (has, had) a trash recycling program; as a result, I now (separate, separated) my trash into recyclable categories. Because glass and metal do not decompose rapidly, recycling these materials (reduces, reduced) the amount of solid waste at our trash dumps. When I took a walk around my neighborhood, I (realize, realized) that every week people (throw, threw) away trash that could easily be recycled. However, I've also learned that some people (think, thought) that recycling trash (is, was) too much work. For instance, when I talked to my neighbor, she (tells, told) me that recycling (is, was) too much trouble.

**5c**

*t*

**5c**  Use present infinitives and participles to express action occurring at the same time as or later than that of the main verb. Use perfect infinitives and past or perfect participles to express action earlier than that of the main verb.

The infinitive and participle forms are as follows:

|  | *Infinitives* | *Participles* |
|---|---|---|
| PRESENT | to begin | beginning |
| PAST | — | begun |
| PERFECT | to have begun | having begun |

Infinitives and participles express only a time that is relative to the time indicated by the main verb of the sentence in which they are used. A present infinitive or participle expresses an action occurring at the same time as or later than that indicated by the main verb. A perfect infinitive or a past or perfect participle expresses a time that is earlier than that indicated by the main verb.

She *wants* [*wanted, had wanted, will want*] *to study* law. [The present infinitive *to study* indicates the same time or time later than that of the main verb *want*.]

She *would have* preferred *to study* [not *to have studied*] law. [The present infinitive *to study* indicates that studying law would occur at the same time or a later time than the expression of her preference.]

She *was* [*is, will be*] glad *to have studied* law. She would like *to have studied* law. [The perfect infinitive *to have studied* indicates that the study occurred earlier than the time indicated by the main verbs *was, is, will be,* or *would like*.]

*Wanting* to study law, she *works* [*worked, had worked, will work*] hard. [The present participle *wanting* indicates the same time or a time later than that of the main verb.]

*Having passed* the entrance exam, she *is celebrating* [*has celebrated, will celebrate*]. [The perfect participle *having passed* indicates that passing the exam occurs before the celebrating.]

*Defeated* in the election, the candidate *retired* [*has retired, had retired, will retire*] from politics. [The past participle *defeated* indicates that the defeat occurred before the time indicated by the main verb *retire*.]

---

**EXERCISE 5c**
In the following sentences and paragraph, choose the infinitive or participle form that is in appropriate sequence. Be prepared to explain your choices. Do any of the sentences have more than one possible answer?

**SENTENCE PRACTICE**

1. I made plans (to go, to have gone) on a trek through a remote and rough area of the Rockies.
2. (Realizing, Having realized) that I may not be in shape for such a trip, I started a conditioning program.
3. I want (to avoid, to have avoided) injury, so a good conditioning program should help me (to prepare, to have prepared) for the trek.
4. After (doing, having done) a lot of research, I realize that the best way (to start, to have started) my program is to climb hills.
5. (Completing, Having completed) my research, I'm ready to start climbing.

**PARAGRAPH PRACTICE**

(After climbing, Having climbed) to altitudes of 8,000 feet or more, many people suffer from altitude sickness. Thus, climbers need (to be, to have been) aware of the symptoms of altitude sickness, symptoms such as headache, nausea, appetite loss, and lethargy. Climbers need (to recognize, to have recognized) these symptoms of altitude sickness, for extreme cases can lead to hallucinations, coma, and death.

---

# VOICE

Voice shows whether the subject performs or receives the action named by the verb. When the subject performs the action, the verb is in the **active voice.** When it receives the action, the verb is in the **passive voice.**

ACTIVE    The elephant *dragged* its trainer.
          The poison *drove* its victim mad.

PASSIVE   The trainer *was dragged* by the elephant.
          The victim *was driven* mad by the poison.

The passive voice is formed by using the appropriate form of the verb *be (am, is, are, was, were, been, being)* with the past participle of the main verb: *was driven, will have been driven, is being driven.* Note that although the passive verb phrase may include other auxiliaries, some form of the verb *be* must always come immediately before the past participle of the main verb.

Only **transitive verbs,** that is, verbs that can take an object, can show both active and passive voices. We can say *The student wrote the paper* or *The paper was written by the student,* but only *He slept,* not *He was slept.*

**5d**   Use the active voice verbs in most situations.

Most written sentences use verbs in the active voice, which is almost always more direct, more economical, and more forceful than the passive (see Sections **33f** and **38a**).

> PASSIVE   The lead role *was played* by the famous British actor, Laurence Olivier.
>
> ACTIVE   Laurence Olivier, the famous British actor, played the lead role.

But in two situations, explained below, the passive voice is both useful and natural.

**5e**   Use the passive voice when the actor is not known.

Consider the following:

> The southside branch of City National Bank was robbed at gunpoint this morning just after ten o'clock.
> The play was first performed in 1591.

The writer of the first of these sentences, presumably not knowing who robbed the bank, was forced to use the passive voice. The only alternative would have been a much less economical construction such as *A person or persons unknown robbed the southside branch.* . . . The second sentence might be written when a record of a play's performance, but not its performers, exists. Otherwise, the sentence might have been written *The Lord Chamberlain's Company first performed the play in 1591.*

**5f**   Use the passive voice when the receiver of the action is more important than the actor.

Consider the following:

> The new bridge was completed in April.
> The experiment was finished on June 16; on June 17 the conclusions were reviewed by the advisory board and reported immediately to the Pentagon.

In these sentences, the writer has focused on the bridge and the experiment rather than on who completed the bridge or who performed the experiment and reported the results.

Problems in the use of voice include awkward and ineffective shifts from one voice to another (see **10a**), and the unnecessary or weak use of the passive (see **38a**).

# MOOD

The mood of a verb indicates whether the speaker or writer regards the action named by the verb as a fact, as a command, or as a wish, request, or condition contrary to fact.

English has three moods: the **indicative,** used for ordinary statements and questions *(He is happy, Is he happy)*; the **imperative,** used for commands *(Be happy)*; and the **subjunctive,** used to express conditions contrary to fact *(If he were happy)* and in clauses following certain verbs. Except for the subjunctive, writers have few problems with mood.

Special forms for the subjunctive have almost disappeared from modern English. The few that do survive are those that appear in *if* clauses expressing unreal conditions; in *that* clauses after verbs expressing requests, recommendations, and demands; and in a few formal idioms.

**5g**    Use the subjunctive to express conditions contrary to fact.

The subjunctive form uses the plain form of the verb (without the *s*), *have* instead of *has*, and *were* or *be* instead of *is, are, was,* or *am.*

> If the rose bush *were* healthy, it would have more buds. [The bush is not healthy.]
>
> Last year, the bush looked as though it *were* going to die. [But it didn't die.]
>
> We prayed that his speech *be* brief. [But it wasn't.]

Note that not all clauses beginning with *if* automatically express a condition contrary to fact.

> If my experiment is successful, I will prove my point. [Here the clause beginning with *if* merely states a condition that, if met, will prove the point.]

**5h**    Use the subjunctive in *that* clauses after verbs expressing wishes, commands, requests, or recommendations.

> I wish I *were* in Rome. [*that* unexpressed]
> The law requires that there *be* a prompt trial.
> I move that the meeting *be* adjourned.
> Resolved, that the auditor *examine* our books.
> The reporter asked that she *repeat* her last reply.

**5i**   **Use the subjunctive in a few surviving idioms.**

Far be it from me.      Long live the Republic!
Suffice it to say.      Come what may.
Heaven help us!         Be that as it may.

Note that except in surviving idioms even the few remaining uses of the subjunctive observed above are often replaced in speech and informal writing by alternative forms. Compare *I wish I was in Rome, The law requires a prompt trial,* or *The reporter asked her to repeat her last reply* with the examples above **(5h)**. In more formal writing, the subjunctive remains quite firm.

---

EXERCISE 5g–i

In the sentences in the following paragraph, choose the appropriate verb form. Be prepared to explain your choices.

Instead of sitting here listening to an economics lecture, I wish I (was, were) lying on the beach. While lying there on the beach, I would request of my friends that I (am, be) left alone to read and relax. If I (was, were) on my ideal stretch of beach, I'd also have palm trees to shade me from the sun and soft breezes to cool me. While I was sitting there daydreaming about my beach, my instructor called my name and recommended that I (pay, paid) more attention in class. I guess I'd better forget about my beach for a while, since my instructor also requested that I (am, be) the person who explains the concept of laissez-faire in class tomorrow.

---

EXERCISE 5a–i

In each of the following sentences, choose the correct form of the verbs, infinitives, or participles from each of the pairs given in parentheses. Do any of the sentences have more than one possible answer? Use each of these sentences as a model to construct a similar sentence of your own.

SENTENCE PRACTICE

1. (Having become, Becoming) interested in astronomy, I wish that I (saw, had seen) the lunar eclipse last week.
2. If I (was, were) a professional astronomer, I could (observe, have observed) the eclipse from an observatory.
3. Last week's eclipse was (to begin, to have begun) at midnight.
4. My friend who stayed up to see the eclipse said that she would (choose, have chosen) (to see, to have seen) a solar eclipse instead.
5. After (seeing, having seen) both types of eclipses, most people say that they (believe, believed) solar eclipses are more spectacular than lunar eclipses.

In the following paragraph, revise the sentences to change the active voice to the passive and the passive voice to the active. Do not change tense in changing verbs. Then determine whether each sentence is improved when you make this change.

PARAGRAPH PRACTICE

The Palomar Observatory in California was visited by my astronomy class. The California Institute of Technology operates the observatory. The members of the class were fascinated by the observatory's major instrument, the Hale reflector. A 48-inch camera telescope is included as a part of the Hale reflector. The camera telescope took photographs of the sky. These photographs were made into a huge photographic atlas.

**5i**

*t*

---

≋ **WRITERS REVISING: VERB TENSE, VOICE, MOOD** *(continued from page 51)*

The rough draft shows a common problem—what verb tense to use when the subject being discussed is historical but has current effects. Is the action past but completed, past but continuing, habitual, or expressing a general truth? These are some of the issues Phil tried to resolve in his second draft.

**Phil's Revision**

R 1   Although Americans ~~are making~~ *have made* blue jeans an

R 2   international fashion, they were not the first on

R 3   the "blue jean scene." Centuries ago, heavy cotton

R 4   cloth called genes was ~~wove~~ *woven* in Genoa, Italy. Henry   **4b**

R 5   VIII ~~buys~~ *bought* a large shipment of the cloth for his

R 6   royal household. Genes is French for Genoa, and   **5a**

R 7   French immigrants ~~bring~~ *brought* the cloth to America.

R 8   The word dungarees ~~comes~~ *came* from Dhunga, India,

R 9   where during the fifteenth century work pants were

R10   made from cloth that was ~~wove~~ *woven* in Nimes, France.   **4b**

R11   About the same time, *the English* the cloth ~~is imported by the~~   **5d**

R12   ~~English~~ and the name serge de Nimes (cloth of

R13   Nimes) ~~is shortened~~ to denim.   **5d**

**Analysis**

Blue jeans are already an international fashion: the action of the opening clause is completed, so *have made* is required rather than *are making*. The principal parts of *wove* (lines R4 and R10) are like *freeze, froze, frozen*—not like *get, got, got*. The event described in the third sentence was completed in the past; hence, the use of past tense *bought* is correct, rather than *buys* in the present tense picked up directly from the student's notes.

In the first clause of the fourth sentence (line R6), the present-tense *is* is correct because it states a continuing general truth. *Brought*, the verb in the second clause (line R7), must be in the past tense to show completed past action. Unlike the opening clause in the fourth sentence (line R6), which expresses a continuing general truth, the action expressed in the opening main clause of the fifth sentence (line R8) is completed. The situations described in the two clauses seem similar but are not.

There is no compelling reason for the use of the passive voice (lines D11 and D12). Also, in the revision (lines R11–R13) the "notetaking" present tense has been replaced by past-tense verbs that correctly signal completed past action.

---

## REVIEW EXERCISE: BASIC GRAMMAR (Sections 1–5)

### PART A
In the following sentences, first identify the basic sentence pattern used (see pp. 7–9); then go back to the sentences and identify the adjectives, adverbs, prepositions, coordinating conjunctions, and subordinating conjunctions.

1. I recently took a ride in a hot-air balloon.
2. Passengers in hot-air balloons drift quietly over fields and rivers.
3. Ballooning is a relaxing way of traveling.
4. The balloon pilot told me the history of hot-air ballooning.
5. The hot-air balloon was invented by two Frenchmen.

### PART B
In the following sentences, identify all phrases—prepositional, infinitive, gerund, or participial; then go back to the sentences and underline each main clause once and each subordinate clause twice; finally, identify each sentence as simple, compound, complex, or compound-complex.

1. Hot-air balloon flights take place in early morning or late afternoon when winds are light.
2. First, a fan fills the balloon with cold air; next a burner, fueled by propane gas, heats the air in the balloon.
3. As the air in the balloon becomes hotter, the balloon becomes bouyant and begins to rise.
4. The balloon pilot can control the altitude of the balloon by heating or cooling the air in the balloon.
5. Even though balloon pilots can control altitude, they cannot control direction, so balloon passengers go where the winds take them.

## PART C

In the following sentences and paragraph, correct in accordance with formal written usage any errors in the use of pronouns, adjectives, adverbs, or verbs.

**5i**

*t*

### SENTENCE PRACTICE

1. George Washington Ferris, whom was an engineer from Pittsburgh, invent the Ferris wheel in 1893.
2. Ferris designs the wheel for the 1893 World's Columbian Exposition in Chicago, and the wheel was the colossolest structure many people had ever saw.
3. The hub of the original Ferris wheel weighed more than seventy tons, making it the larger single piece of steel that had been forged up to that time.
4. Whomever rode on the original Ferris wheel gotten a twenty-minute ride and a view of Lake Michigan.
5. The Chicago Exposition closing, it took workers twelve weeks to have dismantled the giant Ferris wheel.

### PARAGRAPH PRACTICE

I asked my little brother if him and his friends would like to go to the amusement park with my friend and I. My brother said yes quick because he love to ride on roller coasters. My little brother like roller coasters more good than me, for I get scared easy, and I sure don't like being upside down when I'm riding. However, people like my brother seem to love screaming loud as they go up steep inclines and then rapid drop down again. If I was them, I'd get sick because some roller coasters race along the dips and curves at seventy miles an hour. If that doesn't make me feel badly enough, amusement park owners keep building even frighteninger roller coasters; it seems like every week someone advertises the most longest and fastest roller coaster in the world. Anybody whom thinks I'm going to get on one of them roller coasters is crazy. While my brother and his friends spent the afternoon on the roller coaster, I'm going to ride the merry-go-round. I'll sure be the safer of the people at the amusement park.

# COMMON
# SENTENCE
# FAULTS

*sen flt*

*Will [Strunk] felt that the reader was in serious trouble most of the time, a man
floundering in a swamp, and that it was the duty of anyone attempting to write
English to drain this swamp quickly and get his man up on dry ground, or at
least throw him a rope.*

E.B. WHITE, "Introduction to *The Elements of Style*"

**6**

*frag*

$R$eaders have expectations about how sentences should be constructed, expectations based on the system by which our language operates. When you violate this system, you violate your readers' expectations and ask them to work much too hard to understand your meaning—if it can be understood at all. If you want your writing to be understood, you must consider your readers' expectations regarding English grammar.

## WRITERS REVISING: SENTENCE FAULTS

Sentence fragments, comma splices, and fused (run-together) sentences all have one thing in common: a writer's failure to mark accurately for readers the fundamental unit of meaning—a complete thought.

Fran, the student intern at the college placement office, received the following draft of an article for the placement newsletter. The newsletter was due at the printer's that afternoon, and the author of the article was already on her way home for Christmas vacation. Fran had a major editing task ahead of her, one that required interpretation of some badly garbled and incomplete sentences.

As you work through Sections **6** and **7,** see if you can revise the draft, fixing the sentence faults so that the meaning is untangled. Then compare the choices you made with those Fran made as she reworked the article. Her revision appears at the end of Section **7.**

**Draft**

```
                    Leave No Stone Unturned

D 1          These next few months will be crucial.  For

D 2     many students in their search for that first job.

D 3     And despite feelings of despair when considering

D 4     the task that lies ahead, there is a place to

D 5     start.  And a definite path to follow in finding

D 6     the right employer.

D 7          You will find that opportunities do exist.
```

D 8    If you know where to look when looking you should

D 9    leave no stone unturned.  The following are

D10    invaluable sources of help.  Your college

D11    placement office.  It is not only for the

D12    graduating senior, it also offers opportunities

D13    and services for the student who is seeking a

D14    summer internship.  Keep in touch with your

D15    placement counselor.  Also your professors and

D16    department heads, they may prove to be the perfect

D17    contacts for job seekers.

This *Writers Revising* continues on page 77.

6

*frag*

# 6

## SENTENCE FRAGMENT

The usual sentence contains a subject and a verb and at least one independent clause. In writing, we indicate sentences by capitalizing the first word and placing appropriate end punctuation, usually a period, after the last. Any group of words that is set off as a sentence but that lacks a subject, a verb, or an independent clause is a **sentence fragment.**

| | |
|---|---|
| SENTENCE | No thank you. |
| FRAGMENTS | Before we could get there. |
| | Not without a fight. |

Such fragments are common in speech, and they are sometimes used for certain special purposes in writing. But in most writing, the subject-verb sentence is what readers expect, and they will want some special effectiveness if that expectation is not met.

### 6a  Do not punctuate phrases, dependent clauses, and other fragments as sentences.

A fragment is usually an improperly punctuated phrase or dependent clause that is part of the sentence that precedes or follows it.

Thus the fragment can almost always be revised by joining it to that sentence, although other revisions may be possible and sometimes desirable. The most common types of fragments, together with revisions, are illustrated on the following pages.

**6a**

*frag*

**1. Prepositional phrase.** Prepositional phrases consist of a preposition, its object, and any modifiers of the object: *over the mountains, during the long intermission, after eating dinner.* Prepositional phrases usually serve as modifiers. (See **1c.**) The prepositional phrases in the following examples are italicized.

FRAGMENT    For as long as there have been cities, there have been parks. *For the enjoyment of city dwellers.*

REVISED    For as long as there have been cities, there have been parks *for the enjoyment of city dwellers.*

FRAGMENT    Initially parks were for the people in the houses surrounding them. *Not for the city or town as a whole.*

REVISED    Initially parks were for the people in the houses surrounding them, *not for the city or town as a whole.*

Initially parks were for the people in the houses surrounding them—*not for the city or town as a whole.* [Here both revisions join the prepositional phrase introduced by *for* with the main statement, to which it clearly belongs. The dash gives greater emphasis to the phrase. See **23b.**]

**2. Verbal phrase.** Verbal phrases consist of a verbal (infinitive, participle, or gerund), its object, and any modifiers of the object or verbal. (See **1c.**) The verbal phrases in the following examples are italicized.

FRAGMENT    Architects and developers planned urban parks carefully. *To mix the advantages of city and country living.* [Infinitive phrase]

REVISED    Architects and developers planned urban parks carefully *to mix the advantages of city and country living.*

FRAGMENT    Designers borrowed ideas from fashionable country estates. *Featuring elaborate gardens, artificial lakes, and beautiful vistas.* [Participial phrase]

REVISED    Designers borrowed ideas from fashionable country estates *featuring elaborate gardens, artificial lakes, and beautiful vistas.*

FRAGMENT    American parks frequently were designed on British models. *Being patterned after famous London parks.* [Participial phrase]

REVISED    American parks frequently were designed on British models, *being patterned after famous London parks.*

American parks frequently were designed on British models; in fact, some were patterned after famous London parks. [This second revision changes the participial phrase *(being patterned. . .)* to an independent clause. Consequently, the two sentences could be separated by a period, but the semicolon suggests the close relationship between the ideas expressed by the clauses. See **21b.**]

**6a**

***frag***

**3. Subordinate clause.** Subordinate clauses are usually introduced by such subordinating conjunctions as *after, although, because, when, where, while,* or *until* or by a relative pronoun such as *who, which,* or *that.* Subordinate clauses that occur as fragments are almost always modifiers, which properly belong with the preceding or following sentence. (See **1d.**) Subordinate clauses in the following examples are italicized.

FRAGMENT    Wealthy English landowners preferred planned parks to nature's own landscaping. *Which was considered too wild and untamed.*

REVISED    Wealthy English landowners preferred planned parks to nature's own landscaping, *which was considered too wild and untamed.*

FRAGMENT    Regent's Park in London has historical importance. *Because it showed how a large park could be developed within a major city.*

REVISED    Regent's Park in London has historical importance, *because it showed how a large park could be developed within a major city.*

Regent's Park in London has historical importance; *it showed how a large park could be developed within a major city.* [Here the fragment has been made into an independent clause by dropping the subordinating conjunction *because,* but the close relationship of the second clause to the first is suggested by separating the two with a semicolon rather than a period.]

FRAGMENT    Planners intended New York City's Central Park for everyone's enjoyment. *Although mainly the wealthy used its footpaths and carriageways at first.*

REVISED    *Although mainly the wealthy used its footpaths and carriageways at first,* planners intended New York City's Central Park for everyone's enjoyment.

**4. Appositives.** Appositives are words or phrases that rename or explain a noun or a pronoun standing immediately before them. The appositives in the following examples are italicized.

FRAGMENT    Central Park was laid out by F. L. Olmsted. *The same landscape architect who later designed the 1893 World Exposition in Chicago.*

**6a**

**frag**

REVISED    Central Park was laid out by F. L. Olmsted, *the same landscape architect who later designed the 1893 World Exposition in Chicago.*

REVISED    Central Park was laid out by F. L. Olmsted. He was the same landscape architect who later designed the 1893 World Exposition in Chicago. [Here the fragment has been made into an independent clause by adding a subject and a verb. This revision gives greater emphasis to his designing the Chicago exhibition by placing that information in a separate statement.]

FRAGMENT    The Exposition grounds formed one of Chicago's large parks. *Jackson Park along the Lake Michigan shore.*

REVISED    The Exposition grounds formed one of Chicago's large parks, *Jackson Park along the Lake Michigan shore.*

The Exposition grounds formed one of Chicago's large parks—*Jackson Park along the Lake Michigan shore.* [Here the dash rather than the comma gives greater emphasis to what follows. See **23b**.]

FRAGMENT    Both Central Park and Jackson Park were built on seemingly unusable land. *The first being built on garbage-strewn squatters' grounds, the second being dredged from a marshy swamp.*

REVISED    Both Central Park and Jackson Park were built on seemingly unusable land, *the first being built on garbage-strewn squatters' grounds, the second being dredged from a marshy swamp.*

Both Central Park and Jackson Park were built on seemingly unusable land. Central Park was built on garbage-strewn squatters' grounds, and Jackson Park was dredged from a marshy swamp.

## 5. Other fragments.

FRAGMENT    New York City's Parks Department has created fifteen "quiet zones" at city parks and beaches. *And declared them off-limits for radio and tape-deck playing.*

REVISED    New York City's Parks Department has created fifteen "quiet zones" at city parks and beaches and declared them off-limits for radio and tape-deck playing. [Here the fragment is the second half of a compound predicate: *has created . . . and declared. . . .*]

FRAGMENT    The mayor designated some parts of parks for noisy recreation. *But other parts for quiet enjoyment of nature.*

REVISED    The mayor designated some parts of parks for noisy recreation *but other parts for quiet enjoyment of nature.* [Here the fragment is the second part of a compound direct object of the verb *designated.*]

FRAGMENT    *Earphones only.* Music lovers without them may be fined, and their radios may be impounded.

REVISED    *Radios may be played with earphones only.* Music lovers without them may be fined, and their radios may be impounded. [This unusual fragment needs both a subject and a verb. It probably results from a command (*You must use earphones*) and is similar to such phrases as "Nonsmokers only."]

**6b**

*frag*

## 6b  Recognize acceptable incomplete sentences.

Exclamations, commands, and requests have no expressed subject; the subject *you* is always understood. Such sentences as the following are standard sentence patterns rather than incomplete sentences. (See **1a.**)

Look out!                 Let the buyer beware!

Close the door.         Please pass the spinach.

Incomplete sentences are common in the questions and answers of speech and in written dialogue, which imitates speech.

"Where do we go tonight?"
"To the movies."
"When?"
"In about an hour."

In most writing, except for the standard sentence patterns of exclamations and commands, incomplete sentences appear only in the following special situations.

**1. Transitional phrases and a few familiar expressions.** Sometimes experienced writers indicate the conclusion of one topic and the turning to another by using incomplete sentences.

So much for my first point. Now for my second.

In addition, a few familiar expressions such as *The quicker, the better* and *The more, the merrier* occur as incomplete sentences.

**2. Answers to rhetorical questions.** A rhetorical question is one to which the answer is obvious or one that the asker of the question intends to answer. Experienced writers sometimes follow such questions with incomplete sentences.

How much does welfare do for the poor? Not enough.
Who is to blame for accidents caused by drunk drivers? The drivers, always.

**3. Experienced writers sometimes use incomplete sentences for special purposes.** Writers sometimes write verbless sentences deliberately. Intentional fragments can convey emphasis or a sense of the writer's "talking" directly to the reader. They can also be used to create special effects such as haste, suspense, anger, and so forth.

**6b**

*frag*

> I watch the cars go by for a while on the highway. Something lonely about them. Not lonely—worse. Nothing. Like the attendant's expression when he filled the tank. Nothing. A nothing curb by some nothing gravel, at a nothing intersection, going nowhere.
>
> ROBERT M. PIRSIG, *Zen and the Art of Motorcycle Maintenance*

> Every day the farmers raised their eyes to the blazing blue sky. Every day, the same message. No rain.
>
> *Student Essay*

Here is a writer's description of a 400-pound wild boar, found abandoned in the woods as a piglet and raised by an animal-loving family to be a house-broken, leash-trained, affectionate pet:

> I had second thoughts as soon as I saw Unkie. He was a nightmare on the hoof. Massive. Shaped like a World War II tank. A head as big as a beer keg. His grunting sounded like thunder in a bucket and his tusks looked like ivory daggers. "Don't worry, he *loves* visitors," the owners assured me.
>
> JAMES TAYLOR, *Smithsonian*

---

**EXERCISE 6(1)**
In the following sentences and paragraph, eliminate fragments by combining them with a main clause or by making the fragments into complete sentences.

**SENTENCE PRACTICE**
1. In recent years. Statistics show that cats probably outnumber dogs as the most common pets in the United States. Although in the past more people owned dogs than owned cats.
2. For people who live in the city or who are gone all day. A cat can be the ideal pet.
3. Because cats never have to be walked or let outside. These independent creatures can spend the day alone in an apartment.
4. Cats are interesting pets. Being sensitive to the moods of their owners.
5. Cats often have distinct personalities. And may get angry when they seem to be ignored.
6. Researchers have found that cats seem to fall into three basic personality types. The social cat, the shy cat, and the aggressive cat.
7. To help a newly acquired kitten become more comfortable around people. Owners should handle the kitten gently and speak to it frequently.
8. Cats sometimes develop an array of annoying habits. Like clawing the best chair in the house or waking up their owners at three in the morning.

9. Cats can also be stubborn. As any owner knows who has ever had a cat that liked to scratch furniture.
10. Although many people treat their cat as if it had human characteristics. Cat owners need to remember that the cat is an animal. Not another human.

### PARAGRAPH PRACTICE

Over the years, cats seem to have been invested with suprising qualities. Such as having nine lives and always being able to land on their feet. There may be some truth in the idea that cats always land on their feet. Because cats have extraordinary balancing abilities. Also, when they fall from a high place. Cats can often twist themselves around in the air. And land on their feet. As for having nine lives. Most cat owners would rather not have to check the accuracy of that old saying.

---

### EXERCISE 6(2)

In the following paragraph, eliminate fragments by combining them with a main clause or by making the fragments into complete sentences.

The stress associated with our fast-paced and busy lives affects practically everyone. From students to chief executives of large corporations. Stress is not always bad for people, but it can become harmful. If a person isn't able to relax and reduce the negative effects of the stress. People who are experiencing a stressful situation may feel various physical effects. Including headaches, backaches, or stomach aches. To alleviate the negative effects of stress. People should try various methods. Suggested by health experts. One simple stress reliever is to take ten deep breaths. A good way to relax quickly. For those who have to sit at desks or computer terminals all day. Stretching the neck muscles can help relieve stress symptoms. Eating a well-balanced diet and getting plenty of exercise also help to reduce the effects of stress. Although many people overlook these basic but important ways to reduce stress. In addition to a healthy diet and proper exercise. Working at an enjoyable hobby can help to eliminate the symptoms of stress. Finally, people who are feeling tense should remember that a good cry can often help relieve tension. Or a good laugh.

---

# 7

## COMMA SPLICE; RUN-TOGETHER OR FUSED SENTENCE

Readers depend on certain written signals to tell them where one idea stops and another begins. Just as a sentence fragment violates readers' expectations because its capital letter and end punctuation signal a complete thought where none exists, so a comma splice or fused sentence violates expectations because its punctuation signals one complete thought where several exist. Thus readers must untangle ideas, interpret beginnings and endings of thoughts, and decipher relationships among chunks of information that should have been made plain by the writer. The chances for error and misunderstanding increase accordingly.

## 7a   Comma splice: Do not connect two main clauses with only a comma.

Placing a comma between two main clauses without a coordinating conjunction *(and, but, for, or, nor, so, yet)* results in the **comma fault** or **comma splice.** If two main clauses are joined by a coordinating conjunction, a comma must precede the conjunction. If no conjunction is used, the two clauses must be separated by a semicolon or a period.

Comma splices may be corrected in one of the following ways:

1.   Connect the main clauses with a coordinating conjunction and a comma.
2.   Replace the comma with a semicolon.
3.   Make a separate sentence of each main clause.
4.   Change one of the main clauses to a subordinate clause.

COMMA SPLICE    I avoided desserts, I was trying to lose weight.

REVISED    I avoided desserts, *for* I was trying to lose weight.
I avoided desserts; I was trying to lose weight.
I avoided desserts. I was trying to lose weight.
*Because* I was trying to lose weight, I avoided desserts.

The fourth revision would ordinarily be the most effective, for it not only corrects the comma splice but also indicates a specific relationship between the clauses. A good revision of a comma-splice error often entails reworking the sentence rather than merely inserting a punctuation mark. The kind of revision you choose will depend on the larger context in which the sentences occur and the shades of meaning you wish to convey.

A comma is sometimes used between main clauses not connected by a coordinating conjunction if two clauses are in balance or in contrast. Commas are also sometimes used between three or more brief and closely connected main clauses that have the same pattern.

Good nutrition is not just smart, it's vital. [Balanced main clauses]
Some people eat to live, others live to eat. [Contrasting main clauses]
I'm tired, I'm hungry, I'm bored. [Main clauses with the same pattern]

Although such sentences can be very effective, inexperienced writers would be wiser to use semicolons in them.

**7b**  Use a semicolon or a period between two main clauses connected by a conjunctive adverb or a transitional phrase.

Conjunctive adverbs are words such as *accordingly, also, consequently, furthermore, however, instead, likewise, moreover, nevertheless, then, therefore,* and *thus.* Transitional phrases are phrases such as *for example, in fact, on the other hand, in conclusion, in the meantime.* When such words or phrases connect main clauses, they must always be preceded by a semicolon or a period.

**7b**

***cs, fs***

> First we made coffee. Then we cooked breakfast.
> John must be asleep; otherwise he would be here.
> I should drink less coffee; however, the caffeine keeps me alert.
> Caffeine makes the heart pump faster; in fact, people with heart ailments should avoid caffeine.

**7c**  Run-together or fused sentence (run-on): Do not omit punctuation between main clauses.

Such omission results in run-together or fused sentences (run-ons)—that is, two grammatically complete thoughts with no separating punctuation. Correct these errors in the same way as the comma splice.

| | |
|---|---|
| FUSED | Caffeine is a stimulant it gives some people the jitters. |
| REVISED | Caffeine is a stimulant, *and* it gives some people the jitters. |
| | Caffeine is a stimulant; it gives some people the jitters. |
| | Caffeine is a stimulant; *thus* it gives some people the jitters. |
| | Caffeine is a stimulant. It gives some people the jitters. |
| | *Because* caffeine is a stimulant, it gives some people the jitters. |

Be especially careful not to fuse main clauses linked by connecting words and phrases. Punctuation is necessary to signal where one clause ends and another begins (see Sections **7b** and **20a**).

| | |
|---|---|
| FUSED | Coffee contains caffeine furthermore, chocolate, tea, and cola also contain significant amounts of caffeine. |
| REVISED | Coffee contains caffeine; furthermore, chocolate, tea, and cola also contain significant amounts of caffeine. |

FUSED   Many soft drinks have a high caffeine content as a result caffeine-free colas have been developed to respond
to consumers' concerns.

REVISED   Many soft drinks have a high caffeine content. As a result, caffeine-free colas have been developed to respond
to consumers' concerns.

**7c**

*cs, fs*

## EXERCISE 7(1)

Revise the following sentences and paragraph to eliminate comma
splices and fused sentences. Use all four methods of correction.

### SENTENCE PRACTICE

1. Jazz is a uniquely American musical form, however its basic elements of harmony and rhythm are primarily African in origin.
2. Historians trace the beginnings of jazz back to the work songs and spirituals sung by black plantation workers these songs had their roots in the workers' African heritage.
3. New Orleans was an early center of jazz music, there the African elements of jazz came into contact with the varied cultures of that southern city.
4. New Orleans provided a rich mixture of musical cultures, as a result jazz is a blending of the African elements and the French, Creole, and Indian musical influences in the city.
5. By the 1920s, New Orleans had become the center of American jazz music jazz had also become popular throughout the United States and Europe.
6. Classic New Orleans jazz featured the trumpet, the clarinet, and the trombone, although solo playing and improvisation are characteristics of modern jazz, early jazz musicians played together as an ensemble with very little solo playing.
7. Many musical types are related to jazz among these categories of music are the blues and ragtime.
8. The blues, a musical form related to jazz, grew out of the plantation workers' songs, the deep emotion of a blues song and its compact form were influenced by the deep feelings of workers' songs.
9. Ragtime uses fast, syncopated melodies and can be played on various instruments, it is most often performed on the piano.
10. Scott Joplin is the greatest composer of ragtime, he wrote most of his compositions, such as "Maple Leaf Rag," for the piano.

### PARAGRAPH PRACTICE

Rock music, the term used to describe a wide range of musical styles that became popular in the 1950s and 1960s, grew out of a variety of musical traditions, among the greatest influences on rock music are the blues, gospel music, and country and western music. In the 1950s singers such as Chuck Berry, Buddy Holly, and Elvis Presley popularized rock music, in the 1960s groups like the Temptations and the Supremes created the Motown sound from Detroit. In 1962 British groups like the Beatles and the Rolling Stones became incredibly popular however American singers like Bob Dylan and Joan Baez were creating their own folk-rock style of music.

Since its beginnings several decades ago, rock music itself has developed into various genres, for instance some fans flock to heavy metal concerts where the extremely loud music emphasizes the sounds of electric guitars and drums. Some rock fans enjoy innovative new wave music others like experimental electronic music.

---

**EXERCISE 7(2)**
Revise the following paragraphs to eliminate comma splices and fused sentences. Use all four methods of correction.

**7c**

**cs, fs**

Duke Ellington, whose real name was Edward Kennedy Ellington, is one of the most famous names in American music, in fact, Ellington was both a musician and a composer. Born in Washington, D.C., in 1899, Ellington began playing the piano as a young boy in 1918 he formed his own band. Ellington was multi-talented, in his late teens he worked as a commercial artist during the day and played the piano at night. Ellington went to New York he became nationally famous there while appearing in Harlem nightclubs. Ellington's band played at the famous Cotton Club in Harlem, soon his distinctive jazz sound became familiar to radio listeners all over the country. During the Depression, Ellington and his band toured Europe, that trip was a success, Ellington's music became internationally known.

Duke Ellington liked to experiment in his compositions, for example many of his works used dissonant chords or produced new combinations of sounds. Eventually, Ellington's music combined elements of jazz and symphonic music his long concert work "Black, Brown, and Beige" was performed at Carnegie Hall. Duke Ellington died in 1974, he left a range of music that includes thousands of compositions, among them are his most famous songs such as "Mood Indigo," "Solitude," and "Sophisticated Lady."

---

## WRITERS REVISING: SENTENCE FAULTS
*(continued from page 66)*

Fran's revision follows. She has used some of the proofreaders' marks she was learning in her journalism class. A complete list of proofreaders' marks appears on the front endpaper of this book. In the margin of the revision are numbers referring to sections of this handbook.

**Fran's Revision**

```
            Leave No Stone Unturned
                                           y  f
R 1        These next few months will be crucial   for     6a(1)
R 2        many students in their search for that first
```

**7c**

*cs, fs*

R 3    job. And ̶d̶espite feelings of despair when                6a(5)

R 4    considering the task that lies ahead, there is a

R 5    place to start̶ ᵃ̶And a definite path to follow in      6a(5)

R 6    finding the right employer.

R 7        You will find that opportunities do exist̶         6a(3)

R 8    ̶If you know where to look̶ ̶When looking, you           7c

R 9    should leave no stone unturned. The following

R10    are invaluable sources of help. Your college

R11    placement office̶ ̶I̶t̶ is not only for the              6a(4)

R12    graduating senior,ₐit also offers opportunities       7a

R13    and services for the student who is seeking a

R14    summer internship. Keep in touch with your

R15    placement counselor. Also your professors and

R16    department heads̶ ̶t̶h̶e̶y̶ may prove to be the           7a

R17    perfect contacts for job seekers.

## Analysis

To remove the fragment *For many students* . . . (lines D1–2), it is joined to the first sentence (line R1). A sentence may be started with *And* occasionally, but overuse (lines D3 and D5) gives the impression that the writer is incapable of deciding where one idea stops and another begins. Also, the construction at lines D5–6 is not a sentence at all but the second part of a compound subject begun in the preceding sentence. Making the fragment part of the previous sentence corrects the error (line R5).

The run-on *if you know where to look when looking* . . . (lines D8–9) makes nonsense of the meaning. Combining the first part with the preceding sentence and the second part with the following sentence restores meaning (see lines R7–9).

*Your college placement office* (D10–11) is a fragment, probably the first of the "invaluable sources." Joining the fragment to the sentence that follows not only corrects the error but removes a fairly weak *it* and eliminates some unnecessary words. Also, the constructions *It is not only* . . . *it also* on either side of the comma splice seem to suggest a contrast: inserting a conjunction that indicates contrast *(but)* clarifies the meaning in the revision. These changes are shown in lines R11–12.

The draft's final sentence is a fragment fused to a main clause with a comma. There is no way to tell from the incomplete pieces whether the undergraduate meant *stay in touch with your counselor and professor/department heads* or *stay in touch with your counselor* (one thought) and *your professor/department heads may prove perfect contacts* (a separate thought). In her revision (lines R15–17), Fran assumed *they* in the last clause referred to the faculty but not also to the counselor.

# 8

## AGREEMENT

Agreement is a grammatical relationship that signals how pieces of information fit together. For example, subject-verb agreement helps the reader to know which actors and which actions go together, even if there are several possibilities in a sentence. Consider the sentence *Poor reading habits that someone acquires when he or she learns to read often prevent reading enjoyment later in life.* The agreement between the plural subject *habits* and plural verb *prevent* helps the reader pick these two key pieces of information from the lengthy intervening subordinate information. Thus the reader is less likely to become confused about the sentence's main idea.

Agreement relationships pertain to subjects and verbs, pronouns and their antecedents, or demonstrative adjectives *(this, that, these, those)* and the words they modify. Modern English nouns and verbs have few inflections or special endings, so their agreement usually presents few problems. However, there are some grammatical patterns, such as the agreement in number of a subject and verb or a pronoun and its antecedent, that you need to watch carefully so that readers will not be confused about your meaning.

### WRITERS REVISING: AGREEMENT

When Wayne got his literature essay test back, his instructor had marked a number of agreement errors in one answer and instructed him to revise this answer and then read the rest of his exam to discover where he had made similar errors. See if you can discover his problems, and then compare your findings with those of his instructor, shown at the end of Section **8**.

**Exam Draft**

8a

agr

D 1        This scene is found early in the story and

D 2      describe Leo, the manager of the all-night bar and

D 3      grill. While the old man is talking to the boy and

D 5      each of the customers are eating their breakfast,

D 6      Leo takes time to eat a bite. The narrator says

D 7      Leo ''nibbled his own bun as though he grudged it

D 8      to himself.'' This character don't love himself or

D 9      anybody else. More is revealed by the description

D10      of how Leo relates to his customers. That Leo

D11      ''did not give refills on coffee free'' and that

D12      ''the better he knew his customers the stingier he

D13      treated them'' shows that he is not an inherently

D14      generous character. His characterization contrast

D15      the old man in the story who, despite his

D16      difficulties, have learned to love anything and

D17      everything. Also significant is the physical

D18      descriptions of this man. These sort of

D19      descriptions—''a gray face,'' ''slitted eyes,''

D20      and ''a pinched nose with faint blue shadows''—

D21      suggests a weary person, one whose routine has

D22      sapped the very life out of him.

This *Writers Revising* continues on page 91.

**8a**   **Every verb should agree in number with its subject.**

Sometimes a lack of agreement between subject and verb results from carelessness in composition or revision. But more often, writers use a singular subject with a plural verb or a plural subject with a singular verb, not because they misunderstand the general rule, but because they are uncertain of the number of the subject or because other words coming between the subject and the verb obscure the real subject.

**1. Do not be confused by words or phrases that come between the subject and verb. Find the subject and make the verb agree with it.**

The first two *chapters* of the book *were* exciting. [The verb agrees with the subject, *chapters*, not with the nearest noun, *book*.]
The *size* of the bears *startles* the spectators.

FAULTY      *Kittle's* has lowered the prices and *are* offering a free TV to anyone who purchases a new set of bedding.

REVISED     *Kittle's* has lowered the prices and *is* offering a free TV to anyone who purchases a new set of bedding.

Singular subjects followed by such expressions as *with, together with, accompanied by,* and *as well as* take singular verbs. The phrases introduced by such expressions are not part of the subject, even though they do suggest a plural meaning.

FAULTY      The *coach*, as well as the players, *were* happy over the victory.

REVISED     The *coach*, as well as the players, *was* happy over the victory.

FAULTY      *Sally*, together with her friends, *were* here.

REVISED     *Sally*, together with her friends, *was* here.

**2. Be alert to agreement problems with indefinite pronouns used as subjects.**

Indefinite pronouns ending in *-one, -body,* and *-thing,* such as *anyone, everybody,* and *something,* always take singular verbs. The indefinite pronouns *another, each, either, neither,* and *one* also always take singular verbs. (See Section **8a[8]** for use of the phrase *one of the.*)

*Everybody* in the audience *was* enthusiastic.
*Another* of the pesticides *has* proved harmful to birds.
*Each* of the students *needs* individual help.
*Neither* of the books *was* available in the library.

The indefinite pronouns *both, few, many, others,* and *several* always take plural verbs.

*Many use* their football tickets, but *others scalp* them for high prices.

The indefinite pronouns *all, any, most, more,* and *some* may take either a singular or plural verb, depending on the noun to which they refer.

*Some* of the silver *is* missing. [*Some* refers to the singular noun *silver.*]
*Some* of her ancestors *were* pioneers. [*Some* refers to the plural noun *ancestors.*]

The indefinite pronoun *none* can be troublesome. Generally, *none* takes either a singular or plural verb, depending on the noun to which it refers. However, *none* can also mean "not one" and so in some cases may require a singular verb even though the apparent antecedent is plural. The best guide is to choose the verb that exactly conveys your intended meaning to readers.

*None* of the work *is* finished. [*None* refers to the singular *work.*]
*None* of the bees *have* swarmed although the hive is crowded. [*None* refers to the plural *bees.*
*None* of these pies *is* cool enough to eat yet. [*None* refers to (*not one*) *of these pies* and therefore requires a singular verb.]

**3.** **Use singular verbs with collective nouns when the group is considered as a unit acting together. Use a plural verb when the individual members of the group are acting separately.**
    **Collective nouns** have a singular form but name a group of persons or things as a single unit: *audience, band, bunch, class, committee, crowd, family, herd, jury, public, team,* and the like.

Our family *goes* out to dinner weekly. [The family acts together as a single unit.]
The family *have been* arriving all morning. [Members of the family arrived at different times.]
The committee *is* meeting today. [The singular verb *is* emphasizes the committee acting as a unit.]
The committee *are* unable to agree on a plan. [The plural verb *are* emphasizes the members of the committee acting separately.]

**4.** **Use a plural verb with two or more subjects joined by *and.***

A *dog and a cat* are seldom friends.
The *Ohio River and the Missouri River* empty into the Mississippi.

However, use a singular verb when the two parts of a compound subject refer to the same person or thing.

My *friend and benefactor* was there to help me.

**5.** **Use a singular verb with two or more singular subjects joined by *or* or *nor*. When two or more subjects are joined by *or* or *nor*, make the verb agree with the subject closest to it.**

Either the *dean or her assistant* <u>*was*</u> to have handled the matter.
Either *you or he* <u>*has*</u> to be here.
Neither the *farmer nor the chickens* <u>*were*</u> aware of the swooping hawk.

If one of the subjects joined by *or* or *nor* is singular and one plural, as in the last example above, place the plural subject second to avoid awkwardness.

**8a**

**6.** When the verb precedes the subject of the sentence, be particularly careful to find the subject and make the verb agree with it.

***agr***

Do not mistake the expletive *there* for the subject of the verb. (An expletive is a word that signals that the subject will follow the verb. See **1a.**)

> There *are* no *trees* in our yard. [*There* is an expletive. The subject is *trees: No trees are in our yard.*]
> On this question, there *remains* no *doubt*. [The subject is *doubt: No doubt remains on this question.*]

In some sentences beginning with the adverbs *here* and *there* or with an adverbial word group, the verb comes before the subject.

> There *goes* the *man* I was describing. [*There* is an adverb. The subject is the noun *man.*]
> Up the trail *race* the *motorcycles*. [The subject is *motorcycles.*]
> In the chinks between the bricks *grows moss*. [The subject is *moss.*]
> After a big victory *come* the postgame *letdown and fatigue* [The compound subject, *letdown and fatigue*, requires a plural verb.]

An aid for determining correct subject-verb agreement is to rearrange the sentence into normal order, so that the subject comes first: <u>*Moss grows in the chinks between the bricks.*</u>

**7.** The verb should agree with its subject, not with a predicate noun.

> The best part of the program *is* the vocal duets.
> Expensive cars *are* a necessity in his life.

**8.** When the relative pronouns *who, which,* and *that* are used as subjects, use a singular verb when the antecedent is singular, a plural verb when the antecedent is plural.

> They are the employees who *deserve* praise. [*Who* refers to the plural noun *employees;* thus the verb is plural.]
> The book that *was* lost belonged to the library. [*That* refers to the singular noun *book;* thus the verb is singular.]

The phrase *one of the* frequently causes problems in such sentences.

> Sanderson is one of the council members who *oppose* the plan. [*Who* refers to the plural *members;* several council members oppose the plan.]
>
> Sanderson is the only one of the council members who *opposes* the plan. [*Who* refers to *one;* there is only one council member, Sanderson, opposing the plan. Note that the meaning of the sentence would not be changed if the phrase *of the council members* were omitted.]

**9. When the subject is the title of a novel, a play, the name of a business or the like, or a word used as a word, use a singular verb even though the form of the subject is plural.**

> *Romeo and Juliet* <u>is</u> a Shakespearean play.
>
> *Songs and Satires* <u>is</u> a book by Edgar Lee Masters.
>
> *Women* <u>is</u> the plural of *woman.*
>
> *Smith Brothers* <u>is</u> a brand of cough drops.

**10. Nouns such as *economics, news, physics,* and *mathematics* that refer to an art, science, or body of knowledge usually take singular verbs because they are singular in meaning, although plural in form. Plural-form physical ailments such as *measles* or *hives* are treated similarly.**

> *Linguistics* <u>is</u> the study of human speech.
>
> The good *news* <u>has</u> traveled quickly.
>
> *Measles* <u>carries</u> the threat of severe complications.

**11. Some plural-form nouns such as *athletics, hysterics, aerobics, politics, statistics,* and *acoustics* may be either singular or plural, depending on whether they refer to a singular idea or a plural idea. The noun *data,* however, is almost always treated as plural in formal writing.**

> *Aerobics* <u>is</u> an extremely strenuous form of exercise. [Singular meaning]
>
> College *athletics* <u>are</u> responsible for generating thousands of dollars from loyal alumni. [Plural meaning: various collegiate sports]
>
> The *data* <u>indicate</u> that consumers are making more credit card purchases.

**12. Noun phrases indicating fixed quantities or extents (money, time, distance, or other measurements) may be either singular or plural, depending on whether they are being considered as a unit (singular) or as parts of a unit (plural).**

The *majority* in the legislature *is* Republican. [Unit]
The *majority* of the tourists *have* returned to the bus because of the rain. [Individuals]
*Three-quarters* of the money *is* already spent. [ Unit of money]
*Sixty percent* of the trees *were* damaged by the hurricane. [Individual trees]
*Three hundred pounds is* a lot for an amateur to bench-press. [Unit]
*Five-and-a-half liters were* needed to fill the tank. [Parts of unit]

**8a**

*agr*

The expression *the number* takes a singular verb, but *a number* takes a plural verb.

*The number* of candidates for the position *was* large.
*A number* of candidates *were* applying for the position.
*The number* of people moving to the Southwest *is* increasing.
*A number* of business firms *have* moved from New York.

---

EXERCISE 8a
In the following sentences and paragraph, revise any errors in agreement.

SENTENCE PRACTICE
1. Surveys show that stamps and coins is the most popular items that people collect.
2. Serious collectors, as well as the person who spends just an hour or two a week on the hobby, finds enjoyment in sorting through colorful stamps or in acquiring the one coin needed to complete a set.
3. Each of these collectors have special interests; for instance, some stamp collectors specializes in the stamps of only one country.
4. There is lots of people who collect first-day covers, the stamps and envelopes that gets postmarked on the first day of a stamp's issue.
5. A number of countries is known for their colorful stamps; although both Monaco and San Marino is tiny, the two European countries produces colorful and elaborate postage stamps.

PARAGRAPH PRACTICE
    If neither stamp collecting nor coin collecting seem the right hobby, you might enjoy collecting postcards. Statistics shows that this hobby is becoming very popular in the United States as more and more people starts collecting postcards. These collectors often specializes in one particular type of postcard; some collectors tries to acquire postcards with mountain scenery while others might collect only postcards with buildings on them. Everyone who collects postcards face the same problem: finding somewhere to store the cards. Either a small file box or shoeboxes makes a good storage place for the postcard collection.

**8b**   To achieve pronoun-antecedent agreement, use a singular pronoun in referring to a singular antecedent. Use a plural pronoun in referring to a plural antecedent. Avoid sexist pronoun references.

**8b**

*agr*

Most pronoun-antecedent references are straightforward and uncomplicated. Simply make the pronoun agree in number with the word to which it refers.

> The *cat* decided *she* wanted to have her kittens in my closet. [*She* refers to the singular antecedent *cat*.]
>
> My closet *floor* is covered with junk; *it* is littered with shoes, old magazines, and a sleeping bag with a broken zipper. [*It* refers to the singular antecedent *floor*.]
>
> The *kittens* were born on the sleeping bag and played *their* first games among my shoes. [*Their* refers to the plural antecedent *kittens*.]

When agreement problems between pronouns and their antecedents do occur, they usually involve (1) indefinite pronouns, (2) collective nouns, and (3) compound antecedents.

**1. In writing, use singular pronouns to refer to indefinite antecedents such as *person, one, any, each, either, neither,* and compounds ending in *-one, -body,* and *-thing,* such as *someone, anybody,* and *everything.***

Spoken English frequently uses a plural pronoun to refer to indefinite antecedents, but the singular continues to be preferred in writing.

> SPOKEN   *Everyone* at the meeting should be allowed to express *their* opinions before the vote is taken.
>
> WRITTEN   *Everyone* at the meeting should be allowed to express *his or her* opinion before the vote is taken.
>
> SPOKEN   *Each* of the Cub Scouts is to bring *their* own tent to the roundup.
>
> WRITTEN   *Each* of the Cub Scouts is to bring *his* own tent to the roundup.
>
> SPOKEN   *None* [not one] of us actresses wants you to forget *our* performance.
>
> WRITTEN   *None* of us actresses wants you to forget *her* performance.

*He (him, his)* has conventionally been used in English to refer to such antecedents as *one, none, everybody,* and similar indefinite pronouns that designate either male or female. This usage is no longer as common as it once was and is, in fact, offensive to many readers.

For a more complete discussion of sexism and pronoun usage, see Section **8c**.

**2. With a collective noun as an antecedent, use a singular pronoun if you are considering the group as a unit and a plural pronoun if you are considering the individual members of the group separately.**

The *class* finished *their* lab experiments yesterday. [The class members worked as individuals.]

The *sorority* holds *its* rush week in the spring. [The sorority is acting as a unit.]

The *crew* are going about *their* duties preparing the spacecraft for landing. [The members of the crew have separate duties.]

The *crew* is ready for *its* briefing. [The crew is being considered as a unit.]

**3. If two or more antecedents are joined by the conjunction *and*, use a plural pronoun to refer to them. If two or more singular antecedents are joined by the conjunctions *or* or *nor*, use a singular pronoun to refer to them. If one of two antecedents joined by *or* or *nor* is singular and one plural, make the pronoun agree with the antecedent that is closer to it.**

*Dad and Mom* have bought *their* tickets.

Either *my sister or my mother* is missing *her* luggage.

Neither *my parents nor my brother* has confirmed *his* reservation.

Either *Jean or my mother and father* are taking *their* vacation in May.

---

EXERCISE 8b
Revise the following sentences and paragraph to make every pronoun agree with its antecedent in accordance with written usage. Indicate any sentence that would be acceptable in speech.

**SENTENCE PRACTICE**
1. I asked everyone in my office if they would like to go tubing this weekend.
2. I told anyone who didn't know anything about tubing that all they had to do was sit in a large inner tube and float down the river.
3. Of course, I didn't mention that each tuber has little control over their inner tube.
4. Anyone who has tried tubing knows they can try to paddle the tube or try leaning in different directions, but those techniques often make little difference in the direction the tubes goes.
5. After a day of tubing on the local river, the entertainment committee from my office voted unanimously to go tubing again, but they decided to wait at least a few weeks so that everyone could recover from their first attempt at tubing.

**PARAGRAPH PRACTICE**

Because I wanted to start an exercise program, I tried jogging and swimming, but it wasn't the right activity for me. When I asked my friends to join me, nobody wanted to spend their time pounding the streets in a sweatsuit. Also, neither my roommate Alice nor my friend Sarah could find time in their busy schedules to go to the local pool. Finally, I suggested that we try bicycling on the weekends, for I read an article that stated that a person who's looking for a good aerobic exercise should find a level route, get on their bike, and ride. Now that we've been bicycling for a couple of months, each of my friends says that they think bike riding is the perfect exercise for them.

**8c**   Avoid sexism in pronoun-antecedent references.

Pronoun-antecedent agreement can become complicated when you are dealing with so-called *common gender* words, which can refer to either males or females, or when you are dealing with indefinite antecedents. Historically, formal English used masculine pronouns (*he, him, his*) for common gender or indefinite antecedents, assuming them to mean people of either sex: *The applicant should have <u>his</u> SAT scores sent to the College Admissions Office. Anyone who has not taken the SAT should indicate when <u>he</u> plans to do so.*

Today, however, many people consider such usage to be illogical because it ignores realities and, in fact, to be discriminatory (see Section **37b** on derogatory language). For example, college students are as likely to be women as men, so it makes little sense to write as if all the applicants were male. In their style guidelines and manuals, many professional organizations and publications now warn authors to avoid sexist language.

Several alternatives have been proposed for dealing with common gender words. Each has drawbacks:

a.   Use of *he or she* (*hers or his*). This alternative can result in cumbersome, monotonous pronoun repetition: *Anyone who thinks <u>he or she</u> is eligible for financial aid should send <u>his or her</u> application as early as <u>he or she</u> can.*

b.   Alternating pronouns, *she* used in one paragraph, *he* the next. This alternative, although fairly widespread in textbooks, can be confusing to readers, especially if they are skimming paragraphs and do not notice that the alternation is deliberate.

c.   Coined or combined-form pronouns like *s/he* and *his/hers*. The English language is slow to accept such invented words, particularly when their pronunciation is questionable (as with *s/he*). *He/she* and its variant forms have gained some acceptance in business writing, however.

d. Use of plural pronouns to refer to singular common gender or indefinite words: *Anyone who has not taken the SAT should indicate when they plan to do so.* Although common in speech, this alternative is considered by many people to be a grammatical error when it appears in writing.

However, with the following guidelines you can construct clear sentences that are neither awkward nor sexist.

**8c**

*agr*

**1. To avoid monotonous repetition of pronouns, use the plural rather than the singular if the meaning will not be affected.**

An *applicant* who thinks *he or she* is eligible for financial aid should send in *his or her* application forms before December 1.

*Applicants* who think *they* are eligible for financial aid should send in *their* application forms before December 1.

**2. Omit the pronoun altogether to avoid awkward or monotonous pronoun repetition, provided meaning and clarity are preserved.**

Applicants who may be eligible for financial aid should send in the application forms before December 1.

**3. Indefinite pronoun reference choices often become clear if you consider the probable sex of the people about whom you are writing. Rely on available information rather than stereotypes.**

For example, if the person or group is likely to be female, use the feminine pronoun; if the antecedent is likely to be male, use the masculine pronoun.

Each *member* of the college football team had *his* photo taken at the sports banquet.

*Everybody* on the synchronized swimming team performed *her* best at the Olympic trials.

For groups that could be mixed, choose pronouns that do not presuppose only one sex.

NOT    *Anyone* who wants to be on the athletic training staff ought to choose sports medicine as *his* major.

BUT    *Anyone* who wants to be on the athletic training staff ought to choose sports medicine as *his or her* major.

OR    *Anyone* who wants to be on the athletic training staff ought to major in sports medicine.

Be careful not to use feminine pronouns for roles stereotyped as female (nurse, teacher, social worker, secretary, telephone operator, flight attendant, etc.) or masculine pronouns for roles stereotyped as male (engineer, auto mechanic, firefighter, government official, airline pilot, etc.) when, in fact, they are mixed.

## 8d
## *agr*

### EXERCISE 8c
Using the range of available options, revise the following sentences so that pronoun references are nonsexist and reflect reality. Be prepared to discuss your choices.

1. A student who wants to go to medical school should be sure that he has a good background in chemistry and biology.
2. Although his players may not like it, a tennis coach has to schedule long practice sessions each week.
3. A nurse has a demanding job, for she often has to be both an administrator and a caregiver.
4. Anybody who wants to improve his golf game should make sure he has the right size of golf clubs.
5. Those flowers look great, and whoever planted them did a good job because she chose colors that complement each other.

**8d**  A demonstrative adjective *(this, that, these, those)* should agree in number with the noun it modifies.

It can be difficult to choose the correct word to use as a demonstrative adjective with *kind of* or *sort of* followed by a plural noun: *This sort of jogging shoes is expensive.* Remember that the demonstrative adjective modifies the singular noun *kind* or *sort* and not the following plural noun. Thus a singular demonstrative is needed. In most cases, standard usage favors agreement among the demonstrative, the noun being modified, and the noun object following the preposition: where appropriate, make them all singular or all plural.

| | |
|---|---|
| **NONSTANDARD** | Those kind of strawberries taste sweet. |
| STANDARD | Those kinds of strawberries taste sweet. |
| | That kind of strawberry tastes sweet. |
| **NONSTANDARD** | This sort of cakes is delicious. |
| STANDARD | These sorts of cakes are delicious. |
| | This sort of cake is delicious. |
| **NONSTANDARD** | These sort of things happen. |
| STANDARD | These sorts of things happen. |
| | This sort of thing happens. |

### EXERCISE 8a-d
In the following sentences and paragraph, correct every error of agreement in accordance with written usage.

**SENTENCE PRACTICE**

1. Researchers have found that the more hours a day a person wears contact lenses, the more they risk damaging their eyes.
2. Millions of people now use extended-wear contact lenses, but if the wearers leave these sort of lens in his or her eyes too long, eye damage can occur.
3. The Food and Drug Administration has recently announced their recommendation that wearing time for extended-wear contact lenses should be no more than seven days.
4. According to opthamologists, there is several possible dangers in wearing lenses for long periods of time.
5. One of the most serious problems that can occur when contact lenses are worn too long are scratching or abrasion of the cornea.

**8d**

*agr*

**PARAGRAPH PRACTICE**

Anybody who wears contact lenses today should be thankful they don't have to wear the original hard and uncomfortable glass discs that were developed in the 1940s. Another of the early contact lenses' disadvantages were their size, which was about as big as a quarter. Today, neither size nor material are a problem for contact lens wearers: today's contact lens are made of plastic and are about the size of a dime. Extended-wear contact lenses, which were introduced in the early 1980s, and disposable extended-wear lenses, which have become available recently, has given contact lens wearers several new options. Disposable lenses are expensive, though; $300 to $500 per year are a lot for a person to spend on packs of lenses they will throw away.

## WRITERS REVISING: AGREEMENT

(continued from page 79)

Wayne read through the paragraph his instructor had marked and discovered that he had not only been careless with subject-verb agreement, but also with pronoun-antecedent agreement. He would begin by underlining the subjects with one line and the verbs with two and by looking at each pronoun and its antecedent. He thought this might help him to see his errors and correct them.

**Wayne's Revision**

R 1     This scene is found early in the story and

R 2     describe∧the manager of the all-night bar and          8a(1)

R 3     grill. While the old man is talking to the boy

**8d**

*agr*

R 4    and ~~each of~~ the customers are eating their                8c(1)

R 5    breakfast, Leo takes time to eat a bite. The

R 6    narrator says Leo "nibbled his own bun as though

R 7    he grudged it to himself." This character ~~don't~~ *doesn't*          8a

R 8    love himself or anybody else. More is revealed

R 9    by the description of how Leo relates to his

R10    customers. That he "did not give refills on

R11    coffee free" and that "the better he knew his

R12    customers the stingier he treated them" show*s*        8a(3)

R13    that he is not an inherently generous character.

R14    His characterization contrast*s* the old man in the      8a

R15    story who, despite his difficulties, ~~have~~ *has*           8a(8)

R16    learned to love anything and everything. Also

R17    significant ~~is~~ *are* the physical descriptions of this     8a(7)

R18    man. These sort*s* of descriptions—"a gray

R19    face,""slitted eyes," and "a pinched nose with

R20    faint blue shadows"—suggest*s* a weary person,       8a

R21    one whose routine has sapped the very life out

R22    of him.

## Analysis

In lines R1, 7, and 14, the singular subjects *scene, charac-ter,* and *characterization* require the singular verbs *describes, doesn't,* and *contrasts. Each,* the subject in line R4, calls for a singular verb and pronoun reference in line R4. However, the better choice is to make the subject, verb, and pronoun all plural to avoid the his/her modifier. A compound subject consisting of two noun clauses in lines R10–12 calls for the plural verb *show* in line R12. The antecedent of *who,* the relative pronoun in line R15, is the singular subject *man* which requires the singular verb *has* in line R15. The plural verb *are* in line R17 is needed to agree with the plural subject *descriptions,* which follows the verb. *Sort* is made plural in line R18 to agree with the plural demon-strative adjective *these.* This correction calls for the plural verb *suggest* to agree.

# 9

## PRONOUN REFERENCE

A pronoun depends for its meaning on its antecedent, the noun or other pronoun to which it refers. If the antecedents of the pronouns in your writing are not clear, your writing will not be clear. Remember that readers more readily understand information that has been "chunked," that has been delivered in manageable pieces with related bits together. Thus it makes sense that you should place pronouns as close to their antecedents as possible and make all pronoun references exact.

**9**

*ref*

---

### WRITERS REVISING: SHIFTS AND PRONOUN REFERENCE

Fran, the Placement Office intern, read over another student-written article for the placement newsletter. The writer was supposed to have summarized an article originally appearing in *National Business Employment Weekly*. While attempting to adapt the original for readers of the placement newsletter, the student had created shifts and pronoun reference errors. As you work through Sections **9** and **10**, see if you can correct the mismatches; then compare your revision with Fran's version at the end of Section **10**.

**Fran's Article**

D 1      There comes a time when we must make a break

D 2      and rely on ourselves as a career expert. To a

D 3      large degree, you are your own expert because only

D 4      you know best about your interests, challenges,

D 5      and what suits you. This means your own judgment

D 6      and intuition must be trusted, if you are going to

D 7      take the initiative in your job search. They say

D 8      we are often our own worst enemies; if you see

D 9      yourself as a bungling idiot during an interview,

D10      you'll probably behave like it.

This *Writers Revising* continues on page 106.

## 9a    Each pronoun should refer to a single antecedent.

Pronouns can, of course, refer to compound antecedents in such sentences as *Joan and Karen both believed they had performed well,* where the pronoun *they* refers to *Joan and Karen.* However, if a pronoun can refer to either of two possible antecedents, it will be ambiguous, and readers will not know which antecedent is intended.

9a
ref

> AMBIGUOUS    When Kathy visited her mother, she had a cold. [Who had a cold, Kathy or her mother?]
>
> CLEAR    When she visited her mother, Kathy had a cold.
>
> Kathy had a cold when she visited her mother.
>
> Her mother had a cold when Kathy visited her.
>
> AMBIGUOUS    Arthur went with John to the airport, where he took a plane to Phoenix. [Who took the plane, John or Arthur?]
>
> CLEAR    After going to the airport with John, Arthur took the plane to Phoenix.
>
> After Arthur went to the airport with him, John took the plane to Phoenix.

---

EXERCISE 9a
Revise the following paragraph to eliminate the ambiguous reference of pronouns.

> Maureen told the other advertising agency employees that she had several designs for the client's new product and she wanted to get them together the next day. The owner of the agency told Maureen that her job required a great deal of creative ability. When the owner took Maureen to the meeting with the client the next afternoon, she introduced herself. When the client told Maureen the designs were excellent, she was pleased. Maureen told her coworker Carla that the ad agency had been given another ad campaign to plan, so she needed to get busy right away.

---

## 9b    A pronoun should be close enough to its antecedent to ensure clear reference.

In general, the nearer a pronoun is to its antecedent, the more likely it is to be clear. The more remote the antecedent, the more difficulty readers will have in understanding the reference—particularly if other nouns intervene between the antecedent and the pronoun. Readers should never have to search for a pronoun's antecedent.

> REMOTE    Credit cards spread throughout the United States and western Europe during the late 1960s. Card issuers make money from the fees paid by card owners and merchants and from interest charged on unpaid balances. Between 1965 and 1970, *they* increased from

fewer than 5 million in use to more than 50 million. [*Credit cards* is the only antecedent to which *they* can sensibly refer, but the pronoun is too remote from its antecedent for clear, easy reading.]

CLEAR       . . . Between 1965 and 1970, *credit cards* increased from fewer than 5 million . . . [This revision repeats the subject, *credit cards.*]

Credit cards spread throughout the United States and western Europe during the late 1960s, increasing between 1965 and 1970 from fewer than 5 million in use to more than 50 million . . . [The remote reference is eliminated by combining the first and third sentences.]

**9c**

*ref*

**9c**  Avoid the vague use of *this, that,* and *which* to refer to the general idea of a preceding clause or sentence.

The use of *this, that,* and *which* to refer to an idea stated in a preceding clause or sentence is common in informal English in such sentences as *They keep their promises, which is more than some people do.* Although often used by experienced writers when the meaning is unmistakably clear, such broad reference risks confusing the reader. Less experienced writers should ordinarily eliminate any vague use of *this, that,* and *which,* either by recasting the sentence to eliminate the pronoun or by supplying a specific antecedent for the pronoun.

VAGUE    Their credit cards were stolen after they spent all their cash. That was a real shame.

CLEAR    That their credit cards were stolen after they spent all their cash was a real shame. [The sentence has been recast to eliminate the vague use of *that.*]

VAGUE    The disadvantages of credit cards can offset the advantages, which merits careful consideration. [What merits consideration: the advantages, the disadvantages, the offsetting of one by the other?]

CLEAR    The disadvantages of credit cards can offset the advantages, a fact which merits careful consideration. [*Fact* supplies a clear antecedent for *which.*]

CLEAR    Because the disadvantages can offset the advantages, the consequences of using credit cards should be carefully considered. [The sentence has been revised to eliminate the vague use of *which.*]

VAGUE    I announced that I was going to cut up all my credit cards. This caused a shocked silence.

CLEAR    I announced that I was going to cut up all my credit cards. This announcement caused a shocked silence. [*Announcement* clearly indicates the antecedent for *This.*]

**EXERCISE 9b–c**
In the following sentences and paragraph, revise all sentences to eliminate remote or vague pronoun reference.

**SENTENCE PRACTICE**

1. At one time the United States had over two million acres of wetlands, but because these wetlands have been drained to build cities and to create farmland, more than half of them are now gone. This is bad because wetlands provide a home for many species of birds and animals.
2. Destroying wetlands also destroys the wildlife there, which worries conservationists.
3. Wetlands such as ponds, marshes, streams, swamps and estuaries are valuable natural resources and thus need to be preserved. Because they serve as breeding grounds for fish and birds, they are also a vital link in the chain of life.

**PARAGRAPH PRACTICE**

The duck population seems to have suffered the most as the number of America's wetlands has declined. That means that ducks have fewer wetlands in which to breed and live. For example, a mallard duck flying north in the spring may not find the same pond where it spent the previous summer. It will then have no place to make its nest. Conservationists report that the number of ducks flying south each winter has fallen in the last ten years. This has led the U.S. Fish and Wildlife Service to shorten the length of duck hunting season and to lower the number of ducks hunters can kill during the season.

**9d** Do not use a pronoun to refer to an implied but unexpressed noun.

To be clear, a pronoun must have a noun or the equivalent of a noun as its specific antecedent. Modifiers, possessives, and other words or phrases that merely suggest an appropriate noun do not provide clear and specific antecedents. Revise faulty sentences so that each pronoun has a specific noun or noun equivalent as antecedent, or otherwise revise the sentence.

FAULTY    Because we put a wire fence around the chicken yard, they cannot escape. [*Chicken* here functions as an adjective modifying *yard*. It suggests but does not express the necessary antecedent *chickens*.]

REVISED    Because we put a wire fence around the chicken yard, the chickens cannot escape.

FAULTY    When the president's committee was established, she appointed several student representatives. [The possessive *president's* implies but does not express the antecedent *president.*]

REVISED    When the president established the committee, she appointed several student representatives.

FAULTY    The guest speaker for today's class is a banker, and that is a career I want to know more about. [The appropriate antecedent, *banking*, is implied, but it needs to be stated specifically.]

REVISED    The guest speaker for today's class is a banker, and I want to know more about careers in banking.

**9e**

*ref*

---

## EXERCISE 9d
Revise the following paragraph to eliminate all references to unexpressed antecedents.

Physicians recommend that all children be given a rubella vaccination. It is better known by the common name of German measles. Catching German measles is seldom serious, but it is especially dangerous for women who are in the first three months of pregnancy. During that time, the disease can seriously affect the unborn child, so that is something women who have not had German measles should be aware of.

---

**9e**  In writing, avoid the indefinite use of *they* and *it*. Use *you* appropriately.

The indefinite use of *they, it,* and *you* is common at most levels of speech: *In Germany, they drink beer; it says in the dictionary that . . . ; you can never find anything where you're looking for it.* In writing, these pronouns all have a much more restricted use.

**1.** *They* **always requires a specific antecedent in all but the most informal writing.** Correct its use in your writing by substituting an appropriate noun, or revise the sentence.

SPOKEN    In less industrialized areas, *they* do not understand the problems of the city.

WRITTEN    People living in less industrialized areas do not understand the problems of the city.

SPOKEN    *They* said on the late news that Mount St. Helens had erupted again.

WRITTEN    It was reported on the late news that Mount St. Helens had erupted again.

**2.** *It* **in the phrase** *it says* **referring to information in newspapers, magazines, books, and the like, though common in speech, is unacceptable in writing, except in dialogue.**

SPOKEN    *It* says in the newspaper that Monday will be warmer.

WRITTEN    The newspaper says that Monday will be warmer.

**3.** *You* in the sense of people in general is common in informal writing: *Differences of opinion among friends can be healthy if you don't take them too seriously,* or *When you're driving you should always be alert.* More formal writing ordinarily prefers a general noun such as *people* or a *person*, or the pronoun *one*.

**9f**

*ref*

> INFORMAL    Many suburban towns do not permit *you* to drive more than twenty-five or thirty miles an hour.
>
> FORMAL    Many suburban towns do not permit *people* [or *a person* or *one*] to drive more than twenty-five or thirty miles an hour.

*You* is always correct in writing directions or in other contexts where the meaning is clearly *you, the reader.*

> Before turning on your air conditioner, be sure you have closed all your windows.

When using *you* in the sense of *you, the reader,* be sure that the context is appropriate to such use.

> INAPPROPRIATE    In early colonial villages, you had to depend on wood for fuel. [The reader is unlikely to be living in an early colonial village.]
>
> REVISED    In early colonial villages, *people* [or *a person* or *one*] had to depend on wood for fuel.
>
> BETTER    Early colonial villagers had to depend on wood for fuel.

---

EXERCISE 9e
Revise the following paragraph to avoid the indefinite use of *they, you,* and *it.*

> In the United States, they are eating more fish, and as a result, aquaculture, which could be called fish farming, is a growing enterprise. In an article in yesterday's newspaper, it says that natural sources such as oceans and rivers aren't supplying enough fish to meet consumers' demands. To help supply those demands, they are growing fish as well as traditional crops like corn and wheat. Because of the development of aquaculture, that trout you buy for dinner may have come from a special pond on a farm instead of from a stream. In fact, on some fish farms, they let you go out and choose your own fish from the holding ponds.

---

**9f**    Match the relative pronouns *who, which,* and *that* with appropriate antecedents.

In general, use *who* to refer to persons, *which* to refer to things, and *that* to refer to things and sometimes to persons.

Many *students who* major in mathematics today find employment with computer companies.

*Arkansas, which* became a state in 1836, was earlier a part of Louisiana.

Among the *flowers that* (or *which*) grow most easily are petunias and marigolds.

The possessive *whose* is frequently used to refer to things when the phrase *of which* would be awkward.

**9g**

*ref*

*Cinderella* is a story *whose* ending most of us know. [Compare *the ending of which*.]

The relative pronoun *that* can be used only in restrictive clauses, clauses necessary to meaning and thus not set off by commas. *Which* can be used in both restrictive and nonrestrictive clauses, clauses not necessary to meaning and thus set off by commas. (See **20c**.)

The *Eighteenth Amendment, which* forbade the manufacture, sale, import, or export of intoxicating liquors, instituted nationwide prohibition in 1919.

The *amendment that* (or *which*) repealed prohibition was ratified in 1933.

Some writers prefer to introduce all restrictive clauses with *that* and to limit the use of *which* entirely to nonrestrictive clauses.

**9g**  Use the pronoun it only one way in a sentence.

We use *it* as an expletive to postpone a subject (*It is wise to be careful*), in certain idioms (*it is cold*) and colloquial expressions (*He made it to the finish line*), and of course as a definite pronoun referring to specific antecedents. All of these uses are acceptable when appropriate, but sentences in which two different uses occur are likely to be confusing.

> CONFUSING    She put her car in the garage because she never leaves *it* out when *it* is bad weather. [The first *it* refers to *car;* the second is idiomatic.]
>
> IMPROVED    She put her car in the garage because she never leaves it out when the weather is bad [or *in bad weather*].

---

EXERCISE 9f-g
Revise the following sentences so that pronouns are used appropriately.

1.  Five types of plants who eat insects are found in the United States.
2.  Because these plants live in soil that has little nitrogen in it, it is the insect organs that supply the nitrogen the plant needs to survive.

3. The venus flytrap, that is the best known of the carnivorous plants, has leaves that snap shut on insects.

EXERCISE 9a-g
Revise the following paragraph to eliminate the faulty reference of pronouns.

**10**

*shft*

Because most people today take for granted having ice anytime you want it, it is hard to realize that ice has not always been available for chilling drinks or for filling a cooler for a picnic. In the past, it had to be hacked out of frozen lakes and moved to icehouses, where it was kept covered in sawdust. The people that wanted ice bought it from an iceman which delivered blocks of it to hotels, homes, and restaurants. They had to use the ice quickly, for there was no refrigeration. It says in a book about the history of ice in the United States that in 1834 Jacob Perkins invented the first refrigeration unit. This made it possible to store ice for longer periods of time. Refrigeration and icemaking have come a long way since that: today a person can go to your refrigerator door and fill a glass with it without ever having to open the freezer.

# 10

## SHIFTS

Writers keep sentences consistent by using one subject; one tense, voice, and mood in verbs; and one person and number in pronouns, as far as grammar and meaning allow. Unnecessary shifts in any of these elements tend to obscure meaning and make reading more difficult than it has to be. (See Section **42g** for a discussion of consistency within paragraphs.)

**10a** Do not shift the subject or the voice of the verb within a sentence unnecessarily.

Particularly in compound and complex sentences, meaning frequently requires the writer to refer to more than one subject, as in the following sentence:

When the *car* hit their dog, *John* ran home, and *Bill* held the dog until help arrived.

Here the writer is describing an accident involving two boys, their dog, and a car. Meaning clearly requires a shift of subject from one clause to another within the sentence. Such movement of a sentence from one subject to another is perfectly natural.

Less frequently, meaning may justify a shift from active to passive voice within a sentence.

Three men *escaped* from the state prison yesterday but *were captured* before sundown.

Here the writer could have chosen to write *but the police captured them,* changing the subject but keeping the active voice in both main clauses of a compound sentence. But by choosing to use the compound predicate, *escaped . . . but were captured,* the writer keeps attention focused on the important subject, *three men.*

Unlike the shifts in subject and voice in these sentences, the shifts in the following sentences are unnecessary:

> FAULTY  *As the boys approached* the swamp, *frogs could be heard* croaking. [Here the focus of the sentence is on *the boys.* The shift of subject from *the boys* to *frogs* and of the voice of the verb from the active to the passive are unnecessary and distracting.]
>
> REVISED  *As the boys approached* the swamp, *they could hear* frogs croaking.
>
> FAULTY  *Ellen stayed* at a mountain resort, and most of her *time was spent* skiing. [The sentence is about Ellen. The shift of subject from *Ellen* to *time* and the resulting shift from active to passive voice blurs rather than sharpens the sentence.]
>
> REVISED  *Ellen stayed* at a mountain resort *and spent* most of her time skiing.

## EXERCISE 10a

In the following paragraph, correct any unnecessary shifts in subject or voice.

Hikers should choose their hiking boots carefully; a wide variety of boots is offered now as a result of new developments in design and materials. Because of their mountainous locations, Austria and Switzerland have been the leaders in developing new hiking boots, and the wide variety of styles available can be confusing to a hiker. If the hiker plans to do any mountain climbing, the traditional heavy and rigid boots should be worn. However, when the hiker will not be climbing mountains, comfort and protection on rough ground will be given by the new lightweight, flexible hiking shoes. A hiker who plans only to walk through the woods or fields could choose a style that looks like a combination of hiking boot and running shoe, but not much protection on rough ground would be given by this type of shoe.

## 10b  Do not shift person or number unnecessarily.

Just as meaning frequently requires us to refer to more than one subject in a single sentence, it may require us to refer to different persons or to combinations of singular and plural subjects, as in the following sentences:

**10b**

*shft*

> *I* stayed, but *they* left. [*I* is first person singular; *they* is third person plural.]
> The *snake* held its ground until the *coyotes* finally left. [*Snake* is singular, *coyotes* plural.]

But unless meaning clearly requires such changes, keep person and number within a given sentence consistent.

Unnecessary **shifts in person** are frequently shifts from the third person (the person being talked about) to the second person (the person being talked to). They occur principally because in English we can make general statements by using either the second person pronoun *you*, the third person pronoun *one*, or one of various third person general nouns such as the singular *a person* or the plural *people*. Thus any one of the following sentences is consistent:

> If *you* want to play games, *you* must learn the rules.
> If *a person* [or *one*] wants to play games, *he or she* must learn the rules.
> If *people* want to play games, *they* must learn the rules.

Failure to follow one of these possible patterns produces faulty shifts, as in the following:

> **FAULTY**    When *a person* has good health, *you* should feel fortunate.
>
> REVISED    When *a person* has good health, *he or she* should feel fortunate.
> When *you* have good health, *you* should feel fortunate.
> When *people* have good health, *they* should feel fortunate.

A second kind of unnecessary shift frequently occurs in sentences in which the writer starts with the first person and inconsistently shifts to the second. Such sentences are ordinarily more effective when the writer maintains the first-person point of view.

> **WEAK**    I refuse to go to a movie theater where you can't buy popcorn.
>
> IMPROVED    I refuse to go to a movie theater where I can't buy popcorn.

These sorts of shifts are sometimes called **shifts in point of view.** Readers find unnecessary shifts disconcerting because expectations about readers' and writers' roles are disrupted. Readers count on point of view to signal their relationship to the writer and to the information being presented. Think, for example, how startling it is to be reading as a third-party "observer" and then suddenly find the language pointing remarks directly at "you."

**10c**

*shft*

Faulty **shifts in number** within a sentence usually involve faulty agreement between pronouns and their antecedents. (See **8b.**)

FAULTY
I like *an occasional cup* of coffee, for *they* give me an added lift. [Shift from singular to plural. The pronoun should agree with the singular antecedent *cup.*]

REVISED
I like *an occasional cup* of coffee, for *it* gives me an added lift.

I like *occasional cups* of coffee, for *they* give me an added lift.

---

EXERCISE 10b

In the following sentences, correct any unnecessary shifts in person or number.

1. A person's ankle is one of the most frequently used parts of your body.
2. Because the ankle is used so much, they are also frequently injured.
3. People injure their ankles when you run, jump, or turn quickly.
4. I didn't realize that you have just a single anklebone that is connected to the two leg bones.
5. Between the anklebone and the leg bones is a layer of cartilage that protects all of it from damage during normal activity.

---

**10c**  Do not shift tense or mood unnecessarily.

In a sentence such as *Nostalgia is a love of the way things were in our youth,* meaning requires a shift of tense from the present *is* to the past *were.* But except when the meaning or the grammar of a sentence requires such changes in tense, keep the same tense throughout all the verbs in a sentence. (See also Section **5a–c.**)

FAULTY
I *sat* down at the desk and *begin* to write. [The verb shifts unnecessarily from past to present tense.]

REVISED
I *sat* down at the desk and *began* to write.

FAULTY
In Chapter One she *accepts* her first job as a kitchen maid, but by Chapter Three she *was cooking* for an Austrian prince.

REVISED
In Chapter One she *accepts* her first job as a kitchen maid, but by Chapter Three she *is cooking* for an Aus-

trian prince. [In this sentence, the revision uses the present tense in both verbs because it is customary to use the present tense in describing actions in literature. See **5a.**]

Shifts in mood within a single sentence or a series of related sentences are almost never justified. Such shifts often occur in writing directions. Avoid them by casting directions consistently either in the imperative or the indicative mood. (See Section **5** for an explanation of *imperative* and *indicative.*)

> **FAULTY**   *Hold* the rifle firmly against your shoulder, and then you *should take* careful aim. [Shift from imperative to indicative mood.]
>
> REVISED   *Hold* the rifle firmly against your shoulder and then *take* careful aim. [Both verbs are in the imperative mood.]
>
> You *should hold* the rifle firmly against your shoulder and then (you should) take careful aim. [Both verbs are in the indicative. Note that here the second *you should* can be omitted since it will be understood by the reader.]

In general, directions are most economical and effective when they are written in the imperative mood.

---

EXERCISE 10c

In the following paragraph, correct any needless shifts in tense or mood.

> The most common ankle injury is a sprain, which happened when the foot turned over on its side and tore or stretched the ligaments on the outside of the ankle. A sprain heals best when there is little movement of the ankle during the healing process; thus a person who has a sprain should rest that foot, so sit with the foot up or lie down. If a snapping sound occurs when a person had an ankle injury, an X-ray may be needed to determine whether the injury was a sprain or a fracture. Many ankle injuries occur because people don't warm up properly before engaging in sports events or physical activities; always warm up before a sports event or an exercise workout and start any new physical activity gradually. An athlete who wanted to avoid ankle injuries chooses well-designed shoes and may also try taping to help support the ankle.

---

**10d**   Do not shift from indirect to direct quotation unnecessarily.

Direct quotation reports, in quotation marks, the exact words of a speaker or writer. Indirect quotation reports what someone has said or written, but not in the exact words.

| | |
|---|---|
| DIRECT | She said, "I'm psyched up and ready for the game." |
| INDIRECT | She said that she was psyched up and ready for the game. |

The tense in an indirect quotation should ordinarily be the same as the tense of the main verb. Unnecessary shifts between direct and indirect quotation often cause problems in tense.

**10d**

*shft*

| | |
|---|---|
| FAULTY | Lincoln asked the general *whether his army was well supplied* and *is it ready for battle.* [Shift from indirect to direct quotation. In such mixed constructions, the writer usually omits quotation marks from the direct quotation.] |
| REVISED | Lincoln asked the general whether his army was well supplied and whether it was ready for battle. [Indirect quotation] |
| | Lincoln asked the general, "Is your army well supplied? Is it ready for battle?" [Direct quotation] |
| FAULTY | They wondered *if we had missed the train* and *are we trying to telephone them* to let them know. |
| REVISED | They wondered if we had missed the train and if we were trying to telephone them to let them know. [Indirect quotation] |
| REVISED | They wondered, "Have they missed the train, and are they trying to telephone us to let us know?" [Direct quotation] |

---

## EXERCISE 10a–d

Revise the following sentences and paragraph, correcting all needless shifts in tense, mood, voice, person, and number and any shifts from indirect to direct quotation. Be prepared to explain your revisions.

### SENTENCE PRACTICE

1. Although most sharks swim at speeds up to 30 miles per hour, a speed of 60 miles per hour can be attained by the mako shark.
2. The average mako shark is about 12 feet long and weighed up to 1,000 pounds.
3. If you go fishing for mako sharks, a real challenge may be in store for you.
4. A hooked mako shark may fight for hours, and they have also been known to attack boats or even leap into the boat.
5. If you want a challenge, you can fish for a mako shark, but be careful, for its teeth are long, thin, and very sharp.

### PARAGRAPH PRACTICE

When I was swimming at a beach on the southern coast last summer, the lifeguard told me to watch out for sharks and did I

**10d**

*shft*

know what to do if I spotted one in the water. Sharks live in all oceans, but because they are most common in warmer waters, when you swim in warm coastal waters you should be cautious, for people may encounter a shark. Fortunately, not all sharks are predators; the whale shark feeds on plankton, and they do not bother swimmers. The basking shark is another harmless shark species, and plankton is eaten by this shark. Nevertheless, one hears vivid stories of shark attacks, so you tend to become wary when you go into the water.

---

## WRITERS REVISING: SHIFTS AND PRONOUN REFERENCE

*(continued from page 93)*

Fran realized she needed to choose one point of view, and it would be reflected in personal pronouns throughout the article. She could address her audience in either first person plural *(we)* or second person *(you)*. She decided that *we* would encourage readers to identify with the article; the first person plural puts everyone in the same boat—in the scene together. She felt that *you* sounded too much like finger pointing, especially since some negative things were being said *(bungling idiot,* etc.). However, Fran also recognized that she would have to watch agreement carefully so that all the antecedents and verbs were consistent with the plural form.

### Fran's Revision

R 1     There comes a time when we must make a break

R 2     and rely on ourselves as a career expert. To a

R 3     large degree, ~~you~~ *we* are ~~your~~ *our* own expert*s* because only     **10b**

R 4     ~~you~~ *we* know best about ~~your~~ *our* interests, challenges,

R 5     *us. Being our own experts means we must trust our*
        and what suits ~~you. This means your~~ own judgment     **9c**

R 6                                                    *we*
        and intuition, ~~must be trusted,~~ if ~~you~~ are going to     **10a**

R 7                              *our*
        take the initiative in ~~your~~ job search. ~~They say~~

R 8     *can      be                        we*
        ~~We~~ *Ue* ~~are~~ often ~~our~~ own worst enemies; if ~~you~~ see     **9e**

R 9     *ourselves*                              *s*
        ~~yourself~~ as a bungling idiot, during an interview,     **9d**

R10     *we are likely to*          *idiots.*
        ~~you'll probably~~ behave like ~~it~~.

## Analysis

*This*, the first word of the third sentence (line D5), is an unacceptably vague pronoun, referring to the whole idea in the preceding sentence. Furthermore, the passive voice verb (*must be trusted*, line D6), creates an unnecessary shift in voice (**10a**) and results in a weak sentence as well; the revision to active voice (lines R5-6) is consistent and stronger.

*They say. . .* (D7) is an indefinite use of the pronoun and serves no real purpose in the sentence, so Fran eliminated the unnecessary opening phrase. Also, the final pronoun in the sentence, *it* (D10), has no explicit antecedent that agrees with it in number (**9d**), so Fran supplied the unexpressed noun (*idiots*) in her revision (R10). Notice that the plural, *idiots*, maintains consistent use of number with the plural pronoun *we*.

**11**

*mis pt*

# 11

## MISPLACED PARTS

Modern English relies heavily on word order to show relationships among words. *Dog bites man* does not mean the same thing as *Man bites dog*. If the English words are reversed, so is the meaning.

Just as word order helps readers keep subject-verb-object relationships clear, so, too, does word order help readers know which words are the objects of modifiers. Because readers expect modifiers to be next to the words they modify, writers need to be especially careful to place phrases and clauses near the nouns they modify. Otherwise, sentences such as these can occur:

He bought a horse from a stranger with a lame hind leg.
We returned to Atlanta after a week's vacation on Monday.

Context usually—though not always—allows readers to work out the meaning of such sentences. But at best the reader is distracted by the necessary effort; at worst, ludicrous literal meanings can destroy the writer's credibility. Consider, for example, the following misplaced modifier noted by a national magazine·

"While a Legion bugler played 'To the Colors,' the first flag was hoisted on DeVane Park's 30-foot flagpole, followed by David Rinald singing the national anthem." *Lake Placid* (Fla.) *Journal*

Helped him hit the high notes.

*The New Yorker*

## WRITERS REVISING: MODIFIERS

**11**

*mis pt*

Jim, a student in Freshman English, was assigned a personal experience essay. Part of the instructions was to try to achieve variety in sentence construction. When he read over his rough draft, however, Jim noticed that while varying his sentences he had created several dangling and misplaced modifiers. As you work through Sections **11** and **12,** see if you can revise his paragraph, keeping sentence variety but correcting faulty modification. Then compare your version with Jim's retyped revision, which appears at the end of Section **12.**

**Draft**

D 1      Last summer I saw a hot-air balloon race. To

D 2    really understand what is going on, a knowledge of

D 3    hares and hounds is helpful. Taking off first,

D 4    one balloon is designated the "hare" balloon, and

D 5    then all the other balloons--the "hounds"--chase

D 6    it.

D 7      The hare balloon after a while lands in a

D 8    field some distance from the starting point.

D 9    Marked with an "x," the hound balloon that is

D10    able to land on or closest to the hare balloon's

D11    spot wins the race. That balloon takes first

D12    prize and gets congratulations from all the other

D13    balloonists having "caught" the hare. Coming

D14    close to the hare balloon's landing spot is not

D15    easy particularly since hot-air balloons float

D16    with the wind and are difficult to maneuver.

D17      Ballooning is the oldest form of aerial

D18    transportation. First flown in France, that

D19    country celebrated its 200th anniversary for

D20    ballooning in 1983.

This *Writers Revising* continues on page 120.

**11a**   In writing, place adverbs of degree or limitation such as *almost, even, hardly, just, only, nearly* immediately before the words they modify.

In speech we commonly put *only* and similar adverbs before the verb, regardless of what we mean them to modify. To avoid any possible ambiguity in writing, place such modifiers immediately before the words they modify.

| | |
|---|---|
| SPOKEN | I *only* ran a mile. |
| WRITTEN | I ran *only* a mile. |
| | |
| SPOKEN | He *just* wore a smile. |
| WRITTEN | He wore *just* a smile. |
| | |
| SPOKEN | She *almost* read the whole book. |
| WRITTEN | She read *almost* the whole book. |

---

EXERCISE 11a(1)
Revise the following paragraph so that limiting adverbs are placed before the words they modify. Then write five sentences of your own, each using a different limiting adverb (*almost, even, hardly, just, only, practically, precisely, nearly, shortly,* and so on) placed appropriately in the sentence.

When Europeans first settled in America, 30 million buffalo approximately roamed over two-thirds of the continent. However, by the early twentieth century, the buffalo practically was extinct. To protect the disappearing species, conservationists worked to establish public refuges and ranges quickly. Today, the buffalo is safe from extinction, and some public herds have even surplus animals. To keep their herds manageable, public refuges sell their surplus buffaloes often to private breeders.

---

EXERCISE 11a(2)
Move the italicized adverb to a different place in each of the following sentences so that a new meaning is created. Be prepared to explain the differences in meaning between the two sentences. Then write five sentences of your own that change meaning with a repositioning of the adverb.

1. *Actually,* American buffaloes are bison, but the two names are used interchangeably.
2. The *only* true buffaloes live in Asia and Africa.
3. American bison are *usually* gentle, but they can become dangerous and have been known to charge at humans.
4. Seeing *just* one bison can be intimidating, for the shaggy, hump-shouldered creatures are huge.
5. *Often,* a bison will be 5 feet tall and may weigh up to 2,500 pounds.

## 11b    Modifying phrases should refer clearly to the words they modify.

Phrases used to modify nouns must ordinarily be placed immediately after the words they are intended to modify. The following examples show the confusion and misrepresentation created by misplaced modifiers.

> MISPLACED    Joan borrowed a bicycle from a friend *with saddlebags.* [The writer intended the phrase *with saddlebags* to modify *bicycle,* not *friend.*]
>
> CLEAR    Joan borrowed a bicycle *with saddlebags* from a friend.
>
> MISPLACED    "We are committed to eliminating all traces of discrimination in the law *against women,*" Ronald Reagan told some 4,000 members of the American Bar Association meeting in Atlanta. [The law is against women?]
>
> CLEAR    President Reagan said that his administration was committed to eliminating from the law all traces of discrimination *against women.*

Phrases used as adverbs may usually be placed either within the sentence close to the words they modify or at the beginning or end of the sentence. In some sentences, however, their placement requires special thought.

> MISPLACED    The author claims the revolt was caused by corruption *in the first chapter.* [*In the first chapter* seems to modify the noun *corruption* although the writer surely intended it to modify the verb *claims.*]
>
> CLEAR    *In the first chapter,* the author claims the revolt was caused by corruption.
>
> MISPLACED    A huge boulder fell as we rounded the corner *with a crash.* [*With a crash* seems to modify the verb *rounded* although the writer intended it to modify the earlier verb, *fell.*]
>
> CLEAR    A huge boulder fell *with a crash* as we rounded the corner.
>
> MISPLACED    Thank you for the beautiful bowl. Right now it's sitting on our buffet *full of fruit.* [That's a lot of fruit!]
>
> CLEAR    Thank you for the beautiful bowl. Right now it's sitting *full of fruit* on our buffet.

---

EXERCISE 11b
Revise the following paragraph so that the modifying phrases refer clearly to the words they are intended to modify.

Although tofu is a familiar food in the Orient, the soybean product in the United States isn't well known. In the Orient for more than a thousand years tofu has been a staple of people's diets. Tofu with no cholesterol is a versatile food. To make tofu, soybeans are first soaked and then finely ground in water. Because tofu is high in protein, it is often used in dishes such as lasagna as a meat substitute.

## 11c Modifying clauses should refer clearly to the words they modify.

Clauses that modify nouns usually begin with *who, which,* or *that* and follow immediately after the words they modify.

| | |
|---|---|
| MISPLACED | The dog had a ribbon around his neck *that was tied in a bow.* [The ribbon, not his neck, was tied in a bow.] |
| CLEAR | Around his neck the dog had a ribbon *that was tied in a bow.* |
| MISPLACED | The children cautiously approached the deserted house by a winding path, *which was said to be haunted.* [The house, not the path, was said to be haunted.] |
| CLEAR | By a winding path, the children cautiously approached the house *that was said to be haunted.* |

Adverb clauses are introduced by words such as *after, although, because, since,* and *until.* Like adverb phrases, they can usually be placed either within the sentence close to the words they modify or at the beginning or end of the sentence; they can sometimes be confusing unless writers are careful.

| | |
|---|---|
| MISPLACED | The police towed the stolen station wagon to the city garage *after it was abandoned.* [The clause *after it was abandoned* is intended to modify the verb *towed* but seems to modify the noun *garage.*] |
| CLEAR | *After the stolen station wagon was abandoned,* the police towed it to the city garage. |
| | The police towed the stolen station wagon, *after it was abandoned,* to the city garage. |

EXERCISE 11c

Revise the following paragraph to place the modifying clauses in clear relationships to the words they modify.

Indian pudding is a traditional dish served in New England that is made with molasses, cornmeal, eggs, and milk. The native Americans had introduced the colonists to corn, and Indian pudding took its name from the meal ground from this corn, which was called "Indian meal." In colonial times, Indian pudding was often prepared on Saturday so that the Puritans could be free from work on their Sunday Sabbath because the pudding must bake from six to eight hours. Recipes for Indian pudding appear in early American cookbooks that require boiling the pudding for twelve hours, although today the pudding is usually baked. Since Indian pudding requires from six to eight hours of baking, today most people eat Indian pudding in restaurants who enjoy the traditional New England dessert.

**11d**
*mis pt*

## 11d   Avoid squinting modifiers.

A **squinting modifier** is one that may modify either a preceding word or a following word. It squints at the words on its right and left, and leaves the reader confused.

SQUINTING    His physician told him *frequently* to exercise.
CLEAR    His physician *frequently* told him to exercise.
His physician told him to exercise *frequently.*

SQUINTING    The committee which was studying the matter *yesterday* turned in its report.
CLEAR    The committee that was studying the matter turned in its report *yesterday.*
The committee, *which spent yesterday* studying the matter, turned in its report.

SQUINTING    He promised *on his way home* to visit us.
CLEAR    *On his way home,* he promised to visit us.
He promised to visit us *on his way home.*

EXERCISE 11d
Revise the following sentences to eliminate squinting modifiers.

1. In July my neighbors ask me often to go raspberry picking with them.
2. We plan after breakfast to gather our baskets and search out the wild raspberry bushes.
3. We all decided quickly that we needed to get going before the day got too hot.
4. We decided later that day to make fresh raspberry shortcakes.
5. Picking the raspberries was fun, but I frequently had to warn my friends to watch out for mosquitoes and bees.

## 11e   Do not split infinitives awkwardly.

An infinitive is split when an adverbial modifier separates the *to* from the verb. There is nothing ungrammatical about splitting an infinitive, and sometimes a split is useful to avoid awkwardness. But most split infinitives are unnecessary.

AWKWARD    I tried not *to* carelessly *hurt* the kitten.
CLEAR    I tried not *to hurt* the kitten carelessly.

AWKWARD    You should try *to*, if you can, *take* a walk every day.

CLEAR    If you can, you should try *to take* a walk every day.

You should try *to take* a walk every day if you can.

On the other hand, note the following sentence:

The course is designed *to* better *equip* graduates to go into business.

**11f**

*mis pt*

If *better* is placed before *to equip*, it squints awkwardly between *designed* and the infinitive; after *to equip* it modifies *graduates;* at the end of the sentence it is awkward and unnatural, if not entirely unclear. Thus, in this case, the split infinitive is the best choice for conveying the meaning the writer intended.

---

EXERCISE 11e
Revise the following paragraph to eliminate awkward split infinitives.

People who want to improve their diets should be sure to carefully choose their breakfast cereals. Shoppers have a wide variety of cereals to, when they're at the supermarket, choose from. Therefore, consumers have to always be sure to thoroughly read the nutrition information labels on the cereal boxes, for some cereals have high fat, sugar, and salt contents. To accurately determine what's in a box of cereal, shoppers should read the "Nutrition Information" and "Carbohydrate Information" labels. Being careful about the cereals they eat is a good way for people to, if they want, start improving their diets.

---

**11f**    In general, avoid separating a subject from its predicate, a verb from its object, or the parts of a verb phrase from one another. Intentional separations occasionally make a sentence more effective.

As Section 1 on sentence patterns and sentence parts explained, readers rely on related sentence elements and known sentence patterns to help them form the informational "chunks" that aid them in processing a sentence's meaning. Separation of sentence elements requires readers to hold pieces of information "in suspension" so to speak. So when you go against readers' expectations about the order of sentence parts and patterns, you should have a good reason for doing so.

Experienced writers intentionally separate related sentence elements to achieve special effects, such as adding suspense or drama to a sentence by delaying the verb. Nevertheless, effective separation of related sentence elements can be a judgment call, and not everyone will agree on the results. Use such separations only if your subject and purpose warrant the dramatic and artificial impression that separations convey.

EFFECTIVE SEPARATION   The captain, *seeing the ominous storm clouds gathering overhead,* ordered the crew to take in the sail.

And so Pilate, *willing to content the people,* released Barabbas unto them, and delivered Jesus, *when he had scourged him,* to be crucified.

MARK 15:15

Only when a man is safely ensconced under six feet of earth, *with several tons of enlauding granite upon his chest,* is he in a position to give advice with any certainty, and then he is silent.

EDWARD NEWTON

**11f**

*mis pt*

AWKWARD SEPARATION   She *found,* after an hour's search, the *money* hidden under the rug.

CLEAR   After an hour's search, she *found* the *money* hidden under the rug.

AWKWARD SEPARATION   At the convention I saw Mary Ward, whom I *had* many years ago *met* in Chicago.

CLEAR   At the convention I saw Mary Ward, whom I *had met* many years ago in Chicago.

---

EXERCISE 11f
Revise the following paragraph to eliminate unnecessary separation of sentence parts.

    Harriet Tubman, because she worked in the Underground Railroad to lead her people to freedom, came to be called Moses. Harriet Tubman was, in 1820, born a slave, but she, in 1849, escaped and eventually became a "conductor" on the Underground Railroad. Tubman led, while risking great danger to herself, more than 300 slaves to freedom. Individuals like Harriet Tubman were crucial to the success of the Underground Railroad because the system needed, so that it could move slaves north to freedom, brave and dedicated workers.

---

EXERCISE 11a–f
Revise the following sentences and paragraph to eliminate all misplaced parts. Be prepared to explain your revisions.

SENTENCE PRACTICE
1. Writing developed as a means of communication first through the use of pictures to represent the spoken word.
2. Simple pictures were the first forms of writing that were drawn on the walls of caves.
3. These pictures came to eventually represent words.
4. In time these pictures became, when they represented sounds, symbols for syllables.

5. Finally, the alphabet developed when each symbol only represented a single sound.

### PARAGRAPH PRACTICE

The ancient Egyptians developed in about 4000 B.C. a type of writing called hieroglyphic. Hieroglyphics are symbols used to pictorially represent meaning; for instance, two arms reaching together would depict the idea of embrace. Modern scholars were able to at last determine the meaning of hieroglyphics after the Rosetta Stone was discovered by Napoleon's army near the city of Rosetta in northern Egypt. Today the Rosetta Stone is, for those who are fascinated by ancient forms of writing, on display at the British Museum in London.

**12**

*dgl*

# 12
## *DANGLING MODIFIERS*

A modifier must have something to modify. A **dangling modifier** has nothing to modify because the word it would logically modify is not present in its sentence: for example, *Driving through the mountains, three bears were seen.* In this sentence, the modifying phrase has no logical object. The sentence says the bears are driving, but common sense tells us bears can't drive.

Dangling modifiers may be verbal or prepositional phrases (**12a–b**) or elliptical clauses (**12c**). They most commonly come at the beginning of a sentence, but they can come at the end as well. To write *There were three bears, driving through the mountains* still leaves the bears apparently doing the driving. Dangling modifiers often occur in mixed constructions when a writer begins a sentence as if he or she intends to use an active voice verb in the main clause but finishes it by shifting to a passive voice verb instead (see Section **14b**).

Eliminate dangling modifiers (1) by reworking the sentence so that an appropriate word is provided for the modifier to modify—in the case of a mixed construction, by using the same verb voice in both clauses—or (2) by expanding the dangler into a full subordinate clause. The following examples—the first from a student essay, the second from a financial journal—show danglers and how to eliminate them.

| | |
|---|---|
| DANGLING | Driving through the mountains, three bears were seen. |
| REVISED | While driving through the mountains, *we saw* three bears. [Active voice verbs throughout; word to modify supplied] |
| REVISED | *As we were driving through the mountains,* we saw three bears. [Expansion to full subordinate clause] |

**12a**

*dgl*

DANGLING   When asked to explain why they borrowed money from a particular bank, previous good experience and low interest rates were most frequently mentioned as reasons.

REVISED   When asked to explain why they borrowed money from a particular bank, *people* most frequently *mentioned* previous good experience and low interest rates as reasons. [Active voice verbs throughout; word to modify supplied]

Dangling modifiers can also slip into writing when an appropriate object for the modifier is present in an adjacent sentence but not in the sentence containing the dangler. Consider this paragraph from a campus newspaper:

> While wearing a Halloween mask and carrying a handgun, a man entered Marsh Pharmacy and asked for all of the narcotics, said Frank Reinhart, a temporary Marsh employee. According to Reinhart, he was filling in for another pharmacist when a man came up to the desk. *Wearing a green mask and overalls,* Reinhart estimated his height at about 6 feet and his weight at about 150 pounds.

Presumably the would-be thief, rather than Reinhart, was wearing the green mask and overalls. The reporter forgot that a modifier and the word it modifies need to be located in the same sentence:

> According to Reinhart, he was filling in for another pharmacist when *a man* wearing a green mask and overalls came up to the desk.

**12a**   Avoid dangling participial phrases.

A **participle** is a verb form usually ending in *-ing* or *-ed* and used as an adjective to modify a noun or pronoun. A participial phrase consists of a participle, its object, and any modifiers of the participle or object. (See **1b** and **1c**.)

DANGLING   Coming home late, the house was dark. [There is nothing in the sentence that can sensibly be coming home. A revision must identify some person.]

REVISED   Coming home late, we found the house dark. When we came home late, the house was dark.

DANGLING   Being made of glass, Rick handled the tabletop carefully.

REVISED   Because the tabletop was made of glass, Rick handled it carefully. [The participial phrase is expanded into a subordinate clause.]

---

EXERCISE 12a
Revise the following paragraph to eliminate dangling participial phrases.

Mystic, Connecticut, with its historic Seaport Museum and original whaling and fishing schooners, is well worth a detour, touring New England. Founded in 1654 by British colonists, some of the finest ships in the world were built there. Strolling through the town, exhibits on shipbuilding, weaving, and sailmaking can be seen. Being interested in ships, the most popular attractions are the eight large ships anchored in the Seaport. Wanting to learn more about the sealife in the area, the Mystic Marinelife Aquarium displays more than 6,000 marine specimens.

**12b**

*dgl*

## 12b Avoid dangling phrases that contain gerunds.

A **gerund** is an *-ing* form of a verb used as a noun. A gerund phrase consists of a gerund, its object, and any modifiers of the gerund or object. (See **1b** and **1d.**) In typical dangling phrases that contain gerunds, the gerund or gerund phrase serves as the object of a preposition.

Dangling gerunds, like the dangling infinitives discussed in Section **12c,** sometimes occur when the subject of the main clause is not the same as the implied subject governing the gerund phrase. Because a shift of subject is often accompanied by a shift to passive voice, checking the main clause for passive voice verbs is a quick way to test for and correct modifying phrases that may be dangling.

DANGLING     Before exploring the desert, our water supply was replenished. [Who replenished it?]

REVISED      Before exploring the desert, we replenished our water supply.

DANGLING     After putting a worm on my hook, the fish began to bite. [A very accommodating fish that will bait the hook for you!]

REVISED      After I put a worm on my hook, the fish began to bite.

EXERCISE 12b
Revise the following paragraph to eliminate dangling gerund phrases.

Before leaving the Boston area, nearby Cambridge, which is the home of Harvard University and the Massachusetts Institute of Technology, is another interesting city to visit. Located just a few minutes from Boston, Cambridge can be reached quickly by crossing the Charles River. On arriving at the Harvard campus, the long history of the college, which was founded in 1636, can be sensed. After strolling through the historic Harvard Yard, the home of poet Henry Wadsworth Longfellow can be visited on a street near Harvard's campus. After leaving the area around Harvard, the Massachusetts Institute of Technology, famous for its scientific research, should be seen.

## 12c    Avoid dangling infinitive phrases.

An **infinitive** consists of the infinitive marker *to* followed by the plain form of the verb. An infinitive phrase consists of an infinitive, its object, and any modifiers of the infinitive or object.

|  |  |
|---|---|
| DANGLING | To take good pictures, a good camera must be used. [Who will use the camera?] |
| REVISED | To take good pictures, you must use a good camera. |
|  | If you wish to take good pictures, you must use a good camera. |
| DANGLING | To skate well, practice is necessary. |
| REVISED | To skate well, you [or *one*] must practice. |

---

EXERCISE 12c
Revise the sentences in the following paragraph to eliminate dangling infinitive phrases.

> To make a perfect omelet, the eggs should be very fresh. A 5- or 6-inch skillet should be used to make a two- or three-egg omelet. To make sure that the omelet won't be tough, the egg whites and the egg yolks should be mingled together, but not overbeaten. The heat under the pan should be kept at medium-high to cook the eggs without burning them. To put the finished omelet on a serving plate, the pan should be tilted toward the plate as the omelet is pushed out with a fork.

---

## 12d    Avoid dangling elliptical clauses.

An **elliptical clause** is one in which the subject or verb is implied or understood rather than stated. The clause dangles if its implied subject is not the same as the subject of the main clause. Eliminate a dangling elliptical clause by (1) making the dangling clause agree with the subject of the main clause or (2) supplying the omitted subject or verb.

|  |  |
|---|---|
| DANGLING | *When a baby,* my grandfather gave me a silver cup. |
| REVISED | *When a baby,* I was given a silver cup by my grandfather. [The subject of the main clause agrees with the implied subject of the elliptical clause.] |
| REVISED | *When I was a baby,* my grandfather gave me a silver cup. [The omitted subject and verb are supplied in the elliptical clause.] |
| DANGLING | *While rowing on the lake,* the boat overturned. |
| REVISED | *While rowing on the lake,* we overturned the boat. [The subject of the main clause agrees with the implied subject of the elliptical clause.] |

*While we were rowing on the lake,* the boat overturned [*or* we overturned the boat]. [The elliptical clause is expanded into a subordinate clause.]

## EXERCISE 12d
Revise the following sentences to eliminate dangling elliptical clauses.

**12d**

*dgl*

1. When rushed for time, a microwave can save valuable minutes in the kitchen.
2. Children's after-school snacks can be fixed in the microwave, if careful.
3. While cooking, microwaves need to be watched carefully to avoid drying out.
4. Preparing many types of foods is easier in a microwave oven, although not all.
5. Since purchasing a microwave, making breakfast takes only minutes each morning.

## EXERCISE 12a–d
Revise the following sentences and paragraph to eliminate dangling modifiers.

### SENTENCE PRACTICE
1. The number of people who go to bowling alleys has not grown recently, although still the most popular indoor sport in the United States.
2. To attract more customers, computerized scoring systems, restaurants, and child-care centers are being added to modern bowling alleys.
3. When using the new computerized scoring systems, tedious computations of strikes and spares are no longer necessary.
4. To attract young families with children, child-care centers in bowling alleys allow parents to enjoy themselves while their children play in a supervised area.
5. After an evening of bowling, a relaxing dinner can be enjoyed in the bowling alley's full-service restaurant.

### PARAGRAPH PRACTICE
Having experienced a drop in attendance because of the popularity of home video, efforts are being made to encourage customers to return to movie theaters. To make waiting in line before the movie more enjoyable, theater lobbies have been expanded and redecorated. If hungry before or after the movie, some theaters have added cafes and pizza parlors. After getting into the theater itself, comfortable chairs and a temperature-controlled climate are other comforts encountered. To attract moviegoers with sophisticated sound systems at home, high-technology sound equipment has been installed in many movie theaters.

**12d**

*dgl*

## WRITERS REVISING: MODIFIERS
*(continued from page 108)*

### Revision

R 1      Last summer I saw a hot-air balloon race.  To

R 2    really understand what is going on, a knowledge of    **11e**

R 3    hares and hounds is helpful.  Taking off first,

R 4    one balloon is designated the "hare" balloon, and

R 5    then all the other balloons--the "hounds"--chase

R 6    it.

R 7      After a while the hare balloon lands in a    **11f**

R 8    field some distance from the starting point.  The

R 9    hare balloon's landing spot is marked with an    **11b**

R10    "x," and the hound balloon that is able to land on

R11    or closest to that spot wins the race.  Having

R12    "caught" the hare, that balloonist takes first    **11b**

R13    prize and gets congratulations from all the other

R14    balloonists.  Coming close to the hare balloon is

R15    not particularly easy since hot-air balloons float    **11d**

R16    with the wind and are difficult to maneuver.

R17      Ballooning is the oldest form of aerial

R18    transportation.  Hot-air balloons were first flown

R19    in France, where the two-hundredth anniversary of    **12a**

R20    ballooning was celebrated in 1983.

### Analysis

The first sentence of the draft contains no faulty modifiers. Although *To really understand* (lines D1–2) is a split infinitive, the split is not awkward. More importantly, if *really* is to keep modifying *understand,* the only other possibilities are *Really to understand* or *To understand really,* either of which creates a much more awkward sentence. Consequently, Jim wisely made no changes. The third sentence contains no faulty modifiers.

The fourth sentence contains an awkward split of subject and verb (D7–8). As the revision shows (R7–8), moving the modifying phrase to the beginning of the sentence improves the sentence. The opening phrase of the fifth sentence is misplaced (D9). The landing spot, not the hound balloon, is marked with an "x." Anyone not familiar with ballooning would get an entirely incorrect impression. Jim decided that this important information merited its own independent clause, rather than being subordinated, so he completely restructured the sentence (R9–11).

13

om,
comp

In sentence 6 (D11–13), the misplaced modifier *having "caught" the hare* suggests that all the balloonists win, rather than just one. Jim solved this problem by moving the phrase to the front of the sentence, placing it closer to the intended noun (R11–14).

In the seventh sentence (D13–16), *particularly* "squints"—it could be interpreted to mean "not particularly easy" or "not easy, particularly since hot air . . ." Jim transposed the two words (R15).

In the draft's final sentence, France seems to be flying itself, thanks to a dangling phrase. A major revision completely restructures the information; the draft's modifier becomes the main clause—and the major focus—of the last sentence in the revision (R18–20).

Jim located all but one of the misplaced or dangling parts in his draft. He overlooked a subtle error in the second sentence (D1–3)—a dangling infinitive phrase that can be corrected by providing an appropriate subject to perform the action of understanding: *To really understand what is going on, one needs to know something about hares and hounds.*

# 13

## OMISSIONS;
## INCOMPLETE AND ILLOGICAL
## COMPARISONS

A sentence will be confusing if the writer omits words needed for clarity and accuracy. Sometimes, of course, writers omit words through haste or carelessness. This sort of omission can be caught with careful proofreading. Most omissions not caused by carelessness occur in three kinds of constructions: (1) some constructions in which the omission of a preposition or conjunction is common in informal speech, (2) some kinds of compound constructions, and (3) comparisons.

---

**13a**

*om,*
*comp*

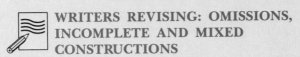

## WRITERS REVISING: OMISSIONS, INCOMPLETE AND MIXED CONSTRUCTIONS

Continuing with the revision of his essay on hot-air ballooning (see pages 108 and 120 for the first part of the essay), Jim checked for omissions, incomplete comparisons, and confused and mixed constructions. As you work through Sections **13** and **14**, see what you can do with the passage that follows, and then compare your revision with Jim's revision at the end of Section **14.**

**Draft**

D 1      I learned ballooning fall semester when I attended

D 2     the Albuquerque International Balloon Fiesta with a

D 3     friend. This event attracts over 700,000 enthusiasts

D 4     interested or skilled at flying the hot-air craft. No

D 5     other ballooning event attracts more spectators and

D 6     participants. Several contests that are held at the

D 7     Fiesta have valuable prizes. One is where balloonists

D 8     try to snag keys hanging from the top of a pole stuck

D 9     into the ground. The keys are to the prize, a new car.

This *Writers Revising* continues on page 131.

---

**13a** Carefully proofread your writing to avoid careless omissions.

The sample sentences below are confusing because they omit necessary words.

> CONFUSING    The opportunities for people television repair are varied.
>
> REVISED    The opportunities for people *in* television repair are varied.
>
> CONFUSING    Many millions people were unemployed last recession.
>
> REVISED    Many millions *of* people were unemployed *during the* last recession.

| CONFUSING | The Kentucky Derby is Louisville's best-known attraction, but far from its only one. |
|---|---|
| REVISED | The Kentucky Derby is *one of* Louisville's best-known attractions, but far from its only one. |

Very probably the writer of the third example thought out the sentence with something like the phrase *one of* in mind and was merely careless in getting the idea down on paper.

## 13b   In writing, express relationships left implied in speech.

Some constructions such as *He left Monday* are idiomatic. In speaking we often extend this pattern to such expressions as *We became friends spring semester,* or *The next few years we'll worry about prices.* In writing, such relationships need to be spelled out.

| SPOKEN | Space travel *the last few years* has been exciting. |
|---|---|
| WRITTEN | Space travel *during the last few years* has been exciting. |

Similes or comparisons such as *I feel like a million dollars* are common in both speech and writing. The construction *feel like* also appears in idiomatic expressions such as *I feel like a cookie,* but in this case no comparison is being expressed. Of course the speaker does not actually *feel* like a cookie (he or she merely wants a cookie to eat); the spoken idiom omits the implied participle *having* or *eating.* In most written contexts, the verbal should be expressed.

| SPOKEN | Do you feel like some popcorn? |
|---|---|
| | She feels like a game of tennis. |
| | I feel like a movie. |
| WRITTEN | Do you feel like *having* some popcorn? |
| | She feels like *playing* a game of tennis. |
| | I feel like *going to* a movie. |

The omission of *that* can sometimes be confusing.

| CONFUSING | He felt completely naked but totally private swimming was indecent. |
|---|---|
| REVISED | He felt that completely naked but totally private swimming was indecent. |

The use of *type, make, brand,* and some other similar words immediately before a noun *(this type show, this brand cereal)* is common in speech but is avoided by most writers.

| SPOKEN | I have never driven this *make car* before. |
|---|---|
| WRITTEN | I have never driven this *make of car* before. |

**13c**

*om,*
*comp*

EXERCISE 13a–b
Revise the following paragraph to correct careless omissions and to supply words that are implied but not stated.

There is such a wide variety of soft drinks on the supermarket shelves today that customers could spend lots of time just deciding what type soft drink to buy. Soft drink consumption has risen the past few years, and manufacturers have created new flavors to appeal to customers. It seems as though every time I go to the store, there's a new brand cola on the shelf. I tried a couple different types of new soft drinks, but I decided to stay with the cola I've drunk for several years. But for people who feel like a new soft drink, all the different kinds carbonated drinks on the shelves must be exciting.

**13c**    Include all necessary words in compound constructions.

When we connect two items of the same kind with coordinating conjunctions such as *and* or *but,* we often omit words that unnecessarily duplicate each other: *She could [go] and did go; He was faithful [to] and devoted to his job.* But such omissions work only if the two items are in fact the same. If they are not, the resulting construction will be incomplete (see also the discussion of parallelism in Section **32**). Such incomplete constructions usually result from omitting necessary prepositions or parts of verb phrases.

| | |
|---|---|
| INCOMPLETE | Tanya was interested and skillful at photography. |
| REVISED | Tanya was interested *in* and skillful *at* photography. [*Interested* idiomatically requires the preposition *in;* if it is not present, we tend to read *interested at.*] |
| INCOMPLETE | My cat never has and never will eat fish. |
| REVISED | My cat never has *eaten* and never will *eat* fish. |
| INCOMPLETE | Tom's ideas were sound and adopted without discussion. |
| REVISED | Tom's ideas were sound and *were* adopted without discussion. [*Were* needs to be repeated here since the two verbs are not parallel; the first *were* is used as the main verb; the second is used as an auxiliary with *adopted.*] |

EXERCISE 13c
Revise the following paragraph to supply the omitted words.

College students have always and continue to want to make their dormitory rooms more comfortable and home-like. Most dorm rooms are clean and functional but not really large, so students have to find ingenious ways to save space. Realizing that dorm rooms never have and never will be large enough, some roommates check with each other about what to bring before moving in; in doing so, the roommates avoid duplicating items such as stereos, refrigerators, and television sets. Students enthusiastic and interested in fitness programs often bring weights and exercise equipment with them when they arrive on campus. Those students who are not skillful and practical in arranging the mass of items they brought for their rooms may spend a year climbing over boxes, bicycles, and books.

## **13d** Make all comparisons complete and logical.

A comparison expresses a relationship between two things: *A is larger than B.* To make a comparison complete and logical, include both items being compared and all words necessary to make the relationship clear, and be sure that the two items are in fact comparable.

**1. Avoid incomplete comparisons.** Sentences such as *Cleanaid is better* or *Weatherall Paint lasts longer* are popular with advertisers because they let the advertiser avoid telling us what the product is better than or lasts longer than. To be complete, a comparison must state both items being compared.

| | |
|---|---|
| INCOMPLETE | Our new Ford gets better mileage. [Better than what?] |
| REVISED | Our new Ford gets better mileage than our old one did. |
| INCOMPLETE | Louisville features more park land per person than any other in the nation. [Any other what?] |
| REVISED | Louisville features more park land per person than any other city in the nation. |

**2. Avoid ambiguous comparisons.** In comparisons such as *He enjoys watching football more than* [*he enjoys watching*] *baseball,* we can omit *he enjoys watching* because only one meaning is reasonable. But when more than one meaning is possible, the comparison will be ambiguous.

| | |
|---|---|
| AMBIGUOUS | I admire her more than Jane. [More than Jane admires her? More than you admire Jane?] |
| CLEAR | I admire her more than I admire Jane. |
| | I admire her more than Jane does. |

**3. Avoid illogical comparisons.** A comparison will be illogical if it compares or seems to compare two things that cannot be sensibly compared.

| | |
|---|---|
| ILLOGICAL | A lawyer's income is greater than a doctor. [The sentence compares an income to a doctor. Logic requires the comparison of income to income or of lawyer to doctor.] |

REVISED    A lawyer's income is greater than a doctor's.
A lawyer's income is greater than that of a doctor.
A lawyer has a greater income than a doctor has.

**4. Avoid grammatically incomplete comparisons.** Comparisons using the expression *as strong as, as good as,* and the like always require the second *as.*

**13d**

*om,*
*comp*

INCOMPLETE    He is as strong, if not stronger than, Bob.

REVISED    He is as strong as, if not stronger than, Bob.
He is as strong as Bob, if not stronger.

In comparisons of items in the same class of things, use *other* or *any other.* In comparisons of items in different classes, use *any.*

INCORRECT    Mount Everest is higher than *any* Asian mountain.

CORRECT    Mount Everest is higher than *any other* Asian mountain.
Mount Everest is higher than *other* Asian mountains. [We are comparing Mount Everest, one Asian mountain, to other Asian mountains.]
Mount Everest is higher than *any* American mountain. [We are comparing Mount Everest, an Asian mountain, with American mountains, a different class.]

---

EXERCISE 13d
Revise the following paragraph to make all comparisons complete and logical.

Today, advances in technology are allowing weather forecasters to make better predictions about the weather. Using devices such as satellites and supercomputers, weather forecasters are able to make predictions that are more reliable than predictions in the past. Factors such as the seasons affect weather forecasting; for instance, weather in summer is less stable. Geography's role in influencing the weather is as important, if not more important than, any factor that affects the climate. Because of the unpredictability of weather patterns, short-range weather forecasters are able to make predictions that are more reliable than long-range forecasters.

---

EXERCISE 13a–d
The following sentences and paragraph all contain incomplete constructions. Revise each to supply words that have been omitted. Be prepared to explain your revisions.

SENTENCE PRACTICE
1. Peppers, either the sweet bell-shaped variety or the hot varieties, have been and continue an important ingredient in many cuisines.

2. For instance, hot peppers such as serrano, jalapeños, cayenne, and poblano are used in the type cooking found in Mexico and in the southwestern United States.
3. For those who are concerned about nutrition, peppers are lower in calories and richer in vitamin C.
4. Green bell-shaped peppers change red and get sweeter as they mature.
5. A person who develops a taste and indulges in dishes containing hot peppers may sometimes feel as though his or her mouth is on fire.

**14**

*awk*

**PARAGRAPH PRACTICE**

Banana peppers, which are native to Louisiana, are often used in Cajun and Creole food, types of cooking that have become popular throughout the United States the past few years. Dishes like jambalaya, gumbo, and shrimp creole are more familiar than any dishes associated with Cajun and Creole cooking. Some dishes, however, aren't as familiar and may take a little getting used to; nevertheless, some people who say they never have and never will eat crawfish change their minds when they encounter crawfish étoufeé, a tasty concoction of crawfish and a savory brown sauce. Visitors to New Orleans find the city is famous for its Cajun and Creole restaurants. In fact, New Orleans most likely has as many, if not more, Cajun and Creole restaurants than any city in the U. S.

# 14
## *MIXED OR CONFUSED SENTENCES*

Sometimes a sentence goes wrong because the predicate says something about the subject that cannot sensibly apply to that subject. Or a sentence goes wrong because it starts with one kind of construction and ends with a different kind of construction. The first of these is called **faulty predication;** the second, a **mixed construction.**

**14a** Combine only subjects and predicates that make sense together.

Not all subjects and verbs make sense together. In each of the following sentences, inappropriate verbs create faulty predication.

The *selection* of the committee *was chosen* by the students.
Many *settlers,* moving into a new part of the country, *expanded* into towns.
Any *member* who failed to do his job on the ship *meant* danger for the whole crew.

**14a**

*awk*

**1. Avoid linking subjects and complements illogically with** *to be*. Illogical combinations of subject and verb are particularly likely to occur when some form of the linking verb *to be (is, are, was, were)* is used. Linking verbs equate what comes before the verb with what comes after it—the subject with the complement: something equals something else. Thus they cannot be used to connect things that are not equal.

FAULTY    An important step in skiing is stopping. [*Step* does not equal *stopping*.]

REVISED    An important step in skiing is learning to stop.

FAULTY    The magician's first trick was a pack of cards. [*Trick* does not equal *pack*.]

REVISED    His first trick was one performed with a pack of cards.

FAULTY    Schools are a serious quarrel today.

In the third example, *schools* clearly is not equivalent to *quarrel*. But revision is not really possible because the subject, *schools,* is itself so vague. Perhaps the writer meant something like *Increased taxes for schools cause serious quarrels today.*

**2. Avoid illogical use of** *is when* **and** *is where*. Predicates that begin with *is when* and *is where* can cause faulty predication. Definitions such as *Drunkenness is when you've had too much to drink* or *Subtraction is where you take one thing from another* are common in speech. Written English, however, ordinarily requires a noun or a word group functioning as a noun as both subject and complement in such definitions.

FAULTY    A documentary is when a movie or a television drama analyzes news events or social conditions.

REVISED    A documentary is a movie or a television drama that analyzes news events or social conditions.

FAULTY    A hasty generalization is when you jump to conclusions.

REVISED    A hasty generalization involves jumping to conclusions. To make a hasty generalization is to jump to conclusions.

Another acceptable revision preserves the *when* or *where* but substitutes another verb for the linking verb *is*. This revision also avoids the over-reliance on *to be* verbs common in much writing.

FAULTY    Frostbite is where skin tissue has been frozen.

REVISED    Frostbite appears where skin tissue has been frozen.

FAULTY    A safety is when a ball carrier gets tackled behind his own goal line.

REVISED    A safety occurs when a ball carrier gets tackled behind his own goal line.

**3. Do not write "the reason is because . . ."** Sentences such as *The reason she didn't come was because she was sick* are common in speech, but *reason is that* is preferred at all levels of writing. *Because* means "for the reason that"; therefore, the expression *the reason is because* is redundant.

**14b**

*awk*

FAULTY     The reason he went to Chicago was because he wanted to visit Kareem.

REVISED     The reason he went to Chicago was that he wanted to visit Kareem.

He went to Chicago because he wanted to visit Kareem.

---

EXERCISE 14a
Revise the following paragraph to eliminate faulty predications.

Bootlegging is where highly taxed or forbidden items are produced illegally. The term *bootlegging* is most often associated with Prohibition; Prohibition was when Congress passed a constitutional amendment in 1919 to limit liquor production and sales. The crime and violence associated with Prohibition meant a big problem for federal law enforcement authorities. One of the reasons that Prohibition was such a problem for federal authorities was because bootleggers such as Al Capone had created a huge illegal liquor industry. The repeal of Prohibition was when the Twenty-first Amendment to the Constitution was passed and ratified in 1933.

---

## 14b  Do not mix constructions.

A mixed construction is one in which a writer begins a sentence in one construction and then shifts to another. The result is a derailed sentence that must be put back on its track to be clear.

MIXED     With every effort the student made to explain his problem got him more confused.

Here the writer began with a prepositional phrase, but was thinking of *every effort* as the subject by the time he or she arrived at the verb *got*. We can untangle the sentence either by giving *got* the subject *he,* or by dropping the preposition *with* and making *every effort* the subject.

REVISED     With every effort the student made to explain his problem, he got more confused.

Every effort the student made got him more confused.

Beginnings such as *the fact that, there are,* and *it is* often cause needless complexity and lead to mixed or confusing sentences.

MIXED     The fact that Louise was a good student she had many offers for good jobs. [*The fact that* as a beginning requires something like *results* or *leads to* as a main verb in the sentence. But the writer has forgotten that as the sentence develops.]

REVISED   The fact that Louise was a good student resulted in her having many offers for good jobs.

Because Louise was a good student, she had many offers for good jobs.

**14b**

*awk*

Unnecessary shifts from active-voice to passive-voice verbs can also create mixed constructions. When the implied or expressed subject of one clause becomes an implied or expressed object in another clause, readers can have a hard time sorting out meaning (see Section **10a**).

MIXED   When they were water-skiing, the tow rope was broken by my friends. [The subject shifts unneccessarily from *they* to *rope*.]

REVISED   When they were water-skiing, my friends broke the tow rope.

### EXERCISE 14b
Revise the following paragraph to eliminate mixed constructions.

The fact that many high school and college sports stars hope to become professional sports stars they often become disappointed when they realize that few athletes actually make it to the pros. When these athletes play in high school or college sports, nonsports careers were not considered by many of them. Although a player is a star on the college tennis team doesn't mean he or she will end up on the professional tennis circuit. Out of the thousands of participants in high school baseball, it may be only a few who ever get to play in the major leagues. By being sure also to plan for a career outside of sports is necessary for anyone who hopes to become a professional athlete.

### EXERCISE 14a–b
Revise the following sentences and paragraph to eliminate faulty predications and mixed constructions. Be prepared to explain your reasons.

#### SENTENCE PRACTICE
1. By studying the problems of office workers it was determined that eyestrain is the most frequent complaint among workers.
2. To prevent eyestrain is a reason health experts suggest that anyone spending hours in front of a video display terminal should take a ten-minute break every hour.
3. When workers take this ten-minute break, something in the distance should be looked at to relax the eyes.

4. The reason so much eyestrain occurs is because office space is often badly designed, and lighting is inadequate or is in the wrong place.
5. The fact that eyestrain can lead to irritability and headaches and those who must spend all day in poorly designed or badly lighted offices can suffer.

**PARAGRAPH PRACTICE**

Another cause of eyestrain is where drivers must spend hours on the road during long trips. Driving at high speeds means concentration for the driver, and that intense concentration often leads to eyestrain. When they drive on long highway trips, stops after the first 200 miles and then after every 100 miles should be made by drivers. Because the sun can cause glare on bright days is a reason drivers should wear sunglasses to reduce that extra strain on their eyes. By taking frequent breaks from driving and by wearing sunglasses makes it possible to avoid eyestrain on long highway trips.

**14b**

*awk*

# WRITERS REVISING: OMISSIONS; INCOMPLETE AND MIXED CONSTRUCTIONS *(continued from page 122)*

**Jim's Revision**

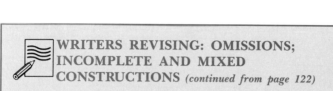

| R 1 | I learned about ballooning during fall semester when I | 13b |
| R 2 | attended the Albuquerque International Balloon | |
| R 3 | Fiesta with a friend. This event attracts over | |
| R 4 | 700,000 enthusiasts interested in or skilled at | 13c |
| R 5 | flying the hot-air craft. No other ballooning | |
| R 6 | event attracts more spectators and | 13d(1) |
| R 7 | participants than the Albuquerque fiesta does. Several contests that are held at | |
| R 8 | the Fiesta have valuable prizes. ~~One is where~~ In one contest | 14a |
| R 9 | balloonists try to snag keys hanging from the | |
| R10 | top of a pole stuck into the ground. The keys | |
| R11 | are to the prize, a new car. | |

**Analysis**

Without the preposition *about*, readers would assume from the first draft sentence that Jim knows how to fly a bal-

**14b**

*awk*

loon—a major misunderstanding of meaning. *During* is also implied; in writing, the relationship should be expressed. The compound construction in the second sentence requires *in* to be complete (see R4). In the third sentence, *than the Albuquerque Fiesta does* completes the comparison *more people*. The fourth sentence (D7–8) is acceptable as written. In the fifth sentence, *One* can't be "where"—"where" means a place. Also, in this sentence *one* is so far from the word to which it refers *(contests)* that the meaning is likely to be unclear (D7–10). These problems are solved in the revision (R8–10). The final sentence requires no revision.

REVIEW EXERCISE: COMMON SENTENCE FAULTS
(SECTIONS 6–14)
Indicate the principal error (faulty agreement, faulty reference, misplaced parts, and so on) in the following sentences and paragraphs. Then revise to eliminate the error.

**SENTENCE PRACTICE**

1. Keeping tropical fish is a rewarding pastime, however aquarium owners need to make sure they don't make several common mistakes that can result in dead fish.
2. One problem that can occur is chlorine poisoning; chlorine poisoning is when chlorine, which is often added to ordinary tap water, gets into the aquarium water and damages the gills of the fish.
3. The wrong pH level in the water, as well as chemicals such as chlorine, also harm fish.
4. Aquarium owners which think they may have problems with pH level can get a kit at pet shops that measures the pH level of the tank water.
5. Some of the biggest problems aquarium owners encounter is caused by dirty tank water.
6. Fish produce waste products that cannot be removed by the best filters even, which results in a buildup of waste that can poison fish. This can be solved by replacing one-third of the water in the aquarium each month.
7. Although lots of different fish swimming around are attractive, fish need plenty of space, so don't overcrowd the aquarium.
8. In the aquarium keeper's manual I read, it says that a good guideline is to have no more than one inch of fish for each gallon of water, which gives fish enough water space to stay healthy.
9. In addition to overcrowding, overfeeding being one of the most common mistakes that aquarium owners make.
10. To make sure that fish are not overfed, several small feedings each day is better than one big feeding.

**PARAGRAPH PRACTICE**

Catfish have become a popular food in the United States diners like to feast on golden brown catfish steaks or filets. Anyone that has ever caught catfish will know that they have to be careful, for catfish have poison glands in their top and forward fins. These kind of glands can give you puncture wounds, so be careful when handling catfish.

The fact that catfish inhabit waters in many parts of the world makes them a common species, indeed, there are 1,000 type catfish. Twenty-eight of which are found in the United States. One peculiar kind of catfish, the armored catfish, has bony plates covering their body. Some of these armored catfish live in Florida, but the ones found in South America are bigger. Living in underwater caves, explorers have found blind catfish. This type catfish find food by using the tastebuds located in their whiskers. It says in a recent science article that there are also electric catfish. The reason a person should be careful about this fish is because it can give you a mild shock. Weighing up to 300 pounds, the jungle rivers of South America contain some of the biggest catfish in the world. A person fishing for catfish would be very surprised to get one of these kind whoppers on their hook.

**14b**

*awk*

# MECHANICS

*Of all forms of symbolism, language is the most highly developed, most subtle, and most complicated. It has been pointed out that human beings, by agreement, can make anything stand for anything.*

S. I. HAYAKAWA, *Language in Thought and Action*

**M**any practices of written English are merely conventions. Logic does not justify them; they simply represent standard ways of doing things—codes of meaning that people recognize and accept. The mechanics of writing numbers and abbreviations, of handling acronyms, initialisms, and clipped forms, and of using word division (syllabication) are such conventions. To ignore these conventions is to be a nuisance to readers.

## WRITERS REVISING: MECHANICS

After an interview with the department chairman, Steve wrote up his notes to use in an oral report on government funding of university research. Then the instructor asked for a written version of the oral report, so Steve had to make some revisions based on the conventions that a general, nontechnical reader would expect. As you work through Sections **15–18**, turn the interview notes into appropriate written form. Then compare your revision with Steve's version, which appears at the end of Section **18**.

**Interview Notes for Oral Report**

N 1    Dr. Brown said NSF $ is used to

N 2    support a lot of research at colleges

N 3    and universities around the U.S. Last

N 4    year they distributed grants worth

N 5    approx. 1.2 billion $. 14 professors,

N 6    forty grad students, and 7 technicians

N 7    are currently supported in our school

N 8    by the National Science Foundation.

N 9    Around the univ. NSF money funds

N10    research in the physical sciences

N11    such as chem., physics, and etc.

N12    Prof. Brown said the analytical chemistry

N13    group has received a 2 hundred thousand

15
*nos*

**136**

N14    $ grant for a lab robotics project, and

N15    grants worth thousands more support

N16    research on cell repro in the bio.

N17    dept. Profs who wish to apply for an

N18    NSF grant must send a grant proposal to

N19    D.C. Over 29,000 50-page proposals

N20    arrive in the Foundation's mail every

N21    yr.

**15**

*nos*

This *Writers Revising* continues on page 148.

# 15

## NUMBERS

Conventions governing the choice between spelling out numbers *(twenty-two)* and using figures *(22)* vary with the kind of writing. You may have noticed that writing in general publications uses spelled-out numbers more frequently than does scientific or technical writing, which favors greater use of figures. Consider the following examples:

> There remained to the seventy-five-year-old King only one great-grandson, a pink-cheeked child of two, the last surviving infant in the direct line. . . . This new little Dauphin remained miraculously alive and lived to rule France for fifty-nine years as Louis XV. On his deathbed, Louis XIV called for his great-grandson and heir who then was five. Face to face, these two Bourbons who between them ruled France for 131 years regarded each other.
>
> ROBERT K. MASSIE, *Peter the Great: His Life and World*

> In alphanumeric mode, the video circuit displays characters in 80 or 40 columns by 25 rows. Sixteen foreground and background colors are available, except with character blinking, which reduces available background colors to eight.
>
> In graphics mode, low resolution provides 16 colors and 160 by 200 pixels, medium resolution provides 4 colors and 320 by 200 pixels, and high resolution offers 2 colors and 640 by 200 pixels.
>
> "The Tandy 1000," *Byte: The Small Systems Journal*

> What is America's biggest regional repertory company, employing as many as 63 actors to mount a dozen productions for a total of 676 performances a year? What company features three spaces ranging from a stripped-down, experimental "black box". . . to a

1,173-seat outdoor Elizabethan playhouse?. . . What company annually attracts more than 300,000 playgoers, 90% of them from more than 150 miles away?. . . The answer in each case is the Oregon Shakespearean festival. . . .

"Only 2,500 Miles from Broadway," *Time*

As different as these passages appear to be in their use of numbers versus figures, each follows a coherent set of guidelines used by writers of general nonfiction (the first example), technical description (the second example), and journalism (the third example).

Your own use of numbers and figures in any given piece of writing should be governed by the conventions of the field for which you are writing. Those conventions can be discovered simply by examining publications in the field or by consulting style manuals published by the professional organizations in the field. The following guidelines explain some of the common conventions governing numbers.

**15a**

**nos**

**15a**  In general, use words for numbers nine and less. Use figures for numbers ten and over. If a discussion contains few numbers, one- or two-word numbers may be spelled out, and other numbers may be represented by figures. Related numbers should all be expressed in the same style.

The larvae of swallow-tail moths feed only on one plant. The leaves, located 15 to 20 meters up into a forest canopy, are difficult to see.

*Chemistry*

Tired volunteers rescued 17 whales beached or stranded Thursday along Cape Cod. . . . Up to 70 scientists and volunteers had worked two days, sometimes in 50-degree water, to aid the giant mammals.

*USA Today*

I wouldn't give you fifty cents for that car, not even if I lived to be one hundred years old. No, not even if I lived to be 199!

The ornithologist reported that 2 of the 50 bald eagles known to be living in Ohio had recently been sighted in Belmont County. The sightings were at 5-, 12-, and 27-day intervals during the three summer months of June, July, and August.

Remember that the words for compound numbers twenty-one to ninety-nine are hyphenated (Section **30d**).

**15b**  Use figures for dates and addresses.

| *Dates* | *Addresses* |
|---|---|
| May 4, 1914 | 13 Milford Avenue |
| 23 April 1978 | 57 East 121st Street |
| 1862–1924 | Route 1 P.O. Box 739 |
| 17 B.C. to A.D. 21 | Apt. 2B |
| | Grinnell, Iowa 50112 |

**Ordinal numbers** (numbers that indicate order: *first, third, twenty-ninth*) or the forms 1st, 3rd, 9th, may be used in dates if the year is not given: *March 1, March first, March 1st.*

In formal invitations, dates are usually written out: *Tuesday, September first, nineteen hundred and eighty-seven.* (See **20i** for the punctuation of dates and addresses.)

**15c**  Ordinarily, use figures to express precise measurements for the following:

| | |
|---|---|
| *Decimals* | 8.72   4.25   13.098 |
| *Percentages* | 72% or 72 percent |
| *Mixed numbers and fractions* | 27½   19⅔   (but *one-half* pound of coffee) |
| *Scores and statistics, numbers being compared* | score of 35-10   vote of 86-53 it was 5-10 degrees warmer |
| *Identification numbers* | Channel 5   Interstate 70 |
| *Volume, chapter, and page numbers* | Volume V, Chapter 7, page 518 |
| *Act, scene, and line numbers* | *King Lear,* 2.1.18–47 |
| *Numbers followed by symbols or abbreviations* | 5 cu. ft.   93° F.   31° C. 55 mph   60 Hz   1200 baud |
| *Exact amounts of money* | $24.98   $3.49   56¢ |
| *Times* | 4:30 P.M.   11:55 A.M.   (but *half past two, quarter of six, seven o'clock*) |

Sums of money that can be expressed in two or three words or in round numbers are sometimes written out: *twenty million dollars in losses, fifty cents on the dollar.*

When writing a compound-number adjective, spell out the first of the two numbers or the shorter of the two to avoid confusing the reader: *sixteen 10-foot poles, 500 one-liter bottles.*

**15d**  Except in legal or commercial writing, do not repeat in parentheses a number that has been spelled out.

COMMERCIAL    The original order was for eight (8) pumps.

STANDARD    Mother dropped six stitches from her knitting.

**15e**  Spell out numbers that occur at the beginning of a sentence.

Although you may frequently see numbers at the beginning of newspaper headlines, such usage is a journalistic space-saving convention.

17 Whales Saved, 11 Killed
*USA Today*

If you use a number to begin a sentence, spell it out or revise the sentence to replace the numeral with a word.

FAULTY    217 bales of hay were lost in the fire.

REVISED   Two hundred and seventeen bales of hay were lost in the fire.

FAULTY    1986 was the year the Chicago Bears won the Super Bowl.

REVISED   In 1986 the Chicago Bears won the Super Bowl.

EXERCISE 15 a-e
In the following sentences and paragraph, make any necessary corrections in the use of numbers. Assume a general audience.

**SENTENCE PRACTICE**

1. Consumers can find up to twelve types of milk and cream on their supermarket shelves, but often shoppers aren't sure just what makes each type of milk different from the others; basically, the main difference in these types of milk is the amount of fat in each.

2. For instance, whole milk has at least three and a quarter percent fat, while lowfat milk, which has had some fat removed, usually contains one or two percent of fat.

3. Skim milk, sometimes called nonfat milk, has less than one percent fat; at the other end of the scale, heavy cream has thirty-six percent fat.

4. The various types of milk and cream on the supermarket shelves have all been pasteurized to destroy bacteria; pasteurizing involves heating the milk or cream at one hundred and forty-five°F. for 30 minutes or at one hundred and sixty-five° F. for 15 seconds.

5. Often, cream is ultrapasteurized, a process in which the liquid is heated at two hundred and eighty ° F. for a minimum of 2 seconds.

**PARAGRAPH PRACTICE**

    Many of the ancient statues, artwork, and buildings of Italy need extensive renovation and restoration to protect them from modern hazards such as pollution, traffic vibrations, and the effects of the 1,000s of tourists who visit them every year. For instance, the Leaning Tower in Pisa, which is over 800 years old, has to be monitored constantly in order to detect any increase in its angle of incline. In another area of Italy, much work is going on at the ruins of Pompeii, the Roman city that was destroyed in A.D. seventy-nine when Mt. Vesuvius erupted. 1966 was a particularly bad year for Italy, for in that year floods innundated Florence and Venice, and much priceless artwork was severely damaged.

# 16

## *ABBREVIATIONS*

Abbreviations are common in writing for specialized audiences. These readers are usually familiar with the abbreviations common to their field and find them a convenient shorthand. When writing for a general audience, however, you will typically want to avoid abbreviations—with some standard exceptions. The following sections describe standard exceptions, as well as some abbreviated forms that should not be used.

**16**

*ab*

**16a**  The following abbreviations are appropriate in both formal and informal general writing.

**1. Titles before proper names.** Use such abbreviations as *Mr., Mrs., Ms., Dr.* only when the surname is given: *Dr. Hart* or *Dr. F. D. Hart.*

> **FAULTY**   He has gone to consult the Dr.
>
> REVISED   He has gone to consult Dr. Hart (*or* the doctor).

Use *St.* (Saint) with a Christian name that refers to a person or place: *St. Theresa, St. Louis.* The plural form of the abbreviation is *SS.: SS. Peter and Paul.*
Use abbreviations such as *Hon., Rev., Prof., Sen.* only when both the surname and given name or initials are given: *The Hon. O. P. Jones,* but not *Hon. Jones.* In more formal usage, spell out these titles and use *The* before *Honorable* and *Reverend.*

> **INFORMAL**   Rev. W. C. Case delivered the sermon.
>
> FORMAL   The Reverend W. C. Case delivered the sermon.

**2. Titles after proper names.** Use the following abbreviations only when a name precedes them: *Jr., Sr., Esq.* Abbreviations of academic degrees and professional certifications *(M.S., Ph.D., L.L.D., M.D., J.D., C.P.A.)* can be used after a name, or they can stand by themselves: *Robert Reese, Jr., has an M.A. in philosophy.* Do not, however, use equivalent titles and/or abbreviations both before and after a name.

> **NOT**   Dr. Carolyn Haas, M.D., is a pediatrician.
>
> BUT   Carolyn Haas, M.D., is a pediatrician.

**3. Abbreviations of terms referring to dates, times, or units of measurement.** These terms should be abbreviated only when they appear with numerals specifying exact figures: *34 B.C., A.D. 1066, 6:54 a.m.* (or *A.M.*), *7:15 p.m.* (or *P.M.*), *$87.59, no. 6* (or *No. 6*), *55 mph.*

Note that *B.C.*, which means "before Christ," is always abbreviated and capitalized and always follows the year. *A.D.*, which means "in the year of our Lord" *(anno Domini)*, is always abbreviated, capitalized, and always precedes the year. Similarly, *a.m.* (*ante meridiem*, "before noon") and *p.m.* (*post meridiem*, "after noon") are always abbreviated.

The use of abbreviations without numbers should be avoided.

16a

*ab*

NOT    We met in the p.m. to check the no. of ft. the river had risen.

BUT    We met in the evening to check the number of feet the river had risen.

See Section **16d** for further discussion of scientific and technical abbreviations.

**4. Latin abbreviations.** Although Latin abbreviations such as *i.e.* (that is), *e.g.* (for example), *etc.* (and so forth) have been common in writing, in formal writing the English equivalent is increasingly used. Do not use *etc.* as a catch-all. It is meaningless unless the extension of ideas it implies is unmistakably clear. Do not write *and etc.;* the *and* is redundant.

CLEAR    The citrus fruits—oranges, lemons, etc.—are rich in vitamin C. [The reader has no difficulty in mentally listing the other citrus fruits.]

INEFFECTIVE    We swam, fished, etc. [The reader has no clues to the implied ideas.]

REVISED    We swam, fished, rode horses, and danced.

**5. The names of agencies, organizations, corporations, and people ordinarily referred to by their initials.**

| | |
|---|---|
| *Agencies* | IRS, FBI, SEC |
| *Organizations* | AMA, YWCA, NOW, NAACP |
| *Corporations* | NBC, IBM, AT&T |
| *People* | JFK, FDR |

If the name of an organization occurs frequently in a paper or article but is likely to be unfamiliar to readers, it should be spelled out in its first use and the abbreviation given in parentheses. Thereafter the abbreviation may be used: *Zimbabwe African National Union (ZANU).* If you are unsure of the meaning of an abbreviation, consult a dictionary of abbreviations and acronyms available in your library's reference collection. See Section **17** for further discussion of words formed from initials.

**16b** Spell out personal names; the names of countries and states; the names of days, months, and holidays; and the names of courses of instruction.

FAULTY     Eliz., a student from Eng, who joined our bio class last Wed., expects to go home for Xmas.

REVISED     Elizabeth, a student from England who joined our biology class last Wednesday, expects to go home for Christmas.

The District of Columbia is spelled out when it is used alone but abbreviated, D.C., when it follows the city name, Washington. The United States and the Soviet Union are commonly abbreviated as the USA (or U.S.A.) or the US, and the USSR (or U.S.S.R.).

**16c** Spell out place names and the words *street, avenue, route, company, corporation,* and the like, as well as references to a subject, volume, chapter, line, or page, except in special contexts such as addresses and footnotes.

FAULTY     The Milano Trucking Co. is near the Michigan St. exit of I-70.

REVISED     The Milano Trucking Company is near the Michigan Street exit of Interstate 70.

FAULTY     The vet. med. students are being tested on chs. 4–7 tomorrow in the Life Sciences Bldg.

REVISED     The veterinary medicine students are being tested on Chapters 4–7 tomorrow in the Life Sciences Building.

Use such abbreviations as *Bros., Ltd.* (for *Limited*), *Co., Corp.,* and the ampersand (& for *and*) only if the firms themselves use them in their official names.

Barnes & Noble, Inc.

Sears, Roebuck and Co.

**16d** When writing for a general audience, spell out most scientific and technical words unless the abbreviations are well known to readers or unless the words would be excessively long and cumbersome in unabbreviated form.

The number of technical and scientific abbreviations in general use—in everyday speech, newspapers, and magazines—increases constantly. Thus we are more likely to recognize the abbreviation DNA than we are its long form, deoxyribonucleic acid.

If you are in doubt about whether to use an abbreviation for a technical word, follow your common sense and prevailing general usage. If you think your readers may be unfamiliar with an abbreviation, first use the full name and then follow it with a brief explanation or with the abbreviation in parentheses. Thereafter, the abbreviation may be used alone.

> Thanks to computer-aided-design and computer-aided-manufacturing (CAD-CAM), automobile companies are able to test new models on the drawing board. CAD-CAM saves thousands of dollars and hundreds of hours in engineering time.

**16e**

**ab**

Whether to use abbreviations for units of measurement in writing for a nontechnical audience or in a nontechnical context can be a judgment call. For instance, most of us probably accept the use of "45 rpm" in the example that follows:

> Record industry analysts say the 45 rpm single will soon be a thing of the past; revolutions per minute don't mean much when your compact disk player holds just one size.

But many readers resist such usage in general writing as the following:

> The canoe was 8 ft long and 3 ft wide. Empty, it weighed 100 lbs.

## 16e Punctuate abbreviations according to the conventions of the field for which you are writing.

In technical writing, the periods are omitted from abbreviations unless they could be confused with words of the same spelling: *The cable is 23 ft 8 in. long.* In general writing, you may omit the periods or not, as you choose, as long as the abbreviations are not confusing and are used consistently throughout the document.

The *MLA Handbook,* the style manual for writing about literature, English, and other modern languages, notes the trend to use neither periods nor spaces between letters of an abbreviation, particularly when the abbreviation is composed of capital letters: *MBA, BC, AD, NY, CPA, USA.* An exception is initials of given names, which require both periods and spacing: *E. F. Hutton, J. Ross Brown.* Periods are recommended for abbreviations composed of or ending in lower-case letters: *a.m., i.e., ft., Dept. of Defense.*

As these examples and others located elsewhere in this text illustrate, conventions regarding abbreviations vary widely between fields and sometimes even within fields. The best advice is to familiarize yourself with the conventions of the group for which you are writing by examining style manuals and periodicals in the field; then apply those conventions with consistency and common sense.

---

EXERCISE 16a–e
Correct any misuse of abbreviations in the following sentences and paragraph.

**SENTENCE PRACTICE**

1. The site for the White House, which is located on Penn. Ave. in Wash., D.C., was chosen by George Washington.
2. Although Washington chose the location for the White House, John Adams was the first pres. who actually lived in the Exec. Mansion.
3. The White House, which was built of stone from Virg., was not originally white, but after being burned by the Brit. in 1814, it was restored and painted white.
4. Although the building had been referred to earlier as the White House, that name finally became official during the time Theo. Roosevelt was in office.
5. Like the White House, the official residence of the Brit. Prime Minister is also a tourist attraction; the house, located at 10 Downing St. in London, can be viewed from several yds. away, but Downing St. itself cannot be entered.

**17**

*init*

**PARAGRAPH PRACTICE**

My Am. hist. prof., Dr. Mary Samuels, Ph.D., asked me to come by her office in the a.m. to discuss my research paper. I need to have this paper finished by the end of Nov., so I have to get my idea approved by this Fri. I plan to do a paper on the work of Dr. Eliz. Blackwell, M.D., the first woman in the USA to receive a med. degree. Dr. Blackwell graduated from medical col. in 1849 and in 1857 helped to start the N. York Infirmary for Women and Children. The Dr. also helped to found the Women's Med. Col. at the Infirmary.

---

# 17

## *ACRONYMS, INITIALISMS, AND CLIPPED FORMS*

Acronyms, initialisms, and clipped forms are types of abbreviations, shortened forms of words. In general writing, the following guidelines should be applied.

**17a**  Spell out acronyms initially if your reader is likely to be unfamiliar with them.

An **acronym** is an abbreviation formed from the initial letters of words. The letters of an acronym are pronounced as a single word, and they are written without periods or spaces between letters.

UNICEF United Nations International Children's Emergency Fund

MADD Mothers Against Drunk Driving

OSHA Occupational Safety and Health Administration

NATO North Atlantic Treaty Organization

If you are unsure of the meaning of an acronym or initialism (**17b**), consult one of the acronym dictionaries in your library.

**17b**

*init*

**17b** Spell out any initialisms that are likely to be unfamiliar to your reader before using them in their abbreviated form.

An **initialism,** like an acronym, is an abbreviation formed from the first letters of words. However, initialisms are pronounced letter by letter rather than as a single word: *SAT* (Scholastic Aptitude Test), *GRE* (Graduate Record Examination), *CRT* (cathode ray tube), *PCBs* (polychlorinated biphenyls).

The Securities and Exchange Commission (SEC) began its investigation of insider trading on Wall Street. According to knowledgeable sources, the SEC has a water-tight case against several brokers.

Some abbreviations are a cross between initialisms and acronyms; the first letter may be pronounced as a letter and the remainder pronounced as a word: *GMAT* (pronounced *gee*-mat, Graduate Management Admission Test).

**17c** Avoid clipped forms in formal writing. Clipped forms are sometimes appropriate in informal writing, if you are striving for a conversational tone and if your audience will understand them.

**Clipped forms** are words from which the beginning or end has been cut to create a shorter word: *dorm* (dormitory), *lab* (laboratory), *prof* (professor), *phone* (telephone), *vet* (veteran). Clipped forms are fairly common in the jargon of particular fields such as business *(sales rep)*, medicine *(lab tech)*, and so forth. Strictly speaking, they are not abbreviations and so are not followed by periods.

---

EXERCISE 17a-c

Write a series of sentences in which you use at least six acronyms, initialisms, and clipped forms. Try to use several from each category, and select several that would not be familiar to some of your audience. Be prepared to discuss whether the clipped forms you have chosen are appropriate for your audience, purpose, and tone.

---

# 18

## SYLLABICATION

When you find that you can write only part of a word at the end of a line and must complete the word on the next line, divide the word between syllables and use a hyphen to indicate the break. Always place the hyphen at the end of the line after the first part of a divided word, not at the beginning of the next line on which you complete the word.

When you are in doubt about the syllabication of a word, consult a good dictionary. Desk dictionaries normally use dots to divide words between syllables. *bank·rupt, col·lec·tive, ma·lig·nant, punc·ture.* Note that not every syllable marks an appropriate point at which to divide a word at the end of a line. (See **18b** and **18c**.) If a word cannot be correctly divided between syllables, move the entire word to the beginning of the next line.

**18a**  Do not divide words pronounced as one syllable.

>   WRONG    thr-ee, cl-own, ycarn-ed, scream-ed
>   REVISED    three, clown, yearned, screamed

**18b**  Do not divide a word so that a single letter stands alone on a line.

>   WRONG    wear-y, e-rupt, a-way, o-val
>   REVISED    weary, erupt, away, oval

**18c**  When dividing a compound word that already contains a hyphen, make the break only where the hyphen occurs.

>   AWKWARD    pre-Dar-winian, well-in-formed, Pan-Amer-ican
>   REVISED    pre-Darwinian, well-informed, Pan-American

---

EXERCISE 18a-c
Which of the following words may be divided at the end of a line? Indicate appropriate divisions with a hyphen. Refer to your dictionary if you have doubts.

| | | |
|---|---|---|
| embezzle | pragmatic | forced |
| await | scanty | gamut |
| duplication | menagerie | unique |
| saved | plague | futility |
| patron | self-sufficient | oily |

---

REVIEW EXERCISE: MECHANICS (Sections 15–18)
Correct any errors in the following sentences and paragraph. Remember to check for faulty syllabication. Assume a general audience.

**18c**

**syl**

### SENTENCE PRACTICE

1. Oktoberfest, which actually begins in Sept., is an international festival that takes place in Munich, W. Germany, every year.
2. During the sixteen days of Oktoberfest, visitors to the city drink beer, eat Bavarian specialities, and enjoy parades, dances, and folk-singing.
3. In large tents that can seat 1,000s of people, Oktoberfest participants drink beer and wine; in fact, the city has 36 large beer gardens and many smaller drinking establishments.
4. 7,000 people can be served at one time at the Hirschgarten, the largest of Munich's beer gardens.
5. After downing several standard-size glasses of Bavarian beer, glasses equal to a little less than 3 12-ounce cans of Amer. beer, a visitor to Oktoberfest might feel rather shaky the next morning.

### PARAGRAPH PRACTICE

Munich is the capital of Bavaria, 1 of the 11 states that made up the Fed. Republic of Germany. In Munich's Marienplatz, its main square, the Glockenspiel clock at the New City Hall goes through an elaborate performance at eleven a.m. each morning and at noon and at five in the p.m. from May through Oct. Munich is a city of museums, including the Bavarian State Picture Galleries, the Bavarian National Mus., and the Deutsches Museum (the Germ. Mus. of Science and Tech.). Much of present-day Munich has been carefully restored after devastating air strikes during W. War II. Thirty-five mi. south of Munich lie the Bavarian Alps and the Zugspitze, Germany's highest mtn., which is nine thousand, seven hundred and nineteen ft. tall.

---

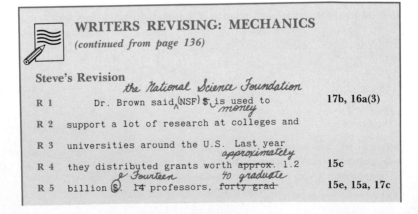

## WRITERS REVISING: MECHANICS
*(continued from page 136)*

**Steve's Revision**

R 1   Dr. Brown said (NSF) $ is used to        17b, 16a(3)

R 2   support a lot of research at colleges and

R 3   universities around the U.S. Last year

R 4   they distributed grants worth approx. 1.2        15c

R 5   billion $. 14 professors, forty grad-        15e, 15a, 17c

| | | |
|---|---|---|
| R 6 | students, and 7 technicians are currently *NSF* | |
| R 7 | supported in our school by the ~~National~~ *university* | |
| R 8 | ~~Science Foundation~~. Around the ~~univ.~~ NSF | 16c |
| R 9 | money funds research in the physical sciences | |
| R10 | such as ~~chem.~~ *chemistry*, physics, and ~~etc.~~ *so forth* | 16b, 16a(4) |
| R11 | ~~Prof.~~ *Professor* Brown said the analytical chemistry | 16a(1) |
| R12 | group has received a ~~2 hundred thousand $~~ *$200,000* | 15c |
| R13 | grant for a ~~lab-~~ *laboratory* robotics project, and | 17c |
| R14 | grants worth thousands more support | |
| R15 | research on cell ~~repro-~~ *reproduction* in the ~~bio. dept.~~ *biology department* | 17c, 16c |
| R16 | ~~Profs~~ *Professors* who wish to apply for an NSF grant | 17c |
| R17 | must send a grant proposal to *Washington,* D.C. Over | 16b |
| R18 | 29,000 ~~50-~~ *fifty-* page proposals arrive in the | 15c |
| R19 | Foundation's mail every ~~yr.~~ *year* | 16a(3) |

**18c**

*syl*

## Analysis

All clipped forms *(grad, prof, lab)* are spelled out for a general
audience. Initialisms may be used throughout a piece of writing
once the name is spelled out as in line R1. Symbols, such as
dollar signs, are used only with a figure as in line R1. Abbreviations are not appropriate when there is no accepted form as in
line R15, nor when there is no number such as *yr.* in line R19.
Numbers are spelled out when they begin a sentence (line R5).
When writing a compound-number adjective, the first of the two
numbers or the shorter of the two is spelled out to avoid confusing the reader as in line R18. Increasingly, writers are using
the English equivalent of Latin terms such as *and so forth* for *etc.,*
when writing to a general audience (line R10).

# PUNCTUATION

*p*

Punctuation [is a] code that serves to signal structural, semantic, and rhetorical meanings that would otherwise be missed by the reader . . . and from the reader's point of view, punctuation provides a map for one who must otherwise drive blindly past the by-ways, intersections, and detours of a writer's thought.

MINA SHAUGHNESSY, *Errors and Expectations*

**W**hen we speak, we use pauses and gestures to emphasize meaning, and we vary the tempo, stress, and pitch of our voices to mark the beginning and end of units of thought. In other words, we "punctuate" our speech. We punctuate writing for the same purposes, drawing on a whole set of conventional devices developed to help readers identify chunks of information and to give them clues to what we are trying to communicate.

The first of these devices is **spacing:** that is, closing up or enlarging the space between letters or words. For example, we do not runwordstogetherthisway. Instead, we identify a word as a word by setting it off from its neighbors. Spacing is the most basic of all punctuating devices. We use spacing also to separate sentences, to set off paragraphs, to list items as in an outline, to mark lines of poetry, and the like.

But spacing, of course, is not the only punctuation we need. What, for example, can you understand from this string of words:

> yes madam jones was heard to say to the owl like old dowager without a doubt the taming of the shrew by shakespeare would be a most appropriate new years present for your husband.

To make this passage intelligible, we need to add two other kinds of punctuation: (1) changes in the size and design of letters, namely, **capitals** and **italics;** and (2) marks or points, namely, **periods, commas, quotation marks, apostrophes,** and other special signs.

> "Yes, Madam," Jones was heard to say to the owl-like old dowager, "without a doubt, *The Taming of the Shrew* by Shakespeare would be a most appropriate New Year's present for your husband."

The example shows four functions of punctuation:

**1. End punctuation.** Capitals, periods, question marks, and exclamation points indicate sentence beginnings and endings.

**2. Internal punctuation.** Commas, semicolons, colons, dashes, and parentheses within sentences show the relationship of each word or group of words to the rest of the sentence.

**3. Direct-quotation punctuation.** Quotation marks and brackets indicate speakers and changes of speaker.

**4. Word punctuation.** Capitals, italics, quotation marks, apostrophes, and hyphens indicate words that have a special character or use.

In questions of punctuation there is often no absolute standard, no authoritative convention to which you can turn for a "correct" answer. But two general rules serve as reliable guides:

1.  Punctuation is a part of meaning, not a substitute for clear and orderly sentence structure. Before you can punctuate a sentence properly, you must construct it properly. No number of commas, semicolons, and dashes can rescue a poorly written sentence.

2.  Observe conventional practice in punctuation. Though many of the rules are not hard and fast, still there is a community of agreement about punctuating sentences. Learning and applying the punctuation rules that follow will help you observe these conventions.

# 19

## *END PUNCTUATION*

19

*p*

Periods, question marks, and exclamation points signal the end of a sentence. Use a *period* after plain statements or commands; use a *question mark* after questions; use an *exclamation point* after strongly emotional expressions.

Ordinarily, the character of the sentence dictates the proper end punctuation; for instance, a clearly interrogative sentence calls for a question mark. Occasionally, however, your readers will not be able to tell from content or structure alone what you intend the meaning of a sentence to be. In such cases, end punctuation is vital to meaning. For example, notice the different intentions of the three sentences below and how the end punctuation contributes to meaning:

> He struck out with the bases loaded.
> He struck out with the bases loaded?
> He struck out with the bases loaded!

## WRITERS REVISING:
## END PUNCTUATION

When Natasha got back an in-class exercise which required an analysis of how sex is sometimes used in advertising, she found her instructor had written "Good analysis, but poor punctuation. Correct it." Revise the end punctuation in Natasha's paper; then compare your version with hers at the end of this section.

**19a**

.

**Natasha's Draft**

D 1         Advertisers often use sex to sell their

D 2   products! Toothpaste commercials illustrate this

D 3   idea the Close-up toothpaste commercial, in which

D 4   a boy is overwhelmed by the smell of a girl's

D 5   breath, is a good example. As a girl searches the

D 6   floor for her lost earring, the boy sniffs her

D 7   breath. Giggling the girl asks, "What are you

D 8   doing." Then the boy asks her what that smell is?

D 9   "Close-up toothpaste," the girl replies. The boy

D10   is amazed that it is toothpaste, and the girl

D11   replies enthusiastically with a lilt in her voice,

D12   "That's why they call it Close-up," the commercial

D13   ends with a bang as the boy kisses the girl,

D14   making the viewer believe that this product is

D15   actually responsible for bringing two people

D16   closer together.

This *Writers Revising* continues on page 157.

## THE PERIOD

**19a** Use a period to signal the end of a statement, a mild command, or an indirect question.

|  |  |
|---|---|
| STATEMENT | She swam the mile with easy strokes. |
| COMMAND | Swim with easy strokes. |
| INDIRECT QUESTION | I asked her where she learned to swim with such easy strokes. |

**19b** Use periods with initials of names and abbreviations ending with lowercase letters.

R. B. Stewart      M. F. K. Fisher      Dr.      Mr.      Mrs.      Ms.
etc.      introd.      Sen.      Switz.

The trend is to omit periods in abbreviations made up of capital letters. Always omit periods in abbreviations that serve as names of organizations and government agencies.

| | | | | | | |
|---|---|---|---|---|---|---|
| RN | CPA | MBA | PhD | BS | NY | CA | CARE |
| PTA | NFL | UNICEF | CIA | | | |

If you are in doubt about whether to use periods in an abbreviation, consult a good dictionary or the style manuals of professional organizations in your field.

## THE QUESTION MARK

**19c**  Use a question mark after a direct question.

Direct questions often begin with an interrogative pronoun or adverb (*who, when, what,* etc.), and usually have an inverted word order, with the verb before the subject.

19c

?

> When did you study chemistry?
> Do you ever wonder what your future will be?
> You want to make a good impression, don't you?

**19d**  Use a question mark inside parentheses (?) to indicate doubt or uncertainty about the correctness of a statement.

The device shows that, even after research, you could not establish the accuracy of a fact. It does not serve as a substitute for checking facts.

> John Pomfret, an English poet, was born in 1667 (?) and died in 1702.

Rather than using (?), you may simply use *about:*

> John Pomfret, an English poet, was born about 1667 and died in 1702.

Do not use a question mark as a form of sarcasm:

> It was an amusing (?) play.

**19e**  Do not use a question mark after an indirect question.

An **indirect question** is a statement implying a question but not actually asking one. Though the idea expressed is interrogative, the actual structure is not: the subject and verb are not inverted.

They asked me whether I had studied chemistry in high school.
He asked me whether I wished to make a good impression.
I wonder what my future will be.

A polite request phrased as a direct question may sometimes be followed by a period rather than a question mark, especially when the
intent is more like that of a mild command than an actual question.

Here is my draft of the committee's report. *When you have finished
adding your comments, would you please return it to me.*

However, if you do not use a question mark, you run some risk of
your reader's failing to realize that a request has been made. The safest practice is to use the question mark with such requests, particularly
if you want a direct response on the reader's part.

**19f**

**!**

With our presentation only a week away, we don't have much preparation time left. *May I have your graphs by Thursday morning, so that
Audio-Visual can make the slides?*

## THE EXCLAMATION POINT

**19f**   Use the exclamation point after an interjection or after a
statement that is genuinely emphatic or exclamatory.

Fire! Help! Oh, no!
Mom! Dad! Guess what! I've been accepted to law school!
The rocket's engines have ignited, and we have liftoff!

**19g**   Do not overuse the exclamation point.

Used sparingly, the exclamation point gives real emphasis to individual statements. Overused, it either deadens the emphasis or introduces an almost hysterical tone in your writing.

War is hell! Think of what it does to young people to have their
futures interrupted and sometimes cut off completely! Think of
what it does to their families! Think of what it does to the nation!

---

EXERCISE 19a–g
Supply the appropriate punctuation marks in the following sentences
and paragraph. If you feel that a choice of marks is possible, state
why you chose the one you did. After completing the sentences, go

back and revise the indirect questions to make them direct questions, and punctuate accordingly.

SENTENCE PRACTICE

1. My roommate asked me last night if I knew what the term *Cinco de Mayo* means
2. According to my history professor, Muriel B. Harrison, *Cinco de Mayo* is a Mexican holiday that celebrates the anniversary of the Battle of Puebla on May 5, 1862
3. Who was involved in the Battle of Puebla
4. Dr Harrison, who has a PhD in Latin American history, told us that the Mexican troops, who were outnumbered three to one, defeated the French troops of Napoleon III
5. Wow Defeating an army when you're outnumbered three to one is quite a feat.

PARAGRAPH PRACTICE

Diego Rivera is one of Mexico's most famous modern painters, but did you realize that you can also see his work at the Detroit Institute of Arts If you ever go to Detroit, be sure to see Rivera's murals in which he painted scenes of industry in America When I was there last spring, a museum guide asked if I had ever seen any of Diego Rivera's paintings in Mexico In fact, I did see his huge murals of Mexican life when I visited the Palace of Fine Arts in Mexico several years ago The murals were fantastic

**19g**

**!**

---

## WRITERS REVISING: END PUNCTUATION

*(continued from page 153)*

Natasha reviewed the material in Section **19** before she began her corrections. She could see, among other things, that she had misused the exclamation point and had failed to distinguish between indirect and direct questions.

### Revision

R 1      Advertisers often use sex to sell their    **19f**

R 2   products Toothpaste commercials illustrate

R 3   this idea The Close-up toothpaste commercial,    **19a**

R 4   in which a boy is overwhelmed by the smell of

R 5   a girl's breath, is a good example. As a girl

```
R 6    searches the floor for her lost earring, the

R 7    boy sniffs her breath. Giggling the girl

R 8    asks, "What are you doing?" Then the boy asks      19c

R 9    her what that smell is? "Close-up                  19e

R10    toothpaste," the girl replies. The boy is

R11    amazed that it is toothpaste, and the girl

R12    replies enthusiastically with a lilt in her

R13    voice, "That's why they call it Close-up!"         19f

R14    the commercial ends with a bang as the boy

R15    kisses the girl, making the viewer believe

R16    that this product is actually responsible for

R17    bringing two people closer together.
```

**19g**

**!**

### Analysis

The exclamation point in line R2 is inappropriate after a statement that is not genuinely emphatic. In line R3 there should be a period after the word *idea* since it ends a complete sentence. The direct question "What are you doing?" ending in line R8 should have a question mark inside the quotation mark since it, and not the sentence, is a question. A period must follow the indirect question in line R9. An exclamation mark would be appropriate following the girl's reply in line R13 since the context indicates a genuinely exclamatory remark.

# 20–24

## *INTERNAL PUNCTUATION*

End punctuation indicates whether a whole sentence should be read as a question, a statement, or an expression of emotion. Internal punctuation indicates the relationships and relative importance of elements within the sentence. Five punctuation marks are used for this purpose: **commas, semicolons, colons, dashes,** and **parentheses.**

Like all punctuation, internal punctuation is a vital way of making the meaning of your sentences clear. In studying the following rules, notice not only how each mark is used but also how it contributes to the total meaning of the sentence.

# 20

# THE COMMA

## WRITERS REVISING: COMMAS

As a punctuation exercise for the high school student whom she was tutoring in English, Paula devised a game she called "Silly Sentences." She wanted to show her tutee that more than merely applying some rules, comma usage determines meaning. As you work through this section, try your hand at removing the nonsense from the following statements by changing the way commas are used. The corrected version appears at the end of Section **20.**

```
At the banquet will be many members of
Congress eating roast beef and members of the
press as well. The waiters will serve the courses
of soup, fish, salad, meat, and vegetables, and
dessert with three wines. For dessert women tend
to prefer sherbet, men, pie and ice cream. Mind
your manners and try not to eat too much pig.
Please try not to drop your spoon, or roll in your
soup. Stay awake during the after-dinner speech,
and if you must yawn do so, quietly.
```

This *Writers Revising* continues on page 175.

**20a**  Use a comma to separate main clauses joined by a coordinating conjunction.

**1. The coordinating conjunctions are** *and, but, or, nor, for, so,* **and** *yet.* **When any one of these conjunctions is used to connect main clauses, it is always preceded by a comma.** The comma acts as a signal that one independent clause has ended and the next is about to begin.

> Half a million colonists remained loyal to the British Crown during the American Revolution, *and* for their loyalty many of them lost their homes, property, and livelihoods.

History books used to portray Loyalists as conniving aristocrats with British connections, _but_ research has revealed that most were ordinary hard-working farmers and tradespeople.

Rebel patriots physically abused some Loyalists, _or_ more often they verbally abused those who would not shift their allegiance.

Loyalists were conservatives who did not want change, _nor_ did they want separation of the colonies from England.

About 36,000 Loyalists eventually emigrated to Nova Scotia in Canada, _for_ this territory was ruled by the British Crown.

Approximately 500,000 of the 2.5 million people in colonial America were Loyalists, _so_ one in every five Americans could be classified as Loyalist.

Nearly 100,000 Loyalist Americans fled the colonies in what was the largest exodus in American history, _yet_ their suffering has been largely unrecognized.

**20a**

**,**

There are, however, two exceptions, noted below.

**2. Some writers omit the comma before the coordinating conjunction when one or both of the main clauses are very short.**

The spirit is willing but the flesh is weak.

Get your coat and let's go.

There is certainly nothing wrong with using a comma in such sentences, and since the comma is sometimes necessary for clarity, it's a good idea simply to establish the habit of using a comma regularly.

**3. When one or both of the main clauses joined by a coordinating conjunction are long or internally punctuated, use a semicolon before the coordinating conjunction.**

The Canadian Mounted Police were established in the 1870s to assure peaceful settlement of the northwest wilderness; and they became symbols of political and social order.

The Mounties, dressed in red tunics and riding well-trained horses, were a familiar sight on the Canadian frontier; but few people in the United States saw Mounties except in the movies.

---

EXERCISE 20a
Combine the following sentences by using a coordinating conjunction and a comma. If one or both of the main clauses are long or internally punctuated, use a semicolon before the coordinating conjunction. If you have a choice of conjunctions, be prepared to explain your selection.

SENTENCE PRACTICE

1. In Amsterdam, the tall and narrow seventeenth-century house where Anne Frank and her family spent two years hiding during World War II is now a museum. Over 500,000 visitors come to the house each year.
2. When they tour the museum, visitors can see permanent displays of photographs of the Frank family, various documents, and World War II materials. The museum also presents changing exhibitions, many of which deal with events of the war and the Holocaust.
3. The German-Jewish Frank family had to go into hiding in rooms in the upper part of the house. The Nazis would have sent them off to the death camps.
4. Anne Frank and her family were discovered on August 4, 1944. Anne and her sister were first sent to Westerbrook, a Jewish transit camp, then to Auschwitz, and finally to Bergen-Belsen, the concentration camp where they died.
5. Anne Frank was only sixteen when she died. She left a diary which is an insightful account of the horrors of war and repression as well as an account of the goodness of people such as those who risked their own lives to hide the Frank family.
6. *The Diary of Anne Frank* was published in 1947 and remains popular today. Editions of the book have been printed in over thirty countries.

**20b**

**,**

Using coordinating conjunctions preceded by commas, combine at least eight of the sentences in the following paragraph. Use a semicolon before the coordinating conjunction if main clauses are long or internally punctuated.

PARAGRAPH PRACTICE

Amsterdam is the capital of the Netherlands. The city is also one of Europe's great commercial and artistic cities. Visitors to Amsterdam should not miss seeing the Rembrandt collection in the Rijks Museum. They should also not leave the city without seeing the Van Gogh collection at the Municipal Museum. Amsterdam is also an important European port. The city is built on two rivers, the Ij and the Amstel. Canals running through the city link it to the North Sea and the Rhine River, one of Europe's most important waterways. Visitors can stroll across some of the bridges that cross Amsterdam's canals. They can wander through the narrow streets and admire the seventeenth-century architecture.

**20b**  Use a comma to separate introductory phrases and clauses from a main clause.

Introductory prepositional or verbal phrases and introductory clauses may be adverbial, modifying the verb in the main clause or the whole main clause; or they may serve as adjectives, modifying the subject of the main clause. Whatever their function, they should always be separated from the main clause by a comma unless they are very short and there is no possibility of misreading.

INTRODUCTORY PREPOSITIONAL PHRASES
*According to legend,* Hercules had enormous strength. [Adverbial]
*After his long exile to France,* Charles II returned to England in 1660. [Adverbial]
*Like any man of sense and good feeling,* I abominate work. [Adjectival]

ALDOUS HUXLEY

INTRODUCTORY VERBAL PHRASES
*To succeed as a long-distance runner,* a person must have strong legs. [Adverbial]
*Announcing a recess,* the judge retired to his chambers. [Adjectival]
*Exhausted by her effort,* the swimmer fell back into the pool. [Adverbial]
*To be quite honest about it,* that dog has been known to climb trees. [Adverbial]

INTRODUCTORY CLAUSES
*As soon as she had finished studying,* she left the library. [Adverbial]
*If your job is to write every day,* you learn to do it like every other job. [Adverbial]

WILLIAM ZINSSER

*Whenever I hear anyone arguing for slavery,* I feel a strong impulse to see it tried on him personally. [Adverbial]

ABRAHAM LINCOLN

Do not confuse verbal modifiers with verbals used as subjects.

VERBAL MODIFIER    *Having been an arbitrator between labor and management for a decade,* he felt confident in tackling one more labor dispute.

VERBAL AS SUBJECT    *Having been an arbitrator between labor and management for a decade* made him feel confident in tackling one more labor dispute.

The comma is frequently omitted after very short introductory clauses or phrases. However, even when the introductory clause or phrase is very short, a comma is necessary if its omission can cause misreading.

CLEAR    When they arrived she was taking the cat out of the piano.
After my defeat I retired from public life.

CONFUSING    When he returned home was not what it used to be.

CLEAR    When he returned, home was not what it used to be.

CONFUSING    After dark fireflies came in large numbers.

CLEAR    After dark, fireflies came in large numbers.

---

## EXERCISE 20b

In the following sentences and paragraph, insert commas wherever they are needed after introductory elements. Then write five sentences of your own containing correctly punctuated introductory elements.

**SENTENCE PRACTICE**

1. According to economics and labor experts a shortage of workers will occur in the 1990s.
2. Because birthrates have dropped since the mid-1960s the number of people entering the labor market in the 1990s will be considerably lower than in recent decades.
3. To find people to fill jobs industries may have to offer more attractive benefits such as flexible hours and improved child-care programs.
4. Since many of these future employees will be unskilled industries will have to create new training programs for them.
5. By learning now what kind of jobs will be plentiful in the 1990s people who will be starting to work during that decade can make sure they have the education and training needed to fill those jobs.

**20c**

**,**

**PARAGRAPH PRACTICE**

In the future service industries will become one of the biggest areas for employment. As manufacturing declines in the United States the number of service industries is growing. Although manufacturing has shown growth in some areas of the country economics and labor experts doubt that it can overtake service industries as the employer of the highest number of workers. In addition to offering the greatest number of jobs in the 1990s the service industry will also offer jobs that provide workers with chances for career advancement. In finding people for these jobs employers will be competing with each other to hire the most highly skilled and educationally qualified people.

---

**20c**  Use commas to set off nonrestrictive elements. Do not set off restrictive elements.

A **restrictive element**—which may be a clause, a phrase, or a word—is an essential modifier. It defines, limits, or identifies the meaning of whatever it modifies. If it is removed from the sentence, the meaning is changed in some basic way. A **nonrestrictive element** may be interesting, but it is incidental to the basic meaning of the sentence. An illustration will help to clarify the difference.

RESTRICTIVE    A person *who is honest* will succeed.

NONRESTRICTIVE    Jacob North, who is honest, will succeed.

In the first sentence the clause *who is honest* identifies the kind of person who will succeed; it restricts the subject of *will succeed* to people *who are honest* as opposed to people *who are not honest*. In other words, the clause is restrictive. It is thus *not* set off with commas. In the second sentence, however, the proper noun *Jacob North* identifies or designates the particular person who *will succeed;* the fact that Jacob North *is honest* is merely amplifying information about a person already sufficiently identified. The clause is nonrestrictive. It *is* set off with commas.

In the illustration just discussed, the meaning is such that there is no question that the clause *who is honest* is restrictive in one sentence and not restrictive in the other. Sometimes, however, a modifying element can be interpreted as either restrictive or nonrestrictive—depending on the particular meaning you intend. In such instances you must decide what you mean. Setting off the modifier or not setting it off is your only way of making your meaning clear to your reader.

**20c**

**,**

The house, built by my grandfather, faced the mountain. [The phrase *built by my grandfather* is nonrestrictive and is thus set off by commas.]

The house built by my grandfather faced the mountain, and the house built by my father stood only a hundred yards away. [In this compound sentence, the two phrases beginning with *built* limit and define the particular houses, distinguishing them from each other.]

Texans, who have oil wells, can afford high prices. [That is, all Texans have oil wells and can afford high prices.]

Texans who have oil wells can afford high prices. [That is, some Texans have oil wells; only they can afford high prices.]

**1. Always use *two* commas to set off a nonrestrictive element unless it begins or ends the sentence. The "opening" comma must have a "closing" comma to balance it.**

NOT    The gate, unlocked and wide-open swung on its hinges.

BUT    The gate, unlocked and wide-open, swung on its hinges.

Unlocked and wide-open, the gate swung on its hinges.

**2. Set off nonrestrictive clauses and phrases with commas. Do not set off restrictive clauses and phrases.**

NONRESTRICTIVE CLAUSE    Wide porches, *which sometimes run along three sides of the house,* are called verandas.

RESTRICTIVE CLAUSE    Houses *that were built in warm climates* often featured verandas.

| | |
|---|---|
| NONRESTRICTIVE CLAUSE | Charleston, South Carolina, *where my grand-mother lived,* has many old homes with lovely verandas. |
| RESTRICTIVE CLAUSE | The town *where I grew up* had few porches and no verandas. |
| NONRESTRICTIVE PHRASE | Grandmother's veranda, *with its enormous length,* was a wonderful place to play. [Prep-ositional] |
| RESTRICTIVE PHRASE | The part *with the most appeal* was filled with wicker furniture. [Prepositional] |
| NONRESTRICTIVE PHRASE | We children, *draping blankets across the furni-ture,* made tunnels and tents. [Participial] |
| RESTRICTIVE PHRASE | Anyone *wanting to sit on a chair* had to dis-mantle childish hide-outs. [Participial] |

**20c**

,

**3. Set off nonrestrictive appositives with commas. Do not set off restrictive appositives.** An **appositive** is a noun or a group of words used as a noun that describes or renames another noun, ordi-narily the noun that comes immediately before it. Like clauses and phrases, appositives may be either restrictive or nonrestrictive, though appositives of more than one or two words are usually nonrestrictive and therefore set off by commas.

NONRESTRICTIVE APPOSITIVES

Davy Crockett, *the most famous man at the Alamo,* was a former Indian fighter.

No treatment, *not even hypnosis or acupuncture,* helped them stop smoking.

The whale, *a cold-water-dwelling mammal,* is protected by a thick layer of blubber.

"Hello, Mitty. We're having the devil's own time with McMillan, *the millionaire banker and close personal friend of Roosevelt.*"

JAMES THURBER

Restrictive appositives limit, define, or designate the noun that they follow in such a way that their absence from the sentence would change its essential meaning. They are often, though by no means always, proper names following a more general noun or identifying phrase.

RESTRICTIVE APPOSITIVES

Robert Frost's poem *"Stopping by Woods on a Snowy Evening"* is one of his best-known poems.

The poet *Bryant* was a leader in New York literary circles.

Do you mean Napoli *the grocer* or Napoli *the doctor?*

The slang term *shrink* is often applied to psychiatrists.

Removing the restrictive appositives from these sentences would create nonsense: *Robert Frost's poem is one of his best-known poems* and *Do you mean Napoli or Napoli?*

---

**EXERCISE 20c**
In the following sentences and paragraph, insert commas to set off nonrestrictive elements. Indicate which sentences are correct as written. Then write five sentences of your own—correctly punctuated—by creating three sentences with nonrestrictive elements and two sentences with restrictive elements.

**SENTENCE PRACTICE**

1. Bread which seems to be a universal food appears in a variety of shapes throughout the world.
2. Anyone who has been to France has seen rows and rows of crisp baguettes in the bakeries.
3. Challah the traditional Jewish braided loaf is a symbol of the ceremonial bread that the priest in the ancient Temple of Jerusalem placed on the table.
4. Pita bread with its handy "pocket" for holding fillings is a traditional Middle Eastern bread.
5. People who think of bread only in terms of plastic-wrapped white loaves don't know what they're missing by not sampling some of these satisfying breads.

**PARAGRAPH PRACTICE**

Some of the most delicious breads in the world come from India where most breads are unleavened. In India the term *roti* means bread, and many of these unleavened breads resemble the tortilla which is a well-known Mexican bread in shape. *Pooris* which puff up like balloons are flattened discs of dough fried in hot oil. The *chapati* a bread made out of finely ground whole-wheat flour is a basic bread that is eaten throughout most of northern India. *Naan* bread one type of leavened bread made in India is baked in a *tandoor* a large clay oven.

---

**20d**  Use a comma to set off adverbial phrases and clauses following the main clause and explaining, amplifying, or offering a contrast to it. Do not set off such clauses if they are closely related to the main clause.

Adverbial phrases and clauses very often *restrict* the meaning of main clauses that follow and are therefore essential to the meaning of the main clause. Restrictive adverbial clauses should not be set off by a comma when they follow the main clause. When adverbial clauses merely introduce additional *nonrestrictive* information, however, a comma is used to indicate that they are not essential to the meaning.

Consider the logic of your sentence and the meaning you intend when deciding whether to set off adverbial clauses and phrases. Note the following:

> We won't miss the beginning of the movie if we hurry.
> We haven't missed the beginning of the movie, even though we're late.

The first of the examples sets up *if we hurry* as the necessary condition for not missing the beginning of the movie. In the second, the main clause makes an unqualified statement of fact; the *even though* clause adds some information but does not change the meaning of the clause.

> Mrs. Jones must have decided not to go outdoors today because the snow hasn't been shoveled from the walk.
> Mrs. Jones must have decided not to go outdoors today, because the snow hasn't been shoveled from the walk.

**20d**

**,**

The first of the foregoing examples states that the unshoveled walk is the reason Mrs. Jones has not gone outdoors. The unshoveled walk is an essential condition for keeping her indoors, as indicated by the lack of a comma before the *because* clause. In the second example, the comma before *because* tells us that the writer intends the clause to be nonrestrictive and the information to be understood as nonessential to the basic meaning of the sentence. The *because* clause merely provides evidence for the fact that Mrs. Jones has not gone outside.

Note that in some constructions a comma or the lack of one determines whether the reader will understand a phrase or a clause as a modifier of a final noun in the main clause or as an adverbial modifier.

> He has visited all the small towns in Pennsylvania.
> He has visited *all* the small towns, in Pennsylvania, in Ohio, in almost every state of the union.

In the first of these examples, *in Pennsylvania* restricts the location of the small towns and is an adjectival modifier of *towns*. In the second, however, the *in* phrase is additional information amplifying the assertion of the main clause but not essential to it.

---

**EXERCISE 20d**
Insert commas in the following paragraph wherever they are needed to set off adverbial clauses or phrases. Indicate which sentences are correct as written. Then write five sentences of your own containing correctly punctuated adverbial clauses or phrases.

> The ingredients and cooking methods involved in making chili often arouse heated debate because everyone seems to have a differ-

ent opinion about what constitutes a perfect pot of chili. Some Texans claim that chili isn't authentic unless it's made with tiny cubes of chopped beef. Others believe that only pure chili powder should be used although many chili cooks use chili seasoning made of a blend of several spices. Some people think chili should contain only beef, tomato, and chili peppers even though many people add onions and beans. Finally there's also a hardy group of chili eaters who think that the concoction is truly authentic only if it's so spicy it burns the mouth.

## 20e   Use commas to set off all absolute phrases.

Absolute phrases consist of a noun or a pronoun followed by a present or past participle: *the sun shining brightly*. These economical but information-rich phrases modify the entire main clause in which they stand rather than any particular word or words in that clause. They are always nonrestrictive, supplying amplifying or explanatory detail rather than essential information. Thus they should always be set off by commas whether they appear at the beginning or end of a sentence or within it.

He was stretched out on his reclining chair in the full sun, *his eyes covered, his head thrown back, his arms spread wide.*

*Other things being equal,* short familiar words are better than long unfamiliar words.

They were waiting for us, *their figures defined by the light from the half-open door.*

The mastiff, *teeth bared, ears standing erect, body tensed,* refused to give ground.

---

EXERCISE 20e
Insert commas in the following sentences to set off absolute phrases. Then write five sentences of your own that contain absolute phrases.

1. Their eyes sparkling in anticipation the children watched as their parents brought the new puppy into the yard.
2. The tiny puppy its legs wobbly and its bark barely audible tried to follow the children when they ran around the yard.
3. Its tail drooping the puppy flopped down on the blanket the children had prepared for their new pet.
4. Head resting on its front paws the puppy slept for several hours.
5. The children settled down for their own naps all the excitement being over for the moment.

---

## 20f   Use commas to set off elements that slightly interrupt the structure of a sentence.

Words, phrases, and clauses that slightly interrupt the structure of a sentence are often called **parenthetical elements.** Although such elements may add to the meaning of the sentence or relate the sentence to a preceding sentence or idea, they are not essential to grammatical structure. Such elements include words of direct address, mild interjections, the words *yes* and *no,* transitional words and expressions, and phrases expressing contrast.

| | |
|---|---|
| DIRECT ADDRESS | Can you show me, *Kathy,* how to punctuate this sentence? |
| | Will you speak a little louder, *George?* |
| MILD INTERJECTIONS | *Well,* no one can do more than his best. |
| | *Oh,* I hate stewed prunes. |
| TRANSITIONAL WORDS AND PHRASES | Sales taxes, *moreover,* hurt poor people severely. |
| | Quakers, *on the other hand,* are opposed to military service. |
| TRANSITIONAL WORDS AND PHRASES | The judge ruled, *nevertheless,* that damages must be paid. |
| | The result, *in short,* was a complete breakdown of discipline. |
| CONTRASTED ELEMENTS | He had intended to write 1868, *not 1968.* |
| | Tractors, *unlike horses,* require gasoline. |
| | Insecticides and garden sprays now available are effective, *yet safe.* |

**20f**

**,**

Note that other elements of a sentence will interrupt its structure and require commas when they are inserted out of their normal grammatical order. Compare the following:

My grandmother always told me that work never killed anyone.

Work, *my grandmother always told me,* never killed anyone.

The exhausted and thirsty construction workers welcomed the cold beer.

The construction workers, *exhausted and thirsty,* welcomed the cold beer.

Always use two commas to set off a parenthetical element unless it begins or ends a sentence.

| | |
|---|---|
| NOT | She noticed, however that tact worked wonders. |
| NOT | She noticed however, that tact worked wonders. |
| BUT | She noticed, however, that tact worked wonders. |
| | She noticed that tact worked wonders, however. |

---

EXERCISE 20f
In the following sentences and paragraph, insert commas to set off parenthetical elements. Then write five sentences of your own that contain parenthetical elements requiring commas.

**SENTENCE PRACTICE**

1. Andrew did you know that Yellowstone National Park covers 2,219,823 acres?
2. Yellowstone unlike some other national parks is actually located in parts of three different states.
3. Old Faithful is Yellowstone's most famous geyser, but the park contains in fact about 200 geysers.
4. Park visitors often see grizzly bears along the roadside; tourists should be very cautious about these bears, for they are fascinating yet dangerous.
5. Some park visitors despite warnings try to approach the bears and thus place themselves in considerable danger.

**PARAGRAPH PRACTICE**

The pronghorn antelope according to experts is the fastest runner among the wild animals living on the western plains. The feet of the pronghorn antelope are padded for running on rocky terrain, and their legs moreover have very strong bones that easily support the animals' weight. These animals a friend from Wyoming tells me even try to race pickup trucks. At one time pronghorn antelopes were very common on the western plains; as settlers moved west however the number of antelopes dropped rapidly as the animals were killed for meat. Today fortunately laws protect the antelope, and lucky travelers may see its distinctive white-haired rump as it leaps across the plains.

**20g** **Use commas to separate the items in a series.**

A series consists of three or more words, phrases, or clauses of equal grammatical rank. The items of such a series are said to be *coordinate:* they have approximately equal importance. Typical series take the form *a, b,* and *c,* or the form *a, b,* or *c.*

She talked *fluently, wittily,* and *penetratingly.* [Three adverbs]

The triathlon is an athletic event involving *swimming, running,* and *cycling.* [Three nouns]

Only a generation ago, the Navaho were *horsemen, nomads, keepers of flocks, painters in sand, weavers of wool, artists in silver,* and *singers of the yei-bie-chai.* [Seven nouns, some modified by prepositional phrases]

EDWARD ABBEY

*Her sails ripped, her engines dead,* and *her rudder broken,* the vessel drifted helplessly. [Three absolute phrases]

The city couldn't *issue birth certificates on time, pay overtime when it was due, maintain its automotive fleets, deliver asphalt to men filling potholes, submit claims for federal and state aid payments, supply diaper pins to obstetric wards,* or *hire key staff.* [Seven predicates, each consisting of a verb and its object]

CHARLES R. MORRIS

After the accident, the driver of the car had no idea of *who he was, where he came from,* or *how the accident happened.* [Three dependent clauses]

And that's the news from Lake Wobegon, *where all the women are strong, all the men are good-looking, and all the children are above average.* [Three dependent clauses introduced by a single conjunction]

GARRISON KEILLOR

Some writers treat three or more short, closely related independent clauses not joined by coordinate conjunctions as a series, separating them by commas rather than semicolons.

Some of the people said the elephant had gone in one direction, some said he had gone in another, some professed not even to have heard of any elephant.

GEORGE ORWELL

**20h**

,

Less experienced writers will be safer using semicolons in such a series.

Some writers omit the comma before *and* in simple *a, b,* and *c* series: violins, flutes and cellos; men, women and children. But since the comma is sometimes vital for clarity, it is preferable to establish the habit of always including it. Note how necessary the final comma is in the following:

Our resort is equipped with comfortable cabins, a large lake with boating facilities, and a nine-hole golf course.

I am interested in a modern, furnished apartment with two bedrooms, kitchenette, living room, bathroom with shower, and garage.

Without the comma after *facilities,* the first sentence seems to suggest that the resort has a lake with a golf course in it. Without the comma after *shower* in the second sentence, the writer seems to be asking for an apartment with a garage in the bathroom.

**20h**   Use commas to separate coordinate adjectives in a series; do not use commas to separate adjectives that are cumulative rather than coordinate.

Adjectives in a series are *coordinate* if each adjective modifies the noun separately. They are *cumulative,* not coordinate, if any adjective in the series modifies the total concept that follows it.

COORDINATE    The British colony of Hong Kong grew up around a *beautiful, sheltered, acccessible* port.

CUMULATIVE    Hong Kong is the *third-largest international financial* center in the world.

In the first sentence, each adjective is more or less independent of the other two; the three adjectives could be rearranged without seriously affecting the meaning of the sentence: *accessible, beautiful, sheltered* port; *sheltered, accessible, beautiful* port. Moreover, the conjunction *and* could be inserted in place of the commas and the basic meaning would remain—*beautiful* and *sheltered* and *accessible* port.

But in the second sentence the adjectives are cumulative and interdependent. Their order may not be changed, nor may *and* be substituted, without making nonsense of the original meaning—*financial third-largest international* center; *third-largest* and *international* and *financial* center. The adjectives in the second sentence constitute, in effect, a *restrictive* phrase, as distinct from the *nonrestrictive* quality of the adjectives in the first sentence, and therefore are not separated from one another by commas.

The same principles apply when only two modifiers precede the word being modified.

**20h**

**,**

*Huge, lumbering* freighters share Hong Kong's *busy deepwater* port with *ancient Chinese* junks.

In actual usage, punctuation of coordinate adjectives varies a great deal. Consider the following sentences:

CUMULATIVE   The *powerful new water-cooled* engine is very fuel-efficient.
COORDINATE   The *powerful, new, water-cooled* engine is very fuel-efficient.

Both sentences may be punctuated correctly: the lack of commas, or their inclusion, signals the writer's intentions and tells the reader how a series of adjectives is to be understood.

---

EXERCISE 20g–h
In the following sentences and paragraph, supply commas where they are needed to separate sentence elements in a series. Then write five sentences of your own containing correctly punctuated elements in a series.

1. The *Mona Lisa* and *The Last Supper* are two of the most famous artworks created by the brilliant multi-talented Italian artist Leonardo da Vinci.
2. Leonardo was born in the Tuscan village of Vinci in 1452 was taken to Florence in 1469 and a few years later became an apprentice in an artist's workshop.
3. Leonardo's notebooks reveal that the painter was interested in fields as varied as geology flight anatomy and architecture.
4. Leonardo's detailed precise drawings include sketches for a self-propelled vehicle flying machines and elaborate anatomical studies.

5.  His attempt to create a flying machine his visions of war machines
    that look like modern missiles and his fascination with automated
    machines reveal Leonardo as a genius whose technological and sci-
    entific thinking was far ahead of his time.

**PARAGRAPH PRACTICE**

Leonardo's fellow Italian artist Michelangelo Buonarroti
painted the ceiling of the Sistine Chapel designed much of St. Pe
ter's Church in Rome created some of the world's greatest sculptures and also wrote poetry. The Sistine Chapel in the Vatican contains not only the huge vividly colored ceiling by Michelangelo but
also his fresco *The Last Judgment,* which is painted on the altar wall.
Michelangelo considered himself primarily a sculptor, and among
his best-known works are the *Pietà* in St. Peter's the huge statue of
Moses in the church of San Pietro in Vincoli in Rome, and the figure
of David now at the Academy in Florence. In the colossal statues of
David and Moses, Michelangelo gives the figures a sense of power
energy and harmony that seems to bring the stone to life. The figures in Michelangelo's ceiling frescoes in the Sistine Chapel exude
that same sense of vibrant energetic power.

**20i**

**,**

**20i** Follow established conventions for the use of commas in
dates, addresses, geographical names, titles, and long numbers.

**1. Dates.** If a date is written as month-date-year, use a comma
between the date and the year. If such a date stands within a sentence,
use a comma after the year.

The German surrender ended World War II in Europe on May 7,
1945.

World War II began on September 1, 1939, when Germany invaded
Poland.

If only the month and year are given, do not use a comma between them or after the year.

The war in the Pacific ended in August 1945.

The war in the Pacific ended in August 1945 after Japan surren-
dered.

If a date is written as day-month-year, use no commas.

17 July 1931    6 August 1982

**2. Addresses.** Standard comma punctuation of addresses is as
follows:

205 Hayes Street, San Francisco, California 94102
39 West 12th Street, Olean, NY 71402

If geographical names or addresses appear within a sentence, use a comma after each element—street, city, state (county or province), country—and use a comma after the final item. Note that no comma is used before the zip code.

ADDRESSES   She gave 39 West 12th Street, Olean, New York 71402, as her forwarding address.

GEOGRAPHICAL NAMES   He spent a month at Bremen, Germany, and the rest of his time in Tunbridge Wells, Kent, a small village in England.

**3. Titles.** Use commas to separate names from titles when the title follows the name. If the name followed by a title occurs within a sentence, use a comma after the title as well as between the name and the title.

Katherine Dugald, M.D.      William Harrington, Sr.

The university recently announced the appointment of Katherine Dugald, M.D., to the faculty of the medical school.

**4. Large numbers.** Use commas in large numbers to indicate thousands, but do not use commas in social security numbers, telephone numbers, zip codes, and the like. These latter should be written as stated.

1,249        Social Security number 391-07-4855
89,129       Telephone number 515-555-7669
1,722,843    Jamaica Plain, MA 02130

**20j** Use a comma to prevent misreading.

Sometimes in a sentence two words fall together so that they may be read two ways. In such instances, a comma may be necessary to prevent misreading even though no standard punctuation rule applies.

Long before, she had left everything to her brother.
Pilots who like to see sunbathers, fly low over apartment houses.
Inside the house, cats are sometimes a nuisance.

The omission of a comma after *before* in the first sentence would be momentarily confusing; we get off to a false start by reading *Long before she had left* without interruption. If there were no comma in the second sentence, we might think we were reading about flying sunbathers. A similar difficulty arises in the third sentence if *house* is not separated from *cats*. Often it is best to rewrite such sentences to avoid confusion.

The following sentences present similar problems:

To John, Smith was a puzzle. [Without the comma, the reader will take the introductory phrase to be *To John Smith*.]

People who can, take vacations in the summer. [Without the comma, the reader is likely to assume that the verb is *can take*.]

For the misuse of the comma, see Section **24**. For the use of commas in quoted material, see Section **25d–f**.

---

EXERCISE 20i–j

In the following sentences and paragraph, insert commas where conventional usage requires them or where they are needed to prevent misreading.

**SENTENCE PRACTICE**

1. Sir Arthur Conan Doyle M. D. created Sherlock Holmes, the fictional detective who is as popular today as he was when he first appeared in the late 1800s.
2. Doyle's first story about Sherlock Holmes appeared in 1887, and since then over 1000 books have been written about the 56 stories and four novels that feature the brilliant detective.
3. Today Holmes's fans try to find the detective's fictional dwelling place at 221-B Baker Street London England.
4. In addition to Sherlock Holmes, Doyle also created John Watson M. D. Holmes's companion and foil.
5. To Watson Holmes often seems to be a genius as he explains to his friend that the deductions he has reached about a complex case are merely elementary.

**PARAGRAPH PRACTICE**

   Edgar Allan Poe, who was born on January 19 1809 in Boston Massachusetts is often called the father of the modern detective story. Poe spent a year at the University of Virginia in Charlottesville Virginia and then entered West Point in July 1930. Poe stayed at West Point less than a year and then went to Baltimore Maryland to live with a relative and work as a journalist. "The Murders in the Rue Morgue," Poe's first detective story, appeared in *Graham's Magazine* in April 1841. Soon after C. August Dupin, the detective Poe had created for the story, became well known among readers for his courage and his deductive powers.

**20j**

,

---

 **WRITERS REVISING: COMMAS**
*(continued from page 159)*

**Revision**

R 1      At the banquet will be many members of

R 2   Congress, eating roast beef, and members of the      **20c(2)**

R 3   press as well. The waiters will serve the

R 4   courses of soup, fish, salad, meat⸝and           **20g**

R 5   vegetables, and dessert⸝with three wines.          **20j**

R 6   For dessert⸝women tend to prefer sherbet; men,     **20a, 20g**

R 7   pie and ice cream. Mind your manners

R 8   and try not to eat too much⸝pig. Please try        **20f**

R 9   not to drop your spoon⸝or roll in your soup.       **20j**

R10   Stay awake during the after-dinner speech,

R11   and if you must yawn⸝do so⸝quietly.                **20b, 20j**

### Analysis

In line R2 a comma is needed to set off the nonrestrictive phrase *eating roast beef*. To punctuate it as a restrictive phrase needing no commas would say that all the senators were eating roast beef when the meaning is that many, not all of them, were eating. To put a comma following *meat* in line R4 indicates that meat and vegetables are two different dishes although they are obviously served together and are another item on a list of dishes served. In line R5, the prepositional phrase *with three wines* is set off to prevent misreading and to indicate that the entire menu, not just the dessert, was served with three wines. In line R8, *pig* is set off because it is a word of direct address, not a dish on the menu. Since it is ludicrous to think that the writer is warning the reader not to fall in the soup, the comma following *spoon* in line R9 is deleted to prevent misreading. A comma sets off the introductory adverb clause *if you must yawn* in line R11. The comma is deleted following *do so* to prevent misreading the sentence to mean that the writer is instructed to yawn.

---

REVIEW EXERCISES: COMMA USAGE (Section 20)

PART A
Insert commas where they are needed in the following sentences and paragraph.

**SENTENCE PRACTICE**
1. *Martial arts* a phrase that refers to various forms of self-defense have become popular today as a method of learning how to protect one's self without a weapon.
2. Although many people think that martial arts refers only to karate a technique using blows with the side of the hand this group of self-defense methods also includes judo and kendo.

**20j**

**,**

3. Created in the 1880s in Japan judo is based upon the principle of jujitsu a term referring to the basic techniques of martial arts.
4. Technically jujitsu skills should enable a smaller weaker person to overcome a larger stronger opponent.
5. Kendo is unusual in the array of martial arts forms leather-covered bamboo sticks being used as weapons by opponents.

**PARAGRAPH PRACTICE**

When modern marathon runners cross the finish line in famous races such as the New York Marathon the Boston Marathon or the Berlin Marathon they are participating in a run that has its roots in ancient Greece. According to tradition the first marathon runner an ancient Greek named Pheidippedes left the city of Marathon Greece to carry to Athens the news of a Greek victory over the Persians. When Pheidippedes made his run in 490 B.C. he covered a distance of 22 miles but today the modern marathon distance has been set at 26 miles and 385 yards. Modern marathons unlike that first run with its single runner include a field of thousands of runners who have an astonishing range of ages, abilities, and nationalities. In a recent New York City Marathon in fact three participants were 90 years old.

**20j**

**,**

**PART B**

In the following paragraphs, insert any necessary commas.

American novelist Willa Cather who was born in the east and grew up in Nebraska wrote of the immigrants who settled the western prairies. Cather was born in Back Creek Valley Virginia but when she was ten years old her family moved to Nebraska. The Cather family settled on the Divide a high area of grassy windblown plains near the Kansas border. In this area which was often affected by blizzards droughts and invasions of insects Willa Cather came to know the various groups of immigrants who had also settled there. The Cathers' neighbors included French Swedish Czech German and Scotch-Irish settlers and several of her early short stories and novels such as *My Antonia* and *O Pioneers!* deal with the prairies and the people who started a new life in this harsh environment.

In 1884 the Cather family moved from the prairie to Red Cloud Nebraska and in 1890 Willa Cather went to the University of Nebraska at Lincoln. Planning to study science Cather however turned to writing. After leaving the university and the plains Cather went first to Pittsburgh and then to New York.

In 1912 Cather visited the southwestern part of the United States an area that continued to draw her back and to influence her later novels. For example Cather's novel *The Professor's House* draws upon experiences she had when she visited Mesa Verde a southwestern national park that could be reached only by wagon when Cather visited in 1915. In addition to *The Professor's House* Cather also set her novel *Death Comes to the Archbishop* in the southwest. In that 1927 novel set in New Mexico Cather writes of Jean Baptiste Lamy who was the first Archbishop of New Mexico. Although she

had spent much of her life in the west Willa Cather spent her last
years on Grand Manon Island which is located off Canada's east
coast and she is buried in Jaffrey New Hampshire.

# 21

## *THE SEMICOLON*

### WRITERS REVISING: SEMICOLONS, COLONS, DASHES, AND PARENTHESES

Susan has written an article for the newsletter of the Department of Dairy Science at State University. Now she must polish her punctuation. See if you can punctuate this exerpt for her; then compare your version with hers on page 190 at the conclusion of Section **23.**

**Susan's Draft**

D 1        There's a whole lot more to dairying these

D 2    days than simply milking Old Bossie twice a day.

D 3    Today's modern dairy farmer is a diverse

D 4    individual, a cross between an engineer and a cost

D 5    accountant. For many, this expanded role is a bit

D 6    too much, consequently, many dairy farmers cannot

D 7    tell you to an appreciable degree whether their

D 8    operation is actually making or losing money.

D 9        A big help in this regard is the Dairy Herd

D10    Improvement Association, DHIA. The DHIA program

D11    combines the efforts of many groups to serve the

D12    needs of dairy farmers and provides educational

D13    information for use in three broad areas, breed

D14    improvement, sire evaluation, and production

D15    records.

D16        Three kinds of production sheets are used by

```
D17   the dairy farmer, the Cow Identification Report

D18   Sheet, the Monthly Report Sheet, and the Herd

D19   Summary Report Sheet. The most informative one of

D20   these sheets is the Barn Sheet, it is used each

D21   month to report production and feed data as well

D22   as other information for each cow and the herd. It

D23   can be divided into two areas, the upper one-

D24   fourth of the form reports on cows as a herd, and

D25   the bottom three-fourths of the form, on the

D26   individual cows.
```

This *Writers Revising* continues on page 190.

**21a**

**21a**   Use a semicolon to separate closely related main clauses not joined by a coordinating conjunction. If the ideas in the main clauses are not closely related, use a period between them.

Coordinating conjunctions (*and, but, or, nor, for, so,* and *yet*) add meaning to sentences, establishing explicit relationships of equality, addition, simultaneity, choice, contrast, and so forth between independent clauses: *Columbus "discovered" America in 1492, but the Vikings got here before that. Norsemen writing to the Vatican reported voyages from Greenland to Canada, and some people believe Columbus was aware of this information.* There may be times, however, when you wish only to suggest relatedness between thoughts, rather than to add meaning. In those instances, a semicolon can be a very effective tool. Compare the following sentences.

Columbus "discovered" America in 1492. The Vikings got here before that. Norsemen writing to the Vatican reported voyages from Greenland to Canada. Some people believe Columbus was aware of this information.

Columbus "discovered" America in 1492; the Vikings got here before that. Norsemen writing to the Vatican reported voyages from Greenland to Canada; some people believe Columbus was aware of this information.

Whereas a period is a full stop, marking a complete break between sentences, a semicolon separates and stops but does not fully break the flow of thought between grammatically independent statements. Also remember that a semicolon may be used only between word groups of equal grammatical rank (see Section **24i**).

> The rabbit is the all-American game; it is everywhere, and everywhere hunted.
>
> JOHN RANDOLPH

> We organize time and myth with music; we mark our lives by it. Music is the way that our memories sing to us across time.
>
> LANCE MORROW

> Initiative in the attack is not much in the nature of the tarantula; most species fight only when cornered so that escape is impossible.
>
> ALEXANDER PETRUNKEVITCH

> Children begin by loving their parents; as they grow older they judge them; sometimes they forgive them.
>
> OSCAR WILDE

> Pay the thunder no mind; listen to the birds.
>
> EUBIE BLAKE

**21b**

**;**

A comma is sometimes used to separate very short main clauses not joined by coordinating conjunctions, particularly if the clauses are parallel, as in *She is not a person, she is a legend* or *Some allow it, some don't.* But the semicolon is always correct in such sentences—and much safer for the inexperienced writer.

**21b**    Use a semicolon to separate main clauses joined by a conjunctive adverb.

Conjunctive adverbs are words like *however, moreover, therefore, consequently, indeed,* and *then* that carry a thought from one main clause to the next. (See p. 601 for a more extensive list; see **7b** for a discussion of semicolons and comma splices.)

> I ordered the concert tickets by mail; *therefore,* I didn't have to stand in line.
> Our muscles were tired and sore; *nevertheless,* we kept on jogging.
> On February 2 the groundhog saw its shadow; *consequently,* according to folk wisdom, we can expect six more weeks of winter weather.

You can recognize conjunctive adverbs and distinguish them from other kinds of connecting words if you remember that they are the only ones that can be moved from the beginning of a clause to another position in that clause without changing the clause's meaning.

> The band struck up a familiar tune; *indeed,* they were playing our song.

The band struck up a familiar tune; they were, *indeed*, playing our song.

When a conjunctive adverb comes within the second main clause instead of at the beginning, the clauses still must be separated by a semicolon and the conjunctive adverb set off by commas. Note that a conjunctive adverb that begins a main clause is followed by a single comma.

Unlike conjunctive adverbs, coordinating conjunctions (*and, but*, etc.) or subordinating conjunctions (*although, because, if, since, when, whereas*, and the like) cannot move from their positions without changing or destroying meaning.

Coordinating conjunctions must stand between the clauses they connect.

21c
;

> **NOT**   Fido barked, we *so* knew he wanted to go out.
>
> **BUT**   Fido barked, *so* we knew he wanted to go out.

Similarly, subordinating conjunctions must stand at the beginning of the clauses they introduce.

> **NOT**   Fido wanted to go for a walk I *whereas* wanted to take a nap.
>
> **BUT**   Fido wanted to go for a walk *whereas* I wanted to take a nap.

## 21c   Use a semicolon to separate main clauses joined by a coordinating conjunction if the clauses are long or internally punctuated.

The meeting last night, the most argumentative and confusing thus far, lasted until midnight; and unless something unexpected happens in the meantime, the next meeting may last even longer.

When New England was first settled, lobsters were plentiful all along the coast; and since the settlers depended heavily on the sea for their food, especially in the early years, they certainly must have eaten lobster frequently.

In some instances, even when relatively short main clauses are joined by a coordinating conjunction, a semicolon instead of a comma may be used for emphasis.

He could hear the excitement of their talk from the next room; but he could not distinguish what they were saying.

**21d**  Use a semicolon to separate the items of a series if the items themselves contain commas.

Compare the following sentences:

At courtside were Mr. Jones, the owner, and the general manager, a referee, the coach, a former star player, and the current trainer of the team.

At courtside were Mr. Jones, the owner and the general manager; a referee; the coach, a former star player; and the current trainer of the team.

As you can see, the number of people at courtside varies considerably, depending on the punctuation. Without semicolons, readers may have difficulty separating items into subsets.

Jean Smith, the cardiologist; Angelo Martinez, the dentist; and Alan Wilson, the psychiatrist, meet for lunch every Tuesday.

In other cases, semicolons help to group items with accompanying lengthy modifying phrases or explanations.

The march had been an extraordinary conglomeration of different types of people: students; young middle-class families with children; punks with stiff green Mohawks; a band of bikers with fifties-style pompadours and big Moto Guzzi motorcycles.

*The New Yorker*

Snobbery has traditionally been founded on birth; knowledge or pseudo knowledge, or merely self-assured ignorance, all of them amounting to the same thing in snob terms; access to power, status, celebrity; circumstances, such as the place one lives or even the things one does not do, such as watch television.

LANCE MORROW

Occasionally, semicolons add an effective emphatic touch as well as provide separation where commas exist.

The bureaucracy consists of functionaries; the aristocracy, of idols; the democracy, of idolators.

G. B. SHAW

You should note that in all the preceding examples semicolons are used to separate items of equal rank—coordinate elements.

EXERCISE 21a–d

PART A
In the following sentence, insert semicolons or substitute them for commas wherever needed.

The itinerary for my trip this summer includes two days in Atlanta, Georgia, where I plan to visit my cousin at Morehouse College, three days in Orlando, Florida, where I want to spend some time at Disney World, a stop at Cape Canaveral, where I hope to get a glimpse of the launch site for the space shuttle, and finally, five days in Key West, where I plan to lie on the beach, do some skin diving, and eat some conch chowder.

## PART B
In the following sentences, insert semicolons or substitute them for commas wherever needed.

1. Soccer is the world's most popular sport, this simple kicking game involves millions of players and probably billions of fans around the world.
2. The game of soccer most likely had its origins in a kicking game played in China 2,000 years ago, what we think of today as modern soccer originated in England in the 1850s.
3. Perhaps the most famous soccer player in the world is Edson Arantes do Nascimento, this Brazilian soccer star who retired in 1977 is much better known by the name of Pelé.
4. Pelé, who began his soccer career at the age of sixteen, helped Brazil's national team win world titles three times, scored over a thousand goals, and brought the attention of the world to Brazilian soccer, and when he signed a contract in 1975 to play for an American team, the New York Cosmos, he also helped to bring soccer to the attention of American sports fans.
5. Soccer's championship series, the World Cup, attracts a tremendous number of fans, although millions of American sports fans tune into the Super Bowl and the World Series, billions of television viewers around the world will watch the World Cup Tournament.

## PART C
Combine at least eighteen of the twenty-two sentences in the following paragraphs by using a semicolon and conjunctive adverb that expresses the correct relationship between the clauses (see p. 000 for a list of conjunctive adverbs). You may need to delete or rearrange some words to achieve smooth sentences.

Earthquakes have always been among nature's most frightening and devastating phenomena. The term *earthquake* describes a trembling or shaking movement of the earth. This trembling or shaking motion occurs because of the movement of opposing plates of rock along fault lines in the earth's crust. Most people have heard of the San Andreas Fault. It is part of a series of faults extending along an area of more than 600 miles in California. When the sections of a fault rub against each other, vibrations move through the earth. An earthquake occurs. These vibrations can also cause a tsunami, or tidal wave. These waves attain tremendous speed and force and can devastate coastal areas. *Tsunami* are often set off by earthquakes. Volcanic eruptions can also set off these giant ocean waves.

**21d**

**;**

Earthquakes terrified and mystified people in the past. Sophisticated systems now allow modern scientists to measure the movements of the earth. These scientists, who are called seismologists, can sometimes predict that an earthquake may occur. Earthquakes themselves are measured on the Richter scale. The Richter scale indicates the amount of energy released at the earthquake's origin deep within the earth.

Not all parts of the earth are subject to frequent or severe earthquakes. Some areas are considered earthquake belts because they are near known fault lines. In the twentieth century, advances in science and technology have enabled city planners in earthquake belts to construct new buildings that can withstand the shock of an earthquake. Today, buildings are less likely to suffer severe damage in an earthquake than they were in the past. Earthquakes still frighten people. These movements of the earth can still cause much damage and destroy life, for scientists have not yet found a way to harness the energy of the earth.

22
:

# 22

## THE COLON

Whereas the semicolon always indicates a full stop, the colon indicates an addition or expectation. It indicates that what follows will explain, clarify, illustrate, or specify detail.

**22a**   Use a colon to separate a main clause and another sentence element when the second explains, illustrates, or amplifies the first.

It is safe to predict what prices will do in the next decade: they will go up.

If you're considering a hat, remember this cardinal rule: never try to wear a hat that has more character than you do.

Charm, in the abstract, has something of the quality of music: radiance, balance, and harmony.

LAURIE LEE

There are two times in a man's life when he should not speculate: when he can't afford it and when he can.

MARK TWAIN

**22b**   Use a colon to set off a list or series, including a list or series introduced by *the following* or *as follows*.

For the most part we are an intemperate people: we eat too much when we can, drink too much, indulge our senses too much.

JOHN STEINBECK

Anything is possible on a train: a great meal, a binge, a visit from card players, an intrigue, a good night's sleep, and strangers' monologues framed like Russian short stories.

PAUL THEROUX

If you are interested in reading further about usage, we recommend the following books: Evans, *A Dictionary of Contemporary American Usage;* Follet, *Modern American Usage;* and Bernstein, *The Careful Writer.*

The recommended treatment for a cold is as follows: plenty of fluids, bed rest, and aspirin for fever.

Make sure that a *complete* statement precedes the colon. **Do not use a colon after a partial statement,** even when that partial statement uses words like *including* or *such as* that indicate a list will follow.

**22c**

:

| NOT | We rented several classic Bogart movies, including: *Casablanca, Key Largo,* and *The Maltese Falcon.* |

BUT    We rented several classic Bogart movies, including *Casablanca, Key Largo,* and *The Maltese Falcon.*

NOT    Tours to Australia feature stops such as: Melbourne, Sydney, and Canberra.

BUT    Tours to Australia feature stops such as Melbourne, Sydney, and Canberra.

OR    Tours to Australia feature such stops as the following: Melbourne, Sydney, and Canberra.

See Section **24k** for more discussion of inappropriate use of colons in lists.

**22c**   Use a colon to introduce a formal quotation.

The Sixteenth Amendment set up the income tax: "The Congress shall have power to lay and collect taxes on incomes, from whatever source derived, without apportionment among the several states, and without regard to any census or enumeration."

In her book *Stress and the American Woman*, Nora Scott Kinzer writes: "Female alcoholism is on the rise. Psychotropic drugs such as Valium and Equanil are widely used by housewives. Harried male and female executives gulp uppers and downers by the handful. Obesity prevents women from obtaining or keeping good jobs—and can destroy lives as effectively as the bottle of liquor or pills. Stress kills via an intermediary."

**22d**   Use a colon according to established conventions to separate items in biblical citations, subtitles and titles, and divisions of time.

BIBLICAL CITATION    Isaiah 40:28–31

SUBTITLES    *2001: A Space Odyssey*
*The Panda's Thumb: More Reflections in Natural History*
DIVISIONS OF TIME    9:20 a.m.    10:10 p.m.

---

## EXERCISE 22a–d
In the following sentences and paragraph, insert colons wherever they are needed. Then write five sentences of your own that use colons in various ways.

**22d**

**:**

**SENTENCE PRACTICE**

1. The fine-grained but exceptionally strong carrara marble has been used for some of the world's most famous buildings the Leaning Tower of Pisa, the Kennedy Center in Washington, D. C., and New York City's World Trade Center.
2. This white marble comes from several marble-quarrying towns in a region of Italy's Apuan Alps, but the beautiful stone is usually referred to by the name of the most well-known of those towns Carrara.
3. For centuries, carrara marble has been quarried and put to artistic and architectural uses the Romans used carrara marble for part of the Pantheon and for Trajan's column.
4. Most of the carrara marble quarried today is sold for nonsculptural purposes slabs are shaped for buildings and tombstones, and the remaining smaller pieces are used for columns of buildings or other adornments.
5. The mountains around Carrara contain about fifty varieties of marble, but the most valued marble is called *statuario* this is the ivory marble that Michelangelo wanted when he visited the quarries in person to choose marble for his sculptures.

**PARAGRAPH PRACTICE**

Jade, a gemstone valued by humankind for thousands of years, appears in two forms nephrite and jadeite. Nephrite, which is more common than jadeite, is found in the following areas China, Australia and New Zealand, Russia, parts of central Europe, South Korea and Taiwan, and in the western parts of North America. According to experts, nephrite is one of the toughest of all rocks in fact, nephrite is even tougher than steel. Jadeite, which is found in Russia, Burma, and Guatemala, occurs in a variety of colors white, black, and lavendar. Jadeite also occurs in the color most people associate with jade bright green. A leading mineralogist states "Jade was used in ancient times to make tools and utensils as well as ornaments, but today we prize jade as a stone for use in jewelry and carved figures."

# 23

## THE DASH AND PARENTHESES

Both dashes and parentheses are used to set off interrupting comments, explanations, examples, and other similar parenthetical elements from the main thought of the sentence. Commas are ordinarily used when parenthetical or other nonrestrictive elements are closely related in the main thought of the sentence. Dashes and parentheses are used when the interruption is abrupt and the element set off is only loosely related to the main thought of the sentence.

Though the choice between dashes and parentheses is sometimes a matter of taste, dashes emphasize more strongly the element being set off and give it greater importance than parentheses do. Parentheses are more commonly used when the element enclosed is an incidental explanatory comment, an aside, or a nonessential bit of information.

A single dash is used following an introductory element or preceding a final sentence element. A pair of dashes is used to enclose an element within a sentence. Parentheses are always used in pairs around the enclosed element. In handwriting, distinguish the dash from the hyphen by making the dash longer. In typewritten copy and computer printouts, use two hyphens, with no spacing between them or on either side, to indicate the dash.

**23**

*int p*

## THE DASH

**23a**   Use the dash or a pair of dashes to mark an abrupt shift in sentence structure or thought.

Could she—should she even try to—borrow money from her aunt?

The Queen of England never carries money—too unseemly—but travels with ladies in waiting who pay from the royal purse for whatever Her Majesty fancies.

That puppy is going to grow up to be enormous—check out the size of his paws—and will eat us out of house and home.

**23b**   Use the dash to set off nonrestrictive appositives and other parenthetical elements for emphasis.

Resorts seeking to expand to other base facilities, such as Winter Park, are also considering the use of funiculars—railroad cars pulled along a track--which can carry up to 5,000 [people] hourly.

*Skiing*

I think extraterrestrial intelligence—even beings substantially further evolved than we—will be interested in us, in what we know, how we think, what our brains are like, the course of our evolution, the prospects for our future.

CARL SAGAN

Of strong constitution himself, Perron—who had not maintained his health in India without an almost valetudinarian attention to the medicinal needs of his body—had even so not been free of the shortness of temper that was one of the side-effects of an overworked and easily discouraged digestive system.

PAUL SCOTT

Each person is born to one possession which overvalues all his others —his last breath.

MARK TWAIN

The student wandered in at 9:30—half an hour after the class began.

The spoken language does not have the same standards as the written language—the tune you whistle is not the orchestra's score.

WILLIAM SAFIRE

**23c**   Use the dash for clarity to set off internally punctuated appositives or other parenthetical elements.

To prevent confusion, use dashes rather than commas to set off appositives containing punctuated items in a series. In the following sentence the word *object* appears to be one item in a series.

Putting a spin on an object, a top, a bullet, a satellite, gives it balance and stability.

But when the commas are replaced by dashes, the meaning is clear.

Putting a spin on an object—a top, a bullet, a satellite—gives it balance and stability.

Here is another example:

Because I have so little regard for most of O'Neill's plays, and especially for those hallowed late plays of his—*A Moon for the Misbegotten, The Iceman Cometh,* and *A Touch of the Poet*—I am relieved to have a chance to repeat my opinion that *Long Day's Journey Into Night* is the finest play written in English in my lifetime.

BRENDAN GILL

## 23d   Use the dash to set off introductory lists or summary statements.

Gather data, tabulate, annotate, classify—the process seemed endless to the research assistant.

Black flies, horseflies, little triangular flies, ordinary house flies, unidentified kinds of flies—those are what I mean when I say I'm sick of flies.

Pound, Eliot, Williams— the course devoted most attention to these poets.

## 23e   Use the dash to show interruption or hesitation in speech.

"Why don't you—" He stopped abruptly and looked away.

"Well, I—uh—we—some of us really want to drop your plan."

# PARENTHESES

## 23f   Use parentheses to set off parenthetical information, explanation, or comment that is incidental or nonessential to the main thought of the sentence.

The lawyer contends (and we can see that the contention has some merit) that this client was convicted on doubtful evidence.

In our society (it's the only one I've experienced, so I can't speak for others) the razor of necessity cuts close.

STUDS TERKEL

More than 1,000 years ago, the Hopis (the word means "the peaceful ones") settled in the mesa-dotted farmland of northern Arizona.

*Time*

Among the narratives in the text, Maya Angelou's (pp. 58–68) is my favorite.

## 23g   Use parentheses to enclose numerals or letters labeling items listed within sentences.

To check out a book from our library, proceed as follows: (1) check the catalog number carefully; (2) enter the catalog number in the upper left-hand corner of the call slip; (3) fill out the remainder of the call slip information; and (4) hand in the call slip at the main desk.

---

EXERCISE 23a–g
In the following sentences and paragraph, insert dashes or parentheses wherever they are needed.

**SENTENCE PRACTICE**

1. Quebec City the city should be given that name to distinguish it from Quebec province is a beautiful and historic city on Canada's St. Laurence River.
2. The city was founded by the French explorer Samuel de Champlain 1567–1635 in 1608.
3. The historic sites of Quebec City the Old Lower Town, the Citadel fortress, and the Parliament Building give visitors a sense of Quebec's French heritage.
4. Some visitiors to Quebec City come for only one reason to dine in the city's French restaurants and cafes.
5. On first arriving in Quebec City, it's a good idea to stop by the Quebec City Office of Tourism 60 d'Auteuil Street to get a guide to the city.

**PARAGRAPH PRACTICE**

Vancouver originally called Granville but renamed Vancouver in 1886 is located on the west coast of the continent and is another of Canada's great cities. Spectacular mountain and sea scenery, mild weather, a varied cultural life all of these aspects of Vancouver make it a pleasant place to live or visit. With its 160 kilometers 100 miles of waterfront, Vancouver has the largest and one of the busiest seaports on the Pacific Coast. Vancouver also has a thriving Chinese section only Chinatown in San Francisco is larger filled with good restaurants and food markets. After enjoying Vancouver's pleasant climate, its beautiful natural setting, and its fascinating neighborhoods, most visitors agree with the name often applied to the city the "Gem of the Pacific."

**23g**

**( )**

## WRITERS REVISING: SEMICOLONS, COLONS, DASHES, AND PARENTHESES
*(continued from page 178)*

As Susan began to read for punctuation, she knew she sometimes confused the use of semicolons and colons. She would have to be especially careful in this paper because it contained a number of lists. She would also check to be sure she hadn't made comma splice errors, which sometimes cropped up in revisions, or any other punctuation errors often made in first drafts.

**Susan's Revision**

R 1     There's a whole lot more to dairying these

R 2     days than simply milking Old Bossie twice a day.

R 3     Today's modern dairy farmer is a diverse

R 4    individual₅—a cróss between an engineer and a cost    **23b**

R 5    accountant. For many, this expanded role is a bit

R 6    too much;/consequently, many dairy farmers cannot    **21b**

R 7    tell you, to any appreciable degree, whether their    **23f**

R 8    operation is actually making or losing money.

R 9         A big help in this regard is the Dairy Herd

R10    Improvement Association (DHIA). The DHIA program    **23f**

R11    combines the efforts of many groups to serve the

R12    needs of dairy farmers and provides educational

R13    information for use in three broad areas: breed    **22b**

R14    improvement, sire evaluation, and production

R15    records.

R16         Three kinds of production sheets are used by    **22b**

R17    the dairyman: the Cow Identification Report Sheet,

R18    the Monthly Report Sheet, and the Herd Summary

R19    Report Sheet. The most informative one of these

R20    sheets is the Barn Sheet; it is used each month to    **21a**

R21    report production and feed data as well as other

R22    information for each cow and the herd. It can be

R23    divided into two areas: the upper one—fourth of    **22a**

R24    the form reports on cows as a herd, and the bottom

R25    three—fourths of the form, on individual cows.

## Analysis

A dash is a good choice of punctuation in line R4 to gain emphasis for the nonrestrictive modifier. In line R6, a semicolon is called for to separate two closely related main clauses joined by a conjunctive adverb. In line R20, the semicolon joins two main clauses not joined by a conjunction. Parentheses set off the parenthetical initialism which will be used in the rest of her paper. In lines R13 and R17, a colon is used to set off lists. In line R23, the colon separates a main clause and a sentence which explains the first.

# 24

## *SUPERFLUOUS INTERNAL PUNCTUATION*

Careful punctuation helps readers separate words and ideas, helps group related words together, and enables writers to set off words or word groups for emphasis. Inadequate punctuation can force a reader to go over a passage several times to get its meaning. But too many marks of punctuation confuse a reader as much as too few marks.

The following sentence, for example, is jarring because of unnecessary and confusing punctuation.

**24**

*int p*

> The people of this company, have, always, been aware, of the need, for products of better quality, and lower prices.

None of the commas in that sentence is necessary. Many of them are undoubtedly the result of pauses in the writer's thinking or reading. Remember that correct punctuation does not derive from such pauses—but from the meaning the writer intended.

Use all the punctuation marks that will make the reader's work easier or that are required by convention. But do not insert marks that are superfluous. Especially avoid the misuses of the comma, the semicolon, and the colon described below.

---

### WRITERS REVISING: SUPERFLUOUS INTERNAL PUNCTUATION

Theo has always had problems with superfluous punctuation. So before he turned in a paper on Ralph Ellison's "Battle Royal," he asked his roommate, who is an English major, to look over his draft and point out excessive punctuation marks. Review Section **24**. Then go over the following excerpt from Theo's paper, make any corrections you think are necessary, and compare your corrections with those of Theo's roommate (see page 198).

**Theo's Draft**

D 1        Years after, the boy's experience at the

D 2    battle royal, he finally discovers, that he is

D 3    ''an invisible man.'' It took many years of

```
D 4    experience in life, and deep thought for this boy

D 5    before he realized, that he was not viewed as an

D 6    individual. While he was growing up, he always

D 7    thought of himself, as special. And because the

D 8    white men in town praised him, he thought, that

D 9    they too, viewed him, as special. However, he

D10    gradually came to the realization, that he was

D11    invisible to these people. They saw him, as an

D12    intelligent black, who must be put in his place,

D13    and sent to a Negro college, so that he would

D14    remain invisible, and never be a threat to them.
```

**24a**

*int p*

This *Writers Revising* continues on page 197.

**24a**  Do not separate a single or a final adjective from its noun.

> NOT   The H.M.S. *Bounty* was a hundred-foot, three-masted, vessel.
>
> BUT   The H.M.S. *Bounty* was a hundred-foot, three-masted vessel.

**24b**  Do not separate a subject from its verb unless there are intervening words that require punctuation.

> NOT   The *Bounty,* had been sent from England by George III in 1787 to Tahiti to trade for breadfruit trees.
>
> BUT   The *Bounty* had been sent from England by George III in 1787 to Tahiti to trade for breadfruit trees.
>
> The *Bounty,* sent from England by George III in 1787 to Tahiti, was to trade for breadfruit trees. [The commas set off a participial phrase.]

Note that here and in **24c** intervening words requiring punctuation use **balanced** punctuation: a pair of commas, dashes, and so forth.

**24c**  Do not separate a verb from its object unless there are intervening words that require punctuation.

> NOT   In April 1789 the ship left, Tahiti with its cargo.
>
> BUT   In April 1789 the ship left Tahiti with its cargo.

NOT   The authoritarian captain gave the crew, the brunt of his temper and sharp tongue.

BUT   The authoritarian captain gave the crew the brunt of his temper and sharp tongue.

The authoritarian captain gave the crew, especially Lieutenant Fletcher Christian, the brunt of his temper and sharp tongue. [The commas set off a parenthetical appositive.]

**24d**   Do not separate two words or phrases that are joined by a coordinating conjunction.

NOT   Captain Bligh called Fletcher Christian a liar, and a scoundrel.

BUT   Captain Bligh called Fletcher Christian a liar and a scoundrel.

NOT   The crew quietly approached Christian, and told him they would follow him if he would lead a mutiny.

BUT   The crew quietly approached Christian and told him they would follow him if he would lead a mutiny.

**24e**   Do not separate an introductory word, brief phrase, or short clause from the main body of the sentence unless clarity or emphasis requires it.

NOT   On April 27, Christian led the crew in the mutiny on the *Bounty.*

BUT   On April 27 Christian led the crew in the mutiny on the *Bounty.*

Occasionally, however, a comma must be inserted to prevent misreading. (See **20j.**)

NOT   For Christian to mutiny was reprehensible in the abstract but somewhat more ambiguous in reality.

BUT   For Christian, to mutiny was reprehensible in the abstract but somewhat more ambiguous in reality.

**24f**   Do not set off a restrictive modifier. (See 20c.)

NOT   They put Bligh and eighteen crewmen, who remained loyal to him, into an open boat.

BUT   They put Bligh and eighteen crewmen who remained loyal to him into an open boat.

**24d**

*int p*

> **NOT** The boat was fitted, with enough provisions and equipment, to give Bligh and his crew a chance, for survival.
>
> **BUT** The boat was fitted with enough provisions and equipment to give Bligh and his crew a chance for survival.

Very often, adverbial phrases and clauses that interrupt or follow a main clause *restrict* the meaning of the word or clause to which they are attached. They are therefore essential to the meaning and should *not* be separated by commas from what they modify. (See also **20d.**)

> **NOT** Bligh and his men sailed their small boat, across 3,600 nautical miles, to what is now Indonesia.
>
> **BUT** Bligh and his men sailed their small boat across 3,600 nautical miles to what is now Indonesia. [The phrases *3,600 nautical miles* and *to what is now Indonesia* restrict the meaning of the verb *sailed,* telling how and where Bligh sailed, and thus are essential to meaning.]
>
> **NOT** Captain Bligh must be called extraordinary, for the skill and willpower with which he directed the crew to a safe landing with eleven days' rations still remaining.
>
> **BUT** Captain Bligh must be called extraordinary for the skill and willpower with which he directed the crew to a safe landing, with eleven days' rations still remaining. [The phrase *for the skill* and the following modifiers restrict the adjective *extraordinary,* explaining the way in which Bligh was extraordinary. On the other hand, *with eleven days' rations still remaining* is a nonrestrictive phrase and so it is set off with a comma.]

**24g** int p

**24g** Do not separate indirect quotations or direct quotations that are part of a sentence's structure from the rest of the sentence.

> **NOT** Before the mutiny Bligh had said, he would drive the crew mercilessly.
>
> **BUT** Before the mutiny Bligh had said he would drive the crew mercilessly.
>
> **NOT** He had called the men, "damned thieving rascals."
>
> **BUT** He had called the men "damned thieving rascals."

**24h** Do not separate a preposition from its object.

> **NOT** Now he had driven a skeleton crew safely through, high seas, broiling sun, and impossible odds.
>
> **BUT** Now he had driven a skeleton crew safely through high seas, broiling sun, and impossible odds.

**24i**   Do not use a semicolon to separate a main clause from a subordinate clause, a phrase from a clause, or other parts of unequal grammatical rank.

> NOT   Christian and the others sailed the *Bounty* back to Tahiti; where they liked the climate, the lifestyle, and the Polynesian women.
>
> BUT   Christian and the others sailed the *Bounty* back to Tahiti, where they liked the climate, the lifestyle, and the Polynesian women.
>
> NOT   Christian, eight of the men, and several Tahitian women eventually traveled further; sailing to the tiny uninhabited island of Pitcairn.
>
> BUT   Christian, eight of the men, and several Tahitian women eventually traveled further, sailing to the tiny uninhabited island of Pitcairn.

**24j**   Do not use a semicolon before a direct quotation or before a list.

> NOT   According to *National Geographic;* "To hide from punishment, the mutineers in 1790 burned their ship in Bounty Bay."
>
> BUT   According to *National Geographic:* "To hide from punishment, the mutineers in 1790 burned their ship in Bounty Bay."
>
> NOT   The new residents of Pitcairn faced still more hardship; loneliness, life in a wilderness, even death.
>
> BUT   The new residents of Pitcairn faced still more hardship: loneliness, life in a wilderness, even death.

**24k**   Do not use a colon between a verb and its object or complement or between a preposition and its object.

Even though the words that comprise the object or complement may be in series, as in a list, a colon is not needed to precede them. A colon precedes a list only when the words before the colon form a complete statement (see Section **22b**).

> NOT   Discovering Pitcairn in 1808, an American ship found: a settlement of women, children, and one man.
>
> BUT   Discovering Pitcairn in 1808, an American ship found a settlement of women, children, and one man.
>
> NOT   By then every man except one had died by: violence, disease, or mishap.
>
> BUT   By then every man except one had died by violence, disease, or mishap.

NOT    Today the descendants of the *Bounty* mutineers number about 1,500; their homes are: Pitcairn Island, New Zealand, Australia, Tahiti, and Norfolk Island near Australia.

BUT    Today the descendants of the *Bounty* mutineers number about 1,500; their homes are Pitcairn Island, New Zealand, Australia, Tahiti, and Norfolk Island near Australia.

---

## EXERCISE 24a–k
In the following sentences and paragraph, eliminate any superfluous commas, semicolons, or colons.

**SENTENCE PRACTICE**

1. The planet, Pluto, is the most distant planet from the sun; and was not discovered until 1930.
2. Pluto has a moon, that was given the name, Charon, when it was discovered on 23 June, 1978, by the astronomer, James Christy.
3. Pluto's name comes from the mythological name, for a deity of the underworld, and is appropriate because of the darkness associated with Pluto's great distance, from the sun.
4. Charon is the name of the ferryman, who took the spirits of the dead across the river Styx, and into the underworld in Greek mythology.
5. Astronomers believe, that Pluto has a rocky core and an atmosphere; containing methane.

**24k**

*int p*

**PARAGRAPH PRACTICE**

    In his book, *Cosmos,* the astronomer, Carl Sagan, describes humankind's ever-present curiosity about their world. Among the subjects he deals with in the book are: the discoveries of the planets, and scientists and astronomers, who helped to shape our modern view of the universe. One of the most interesting chapters, in the book, deals with exploration of the planet: Mars. In 1976, Sagan worked as a member of the Viking Lander Imaging Flight team; collecting data about Mars. Although, a human being has yet to set foot on Mars, scientists have acquired a better understanding of the red planet through expeditions, like the Viking flight.

---

## WRITERS REVISING: SUPERFLUOUS INTERNAL PUNCTUATION
*(continued from page 192)*

    Theo's roommate suggested that Theo look on as he proofed the paper and that the two of them look for patterns of errors. Theo could then use this information to help him proof his own paper next time.

## Theo's Revision

| | | |
|---|---|---|
| R 1 | Years after͜ the boy's experience at the | **24h** |
| R 2 | battle royal, he finally discovers͜ that he | **24c** |
| R 3 | is ''an invisible man.'' It took many years | |
| R 4 | of experience in life͜ and deep thought for | **24d** |
| R 5 | this boy before he realized that he was not | |
| R 6 | viewed as an individual. While he was growing | |
| R 7 | up, he always thought of himself͜ as special. | **24f** |
| R 8 | And because the white men in his town praised | |
| R 9 | him, he thought͜ that they too viewed him͜ as | **24c, 24f** |
| R10 | special. However, he gradually came͜ to the | **24c** |
| R11 | realization͜ that he was invisible to these | **24f** |
| R12 | people. They saw him͜ as an intelligent | **24f** |
| R13 | black͜ who must be put in his place͜ and sent | **24d** |
| R14 | to a Negro college, so that he would remain | |
| R15 | invisible͜ and never be a threat to them. | **24d** |

## Analysis

If Theo were to analyze his errors, he would discover patterns which he could then isolate and learn to look for. He consistently separates restrictive modifiers from his sentences. His roommate pointed this out in lines R7, 9, 11–12, and 13. He also pointed out Theo's tendency to separate two words or phrases that are joined by a coordinating conjunction in lines R4, 13, and 15. Two errors, those in lines R2 and 9, occur when Theo separates a verb from its object. In line R1, he had separated the preposition from its object.

---

## REVIEW EXERCISES: INTERNAL PUNCTUATION (Sections 20–24)

The following sentences and paragraph require various kinds of internal punctuation. Supply the needed punctuation marks, and be prepared to explain your choices.

### SENTENCE PRACTICE

1. Because scuba diving equipment has become lighter safer and easier to use more people are trying out diving for recreation.
2. Before setting off for a diving vacation in a place like Key West Florida however amateur divers should take a scuba diving course.

(margin) **24k**

*int p*

3. These diving schools which usually offer classroom sessions as well as open water instruction are often run by diving shops therefore divers can rent or buy their equipment at the same time they sign up for classes.

4. To make sure a diving school is reputable prospective students should ask if the school is certified and they should also visit a class to see how diving training is conducted.

5. Once people learn to dive they often fall into one of two categories the kind of dedicated diver some might use the word *crazy* who puts on a wet suit to dive in December and the recreational diver who prefers to take off for the warm waters of the southern coast.

6. Some divers do what is called skin diving this popular fairly inexpensive form of diving involves using a face mask and a snorkel to dive just below the surface of the water.

7. If divers wish to go to greater depths they need to use a SCUBA an acronym that stands for Self-Contained Underwater Breathing Apparatus.

8. More serious underwater exploration requires a diving suit these suits were first invented in the seventeenth century but high-tech versions of them are still used by divers today.

9. Once divers learn the technique and feel comfortable underwater they often say they feel as though they have entered another world a world where the human being is the intruder.

10. Divers can participate in various types of group dives for example some diving shops organize tours to Florida or the Caribbean others set up dives to explore shipwrecks and some lead shark dives that allow divers to view sharks from the safety of underwater cages.

**25–26**

**q**

## PARAGRAPH PRACTICE

The Cayman Islands three small islands located in the middle of the Carribean Sea are a diver's paradise for the islands' beaches are protected by barrier reefs. The Cayman Islands the largest of which is Grand Cayman were discovered by Christopher Columbus and today have a population of over 17000. The islands are a British dependency their capital George Town is located on Grand Cayman. The islands' attractions white beaches clear and silt-free water and a tropical climate bring in many tourists each year but the area is still fairly unspoiled by overdevelopment. Short diving courses snorkeling trips and week-long advanced courses the islands' diving operators offer programs for both the inexperienced and the experienced diver.

# 25–26
## *THE PUNCTUATION OF QUOTED MATERIAL*

Direct quotations—that is, direct speech and material quoted word for word from other written sources—must always be set off distinctly from a writer's own words. Quotation marks usually indicate the distinction, although when quotations from written sources are long, the distinction may be shown instead by indentation. Section **25** describes the conventional uses of quotation marks and indentation to set off quoted material; the use and punctuation of explanatory words such as *he said;* the conventions controlling the placement of other marks of punctuation with quotation marks; and the special uses of quotation marks in certain titles and with words used as words.

An explanatory comment inserted in a quotation or the omission of some part of the original quotation calls for the use of brackets or the ellipsis mark. These are discussed in Section **26.**

**25–26**

*q*

## WRITERS REVISING: QUOTATION MARKS, BRACKETS, AND ELLIPSES

To fulfill an assignment in her literature class, Necia has written a paper entitled "Love, Suffering, and Happiness in Bernard Malamud's 'The Magic Barrel.' " Now, she must revise it. Using the material in Sections **25–26,** revise this excerpt from her paper to correct the punctuation marks of quoted material. Then compare your revision with hers, which appears on pages 210–11.

### Necia's Draft

D 1      Through all of his self-searching, Leo

D 2   realizes that his inability to love and his

D 3   unhappiness are a result of his inexperience. He

D 4   believes that this brief time of trial has

D 5   equipped him to find true love. The narrator

D 6   reveals this conclusion to us through Leo's

D 7   thoughts: ''As for his quest of a bride, the

D 8   thought of continuing afflicted him with anxiety

D 9   and heartburn, yet perhaps with this new knowledge

D10   of himself he (Leo) would be more successful than

D11   in the past. Perhaps love would now come to him

D12   and a bride to that love. And for this sanctified

D13   seeking who needed a Salzman''? The search that

D14   Leo pursued was now a: 'sanctified seeking'.

D15  Experience, the suffering, and pain of realizing

D16  this has purified and renewed his search for love.

D17      In his next meeting with Salzman, Leo says,

D18  ''to be frank, I now admit the necessity of

D19  premarital love. That is, I want to be in love

D20  with the one I marry''. He has denied the

D21  ''traditional'' view of love and marriage as

D22  practiced by his family and boldly seeks to find a

D23  woman on his own.

D24      However, time passes and Leo's social life

D25  has not improved. A dust-covered packet of

D26  Salzman's pictures has lain on Leo's table for

D27  almost a month. One morning he tears open the

D28  envelope and discovers a picture that startles

D29  him. Leo is drawn to the girl in the small

D30  snapshot by the intensity in her eyes. He senses:

D31  ''She. . . . .had lived. .had somehow deeply

D32  suffered. . . . .her he desired. .only such a one

D33  could understand him and help him seek whatever he

D34  was seeking. She might, perhaps, love''.

This *Writers Revising* continues on page 210.

# 25
## QUOTATION MARKS
### INDICATING QUOTED MATERIAL

**25a**  Use double quotation marks to enclose a direct quotation from speech or writing.

"Don't dive from that rock," she warned me,

Emerson wrote, "A foolish consistency is the hobgoblin of little minds."

Note that in dialogue, each change of speaker is indicated by a new paragraph.

> "And after dinner, as your personal Mephistopheles, I shall take you up a high hill and show you the second-best place in the world. You agree? A mystery tour?"
> "I want the best," she said, drinking her Scotch.
> "And I never award first prizes," he replied placidly.
>
> JOHN LE CARRE

Remember not to set off indirect quotations.

> She warned me not to dive from that rock.
> Was it Emerson who wrote about foolish consistency being the hobgoblin of little minds, or was it Thoreau?

**25b**

**" "**

**25b**  Use single quotation marks to enclose a quotation within a quotation.

> E. B. White wrote, "As an elderly practitioner once remarked, 'Writing is an act of faith, not a trick of grammar.' "

Notice that the end punctuation of the sentence within single quotation marks serves also as the end punctuation for the entire sentence unit of which it is a part. For the rules governing end punctuation used with quotation marks, see **25g**.

**25c**  Set off prose quotations of more than four lines and poetry quotations of more than three lines by indentation.

**1. Long prose quotations.** Prose quotations of more than four lines should be displayed—set off from the text of a paper and indented from the left-hand margin. In typewritten papers, indent all lines of the quotation ten character-spaces from the left, and double-space it. Do not enclose a displayed quotation in quotation marks. If quotation marks occur *within* material you are setting off, use them as they are in the original: double for double, single for single.

> William Zinsser's comment in his book Writing to Learn is
>
> worth quoting:
>
>> If you think you can dash something off and have it
>>
>> come out right, the people you're trying to reach
>>
>> are almost surely in trouble. H. L. Mencken said
>>
>> that "0.8 percent of the human race is capable of
>>
>> writing something that is instantly

understandable." He may have been a little high.

Beware of dashing. "Effortless" articles that look
as if they were dashed off are the result of
strenuous effort. A piece of writing must be viewed
as a constantly evolving organism.

Zinsser knows what he's talking about.

**2. Quoted poetry.** Single lines of poetry are ordinarily run into the text and enclosed in quotation marks unless the writer wishes to give them particular emphasis by setting them off.

In the line "A spotted shaft is seen," the hissing <u>s</u> sounds
echo Emily Dickinson's subject: a snake.

Two or three lines of poetry may be either enclosed in quotation marks and run into the text or indented ten spaces from the left. If they are enclosed in quotation marks and run into the text, divisions between lines are indicated by a slash mark (/).

Published anonymously in <u>Punch</u> on December 6, 1915, John
McCrae's extremely popular poem "In Flanders Fields" is one
reason poppies have come to symbolize World War I and, in
fact, all British and American war dead: "In Flanders fields
the poppies blow / Between the crosses, row on row, / That
mark our place."


Published anonymously in <u>Punch</u> on December 6, 1915, John
McCrae's extremely popular poem "In Flanders Fields" is one
reason poppies have come to symbolize World War I and, in
fact, all British and American war dead:
    In Flanders fields the poppies blow
    Between the crosses, row on row,
    That mark our place.

Poetry quotations of more than three lines should be double-spaced and set off from the text by indenting ten spaces from the left. Any special spacing or indention appearing in the original should be preserved.

McCrae uses the voice-from-the-grave device to focus on

the ironic contrast between lovers' beds and the soldiers'

graves where "we now lie":

> We are the Dead. Short days ago
>
> We lived, felt dawn, saw sunset glow,
>
> Loved and were loved, and now we lie
>
> In Flanders fields.

---

### EXERCISE 25a–c
In the following sentences, insert double or single quotation marks or slash marks wherever needed.

**25d**

**" "**

1. My younger brother is reading *Hamlet* in his high school literature class, and last night he asked me Do you know what the line To be or not to be—that is the question means?
2. I told him I thought that the line might indicate that Hamlet is thinking of suicide.
3. I recall that when I read *Hamlet* in my English literature class, the professor announced: This play has probably created more critical controversy than any other play ever written.
4. After reading *Hamlet*, I also read Shakespeare's sonnets; my favorite sonnet begins with the lines Let me not to the marriage of true minds Admit impediments.
5. After his class had discussed *Hamlet,* my brother said, I enjoyed that play a lot, even though I had to work hard to understand it, and I think I'd like to see a performance of *Hamlet* on the stage.

---

## PUNCTUATING EXPLANATORY WORDS WITH QUOTATIONS

**25d**   In punctuating explanatory words preceding a quotation, be guided by the length and formality of the quotation.

Explanatory words such as *he said* are ordinarily set off from quotations by a comma when they precede the quotation. However, when the quotation that follows is grammatically closely related, explanatory words may be followed by no punctuation, or when they are relatively long and formal they may be followed by a colon.

|  |  |
|---|---|
| NO PUNCTUATION | I yelled "Stop!" and grabbed the wheel. |
|  | Auden's poem "In Memory of W.B. Yeats" begins with the line "He disappeared in dead of winter." |
|  | The Preamble begins with the words "We, the people of the United States." |
|  | It was President Franklin Roosevelt who said that "the only thing we have to fear is fear itself." |

PUNCTUATION   The old rancher said very quietly, "Under no circum-
WITH COMMA   stances will I tell you where the money is hidden."
             The chairman asked him, "Have I stated your motion
             correctly?"

PUNCTUATION   The speaker rose and began to rant: "The party in
WITH COLON   power has betrayed us. It has not only failed to keep its
             election promises but has sold out to special-interest
             groups." [See also examples in **25c**.]

**25e**   Use a comma to separate an opening quotation from the rest
of the sentence unless the quotation ends with a question mark or
an exclamation point.

"The man is dead," he said with finality.
"Is the man dead?" he asked.
"On, no!" he screamed hysterically. "My brother can't be dead."

**25e**
**" "**

**25f**   When quoted dialogue is interrupted by explanatory words
(*I, you, he, she, we, they said*, or their equivalent), use a comma
after the first part of the quotation. In choosing the proper
punctuation mark to place after the explanatory words, apply the
rules for punctuating clauses and phrases.

"I am not aware," she said, "of any dangers from jogging." [Phrase]
"I have always worked hard," he declared. "I was peddling newspapers when I was eight years old." [Independent clause]
"Jean has great capacities," the supervisor said; "she has energy,
brains, and personality." [Independent clause]

---

EXERCISE 25d–f
In the following sentences, insert appropriate punctuation marks
where necessary to separate quotations from the rest of the sentence.

1. "Do you ever have trouble using your VCR" asked Kevin.
2. "Do I ever" exclaimed Darrell "The instructions make recording a
   movie sound easy" he continued "but I usually end up with the
   wrong film when I'm finished."
3. Kevin said that the instructions for his videocassette recorder state
   "Operating this machine is simple after reading these instructions."
4. "One thing I have discovered" said Kevin "is that the term *simple*
   doesn't mean the same thing to everyone."
5. Maybe Kevin should do what my neighbor did, for he recently told
   me "Whenever I want to record anything on my VCR, I get my
   twelve-year-old daughter to do it for me, and she has no trouble."

# USING OTHER MARKS OF PUNCTUATION WITH QUOTATION MARKS

**25g**  Follow established American conventions in placing other punctuation with quotation marks.

**1. Place commas and periods inside quotation marks.** Commas are generally used to separate direct quotations from unquoted material.

> "There comes a time," said the politician, "to put principle aside and do what's right."

Note that this rule applies regardless of the reason for using quotation marks.

> According to Shakespeare, the poet writes in a "fine frenzy."
> The words "lily-livered coward" derive from an earlier expression, "white-livered," which meant "cowardly."

The only exception to this rule is punctuation of in-text citations using *MLA* style (see Section **46i**).

**2. Place semicolons and colons outside quotation marks.**

> According to Shakespeare, the poet writes in a "fine frenzy"; by "fine frenzy" he meant a combination of energy, enthusiasm, imagination, and a certain madness.

**3. Place a dash, question mark, or exclamation point inside the quotation marks when it applies only to the quotation; place it outside the quotation marks when it applies to the whole statement.**

> She said, "Will I see you tomorrow?"
> Didn't she say, "I'll see you tomorrow"?
> "You may have the car tonight"—then he caught himself abruptly and said, "No, you can't have it—I need it myself."

When a mark applies to both quotation and sentence, use it only once—putting it inside the quotation marks.

> Have you ever asked, "May I come in?"

---

EXERCISE 25g
In the following sentences, insert whatever punctuation marks are appropriate for use with quotation marks.

  1. What do you say to a three-year-old child who asks "Why do the leaves change color and fall off the trees in autumn"

2. "I'd say go look it up" then I realized three-year-olds can't read and said "I'd try to explain that these natural changes take place as the days grow shorter."
3. I'm worried, of course, that the child might then ask "Well, exactly why do plants and tree leaves change color"
4. I guess I'd explain "In the fall, plants stop producing the chlorophyll that makes them green" in addition, I'd try to work in some facts I read in an article explaining the chemical process that occurs when the leaves change color.
5. After all that, the child would probably ask "But what about Jack Frost"

## OTHER USES OF QUOTATION MARKS

**25h** Use quotation marks to set off titles of poems, songs, articles, short stories, and other titles that are parts of a longer work.

For the use of italics for the titles of longer works, see **27a** and **27b**.

Theodore Roethke's poem "My Papa's Waltz" appeared in his book *The Lost Son and Other Poems.*

"The Talk of the Town" has for many years been the opening column of *The New Yorker.*

The song "I Left My Heart in San Francisco" has become an anthem for that city.

"Beowulf to Batman: The Epic Hero in Modern Culture," an article by Roger B. Rollin, originally appeared in the journal *College English.*

**25i** Words used in a special sense may be set off by quotation marks.

When a new book comes into the library, it is first of all "accessioned."

Is this what is known as "functional" architecture?

Do not use quotation marks around common nicknames. Do not use them for emphasis. And do not use them apologetically to enclose slang, colloquialisms, trite expressions, or for imprecise words or phrases when you cannot find the right word. If a word is appropriate, it will stand without apology. If it is inappropriate, replace it. If, however, you wish your reader to recognize a slang term or colloquialism as such (to prevent misunderstanding the usage), then you may need to use quotation marks to indicate that the word is being used in a special sense. In your writing, be careful to distinguish between inappropriate use of slang and colloquialisms (to be avoided) and the necessary and legitimate use of such terms in some types of written discourse.

NOT    Katie got a pair of "totally outrageous" socks for her birthday.

BUT    Katie got a pair of brightly colored, wildly patterned socks for her birthday—socks that received full approval from her pre-teen girlfriends: "Totally outrageous!"

---

EXERCISE 25h–i
In the following paragraph, insert quotation marks wherever they are needed.

Because they believed that the South needed to turn from an industrial to an agricultural economy, a group of prominent southern writers of the 1930s are often referred to as the agrarians. This group included the poets Allen Tate, Robert Penn Warren, and John Crowe Ransom, who wrote the poem Bells for John Whiteside's Daughter. Ransom was also one of the seven founders of *The Fugitive*, a magazine that became a focus for what might be called a southern literary renaissance. Allen Tate's best-known poem is Ode to the Confederate Dead, which was published in 1937 in a volume entitled *Selected Poems*. Robert Penn Warren, who wrote poetry, fiction, and criticism, was a Rhodes Scholar at Oxford; there he wrote the short story Prime Leaf, a story he later developed into the novel *Night Rider*.

**26**

**[ ]**

---

# 26

## *BRACKETS AND THE ELLIPSIS MARK*

Brackets and ellipsis marks signal that a writer has made changes in material being quoted directly. Brackets are used to indicate that a writer has inserted into the quotation some information, comment, or explanation not in the original. The ellipsis mark is used to indicate that something has been deliberately omitted from the material being quoted.

### 26a  Use brackets to set off editorial remarks in quoted material.

You will sometimes want to insert a clarifying word or explanatory comment in a statement you are quoting. By enclosing such information in brackets, you let the reader know at once that *you* are speaking rather than the original author.

John Dryden, a famous English poet, said, "Those who accuse him [Shakespeare] to have wanted knowledge give him the greater commendation; he was naturally learned."

The favorite phrase of their [English] law is "a custom whereof the memory of man runneth not back to the contrary."

RALPH WALDO EMERSON

In bibliographical notations, use brackets to enclose the name of a writer reputed to be the author of the work in question.

[Ned Ward], *A Trip to New England* (1699)

**26b**   Use the word *sic* **("thus it is") in brackets to indicate that a mistake or peculiarity in the spelling or the grammar of a foregoing word appears in the original work.**

The high school paper reported, "The students spoke most respectively [sic] of Mrs. Hogginbottom."

**26c**   Use an ellipsis mark (three spaced periods . . .) to indicate an intentional omission from quoted material.

When you wish to quote from an author but want to omit some word or words within a sentence or to omit one or more sentences, in fairness to the original author and to your readers you must indicate that you have omitted material from the original. Such omissions are indicated by inserting an ellipsis mark at the point of omission.

For an omission within a sentence, use three spaced periods, leaving a space before and after each period. When the omission comes at the end of a sentence, use four periods; the first is the usual sentence period, and the last three are the ellipsis mark. If the quotation continues, leave one space between the last of the periods and the first letter of the next word. If a parenthetical reference, such as a page number or the like, follows the ellipsis mark at the end of a sentence, use three spaced periods and put the sentence period immediately after the final parenthesis.

For example, the first selection below is taken without any omission from Russel Nye's *The Unembarrassed Muse* (New York, 1970). It describes the comic-strip world of Walt Disney's Mickey Mouse. The second selection shows how a writer quoting from the original passage might use the ellipsis.

Mickey's is a child's world, safe (though occasionally scary), non-violent, nonideological, where all the stories have happy endings. Characterization is strong and simple—Mickey is bright and friendly, Minnie eternally feminine, Goofy happily stupid, Donald of the terrible temper a raffish, likeable rascal. No Disney strip ever gave a child bad dreams or an adult anything to ponder.

Mickey's is a child's world, safe . . . nonviolent, nonideological, where all the stories have happy endings. Characterization is strong

and simple—Mickey is bright and friendly, Minnie eternally feminine. . . . No Disney strip ever gave a child bad dreams . . . (157).

If you must omit an entire line or more of poetry or an entire
paragraph or more of prose, use a full line of ellipsis marks to indicate
the omission. The example below is from Edgar Allan Poe's poem
"The Raven."

> Once upon a midnight dreary, while I pondered, weak and weary,
> Over many a quaint and curious volume of forgotten lore—
> While I nodded, nearly napping, suddenly there came a tapping,
> . . . . . . . . . . . . . . . . . . . . . . . . . . . . . . . . . . .
> " 'Tis some visitor," I muttered, "tapping at my chamber door—
> Only this and nothing more."

**26c**

**" "**

## WRITERS REVISING: QUOTATION MARKS, BRACKETS, AND ELLIPSES
*(continued from page 200)*

Necia had typed the rough draft of her paper quickly, interested in capturing her ideas and not bothering to look up
things she was not sure about. Now, she proceeded to revise the
paper, checking every line to correct any inconsistencies or errors.

### Necia's Revision

| | | |
|---|---|---|
| R 1 | Through all of his self—searching, Leo | |
| R 2 | realizes that his inability to love and his | |
| R 3 | unhappiness are a result of his | |
| R 4 | inexperience. He believes that this brief | |
| R 5 | time of trial has equipped him to find true | |
| R 6 | love. The narrator reveals this conclusion | |
| R 7 | to us through Leo's thoughts: | **25d** |
| R 8 | As for his quest of a bride, the | **25c** |
| R 9 | thought of continuing afflicted him | |
| R10 | with anxiety and heartburn, yet | |
| R11 | perhaps with this new knowledge of | |
| R12 | himself [Leo] would be more successful | **26a** |
| R13 | than in the past. Perhaps love would | |

| | | |
|---|---|---|
| R14 | now come to him and a bride to that | |
| R15 | love. And for this sanctified seeking | |
| R16 | who needed a Salzman? | |
| R17 | The search that Leo pursued was now a | 25d |
| R18 | ''sanctified seeking.'' Experience, the | 25a, 25g(1) |
| R19 | suffering, and pain of realizing this has | |
| R20 | purified and renewed his search for love. | |
| R21 | In his next meeting with Salzman, Leo | |
| R22 | says, ''To be frank, I now admit the | |
| R23 | necessity of premarital love. That is, I | |
| R24 | want to be in love with the one I marry''. | 25g(1) |
| R25 | He has denied the ''traditional'' view of | 25i |
| R26 | love and marriage as practiced by his | |
| R27 | family and boldly seeks to find a woman on | |
| R28 | his own. | |
| R29 | However, time passes and Leo's social | |
| R30 | life has not improved. A dust-covered | |
| R31 | packet of Salzman's pictures has lain on | |
| R32 | Leo's table for almost a month. One morning | |
| R33 | he tears open the envelope and discovers a | |
| R34 | picture that startles him. Leo is drawn to | |
| R35 | the girl in the small snapshot by the | |
| R36 | intensity in her eyes. He senses: | 25d |
| R37 | ''She . . . had lived . . . had somehow | 25c |
| R38 | deeply suffered . . . her he desired . . . | 26c |
| R39 | only such a one could understand him and | |
| R40 | help him seek whatever he was seeking. She | 26c |
| R41 | might, perhaps, love''. | 25g(1) |

26c

" "

## Analysis

Lines R8-16 are blocked and indented ten spaces since the quotation takes up more than four lines. When a long quotation is set off, or blocked, no quotation marks are needed. The explanatory words preceding the blocked quotation end in a colon because they present a fairly long and formal introduction. The editorial *Leo* in line R12 is enclosed in brackets, not parentheses. The quoted phrase *sanctified seeking* in line R18 is set off by double quotation marks, and the period falls inside the quotation marks. No mark of punctuation preceding the quotation is necessary in lines R17 and 36 because the quotations are grammatically closely related to the sentences. The periods in lines R24 and 40 are placed inside the final quotation marks. No quotation marks are needed to enclose *traditional* in line R25: the word is used in its usual sense. In lines R37 and 38, three spaced periods are used to mark the ellipses.

**26c**

" "

---

REVIEW EXERCISES: PUNCTUATION OF QUOTED MATERIAL
(Sections 25–26)
In the following sentences and paragraph, supply the appropriate punctuation.

### SENTENCE PRACTICE
1. I went to a Bruce Springsteen concert last night my friend said and the best part of the concert was when Bruce and his band played the song Hungry Heart.
2. Did Bruce let the crowd sing the first stanza and the chorus like he does in the version on his live concert album another friend asked.
3. My friend replied that the crowd sang but he could only remember the first line of the chorus, Everybody's got a hungry heart.
4. I've been taking a nineteenth-century English poetry class, so I thought I'd surprise everyone by telling them that I came across the phrase a hungry heart in a poem entitled Ulysses by Alfred, Lord Tennyson.
5. My friend looked at me and said Are you serious Did you really run across that same phrase in an old poem? I may have to read that poem someday.

### PARAGRAPH PRACTICE
Would you like to go see a production of Lorraine Hansberry's play A Raisin in the Sun at the university theatre this Friday night my sister asked me when I saw her at lunch today. I would I said because I've read the play but I've never seen it performed. I wish I knew where Hansberry got her title for that play my sister said for the title intrigues me. I told her that the title comes from a poem entitled A Dream Deferred by Langston Hughes. In fact, the phrase a raisin in the sun appears in the third line of Hughes' poem.

# 27–30

## WORD PUNCTUATION

Italics, capitals, apostrophes, and hyphens identify words that have a special use or a particular grammatical function in a sentence.

Our two-week reading program, assigned in Wednesday's class, is Shakespeare's *King Lear*.

Here the italics set off the words *King Lear* as a single title. The capitals identify *Wednesday, Shakespeare, King,* and *Lear* as proper names. The apostrophes indicate that *Shakespeare* and *Wednesday* are singular possessives and not plurals. The hyphen between *two* and *week* makes the two words function as a single adjective.

### WRITERS REVISING: ITALICS, CAPITALS, APOSTROPHES, AND HYPHENS

For his business writing course, Clifford is writing a proposal for a new record-keeping computer program at Saco Electric, Inc. In a section on implementation and training, he writes the following paragraph. Check his draft for correct use of italics, capitals, apostrophes, and hyphens as you read through Sections **27-30**. Then compare your conclusions with Clifford's revision at the end of Section **30**.

**Clifford's Draft**

```
D 1      According to ''Info World,'' the weekly

D 2   Computer Magazine, lotus 1-2-3 is the most widely

D 3   used computer spread sheet program in the United

D 4   States. Because of it's popularity, lotus has

D 5   continued to work hard to make it's spreadsheet as

D 6   user friendly as possible. This means that it

D 7   takes very little training to master this package.

D 8   The two Computer Operators could attend a six hour

D 9   training course at the division of continuing

D10   education in Pleasant hall and learn enough to be

D11   fully efficient on lotus 1-2-3.
```

This *Writers Revising* continues on page 228.

# 27

## *ITALICS*

In commercial printing and some computer printer software, italics are typefaces that slope toward the right. In typed or handwritten manuscript, italics are indicated by underlining.

On the printed page: *italics*

In typewritten copy: <u>italics</u>

In handwritten copy: *italics*

**27a**  Italicize the titles of books, newspapers, magazines, and all publications issued separately.

"Issued separately" means published as a single work and not as an article or story in a magazine, nor as a chapter or section of a book. (For the proper punctuation of such titles, see **25h.**)

| | |
|---|---|
| *The New York Times* | *Death of a Salesman* |
| *Commentary* | *Moby Dick* |
| *People* | *Webster's New Collegiate Dictionary* |
| *The Lord of the Rings* | *USA Today* |

Be careful not to add the word *The* to titles unless it belongs there and not to omit it if it does belong.

**NOT**  *The Reader's Digest*
BUT  the *Reader's Digest*

**NOT**  the *Red Badge of Courage*
BUT  *The Red Badge of Courage*

Note that the titles of some very well-known works and documents are not italicized nor placed in quotation marks.

| | |
|---|---|
| the Bible | Psalms |
| the Koran | the Constitution of the |
| the Magna Carta | United States |
| the Declaration of | Matthew |
| Independence | the Bill of Rights |

**27b**  Italicize the names of ships, spacecraft, and aircraft, and the titles of works of art, music, movies, television and radio programs, record albums, and the like.

| | | |
|---|---|---|
| *Titanic* | *Spirit of St. Louis* | *U.S.S. Saratoga* |
| *The Thinker* | *Casablanca* | the *Concorde* |
| *Dallas* | the *Star-Spangled Banner* | *Challenger* |

(sidebar) 27 ital

Note that for ships and the like, the prefix U.S.S. (or H.M.S.) is not italicized: U.S.S. *Nimitz;* H.M.S. *Pinafore.*

**27c**  Italicize letters, words, and numbers used as words.

Your *r*'s look very much like your *n*'s, and I can't decide if this is a *7* or a *1*.

The early settlers borrowed Indian words like *moccasin, powwow,* and *wigwam.*

Quotation marks are also sometimes used to set off words as words (see **25i**). However, if a subject you are discussing in a typewritten or handwritten paper requires you to set off many words as.words, underlining (italics) will make your manuscript look less cluttered.

**27d**  Italicize foreign words and phrases that have not yet been accepted into the English language. Also italicize the Latin scientific names for plants, animals, and so forth.

She graduated *magna cum laude.*

Many of the works of the *fin de siècle* judged so sensational when they were written now seem utterly innocent.

In the fall, the ginkgo tree *(Ginkgo biloba)* produces a yellow fruit that smells indescribably foul.

You may sometimes feel that a foreign word or phrase expresses your meaning more aptly or concisely than an English one. If you are sure that your readers will understand the expression, use it. But overuse of such words is pedantry. Many foreign words have been accepted into the English language and need no longer be italicized. The following words, for example, do not require italics:

bourgeois   milieu   denouement   liqueur

To determine whether a foreign word should be italicized, consult a good dictionary.

**27e**  Use italics to give a word or phrase special emphasis.

*Always* turn off the electricity before attempting to work on the wiring.

We have government *of* the people, *by* the people, and *for* the people; dictatorships have government *over* the people.

**27f**  Avoid the overuse of italics.

Distinguish carefully between a real need for italicizing and the use of italics as a mechanical device to achieve emphasis. The best way to achieve emphasis is to write effective, well-constructed sentences. The overuse of italics will make your writing seem immature and amateurish, as in the following:

> Any good education must be *liberal*.
> America is a *true* democracy, in every sense of the word.
> This book has what I call *real* depth of meaning.

---

EXERCISE 27a–f
Italicize words as necessary in the following sentences and paragraph.

**27f**

*ital*

**SENTENCE PRACTICE**

1. Although Herman Melville's most famous sea novel is Moby Dick, he also wrote a much shorter work set at sea, the novella Billy Budd, Sailor.
2. In this novel written in 1891, Melville's main character, the young sailor Billy Budd, is taken off a merchant ship called the Rights of Man and drafted into service on a British war vessel called the Indomitable.
3. Billy Budd worked as a foretopman on the Indomitable; Webster's Seventh New Collegiate Dictionary defines the word foretopman as "a sailor on duty on the foremast and above."
4. In Billy Budd, Sailor, and his other sea novels such as Redburn and Whitejacket, Melville drew upon his own experiences: according to an article in the New York Times, the writer had spent four years on trading vessels, whaling ships, and U. S. Navy ships in the Atlantic and Pacific.
5. Melville's story of the sailor Billy Budd became the basis for the opera named Billy Budd by British composer Benjamin Britten.

**PARAGRAPH PRACTICE**

The period of the Spanish Civil War, 1936–39, is reflected in both the painting and the literature of Spain during that time, although ironically, one of the most famous works dealing with the war—Hemingway's novel For Whom the Bell Tolls—was written by an American. For those who are interested in twentieth-century art, Picasso's painting entitled Guernica may be the sine qua non, or in other words, the one thing not to be missed. That painting, which hangs in the Prado in Madrid, depicts the agony of the war; in the painting are figures of a mother and her dead child, figures reminiscent of the Madonna and Christ figures in Michelangelo's great sculpture the Pietà. Frederico Garcia Lorca, a contemporary of Picasso's, was assassinated by the Fascists shortly after the Spanish Civil War broke out; Garcia Lorca, whose plays include Blood Wedding and House of Bernarda Alba, is one of Spain's best-known modern writers. Garcia Lorca was born near Granada, but he went to Madrid to study in 1919; there he encountered a circle of artists and intellectuals such as Salvador Dali and Luis Buñuel, a film director who later became famous for such films as The Exterminating Angel and That Obscure Object of Desire.

# 28
## CAPITALS

Modern writers capitalize less frequently than did earlier writers, and informal writing permits less capitalization than formal writing. Two hundred years ago, a famous author wrote:

> Being ruined by the Inconstancy and Unkindness of a Lover, I hope a true and plain Relation of my Misfortune may be of Use and Warning to Credulous Maids, never to put much Trust in deceitful Men.
>
> JONATHAN SWIFT, "The Story of the Injured Lady"

A modern writer would capitalize no letters but the initial *B* and the pronoun *I*.

**28a** Capitalize the first word of a sentence, a line of poetry, a direct quotation that is not structurally part of another sentence, a complete sentence enclosed in parentheses or brackets, or—in some cases—a complete sentence following a colon.

**1. A sentence or a line of poetry.**

Education is concerned not with knowledge but with the meaning of knowledge.
True ease in writing comes from art, not chance,
As those move easiest who have learned to dance.

ALEXANDER POPE, *Essay on Criticism*

Some modern poets ignore the convention of capitalizing each line of poetry, perhaps because they feel that an initial capital letter gives a word unwanted emphasis.

a man who had fallen among thieves
lay by the roadside on his back
dressed in fifteenthrate ideas
wearing a round jeer for a hat

e.e. cummings, "a man who had fallen among thieves"

**2. A direct quotation.**

She thought, "Where shall we spend our vacation—at the shore or in the mountains?"

Notice that the preceding example shows a quotation that is grammatically independent. Before the quotation are words that introduce and attribute it to a speaker, but the quotation itself could stand alone and is, in fact, an independent thought. The capital letter signals this independence.

When a quotation is grammatically incorporated into the sentence in which it appears, the first word of the quotation is not capitalized unless it is a proper noun.

**28a**

*cap*

She knew that "the woods are lovely, dark, and deep," but sun, sand, and sea appealed to her, too.

The newspaper's motto was "all the news that's fit to print," which made me wonder how bad the news had to be before it became unfit.

**3. A complete sentence enclosed in parentheses or brackets.**

The survey shows that cigarette smoking has declined nationally in the last ten years but that smoking among women has increased. (See Table 3 for numerical data.)

"The Black Death killed anywhere between one-third to one-half of the entire population of Europe. [Exact numbers are impossible to derive, given the state of record-keeping in medieval Europe.] Those who survived were often too few to bury the dead."

When a parenthetical or bracketed statement appears within another sentence, the first word is ordinarily not capitalized and the ending period is omitted.

The survey shows that cigarette smoking has declined nationally in the last ten years but that smoking among women has increased (see Table 3 for numerical data).

**4. A complete sentence following a colon.**

Typically, an independent statement following a colon is not capitalized, particularly when it is closely related to the preceding sentence. However, if the writer wishes to emphasize the independence of the statement, a capital letter may be used.

There were fifteen or twenty women in the room: None of them was his mother.

**28b**   Capitalize the pronoun *I* and the interjection *O*.

How long must I wait, O Lord?

Do not capitalize the interjection *oh* unless it is the first word of a sentence.

Oh how we enjoyed the party, but oh how we paid for our fun later.

**28c**   Capitalize proper nouns, their derivatives and abbreviations, and common nouns used as proper nouns.

1. **Specific persons, races, nationalities, languages.**

| | | | |
|---|---|---|---|
| Willa | Bob | Rita Mae Brown | Semitic |
| Asiatic | American | Mongolian | Cuban |
| Canadian | English | Swahili | Zulu |

**28b**

*cap*

Usage varies for the term *black (blacks)* as an ethnic designation. Although it is often not capitalized, and is never capitalized in the phrase "blacks and whites," many authors regularly capitalize other uses in current writing.

2. **Specific places.**

| | | | |
|---|---|---|---|
| Atlanta | Buenos Aires | California | Lake Erie |
| Newfoundland | India | Jerusalem | Snake River |

3. **Specific organizations, historical events and periods, and documents.**

| | |
|---|---|
| National Geographic Society | the French Revolution |
| the Locarno Pact | the Renaissance |
| Declaration of | the Battle of |
| Independence | Hastings |

4. **Days of the week, months, holidays, and holy days.**

| | | | | |
|---|---|---|---|---|
| Thursday | November | Christmas | the Fourth of July | |
| Easter | Good Friday | Hanukkah | Ramadan | Yom Kippur |

5. **Religious terms, deities, and sacred texts.**

| | | | | |
|---|---|---|---|---|
| the Virgin | Allah | Holy Ghost | Jehovah | the Torah |

**6.** **Titles of books, plays, magazines, newspapers, journals, articles, poems, computer software, and copyrighted or trademarked names or products.** Capitalize the first word and all others except articles (*a/an, the*), and conjunctions and prepositions of fewer than five letters. (See also **25h** and **27a.**)

| | | |
|---|---|---|
| *Gone with the Wind* | *The Country Wife* | *Pippa Passes* |
| *Paradise Lost* | *Atlantic Monthly* | *War and Peace* |
| *Ebony* | *Much Ado About Nothing* | *Business Week* |
| *Kleenex* | *Microsoft Word* | *Oreo cookies* |

**7.** **Titles, and their abbreviations, when they precede a proper noun.** Such titles are an essential part of the name and are regularly capitalized. Abbreviations for academic degrees and professional certificates are also capitalized when they follow a proper name.

**28c**

***cap***

| | | |
|---|---|---|
| Professor Berger | Mr. Rothstein | Vice Chairman |
| Dr. Carolyn Woo | Justice Sandra Day | Diaz |
| President Bush | O'Connor | John Leland, PhD |
| Thomas Hass, MD | Valarie Petroski, CPA | Editor-in-Chief |
| Secretary Dole | Associate Dean G. P. | Weil |
| | Bass | |

When a title follows a name, capitalize it only if it indicates high distinction:

> Abraham Lincoln, President of the United States
> John Marshall, Chief Justice of the Supreme Court

> BUT   Sally S. Fleming, director of corporate communications
> J. R. Derby, professor of biology

Often the "in-house" conventions of a particular organization include capitalizing titles after names. For example, in an annual report or employee newsletter you would probably see the following:

> Sally S. Fleming, Director of Corporate Communications

This use of capitals suggests that the concept of high distinction is strongly related to audience and context. Although a title following a name may not warrant the distinctive treatment of capitalization for a general audience (the readers of your paper about corporate research and development), that same title may well be capitalized for a specialized audience (Fleming's coworkers).

**8.** **Common nouns used as an essential part of a proper noun.** These are generic names such as *street, river, avenue, lake, county, ocean, college, church, award.*

| Vine Street | Lake Huron | Hamilton College |
| Fifth Avenue | General Motors Corporation | Pulitzer Prize |
| Pacific Ocean | Penn Central Railroad | Mississippi River |

When the generic term is used in the plural, it is not usually capitalized.

| Vine and Mulberry streets | the Atlantic and Pacific oceans |
| Hamilton and Lake counties | the Catholic and Protestant churches in town |

## 28d   Avoid unnecessary capitalization.

A good general rule is not to capitalize unless a specific convention warrants it.

**1.** Capitalize *north, east, south, west* only when they come at the beginning of a sentence or refer to specific geographical locations, not when they merely indicate direction.

Birds fly south in the winter, some stopping north of South America.

If the United States looks east and west, it sees economic competitors in the Far East and Western Europe.

**2.** The names of seasons need not be capitalized.

fall     autumn     winter     midwinter     spring     summer

**3.** Capitalize nouns indicating family relationships only when they are used as names or titles or in combination with proper names. Do not capitalize *mother* and *father* when they are preceded by possessive adjectives.

> I telephoned my mother.
> BUT   I telephoned Mother.

> My uncle has four children.
> BUT   My Uncle Ben has four children.

**4.** Ordinarily, do not capitalize common nouns and adjectives used in place of proper nouns and adjectives.

> I went to high school in Cleveland.
> BUT   I went to John Adams High School in Cleveland.

> I am a university graduate.
> BUT   I am a Columbia University graduate.

28d
cap

I took a psychology course in my senior year.

BUT    I took Psychology 653 in my senior year.

She received a master's degree in computer science.

BUT    She received a Master of Science degree from the Computer Science Department.

---

### EXERCISE 28a–d

In the following sentences and paragraph, capitalize words as necessary. Remove unnecessary capitals.

**SENTENCE PRACTICE**

1. sojourner truth, whose original name was isabel baumfree, was born in 1797 in hurley, new york.
2. although sojourner truth was born a slave, She was freed by the new york state emancipation act of 1827.
3. Sojourner Truth was one of the first Black women to speak out against Slavery, and later in her life she became a Crusader for Women's rights.
4. After the civil war, truth spoke out for equal treatment for african americans, especially for Equality in Education.
5. even though sojourner truth was Illiterate, she was a powerful speaker; for example, in 1852 she attended the national women's suffrage convention in akron, ohio, and gave the speech that made her famous, a speech entitled "ain't i a woman."

**PARAGRAPH PRACTICE**

women's suffrage, or the right of Women to vote, was first proposed in the united states in 1848. women such as elizabeth cady stanton, susan b. anthony, and lucretia mott led the Fight to win for women the Right to Vote. stanton was a journalist who became President of the national woman suffrage association. Mott was a quaker who had helped slaves come North during the civil war. Anthony, who had organized the daughters of temperance, the first women's temperance association, helped to write the first three Volumes of a work called *the history of woman suffrage*. the Dedication of women such as these three paid off, for in 1920 the constitution of the united states was amended to give women the right to vote.

---

# 29

## THE APOSTROPHE

**29a**  Use an apostrophe to show the possessive case of nouns and indefinite pronouns.

**1. Add an apostrophe and** *s* **to form the possessive of singular nouns, indefinite pronouns, and plural nouns that do not end in** *s*.

| | |
|---|---|
| the woman's decision | the women's decision |
| the child's toy | the children's toys |
| the man's feet | the men's feet |
| someone's sandwich | the people's sandwiches |
| the duchess's ring | |
| James's gym shoes | |
| Keats's famous poem | |

**2. Add only an apostrophe to form the possessive of plural nouns ending in *s*.**

the girls' locker room
the boys' blue jeans
the Smiths' house [Referring to at least two persons named Smith]
The miners' strike lasted three months.

**3. In compounds, make only the last word possessive.**

nobody else's fault
I can't find my brother-in-law's pen. [Singular possessive]
Their mothers-in-law's birthdays are a day apart. [Plural possessive]

**4. In nouns of joint possession, make only the last noun possessive; in nouns of individual possession, make both nouns possessive.**

Margo and Paul's office is down the hall. [Joint possession]
Margo's and Paul's offices are down the hall. [Individual possession]

**29b**   Do not use an apostrophe with the possessive form of personal pronouns. Be particularly careful not to confuse *its* with the contraction *it's* [it is].

The personal pronouns *his, hers, its, ours, yours, theirs,* and the pronoun *whose* are possessives as they stand and do not require an apostrophe.

| | | |
|---|---|---|
| *his* casette player | an idea of *hers* | a friend of *theirs* |

The possessive form of *it* is *its*. **Do not use an apostrophe to form the possessive.** The word *it's* (with an apostrophe) is a contraction for *it is* and is not possessive.

Although we couldn't find *its* nest, we saw the bird. We know *it's* a robin.

**29c**   Use an apostrophe to indicate the omission of a letter or number.

| | | | |
|---|---|---|---|
| can't | cannot | o'clock | of the clock |
| doesn't | does not | blizzard of '89 | blizzard of 1989 |
| it's | it is | will-o'-the-wisp | will of the wisp |

**29b**

**'**

In reproducing speech, writers frequently use an apostrophe to show that a word is given a colloquial or dialectical pronunciation.

"An' one o' the boys is goin' t' be sick," he said.

**29d**  In using apostrophes to form the plurals of letters, numbers, and words used as words, follow the guidelines of writing in your field.

The style manual of the Modern Language Association recommends using an apostrophe to form the plurals of letters but not the plurals of numbers, abbreviations, or words used as words.

> CPAs in the 1990s will have to mind their *p*'s and *q*'s while leading their clients through the *A, B, C*'s—the *if*s, *and*s, and *but*s—of the income tax code.

Other style manuals differ. In fact, many no longer require apostrophes with the plurals of letters.

---

EXERCISE 29a–d
In the following sentences and paragraph, insert apostrophes or a-postrophes plus *s* as necessary. Then write five sentences of your own that use apostrophes in various ways.

**SENTENCE PRACTICE**

1. Because more and more people are taking tours to Antarctica, scientists are becoming concerned about the impact of the increased number of visitors on the regions fragile environment.
2. Scientists concerns involve protecting Antarcticas mosses, grasses, and lichens.
3. Penguins, seals, and seabirds inhabit the Antarctic continents ice shelves and peninsulas, and scientists are also worried that increased tourism will affect these animals habitats.
4. The 1980s were a time of growing interest in travel to Antarctica, and more and more people will journey to the worlds coldest continent in the 1990s.
5. As a result, its vital that the visitors become aware of the importance of preserving Antarcticas unique environment.

**PARAGRAPH PRACTICE**

   Roald Amundsens journey to the South Pole in 1911 made him the first human being to reach the earths southernmost point. Amundsens trek to the South Pole was followed by that of British explorer Robert Scott. Scott didnt achieve the distinction of being the first to reach the South Pole, because Scotts group of five, who had pulled sledges through Antarcticas subfreezing conditions, arrived at the Pole just a month after Amundsen. This second groups return from the South Pole was tragic: Scott and his men suffered

29d

,

from hunger, became ill, and encountered blizzard conditions that resulted in the mens deaths on the return trip. Amundsens and Scotts expeditions to the South Pole opened the way to further explorations of the earths fifth largest continent, although its tragic that the British explorers lives were lost in the effort.

# 30

## THE HYPHEN

In handwriting, distinguish the hyphen from the dash by making the hyphen shorter. In typewriting and word processing, the hyphen is typed immediately next to the letter it follows, with no space in between.

The hyphen has two distinct uses: (1) to form compound words, and (2) to indicate that a word is continued from one line to the next.

Convention in the latter use of the hyphen, called *syllabication* or *word division,* is arbitrarily fixed. (See Section **18**.) However, convention in the use of hyphens with compounds not only shifts rapidly but is unpredictable. As a noun, *short circuit* is spelled as two words; but the verb *short-circuit* is hyphenated. *Shorthand* and *shortstop* are spelled as single words, but *short order* is spelled as two words. *Short-term* in *short-term loan* is hyphenated, but in *the loan is short term* it is spelled as two words.

In such a rapidly changing and unpredictable matter, your only safe recourse is to consult a good, up-to-date dictionary. The following uses of the hyphen in forming compound words are widely accepted.

**30a**   Use a hyphen to form compound words that are not yet accepted as single words.

The spelling of compound words that express a single idea passes through successive stages. Originally spelled as two separate words, then as a hyphenated word, a compound word finally emerges as a single word.

*base ball* became *base-ball* became *baseball*

*post mark* became *post-mark* became *postmark*

Similar words pass through these stages at different rates—and some perhaps not at all. Compare the following words, selected from a recently published dictionary.

| | |
|---|---|
| bull's-eye | bullhorn |
| fire-eater | flame thrower |
| speed-reading | speedboating |

There is no certain way of determining the proper spelling of a compound at any given moment. Your dictionary is your most authoritative reference.

**30b** Use a hyphen to join two or more words serving as a single adjective before a noun.

Do not hyphenate such an adjective if it follows the verb as a predicate adjective.

|          | a well-known speaker |
|----------|----------------------|
| BUT      | The speaker was well known. |

|          | a grayish-green coat |
|----------|----------------------|
| BUT      | The coat was grayish green. |

|          | nineteenth-century American fiction |
|----------|----------------------|
| BUT      | American fiction of the nineteenth century |

Omit the hyphen when the first word is an adverb ending in -ly.

|          | a slow-curving ball |
|----------|----------------------|
| BUT      | a slowly curving ball |

|          | a quick-moving runner |
|----------|----------------------|
| BUT      | a quickly moving runner |

**30c** Use a hyphen to avoid an ambiguous or awkward union of letters.

|          | re-create [for "create again"] |
|----------|----------------------|
| NOT      | recreate |

|          | bell-like |
|----------|----------------------|
| NOT      | belllike |

There are many common exceptions, however.

|          | coeducational | coordinate | cooperate | readdress |
|----------|---------------|------------|-----------|-----------|
| NOT      | co-educational | co-ordinate | co-operate | re-address |

**30d** Use a hyphen to form compound numbers from twenty-one through ninety-nine and to separate the numerator from the denominator in written fractions.

twenty-nine    fifty-five    two-thirds    four-fifths

**30e**  Use a hyphen with the prefixes *self-*, *all-*, *ex-*, and the suffix *-elect*.

self-important      all-conference      ex-mayor      governor-elect

Do not capitalize the prefix *ex-* or the suffix *-elect*, even when used in titles that are essential parts of a name.

ex-Mayor Sanchez      Governor-elect Jones      ex-President Ford

EXERCISE 30
Insert hyphens as needed in the following passage. Then write five sentences containing compound adjectives, some of which precede nouns and some of which follow verbs as predicate adjectives.

**30e**

-

Frederick Douglass, an abolitionist who was an ex slave, is an important figure in nineteenth century American history. Douglass was born in Maryland in 1817 and died in 1895; thus his life spanned almost three fourths of the nineteenth century. His autobiography, *Narrative of the Life of Frederick Douglass, an American Slave*, was published in the mid nineteenth century and is one of the best known accounts of the experiences of pre Civil War slaves. The book quickly became a best seller in its own time. In addition to being a deeply moving account of the young Douglass's life as a slave, the autobiography is also a record of his self discovery of his role as a spokesman for his people.

REVIEW EXERCISES: WORD PUNCTUATION (Sections 27–30)
Supply the necessary italics, capitals, apostrophes, and hyphens in the following sentences and paragraph.

SENTENCE PRACTICE
1. The ever popular movie the wizard of oz was based on L. Frank Baums book the wonderful wizard of oz.
2. The book, which was published in 1900, tells the story of dorothy, an orphan who is blown by a cyclone from her aunt and uncles farm in kansas to Oz, a fantasy land ruled by a wizard named oz.
3. The movie version of the book was filmed in 1939 by mgm and starred judy garland as dorothy.
4. Some of the movies most memorable scenes involve the characters dorothy meets on her way to Oz: a scarecrow, a tin woodman, and a cowardly lion.
5. baum had originally called the book The Emerald City, but he changed the title to the Wonderful world of Oz before the novels publication in may 1900.

PARAGRAPH PRACTICE
    In a recent article about paris in national geographic, the Louvre was described as frances foremost art museum. The mu-

seum is located on the site of a twelfth century fortress built by philip II. Today, a visit to the louvre is usually high on most tourists lists of places to go in paris. inside the vast museum, which is well known for its greek, roman, and egyptian collections, visitors can see world famous sculptures such as the Venus d'Milo and the Victory of Samothrace. One of the most popular attractions is the painting referred to by the title mona lisa, a painting by Leonardo da Vinci.

## WRITERS REVISING: ITALICS, CAPITALS, APOSTROPHES, AND HYPHENS
*(continued from page 213)*

**30e**

Although Clifford had already revised his draft for meaning, he still needed to focus on the mechanics—specifically word punctuation.

### Clifford's Revision

| R 1 | According to ⊙Info World⊙ | 27a |
| R 2 | the weekly Computer Magazine, lotus | 28d(4), 28c(6) |
| R 3 | 1-2-3 is the most widely used | 30b |
| R 4 | computer spread-sheet program in the | 30b |
| R 5 | United States. Because of it's | 29b |
| R 6 | popularity, lotus has continued to | 28c |
| R 7 | work hard to make it's spread sheet | 29b |
| R 8 | as user friendly as possible. This | |
| R 9 | means that it takes very little | |
| R10 | training to master this package. The | |
| R11 | two Computer Operators could attend | 28d(4) |
| R12 | a six-hour training course at the | 30b |
| R13 | Division of Continuing education in | 28c |
| R14 | Pleasant Hall and learn enough to be | 28c(8) |
| R15 | fully efficient on lotus 1-2-3. | 28c(6) |

### Analysis

*Info World* should be italicized since it is the name of a magazine. *Computer magazine* in line R2 and *computer operators* in line R11 are capitalized unnecessarily since they are generic terms and there is no convention for doing so. *Lotus* (lines R2, 6, and 15) should be capitalized because it refers to a particular computer program and is therefore considered a proper noun. *Division of Continuing Education* is capitalized because it refers to a particular division of the university and is thus a proper noun. The word *hall* (line R14) is capitalized because it is an essential part of a proper noun. In lines R5 and R7, *it's* should not have an apostrophe because it is a possessive pronoun. The two-word modifiers *spread-sheet* and *six-hour* in lines R4 and R12 are hyphenated because they serve as single adjectives before nouns.

---

**30e**

-

## REVIEW EXERCISES: PUNCTUATION (Sections 19–30)

### PART A

In the following sentences and paragraph, make all necessary corrections in internal punctuation and in the use of quotation marks, capitals, italics, apostrophes, and hyphens.

#### SENTENCE PRACTICE

1. The american poet langston hughes was born in joplin missouri in 1902 in addition to poetry Hughes who died in 1967 also wrote drama fiction television scripts songs and childrens books.
2. Hughes was one of the prominent figures in the Harlem Renaissance a period in the 1920s marked by a surge of writing and music by black artists many of whom were associated with the harlem section of new york city.
3. Many of Hughes poems deal with Harlem and in his volume of poems entitled Montage of a Dream Deferred Hughes depicts the life of urban black americans.
4. Other writers associated with the Harlem Renaissance include Countee Cullen a poet who used traditional verse forms to express black themes James Weldon Johnson a lawyer who wrote both novels and poetry and Zora Neale Thurston an anthropologist and writer who studied african american folktales.
5. Because of the work of these artists harlem became a literary and artistic center but the period known as the Harlem Renaissance ended with the beginning of the Great Depression in the 1930s.

#### PARAGRAPH PRACTICE

Because i had grown up in a small town in nebraska i was excited by the diversity and overwhelmed by the size of new york city when I made my first but certainly not my last visit there. To get oriented to the huge metropolis I took a guided tour of the city. The two day tour took us to several famous sites the empire state building the world trade center and the statue of liberty. On the first day of the tour our guide said to us I want you to remember that this city which is the largest in the U.S. was established as a dutch settlement in 1624. The tour guide also told us that even before the dutch came to the area the english explorer henry hudson had been there moreover it is believed that Giovanni da Verrazanno 1480–1527 an italian explorer may have been the first european to arrive in the area. Verrazanos name stays in New Yorkers minds today as part of the Verrazano-Narrows bridge. The bridge has a main span of 4260 feet making it the countrys longest suspension bridge used by vehicles. When I saw that bridge at the entrance of new york harbor one word came to mind awesome.

## PART B

In the following paragraphs, insert any needed internal punctuation, as well as capitals, italics, apostrophes, hyphens, and quotation marks.

**30e**

-

When people think of fairy tales the first name to come to mind is probably Grimm the family name of two german brothers who collected and edited over 200 tales and legends. jacob grimm the older of the two brothers was born in 1785 and his brother wilhelm was born in 1786. The brothers studied law but they also became interested in gathering folktales and legends particularly those passed on through the oral tradition. Their first collection of tales was called Kinder-und Hausmärchen a german title that is more familiar to english speakers as Grimm's Fairy Tales. The collections contain such well known stories as Hansel and Gretel Rapunzel Snow White and the Seven Dwarfs and The Frog Prince. Although the Grimms book had been published as a serious scholarly collection of tales it also gained popularity with general readers. Eventually seven editions of Kinder-und Hausmärchen appeared during the brothers lifetime. Today the fairy tales have been translated into seventy languages and characters such as Rumpelstiltskin and the Bremen Town-Musicians as well as many others are favorites of children and adults everywhere.

The grimm brothers became most famous for their work with fairy tales yet they also studied the german language and began work on an etymological dictionary a dictionary which would trace the history of words in the german language. The brothers began work on the dictionary in 1852 however Wilhelm died in 1859 jacob died in 1863 and the dictionary was not completed for over a hundred years.

## PART C

In the following sentences and paragraph, determine which punctuation marks are used correctly, correct any marks used incorrectly, and add any needed punctuation.

**SENTENCE PRACTICE**

1. The Vietnam Memorial an angle of polished black granite situated near the Lincoln Memorial, and the Washington Monument on the

Mall in Washington, D.C., has become one of the most frequently
visited sites in the nations capital.

2. The Memorial was designed by Maya Lin who was an undergraduate, architectural student at Yale when she submitted the winning
   design, for the Memorial in 1981.

3. After considerable controversy over the unusual design construction
   finally began in March, 1982; the 3000 cubic feet of granite for the
   panels came from Barre Vermont.

4. Etched into the granite of the Vietnam Memorial, are nearly 60000
   names of individuals, who were killed in Vietnam, or are listed as
   missing in action.

5. Visitors, to the Vietnam Memorial touch the names of those they
   knew and some leave medals photographs letters and other personal
   mementos.

**PARAGRAPH PRACTICE**

Although over fifty years have passed, since Amelia Earharts
disappearance in the South Pacific in July 1937 the mystery of what
happened on the world famous aviators last flight remains unsolved
today. After the disappearance of the plane, and in the years since
then many searches have been conducted their participants hoping
to find some evidence of Earharts plane. Earhart who had been the
first woman to fly across the Atlantic in 1928 and later the first
woman to fly across the Atlantic alone had set out in 1937 to fly
around the world. On what turned out to be her last flight Earhart
was accompanied by her navigator Fred Noonan. Earhart, and
Noonan, were headed for Howland Island a tiny bit of land in the
Pacific however their plane disappeared somewhere between New
Guinea and Howland Island. The whereabouts of Earhart Noonan
and the plane remain a mystery.

**30e**

**-**

# EFFECTIVE SENTENCES

*sent*

*When you write, you make a point, not by subtracting as though you sharpened a pencil, but by adding. When you put one word after another, your statement should be more precise the more you add.*

JOHN ERSKINE, *"A Note on the Writer's Craft"*

I't's one thing to write sentences that are grammatical; it's another to write sentences that not only convey information but also explicitly establish the relationships among the ideas they are intended to express. Writers sometimes think effective sentences are just a matter of style, a concern important in poetry and novels but not vital to everyday writing.

As the following sample paragraph illustrates, nothing could be further from the truth. The writer, a manager at a large manufacturing company, forgot that one of his roles is to *make meaning*, to show his reader the connections among the chunks of information he presents. As they stand, his sentences are correct, but they give equal emphasis to everything—and, consequently, to nothing. What's more, when he reviewed this paragraph, the writer discovered he had actually subordinated major ideas and stressed minor details. He concluded that, indeed, sentence structure had a lot to do with how a reader perceives meaning. Compare the original version with the revision that follows it.

I usually dislike writing. I particularly dislike writing under pressure. My last four written documents were a plant appropriation request, a business letter, and two personal letters. The plant appropriation request was a thirty-five page report. It was prepared for the department staff's review and approval. I was trying to justify a request for funds to purchase a new computer system. The business letter was addressed to a system designer and confirmed a scheduled project review meeting. This letter also contained a list of issues and questions that I wanted discussed during the review. Both the report and the letter had to be written on short notice, and both involved thousands of dollars in business transactions. Thoroughly disliking the task, I really worried about the effect pressure was having on my writing. The two personal letters were written to friends, and I enjoyed writing them because I could relax.

I usually dislike writing, particularly when under pressure. My last four documents were a plant appropriation request, a business letter, and two personal letters. The plant appropriation request, a thirty-five page report that was prepared for the department staff's review and approval, justified my request for funds to purchase a new computer system. The business letter, addressed to a system designer and confirming a scheduled project review meeting, also contained a list of issues and questions I wanted discussed during the review. Both the report and the letter had to be written on short notice. Because both involved thousands of dollars in business transactions, I really worried about the effect pressure was having on my writing. Consequently, I thoroughly disliked the task. In contrast, because the two personal letters were written to friends, I could relax and enjoy writing them.

Notice that the writer combined some sentences, inserting details previously placed in separate sentences. He also moved some combinations from one sentence to another. For example, instead of leaving the ideas concerning short notice and expensive transactions in a coordinated sentence (the ideas connected by *and*), he decided to develop the cause-and-effect relationship between business responsibility, time pressure, and effective writing. He stressed his dislike of the situation in a short, simple sentence that now varies from the other sentence patterns, thus drawing extra attention to the idea; but he used a connecting word (*consequently*) to show the sentence's relationship to the preceding thought. Because the ideas are now shaped by sentence structures that clarify meaning, the reader is much more likely to understand what the writer intended. An added benefit is that during the revising process the writer was able to edit his sentences so that the number of words in his new paragraph is fewer than in the original. The final result is not only clearer but also less time-consuming for the reader. The following sections discuss ways you can use sentence structure to help make clear to your readers the meaning you intend.

**31**

*sent*

# 31

## COORDINATION AND SUBORDINATION

In a broad sense, **coordination** expresses equality: two things that are coordinate have roughly the same importance, the same rank, the same value. **Subordination** expresses some sort of inequality: when one thing is subordinate to or dependent upon another, it is in some way of lesser importance, rank, or value. Coordination and subordination allow us to indicate relationships between and among ideas by means of grammatical form and placement, without having to say directly "This is equal to that" or "This information is additional, qualifying detail—important, but not as important as the main idea."

### WRITERS REVISING: SUBORDINATION AND COORDINATION

The members of the student council in the business school were asked to nominate a professor for the Outstanding Instructor Award. The nomination was to be presented in writing, with specific discussion of such points as "student evaluations" and "innovations in classroom instruction." Following is a portion of an early draft of their nomination. As you work through Section **31,** revise the draft to eliminate excessive subordination and excessive coordination. Then compare your version with the final draft the business students used to nominate Professor Ashwin Gupta. Their final draft appears at the end of this section. An analysis of the students' revision follows the final draft.

**Draft**

D 1        The extraordinary influence that Professor

D 2    Gupta has had in the professional preparation of

D 3    his students can be seen by the strong ratings he

D 4    has received on course evaluations, which

D 5    frequently place him above the 70th percentile on

D 6    such questions as "ability to achieve a

D 7    conceptual understanding of the material" because

D 8    he creates a close relationship between his class

D 9    and the students' educational goals, and he is

D10    rated above the 80th percentile in the "best

D11    course" and "best instructor" categories.

D12        Although the tremendous importance of the

D13    personal computer to the accounting profession is

D14    now well known, Professor Gupta recognized that

D15    importance very early, and four years ago his tax

D16    accounting course was the school's first

D17    undergraduate course to use a personal computer

D18    frequently in homework assignments and classroom

D19    work, thereby giving business students early and

D20    valuable exposure to the computer applications

D21    that have since become commonplace in the

D22    accounting profession.

This *Writers Revising* continues on page 251.

**31**

*sent*

**31a**   Coordination brings equal, related ideas together.

Coordination allows you to combine equal parts of separate ideas into a single sentence by creating compound subjects, objects, modifiers, or whole predicates.

**1. Using coordinating conjunctions to connect words, phrases, and clauses—and putting them in the same grammatical form—you can express clear relationships between ideas without needless repetition.**

Coordinating conjunctions are the words *and, but, or, nor, so, yet, for.*

Dogs belong to the Canidae family. Foxes belong to the Canidae family. Jackals belong to the Canidae family.

*Dogs, foxes,* and *jackals* belong to the Canidae family. [Coordinate subjects]

Members of the Canidae family possess four legs. They eat meat. They have acute senses of smell.

Members of the Canidae family possess four legs, eat meat, and have acute senses of smell. [Coordinate verbs *possess, eat,* and *have;* coordinate objects *legs, meat,* and *senses*]

**31a**

*coord*

One of the family's general characteristics is a long muzzle. Another is large canine teeth. Another is a long tail.

The family's general characteristics are a long muzzle, large canine teeth, and a long tail. [Coordinate predicate nouns *muzzle, teeth,* and *tail*]

**2. Correlative conjunctions and conjunctive adverbs can be used to join ideas.**

Correlative conjunctions work in pairs: *both—and, either—or, neither—nor, not—but, not only—but also.* Conjunctive adverbs (sometimes called adverbial conjunctions) are words such as *however, consequently, therefore,* and *nonetheless.* Unlike correlative conjunctions, conjunctive adverbs *never* connect words, phrases, or dependent clauses; they coordinate whole sentences only. (See also Section **21b**.)

The domestic species is characterized by its worldwide distribution in close association with humans. It is also characterized by its enormous amount of genetic variability.

The domestic species is characterized not only by its worldwide distribution in close association with humans but also by its enormous amount of genetic variability. [Coordinate adverbial prepositional phrases joined by correlative conjunctions *not only* and *but also*]

The Canidae family is sometimes loosely referred to as the dog family. The term "dog" usually refers only to the domestic species.

> The Canidae family is sometimes loosely called the dog family; however, the term "dog" usually refers only to the domestic species. [Conjunctive adverb *however* coordinating two sentences]

As these examples illustrate, coordination allows you to combine complex ideas and information from several sentences. When the ideas in such sentences are equal and closely related, you aid your readers if you can bring the ideas together into a single, easy-to-follow sentence that reveals those relationships. Compare the following:

> Winter is the season when animals get stripped down to the marrow. Humans also do. Animals can take the winter easy by hibernating. Humans are exposed naked to the currents of elation and depression.
> Winter is the season when *both* animals *and* humans get stripped down to the marrow, *but* many animals can hibernate, take the winter easy, as it were; we humans are exposed naked to the currents of elation and depression.
>
> MAY SARTON, *Plant Dreaming Deep*

**31a**

*coord*

Although the information in both versions is much the same, the first forces the reader to work much harder to discover that animals and humans share the same exposure to winter, but with different effects. May Sarton's single sentence pulls all the relationships tightly and clearly together for the reader by first linking *animals* and *humans* with the coordinating pair *both . . . and*. She then establishes the idea of contrast between them with *but*, and carries out the contrast by linking her statements about animals on the one hand and humans on the other with the semicolon, itself a kind of coordinating link.

---

EXERCISE 31a

In the following sentences and paragraph, combine sentences by using coordinating conjunctions either to form compound sentences or to link similar elements to form compound subjects, objects, predicates, or modifiers. You may need to make slight changes in wording. If appropriate, use a conjunctive adverb to coordinate two sentences. After you have combined the sentences in items 1 through 5, rewrite them as a paragraph. Revise and recombine sentences as necessary to make a smooth, coherent paragraph.

SENTENCE PRACTICE

1. Many public and university libraries provide access to online databases. Some library users don't realize they can use these services. Other users don't know what they can get through an online search.
2. Online searching can save time. It can supply the searcher with the most up-to-date information on a topic. It can provide access to many more databases than are available in one library. It provides the user with a printout listing sources on the particular topic.
3. Online searching is a valuable research tool. It does have its disad-

vantages. It is sometimes expensive. Not all subject areas are completely covered.
4. Some users of online searches get a long list of sources. They discover that the sources are not available in their own library. They are also not available in nearby libraries.
5. Users who can benefit most from online searches are those who need to locate recent articles in periodicals. People who want to avoid duplicating others' research will benefit from online searching. Online searches are also helpful in finding recent consumer information.

**PARAGRAPH PRACTICE**

For a nonsmoker, sitting next to a passenger who is smoking on a crowded plane is not a pleasant experience. It is not a healthy experience, either. Nonsmokers can request a seat in the nonsmoking section of the plane. Smoking is not permitted on U.S. airline flights of six hours or less. Flights longer than six hours allow smoking. They have nonsmoking sections. Often these seats get reserved quickly. Therefore, the nonsmoker on a long flight may have no choice but to sit near the smoking section. People who find themselves sitting next to a smoker can ask the flight attendant to arrange a change of seats. Nonsmokers can politely ask the smoker not to smoke during the flight. Asking a person in the smoking section to put out a cigarette may not work, though. Many smokers feel persecuted by having to sit in a special section. Having someone ask them not to smoke in that section may make smokers quite angry. The nonsmoker may end up enduring the flight in a nonstop cloud of cigarette smoke.

**31b**

*sub*

**31b**  Subordination shows connections between unequal but related information; the central idea appears in the main clause, and less important ideas appear in subordinate constructions.

When you put information into subordinate constructions, you indicate to your readers that these constructions are less important than the main statement, even though they may be vital to the full meaning of the sentence. Subordinating conjunctions, particularly, enable you to express exact relationships among ideas.

The most important relationships, along with the most common subordinating conjunctions expressing them, are illustrated below. Notice how the conjunctions are used to combine ideas so that one idea is subordinated to another.

CAUSE

*because, since*
Many animal species are nearing extinction. They are protected by law.
*Because* many animal species are nearing extinction, they are protected by law.

CONDITION

*if, even if, provided, unless*
Some species can be saved. We can protect their habitats.
Some species can be saved, *if* we can protect their habitats.
*Unless* we can protect their habitats, some species cannot be saved.

CONCESSION

*although, though, even though*
Alligators are protected by law in Florida. Poachers still hunt them for their hide and meat.
*Although* alligators are protected by law in Florida, poachers still hunt them for their hide and meat.

PURPOSE

*in order that, so that, that*
Land has been drained and cleared. It can be used for real-estate development.
Land has been drained and cleared *so that* it can be used for real-estate development.

**31b**
*sub*

TIME

*as long as, after, before, when, whenever, while, until*
The Florida swamps are drained. The alligators lose more of their natural habitat to human intruders.
*Whenever* the Florida swamps are drained, the alligators lose more of their natural habitat to human intruders.

LOCATION

*where, wherever*
New houses now stand on dry ground. Alligators once raised their young amid the sawgrass.
New houses now stand on dry ground *where* alligators once raised their young amid the sawgrass.

The relative pronouns—*who (whose, whom), which,* and *that*—allow you to use adjective clauses for subordinate information and details about nouns.

Humans have legitimate needs. They have come in conflict with the needs of wildlife.
Humans, *who* have legitimate needs, have come in conflict with the needs of wildlife.

Wildlife has given way. Its needs are equally legitimate.
Wildlife, *whose* needs are equally legitimate, has given way.

Land and wildlife management can help save endangered species. It considers the balance between humans and the rest of nature.

Land and wildlife management, *which* considers the balance between humans and the rest of nature, can help save endangered species.

Readers rely greatly on your sentence construction to reveal the meaning you intend. Consequently, the main clause of a sentence should carry your central idea; details, qualifications, and other relevant information that is closely related to but less important than the central idea should be put into subordinate constructions. Deciding which information to subordinate and which to place in the sentence's main clause depends on where you want to focus your reader's attention.

Consider the following sentences as possible topic sentences for a paragraph:

> Gorillas have often been killed to permit the capture of their young for zoos, and humans have recently been occupying more and more of their habitat, and gorillas are now threatened with extinction.

> Because gorillas have often been killed to permit the capture of their young for zoos, and humans have recently been occupying more and more of their habitat, *gorillas are now threatened with extinction.*

**31b**

*sub*

> Even though gorillas have often been killed to permit capture of their young for zoos and are now threatened with extinction, *humans have recently been occupying more and more of their habitat.*

The information in the first sentence is perfectly clear. But it is unclear whether the central concern of the paragraph will be the gorillas' threatened extinction or the causes for that threat, because the coordinating conjunction *and* gives equal emphasis to each of the ideas the sentence expresses. (See also Section **31d**, "Excessive Coordination.")

Either of the other two versions, however, makes the writer's central concern unmistakably clear. In the second sentence, the writer's focus is on the threatened extinction of the gorillas; in the third, the writer's focus is on the current, increasing encroachment on the gorillas' habitat. Neither of these revisions is intrinsically better than the other. Which of them the writer chooses must be determined by the point the writer sees as most important.

---

EXERCISE 31b(1)

In the following sentences and paragraph, combine the pairs of sentences, using subordinating conjunctions that will express the relationships indicated in parentheses. You may need to make slight changes in the wording.

### SENTENCE PRACTICE

1. Tourists in England often visit churches with brass-rubbing centers. They make rubbings of brass plaques found on graves and on the floors and walls of the churches. (location)
2. The brasses date from the thirteenth to the seventeenth centuries. The brasses often show noblemen dressed in armor and their ladies dressed in the costume of their time. (relative pronoun)
3. Many of the original brasses have been worn down or damaged by years of rubbing. Many church officials now refuse to allow visitors to rub the original brasses. (cause)
4. Today, copies of hundreds of these brasses have been created. People can make a rubbing in one of the several brass-rubbing centers in churches and cathedrals throughout the country. (purpose)
5. Tourists may not want to go to the work of making their own brass rubbings. Most centers sell ready-made rubbings. (condition)

### PARAGRAPH PRACTICE

**31c**

**sub**

Historians believe that the practice of placing brasses on a grave or a tomb originated in northern Germany in the early thirteenth century and spread to England later in that century. The practice of placing the brasses on the church wall didn't become common until the early 1500s. (concession) The brasses depict weapons, armor, and clothing of the time. They are a fascinating record of English history. (cause) Unfortunately, many brasses were destroyed in the 1500s. King Henry VIII dissolved the monastaries and converted the Catholic churches to Anglican churches. (time) Other brasses were destroyed during the Civil War in the seventeenth century. Thousands of brasses still exist today in both small churches and magnificent cathedrals. (concession) In England, the oldest brass is a memorial to a nobleman from a town in Surrey. This brass was made in 1277. (relative pronoun)

---

EXERCISE 31b(2)

Examine the sentences and the paragraph in Exercise 31a. Where it makes sense to do so, use subordinating conjunctions to combine sentences, placing one idea in the main clause and subordinating those ideas you think are less important. Then compare your new sentences with the ones you wrote using coordinating conjunctions. What differences in meaning result from these changes?

---

**31c**   Subordinating constructions such as appositives, participial phrases, and absolute phrases add information to sentences.

Although subordinate clauses, simple prepositional phrases, and single-word modifiers are most commonly used for subordinating ideas and details, other subordinate constructions provide good alternatives. Three useful ones are **appositives, participial phrases,** and

**absolute phrases.** With these you can embed information in your sentences, making them economical and tightly knit. These constructions also can add variety to your writing.

Such constructions are even more important to meaning. Participles, for example, are valuable for conveying action; absolutes are valuable for conveying detail; appositives are useful for reducing whole clauses to one or two tightly packed phrases that deliver information quickly. Effective and mature writing typically utilizes such subordinating constructions for their force and precision of expression.

**1. Appositives can be used to replace subordinate clauses or whole sentences.**

An appositive is a word or word group that renames, clarifies, identifies, or expands the meaning of another word or phrase: *Sweden, a Scandinavian country, is very beautiful.* (See also Sections **2a** and **20c.**)

Appositives offer an economical alternative to subordinate clauses or even whole sentences that contain identifying information, as in the following:

**31c**

*sub*

| | |
|---|---|
| TWO SENTENCES | Sven Nilssen has told me much about Sweden. He is my close friend and an accomplished pianist. |
| RELATIVE CLAUSE | Sven Nilssen, *who is my close friend and an accomplished pianist,* has told me much about Sweden. |
| APPOSITIVE | Sven Nilssen, *my close friend and an accomplished pianist,* has told me much about Sweden. |

Generally, any nonrestrictive clause that consists of *who* or *which* as the subject, some form of the verb *to be,* and a complement can be reduced to an appositive:

My mother, *who was the oldest of seven children,* was born in Lima, Ohio.

My mother, *the oldest of seven children,* was born in Lima, Ohio.

Often a series of appositives can be used to bring together several details in a single sentence. In the following passage, each of the last three sentences states a separate observation about the way in which keepers of notebooks are a "different breed altogether."

> Keepers of private notebooks are a different breed altogether. They are lonely and resistant rearrangers of things. They are anxious malcontents. They are children afflicted at birth with some presentiment of loss.

But in the sentence she wrote, Joan Didion used a series of appositives to combine all these observations into a single smooth, clear sentence packed with information:

> Keepers of private notebooks are a different breed altogether, lonely and resistant rearrangers of things, anxious malcontents, children afflicted at birth with some presentiment of loss.
>
> JOAN DIDION, *On Keeping a Notebook*

Although appositives are most commonly noun groups, they can function as adjectives, as in the following:

> A lovely hand tentatively rose. The hand was almost too thin to be seen.
> A lovely hand, almost too thin to be seen, tentatively rose.
>
> HERBERT KOHL, *36 Children*

> She was about thirty-five years old. She was dissipated. She was gentle.
> She was about thirty-five years old, dissipated and gentle.
>
> JOHN CHEEVER, "The Sutton Place Story"

**31c**

*sub*

**2. Participles and participial phrases can replace longer clauses or sentences. They are especially useful for expressing action.**

Participles are nonfinite verb forms; that is, they cannot serve as main verbs in sentences, but they can help form verb phrases or function as adjectives (see Sections **1b, 1c, 4**). Like verbs, participles may be regular or irregular in form. Examples of present and past participles are as follows:

|  | *Regular Verb* | *Irregular Verb* |
|---|---|---|
| PRESENT PARTICIPLE | liv**ing** | blow**ing**, eat**ing**, cling**ing** |
| PAST PARTICIPLE | liv**ed** | bl**own**, eat**en**, cl**ung** |

Like finite verbs, participles can take objects and modifiers to form participial phrases that can be used in place of whole sentences or subordinate clauses to express the same information. Compare the following:

> Writing is a slow process. It requires considerable thought and time.
> Writing is a slow process, *which requires considerable thought and time.*
> Writing is a slow process, *requiring considerable thought and time.*

In contrast to relative clauses, which ordinarily must follow immediately after the nouns they modify, participial phrases can also precede the nouns they modify. Thus, their flexibility of placement often permits you to vary sentence structure to fit a particular purpose in a given paragraph. (See also Section **34c.**)

> The old house, *which was deserted twenty years ago and is said to be haunted,* stood halfway up the hill. [Relative clause]
>
> *Deserted twenty years ago and said to be haunted,* the old house stood halfway up the hill. [Participial phrase preceding subject]
>
> The old house, *deserted twenty years ago and said to be haunted,* stood halfway up the hill. [Participial phrase following subject]

However, when varying the position of the participial phrase, be careful not to create a misplaced modifier (see Section **12a**).

Because they are composed of verb forms, participial phrases are often particularly useful for conveying action, especially for describing events that occur at the same time as those in the main clause. Compare the following:

> The hikers struggled on. They were gasping for breath and nearly exhausted.
>
> The hikers, gasping for breath and nearly exhausted, struggled on.

In the following sentence, notice how author John Updike uses a pair of present participial phrases to suggest that his walking through the yard and his clutching the child's hand both occur at the same time as his thinking that "It was all superstition."

> [It was all] superstition, I thought, walking back through my yard, and clutching my child's hand tightly as a good luck token.
>
> JOHN UPDIKE, "Eclipse"

**31c**

*sub*

**3. Absolute phrases are both economical and flexible.**

Absolute phrases consist of a subject, usually a noun or a pronoun, and a participle, together with any objects or modifiers of the participle. They may be formed from any sentence in which the verb phrase contains a form of the verb *be* followed by a present or past participle by simply omitting the *be* form. In other sentences they may be formed by changing the main verb into its *-ing* form. Note the following:

| | |
|---|---|
| SENTENCE | Her thoughts were wandering |
| ABSOLUTE | Her thoughts wandering . . . |
| SENTENCE | The wind blew with increased fury, and the drifts rose ever higher. |
| ABSOLUTE | The wind blowing with increased fury, and the drifts rising ever higher . . . |

When the participle of an absolute phrase is a form of the verb *be*, the verb is frequently omitted entirely, so that the absolute consists simply of a noun followed by adjectives.

The pianist played beautifully. Her technique *was* flawless, and her interpretation *was* sure and sensitive.

The pianist played beautifully, *her technique flawless, her interpretation sure and sensitive.*

Because of its speed and compression, an absolute phrase allows you to add specific, concrete detail to a general statement with greater economy than most alternative constructions. Extremely flexible besides, it can be placed at the beginning or end of a sentence, or often in the middle:

*The rain having stopped,* we went to the beach.

*Slouched in our seats,* we listened to the soothing music, *eyes closed.*

The driver of the wrecked car, *one leg trapped beneath the dashboard, body pinned against the steering wheel,* waited for the rescue squad.

**31c**

*sub*

EXERCISE 31c

In the following sentences and paragraph, combine the sets of sentences, expressing in the main clause what you consider to be the most important idea and using appositives, participial phrases, or absolute phrases to subordinate other ideas. After you have combined the sentences in items 1 through 5, rearrange, revise, and recombine them to create a smooth, coherent paragraph.

**SENTENCE PRACTICE**

1. Mt. Everest is one of the highest mountains in the Himalayas. Its snow-covered peak rises to 29,028 feet.
2. The people of Nepal and Tibet live in the shadow of the mountain. The Nepalese call the mountain "sky head," and the Tibetans call it "goddess mother to the world."
3. The temperatures on Mt. Everest fall much below freezing. The winds on Mt. Everest blow at 150 miles an hour or more. The mountain has long presented the ultimate challenge to climbers.
4. George Leigh Mallory explored the first practical route up Mt. Everest in 1921. Mallory was a British climber. He died in 1924 in an attempt to reach the mountain's summit.
5. The summit was finally reached in 1953 by Tenzing Norgay and Edmund Hillary. Tenzing Norgay was a Sherpa from Nepal. Edmund Hillary was from New Zealand.

**PARAGRAPH PRACTICE**

Mt. Everest is situated between Nepal and Tibet. Mt. Everest has drawn more and more climbers and tourists each year to those two countries. Nepal is often called "the roof of the world." Nepal was once an isolated mountain kingdom. Today Nepal receives almost a quarter of a million visitors each year. Nepalese authorities have realized that they have to do something to protect their region. They established the Everest National Park in 1976. The park covers 480 square miles. The Tibetan side of the Himalayas is isolated and remote from commercial or tourist centers. Tibet has not suffered quite as badly from the growth of tourism as has Nepal.

---

**31d**  Excessive or faulty coordination and subordination hinder meaning.

Too much of a good thing is no good at all. Too much subordination and coordination, or subordination and coordination used incorrectly, may show the writer's skill at jamming information into dense constructions but is not necessarily easy or pleasant to read. Such sentences force too many chunks of information on the reader at once. Your goal in the use of coordinating and subordinating constructions should be to clarify meaning.

**1. Excessive coordination results in "primer style."**
Paragraphs composed mainly of short, simple sentences can make writing sound childish. Such sentences are sometimes called "primer" sentences because they resemble those of children's first reading books. Not only are primer sentences monotonous and choppy but they are also indiscriminate, giving equal weight and importance to all the facts and ideas. Sentences strung together with a series of *ands* and *buts* are just as ineffective as a series of short, choppy sentences and sound equally childish. These types of sentences also give equal emphasis to all the ideas, with no clue as to which information is more or less important.

**31d**

*sub*

| | |
|---|---|
| **PRIMER STYLE** | He stood on a street corner. The wind was blowing. He peered into the darkness. The stranger had no place to go. |
| **EXCESSIVE COORDINATION** | He stood on the street corner and the wind was blowing and he peered into the darkness, but he was a stranger so he had no place to go. |

Help your readers understand which ideas are important and which are minor by reworking primer sentences into more complex ones that use both coordination and subordination to reflect meaning. The following revisions illustrate two different meanings that emerge from the preceding primer sentences.

| | |
|---|---|
| REVISED | Standing on a windy street corner and peering into the darkness, the stranger had no place to go. |
| REVISED | Standing on a windy street corner, the stranger peered into the darkness. He had no place to go. |

Notice the slightly different effects, and thus different meanings, created by the two revisions. The first revision uses the main clause to emphasize the stranger's having no place to go. The second revision gains two points of emphasis by means of the two main clauses *the stranger peered into the darkness* and *He had no place to go.* The concluding short, simple sentence achieves extra impact because its structure differs from the preceding sentence.

### 2. Excessive subordination obscures important information.

Like excessive coordination, excessive subordination occurs when you include in a sentence details that are inessential or only loosely related to the main line of thought. It also occurs when successive dependent clauses are strung together, each attached to the preceding one without a clear relationship to the main clause. The sentences below show how one writer decided what he really meant to say and restructured the information to convey that meaning.

**31d**

*sub*

| | |
|---|---|
| EXCESSIVE SUBORDINATION | My fishing equipment includes a casting rod *which my Uncle Henry gave me many years ago* and which is nearly worn out, and an assortment of lines, hooks, and bass flies, which make good bait *when I can get time off from work to go bass fishing* at Harwood Lake. |
| REVISED | My fishing equipment includes an old casting rod and an assortment of lines, hooks, and bass flies—which make good bait. When I can get time off from work, I like to go bass fishing at Harwood Lake. |

In the following sentence the successive details are all essential, but the structure of the successive dependent clauses makes their relationship hard to grasp.

| | |
|---|---|
| EXCESSIVE SUBORDINATION | We walked down Fifth Avenue, which led us to Washington Square, where we saw the memorial arch, which resembles the *Arc de Triomphe* which is in Paris. |

Such a sentence can often be improved by changing some of the clauses to modifying phrases.

| | |
|---|---|
| REVISED | We walked down Fifth Avenue to Washington Square, where we saw the memorial arch resembling the *Arc de Triomphe* in Paris. |

Sometimes effectiveness requires that you rework a sentence as two separate sentences. Even when relationships to the main clause are clear, using too many subordinate constructions can overload readers. It may be challenging to see how much information you can pack into a single sentence, but if the meaning becomes too complex many readers will simply stop trying to comprehend it.

**3. Faulty coordination connects ideas having no logical relationship.**

Faulty coordination occurs when you coordinate two or more facts or ideas that have no logical connection.

> **FAULTY** The poet John Keats wrote "The Eve of St. Agnes," and he died of tuberculosis.

The connection between two such unrelated facts would not be improved even if one were subordinated to the other. Readers will continue to scratch their heads—unless perhaps they are given some such meaningful context as the following:

> She could remember only two facts about John Keats: He wrote "The Eve of St. Agnes," and he died of tuberculosis.

Sometimes faulty coordination occurs when writers leave out important information that is evident to them but not to the reader.

> **FAULTY** My uncle was in the army in World War II, but he didn't have enough money to finish college.
>
> **REVISED** Although my uncle's service in World War II entitled him to some education under the G.I. bill for veterans, he didn't have enough money to finish college.

**31d**

*sub*

A somewhat different kind of faulty coordination occurs when a writer coordinates items from overlapping classes. In the following sentence, for example, the four-item coordinate series makes it appear that there are four different kinds of animals or birds in the pet show the writer is describing. But clearly there are only three: dogs, parrots, and monkeys. The "mangy cocker spaniel" belongs among the dogs.

> **FAULTY** Entered in the pet show were several dogs, two parrots, three monkeys, and a mangy cocker spaniel.
>
> **REVISED** Entered in the pet show were two parrots, three monkeys, and several dogs, one of which was a mangy cocker spaniel.

**4. Faulty subordination incorrectly places the most important information in the dependent clause.**

If you write *While Lincoln was still President, he was shot*, you emphasize the assassination. If you write *When he was shot, Lincoln was still President*, you emphasize the fact that he was still in office. Your intentions as writer and the demands of a particular context should determine which idea you place in a main clause and which in a subordinate clause. Only these factors make one version preferable over the other.

Even so, remember that readers apply the logic of normal expectation to most sentences. When you contradict the reader's sense of the relative importance of two ideas, the logic will seem to be "up-side-down," the subordination faulty. Compare the sentences that follow.

|   |   |
|---|---|
| **FAULTY SUBORDINATION** | She happened to glance at the sidewalk, noticing a hundred-dollar bill at her feet. |
| REVISED | Happening to glance at the sidewalk, she noticed a hundred-dollar bill at her feet. |

Ordinarily, the finding of one hundred dollars would be the logically emphasized fact: readers would expect the sentence to be constructed to achieve that emphasis, with the finding of the bill in the main clause. If you violate readers' normal expectations, you need to have a good reason for doing so, a reason that your readers will comprehend.

**31d**

**sub**

EXERCISE 31d(1)
Revise the first passage to eliminate excessive coordination and excessive subordination. Revise the second passage, using both coordination and subordination where appropriate to eliminate choppy, ineffective sentences. Your revisions should create meaningful relationships between ideas.

1. My ten-year-old brother plays the violin in his elementary school orchestra, and he's been playing for two years, so last week he invited me to go to the spring concert at his school. I agreed to go, but I am not really looking forward to the concert because I've heard my brother, whose name is Chris, practice while he's here at home, and he's not a very good violinist. He practices in his room, and he keeps the door shut, but screeches and squeaks still disturb everyone who is in the house when he plays. I asked him one time if he had tuned his violin before he played, but he told me only his music teacher could tune the instrument correctly, and she wasn't there. When Chris is practicing at home when I'm studying, I have to put cotton in my ears, and I try to get far away from his room so that I can concentrate. Nevertheless, I knew he really wanted me to go to the concert, and I agreed to go, but I don't think I'm going to feel like I'm at Carnegie Hall.

2. The night of the concert arrived. I took Chris to his school. He was dressed for the concert. He had on a white shirt and a red bow tie. He hated the tie. He said it affected his playing. I don't see how a tie could make his playing any worse. Chris had to get to the school early. The violinists had to practice one more time before the performance. I dropped him off at the music room. I said to him, "I'm sure you'll do fine." I went to the auditorium. I wanted to get a seat in the front. I wanted to be able to see Chris. The auditorium was crowded. Parents had all flocked to the front rows. They had cameras and tape recorders. They wanted to get pictures of their young

musicians. They wanted to record the concert. I had to sit in the back of the auditorium. I could barely see the stage.

## EXERCISE 31d(2)
Revise the following passage, eliminating faulty coordination and faulty subordination. Add information as necessary to establish logical, meaningful relationships.

At last the concert began, and Chris was sitting in the front row of the violin section with the other players who were all fifth graders like him. I was in the back of the auditorium since I could barely see the stage, but Chris stood out among the other violinists because he had on that red bow tie. The orchestra was going to play four songs, and then the concert band, which is a separate group and was sitting on the other side of the stage, was going to play four songs, but then the two groups were going to play one final song together. Because the orchestra began playing, I was nervous since I knew what Chris's playing sounded like at home, and being with a larger group of players must have helped him because I didn't hear any screeches or squeaks as everyone seemed to be playing well, although all four songs sounded good. I applauded when the orchestra stood up when they had finished their performance. I got a big surprise when the concert band started playing because they sounded terrible, and my ears hurt from the noise. The clarinets squeaked, and the trumpets blared, so the trombones played completely off key. When I clapped politely, the concert band had finished all its four songs. I thought they were awful, because I dreaded having to hear them play one more song with the orchestra. Fortunately, because the last song was better, the orchestra had drowned out the awful sound of the band when they played together. When I decided that Chris perhaps had some potential as a violinist after we got home from the concert, I said to him, "Stick with the violin because I couldn't stand to hear you practicing a trumpet or a clarinet or a trombone."

**31d**

*sub*

## WRITERS REVISING: SUBORDINATION AND COORDINATION
*(continued from page 235)*

The major flaw in the first draft is excessive use of coordinating conjunctions, particularly *and*. Each lengthy, strung-together sentence lacks focus and contains too many ideas. Notice that each paragraph, although several lines long, contains only a single sentence. So that readers can focus on points of emphasis and understand the relationships between ideas, the revision breaks the two long sentences into six shorter ones.

## Revision

R 1     The extraordinary influence that Professor

R 2   Gupta has had in the professional preparation of

R 3   his students can be seen by the strong ratings he

R 4   has received on course evaluations. ~~which~~ *His course evaluations*   **31b**

R 5   frequently place him above the 70th percentile on

R 6   such questions as "ability to achieve a

R 7   conceptual understanding of the material", ∧ because *no doubt*   **31b**

R 8   he creates a close relationship between his class

R 9   and the students' educational goals ~~and~~ *Furthermore,* he is   **31d**

R10   rated above the 80th percentile in the "best

R11   course" and "best instructor" categories.

R12     Although the tremendous importance of the

R13   personal computer to the accounting profession is

R14   now well known, Professor Gupta recognized that

R15   importance very early. ~~and~~ ~~F~~our years ago his tax   **31d**

R16   accounting course was the school's first

R17   undergraduate course to use a personal computer

R18   frequently in homework assignments and classroom

R19   work, ~~thereby giving~~ *Thus he gave* business students early and   **31d**

R20   valuable exposure to the computer applications

R21   that have since become commonplace in the

R22   accounting profession.

## Analysis

The first sentence in the revision (R1–4) focuses on Gupta's influence as reflected in course evaluations. The second sentence (R4–9) is constructed from the "which" dependent clause in the first draft (D4–7). Thus, rather than burying the numerical information about Gupta's good ratings in a subordinate clause, the revision focuses on the ratings (in the main clause). The reason for these ratings (close relationship between class and goals) is placed in a dependent clause *(because . . . .)* (R7–9),

**31d**

*sub*

the writer having chosen to subordinate the explanation to the numbers. The third sentence (R9–11) achieves much more emphasis for the 80th percentile ratings by placing the information in a separate sentence (compare lines D9–11 and R9–11). The connection between this idea and the previous sentence is achieved with the transition *furthermore.*

The fourth sentence (R12–15) subordinates the importance of the personal computer (*although* dependent clause, R12–14) to the main clause about Professor Gupta's having *recognized* its importance (R14), thus focusing the reader's attention on the professor rather than the personal computer. However, because the dependent clause occurs first in the sentence, it receives some secondary emphasis. The evidence for the claim stated in the fourth sentence appears in a separate sentence (R15–19) so that both the claim and the evidence will make equally emphatic impressions on the reader's mind. The results—giving students early and valuable exposure to computers—benefit from the focus achieved with a separate sentence (R19–22). The transition word *Thus* provides the cause-and-effect link to the foregoing sentence.

# 32
## *PARALLELISM*

When you coordinate two or more elements in a sentence, readers expect you to make them *parallel,* that is, to state them in the same grammatical form. Noun should be matched with noun, verb with verb, phrase with phrase, and clause with clause.

A lawyer must be *articulate* and *logical.* [Parallel and coordinate adjectives]

She *closed the door, opened the window,* and *threw herself* into the chair. [Three coordinate and parallel predicates, each consisting of verb plus direct object]

*The otter's fur is dark-chocolate brown,* and *its eyes are small and black.* [Two coordinate and parallel independent clauses]

Parallelism is a basic principle of effective writing and speaking. Equal form reinforces equal meaning. By putting equally important parts of a sentence or of successive sentences into equal grammatical constructions, you emphasize their relationship to one another. The parallelism confirms the coordinate relationship, the equal importance of the coordinate parts.

# WRITERS REVISING: MORE EFFECTIVE SENTENCES

Library users were being asked to share their thoughts on a book that had made a difference in their lives—not just a favorite book, but one that had changed their thinking or their actions. People were being asked to write a page about this book for display in a loose-leaf binder that would be part of a special exhibit during National Library Week. To start the ball rolling, each library staff member had been asked to write a contribution for the binder.

Stacy, who worked part-time in the library, drafted several paragraphs, but she wasn't very happy with them. She was challenged by the topic but felt she hadn't effectively conveyed her feeling about it. Her sentences seemed monotonous and uninteresting, without energy and lacking the emotion she felt about the subject.

Although you, of course, cannot bring the same experience to the following draft, experiment with some sentence revisions that help to emphasize the feelings Stacy discusses. Then turn to the end of Section **34** to see what she did in the final version she submitted for the library display. Notice in Stacy's retyped version how her thoughts evolved and how the meaning emerged with the changing sentences.

**32**

**∥**

### Stacy's Draft

D 1        A book that has made a difference in my life

D 2    is Anne Frank's The Diary of a Young Girl.

D 3    Actually, two books have made a difference in my

D 4    life. One is The Diary of a Young Girl by Anne

D 5    Frank and the other is the diary my Aunt Betty

D 6    gave me at Christmas when I was twelve years old.

D 7    That fall I had read the diary of Anne Frank, the

D 8    young Jewish girl only a few years older than I

D 9    who died at Belsen, a Nazi concentration camp, in

D10   1945 during World War II. Then at Christmas, I

D11   received my own diary.

D12      I had never kept a diary before, but Anne

```
D13   Frank's diary inspired me and served as a model.

D14   Of course my life was very mundane compared to

D15   hers and certainly did not contain the tragedies

D16   she experienced while hiding from the Nazis, but I

D17   understood and appreciated her need to write

D18   things down. Writing was the way she came to

D19   terms with her life, she tempered suffering by

D20   writing about it, and she also kept hope alive

D21   through writing. With my own diary, I had the

D22   opportunity to use writing as a way of

D23   understanding what was happening in my life. I

D24   have kept a diary ever since receiving that first

D25   one when I was twelve. Anne Frank and Aunt Betty

D26   helped me find my voice as a writer, so you can

D27   see why I think the two books made a lot of

D28   difference.
```

**32a**

‖

This *Writers Revising* continues on page 276.

## 32a  Parallelism makes coordinate relationships clear.

**1. In single sentences.** Putting equal ideas in a sentence in parallel constructions will help you make their coordinate relationship more immediately clear to your reader. Compare the following sentences:

> If they buy the assigned books, students can usually be successful, but they must read them and careful notes must be taken.
> Students can usually be successful if they *buy the assigned books, read them,* and *take careful notes.*

The first sentence really sets three conditions for a student's success: buying the books, reading them, and taking notes. But the sentence muddies this equal relationship by putting the first in an *if* clause separate from the other two; and although the last two conditions—reading the books and taking notes—are coordinated by *and*, the first is active and the second passive, thus further weakening their coordinate relationship. The revised sentence brings the three conditions neatly and clearly together in a single parallel series of predicates.

> The most overworked word in English is the word "set," which has 58 noun uses, 126 verbal uses, and 10 as a participial adjective.
>
> *Environmental Engineering News*

So strong is our desire for parallelism in series that as soon as we see the first two items in the preceding sample sentence, it is very likely that our minds will "fill in" the third phrase—even before we have actually read it. Consequently, when we realize that the sentence does not say . . . *and 10 participial adjective uses,* we may feel annoyed or cheated: the sentence's rhythm has been thwarted, as have our expectations.

**2. Among successive sentences.** Many times you can increase the coherence of your writing by combining several successive sentences into a single sentence that uses parallelism carefully. (See also Section **42c**.)

Suppose you are trying to get together your ideas about the things necessary for good writing and that you have written the following in a first draft:

> Logical thinking is one of the things necessary for good writing. Good writers also have to organize their ideas coherently. And finally, anyone who wants to write well must express his or her ideas clearly.

Look at this draft closely; *thinking, organizing,* and *expressing* are the main related processes here. Parallel structure can help you knit these together tightly and emphasize them clearly. Compare the following single sentences with the three original sentences:

Thinking logically,
organizing ideas coherently,
and
expressing ideas clearly
} are three requirements of good writing.

or

Logical thought,
coherent organization,
and
clear expression
} are the major ingredients of good writing.

or

**32a**

‖

|                                              |                                                           |
| -------------------------------------------- | --------------------------------------------------------- |
| Anyone who wishes to write well must learn   | to think logically, to organize ideas coherently, and to express them clearly. |

Each of these versions of the first draft pulls the ideas together into a single economical unit and gives emphasis to the three major items.

Notice how parallelism helps to keep the following sentences clear and to emphasize the relationship between the ideas.

|                                              |                                                           |
| -------------------------------------------- | --------------------------------------------------------- |
| Strikes, though sometimes necessary, mean    | loss of wages for workers, interference with production for managers, and disruption of services for consumers. |

|                                   |            |                                         |
| --------------------------------- | ---------- | --------------------------------------- |
| Political language is designed    | to make    | lies sound truthful and murder respectable |
|                                   | and to give an appearance of solidity to pure wind. |

**32a**

‖

**3. In whole paragraphs.** Just as you can often make single sentences clearer by coordinating equal ideas and putting them in parallel constructions, so you can often use roughly parallel sentences to increase the coherence of an entire paragraph. (See also Section **42d[2].**) Study the following paragraph:

> Otters seem to improvise. *When swimming along* in a lake or a stream, *one may push* a leaf or twig ahead of it. Or *it may drop* a pebble, then chase it through the sparkling water, catching it before it touches bottom, only to bring it to the surface and drop it again *Underwater, it may balance* a rock or mussel on its head as it swims, *or play* cat and mouse games with its prey. *In captivity, it plays* games with every moving object and explores all corners and crevices for string to pull, wires to loosen, latches to open, and new mysteries to solve.
>
> GEORGE LAYCOCK, "Games Otters Play," *Audubon*

The structure of this paragraph is kept unmistakably clear by its careful coordinating and confirming parallelism throughout. The simple topic sentence, *Otters seem to improvise*, is developed by a series of details of their improvisation in three situations: in the water, underwater, or in captivity.

Not only does parallelism provide connecting links between ideas in this paragraph, it also binds information within sentences. A case in point is the final sentence, which uses parallel prepositional objects: *for string to pull, wires to loosen, latches to open, and new mysteries to solve.*

As is true for all the sentence-writing techniques we have been examining, parallelism can be overdone. While two or three parallel sentences in a paragraph may set up a nice rhythm, nine or ten sentences using the same parallel structures can amount to overkill. Monotonous repetition of constructions bores readers, blunting their attention to meaning. To write effective sentences, you also need to pay attention to emphasis and variety (see Sections **33** and **34**).

---

**EXERCISE 32a**
Using parallelism and subordination, revise the following passages, combining sentences as necessary.

**32b**

**‖**

1. The tiny hummingbird has always fascinated humans. Hummingbirds are like miniature helicopters. They have incredible ability to stop and hover in their flight. They maneuver easily from flower to flower. They fly fast. It doesn't even look like they move their wings.

2. The hummingbird uses enormous amounts of energy. The hummingbird has a high rate of metabolism. It has to take in enough food to equal more than half its body weight each day. Hummingbirds eat nectar from blooms of plants. They eat insects. They stop in mid-flight and catch insects.

3. Some people want to attract hummingbirds to their yards. These people should put an artificial hummingbird feeder in their garden. The feeder should be filled with a mixture of sugar and water. The mixture should be changed every few days. The feeder should be washed with water. Dishwashing detergent or soap should not be used when washing the feeder. People can also plant flowers that attract hummingbirds. Honeysuckle and fuschia are two flowers that appeal to hummingbirds. Hummingbirds are territorial birds. They will chase other birds away from their area. They will even chase away bigger birds. Hummingbirds do not seem to fear other birds. They don't appear to fear humans. They stay away from bees and wasps.

---

**32b** **Make elements joined by coordinating or correlative conjunctions parallel.**

**1. Coordinating conjunctions.** Parallelism is useful for constructing effective sentences, for combining successive sentences to achieve economy and clarity, and for maintaining coherence throughout an entire paragraph. On the other hand, lack of parallelism can throw a reader off and produce ineffective sentences. To keep your sentences clear, as well as grammatically correct, make sure the structural patterns of the coordinate elements match one another.

| | |
|---|---|
| FAULTY | As an industrial designer, Pam enjoys *her work* with engineers and *creating* the shape of mass-produced products. |
| PARALLEL | As an industrial designer, Pam enjoys *working* with engineers and *creating* the shape of mass-produced products. |
| FAULTY | Industrial designers are *highly trained, with creative ideas,* and *have knowledge* of ergonomics. |
| PARALLEL | Industrial designers are *highly trained, creative,* and *knowledgeable* in ergonomics. |

When you are coordinating prepositional phrases or infinitives, clarity will sometimes require you to point up parallel structure by repeating prepositions.

**32b**

||

| | |
|---|---|
| AMBIGUOUS | A poorly designed telephone may be identified by the trouble it gives you with dialing or holding the receiver. [Dialing the receiver?] |
| CLEAR | A poorly designed telephone may be identified by the trouble it gives you *with* dialing or *with* holding the receiver. |
| AMBIGUOUS | Industrial designers are trained to study the way people will use a product and then create the most attractive but functional form. [People use and then create?] |
| CLEAR | Industrial designers are trained *to* study the way people will use a product and then *to* create the most attractive but functional form. |

**2. Correlative conjunctions.** Correlative conjunctions are coordinating pairs: *either. . .or, neither. . .nor, both. . .and, not. . .but, not only. . .but also.* Parallelism requires that the structure following the second part of the correlative be the same as that following the first part.

| | |
|---|---|
| FAULTY | A well-designed office chair *both should be* attractive to look at *and comfortable* to sit in. |
| PARALLEL | A well-designed office chair should be *both attractive* to look at *and comfortable* to sit in. |
| FAULTY | Industrial designers work *on not only* office furniture and equipment, bathroom fixtures, kitchen appliances, |

beds, lamps, and cookware *but also on* cars, camping gear, and cameras.

PARALLEL     Industrial designers work *not only on* office furniture and equipment, bathroom fixtures, kitchen appliances, beds, lamps, and cookware *but also on* cars, camping gear, and cameras.

If you are uncertain of the parallelism with correlative conjunctions, try recasting your sentence as two sentences. Take, for example, the sentence *Not only is Pierre Cardin famous for his fashion designs but also the industrial designs that bear his name.* Recast as separate sentences, this becomes

Pierre Cardin is famous for his fashion designs.

Pierre Cardin is famous for the industrial designs that bear his name.

When you combine the common parts of these two sentences to get *Pierre Cardin is famous for,* it is clear that the two distinct parts that belong in parallel form are *his fashion designs* and *the industrial designs that bear his name.* The correct forms of the sentence are as follows:

Pierre Cardin is famous for *not only his fashion designs but also the industrial designs* that bear his name.

OR     Pierre Cardin is famous *not only for* his fashion designs *but also for* the industrial designs that bear his name.

**32c**  **Avoid faulty parallelism with *and who, and which, and that.***

Do not use *and who, and which,* or *and that* to introduce a clause in a sentence unless you have already used a parallel *who, which,* or *that.* (So too with *but* and *who, which,* or *that.*)

FAULTY     We met Abner Fulton, a brilliant biologist and who is also an excellent pianist.

PARALLEL     We met Abner Fulton, who is a brilliant biologist and who is also an excellent pianist.

PARALLEL     We met Abner Fulton, who is both a brilliant biologist and an excellent pianist.

FAULTY     I like a detective novel with exciting action and that keeps me guessing.

PARALLEL     I like a detective novel that has exciting action and that keeps me guessing.

---

EXERCISE 32b–c(1)

In the following sentences and paragraph, revise and reword as necessary to express coordinate ideas in parallel form.

SENTENCE PRACTICE

1. Because playing video games has become very popular, some parents worry that their children may be spending too much time in front of the video screen and their homework or reading is neglected.

2. Educational experts agree that parents should be concerned if a child sits for hours playing video games, but these experts also point out that video games are valuable in improving hand-eye coordination and for the development of visual-spatial skills.

3. These experts also advise parents who are worried that their children spend too much time playing video games to encourage other activities such as reading a book, to go outside and play with friends, and games like chess and Scrabble.®

4. Educational psychologists warn that parents should screen video games carefully, for children may encounter violence on television but also may see violence in some video games.

5. One contrast that experts make between television and video games is that watching television is a normally passive activity, but to play a video game requires the child to make responses.

PARAGRAPH PRACTICE

Lovers of electronic games can engage in an individual contest with a computer, or a computer game can be played among several people. Games involving finding one's way through a maze, surviving in an adventure world, or how to win a battle in outer space are favorites. Sports games are also popular; in these games either the computer is the opponent or another player. To be successful at maze games, a player needs to have tactical skill and with good hand-eye coordination. In role-playing games in which the player develops a character to participate in an adventure world, the player both needs to be good at strategy and logic.

**33**

*emp*

---

EXERCISE 32b–c(2)

Write at least five sentences, each containing parallel, coordinate elements.

---

# 33

## *EMPHASIS*

Effective sentences emphasize main ideas and keep related details in the background. The careful use of coordination, subordination, and parallelism enables you to stress your most important ideas without losing track of less important but related ideas and information. Sentence variety enables you to emphasize important ideas by changing the pace and rhythm of a passage. In addition to these useful strategies, you can also emphasize ideas within a single sentence by controlling the arrangement of its elements and by using repetition carefully.

As you revise sentences to achieve the emphasis you want, keep in mind that any sentence is part of a paragraph and of a larger whole. To determine what to emphasize in a given sentence, always look at the sentence in relation to its context and in relation to your audience and overall purpose.

## 33a   Emphatic positions in a sentence highlight important ideas.

The position of a word or idea within a sentence usually determines the emphasis it receives. Generally, the most emphatic place in the sentence is at its end; the next most emphatic, its beginning; the least emphatic, its middle. Consider the following sentence:

> Brunhilda, our Great Dane, loves to play with the neighborhood children, but she is bigger than most of them.

**33a**

*emp*

The end position of *bigger than most of them* gives that information the heaviest stress in the sentence. As the topic sentence of a paragraph that contrasts the dog's love of children with their fear of her size, the sentence is effective.

If, however, the sentence introduces a paragraph that focuses on Brunhilda's love of children, it must be revised.

> Brunhilda, our Great Dane, although bigger than most of the neighborhood children, loves to play with them.

In this version, the information about the dog's size is subordinated and placed in the middle of the sentence. Such placement of modifying phrases and clauses delays the predicate, the sentence's action, for the final position in the sentence, thus emphasizing the dog's love of children.

Sometimes you can increase the emphasis on a single-word adverb or a brief adverbial phrase by moving it to the initial position in a sentence.

> Debra reached sleepily for the alarm clock.
> Sleepily, Debra reached for the alarm clock.

On the other hand, don't weaken emphasis by placing minor qualifying phrases before your subject or at the end of the sentence. Be sure any qualifying words or phrases placed at the very beginning or the very end of a sentence are worth emphasizing. Otherwise they may seem distracting, illogical, or tacked on. When such words do not merit emphasis, bury them within the sentence or omit them.

| WEAK | Such matters as incorrect spelling and unconventional punctuation can distract a reader's attention even in otherwise good writing. |
|---|---|
| EMPHATIC | Incorrect spelling and unconventional punctuation can distract a reader's attention even in otherwise good writing. |
| WEAK | The history of English vocabulary is the history of English civilization, in many ways. |
| EMPHASIS ON HISTORY | The history of English vocabulary is in many ways the history of English civilization. |
| EMPHASIS ON QUALIFIER | In many ways, the history of English vocabulary is the history of English civilization. |

## EXERCISE 33a

Write ten pairs of sentences using the phrases listed below. In the first sentence, place the phrase in the emphatic position. In the second, place it so that it is de-emphasized.

1. with tears in their eyes
2. last year
3. the driver of the truck
4. laughing loudly
5. as soon as you can
6. staring in disbelief
7. if you want to
8. on the other hand
9. in the future
10. fearfully

**33b**

*emp*

## 33b  Different sentence structures create different emphases.

The position of subordinate or modifying material can have a definite impact on where the emphasis falls in a sentence (see Section **33a**). There are four basic sentence structures for handling modifying material: the periodic, or left-branching, sentence; the mid-branching sentence; the balanced sentence; and the loose, or right-branching, sentence.

A **periodic** or **left-branching sentence** places a modifying clause at the beginning and holds the main idea until the end. This pattern creates anticipation, first setting up the reader's expectations with background information or qualifying details and then presenting the subject dramatically in the main clause at the end.

PERIODIC, LEFT-BRANCHING  *When her mother was in the hospital for two months and her father was on the edge of a breakdown,* Brenda showed great courage.

Because the structure of a periodic sentence contains built-in suspense, it can be extremely effective. However, it also contains inherent risk. The longer readers must wait to discover the subject, the greater the likelihood that they will become impatient or confused. Consequently, the delivery of the subject in the final clause should have a strong clarifying effect and should be worth the reader's wait.

A **mid-branching sentence** places modifying material between the subject and the verb. Again, you are asking the reader to suspend normal thought patterns and expectations about the way information is delivered. The subordinate information amounts to an interruption, as you imbed detail, before the main idea is carried to completion. This structure can be used to create drama and suspense, or it can be used to de-emphasize information by sandwiching it between the more powerful parts of the sentence—the subject and the verb.

EMPHASIZED  Death Valley—*without a doubt the hottest spot in the country*—comes by its name honestly.

DE-EMPHASIZED  Death Valley, *the nation's hot spot,* comes by its name honestly.

**33b**

*emp*

Notice in the preceding examples that the punctuation and word choice combine with sentence structure to provide additional cues that reinforce the meaning the writer intended.

A **balanced sentence** is a compound sentence in which the independent clauses are exactly, or very nearly, parallel in all elements.

We always like those who admire us; we do not always like those whom we admire.

LA ROCHEFOUCAULD, *Maxims*

Grammar maps out the possible; rhetoric narrows the possible down to the desirable and effective.

FRANCIS CHRISTENSEN, *Toward a New Rhetoric*

It is as natural to die as to be born; and to a little infant, perhaps, the one is as painful as the other.

FRANCIS BACON, "Of Death"

As these three examples illustrate, the balanced sentence is useful for stating contrasts and distinctions. Because it holds two coordinate ideas before the reader, its structure naturally emphasizes meanings involving weighing or choice.

A **loose** or **right-branching sentence,** sometimes called a **cumulative sentence,** completes its main statement and then adds subordinate details. This structure follows the most common pattern of human thought, identifying key informational elements (the subject and verb) first and then providing qualifying material.

LOOSE, RIGHT-BRANCHING        Brenda showed great courage *when her*
*mother was in the hospital for two months and*
*her father was on the edge of a breakdown.*

Because it follows our usual thought patterns, the loose sentence is
easy to read and satisfies readers' expectations about normal emphasis
in sentences. For the same reason, it does not lend itself to special
emphasis and can lead to rambling lists of details that are simply piled
on after the subject and verb without regard for effectiveness. Consider the following example, the opening sentence from a newspaper
article:

> A bid to set the altitude record for hot-air balloons suffered a
> setback Saturday when one of the two British crewmen was hurt in
> a fall and a gust of wind tore the balloon at the Royal Air Force base
> in Watton, England.

Journalists attempt to include as much pertinent information as possible in the opening sentence of a story: who, what, when, where, why,
and how. The foregoing example covers all the bases, but its listlike
construction offers little emphasis.

> **33c**
>
> *emp*

Strictly speaking, any sentence consisting of a main clause followed by an adverbial phrase or clause is loose and can be made periodic simply by moving the adverbial modifier to the beginning. Often, periodic and loose constructions are more or less equally effective.
Your choice should be guided by the particular emphasis and effect
you want and by the relation of your sentence to those before and
after it. In the following passage from a student paper, notice how the
writer uses a periodic sentence between two loose, cumulative sentences to emphasize his sense of loss after his mother's death.

> I became aware of myself—who I was and what I was—during
> the weeks following her funeral. After the relatives had all left and
> the sympathy cards stopped coming, I was left alone. I had to be
> independent, find others to shed my tears upon, and look elsewhere
> for a scolding.

### EXERCISE 33b

Write a paragraph describing an accident. Include at least one each
of the following sentence structures: periodic, mid-branching, bal
anced, and loose. Be sure, in each case, that the sentence's structure appropriately reflects the content, meaning, and emphasis you
intend.

## 33c  Expletive constructions can be used to regulate the pace and emphasis of a sentence.

Expletives such as *there are, there was, it is,* and *it was (there* or *it*
together with forms of the verb *to be)* can be wordy time-wasters that

weaken the emphasis on a sentence's true subject (Section **39a[3]**). On the other hand, it should also be recognized that expletive constructions can affect the pace, and thus the emphasis, of a sentence.

For example, compare the following two passages, and notice how the expletives in the second add to the suspense by delaying the delivery of information.

> Dead silence prevailed for about a half a minute, during which we might have heard the falling of a leaf, or a feather. A low, but harsh and protracted grating sound which seemed to come at once from every corner of the room interrupted the silence.

> There was a dead silence for about a half a minute, during which the falling of a leaf, or of a feather might have been heard. It was interrupted by a low, but harsh and protracted grating sound which seemed to come at once from every corner of the room.
>
> EDGAR ALLAN POE, "Hop-Frog"

**33d**

*emp*

As the preceding example shows, expletives sometimes occur as part of passive voice constructions—verb forms which de-emphasize the actor in a sentence and focus on the receiver of the action or the result (see Section **33f**). By themselves, expletives can also focus the reader's attention on the outcome of some action rather than on the actor. Compare the following:

> You have no excuse for missing the meeting. You chose to set the time for last night at eight.
> There is no excuse for your missing the meeting. It was your choice to set the time for last night at eight.

When you hear expletives in speech, notice that they are often used in preparation for heavier spoken emphasis on the words that follow them—on the grammatical subject of the sentence. Expletives can have a similar effect in writing. They are relatively content-free themselves, but like the wind-up before a pitch, expletives can help readers anticipate and prepare for the delivery of meaning. Thus in some circumstances they can help to achieve emphasis and variety.

---

EXERCISE 33c
Write five pairs of sentences in which the principal difference between the first sentence and the second sentence in each pair is the use of expletives. Try to create sentences that benefit from the use of the expletive construction to delay information.

---

**33d**   Items in parallel series create cumulative emphasis.

When items are arranged in a parallel series, emphasis tends to fall on the last item, simply because it is last. Because readers expect order of increasing importance in parallel series, meaning can be especially enhanced in cumulative series. For example:

> Their lives were brief, pitiable, and tragic.
> The life of man [is] solitary, poor, nasty, brutish, and short.
>
> THOMAS HOBBES, *Leviathan*

The first sentence mentions life's brevity but emphasizes its tragic nature, whereas the second sentence puts the full weight of the cumulative effect on the word *short*. In the first sentence, the words and structure combine to emphasize a more sympathetic view of human beings than that of the second sentence.

The arrangement of a series in descending order of importance can sometimes be used for surprise, humor, or irony.

> If once a man indulges himself in murder, very soon he comes to think little of robbery; and from robbing he next comes to drinking and Sabbath-breaking; and from that to incivility and procrastination.
>
> THOMAS DE QUINCY

**33d**

*emp*

In many series some other principle dictates the arrangement: order of events, increasing or decreasing size, spatial order, or some other order that fits the logic of the writer's purpose. In the following paragraph, for example, author Joan Mills uses parallel series extremely effectively in capturing a sense of her childhood:

> Children are spoiled by overindulgence; but never by love. It was a day's work for me to spend 12 hours inside my own littleness: dragging a stool around to see the top of things; living with my daily failures—shoelaces all adraggle again, the peas rolling off the spoon, my sweater on backward; worrying about goblins long past Halloween. But love let me know all was right with the world, and with me.
>
> JOAN MILLS, "The One, the *Only . . . Joanie!*"

---

EXERCISE 33d
Revise the following sentences by arranging parallel items in what seems to you to be a more logical order.

1. Getting stuck in a traffic jam, getting fired when I finally did get to work, and forgetting to take my lunch this morning—nothing went right for me today.
2. My roommate's goals include becoming a partner in an accounting firm, passing her CPA exam on the first try, and earning a bachelor's degree in accounting.
3. The marathon runner finished last in the race and was exhausted after the first ten miles.

4. During vacation, I read a bestseller that had everything I like in a novel: exotic locations, a murder, romance, fast-paced action, and good dialogue.
5. My college basketball team won the NCAA Championship and finished first in our conference.

Write sentences containing parallel series of items using the following principles of arrangement:

6. Time order
7. Spatial order
8. Order of increasing importance
9. Order of decreasing importance (for humorous effect)
10. Series arranged for contrasting effect

**33e** Key words and ideas can be repeated for emphasis.

Careless and awkward repetition of words makes sentences weak and flabby (see Section **39a[6]**), but careful, deliberate repetition of key words, when not overdone, can be an effective way of gaining emphasis, as in the following sentences:

A *moderately* honest man with a *moderately* faithful wife, *moderate* drinkers both, in a *moderately* healthy home: that is the true middle class unit.

G. B. SHAW

Don't *join* too many gangs. *Join* few if any. *Join* the United States and *join* a family—but not much else in between, unless a college.

ROBERT FROST

It is the *dull* man who is always *sure,* and the *sure* man who is always *dull.*

H. L. MENCKEN

As you can see from the examples, repetition frequently appears in combination with parallel constructions. This is not surprising, since repeated words are naturally reinforced and emphasized by repeated constructions. (For a discussion of ways in which repetition of words and ideas links sentences within a paragraph, see Section **42**).

EXERCISE 33e
Discuss the effectiveness of repetition of words and phrases in each of the sentences below.

1. Grandmother was by nature lavish, she loved leisure and calm, she loved luxury, she loved dress and adornment, she loved to sit and talk with friends or listen to music; she did not in the least like pinching or saving and mending and making things do, and she had no patience with the kind of slackness that tried to say second-best was best, or half good enough.

KATHERINE ANNE PORTER

2. Some books are to be tasted, others to be swallowed, and some few to be chewed and digested; that is, some books are to be read only in parts; others to be read, but not curiously; and some few to be read wholly, and with diligence and attention.

FRANCIS BACON

3. No one can be perfectly free till all are free; no one can be perfectly moral until all are moral; no one can be perfectly happy until all are happy.

HERBERT SPENCER

## 33f Verbs in the active voice create more emphasis than verbs in the passive voice.

The **active voice** puts the subject (the actor) first, following it with the active verb, and then the object (the receiver of the action): *The cat killed the rat.* The **passive voice** turns things around, putting the receiver in front, then the verb, and finally the actor: *The rat was killed by the cat.* (See Section **5.**)

Of the two, the active is almost always more direct, more forceful and emphatic, and also more economical. Therefore, if your goal is to emphasize the actor and the action itself, the active voice is the better choice. If you want to emphasize the receiver or result of the action, downplaying the action and its initiator, the passive voice is usually preferable.

**33f**

*emp*

ACTIVE The firefighter saved the terrified child.

PASSIVE The terrified child was saved by the firefighter.

The first example sentence focuses our attention on the rescue; the second focuses on the object of the rescue, the child. Bear in mind that, as its name implies, a sentence in the passive voice will always be less forceful than one in the active voice, and longer as well. If your goal is economy and directness, choose active-voice verbs.

PASSIVE It was voted by the faculty that all students should be required to take mathematics. [15 words]

ACTIVE The faculty voted to require that all students take mathematics. [10 words]

EXERCISE 33f
Write five pairs of sentences, using active and passive voices as appropriate to emphasize the actor in the first sentence and to emphasize the recipient of the action in the second sentence. To get you started, try writing a pair of sentences about Congress passing legislation and then a pair about a pilot flying a plane.

# 34

## VARIETY

A long series of sentences identical or very similar in length and structure is monotonous. But a series of well-written, varied sentences provides the reader with more than mere absence of monotony. It reflects the writer's careful molding of form to thought and the careful choice of length and structure to supply emphasis that creates meaning.

**34a**   Varying sentence structure and length creates emphasis and accentuates meaning.

Consider the following paragraph by Jane Howard. Notice the variety in length and structure of the eight sentences that make up the paragraph.

> The trouble with the families many of us were born into is not that they consist of meddlesome ogres but that they are too far away. In emergencies we rush across continents and if need be oceans to their sides, as they do to ours. Maybe we even make a habit of seeing them, once or twice a year, for the sheer pleasure of it. But blood ties seldom dictate our addresses. Our blood kin are often too remote to ease us from our Tuesdays to our Wednesdays. For this we must rely on our families of friends. If our relatives are not, do not wish to be, or for whatever reasons cannot be our friends, then by some complex alchemy we must try to transform our friends into our relatives. If blood and roots don't do the job, then we must look to water and branches.
>
> JANE HOWARD, *Families*

Such variety of length and structure is by no means accidental. In the paragraph immediately before this one, Howard has set her thesis: all of us need to belong to a clan, a tribe; if our families don't fit that need, we will find a substitute that does. The quoted paragraph develops that thesis. Its pivotal point falls at the cluster of three comparatively short, subject-verb-object sentences—seven, sixteen, and ten words, respectively—that comes at the approximate center of the paragraph: our blood families often are remote; thus they cannot "ease us from our Tuesdays to our Wednesdays"; for this we need friends. By using shorter, simpler sentences, Howard focuses the reader's attention, emphasizing those ideas that are in an ordinarily unemphatic, mid-paragraph location.

There is no formula for the "right" variety of length and form among the sentences of a paragraph or a paper. The variety of Jane Howard's paragraph above comes from choosing the length and form best suited to the meaning and emphasis she intended to convey to her readers.

Such fitting of form to meaning is unlikely to come in the first draft of a paragraph or paper. It comes with revision. When you turn to revising the early drafts of your writing, be wary if many or most of your sentences are either short or long or if some single structure seems to recur overfrequently. You will need relatively long and complex sentences to relate ideas clearly to one another and to subordinate minor detail; short sentences to give you emphasis where you want it; variety to avoid monotony. Be aware, too, that the kind of sentences that will be appropriate if you are writing a sports column or a set of simple directions will differ from the kind you will need to explain a complex idea.

Most important, always keep in mind that sentence variety is not an end in itself. Your choice of length and structure for any one sentence must always depend upon your meaning and upon the relationship of that sentence to those that stand before and after it.

**34b**   Short, simple sentences and longer, more complex sentences can work together to achieve variety that enhances meaning.

**34b**

*var*

If you are effectively using coordination, subordination, parallelism, and other sentence structures discussed in Sections **31–33**, your writing will already contain a good deal of variety. You will have discovered, for instance, that short sentences are good for introducing a topic or summing up a point and that longer sentences lend themselves to elaboration, detailed explanation, or qualification of a main idea. Notice how the following passages use this "push, pull" technique to advantage.

> My biology final flopped on my desk. A big, fat *D* stared up at me. Refusing to believe what my eyes had seen, my mind uncomprehending, I scooped up the paper, lunged through the door, and took off across the parking lot. I drove home, cursing the white car that drove so slow I had to pass it and damning the blue truck that drove so fast it had to pass me.
>
> *Student paragraph*

> When I was nine, we moved to Boston. I grew up; got my schooling; larked about a while as a reporter; married, and had a little girl of my own. I adored her. . . . Raising three in the baby boom was louder, funnier, messier; more alarming, marvelous, tearful and tender than any prior experience of mine. My children spent emotions and energies over a range I'd never known in my childhood. So did I.
>
> JOAN MILLS, "The One, the *Only?*"

Both writers take advantage of sentence structure to build details, move their readers forward through the meaning with vigor and energy, and stop them short to make points memorable. The writing is effective not only because the authors have something interesting to say but also because they align the structure of their sentences to the content of those sentences—piling and building, adding and combining, balancing or contrasting, pausing and breaking—in ways that reinforce their thoughts.

**34c** Changing the word order, the sentence pattern, or the sentence type can add variety.

*Word Order*

Certain modifiers, called **free modifiers,** can be moved from one position to another in a sentence. Prepositional phrases, clauses, and single words that modify nouns should be placed next to or very close to the nouns they modify; their position is relatively fixed. But adverbs, adverbial phrases and clauses, many participial phrases, and absolute phrases can often be placed at different positions in a sentence; these are free modifiers. Moving such modifiers into varying positions can help you place emphasis where you want it and increase sentence variety. As you read the examples below, note the cases in which free modifiers are set off with commas. (See also Sections **20c–e.**)

ADVERBIAL PHRASES AND CLAUSES

Westerners and Arabs still do not understand each other, *in spite of two thousand years of contact.*

*In spite of two thousand years of contact,* Westerners and Arabs still do not understand each other.

Westerners and Arabs, *in spite of two thousand years of contact,* still do not understand each other.

The defendant changed his plea to guilty *because the prosecutor had built up such convincing evidence against him.*

*Because the prosecutor had built up such convincing evidence against him,* the defendant changed his plea to guilty.

The defendant, *because the prosecutor had built up such convincing evidence against him,* changed his plea to guilty.

The bank's vice president kept juggling several customers' large deposits *to cover his own embezzlement.*

*To cover his own embezzlement,* the bank's vice president kept juggling several customers' large deposits.

The bank's vice president, *to cover his own embezzlement,* kept juggling several customers' large deposits.

**34c**

*var*

PARTICIPIAL PHRASES

The deer, *grazing peacefully in the valley,* were unaware of the approaching hunters.

*Grazing peacefully in the valley,* the deer were unaware of the approaching hunters.

*[Being] unaware of the approaching hunters,* the deer were grazing peacefully in the valley.

*Gasping for air,* the diver came to the surface.

The diver, *gasping for air,* came to the surface.

The diver came to the surface, *gasping for air.*

Note that in placing participial modifiers, you must be alert to the possibility of creating a misplaced modifier (see Section **12a**). Participial phrases can almost always be placed either before or after the nouns they modify. But whether they can be more widely separated will depend upon the sentence. In the example above, *gasping for air* can logically modify only *diver,* not *surface;* and since the sentence is brief, the phrase can comfortably be placed at its end. But in the previous example, if the *grazing* phrase were moved to the end of the sentence, it would modify *hunters* rather than *deer.*

Absolute phrases, since they always modify the entire sentence in which they stand, can usually be placed either at the beginning or end of a sentence or within it.

**34c**

*var*

ABSOLUTE PHRASES

*His hair cut close, his arms and legs tanned, his face freckled,* Jonathan seemed the typical country boy in summer.

Jonathan, *his hair cut close, his arms and legs tanned, his face freckled,* seemed the typical country boy in summer.

Jonathan seemed the typical country boy in summer—*his hair cut close, his arms and legs tanned, his face freckled.*

Sarah settled back for a quiet evening, *the work day over, the bills paid, some letters written.*

*The work day over, the bills paid, some letters written,* Sarah settled back for a quiet evening.

Sarah, *the work day over, the bills paid, some letters written,* settled back for a quiet evening.

## Sentence Patterns

The subject-verb-object pattern of the basic English sentence is so strongly established that any shift in it causes unusually heavy emphasis. Sentences such as *Over the fence jumped Oscar* or *Siamese cats she adores* are rather infrequent in most modern writing. But such **inver-**

**sion,** when context justifies it, can be effective. Consider the following example from a student's essay about his mother's death:

> No longer did I have the security of someone being there to greet me when I arrived home from school—all I had was a high-strung Yorkshire terrier with a bladder problem. What I had to do was fend for myself and take on new responsibilities.

The student might have written "I no longer had the security . . .," but because he inverted the word order a bit at the opening of his paragraph, its contrast with the parallel "all I had" and "what I had" of the next two independent clauses highlights the change his mother's death brought to his life.

Notice how the next example uses inversion to emphasize the desire for wealth.

> Throughout Dawson's life his great obsession had been to secure wealth, great wealth, wealth that would enable him to indulge his wildest fantasies. Such wealth he constantly dreamed of; and such wealth he was determined to get at all costs.

**34c**

**var**

A more common and much less emphatic inversion occurs when the subject and verb are reversed in a sentence opening with a long adverbial modifier.

> Across the boulevard where a milk truck scurries to more lucrative fields lies the sea and miles of empty beach.
>
> JOHN J. ROWLAND, *Spindrift*

## Sentence Types

Except in dialogue, the overwhelming majority of written sentences are statements. But questions, commands, and occasionally even exclamations are useful for achieving emphasis and variety when the context warrants them.

**Questions** at the beginning of a paragraph can point its direction. The following sentence opens a paragraph in which the author argues that television news coverage is superior to that of all but the best newspapers.

> Why do I think network TV does a better job of informing than [most] newspapers?
>
> MARYA MANNES, "What's Wrong with the Press?"

Or a question may open a paragraph of definition.

> What is civilized man? By derivation, he is one who lives and thinks in a city.
>
> BERNARD IDDINGS BELL

**Imperative sentences** are the staple sentences of writing that gives directions. But occasionally they are useful in other contexts.

Observations indicate that the different clusters of galaxies are constantly moving apart from one another. To illustrate by a homely analogy, think of a raisin cake baking in an oven.

If not overused, an **exclamation** is a sure attention-getter that will change the flow of a paragraph momentarily. Notice how the following student paragraph mixes exclamations and questions to create an informal, breezy, comic tone.

Now we all know that college presents many new and exciting experiences to be sampled in the name of education. You want culture and a foreign flavor? There are hundreds of exotic beers and wines to be tasted, especially the foreign ones. Skoal! You want social graces? There are dozens of events to attend where the fine art of genteel behavior can be practiced. Food fight! What about homework? You would ask. Mom, Dad . . . would a well-brought-up son of yours flunk out of school? Get serious!

Avoid the temptation to vary sentences just for the sake of change. As the sections on parallelism and effective repetition explained, sameness can be a strength in your writing, just as variety can be. The important thing is to clarify and reinforce your meaning and aid your reader's understanding. Observe how author William Zinsser uses similar sentence structures to suggest the dreamlike quality of a reverie and then introduces sentence variety to shift from the imaginary to the real.

**34c**

*var*

Pagination! I have always loved the word and been sorry that it doesn't mean all the things I think it ought to mean. Its sound wafts me to romantic or faraway worlds. I think of the great voyages that paginated the Indies. I watch the moonlight playing across the pagination on the Taj Mahal. I hear glorious music (Lully's pagination for trumpets). I savor gourmet meals (mussels paginated with sage). I see beautiful women—the pagination on their bodice catches my eye—and dream of the nights we will spend in torrid pagination. The wine that we sip will be exquisitely paginated—dry, but not too dry—and as the magical hours slip away we will . . .

But why torture myself? The fact is that it's a dumb word that means just one thing: the process of arranging pages in their proper sequence and getting them properly numbered.

WILLIAM ZINSSER, *Writing with a Word Processor*

---

EXERCISE 34a–c(1)
Practice the following techniques for achieving sentence variety.

1. Write two sets of sentences in which a short, simple sentence works together with longer ones that elaborate on the subject of the short sentence and provide details about it.

2. Write two sets of sentences in which several of the sentences use inverted word order effectively.
3. Write pairs of sentences containing free modifiers. In the sentences, move the free modifier to a different position to achieve a change in the meaning of the sentence.
4. Write two sets of sentences in which you vary the second sentence by recasting some declarative statements as questions, commands, and/or exclamations.
5. Write a paragraph that uses at least four of the techniques for varying sentences that are discussed in Section **34.** Then write a paragraph explaining why you chose those particular techniques, how you used them, and what effect you wanted to achieve.

---

EXERCISE 34a–c(2)
Revise the following paragraph by introducing greater sentence variety to enhance meaning.

**34c**

*var*

> Mary had been looking forward to her ski trip during Christmas break. She was worn out from a heavy class load and she needed a vacation. She was an experienced skier. She thought a week at a ski resort in Utah would be great. Mary asked two friends to go with her. They arrived at the resort to find the snow melting. The temperatures were in the fifties. The ski lodge manager said the weather was supposed to change, so Mary and her friends decided to stay for the week. They hoped for the best. The weather changed and got even warmer. More snow melted. Mary and her friends swam in the hotel's heated pool. They went to movies. They browsed in every shop in the town. They didn't have enough money to make any purchases. At the end of the week the weather was still warm. Almost no snow remained on the slopes. Mary and her friends had to go back to school. They had spent all their money on their trip to Utah. They hadn't even put on their skis.

---

 **WRITERS REVISING: MORE EFFECTIVE SENTENCES**
*(continued from page 254)*

**Stacy's Revision**

| | | |
|---|---|---|
| R 1 | Two books—Anne Frank's The Diary of a | **31c, 33b** |
| R 2 | Young Girl and a diary given to me by my | |
| R 3 | aunt—have made a tremendous difference in my | |
| R 4 | life. When I was twelve, I read the diary of | **34a, 34b** |

R 5    Anne Frank, a Jewish girl only a few years

R 6    older than I when she wrote her diary. Anne

R 7    died at Belsen, a Nazi concentration camp.          **33b**

R 8         That Christmas, I received a diary of my

R 9    own. Although I had never kept a diary              **33a**

R10    before, Anne Frank's diary provided me with

R11    both model and inspiration. Compared to her

R12    life, mine was very mundane, of course,

R13    containing none of the tragedies she

R14    experienced while hiding from the Nazis.

R15    Nevertheless, I did understand and appreciate

R16    her need to write things down. Writing was

R17    the way she came to terms with her life, the

R18    way she tempered suffering, the way she kept

R19    hope alive.

R20         Gradually, writing also became my way of

R21    understanding what was happening in my life.

R22    Those two books received when I was twelve—

R23    one filled, one blank—helped me find my

R24    voice as a writer. I have kept a diary ever

R25    since. It has made all the difference.

**34c**

*var*

## Analysis

Most of the information in the first three draft sentences (D1-6) has been compressed into the first revision sentence (R1-4). Now the paragraph gets off to a faster, smoother start. Stacy decided that, for her readers, her aunt's name was unimportant. She also decided that the information identifying the two books would be more effective in an appositive (**31c, 33b**) than in separate sentences.

The fourth draft sentence (D7-10) contains a long string of information delivered in prepositional phrases and other modifiers. Some information concerns a comparison between Stacy and Anne Frank, some of it concerns the circumstances of

Anne's death. The revision (R4-7) separates the two sets of information, first, so that the reader is not confronted by so many unrelated bits and, second, so that the statement about Anne Frank's death can achieve greater impact (**34a**, **34b**). The contrast between the periodic sentence (R4-6) and the loose sentence (R6-7) in the revision also helps to emphasize the brutal fact of Anne Frank's death. The relatively short, right-branching sentence that concludes the paragraph (R6-7) makes this information easily accessible (**33b**). Also for the sake of emphasis, Stacy chose to move the fifth draft sentence (D10-11) to the beginning of the revision's second paragraph (R8), where it would not detract from the starkness of the first paragraph's ending.

Notice that the sixth draft sentence (D12-13) is a compound sentence, but in the revision (R9-11), Stacy subordinates the information that previously appeared in an independent clause. This change places full emphasis on the idea of Anne Frank's diary as a model and inspiration for Stacy—emphasis achieved both by situating the main idea in an independent clause (**33a**) and by placing it at the end of the sentence (**33a**) (R10-11).

Take over the analysis of Stacy's revision. What are the effects of the changes she has made? Also analyze her revision in relation to yours. Which choices do you prefer?

**34c**

*var*

---

REVIEW EXERCISES: EFFECTIVE SENTENCES (Sections 31–34)

PART A
Indicate what you consider to be the principal detraction in the following sentences and paragraph (excessive coordination, faulty subordination, lack of emphasis, lack of parallelism, etc.), and then revise the sentences and paragraph.

**SENTENCE PRACTICE**
1. The Alps form the greatest mountain range in central Europe. The Alps are about 500 miles long. The Alps are about 100 miles wide.
2. During the ice age, glaciers shaped the mountains, creating U-shaped valleys, and many lakes were formed.
3. Because passage through the Alps that opens up new areas for trade has always been crucial, ancient peoples such as the Celts and the Romans, who built paved roads, created early routes through the mountains which are dangerous.
4. Hannibal marched his army through the Alps, Augustus Caesar's army crossed the Alps. Charlemagne led his men across the Alps. Napoleon's troops crossed the Alps.

5. Those who live on the Alpine mountainsides today must cope with long, cold winters and difficult farming conditions, but winter sports activities and a huge tourist industry help bolster the local economy, fortunately.

6. The Alps offer visitors magnificent snow-capped peaks and isolated valleys and rustic chalet-style hotels, but the Alpine area also includes sophisticated spas and casinos and internationally famous resorts.

7. Experienced mountaineers can climb the Matterhorn, or the famous peak can be gazed at by less brave visitors from the comfort of a hotel balcony in Zermatt, a nearby town.

8. Mont Blanc near Chamonix in the French Alps is the highest Alpine peak at 15,771 feet, and not even the Matterhorn is higher.

9. Approximately 2,000 people attempt to climb Mont Blanc every year, although the climb isn't easy since only about 300 of those who attempt the ascent eventually reach their goal.

10. The first person to reach the summit of Mont Blanc was Michel Gabriel Pacard, and he was a doctor from Chamonix, and he climbed the mountain in 1786.

**PARAGRAPH PRACTICE**

The highest mountain in North America is Mount McKinley. It is in Alaska. It is 20,320 feet tall. At one time Mount McKinley was part of McKinley National Park, but Denali National Park is the present location of the famous mountain. Mount McKinley National Park, which was established in 1917 and which was at the time a national park, became a part of a larger area which is called Denali National Park, which was given that name in 1980. The huge park, which covers 4,065,493 acres, is inhabited by a variety of wildlife: sheep, even grizzly bears, moose, and caribous.

**34c**

*var*

PART B

Go over a paper you have written recently, revising several paragraphs in which the sentences can be written more effectively.

# WORDS

*wds*

*In searching for the precise word, in reaching for the accepted form,
and in knowing the rules well enough to break them consciously and for effect,
the writer and reader can luxuriate in the language. Fighting the good fight for
the good word leads to the good life of the mind.*

           **WILLIAM SAFIRE,** *What's the Good Word?*

# 35

## THE DICTIONARY

A good dictionary is more than a source for checking spelling, pronunciation, and meaning; it also records word history (**etymology**), part of speech, and, when necessary, principal parts, plurals, or other forms. Frequently it records the level of current usage. Often the dictionary offers other information as well—lists of abbreviations, rules for punctuation and spelling, condensed biographical and geographical information, the pronunciation and source of many given names, and a vocabulary of rhymes. For writers and readers a dictionary is an invaluable resource and an indispensable tool.

Dictionaries are not born; they are made. The various editorial staffs, contributors, consultants, and panels who work together to produce a first-rate dictionary are interested in where a word has come from, its current meaning and actual usage, and its latest important developments. As William Morris explains in his introduction to the first edition of *The American Heritage Dictionary:* "We have engaged the services of hundreds of authorities in every range of human endeavor and scholarship, from archaeology to space research, from Indo-European to computer programming . . . many thousands of definitions were sent to these specialists for emendation or approval." Good dictionaries record the way our language changes and provide guidance about its most effective use in our speech and writing.

**35a** General dictionaries are of two types: abridged and unabridged.

**1. Abridged dictionaries.** Also known as desk dictionaries, abridged dictionaries usually list between 150,000 and 200,000 entries and conveniently serve most people's daily reading and writing needs. Of the many dependable ones available, five reputable abridged dictionaries are described below. Although they differ in important ways, all contain more than 150,000 entries, provide careful etymologies (word histories) and basic grammatical information about each entry, and specify distinctions among synonyms. All but *Webster's New Collegiate* provide helpful style or usage labels.

*Webster's New Collegiate Dictionary.* 9th ed. Springfield, MA: Merriam, 1983.

Based upon the *Third New International,* this desk dictionary profits from its extensive scholarship. The order of definitions under any one word is historical; a date notes the first instance of use. It has relatively full etymologies, a wide range of synonymies, and full pref-

atory material (including explanatory notes, history of English, pronunciation guide and symbols, spelling guide, and list of abbreviations). Abbreviations, biographical names, and place names are listed
separately at the end of the dictionary. Some users find inconvenient
the lack of the label *colloquial* or its equivalent, *informal,* and sparse
use of the label *slang.*

> *Webster's New World Dictionary.* 2nd college ed. New York: Simon,
> 1982.

This dictionary emphasizes simplified definitions even of technical terms and includes a large number of words and phrases that
are relatively informal. Usage labels are generously used. Synonymies
and etymologies are full and thorough. The sequence of definitions is
historical, except that common meanings are placed first before specialized ones. All words are contained in the main alphabetical list.
Identification of Americanisms and attention to the origin of American place names are special features. Foreign words that need to be
italicized are clearly labeled by double-daggers in the margin. This
dictionary is fairly liberal in allowing for variant spellings.

> *The American Heritage Dictionary of the English Language.* 2nd college
> ed. Boston: Houghton, 1982.

The distinguishing features of this dictionary are its numerous
illustrations and its usage notes based upon a consensus of a panel of
some one hundred writers, editors, poets, and public speakers. The
initial definition of an entry offers what the editors judge to be the
central meaning, and it serves as the base for the arrangement of
other senses of the word. Synonymies are generous but lack cross-
references. Abbreviations and biological and geographical entries are
listed in separate sections. An appendix of Indo-European roots is a
special feature.

**35a**

*dict*

> *The Random House Dictionary of the English Language.* College ed. New
> York: Random, 1984.

This dictionary is based on the unabridged *Random House Dictionary of the English Language.* Definitions are ordered by frequency of
use; recent technical words receive careful attention. A single alphabetical listing incorporates all biographical and geographical as well as
other entries. Among its prefaces, that by Raven I. McDavid, Jr., on
usage, dialects, and functional varieties of English, is a particularly
valuable summary.

> *Webster's II: New Riverside University Dictionary.* Boston: Houghton,
> 1984.

This dictionary features some 200,000 definitions and is an updated and slightly condensed version of the same publisher's *American Heritage Dictionary, 2nd College Edition*. Special strengths include clear and adequate usage labels, numerous word histories, and excellent usage notes. Definitions are ordered neither historically nor by frequency of occurrence. Rather, they are ordered according to central meaning clusters from which related meanings and additional meanings may evolve. Reviewers have compared *Webster's II* to the now-out-of-print second edition of *Webster's New International Dictionary* because it is prescriptive rulings on what is acceptable or unacceptable usage in the notes.

**2. Unabridged dictionaries.** Unabridged dictionaries contain the most complete and scholarly description of English words. The three described below are available in most libraries and are the unabridged dictionaries most frequently used.

*The Oxford English Dictionary.* 2nd ed. New York: Oxford UP, 1989.

Commonly referred to as the *OED*, this is the greatest dictionary of the English language. Listing a total of 616,500 word forms, the second edition of the *OED* amalgamates the text of the first edition, twelve volumes published in 1933, and the four supplementary volumes published between 1972 and 1986. The 1933 edition was itself a reprint of the ten-volume *New English Dictionary on Historical Principles* originally published in parts between 1884 and 1928.

The second edition contains about 5,000 new words or new senses of existing words not previously published in earlier editions, and the total number of main entries has increased by about 15 percent. Definitions are ordered historically. The *OED* is distinguished by approximately 2,400,000 quotations dated to illustrate meaning and spelling for a given word at particular times in its history. A single word may occupy several pages. *Set,* for example, occupies twenty-five pages, and a single one of its more than 150 definitions is illustrated by nineteen quotations from writings beginning in 1205 and extending to 1974. The pronunciation system used in the first edition has been replaced by the International Phonetic Alphabet, in which stress marks are placed before the syllable.

*Webster's Third New International Dictionary of the English Language.* Springfield, MA: Merriam-Webster, 1981.

This is the unabridged dictionary that people who live in the United States are most likely to be familiar with. Issued originally in 1909, it was revised in 1934. The current edition, thoroughly revised, has 460,000 entries and was first published in 1961. Though not as exhaustive as the *OED*, its definitions are scholarly and exact and fre-

**35a**

*dict*

quently supported by illustrative quotations. Since the 1961 edition uses style labels such as *slang* infrequently and does not use the label *colloquial,* some readers continue to prefer the second edition.

*Random House Dictionary of the English Language.* 2nd ed. New York: Random, 1987.

With only 315,000 entries, the *Random House Dictionary* is considerably briefer than most unabridged dictionaries. But it is a sound and scholarly dictionary with especially up-to-date entries. It is the only entirely new unabridged dictionary to be published in recent years.

Other unabridged dictionaries of English are the *New Standard Dictionary of the English Language, Webster's New Twentieth-Century Dictionary,* and the *Dictionary of American English* (four volumes), which is made on the same plan as the *OED* and follows the history of words as they were used by American writers between 1620 and 1900.

**3. Special dictionaries.** General dictionaries bring together in a single reference all of the information you ordinarily need about a word. Special dictionaries, because they limit their attention to a single kind of information about words or to a single category of words, can give more detailed, complete information. Thus a dictionary of slang can devote an entire page to the word *hip,* in contrast to the general dictionary, which can afford no more than four or five lines. A medical dictionary can include thousands of specialized medical terms of which only a few hundred might be included in a general dictionary.

Specialized dictionaries abound: dictionaries for engineers, psychiatrists, scholars of music, nurses, economists, auto mechanics—just about any field that has a specialized vocabulary. You would do well to familiarize yourself with specialized dictionaries in the fields you are studying. Instructors and practitioners in these fields, as well as reference librarians, can point such dictionaries out to you. (See also the lists of reference books in Section **44,** "Locating and Working with Sources.")

Dictionaries of usage and of synonyms can help you a great deal with your writing. When you need specialized information about words, check the most recent edition of one of the following dictionaries:

Bernstein, Theodore M. *The Careful Writer: A Modern Guide to English Usage.*

Follett, Wilson. *Modern American Usage.*

Fowler, H. W. *Dictionary of Modern English Usage.* Rev. and ed. Sir Ernest Gowers.

*Harpers Dictionary of Contemporary Usage.*

Partridge, Eric. *A Dictionary of Slang and Unconventional English.* Ed. Paul Beale.

**35a**

*dict*

*Webster's College Thesaurus.*
*Webster's Dictionary of English Usage.*
*Webster's New Dictionary of Synonyms.*
Wentworth, Harold, and Stuart Berg Flexner. *Dictionary of American Slang.*

## 35b Become familiar with the features of a dictonary entry.

Because dictionaries must say a great deal in a very brief space, they use systems of abbreviations, symbols, and typefaces to condense information. Although such systems vary from dictionary to dictionary, their format is quite similar. Taking the time to read a dictionary's explanatory pages will save you some puzzlement later; and once you have become familiar with the system in one dictionary, you will find reading any dictionary's entries fairly easy.

The following sample entry, from *Webster's Third New International Dictionary,* shows most of the principal features to be found in a dictionary entry. These are labeled and numbered to correspond with the more detailed descriptions that follow.

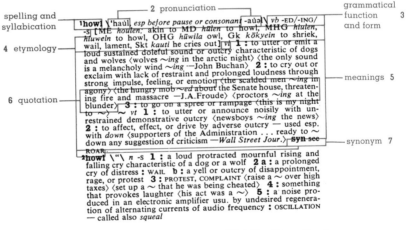

35b

dict

By permission. From *Webster's Third New International Dictionary.* © 1986 by Merriam-Webster, Inc., publisher of the Merriam-Webster® dictionaries.

**1. Spelling and syllabication.** The main entry of a word in a dictionary shows the spelling and syllabication, using centered dots between syllables to show how to separate the word properly at the ends of the lines (see "Syllabication," Section **18**). The entry also gives the proper spelling of compound words—properness depends on whether the editors found them more often written as two single words (**half broth·er**), as a hyphenated compound (**quar·ter-hour**), or as one word (**drug·store**). Dictionaries also indicate foreign words that require italics (in manuscript, underlining) either by labeling them as foreign (*French, German,* etc.), printing them in boldface italics, or using a symbol such as a double dagger (‡).

Any variant spellings will also be listed in the main entry. Usually, the first listing is, in the opinion of the editors, the more common; some dictionaries indicate that two variants are equally common by joining them with *or* (**cad·die** *or* **cad·dy**) or that one is less common than the other by joining them with *also* (**wool·ly** *also* **wool·y**). In general, choose the first listed variant unless there is a special reason for choosing the second.

The main entry for *howl* shows that it is a one-syllable word, which cannot be divided at the end of a line; that it is not normally capitalized; and that it has no variant spelling.

---

EXERCISE 35b(1)

Referring to a dictionary, give the preferred spelling of each word.

1. judgement
2. favour
3. practise

4. ambiance
5. orthopaedic
6. modelled

7. blonde
8. skilful
9. sceptic

---

EXERCISE 35b(2)

Rewrite the following compounds, showing which should be written as they are, which hyphenated, and which written as two or more separate words.

1. paperback
2. circuitbreaker
3. toothpaste

4. crossreference
5. aircooled
6. carpool

7. nativeborn
8. coldfront
9. habitforming

**35b**

*dict*

---

EXERCISE 35b(3)

Copy the following foreign words, underlining those that require italics and supplying accents where needed.

1. laissez faire
2. gemutlich
3. sine qua non

4. simpatico
5. bourgeosie
6. tete a tete

7. paparazzi
8. nouveau riche
9. coup d etat

---

**2. Pronunciation.** Dictionaries indicate the pronunciation of words by respelling them with special symbols and letters. Explanation of the symbols is given either at the bottom of the page on which the entry appears or in the prefatory pages or both.

In *Webster's Third* the pronunciation appears between slant lines called reverse virgules; some other dictionaries use parentheses. Stressed syllables are indicated by accent marks (´ or '). In most dictionaries, the accent mark follows the stressed syllable. Notice, however, that *Webster's Third* (as well as *Webster's New Collegiate,* based on the *Third*) places the accent mark immediately before the stressed syllable.

Dictionaries show frequently occurring variant pronunciations as they do variant spellings. In the *Webster's Third* sample entry, for instance, you can see that an unabridged dictionary may even show variant pronunciations for such a simple word as *howl*. As with variant spellings, the first pronunciation is sometimes said to be preferred. However, unless there is a limiting label or comment attached to one or more variants, they are all equally correct. Your preference should be determined by the pronunciation you hear in conversation around you.

---

EXERCISE 35b(4)
Copy the dictionary pronunciations for the following words. If there is variant usage for any, underline the pronunciation that you are accustomed to.

| | | |
|---|---|---|
| 1. exquisite | 4. kindergarten | 7. aunt |
| 2. presentation | 5. abdomen | 8. negate |
| 3. either | 6. promenade | 9. irrefutable |

---

**35b**

*dict*

**3. Grammatical functions and forms.** All dictionaries indicate the part of speech to which a word belongs. If a word can serve as more than one part of speech, most dictionaries include all its functions and meanings under a single entry, grouping the meanings separately for each function. A few dictionaries list a separate entry for each part of speech—as does *Webster's Third*, which groups the intransitive *(vi)* and transitive *(vt)* verb forms in the first entry and the noun form *(n)* in the second.

Dictionaries also show a word's inflected forms, especially if they are irregular or if they might cause spelling problems (as in *travel, traveled, traveling* or *travelled, travelling*). Thus the entry for the verb *drink* lists the irregular past tense *drank* and the past participle *drunk*. The entries for the singular nouns *child* and *alumna* give the plural forms *children* and *alumnae*. Most dictionaries do not show plurals for nouns that are regular, forming their plurals with *-s*. Most dictionaries also show *-er* and *-est* for the comparative and superlative forms of adjectives and adverbs. Where this information is not supplied, you can assume the comparative and superlative forms require the addition of *more* and *most*. *Webster's Third* is one of several dictionaries that also show the regular as well as irregular forms for various parts of speech.

Other parts of speech formed from the word being defined, and related in meaning, are listed at the end of the entry. They are spelled, divided into syllables, and identified by part of speech, but not defined.

---

EXERCISE 35b(5)

Write the past tense and the past participle of each of these verbs. Use a dictionary as necessary.

|   |   |   |   |   |   |
|---|---|---|---|---|---|
| 1. | lend | 4. | burst | 7. | bear |
| 2. | forecast | 5. | strive | 8. | dive |
| 3. | hide | 6. | occur | 9. | take |

---

EXERCISE 35b(6)

Write the plural (or plurals) of each of the following. Use a dictionary as necessary.

|   |   |   |   |   |   |
|---|---|---|---|---|---|
| 1. | phenomenon | 4. | syllabus | 7. | wolf |
| 2. | crisis | 5. | criterion | 8. | medium |
| 3. | fungus | 6. | sister-in-law | 9. | radius |

---

EXERCISE 35b(7)

Write the comparative and superlative forms of each of the following. Use a dictionary as necessary.

|   |   |   |   |   |   |
|---|---|---|---|---|---|
| 1. | scarce | 4. | early | 7. | often |
| 2. | bad | 5. | horrible | 8. | swiftly |
| 3. | concise | 6. | pitiful | 9. | inferior |

---

**4. Etymology.** A word's history—its origin and derivation— often helps clarify its present meaning, forms, and spelling. Because the course of history changes, restricts, or extends meanings, many original ones have been lost entirely. *Presently*, for example, formerly meant *at once, immediately;* it now usually means *shortly, in a little while.*

The etymology of a word can be very useful in discriminating between synonyms, so that you can select the one that comes closest to the meaning you intend. Dictionaries place etymologies after the initial grammatical label or at the very end of the entry. When they contain symbols, abbreviations, and different typefaces, you should check the key and explanation provided in the dictionary's opening pages.

The material between the brackets in the *Webster's Third* entry for *howl* shows the origin or etymology of the word: *howl* comes from a word in Middle English (ME) spelled *houlen,* and is related to Middle Dutch (MD) *hūlen* and Middle High German (MHG) *hiulen* or *hiuweln,* all meaning "to howl"; to the Old High German (OHG) word *hūwila* meaning "owl"; to the Greek (Gk) *kōkyein* meaning "to wail" or "lament"; and to the Sanskrit (Skt) word *kauti* meaning "he cries out."

**35b**

*dict*

---

EXERCISE 35b(8)

Explain the etymology of each of the following.

|   |   |   |   |   |   |
|---|---|---|---|---|---|
| 1. | ghastly | 4. | livid | 7. | paradox |
| 2. | fervent | 5. | mawkish | 8. | zone |
| 3. | debris | 6. | sabotage | 9. | jacket |

---

EXERCISE 35b(9)
From what specific names have the following derived?

| | | |
|---|---|---|
| 1. serendipity | 4. fuchsia | 7. volt |
| 2. dalmatian | 5. vulcanize | 8. frankfurter |
| 3. bowdlerize | 6. quixotic | 9. plutonium |

EXERCISE 35b(10)
From what language did each of the following words originally come?

| | | |
|---|---|---|
| 1. chrome | 6. walrus | 11. marimba |
| 2. chutney | 7. kowtow | 12. pigment |
| 3. hammock | 8. juggernaut | 13. aardvark |
| 4. sherbet | 9. yogurt | 14. yo-yo |
| 5. tycoon | 10. persimmon | 15. okra |

5. **Meanings.** Strictly speaking, dictionaries do not *define* words; they record meanings that actual usage, past and present, has attached to words. When more than one meaning is recorded for a single word, *Webster's Collegiate* (and *Webster's Third*) lists them in order of historical use, earliest meaning first. Most other dictionaries list the most common or frequently used, most general, or most basic meaning first. Thus it is important to know a dictionary's system of arrangement, explained in the volume's prefatory pages, and to read *all* the meanings in an entry before choosing the one that best suits the context in which you plan to use the word.

Senses of a word within a single part of speech are shown by means of boldface numbers. Where the sense of a word can be subdivided into further shades of meaning (different but related senses), boldface, lower-case letters are used. Words in small capitals (WAIL in meaning 2 of the noun form of *howl*, for example) are both synonyms and also main entries where further related definitions can be found. Special and technical meanings are clearly indicated.

**35b**
*dict*

EXERCISE 35b(11)
For each of the following words, (1) indicate the total number of meanings you can find, and (2) write three sentences that illustrate three meanings.

| | | |
|---|---|---|
| 1. deck | 4. school | 7. date |
| 2. scrape | 5. left | 8. closet |
| 3. troll | 6. nurse | 9. fortune |

EXERCISE 35b(12)
Explain the changes in meaning that have taken place in each of the following words, using etymologies where helpful.

| 1. vaccine | 6. slogan | 11. mayhem |
| 2. decimate | 7. hectic | 12. quarantine |
| 3. scold | 8. mundane | 13. dilemma |
| 4. frantic | 9. glamour | 14. libel |
| 5. shambles | 10. foible | 15. dally |

**6. Quotations.** Quotations form a major part of a definition by illustrating actual usage, the context for a word. They are extremely valuable in showing differences in synonyms, distinguishing between closely related meanings, or illustrating unusual uses of a word. Those labeled by authors' names or by sources are actual quotations; those not so labeled are typical phrases created by the dictionary editors. Illustrative quotations are usually enclosed in angle brackets (< >) or set off by a colon and italicized.

Under meaning 2 of *howl* as a transitive verb, a usage note states that in this meaning *howl* is used especially with *down* in the phrase *howl down,* and an example from *The Wall Street Journal* is provided. *Webster's Third* uses a swung dash (~) in quotations to replace the word itself.

**7. Synonyms and antonyms.** A **synonym** is a word having approximately the same general meaning as the main-entry word. An **antonym** has approximately the opposite meaning. For practical reasons, not all entries show synonyms and antonyms. Paragraph-length discussions of groups of synonyms are usually located at the end of certain entries and cross-referenced at related entries. For instance, at the end of meaning 2 in the *Webster's Third* transitive verb entry for *howl,* "syn see ROAR" means that the entry for *roar* contains a discussion of the synonyms for *howl.* That synonym group is reproduced below.

From *Webster's Third,* for *howl:*

**35b**

*dict*

**syn** HOWL, ULULATE, BELLOW, BAWL, BLUSTER, CLAMOR, VOCIFERATE: ROAR suggests the full loud reverberating sound made by lions or the booming sea or by persons in rage or boisterous merriment ⟨far away guns *roar* —Virginia Woolf⟩ ⟨the harsh north wind . . . *roared* in the piazzas —Osbert Sitwell⟩ ⟨*roared* the blacksmith, his face black with rage —T.B.Costain⟩ HOWL indicates a higher, less reverberant sound often suggesting the doleful or agonized or the sounds of unrestrained laughter ⟨frequent *howling* of jackals and hyenas —James Stevenson-Hamilton⟩ ⟨how the wind does *howl* —J.C.Powys⟩ ⟨*roared* at his subject . . . *howled* at . . . inconsistencies —Martin Gardner⟩ ULULATE is a literary synonym for HOWL but may suggest mournful protraction and rhythmical delivery ⟨an *ululating* baritone mushy with pumped-up pity —E.B.White⟩ BELLOW suggests the loud, abrupt, hollow sound made typically by bulls or any similar loud, reverberating sound ⟨most of them were drunk. They went *bellowing* through the town —Kenneth Roberts⟩ BAWL suggests a somewhat lighter, less reverberant, unmodulated sound made typically by calves ⟨a woman *bawling* abuse from the door of an inn —C.E.Montague⟩ ⟨the old judge was in the hall *bawling* hasty orders —Sheridan Le Fanu⟩ BLUSTER suggests the turbulent noisiness of gusts of wind; it often suggests swaggering and noisy threats or protests ⟨expressed her opinion gently but firmly, while he *blustered* for a time and

*(continued on p. 292)*

then gave in —Sherwood Anderson⟩ ⟨swagger and *bluster* and take the limelight —Margaret Mead⟩ CLAMOR suggests sustained, mixed and confused noisy outcry as from a number of agitated persons ⟨half-starved men and women *clamoring* for food —Kenneth Roberts⟩ ⟨easy ... for critics ... to *clamor* for action —Sir Winston Churchill⟩ VOCIFERATE suggests loud vehement insistence in speaking ⟨was not willing to break off his talk; so he continued to *vociferate* his remarks —James Boswell⟩

By permission. From *Webster's Third New International Dictionary*. © 1986 by Merriam-Webster, Inc., publisher of the Merriam-Webster® dictionaries.

**8. Labels.** Dictionaries label words or particular meanings of words to indicate that they are in some way restricted. Words and meanings not so labeled are appropriate for general use. Although the particular labels that dictionaries use vary somewhat, all labels can be divided into four general categories: *geographic* labels, *time* labels, *occupational* or *subject* labels, and *usage* or *style* labels.

**Geographic labels** indicate that the word or meaning is limited to a particular area. Typical labels of this sort are *British, Australian, New England, Southern U.S.*, and the like. Thus *Webster's Collegiate* labels *lift*, in the meaning of "elevator," *British*, and *outbye*, meaning "a short distance away," *Scottish*. *Webster's New World* labels *corn pone*, a kind of corn bread, *Southern U.S.* The label *dialectal* or *regional* usually suggests a specialized local or provincial word, often traditional. Thus *larrap*, meaning "a blow" or "to flog," is labeled *dialectal* by *Webster's Collegiate* and *regional* by *American Heritage*.

**Time labels** indicate that the labeled word has passed out of use entirely or no longer occurs in ordinary contexts. *Obsolete* means that a word has passed out of use entirely, as for example *absume* and *enwheel*, words that have not been used for 200 years. *Archaic* means that the labeled word or meaning is no longer generally used although it may still be seen occasionally in older writing, as for example *belike*, meaning "probably," and *outland*, meaning "a foreign land."

**Subject labels** indicate that a word or a particular meaning belongs to a special field such as law, medicine, baseball, finance, mathematics, or psychology. Thus *Webster's New World* identifies *projection* as a psychiatric term *(Psychiatry)* when used to mean the process of assigning one's own undesirable impulses to others and as a photographic term *(Photog.)* when used to mean projecting an image on a screen. *American Heritage* labels as *Law* the meaning of *domain* in the sense of ownership and rights of disposal of property.

**Style labels** indicate that a word or meaning is restricted to a particular level of usage. Typical style labels are *slang, colloquial, informal, nonstandard, substandard, illiterate,* and *vulgar*. (See also Section **36a–c** for further discussion of standard, nonstandard, and slang usage.) Variations among dictionaries are greatest in their choice of

35b

*dict*

labels and in the words and meanings to which they apply them. Nonetheless, there is broad agreement on the meanings of the labels themselves.

*Slang* indicates that a word, though widely used, has not yet been accepted in the general vocabulary. Slang terms and meanings often are used humorously; are likely to be short-lived, limited to a particular group of people; and are used almost entirely in speech rather than writing. Typical examples are *gross out* (to fill with disgust), *shaft* (to treat in a harsh, unfair way), *shades* (sunglasses), *snow* (cocaine or heroin), and *megabuck* (a million dollars). Of the dictionaries described, *Webster's Collegiate* is by far the most sparing in its use of the label, allowing many entries labeled *slang* by others to pass without any label.

*Colloquial* and *informal* are almost synonymous terms. They both indicate that a word is characteristic of speech or of quite informal, rather than more formal, writing. The *American Heritage* and *Webster's II* use the label *informal; Webster's New World* uses *colloquial. Webster's Collegiate* uses neither label and thus may be less useful for those who need to determine how appropriate a word is for a particular writing context.

*Illiterate, substandard,* and some other similar terms are labels indicating that a word is limited to uneducated speech, as *drownded* for the past tense of *drown.* Though dictionaries vary somewhat in the particular labels they use, their agreement in classifying a word as being limited to uneducated speech is much greater than their agreement in labeling a word *slang, colloquial,* and so on.

**35b**

*dict*

To use your dictionary wisely as a guide to usage, you will have to examine carefully the explanatory notes in it to determine exactly what labels are applied and how they are interpreted by the editors.

---

EXERCISE 35b(13)

Which of the following are standard English and which also have colloquial, informal, or slang usages, according to your dictionary? If possible, check more than one dictionary to determine if they agree.

| | | |
|---|---|---|
| 1. grind | 5. lemon | 9. lousy |
| 2. fishy | 6. champ | 10. dive |
| 3. belt | 7. lump | 11. square |
| 4. punk | 8. groove | 12. cinch |

---

EXERCISE 35b(14)

In what areas of the world would you be likely to hear the following?

| | | |
|---|---|---|
| 1. kuchen | 5. mahout | 9. petrol |
| 2. sarong | 6. dingo | 10. boccie |
| 3. troika | 7. origami | 11. kibbutz |
| 4. queue | 8. pita | 12. piñata |

EXERCISE 35b(15)

Any of the desk dictionaries discussed in this section will help you answer the following questions. Look up the meanings of *etymology*, *homonym*, and *synonym*, if necessary, before answering the questions.

1. What is the etymology of the word *campaign?*
2. What are three homonyms for the word *right?*
3. What is the syllabication of the word *extemporaneous?*
4. What are some synonyms for the adjective *authentic?*
5. Give the meanings of these abbreviations: DNB, kg, q.v., RSVP

**35c**   Increasing your vocabulary can improve the effectiveness of your writing.

The English language contains well over a million words. Of these, about two-fifths belong almost exclusively to special fields: e.g., zoology, electronics, psychiatry. Of the remaining three-fifths, unabridged dictionaries list 500,000 or more, desk dictionaries between 150,000 and 200,000. Such wealth is both a blessing and a curse. On the one hand, many English words are loosely synonymous, sometimes interchangeable, as in *buy* a book or *purchase* a book. On the other hand, the distinctions between synonyms are fully as important as their similarities. For example, a family may be said to be living in *poverty*, or in *penury*, or in *want*, or in *destitution*. All these words are loosely synonymous; but each in fact indicates a slightly different degree of need, *want* describing the least severe and *destitution* describing the most severe degree. Thus only one of the words will portray the family exactly as you see it and wish your reader to see it. In short, as a writer of English you must use words carefully in order to be precise.

We all have two vocabularies: a **passive**, or **recognition**, **vocabulary**, which is made up of the words we recognize in the context of reading material or conversation but do not actually use ourselves; and an **active vocabulary**, which consists of "working" words—those we use daily in our own writing and speaking. A good vocabulary is the product of years of serious reading, of listening to intelligent talk, and of trying to speak and write forcefully and clearly. This does not mean other methods of vocabulary building are ineffective, but it does mean that acquiring a good vocabulary is inseparable from acquiring an education.

**1. Increase your recognition vocabulary by learning the meaning of common prefixes and suffixes.** English includes many words derived from other languages. Consequently, it has a number of words based on common root forms to which different prefixes or suffixes have been added. The root form *spec-*, for example, from the Latin *specere (to look)*, appears in *specter, inspection, perspective, aspect,*

**35c**

**dict**

*introspection, circumspect, specimen, spectator.* Knowing the common prefixes and suffixes will help you detect the meanings of many words whose roots are familiar.

## Prefixes

| Prefix | Example | Meaning |
|---|---|---|
| ab- | absent | away from |
| ad-* | adverb | to *or* for |
| com-* | combine | with |
| de- | degrade, depart, dehumanize | down, away from *or* undoing |
| dis-* | disparate, disappoint | separation *or* reversal |
| ex-* | extend, ex-president | out of *or* former |
| il-* | illogical | not |
| im- | immobile | not |
| in-* | input | in *or* on |
| in-* | inhuman | not |
| ir- | irrefutable | not |
| mis- | misprint | wrong |
| non- | non-Christian, nonsense | not |
| ob-* | obtuse | against |
| pre- | prevent, precondition | before |
| pro- | proceed | for *or* forward |
| re- | repeat | back *or* again |
| sub-* | subcommittee | under |
| trans- | transcribe | across |
| un- | unclean | not |

**35c**

*dict*

*The spelling of these prefixes varies, usually to make pronunciation easier. *Ad* becomes *ac* in *accuse*, *ag* in *aggregate*, *at* in *attack*. Similarly, the final consonant in the other prefixes is assimilated by the initial letter of the root word: *colleague* (*com* + *league*); *illicit* (*in* + *licit*); *offend* (*ob* + *fend*); *succeed* (*sub* + *ceed*).

---

## EXERCISE 35c(1)
Write words denoting *negation* of the following.

EXAMPLE     movable—able to be moved

            immovable—*not* able to be moved

1. visible
2. sanitary
3. ambiguous
4. legitimate
5. existent
6. passive
7. moderate
8. rational
9. significant

## EXERCISE 35c(2)
Write words denoting *reversal* of the following.

EXAMPLE     accelerate—to move at *in*creasing speed

            decelerate—to move at *de*creasing speed

            increase—to grow *larger*

            decrease—to grow *smaller*

| | | |
|---|---|---|
| 1. infect | 4. classify | 7. generate |
| 2. compose | 5. please | 8. honor |
| 3. bend | 6. cut | 9. personalize |

**Suffixes.** These fall into three groups: noun suffixes, verb suffixes, adjectival suffixes.

Noun suffixes denoting *act of, state of, quality of* include the following:

| Suffix | Example | Meaning |
|---|---|---|
| -dom | freedom | *state of* being free |
| -hood | manhood | *state of* being a man |
| -ness | dimness | *state of* being dim |
| -ice | cowardice | *quality of* being a coward |
| -ation | flirtation | *act of* flirting |
| -ion | intercession | *act of* interceding |
| ⌈-sion | scansion | *act of* scanning |
| ⌊-tion | corruption | *state of* being corrupt |
| -ment | argument | *act of* arguing |
| -ship | friendship | *state of* being friends |
| ⌈-ance | continuance | *act of* continuing |
| ⌊-ence | precedence | *act of* preceding |
| ⌈-ancy | flippancy | *state of* being flippant |
| ⌊-ency | currency | *state of* being current |
| -ism | baptism | *act of* baptizing |
| -ery | bravery | *quality of* being brave |

35c
dict

Noun suffixes denoting *doer, one who* include the following:

| Suffix | Example | Meaning |
|---|---|---|
| -eer (general) | auctioneer | *one who* auctions |
| -ist | fascist | *one who* believes in fascism |
| -or | debtor | *one who* is in debt |
| -er | worker | *one who* works |

Verb suffixes denoting *to make* or *to perform the act of* include the following:

| Suffix | Example | Meaning |
|---|---|---|
| -ate | perpetuate | *to make* perpetual |
| -en | soften | *to make* soft |
| -fy | dignify | *to make* dignified |
| -ize, -ise | sterilize | *to make* sterile |

Adjectival suffixes include the following:

| Suffix | Example | Meaning |
|---|---|---|
| -ful | hateful | full of |
| -ish | foolish | resembling |
| -ate | affectionate | having |
| -ic, -ical | angelic | resembling |
| -ive | prospective | having |

| Suffix | Example | Meaning |
|---|---|---|
| -ous | zealous | full of |
| -ulent | fraudulent | full of |
| -less | fatherless | without |
| -able, -ible | peaceable | capable of |
| -ed | spirited | having |
| -ly | womanly | resembling |
| -like | childlike | resembling |

## EXERCISE 35c(3)

Make words indicating *act of, state of, or quality of* from the following words.

| | | |
|---|---|---|
| 1. child | 4. fellow | 7. imprison |
| 2. disrupt | 5. fluent | 8. object |
| 3. excite | 6. ignore | 9. shrewd |

## EXERCISE 35c(4)

Make nouns indicating *doer* from the following.

| | | |
|---|---|---|
| 1. labor | 4. philanthropy | 7. pamphlet |
| 2. wander | 5. dwell | 8. ideal |
| 3. act | 6. violin | 9. promote |

## EXERCISE 35c(5)

Make verbs indicating *to make* or *to perform the act of* from the following nouns and adjectives.

| | | |
|---|---|---|
| 1. active | 4. caliber | 7. equal |
| 2. light | 5. motor | 8. length |
| 3. sharp | 6. system | 9. pulse |

**35c**

*dict*

## EXERCISE 36c(6)

Make adjectives of the following words by adding a suffix.

| | | |
|---|---|---|
| 1. like | 4. sorrow | 7. prince |
| 2. hero | 5. reason | 8. nutrition |
| 3. odor | 6. waste | 9. wonder |

**2. Increase and strengthen your active vocabulary by transferring words to it from your recognition vocabulary.** When you acquire a new word, find opportunities to use it so that it will come to feel natural and comfortable in your speech and writing.

An excellent way to strengthen your vocabulary is to study dictionary discussions of synonyms. As you add words to your vocabulary, look them up in a dictionary to be certain of their meaning and usage, and examine their synonyms at the same time. That way you will be able to increase your vocabulary by not one but several related words at a time. Furthermore, you will have learned the distinctions in meaning that will make your use of these words accurate and effective. Synonym dictionaries and thesauruses, devoted exclusively to the grouping and differentiating of synonyms, are also good sources. Although the various editions of *Roget's Thesaurus* are valuable for long lists of closely related words, they must be used cautiously because they do not discuss distinctions in meaning and offer no guiding examples. A thesaurus should be used in conjunction with a dictionary so that you will be sure of selecting the synonym with the shade of meaning you need.

---

EXERCISE 35c(7)
Indicate the distinctions in meaning among the words in each of the following groups.

1. absurd, silly, preposterous, ridiculous, ludicrous
2. eccentric, anomalous, abnormal, odd, singular
3. mournful, sorrowful, sad, grievous, lugubrious
4. vacant, void, vacuous, empty, unoccupied
5. rude, uncouth, churlish, insolent, impudent

---

# 36

## APPROPRIATENESS

**36**

*appr*

Several thousand years ago, the Greek philosopher Aristotle wrote that a speech is composed of three things: the speaker, the subject on which he speaks, and the audience he is addressing. Contemporary author and teacher William Zinsser states that good writing is a personal transaction between a reader and a writer. Both Aristotle and Zinsser point to the importance of choosing words that are appropriate. Your language reflects your attitude toward the subject, your attitude toward yourself, and your attitude toward your listeners or readers. If the words you choose are inappropriate, you will end up alienating your audience.

There are no words in the English language that cannot be used somewhere, sometime. Consider the range of choices involved in describing the same event to different audiences. The words you use to describe a campus party in a letter to a friend and in a paper for a psychology class will differ considerably. The writing in the letter would appropriately be informal and colloquial—easy, loose, and full of jargon and slang: *The mixer was a blast, everybody just hanging out and generally blowing off steam after too many all-nighters and heavy-duty midterms.* In the psychology paper the writing would appropriately be more formal, edited, standard English—the "public" writing of the professions and most college courses: *Many college students release the tension and pressure resulting from concentrated study by attending parties after their exams are over.* (Section **36 a–c** discusses the differences between standard and nonstandard, formal and informal English.)

Both examples are right for their situations. But the audience for the first is much more limited than the audience for the second. When you write, remember that the more diverse and general your audience, the more you need to rely on standard, formal English, which offers a huge vocabulary of widely understood words. In contrast, the vocabularies offered by slang, jargon, colloquialisms, regionalisms, and the like are narrow and specialized, limited to relatively small groups of readers, and therefore much more likely to be misunderstood. Consequently, their use should generally be limited to special contexts, audiences, and purposes.

## WRITERS REVISING: EFFECTIVE WORDS

Ricky has become politically active recently concerning environmental issues and wants to encourage more funding for his state's Department of Environmental Quality. He has decided to write to his county representative in the legislature, asking the representative to support increased funding for DEQ. Before he mails his letter, he asks his English instructor, who is also interested in environmental issues, if she will critique it. She agrees and marks his letter with references from Sections **36–38**. Read the following excerpt from Ricky's letter and critique it. Then compare your critique with the one Ricky's instructor marked, which appears at the end of Section **38**.

**36**

*appr*

### Ricky's Draft

Dear Representative Maxey:

D 1       For many, many years our state has referred

D 2    to itself as the ''Sportsman's Paradise.'' This

D 3    environmental turf, which is our state, has

D 4    longtime been a haven for both hunters and

D 5    fishermen to enjoy their pastimes respectfully.

D 6    But Louisiana is presently in the wake of an

D 7    enormous and tremendous environmental crisis which

D 8    poses great potential harm for all of us citizens

D 9    who live and work here and love our state dearly.

D10   The only sure solution to this crisis is to begin

D11   the cleaning up of our environment and to support

D12   sufficiently those state agencies which specialize

D13   in this area. With the establishment of the

D14   Department of Environmental Quality in 1983, and

D15   under the guidelines of the 1980 Environmental

D16   Affairs Act, we have a proper base to commence to

D17   begin saving our state. However, establishment is

D18   not enough. Instead of pinching pennies, we must

D19   properly fund the DEQ to allow for this process to

D20   begin. Therefore, the legislature should push for

D21   increased general funding for the DEQ from our

D22   state.

This *Writers Revising* continues on page 330.

## 36a
## appr

**36a**   Choose the variety of English appropriate to your writing task.

Spoken language varies widely at any given time—from one geographical area to another and from one occupational and social group to another. Further, the language each of us uses varies from situation to situation—depending on our audience and purpose. Typically, written language varies less because we expect it to conform to certain standards. Two recognized categories of variation are **standard** and **nonstandard** English.

**1. Standard English.** The term *standard English* applies to the written and spoken language of educated people. It is the language of their social discourse and also of the professions: business, journalism, law, education, medicine, politics, engineering, and so forth. Standard English is accepted as the norm for public speech and writing: it is the language shared by a wide audience of literate people. One purpose of the *Prentice Hall Handbook for Writers* is to present the principles and conventions comprising standard American English.

**2. Nonstandard English.** This is language that varies from the standard, differing in verb and pronoun forms and in the use of double negatives: *he give, growed; I seen, have saw; she be going; him and me* *is; hern, youse, can't never.* Nonstandard is also characterized by a relatively narrow range of vocabulary, deviant pronunciation and spelling, and often by a heavy dependence on a small variety of sentence structures. (See also **36b.**) Historically, users of nonstandard English have been stigmatized as uneducated and possibly illiterate. This view continues to be held by the majority of educated people. Unless you are deliberately trying to replicate nonstandard English, as for in stance in dialogue, your writing should use standard English.

The following passages illustrate standard and one form of nonstandard English. Since nonstandard language is primarily spoken, the illustration can only approximate it.

STANDARD

While no country boasts the highest standards in every field, other cultures are more demanding of some services than America is. Most European countries insist on timely and efficient service on their railroads and airlines, which receive state subsidies to assure that performance. Americans who visit London typically come away with fond memories of the city's excellent taxicabs and subway system. The shortage of personal attention comes just when U.S. consumers are enjoying a cornucopia of novel products and services. . . . Shoppers can now find ten kinds of mustard and a dozen varieties of vinegar in a supermarket, but where is a clerk who can give a guiding word about these products?

STEPHEN KOEPP, *Time*

**36a**

*appr*

NONSTANDARD

"Well," he said at last, "I got in your springhouse for a fact and drank me some milk." He made a gesture toward the cement sack with his forefinger. "If you look in my poke yonder, you'll find two turnips and a handful of pole beans I grubbed outta your garden." He inclined his head toward the far-off field. "I expect that haystack I bedded down in needs fixin' if it ain't to molder." He took a deep breath and raised his eyebrows quizzically. "I think them's the damages," he said. "I trust they ain't none of em shootin' offenses."

JOHN YOUNT, *Hardcastle*

**3. Informal and formal English.** Standard English is divided according to use into **functional varieties,** the most general variations being informal and formal. **Informal English** is everyday speaking and writing, casual conversation between friends and associates, personal letters, and writing close to general speech. **Formal English** is the language of scholarly books and articles; business, scientific, and governmental reports; legal writing; and most literary prose. You will use both varieties in school and on the job. For example, a research paper or feasibility study will typically require formal English, whereas a first-person-experience essay or a short memo to a colleague at work might appropriately use somewhat more informal language.

Because *informal* and *formal* each encompass wide ranges of degree, what may seem relatively formal to one listener or reader may strike another as fairly informal. Perceived formality or informality is often highly dependent on purpose, subject matter, and audience expectations.

In general, as language moves closer to casual speech, it becomes more informal. Free use of contractions, loose sentence structures, and conversational, everyday words and expressions (such as *shape up* and *get going*) characterize informal language. As formal language moves away from the conversational, its sentence structures become more complex, elaborate, and rigid, its vocabulary often more Latinate, and its tone more serious, less relaxed. The examples that follow illustrate the range possible within formal and informal writing. The first example is quite formal, the second more informal, and the third quite informal.

**FORMAL**

The enduring social unit is a female [polar bear] and her cubs. They are usually together for two years, during which time the female teaches the cubs to hunt. Their social interaction is constant and intense. Older bears infrequently make sounds—they hiss loudly, growl, and champ their teeth when they are irritated; and when they are agitated they make a soft chuffing sound. Cubs, on the other hand, have an impressive vocal repertoire.

BARRY LOPEZ, *Arctic Dreams*

**36a**

*appr*

**INFORMAL**

The colossal success of the supermarkets is based upon the fact that nobody, but nobody, can sell you something as well as you can by yourself. As a result, supermarkets now stock clothing, appliances, plastic swimming pools, and small trees. The theory is that if you succumb to an avocado today, tomorrow you may fall for an electronic range or a young poplar.

ELAINE KENDALL, "An Open Letter to the Corner Grocer"

Of all the common farm operations none is more ticklish than tending a brooder stove. All brooder stoves are whimsical, and some of them are holy terrors. Mine burns coal, and has only a fair record. With its check draft that opens and closes, this stove occupies my dreams from midnight, when I go to bed, until five o'clock, when I get up, pull a shirt and a pair of pants on over my pajamas, and stagger out into the dawn to read the thermometer under the hover and see that my 254 little innocents are properly disposed in a neat circle around their big iron mama.

E. B. WHITE, *One Man's Meat*

**4. Colloquial and edited English.** The terms *colloquial* and *edited* are often used in discussing varieties of English. Loosely synonymous with informal, **colloquial** means *characteristic of conversation*. It describes the everyday speech of educated people and writing that uses easy vocabulary, loose constructions, contractions, and other characteristics of that speech. The informal writing styles of E. B. White and Elaine Kendall illustrated above are colloquial writing styles.

**Edited English** is the *written* language of many books, magazines, and newspapers. It may be more or less formal or informal, but it is always marked by its observation of the conventional standards of spelling, punctuation, grammar, and sentence structure accepted by literate people.

That English contains such variety means there can be no rigid standard of correctness. But this does not mean there are no standards. We choose a standard according to its appropriateness for the speaking or writing situation, paying careful attention to the demands of the subject, the purpose in speaking or writing about it, and, particularly, the characteristics and expectations of the audience. Having considered these factors, we select the level of language that will communicate most effectively.

## 36b Regional or nonstandard language is inappropriate in most writing.

**Regional words** (sometimes called **provincialisms** or **localisms**) are words whose use is generally restricted to the speech of a particular geographical area. Examples are *tote* for *carry, poke* for *bag, spider* for *frying pan* or *skillet*. **Nonstandard** words and expressions generally occur only in the language of uneducated speakers. Examples are *ain't, could of, she done,* and double negatives such as *can't never, scarcely none,* and *don't have no.* Dictionaries label such words *nonstandard* or *illiterate.* These have no place in your writing unless you are presenting dialogue or characterizing actual speech that uses such words.

**36b**
*appr*

REGIONAL She *redded up* the house for our *kinfolk.*
GENERAL She cleaned the house for our relatives.

NONSTANDARD They *didn't ought to have* spent the money.
STANDARD They shouldn't have spent the money.

NONSTANDARD I wish *I'd of drove more careful.*
STANDARD I wish I had driven more carefully.

---

EXERCISE 36b
If you are a native of the region in which your college is located, ask a classmate from another region to give you a list of words or expressions that strike him or her as being regionalisms in your speech. If you come from another area yourself, make up your own list of regionalisms of the college area and compare it with a classmate's.

**36c**   Use slang only when it suits the audience and purpose for which you are writing.

Slang consists of the rapidly changing words and phrases in popular speech that people invent to give language novelty and vigor. Slang words, in fact, are fun—unless you don't happen to know what they mean. Then they can seem like the strange tongue of a secret sect.

Slang often is created by the same process we use to create most new words: by combining two words *(ferretface, blockhead);* by shortening words *(pro, prof, vet, max);* by borrowing from other languages *(kaput, spiel);* and by generalizing a proper name *(the real McCoy).* Often slang simply extends the meaning of phrases borrowed from other activities *(lower the boom* from sailing; *tune in, tune out* from radio; *cash in your chips* from poker). A great deal of slang gives a new range of meaning to existing words *(tough, heavy, high, joint, turned on, bombed out).*

Slang is—and has always been—part of the current language, adding spontaneity, directness, color, and liveliness. Over three hundred years ago, Pilgrim youngsters were inventing slang terms, turning the traditional farewell—"God be with you"—into the flippant "good-by." Thus slang often contributes directly to the growth of the language as slang terms move gradually into general use. Words like *rascal* and *sham* were originally slang terms; shortened forms such as *A-bomb, ad, gym,* and *phone* are now appropriate to most informal writing. Reports on education routinely refer to high school *dropouts.* To see soft drinks and potato chips called *junk food* in the pages of a magazine surprises no one. When slang is clear, precise, vivid, and descriptive in ways that more standard words are not, it tends to enter general usage. In informal writing, well-chosen slang terms can be very effective:

36c
*appr*

> Has Harold Wilson *Lost His Cool?*
>
> Headline, *New York Times*

> Heaven knows there are large areas where a shrewd eye for the *quick buck* is dominant.
>
> FREDERICK LEWIS ALLEN, *The Big Change*

But slang has serious limitations. It is often imprecise, understandable only to a narrow social or age group, and usually changes very rapidly. You may be familiar with the latest slang, but who remembers *lollapalooza, balloon juice,* or *spooning?* The fact that *hep* became *hip* within a few years suggests how short-lived slang can be.

Enjoy slang for the life it can sometimes give to speech. But even in conversation, remember that it may not be understood and that a little goes a long way. If you rely on *nifty, lousy, tough,* and *gross* to describe all objects, events, and ideas, you don't communicate much.

In writing, use slang primarily when it serves some legitimate purpose, such as capturing the flavor of conversation.

> The bouncer told the drunk he had better back off or he was likely to get his lights punched out. Then he firmly steered the drunk through the door and out of the bar.

Except in carefully controlled contexts, slang and standard language usually make an inappropriate mixture:

> The very notion of venture capital is so alien in Communist China that no government official was willing to risk giving the two [young Chinese entrepreneurs] permission to set up shop. The decision was bucked up all the way to Premier Zhao Ziyang. He flashed the go-ahead last year, and the company began operation in January.
>
> *Business Week*

While we are not likely to resist such usages as *set up shop* in a magazine aimed at a fairly broad, general business audience, the slang expressions *bucked up* and *flashed the go ahead* here seem out of place in a news story concerning the head of the Chinese government. The best rule of thumb is to assess your audience and purpose carefully in deciding whether a slang term is appropriate.

---

**EXERCISE 36c(1)**
Almost everyone has favorite slang terms. Make a list of your own slang expressions and compare the list with those of your classmates to see how "original" your slang is. Then ask an individual from an older generation for a list of slang terms to see how expressions for similar things vary from age group to age group.

**36d**

*appr*

**EXERCISE 36c(2)**
For a week or two, keep a list of slang terms you find in a daily newspaper or a weekly news magazine. Which terms strike you as appropriate and effective? Which as poor usage? Why? Here's an example from *Time* to get you started.

> Thousands of U.S. companies have learned that if their products are second rate, customers will quickly turn to those that are first rate. Brand loyalty still has its allure but no longer counts for everything in an increasingly crowded global marketplace, in which armies of manufacturers are jostling for the customer's eye and U.S. products are being pushed off store shelves by rival goods from every part of the world.

---

**36d** **For a general audience, jargon should be used sparingly.**

The term **jargon** has several meanings (see Section **38b**). In a famous essay, "On Jargon," Sir Arthur Quiller-Couch defined the term as vague and "woolly" speech or writing that consists of abstract words, elegant variation, and "circumlocution rather than short straight speech." Linguists often define jargon as hybrid speech or dialect formed by a mixture of languages, for example the English-Chinese jargon known as pidgin English.

To most people, however, jargon is the technical or specialized vocabulary of a particular trade, profession, or field of interest—for example, engineering jargon, computer jargon, or horticultural jargon. Naturally, members of a specialized group use their jargon when communicating with one another. It is their language, so to speak, and its terms are often more precise, more meaningful, and more quickly comprehended than non-jargon expressions would be.

The following example shows how the author of a computer manual carefully defines terms, even though some of his readers may be very familiar with computer jargon. The author knows that the Macintosh computer is relatively new to a significant number of his readers; hence, he is careful to establish meanings for Macintosh jargon.

**36d**

*appr*

> The Macintosh makes a useful distinction between *applications* and *documents*, the first being used to create the second. Applications can also be thought of, more generally, as *tools* since the Macintosh manual uses the former term somewhat restrictively. Programs, such as MacWrite and MacPaint, are what are formally referred to as applications. . . . The pointer is a tool, whose use will vary from place to place; the keyboard and mouse are physical tools, as is the video screen on which you see the development of your labors. . . . Documents, on the other hand, are the end result of the process of computing, the reason you bought a computer in the first place.
>
> JOHN M. ALLSWANG, *Macintosh: The Definitive Users Guide*

Technical jargon is inappropriate when you are writing for a general audience unless, of course, the terms have entered everyday language and are widely understood. The mass media have broadened our understanding of many technical terms, especially those relating to newsworthy topics. *Countdown* and *liftoff* from space exploration, *carcinogenic* and *biopsy* from medicine, *printout* and *terminal* from computer technology are but a few of the words that have moved from jargon into fairly general usage. Nevertheless, you should use jargon with care, defining the terms if you think your readers might not know the meanings.

Unfortunately, jargon impresses some people simply because it sounds involved and learned. We are all reluctant to admit that we do not understand what we are reading. What, for example, can you make of the following passage?

### THE TURBO-ENCABULATOR IN INDUSTRY

. . . Work has been proceeding in order to bring to perfection the crudely conceived idea of a machine that would not only supply inverse reactive current for use in unilateral phase detractors, but would also be capable of automatically synchronizing cardinal grammeters. Such a machine is the Turbo-Encabulator. . . . The original machine had a base plate of prefabulated amulite surmounted by a malleable logarithmic casing in such a way that the two spurving bearings were in a direct line with the pentametric fan. . . . The main winding was of the normal lotus-o-delta type placed in a pan-endermic semiboloid slot in the stator, every seventh conductor being connected by a non-reversible tremie pipe to the differential girdlespring on the "up" end of the grammeters. . . .

> Reprinted by permission of the publishers,
> Arthur D. Little, Inc., Cambridge, Mass.

This new mechanical marvel was a joke, the linguistic creation of a research engineer who was tired of reading jargon. The point is, you should avoid unnecessary jargon in your writing, words used merely to impress, words that clutter rather than clarify.

---

EXERCISE 36d(1)

Make a list of twenty words and/or phrases that constitute jargon in a field you know. Define these terms in a way that a general reader could understand. Finally, explain whether you think each term is a justifiable use of jargon in your field or whether a "plain English" term would work just as well.

---

EXERCISE 36d(2)

From an issue of a magazine or newspaper written for a general audience, list technical or specialized terms that have ceased to be jargon and have entered the general usage. From what fields did these terms originally come? How many of them are at least partially defined within the context of the articles in which they appear?

---

**37**

**ex**

# 37

## *EXACTNESS*

Once you have determined the type of language that is appropriate for your subject and audience, you will want to choose words that most precisely convey the meaning you intend. To write with precision, you need to know both the denotation and the connotation of words. **Denotation** is the core of a word's meaning, sometimes called the "dictionary" or literal meaning: for example, a *tree* is "a woody perennial plant having a single stem or trunk." **Connotation** refers to the reader's emotional response to a word and to the associations the word carries with it. Thus, *tree* may connote shade or coolness or shelter or stillness or strength.

If you have misunderstood the denotation of a word you are

using, you are quite likely to confuse your readers. For example, the student who wrote *The firefighters who risked their lives to rescue the child were praised for their heroics* chose the wrong word. *Heroics* means "melodramatic behavior or language," quite different from *heroism,* the word the writer surely intended.

Errors of connotation are more subtle because individual responses to words differ and meanings can change over time. For example, *gay* commonly means "exuberant," but its secondary definition, "homosexual," has no doubt affected the word's connotative impact. Nonetheless, many words have quite stable connotations. *Home* generally suggests security, a sense of one's own place. Most of us would prefer a *cozy* robe and slippers to *snug* ones.

Your words should also connotatively fit other words in the same sentence and the larger context. Consider the following:

> *Brandishing* a gun and *angrily demanding* the money, the thief *yelped threateningly* at the frightened teller, "Empty the cash drawer."

The verb *yelped* suggests animal-like anger and abruptness, perfectly appropriate to the situation being described. Yet the connotations seem to conflict with the adverb *threateningly. Yelped* also connotates alarm and pain. Since the thief appears to have the upper hand in the situation, for most of us *snarled* would suggest connotations more in keeping with the other words in the sentence.

Many words stand for abstractions: *democracy, truth, inadequacy, challenge, beauty.* Because the connotations of such words are both vague and numerous, state specifically what you mean when you use them, or make sure that the context clarifies their meaning (see Section **37f**). Otherwise, readers will think they understand your terms when they do not.

**37a**   **ex**

## 37a   Distinguishing among synonyms increases exactness.

English is rich in **synonyms,** groups of words that have nearly the same meaning: *begin, start, commence; funny, comic, laughable.* But most synonyms differ in connotation. By observing their precise shades of meaning and choosing carefully among them, you can more accurately express your ideas. Occasionally, the difference in meaning between two synonyms is so slight that it makes little difference which you choose: you can *begin a vacation* or *start a vacation*—either will do. But usually the differences will be much greater. To *commence a vacation,* for example, connotes far more formality than ordinarily goes with vacations. And it makes a much more important difference whether you describe a movie as *funny, comic,* or *laughable.*

If you increase the number of synonyms in your vocabulary (see Section **35c**) and distinguish carefully among them when you write, your use of language will be more precise and therefore a greater aid to your readers. Knowing that *fashion* and *vogue* are synonyms for *fad*, or that *renowned* and *notorious* are synonyms for *famous*, gives you the chance to make your writing more exact by selecting the synonym connoting the precise shade of meaning that best expresses your idea. On the other hand, careless use of synonyms not only makes writing inexact, but also often distorts meaning. Notice the importance of connotation in the following sentence:

> Capone was a *renowned* gangster. [*Renowned* has favorable connotations that the writer probably did not intend. *Famous* would do, but it is not very exact. *Notorious*, "known widely and regarded unfavorably," would be exact.]

---

EXERCISE 37a

Explain the differences in meaning among the italicized words in each of the following groups.

1. an *impossible*, an *absurd*, an *unreasonable*, an *impractical* plan
2. a *stingy*, a *miserly*, a *mercenary*, a *penurious* person
3. a *precept*, an *instruction*, a *maxim*, a *prescription*
4. to *diminish*, to *dwindle*, to *decrease*, to *decline*
5. a *disrespectful*, a *supercilious*, a *contemptuous*, a *disdainful* attitude

For each of the following sentences, choose the italicized synonym that seems to connote the most appropriate and precise shade of meaning for the context.

**37b**

*ex*

1. The first grader's parents told him not to *tarry, dawdle, linger, lag* on the way to school.
2. The mayor had to resign after the *revelation, exposure, disclosure, divulgence* of her income tax evasion.
3. Because he was so *unskillful, incompetent, awkward, maladroit*, the juggler dropped all the plates the first time he tried to juggle them.
4. The mountain climber showed much *obstinacy, tenacity, perseverance, resolution* as he spent ten days climbing the snow-covered cliffs.
5. Wondering if they would ever get home, the dinner guests spent an hour and a half listening to the speech of the *garrulous, chatty, fluent, glib* guest of honor.

---

## 37b Derogatory references to sex, race, ethnicity, or religion are both inaccurate and offensive.

Language that relies on stereotypes as do derogatory terms and language with negative connotations referring to women or men or members of racial, ethnic, religious, or other groups—is both inappropriate and inaccurate. Broad-brush stereotypes—for example, that men are insensitive, women prone to hysteria, or Scots tight with their money—will reveal your thinking and your writing to be based on biased, insupportable generalizations. Make sure that the language you choose does not reflect these types of narrow-minded, offensive biases.

The reasons for the nonsexist use of personal pronouns have been discussed elsewhere in this book (see **Section 8c**). But eliminating sexist language from your writing involves more than removing common-gender pronoun references. You need to be sure that you refer to men and women in the same way when the circumstances are similar. For example, two faculty members in the biology department should be referred to as Professor Winston and Professor Levitz, not Professor Winston and Mrs. Levitz. The two poets Richard Wilbur and Sylvia Plath should be referred to as Wilbur and Plath (once their full names have been given), not as Wilbur and Sylvia (or Miss Plath or Mrs. Hughes).

Be aware, also, that professions and occupations once viewed as typically male or typically female now usually employ both sexes. Do not use terms like *nurse* and *doctor* in ways that suggest nurses are always women and doctors always men, for instance. Our language is changing to reflect the awareness that stereotypes are usually inaccurate and frequently discriminatory or demeaning. *Police officer* instead of *policeman, mail carrier* instead of *mailman,* and *flight attendant* instead of *stewardess* are words that have gained widespread use as people come to terms with sexism both as a habit of mind and as a habit of language.

**37c**

*ex*

---

EXERCISE 37b
Put together a list of words that show how standard English is reflecting elimination of stereotyping. Be ready to discuss whether you think the new or preferred term is accurate and/or justified.

---

**37c**  Be careful not to confuse words that have similar sound or spelling but different forms or meanings.

Some words are **homonyms;** that is, they have the same pronunciation but different meanings and different spellings (*idol, idle, idyll; aid, aide; aisle, isle*). Other words are sufficiently similar in sound and spelling to be confusing *(marital, martial).* Treat all these words as you would any other unfamiliar term: learn the correct spelling and meaning of each as an individual word.

Many words have two, sometimes three, adjectival forms, each having a distinct meaning: for example, a *changeable* personality, a *changing* personality, a *changed* personality. A roommate whom you *like* is not necessarily a *likeable* roommate, nor is a *matter of agreement* necessarily an *agreeable matter.* Be careful not to substitute one form for the other.

| UNACCEPTABLE | The cook served our *favorable* dessert. |
| ACCEPTABLE | The cook served our *favorite* dessert. |
| UNACCEPTABLE | He is a good student; he has a *questionable* mind. |
| ACCEPTABLE | He is a good student; he has a *questioning* mind. |

## EXERCISE 37c
What are the differences in meaning in each of the following pairs of words?

1. accept, except
2. affect, effect
3. elude, allude
4. credible, creditable
5. discreet, discrete
6. flaunt, flout
7. illicit, elicit
8. mitigate, militate
9. moral, morale
10. ordinance, ordnance
11. principle, principal
12. populace, populous

13. an *ingenious* person
    an *ingenuous* person
14. a *distinctive* book
    a *distinguished* book
15. an *effective* plan
    an *efficient* plan
16. an *imaginary* friend
    an *imaginative* friend
17. a *laudable* speech
    a *laudatory* speech
18. a *masterly* performance
    a *masterful* performance
19. an *ornate* table
    an *ornamental* table
20. a *valuable* painting
    a *valued* painting

## 37d  Invented words tend to confuse meaning.

A **coined word** is a new and outright creation (like *gobbledygook, blurb*). A **neologism** is either a new word or a new use of an old word or words (like travel agents' *package tours* or the traffic department's *gridlock*). A **nonce-word,** literally **once-word,** is a word made up to suit a special situation and generally not used more than once ("My son," he said, "suffers from an acute case of televisionitis"). Though most neologisms and nonce-words are short-lived, they are among the ways by which new words and new functions for old words are constantly working their way into a changing language. *Motel,* for example, an invented word formed from *motor* and *hotel,* is now a permanent fixture in our language.

English is relatively free in shifting words from one part of speech to another. This process, called **functional shift,** is one of the many ways in which our language grows. The noun *iron* is used as an adjective in *iron bar,* and as a verb in *iron the shirts.* The space age has given us *All systems are go,* using the verb *go* as a modifier. *River, paper,* and *tennis* are clearly nouns in form, but we commonly use them as modifiers in *river bank, paper bag,* and *tennis elbow.*

But the fact that such changes are common in English does not mean that there are no constraints on functional shift. In *The jury opinioned that the defendant was guilty, opinion* is used as a verb, a grammatical function to which it is entirely unaccustomed. The meaning may be clear, but the use is not accepted. We *punish* a person. There is perhaps no good reason why we should not speak of *a punish*, but we don't: if we want a noun, we use *punishment*. Advertisers talk about *winterizing* our cars with antifreeze and snow tires, but most of us draw the line at *skiierizing* our automobiles with the addition of a ski rack.

Devote most of your attention to learning and using words whose meanings are already established by usage. Invented words probably confuse readers and obscure meaning more often than they succeed. Still, don't be afraid to try a new coinage if it seems to suit your purpose and audience. Do be careful, however, to avoid unintentional inventions—words that you "invent" because of spelling errors *(disallusion* for *disillusion)* or an inexact knowledge of word forms and functions *(understandment* for *understanding)*. If you have any doubt about the accepted grammatical functions of a word, consult your dictionary.

---

**37e**

**ex**

### EXERCISE 37d
Correct the italicized words that seem to you needlessly invented. When necessary, check your dictionary to determine whether a particular word is an accepted form as used.

1. The *pathetical* sight of the burned house caused *despairment* to its owners.
2. The legislators were concerned about how the tax increase would *impact* on the average citizen.
3. We decided to *bike* through the countryside, but the *uncertainment* of the weather caused us to delay our trip.
4. The *illiterateness* of a significant number of the population worries educators and has *prompted* them to emphasize reading instruction.
5. The child had a *perplexical* look on his face as he asked his father what seemed like *unnumerable* questions about nature.

---

## 37e Follow accepted usage for idioms that include prepositions.

An **idiom** is an expression that does not follow the normal pattern of the language or that has a total meaning not suggested by its separate words: *to catch fire, strike a bargain, ride it out, lose one's head, hold the bag.** Such expressions are a part of the vocabulary of native speakers. In fact, we learn them in the same way we learn new

*The term *idiom* is also used to mean the characteristic expression or pattern of a dialect or language. In this sense of the word, we can speak of the *idiom* of speakers from South Boston, or we can compare English *idiom* with German or French.

words—by hearing them in the speech around us and by reading them in context. For the most part they give no more, and no less, difficulty than vocabulary itself gives us. Dictionaries usually give the common idiomatic expressions at the end of the definition of a word entry. Usage dictionaries, such as those listed in Section **35a[3]**, also provide detailed information about using idioms.

For many writers the most troublesome idioms in English are those that require a particular preposition after a given verb or adjective according to the meaning intended. The following list contains a number of such combinations that frequently cause trouble.

| | |
|---|---|
| ABSOLVED BY, FROM | I was *absolved by* the dean *from* all blame. |
| ACCEDE TO | He *acceded to* his father's demands. |
| ACCOMPANY BY, WITH | I was *accompanied by* several advisors. |
| | The terms were *accompanied with* a plea for immediate peace. |
| ACQUITTED OF | He was *acquitted of* the crime. |
| ADAPTED TO, FROM | This machine can be *adapted to* farm work. |
| | The design was *adapted from* a previous invention. |
| ADMIT TO, OF | The clerk *admitted to* the error. |
| | The plan will *admit of* no alternative. |
| AGREE TO, WITH, IN | They *agreed to* the plan but *disagreed with* us. |
| | They *agreed* only *in* principle. |
| ANGRY WITH, AT | She was *angry with* me and *angry at* the treatment she had received. |
| CAPABLE OF | This paint is *capable of* withstanding vigorous scrubbing. |
| CHARGE FOR, WITH | I expected to be *charged for* my purchase, but I didn't expect to be *charged with* stealing something. |
| COMPARE TO, WITH | He *compared* the roundness of the baseball *to* that of the earth. [to liken] |
| | He *compared* the fuel economy of the Ford *with* that of the Plymouth. [to examine for resemblances and differences] |
| CONCUR WITH, IN | We *concur with* you *in* your desire to use the revised edition. |
| CONFIDE IN, TO | My friend *confided in* me. She *confided to* me that she was interviewing for another job. |
| CONFORM TO, WITH | The specification *conformed to* (or *with*) the architect's original plans. |
| CONFORMITY WITH | You must act in *conformity with* our rules. |
| CONNECT BY, WITH | The rooms are *connected by* a corridor. |
| | That doctor is officially *connected with* this hospital. |

**37e**

*ex*

| | |
|---|---|
| CONTEND FOR, WITH | Because she needed to *contend for* her principles, she found herself *contending with* her parents. |
| DIFFER ABOUT, FROM, WITH | We *differ about* our tastes in clothes. My clothes *differ from* yours. We *differ with* one another. |
| DIFFERENT FROM* | Our grading system is *different from* yours. |
| ENTER INTO, ON, UPON | She *entered into* a new agreement and thereby *entered on* (or *upon†*) a new career. |
| FREE FROM, OF | The children were *freed from* the classroom and now are *free of* their teachers for the summer. |
| IDENTICAL WITH | Your reasons are *identical with* ours. |
| JOIN IN, WITH, TO | He *joined in* the fun *with* the others. |
| | He *joined* the wire cables *to* each other. |
| LIVE AT, IN, ON | The Wamplers *live at* 14 Neil Avenue and *live in* a Dutch colonial house. They *live on* Neil Avenue. |
| NECESSITY FOR, OF NEED FOR, OF | There was no *necessity (need) for* you to lose your temper. There was no *necessity (need) of* your losing your temper. |
| OBJECT TO | I *object to* the statement in the third paragraph. |
| OBLIVIOUS OF | When he held her hand he was *oblivious of* the passing of time. |
| OVERCOME BY, WITH | I was *overcome by* the heat. I was *overcome with* grief. |
| PARALLEL BETWEEN, TO, WITH | There is often a *parallel between* fantasy and reality. This line is *parallel to* (or *with*) that one. |
| PREFERABLE TO | A leisurely walk is *preferable to* no exercise at all. |
| REASON WITH, ABOUT | Why not *reason with* them? Why not *reason about* the matter? |
| REWARD BY, WITH, FOR | They were *rewarded by* their employer *with* a raise *for* their work. |
| VARIANCE WITH | This conclusion is at *variance with* your facts. |
| VARY FROM, IN, WITH | The houses *vary from* one another. They *vary in* size. |
| | People's tastes *vary with* their personalities. |
| WAIT FOR, ON | They *waited for* someone to *wait on* them. |
| WORTHY OF | That candidate is *worthy of* our respect. |

---

## EXERCISE 37e
Provide the idiomatic expressions needed in the following sentences and paragraph.

*\*Different than* is colloquially idiomatic when the object of the prepositional phrase is a clause:

FORMAL    This town looks *different from* what I had remembered.

COLLOQUIAL    This town looks *different than* I had remembered it.

†In many phrases, *on* and *upon* are interchangeable: *depend on* or *depend upon; enter on* or *enter upon.*

37e
ex

**SENTENCE PRACTICE**

1. Some people are hesitant to enter _____ the spirit of adventure and try new or unusual foods.

2. In fact, many people object _____ any food that is not familiar; these people are hard to reason _____, for they're adamant that they would never try something like fried squid or goose liver.

3. These picky eaters seem oblivious _____ the possibilities of discovering new foods because they feel their old favorites like meat and potatoes are preferable _____ something exotic like goat meat stew.

4. Actually, people who never vary _____ their standard dishes are missing a lot, for if they would only agree _____ trying an unusual food like squid, they might find they like it.

5. Those diners who are capable _____ putting aside their qualms about eating unusual foods are usually rewarded _____ a tasty experience.

**PARAGRAPH PRACTICE**

When my Japanese friend invited me to have dinner at a sushi restaurant, I had to admit _____ almost total ignorance about sushi. I told my friend that I thought sushi was identical _____ raw fish; when my friend heard that, she laughed and confided _____ me that most westerners make the same mistake. In fact, she said, in Japan raw fish is called sashimi, and sashimi is different _____ sushi in many ways. To the Japanese, sushi refers to vinegared rice. Perhaps people get sushi and sashimi confused because sashimi is normally accompanied _____ sushi when the dish is served. After my friend had made clear to me how sushi varies _____ sashimi, we joined _____ a wonderful feast of sushi and sashimi _____ several other friends.

**37f**

**ex**

## 37f Concrete and specific words contribute exactness to abstract and general language.

**Abstract words** name qualities, ideas, concepts: *honesty, virtue, poverty, education, wisdom, love, democracy.* **Concrete words** name things we can see, hear, feel, touch, smell. *Sweetness* is abstract; *candy, honey, molasses,* and *sugar* are concrete. To describe people as *reckless* is to describe them abstractly; to say *they ran two traffic lights in the center of town and drove eighty-five miles an hour in a restricted zone* is to pin that recklessness down, to make it concrete.

**General words** refer to all members of a class or group. **Specific words** refer to the individual members of a class. *Vegetation* is general; *grass, shrubs, trees, flowers,* and *weeds* are specific. *Animal* is general; *lions, elephants, monkeys, zebras, cats, dogs, mice,* and *rabbits* are specific.

The classes abstract and concrete, and general and specific over-

**316** WORDS

lap with each other, and both are relative. The verb *communicate* is both abstract and general. *Speak* is concrete and specific relative to *communicate*, but it is general compared to *gasp, murmur, rant, rave, shout,* and *whisper*. *Music* is concrete and specific relative to *sound* but general compared to *classical music,* which in turn is general compared to *Beethoven's Fifth Symphony. Dwelling* is a general word; *apartment, cabin, barracks, house, hut, mansion, shack,* and *tent* are specific. But *dwelling* is more specific than *building,* which includes not only *dwelling* but also *church, factory, garage, school,* and *store.*

All effective writing will use both abstract and concrete words, both general and specific. There are no substitutes for such abstractions as *fairness, friendship, love,* and *loyalty.* But all abstractions need to be pinned down by details, examples, and illustrations. When not so pinned down, they remain vague and always potentially confusing. We can all quickly agree that taxes and justice should be *fair.* But until each of us has narrowed down by detail and example what he or she means by *fairness* in these matters, we will not understand each other in any useful way.

Similarly, we cannot do without general terms. We would be hard-pressed to define *cat* if we could not begin by putting cats in the general class *animal.* But as soon as we have done so, we must then name the specific characteristics and qualities that distinguish cats from, say, armadillos or raccoons. To say *Tom enjoys reading* tells readers very little until we know whether the reading consists of *Sports Illustrated, People,* and *Masters of the Universe* or of Dickens and Dostoyevsky.

Effective writing constantly weaves back and forth between abstract and concrete, between general and specific. It is the writer's use of the abstract and general that guides the reader, but it is the concrete and specific that allow the reader to see, feel, understand, and believe. *This lamp supplies insufficient light* informs us; *this fifteen-watt bulb gives no more light than a firefly in a jam jar* makes us understand what the writer means by *insufficient.*

Whenever you use abstract words, give them meaning with concrete details and examples. Whenever you use general words, tie them down with specific ones. Try constantly to express yourself and your ideas in concrete terms; search for the most specific words you can find.

| | |
|---|---|
| GENERAL | The flowers were of different colors. |
| SPECIFIC | The chrysanthemums were bronze, gold, and white. |
| GENERAL | The cost of education has increased greatly. |
| SPECIFIC | Tuition at many private universities has increased as much as 1,000 percent in the past three decades. |
| MORE SPECIFIC | Tuition at Boston University was $300 in 1947; forty years later it was more than $10,000. |

SPECIFIC    Mateo was a stocky man, with clear eyes and a deeply tanned face. His skill as a marksman was extraordinary, even in Corsica, where everyone is a good shot. He could kill a ram at one hundred and twenty paces, and his aim was as accurate at night as in the daytime.

MORE SPECIFIC    Picture a small, sturdy man, with jet-black, curly hair, a Roman nose, thin lips, large piercing eyes, and a weather-beaten complexion. His skill as a marksman was extraordinary, even in this country, where everyone is a good shot. For instance, Mateo would never fire on a wild ram with small shot, but at a hundred and twenty paces he would bring it down with a bullet in its head or shoulder, just as he fancied. He used his rifle at night as easily as in the daytime, and I was given the following illustration of his skill, which may seem incredible, perhaps, to those who have never travelled in Corsica. He placed a lighted candle behind a piece of transparent paper as big as a plate, and aimed at it from eighty paces away. He extinguished the candle, and a moment later, in utter darkness, fired and pierced the paper three times out of four.

PROSPER MÉRIMÉE, *Mateo Falcone*

---

## EXERCISE 37f

Revise the following paragraph, supporting the generalizations and abstractions with concrete and specific details so that the meaning of the paragraph is clearer and the language more exact. Before you begin to revise, list the abstract or general words you think need sharper focus.

**37g**

***ex***

Recently my friend and I have been looking for a new place to live. We don't like our present place, so we have decided to find something that suits us better. We don't like the location of where we live now, our neighbors are too noisy, and we don't have enough room. Because of our financial situation, we have to find something fairly cheap, but we also want a bigger place and more conveniences. We'd also like to be closer to work and school. So far, we haven't seen anything we like, and we're worried that we may have trouble finding the right place. In fact, we're getting pretty anxious about the whole situation.

---

## 37g  Apt figurative language can increase exactness.

Like concrete and specific words, figurative language can help readers understand your ideas. The basis of most figurative language lies in the comparison or association of two things essentially different but nonetheless alike in some underlying and surprising way. Inexperienced writers sometimes think figurative language is the monopoly of poets and novelists. In fact, it plays an important part in much prose and is one of the most effective ways of making meaning concrete. Notice how the following passage uses figurative language to illustrate a point about consumer spending:

> Any significant business recovery has to have the consumer's support, because the consumer sector accounts for two-thirds of GNP [Gross National Product]. So far there is no solid support—consumer spending is not advancing. And for good reason: Consumer incomes are growing slowly. . . . So consumers are not exactly dragging their feet. They are dancing as fast as can be expected.
>
> *Business Week*

The two most common figures of speech are simile and metaphor. **Similes** make direct and explicit comparisons, usually introduced by *like, as, as if,* or *as when,* as in *Jess is as changeable as the New England weather.* **Metaphors** imply comparisons, as in *Prisoned in her laboratory, she ignored the world.* The figure of speech used in *Business Week* above is a metaphor that compares consumers to dancers in step with the slow growth in personal income.

Both simile and metaphor require that the two things compared be from different classes so that their likeness, when pointed out, will be fresh and surprising. The consumer–dancer metaphor accomplishes this goal because we do not usually think of consumers as dancers stepping to the tune of the economy. The image adds liveliness to the economic discussion and helps personify the generalization *consumers,* increasing our understanding of the relationship between spending and income. If similes and metaphors are extended they must also be consistent.

**37g**

**ex**

> Up scrambles the car, on all its four legs, like a black beetle straddling past the schoolhouse and the store down below, up the bare rock and over the changeless boulders, with a surge and a sickening lurch to the skybrim, where stands the foolish church.
>
> D. H. LAWRENCE, *Mornings in Mexico*

> Writing a story or a novel is one way of discovering *sequence* in experience. . . . Connections slowly emerge. Like distant landmarks you are approaching, cause and effect begin to align themselves, draw closer together. Experiences too indefinite of outline in themselves to be recognized for themselves connect and are identified as a larger shape. And suddenly a light is thrown back, as when your train makes a curve, showing that there has been a mountain of meaning rising behind you on the way you've come, is rising there still, proven now through retrospect.
>
> EUDORA WELTY, *One Writer's Beginnings*

In the foregoing passage, Eudora Welty compares meaning to a mountain and writing to a journey—specifically, a train trip—a simile she uses frequently in *One Writer's Beginnings*. Extended throughout the book is the metaphor of memory, and life itself, as a journey: "*The memory is a living thing—it too is in transit.*"

Apt figures of speech can do much to make writing concrete and vivid, and, by making one experience understandable in terms of another, they can often help clarify abstractions. But be careful when creating figures of speech; if they strain too hard, as in the first example below, they will miss their mark, falling flat or seeming too contrived. When two figures are *mixed* so that they create clashing images (sometimes called *mixed metaphors*), as in the final four examples, readers will not only miss your point, they will find your writing ludicrous.

Her smile was as warm as an electric blanket.

Does your life have to be on the rocks before you will turn over a new leaf?

She made her reputation as a big star early in her career, but she has been coasting on her laurels for the past ten years.

He held the false belief that in a capitalist democracy we can peer deep into the veil of the future and chain the ship of state to an exacting blueprint.

He [artist Thomas Hart Benton] was flat-out, lapel-grabbing vulgar, incapable of touching a pictorial sensation without pumping and tarting it up to the point where the eye wants to cry uncle.

*Time*

**37g**

**ex**

EXERCISE 37g(1)

Collect several examples of figurative language from newspapers and magazines. Look for some that are effective and some that are mixed metaphors. Identify what is being compared, what image is being created. Then analyze why the effective ones work and why the ridiculous ones do not. You can begin by practicing on the following paragraphs from the sports pages of a newspaper.

A Harvard team that could do no wrong upset a Yale team that did almost everything wrong today before a crowd of 59,263 in the Yale Bowl. This victory, by a 37–20 score, deprived the Bulldogs of an outright Ivy League championship. They had to share the title with Princeton, both finishing with 6–1 records.

For Harvard, there was the exquisite satisfaction of snatching a jewel away from its old rival and staining an otherwise respectable season. It was the fifth time since 1974 that a Harvard triumph in the finale took away from Yale either an outright or shared Ivy title.

EXERCISE 37g(2)

Replace the mixed or incongruous figures of speech in the following sentences and paragraph with more appropriate comparisons. Be prepared to explain why the original similes or metaphors are inappropriate.

**SENTENCE PRACTICE**
1. My neighbor was green with envy when he saw my new red sports car.
2. The children went limp with fear at the sight of the monster and then froze in horror as it let forth a gigantic roar.
3. My brother didn't like playing second fiddle to the leader of the clarinet section, so he dropped out of the band.
4. The president tried hard to steer the ship of state through the latest diplomatic crisis, but because of bad advice from his cabinet members, he had a hard row to hoe.
5. The sales director needed information about our earnings for the year, so she asked us for a ball park figure so that she could run it up the flagpole at the next budget meeting.

**PARAGRAPH PRACTICE**

The cook had egg on his face when the chocolate souffle he had prepared for the special dinner fell flat as a pancake. As if that weren't enough, he flipped his lid when he lifted the cover of the soup pot and discovered that he'd forgotten to turn on the heat under the pan. When he realized the soup was ice cold, the cook decided this dinner wasn't going to be a bowl of cherries. He knew he had failed the acid test when he mistakenly put too much vinegar in the salad dressing. He finally threw in the towel when he realized that even though the dinner was ruined, he'd still have to spend half the night cleaning up the kitchen.

**37h**

**ex**

## 37h  Trite expressions obscure meaning.

A trite expression, sometimes called a **cliché,** or a **stereotyped** or **hackneyed phrase,** is an expression that has been worn out by constant use, as *burning the midnight oil, Father Time, raving beauties, man about town.* Many trite expressions are examples of figurative language that once was fresh but has lost its power because we have heard it too often. Several of the metaphors and similes in Exercise 37g(2) are trite expressions: *flat as a pancake* and *threw in the towel,* for example.

Words in themselves are never trite—they are only used tritely. We cannot avoid trite expressions entirely, for they sometimes describe a situation accurately, capturing a writer's or speaker's intended meaning precisely. But such expressions can also be the crutch of a lazy thinker who chooses the worn cliché rather than searching for the exact words that will best express an idea.

> But when inflation came down last year and the lingering recession and a strong dollar forced even the wealthiest business executives and foreign travelers to pinch pennies, the financial feasibility of scores of new hotel projects went down the tubes.
>
> *Business Week*

The writer of the above example has chosen expressions that accurately capture the meaning. But the *pinch pennies* metaphor and the slang phrase *down the tubes* have been so overworked that they cease to be effective. Together these expressions create a mixed image (pennies down the tubes) that is likely to strike many readers as funny—probably not the effect the writer intended.

What is your estimate of the person who wrote this?

> A college education develops a *well-rounded personality* and gives the student an appreciation for *the finer things of life*. When he or she finally graduates and leaves *the ivory tower* to *play in the game of life,* the student will also have the necessary *tools of the trade.*

This writer's language suggests that her thinking is not only trite but imprecise as well. The expressions *well-rounded personality* and *finer things of life,* for example, are so abstract and vague that readers will surely wonder just what, exactly, the writer means.

Effectively used, triteness can be consciously humorous. The string of trite expressions in the example below explodes into absurdity when the writer deliberately transposes the words in the two clichés in the last clause.

> A pair of pigeons were cooing gently directly beneath my window; two squirrels plighted their troth in a branch overhead; at the corner a handsome member of New York's finest twirled his night stick and cast roguish glances at the saucy-eyed flower vendor. The scene could have been staged only by a Lubitsch; in fact Lubitsch himself was seated on a bench across the street, smoking a cucumber and looking as cool as a cigar.

> S. J. PERELMAN, *Keep It Crisp*

**37h**

*ex*

---

EXERCISE 37h

Identify all the clichés in the following passage. Then revise the passage, eliminating those expressions you think are too hackneyed to be effective and substituting fresher, more meaningful language.

> When I decided at long last to have a party and invite all my friends, I was determined to go the whole nine yards and do it up big. Because my house was a real disaster area, I worked for a week to get the place shipshape. I also slaved over a hot stove for several days so that the food would be first rate. The day before the party, I bought beer and soft drinks so that my friends could eat, drink, and be merry. Finally, I asked several friends to bring their favorite records and tapes so that we could dance the night away. Little did I think when I was making all these preparations that the roof might fall in. First, it was raining cats and dogs the night of the party, and all the guests arrived looking like drowned rats. My friends forgot to bring their records and tapes, so we all sat around staring at the

ceiling. The food was the only bright spot in the evening, so at least
I hit a home run in that area. When the evening was over, I
breathed a big sigh of relief. I've decided that you live and learn,
and I've learned that giving parties may not be my cup of tea.

# 38

## DIRECTNESS

The challenge to directness comes from two fronts—wordiness
and vagueness. A wordy writer uses more words than are necessary to
convey meaning; a vague writer fails to convey meaning sharply and
clearly. Wordiness and vagueness are found together so often as to be
nearly indistinguishable, as the following example shows:

WORDY AND VAGUE   He attacks the practice of making a profitable business out of college athletics from the standpoint
that it has a detrimental and harmful influence on
the college student and, to a certain degree and extent, on the colleges and universities themselves.

IMPROVED   He attacks commercialization of college athletics as
harmful to the students and even to the universities
themselves.

Sometimes wordiness is just awkwardness; the meaning is clear, but
the expression is clumsy.

AWKWARD   The notion that present-day Quakers wear flat-brimmed
dark hats or black bonnets and long dresses is a very
common notion.

IMPROVED   Many people think that present-day Quakers wear flat-
brimmed dark hats or black bonnets and long dresses.

Wordiness and vagueness obscure meaning. Your goal as a
writer should be to say things as directly and economically as possible
without sacrificing clarity and completeness. Readers are always grateful for writing that is concise, that makes every word count. The following sections discuss ways to spot and eliminate wordiness and
vagueness in your writing.

### 38a  Wordy writing wastes readers' time and contributes nothing to meaning.

Constructions that contribute to wordiness often appear in clusters. Where you find one sort, you are likely to find another. Two that
frequently appear as a pair are **nominals** and **weak verbs**. Other con-

**38**
**dir**

tributors to wordiness are **roundabout constructions, unnecessary phrases and clauses, redundancy,** and **awkward repetition.**

**1. Nominals.** Nominals are nouns created by adding suffixes to verbs: *establishment, completion, deliverance.* While there is certainly nothing wrong with these words, using unnecessary nominals in your writing tends to make it ponderous and slow-moving. The reason is that the verb, the word that conveys action in the sentence, has been transformed into a noun, an object. Learn to spot nominal suffixes such as *-ment, -tion, -ance* (also sometimes *-ity, -ize, -ness*) in your writing and to change unnecessary nominals back into verbs. Your sentences will be shorter and more vigorous.

| | |
|---|---|
| **WORDY NOMINALS** | Strict *enforcement* of the speed limit by the police will cause a *reduction* in traffic fatalities. |
| REVISED | If the police strictly enforce the speed limit, traffic fatalities will be reduced. |

**2. Weak verbs.** Vague, weak verbs such as *make, give,* and *take* often occur in combination with nominals as replacements for the stronger, more energetic verbs that have been changed into nouns. Another weak verb form, the passive-voice verb, also lengthens sentences and reduces vigor because it involves things being *done to* rather than things *doing.* Consequently, a sentence using a passive-voice verb requires a prepositional phrase to identify the agent, or *doer* of the action. Your writing will be less wordy if you choose specific, concrete, active-voice verbs.

**38a**

*dir*

| | |
|---|---|
| **WEAK VERB** | At the next meeting, the city council *will take* the firefighters' request for a raise under consideration. |
| REVISED | At the next meeting, the city council will consider the firefighters' request for a raise. |
| **PASSIVE VOICE** | A decision *was reached* by the council members to amend the zoning laws. |
| REVISED | The council members reached a decision to amend the zoning laws. |
| | The council members decided to amend the zoning laws. |

**3. Roundabout constructions.** Indirect and circuitous wording annoys readers and wastes their time because it detracts from quick, clear understanding of your meaning. As you revise your writing, you will often be able to strike out obviously unnecessary words or gain directness with slight changes. Words such as *angle, aspect, factor,* and *situation,* and phrases such as *in the case of, in the line of, in the field of* are almost never necessary and are common obstacles to directness.

| WORDY | I am majoring in the field of biology. |
|---|---|
| REVISED | I am majoring in biology. |

| WORDY | Another aspect of the situation that needs to be examined is the matter of advertising. |
|---|---|
| REVISED | We should also examine advertising. |

Expletives *(there is, there are, it is, it was)* frequently add unnecessary words and weaken the emphasis on a sentence's true subject. (See Section **33c**.) Your sentence may be more effective if you simply begin with the true subject. In other instances, a one-word modifier may convey meaning more economically.

| WORDY | There were fourteen people in attendance at the meeting. |
|---|---|
| REVISED | Fourteen people attended the meeting. |

| WORDY | It is apparent that we can't agree. |
|---|---|
| REVISED | Apparently, we can't agree. |

Weak and wordy constructions such as *because of the fact that, it was shown that,* and *with regard to* can often be reduced to a single word or eliminated.

**38a**

*dir*

| WORDY | Due to the fact that the plane was late, I missed my connecting flight to San Antonio. |
|---|---|
| REVISED | Because the plane was late, I missed my connecting flight to San Antonio. |

| WORDY | With regard to the luggage, the airline will deliver it to our hotel this afternoon. |
|---|---|
| REVISED | The airline will deliver the luggage to our hotel this afternoon. |

**4. Unnecessary phrases and clauses.** Wordiness often results from using a clause when a phrase will do, or a phrase when a single word will do. Needless constructions waste readers' time and lengthen sentences without adding meaning. Learn to spot such constructions, especially several piled together. Where appropriate, try reducing clauses to participial or appositive phrases or to single-word or compound modifiers. Try reducing phrases to single-word or compound modifiers, verbals (verb root plus *-ing*), or possessives with *-'s;* or leave them out if they don't contribute to meaning.

| WORDY | This shirt, *which is made of wool,* has worn well for eight years. |
|---|---|
| REVISED | This *woolen* shirt has worn well for eight years. [The meaning of the wordy clause *which is made of wool* is con- |

veyed as accurately, and more economically, by *woolen,*
a single-word modifier.]

**WORDY**    The football captain, *who is an All-American player,*
played his last game today.

REVISED    The football captain, *an All-American,* played his last
game today. [The meaning of the clause modifying *captain* is more economically expressed as an appositive
phrase.]

**WORDY**    The conclusions *that the committee of students* reached are
summarized in the newspaper *of the college that was published today.*

REVISED    The conclusions *reached by the student committee* are summarized in *today's college newspaper.* [One-word modifiers
*(student, college),* a possessive *(today's),* and a participle
*(reached)* have replaced wordy clauses and phrases.]

**5. Redundancy.** Expressions such as *I saw it with my own eyes* and
*audible to our ears* are **redundant;** they say the same thing twice. Re-
dundancies don't clarify or emphasize; they just sound stupid—especially ones with words that are already absolute and cannot logically
be further qualified *(unique, perfect, dead,* for example). Typical examples include the following:

| *Redundant* | *Direct* |
|---|---|
| advance forward | advance |
| continue on | continue |
| completely eliminate | eliminate |
| refer back | refer |
| repeat again | repeat |
| combine together | combine |
| circle around | circle |
| close proximity | close |
| few in number | few |
| cheaper in cost | cheaper, less costly |
| disappear from view | disappear |
| past history | history, the past |
| important essentials | essentials |

**38a**

*dir*

Sometimes sentences become wordy through a writer's careless repetition of the same meaning in slightly different words.

**WORDY**    As a rule, I usually wake up early.
REVISED    I usually wake up early.

**WORDY**    In their opinion, they think they are right.
REVISED    They think they are right.

**WORDY**    After the close of the office at 5 P.M. this afternoon,
Jones's farewell party will begin.

REVISED   After the office closes at 5 P.M., Jones's farewell party will begin.

WORDY   She is attractive in appearance, but she is a rather selfish person.

REVISED   She is attractive but rather selfish.

Similarly, some expressions are simply redundant or roundabout ways of saying things that could be stated in a single, precise word.

| *Wordy* | *Direct* |
| --- | --- |
| call up on the telephone | telephone |
| this day and age | today |
| of an indefinite nature | indefinite |
| at this point in time | now, today |
| by means of | by |
| destroy by fire | burn |
| at all times | always |
| in the near future | soon |

**6. Awkward repetition.** Repetition of important words can be a useful way of gaining emphasis and coherence in your writing (see Section **42d**), but careless repetition is awkward and wordy.

**38a**

*dir*

AWKWARD   The investigation revealed that the *average teachers teaching* industrial arts in California have an *average* working and *teaching* experience of five years.

REVISED   The investigation revealed that industrial arts teachers in California have an average of five years' experience.

AWKWARD   Gas mileage of American cars is being *improved* constantly in order to *improve* efficiency.

REVISED   Gas mileage of American cars is being improved constantly to increase efficiency.

---

EXERCISE 38a(1)
Revise the following sentences and paragraph to reduce wordiness.

SENTENCE PRACTICE
1. The establishment of a new supply system to supply the university's offices with paper needs to be instituted.
2. Due to the fact that delivery trucks are fewer in number than in past years, we don't have enough trucks to deliver supplies each week.
3. At this point in time, some offices run out of paper by the end of the working week, and then they call us on the telephone and complain.
4. In fact, one office manager called yesterday and said that if we didn't make delivery of paper to the Sociology Department in the near future, they wouldn't be able to copy the final exams on the copying machine.

5. We have issued a report to all university departments, reporting to them that our future goal is the implementation of a successful new paper delivery system.

**PARAGRAPH PRACTICE**

    I was late yesterday morning, so I had to run hurriedly down the street in order to get to the bus stop on time. There were a dozen other people standing there waiting for the bus at the bus stop when I arrived there. We waited for at least half an hour more for the bus to make its appearance, and it's my personal opinion that buses should be more prompt in arriving on time. As a result of the bus arriving so late, I arrived late at my office and missed the staff meeting we have every morning. My boss told me that in the event that I repeat my lateness again, I might face future problems keeping my employment at my present job.

EXERCISE 38a(2)
Revise the following paragraph to eliminate wordiness and awkwardness.

    Yesterday, a date was decided upon by our committee for our annual picnic we hold once a year. There were fourteen members of the committee present at the meeting, and all the members of the committee voted unanimously to hold the picnic on June 15. To have a successful picnic, it is very essential to have funds in the amount of $250.00. At this particular point in time, we have a budget of $50.00, so the creation of money-making projects was a vital necessity for the committee. If past history is any indication of ways we can succesfully make money, we should have a bake sale or a raffle, for those kinds of events have been successful in past years. We held a discussion for one hour, and after sixty minutes, a decision was made to have weekly bake sales to make money for the picnic. The chairman of the committee said he was sure we could earn enough money by means of the bake sales and that we would want to meet again in the near future to discuss final plans for the picnic.

**38b**
*dir*

## 38b Vague, pretentious, artificial diction obscures meaning.

    Journalist Edwin Newman, well known for his writing about the English language, has noted that "direct and precise language, if people could be persuaded to try it, would    help to substitute facts for bluster . . . and it would promote the practice of organized thought and even of occasional silence, which would be an immeasurable blessing." Never be ashamed to express an idea in simple, direct language. Complicated, pretentious, artificial language is not a sign of superior intelligence or writing skill. If alternative forms of the same word exist, use the shorter. Choose *truth* and *virtue* over *truthfulness* and *virtuousness*. Choose *preventive* rather than *preventative*.

    As many of the examples in Section **38a** illustrated, wordy language is frequently also pretentious language; diction becomes more elaborate, showy, and self-conscious than the subject requires. Vague, abstract terms and euphemisms are other characteristics of pretentious language. Instead of *we decided against it,* someone writes *we have assumed a negative posture on the matter*—as if these words were better than simply saying no.

We all are familiar with this kind of diction—the pompous language of many government documents, military reports, scholarly articles, and business executives' defenses of a poor product or unprofitable year. Pretentious diction is all too frequently a means of disguising the truth rather than revealing it. Instead of admitting he wants to raise taxes, the President talks about "revenue enhancement." Rather than a press office, the Environmental Protection Agency has an "Office of Public Awareness." The military refers to a bombing raid as a "protective reaction strike," and the MX missile is named "the Peacekeeper." Instead of saying "You're fired," the boss explains that an employee is "the next candidate for staff reduction." Even when such language is meant to convey information honestly, we react negatively because we are used to associating it with bureaucratic smokescreens. It's no wonder artificial diction of this type has come to be called *businessese, bureaucratese, gobbledygook,* and *bafflegab.* In his novel *1984,* George Orwell termed such doubletalk "Newspeak"—a language designed to supplant truth with vagueness. Following Orwell's lead, since 1974 the Committee on Public Doublespeak, a group affiliated with the National Council of Teachers of English, has presented annual Doublespeak Awards to public figures for language that is "grossly deceptive, evasive, euphemistic, confusing, or self-contradictory."

**38b**

*dir*

Preferring simplicity does not mean you must make *all* writing simple. Naturally, highly complex or technical subjects call at times for complex and technical language—the jargon and style appropriate to the subject and audience (see Section **36d**)—as the following passage illustrates.

> One of the simplest ways of evolving a favorable environment concurrently with the development of the individual organism, is that the influence of each organism on the environment should be favorable to the *endurance* of other organisms of the same type. Further, if the organism also favors *development* of other organisms of the same type, you have then obtained a mechanism of evolution adapted to produce the observed state of large multitudes of analogous entities, with high powers of endurance. For the environment automatically develops with the species, and the species with the environment.
>
> A. N. WHITEHEAD, *Science and the Modern World* [his italics]

Within the context of its subject, purpose, and audience, this passage is neither vague, pretentious, nor artificial. It conveys its meaning directly. On the other hand, the following examples are wordy and vague.

| | |
|---|---|
| ARTIFICIAL | Due to the fact that the outlet mechanism for the solid fuel appliance was obstructed by carbon, the edifice was consumed by fire. |
| DIRECT | Because the flue for the wood-burning stove was clogged with soot, the house burned down. |
| ARTIFICIAL | The athletic contest commenced at the stipulated time. |
| DIRECT | The game began on time. |
| ARTIFICIAL | It still looks favorable for beneficial crop moisture in central Indiana. |
| DIRECT | Chances for rain in central Indiana still look good. The soybeans could use a soaking. |

**Euphemisms,** words or phrases substituted for those that are, for some reason, objectionable, have their place in effective writing. They express unpleasant things in less harsh, less direct ways: *perspire* for *sweat, elderly* for *old, intoxicated* for *drunk.* Most common euphemisms are associated with the basic facts of existence—birth, age, death, sex, body functions—and often seem necessary for politeness or tact. We may be more comfortable describing a good friend as one who is *stout* and *likes to drink* rather than as a *fat drunk.* In such contexts these terms are harmless.

But using euphemisms to distract readers needlessly from the realities of work, unemployment, poverty, or war is at best misleading and at worst dishonest and dangerous. Today we take for granted terms such as "sanitation engineer" (garbage collector), "funeral director" (undertaker), and "maintenance staff" (janitors). Such terms perhaps help protect the feelings of individuals and give them status; but the individuals themselves still have to pick up garbage, prepare bodies for burial, and sweep floors—in short, do work that is hard or unpleasant. And if the terms make us forget that reality, they are misleading. It is but a short step to language consciously intended to deceive. Such language gives us "peace-keeping force" (military troops), "servicing the target" (killing the enemy), "strategic redeployment" (retreat), "visual surveillance" (spying), and "inoperative statements" (lies). Such phrases are downright dishonest, created for the sole purpose of distracting us from realities we need to know about. Slums and ghettos are no less slums and ghettos because a writer calls them the "inner city." And if you're fired, you're out of a job even if you've been "terminated" or "de-selected."

Keep your own writing honest and direct. Be alert to dishonesty and pretentiousness in the writing of others. Use euphemism if tact and genuine respect for the feelings of your audience warrant it, but

**38b**

*dir*

resist temptations to slide into artificial diction that veils, rather than conveys, meaning.

---

**EXERCISE 38b(1)**
Supply more direct words or phrases for the following euphemisms.

1. golden years
2. blessed event
3. interment
4. waste disposal facility
5. obsequies
6. correctional facility
7. powder room
8. indigent
9. substance abuse
10. preowned automobile
11. hairpiece
12. misspeak

---

**EXERCISE 38b(2)**
Find several examples of "gobbledygook" or pretentious, artificial diction in newspapers and magazines. Translate these into direct, natural language.

---

**EXERCISE 38b(3)**
Revise the following passage, substituting more direct, natural language for the wordy, artificial diction and unnecessary euphemisms.

**38b**

*dir*

> At the commencement of business this morning, it was discovered that the computer system at the banking facility was in a nonoperational mode. As a result of this negative situation, the bank manager had to establish a dialogue with the supervisor of the computer department in order to determine the most advantageous method of serving the bank's customers. After the termination of this meeting, the bank manager informed the tellers that in order to effect maximum efficiency of operation, they would be required to check each customer's account before issuing payment for a check. When plans for operating had been finalized, the manager said that it was her observation that, customerwise, the bank could operate in a productive posture until repair of the computer system could be implemented.

---

**WRITERS REVISING: EFFECTIVE WORDS**
*(continued from page 299)*

Ricky's instructor asked him to go over his paper with her. When he read the paper along with her, he saw his language problems were primarily wordiness and imprecise word choice.

## Ricky's Revision

```
        Dear Representative Maxey:
                    decades
R 1         For many, many years our state has          38a(5)

R 2     referred to itself as the ''Sportsman's

R 3     Paradise.'' This environmental turf, which

R 4     is our state, has longtime been a haven for

R 5     both hunters and fishermen to enjoy their
            respective
R 6     ∧pastimes respectfully. But Louisiana is       37c

R 7     presently in the wake of an enormous and       38a(5), 38b
            a great
R 8     tremendous∧environmental crisis which poses

R 9     potential harm for all of us citizens who      38a(4)

R10     live and work here and love our state          37h

R11     dearly. The only sure solution to this
                            clean
R12     crisis is to begin the cleaning∧up of our      38a(4)

R13     environment and to support sufficiently

R14     those state agencies which specialize in

R15     this area. With the establishment of the

R16     Department of Environmental Quality in

R17     1983, and under the guidelines of the 1980

R18     Environmental Affairs Act, we have a proper

R19     base to commence to begin saving our state.    38a(5)

R20     However, establishment is not enough.

R21     Instead of pinching pennies, We must           37h

R22     properly fund the DEQ to allow for this

R23     process to begin. Therefore, the

R24     legislature should push for increased

R25     general funding for the DEQ from our state.     38a(5)
```

**38b**

*dir*

## Analysis

In line R1, *decades* replaces the redundant *many, many years*. In line R6, the incorrect word *respectfully*, meaning "to show regard," is replaced by *respective,* meaning "relating to particular persons or things," to precede *pastimes.* In lines R7–8 the redundant *enormous and tremendous* is replaced by one word, *great.* In lines R9–11 the wordy *of us* and the trite expression *love our state dearly* are deleted. In line R12 two words, *clean up,* replace five. In line R19, the awkward and wordy *commence to* is deleted. Finally, the trite expression *pinching pennies* in line R21 is omitted, as is the redundant phrase *from our state* in line R25.

# 39

## *SPELLING*

Language existed first as speech, and the alphabet is basically a visual device to represent speech. When letters of the alphabet have definite values and are used consistently, as in Polish or Spanish, the spelling of a word is an accurate index to its pronunciation, and vice versa. Not so with English. The alphabet does not represent English sounds consistently. The letter *a* may stand for the sound of the vowel in *may, can, care,* or *car; c* for the initial consonant of *carry* or *city; th* for the diphthong in *both* or in *bother.* Different combinations of letters are often sounded alike, as in *rec(ei)ve, l(ea)ve,* or *p(ee)ve.* In many words, moreover, some letters appear to perform no function at all, as in *i(s)land, de(b)t, of(t)en, recei(p)t.* Finally, the relationship between the spelling and the pronunciation of some words seems downright capricious, as in *through, enough, colonel, right.*

Much of the inconsistency of English spelling may be explained historically. English spelling has been a poor index to pronunciation ever since the Norman conquest, when French scribes gave written English a French spelling. Subsequent tampering with English spelling has made it even more complex. Early classical scholars with a flair for etymology added the unvoiced *b* to early English *det* and *dout* because they mistakenly traced these words directly from the Latin *debitum* and *dubitum* when actually both the English and the Latin had derived independently from a common Indo-European origin. Dutch printers working in England were responsible for changing English *gost* to *ghost.* More complications arose when the pronunciation of many words changed more rapidly than their spelling. The *gh* in *right* and *through,* and in similar words, was once pronounced much like the German *ch* in *nicht. Colonel* was once pronounced *col-o-nel.* The final *e* in words like *wife* and *time* was long ago dropped from actual speech, but it still remains as a proper spelling form.

The complex history of the English language may help to explain why our spelling is illogical, but it does not justify misspelling. Society tends to equate bad spelling with incompetent writing. In fact, only the misspellings tend to be noticed, not the quality of the writing, and correct spellings sometimes render faulty constructions invisible.

## WRITERS REVISING: SPELLING

Janet's boss asked her to write a letter inviting customers to attend a barbecue sponsored by the company. Since she is a poor speller, Janet asked her office mate Sylvia to check her draft. Here is the first paragraph of the letter. Proof it for spelling errors and find the rules that apply in Section **39**; then check your proofreading against Sylvia's corrections, which appear at the end of this section.

**39**

*sp*

**Janet's Draft**

Dear Customer:

D 1      We are happy to announce that High Tech Photo

D 2    Industries will be haveing an employee/client

D 3    barbecue this year. We hope this barbecue will

D 4    become an anual event at H. T. We are getting

D 5    togather to show our appreciateion of you, the

D 6    customer, and to get to know you better.

D 7      There will be plenty of food and games, so

D 8    bring your family and come ready to have fun. You

D 9    can leave your breifcase at home, because this day

D10    will be devoted to haveing a good time—no business

D11    allowed!

D12      The barbecue will be held on Saturday, March

D13    25, begining at 2:00 p.m. The home of High Tech

D14    Photo Industries president, Johnny Miller, is the

D15    cite of the event.

This *Writers Revising* continues on page 341.

## 39a    Use preferred spellings.

Many words have a secondary spelling, generally British. Though the secondary spelling is not incorrect, you should use the spelling more widely accepted in our society, the American spelling. Here is a brief list of preferred and secondary spelling forms; consult a good dictionary for others.

*1. American e*
anemia
anesthetic
encyclopedia
fetus

*British ae, oe*
anaemia
anaesthetic
encyclopaedia
foetus

*2. American im-, in-*
impanel
incase
inquiry

*British em-, en-*
empanel
encase
enquiry

*3. American -ize*
apologize
civilization

*British -ise*
apologise
civilisation

*4. American -or*
armor
clamor
color
flavor
labor
odor
vigor

*British -our*
armour
clamour
colour
flavour
labour
odour
vigour

*5. American -er*
center
fiber
somber
theater

*British -re*
centre
fibre
sombre
theatre

*6. American o*
mold
plow
smolder

*British ou*
mould
plough
smoulder

*7. American -ction*
connection
inflection

*British -xion*
connexion
inflexion

*8. American l*
leveled
quarreled
traveled

*British ll*
levelled
quarrelled
travelled

*9. American e omitted*
acknowledgment
judgment

*British e*
acknowledgement
judgement

## 39b  Proofreading your manuscripts carefully helps eliminate misspelling.

In writing a first draft, you form words into sentences faster than you can write them down. You concentrate not on the words you are writing, but on the words to come. A few mistakes in spelling may easily creep into early drafts. Always take five or ten minutes to proofread your final draft for spelling errors.

Lack of proofreading accounts for the fact that the words most often misspelled are not, for example, *baccalaureate* and *connoisseur*, but *too, its, lose, receive, accommodate,* and *occurred.* Most of us think we can spell a familiar word. Either we never bother to check the spelling in a dictionary, or we assume that a word pictured correctly in our mind will automatically transfer to our writing. This thinking accounts for such errors as omitting the final *o* in *too,* confusing the possessive *its* with the contraction *it's,* and spelling *loose* when *lose* is meant. You will never forget how to spell *receive, accommodate, occurred* if you will devote just a few moments to memorizing their correct spellings.

## 39c  Careful pronunciation aids correct spelling.

Many words are commonly misspelled because they are mispronounced. The following list of frequently mispronounced words will help you overcome this source of spelling error.

| accident*al*ly | | note the *al* |
|---|---|---|
| accu*r*ate | | note the *u* |
| bus*i*ness | | note the *i* |
| can*d*idate | | note the first *d* |
| envir*on*ment | | note the *on* |
| Feb*r*uary | | note the *r* |
| gover*n*ment | | note the *n* |
| incident*al*ly | | note the *al* |
| libra*r*y | | note the *r* |
| math*e*matics | | note the *e* |
| proba*bl*y | | note the *ab* |
| quan*t*ity | | note the first *t* |
| represen*ta*tive | | note the *ta* |
| soph*o*more | | note the second *o* |
| su*r*prise | | note the first *r* |
| ath*l*etics | NOT | ath*e*letics |
| disas*tr*ous | NOT | disas*te*rous |
| heigh*t* | NOT | heigh*th* |
| gri*e*-vous | NOT | gre-*vi*-ous |
| ir-*rel*-e-*v*ant | NOT | ir-*rev*-e-*l*ant |
| mis-chi*e*-vous | NOT | mis-che-*vi*-ous |

However, pronunciation is not an infallible guide to correct spelling. Although, for example, the last syllables of *adviser, beggar,* and *doctor* are all pronounced as the same unstressed *ur,* they are spelled differently. Proceed cautiously when using pronunciation as a spelling aid, and check your dictionary whenever you doubt either your pronunciation or your spelling.

## 39d    Distinguish among the spellings of words that are similar in sound.

English abounds in **homonyms,** words whose sound is similar to that of other words but whose spelling is different: for example, *rain, rein, reign.* Some of the most troublesome homonyms are listed below.

*all ready:* everyone is ready
*already:* by this time

*all together:* as a group
*altogether:* entirely, completely

*altar:* a structure used in worship
*alter:* to change

*ascent:* climbing, a way sloping up
*assent:* agreement; to agree

*breath:* air taken into the lungs
*breathe:* to exhale and inhale

*capital:* chief; leading or governing city; wealth, resources
*capitol:* a building that houses the state or national lawmakers

*cite:* to use as an example, to quote
*site:* location

*clothes:* wearing apparel
*cloths:* two or more pieces of cloth

*complement:* that which completes; to supply a lack
*compliment:* praise, flattering remark; to praise

*corps:* a military group or unit
*corpse:* a dead body

*council:* an assembly of lawmakers
*counsel:* advice; one who advises; to give advice

*dairy:* a factory or farm engaged in milk production
*diary:* a daily record of experiences or observations

*descent:* a way sloping down
*dissent:* disagreement; to disagree

39d

*sp*

*dining:* eating
*dinning:* making a continuing noise

*dying:* ceasing to live
*dyeing:* process of coloring fabrics

*foreword:* a preface or introductory note
*forward:* at, near, or belonging to the front

*forth:* forward in place or space, onward in time
*fourth:* the ordinal equivalent of the number 4

*loose:* free from bonds
*lose:* to suffer a loss

*personal:* pertaining to a particular person; individual
*personnel:* body of persons employed in same work or service

*principal:* chief, most important; a school official; a capital sum (as distinguished from interest or profit)
*principle:* a belief, rule of conduct, or thought

*respectfully:* with respect
*respectively:* in order, in turn

*stationery:* writing paper
*stationary:* not moving

*their:* possessive form of *they*
*they're:* contraction of *they are*
*there:* adverb of place

*whose:* possessive form of *who*
*who's:* contraction of *who is*

*your:* possessive form of *you*
*you're:* contraction of *you are*

**39e** sp

**39e** Knowing spelling rules aids correct spelling.

**1. Distinguish between *ie* and *ei*.** Remember this jingle:

Write *i* before *e*
Except after *c*
Or when sounded like *a*
As in *eighty* and *sleigh*.

| *i before e* | *ei after c* | *ei when sounded like a* |
|---|---|---|
| thief | receive | weigh |
| believe | deceive | freight |
| wield | ceiling | vein |

Neither sovereigns nor financiers forfeit the height of their surfeit leisure to seize the weird counterfeits of feisty foreigners.

CHRISTOPHER W. BLACKWELL

**2. Drop the final e before a suffix beginning with a vowel but not before a suffix beginning with a consonant.**

**a. Suffix beginning with a vowel, final e dropped:**

```
please + ure  = pleasure
ride + ing    = riding
locate + ion  = location
guide + ance  = guidance
```

EXCEPTIONS:

In some words the final e is retained to prevent confusion with other words.

dyeing (to distinguish it from *dying*)

Final e is retained to keep c or g soft before a or o.

```
                notice + able  = noticeable
                change + able  = changeable
        BUT     practice + able = practicable (c has sound of k)
```

**b. Suffix beginning with a consonant, final e retained:**

```
sure + ly       = surely
arrange + ment  = arrangement
like + ness     = likeness
entire + ly     = entirely
entire + ty     = entirety
hate + ful      = hateful
```

EXCEPTIONS:

Some words taking the suffix -*ful* or -*ly* drop final e:

```
awe + ful = awful
due + ly  = duly
true + ly = truly
```

Some words taking the suffix -*ment* drop final e:

```
judge + ment       = judgment
acknowledge + ment = acknowledgment
```

**39e**

*sp*

The ordinal numbers of *five, nine,* and *twelve,* formed with *-th,* drop the final *e. Five* and *twelve* change *v* to *f.*

fifth      ninth      twelfth

**3. Final *y* is usually changed to *i* before a suffix, unless the suffix begins with *i.***

defy + ance   = *defiance*
forty + eth   = *fortieth*
ninety + eth  = *ninetieth*
rectify + er  = *rectifier*
BUT   cry + ing   = *crying* (suffix begins with *i*)

**4. A final single consonant is doubled before a suffix beginning with a vowel when (a) a single vowel precedes the consonant, and (b) the consonant ends an accented syllable or a one-syllable word. Unless both these conditions exist, the final consonant is not doubled.**

stop + ing   = *stopping* (*o* is a single vowel before consonant *p* which ends word of one syllable.)

admit + ed   = *admitted* (*i* is single vowel before consonant *t* which ends an accented syllable.)

stoop + ing  = *stooping* (*p* ends a word of one syllable but is preceded by double vowel *oo*.)

benefit + ed = *benefited* (*t* is preceded by a single vowel *i* but does not end the accented syllable.)

**39e**

*sp*

---

EXERCISE 39e(1)
Spell each of the following words correctly and explain what spelling rule applies. Note any exceptions to the rules.

| | | | |
|---|---|---|---|
| 1. delegate + ion | = ? | 9. omit + ed | = ? |
| 2. drop + ing | = ? | 10. qualify + er | = ? |
| 3. eighty + eth | = ? | 11. rake + ing | = ? |
| 4. fascinate + ion | = ? | 12. relate + ion | = ? |
| 5. hurry + ed | = ? | 13. score + ing | = ? |
| 6. knowledge + able | = ? | 14. believe + able | = ? |
| 7. lonely + ness | = ? | 15. compare + ing | = ? |
| 8. occur + ed | = ? | 16. comply + ance | = ? |

---

**5. Nouns ending in a sound that can be smoothly united with *-s* usually form their plurals by adding *-s*. Verbs ending in a sound that can be smoothly united with *-s* form their third person singular by adding *-s*.**

| Singular | Plural | Some Exceptions | | Verbs | |
|----------|--------|-----------------|---|-------|---|
| picture | pictures | buffalo | buffaloes | blacken | blackens |
| radio | radios | tomato | tomatoes | criticize | criticizes |
| flower | flowers | zero | zeroes | radiate | radiates |
| chair | chairs | | | | |
| ache | aches | | | | |
| fan | fans | | | | |

**6.** Nouns ending in a sound that cannot be smoothly united with -*s* form their plurals by adding *es*. Verbs ending in a sound that cannot be smoothly united with -*s* form their third person singular by adding -*es*.

| Singular | Plural | Verbs | |
|----------|--------|-------|---|
| porch | porches | pass | passes |
| bush | bushes | tax | taxes |

**7.** Nouns ending in *y* preceded by a consonant form their plurals by changing *y* to *i* and adding -*es*. Verbs ending in *y* preceded by a consonant form their third person singular in the same way.

| Singular | Plural | Verbs | |
|----------|--------|-------|---|
| nursery | nurseries | pity | pities |
| mercy | mercies | carry | carries |
| body | bodies | hurry | hurries |
| beauty | beauties | worry | worries |

EXCEPTIONS:

The plural of proper nouns ending in *y* is formed by adding -*s* (*There are three Marys in my history class*).

**8.** Nouns ending in *y* preceded by *a, e, o,* or *u* form their plurals by adding -*s* only. Verbs ending in *y* preceded by *a, e, o,* or *u* form their third person singular in the same way.

| Singular | Plural | Verbs | |
|----------|--------|-------|---|
| day | days | buy | buys |
| key | keys | enjoy | enjoys |
| guy | guys | | |

**9.** The spelling of plural nouns borrowed from French, Greek, and Latin frequently retains the plural of the original language.

| Singular | Plural |
|----------|--------|
| alumna (*feminine*) | alumnae |
| alumnus (*masculine*) | alumni |
| analysis | analyses |
| basis | bases |

**39e**

*sp*

| Singular | Plural |
|----------|--------|
| crisis | crises |
| criterion | criteria |
| datum | data |
| hypothesis | hypotheses |
| medium | media |
| phenomenon | phenomena |

The tendency now, however, is to give many such words an an-glicized plural. The result is that many words have two plural forms, one foreign, the other anglicized. Either is correct.

| Singular | Plural (foreign) | Plural (anglicized) |
|----------|------------------|---------------------|
| appendix | appendices | appendixes |
| chateau | chateaux | chateaus |
| focus | foci | focuses |
| index | indices | indexes |
| memorandum | memoranda | memorandums |
| radius | radii | radiuses |
| stadium | stadia | stadiums |

---

EXERCISE 39e(2)

Spell the plural of each of the following words correctly and explain what spelling rule applies. Note any exceptions to the rules.

1. accompany
2. booth
3. church
4. convey
5. cry
6. delay
7. gas
8. hero
9. luxury
10. pass
11. publicize
12. receive
13. rely
14. surprise
15. synopsis
16. try
17. transfix
18. use
19. valley
20. taco

**39f**

*sp*

---

**39f**  Spell compound words according to current usage.

Compound words usually progress by stages from being written as two words, to being hyphenated, to being written as one word: for example, *door mat, door-mat, doormat.* Since these stages often overlap, the correct spelling of a compound word may vary. For the current spelling of a compound, take the advice of a good dictionary. (For more examples and a discussion of the general use of the hyphen in compounds, see "Hyphen," Section **30.**)

---

**WRITERS REVISING: SPELLING**
*(continued from page 333)*

To speed up her proofing and insure that she looked at every word carefully, Sylvia read the letter backwards. Try this strategy for correcting Janet's spelling.

**Janet's Revision**

```
        Dear Customer:
```

R 1        We are happy to announce that High Tech

R 2    Photo Industries will be having an employee/        **39e(2a)**

R 3    client barbecue this year. We hope this

R 4    barbecue will become an annual event at H. T.

R 5    We are getting together to show our                 **39c**

R 6    appreciation of you, the customer, and to get       **39e(2a)**

R 7    to know you better.

R 8        There will be plenty of food and games,

R 9    so bring your family and come ready to have

R10    fun. You can leave your briefcase at home,          **39e(1)**

R11    because this day will be devoted to having a        **39e(2a)**

R12    good time—no business allowed!

R13        The barbecue will be held on Saturday,

R14    March 25, beginning at 2:00 p.m. The home of        **39e(4)**

R15    High Tech Photo Industries president, Johnny

R16    Miller, is the site of the event. . . .             **39d**

**Analysis**

In lines R2, R6, and R11, Janet fails to drop the final *e* before a suffix beginning with a vowel. In line R5 she probably misspelled *together* because she does not pronounce it carefully **(39c).** She reverses *ie* in misspelling *briefcase* **(39e).** On line R14, she fails to double the final consonant before a suffix beginning with a vowel in her spelling of *beginning* **[39e(4)].** Finally, she mistakes the homonym *cite* for *site* **(39d).**

**39f**

*sp*

---

REVIEW EXERCISES: WORDS (Sections 35–39)

PART A
Use your dictionary to help you answer the following questions.

1. What is the etymology of the word *virus?*
2. How many meanings can you find for the word *sack?*

3. What are some synonyms for the word *elegance?*
4. What are two homonyms for the word *you?*
5. What do the abbreviations EDT, i.e., and HMS mean?

## PART B

Rewrite the following sentences and paragraph, eliminating poor usage of slang, inappropriate words, clichés, euphemisms, needlessly invented words, incorrect idioms, vagueness and wordiness, mixed or incongruous metaphors, and misspellings.

### SENTENCE PRACTICE

1. The personal director of the manufacturing company said she was looking for a person to fill a management position: the right person would have a degree in computer science, would have knowledge of goverment regulations, and would have experience in the business world.
2. Niether of the first two canidates she interviewed had the right stuff, so she went back to square one and ran an ad in the newspaper.
3. The next person who came to apply for the job had been involuntarily terminated from his previous position.
4. The next applicant was very eager and enthusiastic about the job; she wanted to get on the fast track to success right away, but she didn't have any managerial experience.
5. Finally, just when the personal director was ready to throw in the towel, the perfect applicant arrived; this person had worked in a management position in a goverment agency for five years, had recieved a degree in computer science, and showed poise, good judgement, and enthusiasm in the job interview.

**39f**

*sp*

### PARAGRAPH PRACTICE

When I decided to take college classses at night, I knew I would have to have self-disipline since I also work full-time during the day. Nevertheless, I knew that if I wanted to climb the ladder of success, I had to dive right in and get to work on my degree. Now that I have been attending classes for a while, I'll agree to those people who told me that working full-time and going to school would effect my life. The biggest problem I have is time; when I think back to my life before I became a student, I realize I had every night to relax after work. Now I rush home, change cloths, grab a quick snack, and go to class. Sometimes, when I'm burning the midnight oil, I feel overwhelmed, but I tell myself to chill out because the attainment of a degree is worth the effort. My moral does get a little low at times also, but I always feel better when the semester is over, and I see what I have acheived.

# THE
# WRITING
# PROCESS

*Almost all Americans can read and write. Thus we seem to be equal. But very few Americans possess discipline in the habits of language necessary for its advantageous use, and those few who do effectively control the many who do not.*

ROBERT PATTISON, On Literacy: The Politics of the Word
from Homer to the Age of Rock

# 40

## PREPARING TO WRITE

To write well, you must first think critically about your topic and make a number of choices that will affect the written product. You need to think carefully not only about the end result—the words on the page—but also about *how* you get those words on the page. The *how* is known as the **writing process.** This chapter describes the writing process in its initial phases, examines many of the choices that precede actual writing, and shows the choices two writers, Tina Rodriguez and Brad Bolton, made as they started writing assignments.

### 40a An overview of the writing process.

By studying what writers think about and do when they write, researchers have learned that writing is a process involving a number of interrelated activities. These activities, or subprocesses, can be grouped under the general headings of **planning, drafting,** and **revising.**

#### 1. Planning

**a.** Generating ideas about the paper to be written. This activity is sometimes called "invention" or "the discovery process" because it helps writers find out what they know about a subject or need to learn about it before they write.

**b.** Creating goals for the paper and for the writing activity as a whole. Goals may be as global as "I want to convince my readers that geology is an exciting major" or as narrow as "I have too many topics in this paragraph; I need to focus it more." Plans and goals should respond to the needs that prompted the writing activity in the first place.

**c.** Grouping and organizing concepts and ideas. This activity helps the writer explore topics and think about possible ways to present them.

#### 2. Drafting

**a.** Making ideas visible and available to readers, whether on paper, on the computer screen, or through some other medium; using the brainstorming notes, outlines, or other results of planning activities to produce text.

**b.** Presenting your meaning in a form that is accessible and meaningful to your readers. This complex drafting activity involves everything from the physical act of shaping letters or making key strokes to the mental process of choosing words, forming sentences, arranging paragraphs, and structuring the organization of the document.

### 3. Revising

**a.** Rereading and evaluating your writing, either as it is being created or later, to test it against your plans and goals.

**b.** Changing your writing if your evaluation indicates that the changes will help you meet your goals. Revision may involve changes in meaning (the addition or deletion of information), changes in surface features (such as spelling and punctuation), or both.

Sometimes these activities seem to be **embedded** in one another, occurring almost simultaneously. For example, while *drafting* a sentence, writers may *reread* several previous sentences to help recall how they intended to develop an idea *(planning)*. Or, while thinking about how to conclude an essay *(planning)*, writers may try out several final sentences *(drafting)*, *evaluating* and crossing out false starts until they are satisfied with the thought and its expression.

Not only are the activities of the writing process embedded in one another, they are also **recursive**—they occur over and over as writers work their way toward a finished product. Writers change their plans, set new goals, and discover new ideas as they are reading for revision. The process of writing is *not* a straight line from planning through writing and revision. These activities can take place in any order, and again and again, as writers generate and test their words and ideas.

Through the remainder of this section and Section **41**, we will follow the writing process of two writers: Tina Rodriguez, an office employee who needs to let her coworkers know about an upcoming meeting; and Brad Bolton, a student who needs to write a personal experience essay for his English composition class. Read Tina's and Brad's rough drafts now, before continuing this section. They appear on pages 379 and 381–84 at the end of Section **41**.

### 40b  Make preliminary decisions.

Writers write from need—either their own internal motivation or external motivation from others, or both. The result is **text:** a personal diary, a memo to a coworker, a newspaper article, a poem, an essay exam, a legal brief, a Broadway play, and a lab report are all forms of text that orginated from someone's need for writing.

As you begin the activities that comprise the writing process, it is important that you think critically about the needs which motivated your writing in the first place, because you will he making writing decisions based on your "needs assessment." The following four questions will help you identify the fundamental needs to which your text should respond:

- **Audience:** Who will read this text? Will there be different readers with different needs?

- **Writer's role or voice:** Should the writer's personality be evident in the text? Which aspects?
- **Subject:** What should this text be about?
- **Purpose:** What will this text be used for? What is its aim or goal?

These questions are interrelated, so they can be addressed in any order. Start with the one you find easiest to answer. Also, remember the recursive nature of the writing process. As your writing progresses, you may make discoveries that cause you to redefine your audience, role, subject, or purpose.

## 40c   Analyze your audience.

Planning with your audience in mind will make your writing more effective. Try to picture your audience. What do you know about your readers? What do they know about you? About your subject? To communicate effectively, you will need to adjust your subject matter, your point of view, the kinds of details and explanations you use, even the words you choose to the audience for whom you are writing. In analyzing your readers, ask yourself such questions as

- What are the *common denominators?* What characteristics do I share with my readers: education, occupation, age, beliefs and attitudes, levels of knowledge about and interest in the subject? Are there any other factors that have a bearing on my assumptions about the common ground shared with my readers?
- What are the crucial *differences* between me and my readers? What steps will I need to take to overcome or minimize the effects of these differences? Will I need to define terms, use analogies, include more explanation or background, provide more evidence and examples, use a special tone? Are my readers likely to be sympathetic, hostile, or indifferent? How will that affect what I write?

The preceding questions will help you to decide whether you are writing for a specialized audience or a general audience and to shape your text appropriately.

**1. Specialized audiences.** These readers already know a good deal about a subject, so writers can take for granted a certain level of knowledge as well as the audience's interest in the subject. Attorneys who write articles for the *Harvard Law Review* do not have to define the legal terms they use: their readers, other attorneys, already know them.

What is true for the authors writing for specialized journals and magazines is true for you as well. The professor reading your political science paper, the friend reading your letter about a recent rock concert, and the insurance agent reading your inquiry about a medical bill all have expertise that makes them specialized audiences in the subjects you address to them. Tina Rodriguez, whose memos appear on pages 279–80 in Section **41**, has written for specialized readers, co-workers who are familiar with the company and its procedures. Thus, she does not have to explain "new staffing needs" or other business-related terms.

    **2. General audiences.** General readers may work in highly specialized professions and have many particular interests, but when they turn to general-interest publications such as *Ebony, Newsweek,* or *Sports Illustrated,* they expect to find articles in standard nontechnical language that can be easily understood, with definitions and explanations supplied for unfamiliar things. Writing aimed at the general reader assumes no special degree of knowledge about a subject or issue. These readers are like yourself; they wish to be informed without having to become experts in a subject to achieve a general understanding about it.

    Brad Bolton, whose essay appears at the end of Section **41**, decided to write about his experiences during a European summer exchange program. When he shifted from brainstorming in a letter to Judy, the leader of his exchange trip, to writing the essay for an audience of his college classmates, he found he needed to change his approach. Judy's familiarity with European travel and student exchange programs made her a specialized audience. On the other hand, Brad could not count on his English instructor and classmates having a similar background. Because they comprised a more general audience, he had to include more description and explanation in his essay.

---

**EXERCISE 40c**
Write three short letters in which you explain the reasons why you missed a final exam. Write the first letter to your instructor and explain your reasons and ask for a chance to make up the exam. Write the second letter to your parents explaining why you missed the exam and asking their understanding if your instructor does not let you make up the exam. Write the third letter to a friend you have known for a long time. Share your letters with a classmate, explaining the approach you used for each and what considerations about the audience played a role in your approach

---

**40d**   Choose an appropriate voice or role.

    **Voice** refers to the way we as writers "sound" to our readers, the way we present ourselves to our audience, the authorial role we have chosen. In many types of writing a scientific journal article on the moons of Saturn, for example, or a newspaper story about a train

**40d**

*plan*

wreck—the writer seems transparent, absent except as a channel for information. The facts are at the forefront. In other types of writing, the author's presence can be detected more strongly. We feel that someone is "speaking" to us, even if the writer is not using the *I* of the first person pronoun. As a contributing editor of *Smithsonian* magazine says, "A good writer is, above all, a voice, a distinctive voice that we recognize instantly, and sometimes a voice that can sound in the heart of memory."

Some of the things that help to create the voice in a piece of writing are as follows:

1. **Word choice.** Slang, jargon, standard or nonstandard language, formal or informal language, and figurative language all affect the way writing sounds to readers (see Sections **35–38**). Your task is to select the words that create the voice appropriate for your audience, purpose, and subject.

2. **Verbs.** Using either active-voice or passive-voice verbs can also influence whether the writing sounds lively and emphatic or dull and distant (see Section **33f**).

3. **Point of view.** Have you taken on the role of a writer who has an opinion on the subject about which you are writing, or are you simply a transmitter of information? Do you want to project the image of an authority or just an observer? Are you a participant in the situation about which you are writing? If so, does it make sense to use the first person pronoun *I,* or do you wish to remain anonymous and use third person pronouns—writing about what happened rather than your role or reaction?

**40d**

*plan*

Your decisions about these issues will determine the authorial voice in a given piece of writing. How you choose to present yourself to your readers can have a definite impact on the way they perceive your message.

In his essay, Brad's voice is that of a peer to his classmates. In writing about his personal experiences, he uses standard though informal English, without a great deal of slang, because he wants to be understood clearly and also because an important person in the audience is his instructor, who may not be familiar with teenage slang. Brad's first draft contained some slang *(freaked out, wow)*. His instructor's comments note a conflict in tone between the slang and the sophisticated vocabulary of the next sentence *(conversation that ensued)*. She wrote *voice* in the margin of his paper not so much because she objected to his use of slang but to indicate that he was presenting himself as an inconsistent narrator. Read Brad's revision-in-progress now (pages 384–88) if you have not already done so, and analyze how he creates his role in the essay.

While revising her memo, Tina also encountered a problem with voice. She realized that her original tone was too stiff and formal for a memo addressed to her colleagues. Her goal was to encourage her coworkers to act as a team, but her tone sounded as if she were giving orders to subordinates rather than offering suggestions to peers. In contrast to Brad's essay, where the use of first person pronouns helps readers feel they are seeing things through the writer's eyes, the frequent use of *I* in Tina's memo made her writing sound inappropriately self-centered. To avoid giving the impression that she was trying to seize control of the group, she adopted a more casual, conversational voice in the final draft, using more plural pronouns *(we, us)* to emphasize teamwork. Read Tina's first draft and final draft now (pages 379–80) if you have not already done so, and notice the revisions she makes to change the voice in her memo.

---

EXERCISE 40d

Practice using different authorial voices by writing two paragraphs as follows: (1) for a new manual to be used in the driver's education class at your old high school, explain how to change a tire; (2) for a friend, describe how you had to change a tire for the first time on the shoulder of an interstate highway. (Use your imagination if you have never actually changed a tire.) To what extent would each paragraph make the reader aware of you the author, as distinct from you the participant? Why?

---

## 40e  Determine your subject.

Sometimes your subject is predetermined by the needs of the writing situation, perhaps a class assignment or work assignment: *Write an essay on the causes of World War I. Prepare a sales forecast for the next quarter. Discuss the question of whether our club should choose the Sunshine Day Care Center or the Grovemont Nursing Home for this year's service project.* At other times you may need to develop the subject yourself: *Write a personal experience essay. Write a term paper on the nineteenth-century American novel of your choice. Identify a business problem in the company you are studying and write a report about it.*

Later, in the sections on planning (40g–i), we will more thoroughly explore the process of choosing a subject and generating ideas about it. For now, think about how the needs of the writing situation help to shape a subject. For example, Tina wrote *Subject: Agenda for Tuesday's Meeting* at the top of her planning sheet. However, as she generated ideas for her memo, she realized that her goal was to encourage the staff to prepare for the meeting. Although she left the memo's subject line more or less as she had first drafted it, the major topic Tina addressed in the text was the need for people to do some preliminary thinking about the agenda issues.

Brad's assignment, to write a personal experience essay, was more open-ended. He needed to set some boundaries for the subject. His planning began with the question "Which personal experience?"

and progressed through a series of focusing activities. He finally settled on a recent and powerful experience, his summer trip as an ambassador in a youth exchange program. Because the broad subject "my trip to Europe" demanded more space than the three or four pages his instructor had allotted, Brad knew he must narrow his focus. He then chose the more limited subject "my most memorable experiences in Europe" for further planning and initial drafting.

Both Tina and Brad discovered the necessary constraints of their writing tasks and adjusted their subjects accordingly. Tina broadened her task from *deliver the agenda* to *encourage thinking about the agenda.* Brad narrowed his task from *tell about trip to Europe* to *tell about most memorable parts of trip.*

## 40f   Identify your rhetorical purpose.

Writers sometimes find themselves at cross-purposes with their subjects, audiences, and the needs of the writing task. Ask yourself just what your writing ought to accomplish. What is your aim? If your answer to this question is unclear, or if it disregards the needs of your audience or subject matter, you are likely to have trouble creating a satisfactory text.

For example, if a question on a history exam asks you to *defend* the Loyalists' actions during the American Revolution, then the rhetorical purpose of your answer must be to *argue for* the validity of their viewpoint. If your answer only *explains* what the Loyalists did during the Revolution, you are likely to receive poor marks—because you have misunderstood the task the question set before you, which was both to explain and to persuade.

One way to see if you have identified your purpose correctly is to compare what you have written to four categories of prose known as the **rhetorical modes: narration, description, exposition,** and **argumentation.** Each of these modes fits a different rhetorical purpose.

**1. Narration.** The purpose of narration is to tell a story, to recount a sequence of events, to tell "what happened." The appeal of narrative is universal: it is the first kind of discourse that children learn, in bedtime stories and tales relatives tell about their childhood. We use narration constantly in our writing: on an insurance claim to recount how an accident happened; on the job, to report monthly sales calls; for an economics paper, to outline the events that led to the 1987 stock market crash.

Brad used narration in sections of his essay. It suited his purpose quite well—to tell what he did on his free day in London. But for Tina, the narrative opening paragraph in the first draft of her memo was an important clue that she had misdefined her purpose. Since people already knew the sequence of events leading up to the staff meeting, why repeat them? Tina had to ask herself what she was really trying to accomplish and what her readers really needed to know. Thus the final draft of the memo contains much less narrative, because its purpose is mainly persuasive.

**2. Description.** The purpose of description is to make readers see, feel, hear what the writer has seen, felt, or heard. Description often appears in combination with other modes and provides an important sense of immediacy—"you are there"—that readers need in order to fully grasp a writer's meaning. Brad's instructor commented on an early draft of his essay that he needed to "put flesh on the bones" of his experience. Referring to paragraph 4 about a famous British department store, she wrote, "We need to see concrete examples to understand why you were overwhelmed" (see p. 385). Without using the term, she was asking him to supply more description.

Description can be of two kinds: **objective** (or **technical**) and **suggestive** (or **impressionistic**). The first requires writers to reproduce, as a camera would, what they see. An appraiser for a mortgage company provides an objective description of a house:

> Lot size 120 feet wide by 150 feet deep. Exterior dimensions of house: 84 feet by 27 feet. Living area 1,620 square feet; 648 additional square feet in two-car garage. Seven rooms: three bedrooms, living room, dining room, kitchen, den; two baths. One brick fireplace. Central heat (gas); central air (electric). R-19 insulation rating. Three years old.

The appraisal contains no emotional reaction, no judgment of the house's appeal. The goal of the appraiser's objective description is to enable the mortgage company to set a fair loan value on the house.

The homeowner who wishes to sell the same house writes up a description that reads as follows:

**40f**

*plan*

> Practically new three-bedroom, two-bath, ranch-style brick home situated on a shade-tree-covered half-acre lot. Over 1,600 square feet of living area. Modern kitchen with built-in appliances. Walnut-panelled family room with brick fireplace and beamed ceiling. Formal living and dining rooms for gracious entertaining. Master bedroom suite with adjoining full bath. Oversized two-car garage. Large patio with gas grill. All of this is nestled beneath stately maples on beautiful, easily maintained grounds and is available with a mortgage at 10½% interest.

This description creates a much different impression from the appraiser's. The second description may not be merely the product of the owner's desire to sell the house; it no doubt reflects an emotional attachment to the house.

**3. Exposition.** The purpose of exposition is to inform, to explain, to clarify—to make readers know or understand something about a subject. Exposition may sometimes appeal to emotions, as narration and description often do, but the primary purpose of exposition is to inform. Exposition is the principal mode used to write a manual for automobile owners, a recipe for Southern fried chicken, a physics textbook, a magazine article about the campaigns of presidential candidates.

Both Tina and Brad had expository purposes for sections of their text. Brad wanted to explain why certain experiences on his trip were especially memorable. Tina needed to inform her colleagues of what was planned for the Tuesday meeting.

**4. Argumentation.** The purpose of argumentation is to persuade the audience—to convince them of the rightness of a point of view and/or course of action. We encounter argumentation in debates and editorials. Most political speeches are a form of argumentation.

Argumentation often has an emotional component, as is the case in political speeches, for example. But truly persuasive arguments are based primarily on adequate evidence, sound logic, and a thorough understanding of opposing positions. (See Section **43** for a more developed discussion of persuasive writing.)

Tina wanted to persuade her readers to think about the agenda items. Consequently, her memo contains argumentative sections where she provides reasons for the action she is trying to convince her readers to take (see her final draft, paragraphs 2 and 3).

Knowing the characteristics and purposes of narration, description, exposition, and argumentation will help you recognize when and where they are appropriate in your writing. You will be better able to judge which mode is most effective for what you are trying to accomplish.

**40g** Planning: techniques for generating and joining ideas

Planning occurs throughout the writing process, and especially at the outset when the initial goals are being set—when the audience, author's role, subject, and purpose are being identified, developed, and shaped. The generative aspects of planning—invention, and exploration—are fundamental to retrieving from memory knowledge and information about a subject. Thus, many writers need a rather unstructured period during the planning activity, when ideas are allowed to flow freely. At other times, more systematic planning techniques can be used. The following discussion explains both unstructured and structured techniques that can be used in planning activities.

**1. Free association.** This technique uses no writing at all, but simply lets the mind range freely over a subject to see what bubbles up from the memory. Free association can work well when you have a wide-open assignment. It also can be helpful if you are experiencing writer's block and need to stop trying to compose sentences. Instead of trying to impose structure on your ideas before they may be ready for order, just see what percolates from your thoughts.

**2. Brainstorming.** This technique can be a good step to follow free association—when your mind is generating enough potentially useful ideas that you want to get some of them down on paper. Brainstorming does not involve a mental censor. Concentrate on your subject or some aspect of it. Then write down what comes from brainstorming, without censoring ideas as to their importance. You are trying to see what mental information is available, trying to encourage a focus without forcing it. Your jotting might take the form of a list, a series of random notes, some key words, questions, or whatever will help you recall ideas later.

**3. Free writing.** Free writing, like free association, is meant to help you generate ideas by simply letting them flow without censorship or interruption. Do not worry about spelling, punctuation, grammar, or form. Just start writing, including everything that goes through your mind, to see what you may have to say.

Free writing can be helpful when you have a wide-open subject and also when you are searching for a subject. It can also help when you have too much information to deal with and cannot seem to get it under control. Rather than struggling, relax and free write about the subject for five or ten minutes. Useful groupings and relationships may emerge. If not, give yourself a break and return to brainstorming when you are refreshed.

**40g**

**plan**

The following is a portion of Brad's free writing, done on a computer with a word-processing program. He often used the computer when generating ideas, sometimes dimming the monitor's screen so he would not be tempted to censor or to correct what he was writing. In this case, Brad believed it might be easier to get the ideas flowing if he addressed his thoughts to someone, so his free writing took the form of a letter to the leader of his summer trip. You may find that this method of "talking" to someone, either in person, on screen, or on paper, helps you, too. Compare Brad's free writing with his essay drafts at the end of Section **41**. Note which ideas Brad used in each draft and how he developed those ideas. For example, notice how he expanded a nine-word note about French students to five paragraphs in the first draft (paragraphs 7–11), but that another note about a cookout that he expanded to a long paragraph in the first draft (paragraph 12) was eliminated in the final draft.

*Free writing*

> Dear Judy,
>     We're supposed to write a personal experience essay for
> English class and I decided to write about last summer on the
> student ambasador trip. That sure was a lot of fun and I
> learned an awful lot about other people and countries. The
> trip was awesome—absolutely the most interesting thing that
> has happened in my life. Also learned a lot of things about
> myself. should I write about that? what I learned about
> people during our homestays or when we were traveling. Or
> should I stick to what I learned about myself? I suppose the
> two things are realy connected, maybe I can separate them—
> should they be separated? Anyway the parts of the trip that
> come to mind right now are shopping in London and . . . .
> what else? . . . talking to french students on park bench in
> Paris . . . . . Bavarian homestay cookout . . . . Austrian
> homestay family . . . . the bike ride I took with Peter and
> Patrick. Why these? anything in common??? What? What?? Judy,
> you told us one of the most important things we would do as
> student ambassadors would be talk to people. You were right.
> What sticks in my mind the most is times where I <u>really</u>
> communicated with people, never mind language barriers. Times
> when I really exchanged viewpoints with people and learned
> new things. Maybe I can write my essay around that idea.

**4. Mind mapping.** This technique is more structured than free writing but less structured than some other techniques. Mind mapping emphasizes the free flow of ideas, but it also allows you to show relationships among ideas without forcing them into an organizational scheme. Start with the subject circled in the center of a page. Then, as you think of other ideas, add new circles radiating outward on the page. If ideas are related to one another, place them in overlapping

**40g**

**plan**

*Mind map*

circles, or connect the circles with lines. Your mind map can be as simple or as detailed as you choose. The mind map on page 356, used to plan this section of the *Prentice Hall Handbook*, shows how the technique is done.

Mind mapping is especially helpful if you want to collect ideas about aspects of a subject but find yourself stalled by the best order in which to present them. Seeing the ideas without a superimposed structure but in relationship to one another can help postpone the need to organize them until you have finished idea collection and are ready to think productively about organization.

**5. Idea trees.** This technique is a bit more structured than mind mapping; it represents ideas not only in relation to one another but also in hierarchical arrangements. Various arrangements could be from greater to lesser, general to specific, main idea to supporting idea, and so forth, depending upon the subject and purpose of the tree. As the following example illustrates, idea trees can be useful for exploring the parts of a subject and also for organizing the presentation of ideas.

**Idea tree**

**40g**

*plan*

**6. Heuristics.** *Heuristics* refers to procedures for thinking systematically about a subject. Except for outlining, heuristics are the most structured planning techniques we will examine. Among the many heuristics available, two popular ones are Burke's pentad and Aristotle's topics.

**a. Burke's pentad.** This procedure involves exploring a subject as if it were a drama, using the five categories *act, scene, agent, agency,* and *purpose.* We can ask the following questions about a subject: "What happens to or with the subject *(act)*? When and where does the action take place *(scene)*? Who causes the action *(agent)*? How is the action carried out—who or what, by what means *(agency)?* Why does the action occur *(purpose)?* These "who, what, when, where, why, and how" questions can be helpful in discovering how much you know about a subject and whether there is anything you need to find out before you can start writing.

The pentad can also be quite helpful in checking what you are writing against the purpose you have identified. For example, if your purpose is to discuss the causes of teenage suicide but you find that most of your paper concentrates on the methods teenagers use to attempt suicide, the pentad will show you that you have emphasized agency rather than purpose. You will need to adjust the focus of the paper, condensing the material on methods and developing material on reasons and motivations.

**b. Aristotle's topics.** The Greek philosopher Aristotle identified four "common topics" to be used as keys for exploring the nature of a subject. These points of departure include (a) *definition:* what is it?; (b) *chronology:* what happened and in what order did things happen?; (c) *comparison and contrast:* what are the similarities and the differences?; (d) *cause and effect:* what are the reasons and the results? The topics can provide helpful categories for organizing ideas as well as means for generating and exploring them. For example, if Brad Bolton had used Aristotle's topics as a heuristic for generating ideas about his essay assignment, he might have come up with something like the following.

**40g**

*plan*

| | |
|---|---|
| DEFINITION: | What is my most memorable experience? What do I mean by memorable? What are the components required for a memorable experience? |
| CHRONOLOGY: | What happened that made my student-ambassador experience memorable? |
| COMPARISON/CONTRAST: | How was my student-ambassador experience more memorable than other experiences? How was I different when I came back from the trip than before I left? |
| CAUSE/EFFECT: | Did some event(s) or person(s) on the trip cause me to change? What was responsible for making the trip so memorable? What have been the results of this trip that made it more memorable than other trips? |

---

## EXERCISE 40g

1. Assume that you have been given an essay-writing assignment. The choice of subject is up to you. Applying the idea-generating technique that you think will work best, come up with a subject and some ideas for a three-to-four page essay.

2. You have been assigned an essay on the subject of homelessness in America. Use another of the techniques described in Section **40g** to generate ideas on this subject.

---

## 40h   Planning: using a formal outline

Notes, lists, and idea trees are types of **informal outlines** that can be used very effectively for generating ideas and preliminarily planning their arrangement. A **formal outline** will serve you best at a slightly later stage of your planning, after you have arrived at a fairly well-developed scheme for organizing your ideas—perhaps even after you have formulated a thesis statement (see Section **40i**).

A well-developed informal outline can be especially valuable when you must write against a deadline—an in-class essay or exam, for instance. It can keep you from discovering too late that you have confused issues, wandered from the main line of argument, left out important points, or maybe even failed to understand the question.

Some writers use a formal outline as a blueprint for the paper they will write. For example, one business student always prepares a fairly detailed outline as part of his writing process. In fact, the outline virtually serves as his first draft. Once he is satisfied with the outline, he simply fleshes it out for the final draft. Other writers use an outline as part of the revision process, preparing it after their paper has been written as a means of checking the structure and the development of ideas. Some assignments, such as research papers or long reports, even require that a formal outline be submitted as part of the document.

The conventions of **formal outlining** are as follows:

**1. Number and indent headings and subheadings consistently; do not use single headings or subheadings.** Follow the rule "for every *I*, there must be a *II;* for every *A*, there must be a *B*." Any category of heading or subheading must have at least two parts. Here is a portion of Tina's working outline.

```
    I. Reasons for agenda
       A. Structure at meeting
          1. More efficient approach to business
             a. Most important topics first
             b. Least important topics if time
          2. Fewer irrelevant topics
       B. Preparation for meeting
   II. Agenda items for Tuesday
```

**40h**

*plan*

The following outline is **not** in correct form. It contains single subheadings, an indication of poor organization or incorrect partition. You cannot logically divide something into just one part. A single subheading should be incorporated into the heading of which it is logically a part, or it should be divided in two.

    I.  Reasons for agenda
        A.  Structure at meeting
   II.  Agenda items for Tuesday
        A.  Criteria for new staff jobs
        B.  Growth areas
            1.  data processing
               a.  sales
        C.  Proposal to Department Head

Also note that the incorrect outline contains same-level headings that do not represent the same classification principle. Items II. A. and B. are not of the same class; II. B. should be a subcategory of II. A. Items B. 1. and B. 1. a. are of the same class; they should have same-level headings. More logical divisions for the last part of the outline would be as follows:

   II.  Agenda items for Tuesday
        A.  Criteria for new staff jobs
            1.  Anticipated growth areas
               a.  data processing
               b.  sales
            2.  Currently overburdened area: accounting
        B.  Proposal to Department Head

**2. Follow either topic, sentence, or paragraph style throughout an outline, and use parallel grammatical structure.** A *topic outline* uses a noun (or noun substitute) and its modifiers for each heading, as in the foregoing example. A *sentence outline* follows the same structure but uses a complete sentence for each heading. For an example of a sentence outline, see the sample research paper in Section 46. A *paragraph outline* gives a summary sentence for each paragraph of the paper and does not divide and subdivide headings into subordinate parts. Do not mix types in the same outline.

Remember also to make all parts within the same level or degree of the outline parallel in grammatical structure. Using consistent grammatical form emphasizes the logic of the outline as well as providing clarity and smoothness. Notice that in the last part of her revised outline, Tina wrote the modifier-noun phrase *Anticipated growth areas* and then the parallel modifier-noun phrase *Currently overburdened area*—not an unparallel construction such as *add to area currently overburdened.*

**3. Avoid vague outline headings such as Introduction, Body, and Conclusion.** These headings will not help you in planning, because they do not provide content clues. Also, if you are asked to submit an outline with your paper, such headings do not help your readers. Indicate in the outline what the introduction will include. If your paper is to have a formal conclusion, show in the outline what conclusion you will draw. Think of the outline as a table of contents for the reader, a preview of important information and its organization. Because it does provide such an overview, a formal outline often begins with a statement of the paper's thesis, as does the outline for the research paper in Section **46j**.

## 40i  Planning: Bringing the subject into focus

**1. Setting the boundaries of your subject.** Many of the idea-generating techniques previously discussed contain built-in methods for setting the boundaries of a general subject so that it fits the constraints of the writing task. An idea tree, for instance, is designed to move from general to particular aspects of a subject, from the whole to its parts, or from main idea to related supporting ideas. At some point in your planning activities you need to move from expanding the field of ideas to focusing on a few of them. You must choose those that look most promising for development and disregard the rest.

Brad set boundaries and focused his ideas when he decided which of his life's experiences he wanted to explore for his personal experience essay. He settled on his European trip and then focused on the few incidents that fit two important constraints. One constraint was external: the page limit set by the instructor. The other Brad eventually set himself: the **controlling idea,** or **thesis,** he was developing for his essay.

In planning his essay, Brad had to answer the question "*What* about the trip?" He had to refer to larger goals involved in the writing task. What, exactly, would be the **purpose** of the paper? Brad narrowed his purpose to **explaining** why the trip was his most memorable experience. He expressed this purpose as the **controlling idea** of his paper: *Probably the most memorable experience in my life is the trip I took to Europe . . . [because it] contributed to [my] general maturing. . . ."* Thus, Brad needed to select incidents that illustrated and supported the controlling idea.

His first draft shows that he initially chose four incidents for the essay—one each in London, France, Bavaria, and Austria. By the final draft, he had reduced the incidents to three. Brad omitted Bavaria not because it added too much length but because it did not add anything new to his illustration of the essay's controlling idea. This example shows how the focusing process is likely to be ongoing as you plan, write, and revise.

**40i**

*plan*

EXERCISE 40i(1)

For each general subject that follows, list three different, more focused subjects that could be derived from the general one. Then, for each of those resulting subjects, list two even more limited subjects. Put your lists in the form of an idea tree. The general subjects are:

1. cooking
2. recreation
3. sports
4. cars
5. a subject of your choice

Following is an example of an idea tree using one general subject.

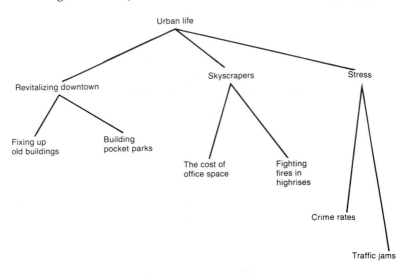

2. **Expressing the controlling idea as a thesis statement.** Readers are notoriously impatient. They like to know what's going on. They appreciate being notified early in a paper about the subject and the direction you plan to go with it. In fact, it is to your advantage as a writer to indicate your goals and purposes early because sharing them not only makes your readers more attentive but also prepares them to understand the ideas you present.

A thesis statement is the most efficient means by which you can communicate your subject, goals, and purposes. It sets forth in a sentence or two the paper's **controlling idea**—its **thesis.** A thesis statement is *not* simply a statement of the paper's subject. "This paper is about the effects of industrialization on developing nations" is not a thesis statement. A thesis statement is an **assertion**; it answers the questions *What point does this paper make? What opinion does it offer? What stand does the writer take? What does the writer want us to focus on as we read this paper?* A carefully stated thesis introduces and summarizes the entire paper—puts into a nutshell the central idea, which the rest of the paper explores and develops.

Like any other statement, a thesis statement consists of a subject and a predicate. Your main topic is the subject. Writing a thesis statement is a matter of writing a predicate to go with that subject, a matter of stating the assertion you wish to make about the subject.

The opening paragraph from Brad Bolton's essay follows. His thesis is expressed in two related sentences. See if you can identify the thesis sentences.

> Probably the most memorable experience of my life is the six-week trip I took to Europe last summer as a student ambassador in a youth exchange program. In Europe I explored new surroundings, made lasting friends, and experienced new cultures. All of this contributed to a general maturing that took place in me over the course of the six weeks. Here is a small portion of how it happened.

Brad's thesis asserts that his trip to Europe (subject) added to his maturity (predicate), and thus the trip (subject) is the most memorable experience of his life (predicate). Notice that his opening paragraph also indicates his purpose (to explain why by telling the reader what happened), the main rhetorical modes he will use (exposition and narration) to carry out that purpose, and the probable organization of the paper (cause and effect overall, chronology within sections).

A well-formed thesis statement has four main characteristics:

a.   **Unity:** the thesis states a *single controlling idea.* The idea may be complex and have several parts, but it should be one idea nevertheless.

b.   **Focus:** the thesis should be restricted and specific enough for the reader to gain a clear idea of the subject and direction of your paper.

c.   **Organization:** if the thesis is sufficiently focused, it will provide a basis for decisions about what to include and what to exclude. As a result, it will help you organize your ideas.

d.   **Dramatic interest:** the thesis serves as the writer's promise to readers to make a clear point—in Brad's case, to show why his trip was memorable. Thus, even in a paper whose general purpose is to explain or describe, the thesis can provide a kind of argumentative edge that will sharpen the reader's interest in your subject.

The most common problems that weaken a thesis statement are lack of unity and lack of focus. The "original" sentences that follow have neither unity nor focus.

**40i**

*plan*

| ORIGINAL | My difficulties in philosophy are unbelievable, but I'm doing OK in biology. |
|---|---|
| REVISION | Because I seem to be more comfortable with concrete things like frogs than with abstract ideas like existence, I am getting better grades in biology than in philosophy. |

ORIGINAL    Kids face a lot of problems today and need help.

REVISION    Although being a teenager has never been easy, drug use, suicide, parental divorce, and unwanted pregnancy mean we need many more teenage counseling programs than are currently available.

The first sentence fails the test for unity because it contains two separate ideas with no indication of how—or if—they will be brought together. The paper that results from this thesis is likely to break into unconnected halves: one half devoted to biology, one half to philosophy. The second sentence remedies this problem by subordinating the ideas in a cause-and-effect relationship.

The first sentence also fails the test for focus because it uses vague generalities such as "are unbelievable" and "doing OK." Predicates that consist of *is* or *are* plus a vague modifying phrase or complement such as *good, interesting,* or *a serious problem* are usually too imprecise to be useful. Although general terms can be narrowed and defined elsewhere in a paper, readers appreciate a thesis assertion (such as that in the second, revised sentence) that supplies a specific subject and clear direction as quickly as possible.

Keep in mind that not every kind of writing needs an explicit thesis statement. Tina's memo, for instance, has a purpose statement that tells her readers why they have received the memo, but no actual thesis statement. The first sentence of the second paragraph, which expresses her goal of persuading her readers to prepare for the meeting, is the closest thing in the memo to a thesis sentence.

Some types of writing, such as business or technical reports, may have an overall purpose and clear goals that respond to needs known to writer and readers, but no single controlling idea that appears in a single statement. In fact, there may be different controlling ideas for different parts of a report. However, especially in essays that explain or argue a point, a clear thesis sentence is a great aid to the reader's understanding and recall.

Where you place a thesis sentence depends on your goals, your audience, the purpose of the essay, and how you intend to organize it. The most common position for the thesis statement in short expository and persuasive essays is in the opening paragraph. It may appear early in the opening paragraph, followed by sentences that further define or explain the assertion that the thesis makes. Or the thesis statement may be positioned at the end of the paragraph, following an introduction of the subject and some background information.

Although other locations for the thesis statement can work, remember that readers like a clear sense of what is going on. Be sure that your controlling idea is indeed controlling the paper, wherever the thesis is located. The principal argument for its early appearance in an essay is that readers will understand the relevance of your dis-

**40i**

*plan*

cussion better if you first tell them the main idea behind that discussion.

---

### EXERCISE 40i(2)

For practice in writing unified, focused thesis statements, revise the following thesis statements. If any of them are satisfactory as written, explain why.

1. The problem of homelessness in America can be traced to the decline of the job market for unskilled laborers, the large number of mentally ill people without family and institutional support, drug abuse, and the lack of affordable housing.
2. Our downtown area is a disgrace and needs help.
3. There are five steps in growing a garden: preparation of the soil, planting the seed, watering and fertilizing the plants, and harvesting.
4. Learning disabilities take many forms as well as many degrees of severity.
5. People's attitudes can often be seen in the way they treat others.

---

### EXERCISE 40i(3)

Look for the thesis statement in (1) several editorials and letters to the editor in a local newspaper, (2) the "Essay" in *Time* magazine or an opinion article in another news magazine, (3) an informative article in a magazine for specialized readers. Choose one of them, write the thesis statement at the top of a page, and then make an outline of the editorial, letter, or article. How well does the author's thesis statement serve as the controlling idea?

---

### EXERCISE 40i(4)

Using the subject you chose for an idea tree in Exercise 40i(1), write two unified, focused thesis statements for essays on that subject. These two statements should result in essays that go in different directions.

**41**

*draft*

# 41

## DRAFTING AND REVISING

Most writers begin their first draft with a general notion of the order in which they want to present their points, an order that fits their purpose. After all, constructing a message for readers is not simply a matter of filling a sack with ideas. As you plan your essay, your ideas will begin to group together into an organizational scheme. In fact, when you use an idea tree or an outline in your planning you are already shaping your material.

More detailed organizing often occurs while drafting and revising are underway. Tina, for example, made major changes in the structure of her memo after she had written her first draft because it did not satisfy her plans as they developed while she was writing. This "change of plans" happens to writers all the time: it is normal. Preliminary plans and goals are very important in helping you start to write, but do not be afraid to change them if something else seems to work better. As you draft your paper, you may find that you need to revise your thesis statement if your thoughts and the structure of your essay take a new turn. In truth, the writing process is not only a recursive process, it is also a discovery process.

**The main thing to keep in mind as you write is that all the parts of your essay—every paragraph—should be related to the controlling idea that governs your paper.** Each sentence should in some important way increase the reader's understanding of your main point. As you plan, draft, and revise, you will want to check your organization and development of ideas to be sure you have (1) eliminated things that are irrelevant to your focus and (2) made clear to your readers connections between ideas and paragraphs.

## 41a  Organizing your material

When they are trying to accomplish certain kinds of purposes, writers naturally create certain organizational structures. Knowing the following common structures can help you shape your ideas to fit the particular purpose you have chosen for your essay. Sample paragraphs of each type of organization appear in Section **42**.

**1. Time.** If you are writing narration—telling what happened— time order (also called chronological order) is a natural structure. When you write about an automobile accident or a historical event, you are likely to relate the events in the sequence in which they happened. Brad used chronological order for the sections of his essay dealing with events in London, Paris, and Austria. A chronology is also the appropriate structure for instructions: how to write a computer program, how to make a Caesar salad, how to use the library or overcome a fear of flying on airplanes.

**2. Space.** If you need to describe a scene or object, spatial order may be appropriate. You may focus the scene from where either you or the readers are located, and then move from left to right, top to bottom, front to back, inside to outside, or whatever spatial arrangement suits your purpose. Spatial order closely follows the order in which the eyes see or movie cameras move. One bit of information relates to the next in terms of position.

If you want to create an unusual descriptive effect, deliberately departing from normal spatial order might be your choice. Horror movies frequently violate the audience's spatial expectations to create

41a

draft

a special atmosphere. The camera may first focus on glazed eyes, then on sprawled legs, then on a gaping mouth, and ultimately on a knife protruding from the chest to create the feelings of suspense, fear, and shock associated with a murder. You can use words in the same way.

**3. General to particular / particular to general.** If you are explaining an idea or a concept, one of these structures can be useful. You might state the *general* idea first and then explain it by citing *particular* instances or examples of the generalization. The reverse is also possible: instances and examples first, summed up by a general statement. In his final draft, Brad used a particular-to-general organization when he first described his encounter with the French student and then concluded that the encounter was the reason he would never forget the evening in Paris (pp. 390-91).

These two organizational structures sometimes go by another name. Especially when applied to persuasive writing or logical analysis, the general-to-particular order may be called **deductive** organization (from a Latin word meaning "lead away from"). The particular-to-general order may be referred to as **inductive** organization (from a Latin word meaning "lead into"). When writers give reasons and explanations first and then present the central idea or conclusion to be drawn, they are using an inductive structure. If they present the conclusion/generalization/main idea first and then follow it with reasons and other explanatory detail, they are using deductive organization. Tina switched from an inductive structure to a deductive structure for the final draft of her memo because she decided that she needed a more direct approach for her readers and subject matter (pp. 379 and 380). Section **43** contains further discussion of deduction and induction.

**4. Climax.** If you are writing to persuade your readers, the order of climax can be very effective. Arranging evidence from least important to most important is a strategy used routinely in arguments and debates. When someone says "and last, but not least," you know he or she is about to deliver the crushing blow. Because climactic order, like a well-constructed play, achieves its big moment at the end, it also works well when you want to create suspense. Its drawback is that readers may get tired of waiting for you to come to the point.

**5. Comparison and contrast.** Writing that points out similarities compares; writing that notes differences contrasts. Frequently, but not always, comparison and contrast coexist in the same paper. Brad compared himself with the French student and noted a difference he found unusual: he doesn't care what language he speaks, but the French love to speak, and hear the sound of, their own language (p. 391).

Comparison and contrast are two of the most common struc-

**41a**

*draft*

tures for writing. This is not surprising when you remember that the principal way our minds process new information is to attach it to old information. We learn about the unknown by viewing it in terms of what we already know: how is it the same as (compared to) or different from (contrasted with) our previous experience? It makes sense, then, that writers naturally rely a good deal on comparison and contrast to communicate their ideas.

Extended comparisons usually use one of two organizational patterns: either point-by-point or parallel order. In point-by-point organization the things being compared are discussed one point at a time, first point of *A* followed by first point of *B* and so on. Parallel order requires that all points of *A* be discussed, followed by all points of *B*, with the points of each in the same order.

| *Point-by-Point Organization* | | *Parallel Order Organization* |
|---|---|---|
| *A* | *B* | *A* |
| first point | first point | first point |
| second point | second point | second point |
| third point | third point | third point |
| etc. | etc. | etc. |
| | | *B* |
| | | first point |
| | | second point |
| | | third point |
| | | etc. |

A special kind of comparison, called **analogy,** uses similarities between two things to imply other similarities or resemblances. To show how working for Company X is like belonging to a big family is to compare by analogy. For a more complete discussion of analogy, see Section **42.**

**41a**

*draft*

**6. Analysis and classification.** Analysis is the conscious process of trying to understand something by taking it apart, breaking it down into its smaller parts. Analysis is also sometimes called partition or division. For example, if you have decided on a career in nursing, at some point you will need to analyze the field—look at the kinds of nursing available—in order to decide which one—obstetric, pediatric, geriatric, surgical—you wish to practice. If you are trying to determine the cause of a business problem, you may want to analyze the business according to its components—manufacturing, distribution, marketing and sales, finance and accounting—to see where the problem lies. An important adjunct of analysis is classification; in fact, analysis makes classification possible. If you want to group items according to a common principle or characteristic, you classify them—put them into categories.

Suppose you were assigned an essay on the student body at your school. You would first analyze, then classify. In brainstorming about the subject, you would have to consider a variety of ways to distinguish one student from another. You could do so in terms of those who study diligently, those who study just enough to get by, and those who demonstrate no interest in their studies. When you assign several individuals to each of these categories, you are classifying according to study habits, a principle common to all students. Other classifications are possible: you might divide students according to their place of residence or their choice of career. Whatever classification you select for a paper depends on your purpose and derives from careful analysis.

Classification without analysis is called **stereotyping.** You stereotype if you classify a person or group without systematic and valid analysis. The outcome of stereotyping is often prejudice directed toward members of ethnic, political, sexual, racial, or religious groups. Before you put people or things into categories, be sure that you have fully and fairly examined the components that make up those people or things and have drawn valid conclusions about them. (See also Section **43f(1)**.)

**7. Definition.** If your purpose is to explain an abstract concept or something unfamiliar to your audience, you may find that definition is an appropriate organizational structure. If definition provides the overall structure for much or all of your paper, you will be writing an **extended definition.**

Definition is actually a form of comparison, beginning with the thing to be defined (the unfamiliar or unknown) and describing it in terms of things with which the reader is familiar. In addition, definition uses classification, first placing the thing to be defined within a broad category *(genus)* and then within narrower and narrower categories *(differentia)*. In the sentence definition A *crumpet is a light, soft bread similar to a muffin,* for example, *crumpet* (the unfamiliar) is compared to *bread* (the familiar) and further classified under the narrower categories *light* and *soft* to differentiate it from other types of bread. Section **43**, "Critical Thinking and Argument," contains a full discussion of various types of definition.

**41a**

*draft*

**8. Cause and effect.** If your chemistry professor asks you to discuss the results of combining certain chemicals, you will develop your answer by the cause-and-effect method. If your English instructor asks you to write a paper on why you selected the college you attend, you will be expected to develop the paper using an effect-to-cause relationship. The decision is an effect, an already accomplished action; the reasons for your decision are the causes.

Cause-and-effect organization quite naturally falls into the pattern of (1) stating causes and describing or arguing what their consequences will be, or (2) identifying a problem or consequence and then explaining the causes. An organizational structure related to cause and effect is the *problem-solution pattern*. In analyzing the problem, you would first discuss causes and effects. Then you would probably switch to a thesis-support approach to present your solution and prove its validity.

**9. Detail and example / thesis–support.** If your purpose is to explain or persuade, it is very likely that a thesis supported by examples and details will provide the overarching structure for your paper. In fact, many of the papers you write in college can be effectively structured this way because many of your writing tasks will call for you to explain things to your readers or convince them of a point of view.

Even though you will frequently need to use cause-and-effect, comparison and contrast, definition, or one of the other types of organization discussed in this section, in many cases these structures will be subordinated to the larger goal of supporting your paper's thesis. They will often be a part of the larger web of details and examples you will need to get your point across clearly to your audience.

Because it is so basic to effective writing, detail and example/ thesis–support fits quite comfortably with other types of organization. A very common combination is detail and example with general-to-particular/particular-to-general order. Brad's paper illustrates another common combination: he used details and examples along with cause-and-effect to support his thesis that his trip to Europe was his most memorable experience because it helped him to gain maturity.

---

**EXERCISE 41a**
Study the thesis statements you wrote for Exercise 40i(4). Which organizational structures seem appropriate for each statement? Why? Explain how the organization would support the thesis.

---

**41b**
*draft*

## 41b   Drafting effective beginnings and endings

The beginning of a paper serves as a springboard into its subject and the assertion you are making about that subject. While there is no need to be "cute" in the introduction, it is important to think about the needs of your audience, purpose, and subject. The beginning should be strong enough to interest your audience in the subject and make them want to continue reading.

Journalists think in terms of writing a "hook" that will attract readers' attention and draw them into the story. Business people, on the other hand, write to get things done. For business readers, then, an effective beginning is one that clearly announces the subject and purpose of a document. Whereas an entertaining anecdote might be a good beginning for a magazine article, it probably would not be appropriate for the opening of a progress report from a manufacturing manager to corporate headquarters. The best advice is to consider the needs of your audience and purpose when evaluating the merits of a particular beginning or ending.

Important as a good beginning is, do not be overly concerned about it in your rough draft. If you think of a strong beginning, fine; but you may find that after drafting the paper your purpose is clearer and writing the opening is easier. Some people habitually compose the opening paragraph last, with good results. At least be prepared to perform major surgery on your opening. You may discover that the first few sentences you wrote in the rough draft were warm-ups and that a little revising will transform the third or fourth sentence into a good beginning.

**1. Effective beginnings.** The following strategies can be used to begin papers effectively.

**a.** *Consider beginning with a statement of fact, a startling statement, or an unusual detail.*

FACTUAL STATEMENT    Ninety-two percent of the students at State College live at home and commute.

STARTLING STATEMENT    There's a fine line between cheap and sleazy. I know. I recently drove right along it. Let me explain.
CARRIE DOLAN, " 'Little Lady' Suffers a Lapse of Luxury to Prove Boss Right"

UNUSUAL DETAIL    Grandmother Gardner didn't drink tea; she drank beer.

**b.** *Consider beginning with a firm statement of opinion or a directly stated proposition.*

OPINION    Stray dogs and cats are a nuisance, and they should be exterminated.

DIRECTLY STATED PROPOSITION    Because people who rarely talk together talk differently, differences in speech tell what group a man belongs to.
JAMES SLEDD, "Bi-Dialectalism: The Linguistics of White Supremacy"

**c.** *Consider beginning with a brief anecdote or incident that leads directly into your main topic.*

BRIEF ANECDOTE    When Mark Twain left home at an early age, he had no great respect for his father's intelligence. When he returned a few years later, he was astonished at how much his father had learned in the meantime. I have been similarly astonished at how much both my father and mother have learned in the time I have been away from home.

**41b**

*draft*

**2. Ineffective beginnings.** A poor beginning that bores, confuses, or otherwise alienates readers will cause them to quit before you have even begun to discuss your subject. Following are some beginning strategies to avoid.

**a.** *Avoid beginnings that are not self-explanatory.* Don't make a reader refer to the title to find out the meaning of your paper's opening sentence. For example, a paper entitled "Nuclear Energy" that begins *Everyone is against it* opens vaguely, as does a paper giving instructions for building a model airplane that starts *The first thing to do is to lay all the parts on the table.* In both instances, readers will wonder what is being referred to.

**b.** *Avoid beginnings that start too far back.* If you are writing a paper describing last Saturday's football game, get directly to the description; don't begin by explaining how you happened to go to the game. The writer of the following paragraphs should have begun with the second paragraph:

### FATHER KNOWS BEST

You probably wonder from my title what I am going to write about. Well, it's a long story. It started when I was born. My mother announced to my father that I was a boy! "We're going to send him to State University!" my father exclaimed. So here I am at State, a member of the freshman class.

It was my father's idea from the first that I should come to State. He had been a student here in the 1960s when he met my mother. . . .

**c.** *Don't complain about an assigned topic or apologize for what you have written.* If you want to complain or apologize, do so in a note attached to your paper. Never include such material in any part of the paper itself.

COMPLAINT Describing a building accurately is a very difficult task. Though it is a good assignment because it makes you look closely and observe details you would not otherwise notice, it takes considerable time and does not leave the student enough time to write the actual paper. I discovered this when I tried to observe and describe the university chapel.

APOLOGY After trying unsuccessfully to write a paper describing my roommate, and then attempting to gather some new ideas on books I had read during the summer, I gave up and decided to write on my experience in reading *The Grapes of Wrath* by John Steinbeck. I hope this fits the assignment.

**41b**

*draft*

**3. Effective endings.** A decisive ending lends your paper a finished, polished note. It echoes your introduction and brings your paper to a logical conclusion.

Just as the nature of an introduction depends on the length and complexity of the paper, so too does the conclusion. A paper of 500 words may require only a concluding sentence or two, whereas a paper of two or three times that length will probably need a paragraph to summarize its contents. Following are several types of effective endings that you may wish to adapt to your essays.

**a.** *Consider concluding with a restatement of your thesis statement or with a quotation that clearly illustrates the thesis.* Keep in mind, however, that a restatement of your thesis does *not* mean a word-for-word repetition of it—which will simply bore your readers and make them wonder at your lack of originality.

THESIS
RESTATED

Now that I have been here and have seen the school for myself, I am convinced that Father *does* know best. I have decided to enroll at State next term.

QUOTATION
REFLECTING
THESIS

I realize the image of chemistry is in such disrepair that it would take a major effort on all our parts to turn this around. . . . Most important, surely, is that we reach the general public and the politicians with the message that chemistry is absolutely essential to our modern way of life. Let's revive the spirit once contained in the slogan, "Better things for better living through chemistry."

FRED BASOLO, "Let's Be Positive About Chemistry"

**b.** *Consider summarizing the major ideas that you developed in your paper.* A summary serves the double purpose of bringing your paper to a conclusion and of reminding your readers of the paper's major points.

**41b**

*draft*

SUMMARY

As I have shown, all you need to build a model plane is a model to assemble, a little ingenuity, and a lot of patience. With these ingredients you can fill the friendly skies of your bedroom.

**c.** *Consider a conclusion drawn from the facts you present.* Especially if your purpose in the paper has been to argue a point of view, you need to write a conclusion that derives from the evidence you presented.

CONCLUSION
BASED ON
PRESENTED
FACTS

The fact that a state judge could seem almost casual about rape shows that beneath the new surface sensitivity, many of the cultural prejudices linger. "What we do in our society, whether it's in photography, films or lan-

guage, is devalue sex," says Psychologist Groth, "and
that gives the message that sex can become a weapon to
degrade somebody." Such moral carelessness is what
has made the U.S. violent in private, as well as in public.

MAUREEN DOWD, "Rape: The Sexual Weapon"

**d.** *Consider ending with a punch line.* The punch-line ending
usually contains an element of surprise or irony. It provides a twist,
often somewhat humorous, that can be appealing, especially if it is
consistent with the voice and tone of the rest of your paper. The following ending effectively concludes an essay that argues that exercise
can be a good remedy for writer's block.

PUNCH LINE   Give it a fair trial—three months, say, long enough
for the novelty to wear off and for it to become a part
of your routine. You may find, as I have, that exercise
helps create a climate for the solution of writing problems. You may find only that it makes you feel better.
On the other hand, it may be that all you get for your
troubles is better health and longer life.
Listen, you can't win 'em all.

LAWRENCE BLOCK, "Fiction: Huffing and Puffing"

**4. Ineffective endings.** A poor ending can spoil the momentum
and reader interest you have worked so hard to create in the body of
the paper. Following are three of the most common ineffective endings.

**a.** *Don't end your paper by branching off into another aspect of
the topic or by introducing new material.* Readers are distracted and
frustrated when a new, undeveloped idea is presented at the end of
the paper. Don't conclude an essay describing how autumn appeals to
you with the statement "Even though autumn is a beautiful and exhil-
arating time of year, spring is still my favorite season." Such a sentence
makes your readers wonder why you wrote about autumn in the first
place.

**b.** *Don't leave your paper hanging in mid-air.* An essay should
provide readers with a sense of closure—the sense that things have
drawn satisfactorily to their conclusion. Papers that "just quit" leave
the audience with an uneasy feeling of unfinished business, as is the
case with the following ending to a magazine article about the battle
between the Coast Guard and shrimp fishermen over the use of TEDs
(Turtle Extruder Devices) on shrimp nets.

INEFFECTIVE   The flip-flopping through the summer made an already
difficult situation worse. One shrimper spoke angrily at
a meeting with the Coast Guard: "It's the on-again, off-
again, on-again stuff we can't stand. If they'd have

**41b**

*draft*

made us put on TEDs—and leave us alone—we'd either get by, starve or go bankrupt, but there wouldn't be this misery of jerking us around." "This whole thing is terrible," agreed one woman.

**c. Finally, never end your paper with an apology.** Statements like "This is only my opinion, and I'm probably not really very well qualified to speak" or "I'm sorry this isn't a better paper, but I didn't have enough time" destroy the effect of whatever you have written. If you say that you have failed, your reader will probably agree with you.

---

EXERCISE 41b(1)
Look at articles in at least two different magazines (only one may be a news magazine). What sorts of beginnings and endings do you find? Do any of them fit the types discussed in Section 41b? Look at the beginning and ending of Brad's first draft (pp. 381 and 384). Do they fit any of the types discussed in Section 41b?

---

EXERCISE 41b(2)
Using one of the thesis statements you developed for Exercise 40i(4), write the rough draft of an essay. Try to notice the times when you stop drafting to do more planning or to reread and revise. In other words, try to become conscious of your own writing process—what you are doing when the writing goes well and what is happening when it does not.

---

**41c** Revising: reviewing, evaluating, and rewriting

Throughout the writing process you will review what you have created, evaluate it to see if it fulfills the goals and purposes you established during planning activities, and rewrite those portions that do not measure up. Changes that result from revision are of two related types: *surface changes* and *meaning changes.*

**41c**

*draft*

1. **Surface changes.** These are largely sentence-level matters of correctness, convention, and style. Spelling, grammar, punctuation, sentence construction, word and sentence order, and vocabulary choice are types of surface changes. Most of the changes in paragraphs 5–11 of Brad's revision-in-progress (pp. 385–86) are surface changes.

2. **Meaning changes.** These involve major additions of new content or deletions of existing content. Typical meaning changes include major changes in sentence and paragraph content, in the controlling idea and thesis statement, in organizational structure, in the authorial voice, in the purpose, or in the conception of the audience. The long note Brad wrote next to paragraph 12 of his revision-in-progress (p. 386–87) indicates that he evaluated that paragraph and decided on a meaning change.

Sometimes revisions involving surface changes are referred to as **editing** and **proofreading,** while the term *revision* is reserved for activities involving meaning changes. However, sentence-level surface changes can certainly result in meaning changes.

American children who typically attend public school receive poor educations in science and math.

American children, who typically attend public school, receive poor educations in science and math.

As the foregoing example shows, the addition of a pair of commas that changes a restrictive modifier to a nonrestrictive one can substantially alter the meaning of a sentence (from *some American children* to *all American children*) and thus the whole focus of a paragraph. For this reason, revision here refers to any and all changes that result from reviewing and evaluating text—including proofreading for correctness and editing for word choice, sentence arrangement, paragraph construction, and so forth.

**3. When to revise.** Most people do some revising while they are drafting. Some people alternate between revising and drafting, especially when they are having a difficult time generating text. Reviewing previously written text can be a way of "priming the pump" and getting ideas to flow again.

Many writers like to make major revisions after they have finished all or a substantial part of their first draft. If the paper is long, they may revise after writing each section and then again when they have completed the entire paper. That way they can get a clearer sense of whether the text as a whole is measuring up to the goals they have set.

Many writers also find it useful to separate reviewing for surface changes from reading for meaning changes. That way they don't fall victim to "memory overload," the problem of trying to pay attention to too many things at once.

The key to revising is being able to see your paper critically. To *revise* means "to see again." Sometimes you may need at least a few hours, or even a few days, away from your paper to be able to revise it effectively. Being too closely involved with what you are writing can be a disadvantage to reading it critically and finding the weak spots. At other times, you may recognize the nagging sensation of "something wrong" while you are writing, and may find stopping right then and puzzling out the problem to be the most effective method. If you are afraid that stopping will cause you to lose an important train of thought, put a check mark, a key word, or a brief note in the margin as a reminder for later revision, and go on with your writing.

**4. Peer review.** Asking another person to read your draft and to point out surface errors or poorly written spots can be very helpful

**41c**

*draft*

in revising your paper. Ask your peer reader to evaluate your ideas, their organization, and the validity of the evidence you use to support assertions. Faulty logic and weak connections between thoughts may be invisible to you but quite evident to a critical reader. If you can develop a buddy system with another writer, not only will both of you gain a critical reader but both of you will undoubtedly benefit from seeing how another person's writing process works.

The revision checklist at the end of this section will serve equally well as a guide for critiquing someone else's paper or for critiquing your own writing. If you are asked to provide a peer review, the following tips will also be helpful.

**a.** *Read the paper carefully several times, and do not respond before you have thought about what to say.* It is important to get the "big picture" and try to determine the writer's goals, audience, purpose, and so forth. You should also be sure you understand the assignment the writer is responding to.

**b.** *Be honest, but fair and tactful.* It is important to say what you think and not mislead the writer about a paper's strengths—or its weakness. Also remember that writers tend to take criticism personally, so talk in terms of the ideas, sentences, and paragraphs—in other words, about the writing itself, not about the writer. Say "This thought doesn't follow from the previous one" rather than "You don't make sense here" or "Your ideas about this subject are all screwed up."

**c.** *Be as specific as possible about problems, and suggest priorities.* Are some problems bigger than others? Which one should be tackled first? Which one is the key to others? If you are being critical, you should also try to suggest alternatives if you can.

**d.** *Point out strengths as well as weaknesses.* It is important to build a writer's confidence. Nearly everybody's paper has something admirable in it, even if there are many poor spots. How will writers know where their text works well if no one tells them?

**e.** *Remember that peer review is not the same as editing or rewriting another person's paper for him or her.* You should not be asked, nor should you volunteer, to act as another person's "ghost writer." People may expect a thoughtful critique, but they must not expect someone to "fix" their writing when the assignment calls for independent, individual work. Such editing, when carried too far, amounts to plagiarism—submitting the writing of another instead of one's own. It is dishonest and can result in academic penalties.

At the end of this section you will find the various drafts written by Tina Rodriguez and Brad Bolton. Look at how they revised their texts between the first and final drafts. In Brad's case, in addition to his own notes, you will be able to see some of the comments his instructor wrote on his first draft and how he rewrote his paper in view of those comments.

**41c**

*draft*

## 41d   Revision Checklist ☑

Keeping these questions in mind will help you evaluate your writing as you work through your writing process.

*Meaning changes:*

☑ **Subject.** Is the subject clear? Are the ideas in the paper all related to the subject?

☑ **Focus.** In addition to the subject, does the paper have a clear controlling idea? Are all the paragraphs in the paper related to the controlling idea?

☑ **Thesis.** Is there a thesis statement that expresses the controlling idea? If not, should one be added?

☑ **Development.** Are the thoughts in the paper adequately developed?

☑ **Organization.** Do the ideas, the paragraphs, in the paper progress in an organized fashion?

☑ **Logic.** Are assertions adequately supported with evidence? Are ideas presented fairly? Is credit given to others where credit is due?

☑ **Audience.** Has the paper taken its audience into account appropriately?

☑ **Opening and closing.** Does the paper have an effective beginning and a strong conclusion?

☑ **Purpose.** Does the paper have an apparent aim? Has that purpose been fulfilled?

☑ **Title.** Does the paper have a title that captures the reader's interest and clearly indicates what the paper is about?

*Surface changes:*

☑ **Grammar, punctuation, spelling.** Has proofreading for grammar, punctuation, and spelling mistakes been thorough? Have mistakes been corrected?

☑ **Mechanics.** Have the conventions of capitalization, use of abbreviations, numbers, and so forth that are appropriate for the subject and audience been observed?

☑ **Level of language.** Is word choice precise and appropriate for the subject and the audience?

☑ **Wordiness.** Have words been used economically and effectively, avoiding wordiness and vagueness?

☑ **Sentence structure.** Are sentences logical, well constructed, and effective in their use of subordination, variety, parallelism, and emphasis?

**41d**

*rev*

## Tina's memo: first draft with her notes for revisions

```
         To:      Task force members
         From:    Tina Rodriguez
         Date:    March 14, 199–
         Subject: Agenda for Tuesday's Meeting

         As you know, the company has been experiencing
healthy growth over the past year. Orders have
been increasing since October. In January,
laid-off production employees were called back
to work. Simultaneously, staff work has also
increased. Earlier this month upper management
decided to allocate new staff positions. Last
week the vice president of human resources
asked us to serve on a task force to
investigate the staffing situation and
recommend where new positions are critically
needed. She says the budget allows for the
creation of a total of six new jobs. I have
been asked to set the agenda for our first
meeting, which will be held on Tuesday at 9:30
a.m. in the third floor conference room.
    I know some of you are probably not used to
working from a set agenda. However, I feel that
an agenda will provide structure for the
meeting, promoting efficient handling of
business. More important topics can be talked
about first and less important matters can be
delt with if time permits. I also think that an
agenda keeps people from spending time on
irrelevant matters. An agenda distributed in
advance also gives people the chance to think
about topics beforehand and thus make better
contributions to the meeting.
         Here is the agenda I have set for Tuesday,
along with time and decision goals:

         * Develop criteria for creating new staff
           jobs
           Goal:  Devise a formula for deciding
                  how positions will be allocated
           Time:  30 minutes

         * Identify areas for new staff positions
           Goal:  Choose areas that best fit
                  criteria
           Time:  30 minutes

         * Select task force members to write
           report to vice pres.
           Goal:  Pick best author for each
                  section
           Time:  15 minutes

         * Other business:  15 minutes

         I look forward to seeing each of you on Tuesday
         morning.  If you have questions, please do not
         hesitate to ask.
```

Handwritten annotations:

- very busy people! memo too unfocused - wastes time!!
- redo first ¶ / condense
- too much background
- background / readers know this stuff
- or omit
- memo starts too slowly - readers will quit before they get to important info!
- ← essential meeting info buried - move
- awfully patronizing tone
- dealt
- irrelevant
- too many "I"'s / too much ego / Team="we."
- sounds pretty dictatorial
- move some of these / reasons
- this part O.K.
- not enough time allotted here.
- president
- stuffy / business / cliché
- whole memo too long-winded - / organization too round-about
- tired jargon.

**Tina's memo: final draft after revision**

To:      Task force members
From:    Tina Rodriguez
Date:    March 14, 199–
Subject: Agenda for March 18 meeting

The purpose of this memo is to let you know the agenda for our first task force meeting, which is scheduled for next Tuesday at 9:30 a.m. in the third-floor conference room. The vice president for human resources asked me to write up an agenda based on the directions she gave us last week.

Since we will be trying to formulate some firm recommendations about new staffing needs, this outline can help prepare us to accomplish as much as possible on Tuesday morning. Below are the major agenda items, along with time and decision goals:

  * Develop criteria for creating new staff jobs
      Goal:  Devise a formula for deciding how positions will
             be allocated
      Time:  30 minutes

  * Identify areas for new staff positions
      Goal:  Choose those areas that best fit criteria
      Time:  40 minutes

  * Select task force members to write report to vice
    president
      Goal:  Pick best author for each section of report
      Time:  10 minutes

  * Schedule date for next meeting. Other business.
      Goal:  Allow sufficient time for drafting report
      Time:  10 minutes

Having the agenda ahead of time should give everyone the chance to think about issues beforehand. Also, a plan for the meeting may help us handle business more efficiently and keep us from going off on tangents.

Please call me at extension 523 if you have comments or questions. See you all on Tuesday morning.

**41d**

*rev*

## Brad's essay: first draft

1
My Most Memorable Experience

Probably the most memorable experience in my life
is the trip I took to Europe for six weeks. It is
memorable for several reasons. They are: I explored new
surroundings; I made lasting friends; and I experienced
new cultures. All of this contributed to a general
maturing that took place in me over the course of the
six weeks that I spent in Europe. Here is how it
happened.

2
London, England is the one city that I remember for
the exploring that I did while there. In London on the
last thursday of the trip I did some "real" exploring.

3
That morning at breakfast Judy, our teacher-leader,
told us that we had the entire day free. We could do
what ever we wanted. We were given our sack lunches and
sent off. I, being an inexperienced shopper, don't like
to shop for things that don't interest me. Consequently
I went alone on this excursion. I planned to do some
serious shopping, and I didn't want to waste time
shopping for someone elses "important" items.

4
My first stop took me to that famed shopping
extravaganza, Harrods. Harrods is a stately, old
department store that just happens to serve the British
Royal family. I was overwhelmed at the selection and
quality of the merchandise that was on display there. I
can imagine what the employees thought of me as I gaped
at the fine merchandise on display. Such finery I had
never seen.

5
After purchasing two sweaters and thourghly

**41d**

*rev*

examining the first floor, I was hungry. I pulled out
my trusty map of London. Where to eat? Hmmn. . . ? Oh!
yes I've got a sack lunch. I almost forgot. I noticed
Hyde park was nearby, so I decided to walk there and
brown bag it in style.

6    As I look back, I realize that the day I spent in
London helped me to gain an independence that I had
never had before. I could actually take care of myself!
This, I feel, is an important step in my maturation
process.

7    As I look back, I can easily remember the night
Patti and I met a group of French students in Paris. We
were having a deep discussion on some important topic
when I noticed a group of students approach the area we
were sitting in the park. I became nervous. Since I
didn't speak French I had no way to communicate with
them. At first I thought that they were going to mugg
us. One of them asked me a question (in French of
course). I was astounded.

**41d**

*rev*

8    I replied, "I don't speak any French." This seemed
to puzzle them.

9    However, one replied, "Are you American?"

10   I almost freaked out! I couldn't believe that he
spoke English. I replied, "You speak English! WOW! How
old are all of you? . . ."

11   From the conversation that ensued Patti and I
learned much about France and the French. We talked of
favorite rock groups, favorite languages, and common
pasttimes. During the whole conversation the one that
spoke English acted as a translator. Now as I look
back, I realize, I realize that this particular
experience helped to broaden my people-meeting skills.

This experience was, fairly tipical. In almost every
city we were in we met and talked to total strangers.
These spontaneous talks I will never forget.

12          At our homestay in Bavaria (Germany), our hosts
threw a going away cookout party on the last night of
our stay. At the cookout we had steaks, baked potatoes,
bratwurst, pretzels, and of course beer. I think that
this particular experience is memorable because of the
good time that was had by all. We had a bon-fire,
around which we told tall tales and ghost stories until
the wee hours of the morning. Besides the tall tales, I
enjoyed talking with my hosts. The neatest thing was
their command of languages. The German youths could
speak at least two languages fluently, and they often
were knowledgable in a couple of other languages. I
remember we talked of politics, rock music, and common
interests. At the end I can remember many of my hosts
and travel companions crying because they all knew they
wuld mis their new friends and might never see them
again.

13          In Austria I spent an unforgettable week with the
Staudlbauer family. As I look back now I realize that
the entire week I was learning about their culture. At
the time, however, I didn't think of the significance of
this particular homestay. One evening my homestay
mother cooked cooked a typical Austrian meal that
included Rindsbraten (pork roast), sauerkraut, knudel
(dumplings), and a salad. After dinner my homestay
father, Peter, and brother, Patrick, and I took a
liesurely bike ride on some of the nearby country roads.
While riding we spoke of politics, business, athletics,
farming, and life in general. The irony was that my

**41d**

*rev*

father said he didn't speak any English, but the entire conversation was in English. I spoke very slowly and he followed along the best he could, nodding where it was appropriate. Occasionly he would say, "Ja." I think that he knew more English than he led me to believe. As time progressed I became very fond of Austrian customs and my homestay family. On the last day of the homestay I can remember seeing tears in Peter's eyes. I resolved to someday go back and visit. As our bus left the small town of 5,000 I can remember feeling a pang in my throat. I, too, would miss the Staudlbauers.

In summation I feel that the trip did several
things for me. It helped to broaden my views through showing me different view points. It helped to increase my independence through my exploration of the big cities I visited. As I look back I realize that I am now more mature. I'm not really sure if there was one incident that has made me more mature, but instead I think it was a more gradual process in which the entire trip played a good part. All of this has made the trip a very unforgetable part of my life.

14

**41d**

*rev*

**Brad's revision-in-progress (blue), with instructor's comments
(green)**

*boring title!*
My Most Memorable Experience

*combine sentences*

Probably the most (memorable experience) in my life

*When? Reader will want to know*

is the trip I took to Europe for six weeks) (It is)

22B

(memorable) for several reasons. They are: I explored new surroundings; I made lasting friends; and I experienced new cultures. All of this contributed to a general maturing that took place in me over the course of the

six weeks that I spent in Europe. Here is how it

happened.

2      London, England, is the one city that I remember
*redundant*

for the (exploring that I did while there.) In London on

the last Thursday of the trip (I did some "real" *25i*

(exploring.)
*no new ¶ (same topic)*

3      That morning at breakfast Judy, our teacher-leader, *20b*

told us that we had the entire day free. We could do
*whatever*
~~what ever~~ we wanted. We were given our sack lunches and

sent off. ~~I, being an inexperienced shopper, don't like~~

~~to shop for things that don't interest me.~~ Consequently

I went alone on this excursion. I planned to do some *Order of*
*ideas:*
serious shopping, and I didn't want to waste time *is this*
*chronology*
shopping for someone elses "important" items. *logical?*

4      *was*
My first stop ~~took me to~~ that famed shopping

extravaganza, Harrods. Harrods is a stately, old
*tone: attempt at humor may seem like snobbery to some*
department store that just happens to serve the British *readers*

Royal family. I was overwhelmed at the selection and

quality of the merchandise that was on display there. I

can imagine what the employees thought of me as I gaped

at the fine merchandise on display. Such finery I had
*Put some flesh on these bones, Brad. We need to see*
*concrete examples to understand why*
never seen.
*you were* After purchasing two sweaters and ~~thourghly~~ *thoroughly*
*overwhelmed.*

5      examining the first floor, I was hungry. I pulled out

my trusty map of London. Where to eat? Hmmn. . . ? Oh
*effective use of present-tense "thoughts" to pull reader into the*
yes! I've got a sack lunch. I almost forgot. I noticed *picture*

Hyde Park was nearby, so I decided to walk there and

brown bag it in style. *What made it stylish? not clear.*

6      *Notice how* (As I look back) (I realize) that the day I spent in
*often you*
*repeat* London helped me to gain an independence that I had *not enough previous evidence*
*these* *to support*
*phrases* never had before. I could actually take care of myself! *generalization*

*wordy—why I remember London so well*

This, I feel, is an <u>important step in my maturation</u>

process.

As I look back, I can easily remember the night

*another student ambassador*

Patti_ and I met a group of French students in Paris. We

*sitting on a park bench*

were having a deep discussion <u>on some important topic</u>

*ing us*

when I noticed a group of students approach <u>the area we</u>

<u>were sitting in the park</u>. I became nervous. Since I

didn't speak French I had no way to communicate to them, *20b*

*mug — why did*

At first I thought that they were going to <u>mugg</u> us. One *you*

*think*

of them asked me a question (in French of course). I *so?*

*Give*

was astounded. *Why? Explain* *reason.*

I replied, "I don't speak any French." This seemed

to puzzle them. *dialogue draws*

*reader into*

However, one replied, "Are you American?" *scene. Good!*

I almost <u>freaked out</u>! I couldn't believe that he

spoke English. I replied, "You speak English! WOW! How

old are all of you? . . ." *voice: conflicting tones here—*

*In* *we discussed* *slang*

<u>From</u> the conversation that <u>ensued</u> <u>Patti and I</u> *jars with*

*sophis-*

<u>learned much about France and the French. We talked of</u> *ticated*

*vocabulary*

favorite rock groups, favorite languages, and common

*sp.* (pasttimes.) During the whole conversation the one that

spoke English acted as a translator. (Now as I look)

(back), (I realize) <u>I realize</u> that this particular

*not really the point*

experience helped to broaden my people-meeting skills.

*typical*

This experience was fairly tipical. In almost every

city we were in we met and talked to total strangers.

*here's the point!*

These spontaneous talks I will never forget.

*audience: what's a homestay?*

At our (homestay) in Bavaria (Germany), our hosts

*30b*

threw a going away cookout party on the last night of

our stay. At the cookout we had steaks, baked potatoes,

bratwurst, pretzels, and of course beer. I think that

this particular experience is memorable because of the

**41d**

*rev*

7

8

9

10

11

12

*yuck! horrible cliché – says nothing*    *sp*

good time that was had by all. We had a ~~bon-fire~~, *this # goes*
                                                        *nowhere.*
around which we told tall tales and ghost stories until *French*
*another cliché*                                        *+ Austrian*
the wee hours of the morning. Besides the tall tales, I *examples*
                                    *37b*        *make some*
enjoyed talking with my hosts. The neatest thing was   *point*
                                               *with better*
their command of languages. The German youths could *detail.*
                                                        *cut!*
speak at least two languages fluently, and they often
                    *sp*
were ~~knowledgable~~ in a couple of other languages. ~~I~~

~~remember~~ we talked of politics, rock music, and common

interests. At the end ~~I can remember~~ many of my hosts

and travel companions crying because they all knew they
*would miss*
~~wuld mis~~ their new friends and might never see them

again.

3        In Austria I spent an unforgettable week with the

Staudlbauer family. ~~As I look back now I realize~~ that

the entire week I was learning about their culture. At

the time, however, I didn't think of the significance of
*Brad, this paragraph is mostly unfocused narrative*
this particular homestay. One evening my homestay

mother cooked ~~cooked~~ a typical Austrian meal that *too many*
                                                        *topics*
included Rindsbraten (pork roast), sauerkraut, knudel *in #*
                                                    *controlling*
(dumplings), and a salad. After dinner my homestay   *idea?*

father, Peter, and brother, Patrick, and I took a
*leisurely*
~~liesurely~~ bike ride on some of the nearby country roads.
            *We*
~~While riding~~ spoke of politics, business, athletics,
                                            *conversation)*
farming, and life in general. ~~The irony was that~~ My *not father'*
                                            *ironically    ironic*
father said he didn't speak any English, but the entire

conversation ~~was~~ in English. I spoke very slowly and he

followed along the best he could, nodding where it was
*What's your*      *Occasionally*          *audience: will readers know*
*point*  appropriate. ~~Occasionly~~ he would say, "Ja." I think  *what*
*here?*                                              *this word means?*
that he knew more English than he led me to believe. As
        *Ideas not related - need transition*
time progressed I became very fond of Austrian customs

and my homestay family. On the last day of the homestay

~~I can remember~~ seeing tears in Peter's eyes. I resolved

to someday go back and visit. As our bus left the small

town of 5,000 (I can remember) feeling a pang in my

throat. I, too, would miss the Staudlbauers. *with other*

*voice: very pompous language, not consistent* made me *vocabulary*

In summation I feel that the trip ~~did several~~    14

~~things for me~~. It helped to broaden my views through

showing me different view points. It helped to increase

my independence through my exploration of the big cities

I visited. (As I look back)(I realize) that I am now (more)

(mature). I'm not really sure if there was one incident

*say something about friendships*

that has made me more mature, but instead I think it was

*awful!*

a more gradual process in which the entire trip played a

good part. All of this has made the trip a very

unforgetable part of my life. *A weak ending, Brad. Also, check*

*your final paragraph against your thesis paragraph. Consistent?*

*Purpose fulfilled?*

## Brad's final draft

**41d**

*rev*

Truly a Learning Experience    1

Probably the most memorable experience in my life

is the six-week trip I took to Europe last summer as a

student ambassador in a youth exchange program. In

Europe I explored new surroundings, made lasting

friends, and experienced new cultures. All of this

contributed to a general maturing that took place in me

over the course of the six weeks. Here is a small

portion of how it happened.

London, England, is the one city that I remember    2

for the exploring that I did while there. In London on

the last Thursday of the trip, Judy, our teacher-leader,

told us at breakfast that we had the entire day free.

We could do whatever we wanted. We were given our sack

lunches and sent off. I planned to do some serious
shopping, and I didn't want to waste time shopping for
someone else's "important" items. Consequently, I chose
to go alone on my excursion.

3 My first stop was that famed shopping extravaganza,
Harrods. Harrods is a stately, old department store
that serves the British Royal family. I figured that if
it was good enough for Charles and Di, then it must be
good enough for me. I had been told what a fine store
Harrods was, but words just didn't do it justice.

4 Remembering Harrods now is like remembering
Christmas as a little boy. As I walked into this place,
a feeling of awe came over me. I simply stared in
wonder. But soon, like a boy at Christmas, I wanted to
examine the goodies. Browsing the first floor, I found
the men's section. In this area I saw the finest
clothing I had ever seen: pure cashmere sweaters in the
trendiest styles, velour robes that only wealthy
businessmen could afford to wear. Anything a man would
want, it was here.

**41d**

*rev*

5 I must have looked rather strange as I gaped at all
of the fine merchandise. I'm sure I looked much like
the Russians shopping in New York at Bloomingdale's in
the movie <u>Moscow on the Hudson.</u>

6 I had only covered one of Harrods six floors when
my stomach reminded me that I was starved. Leaving the
store in search of a place to eat, I pulled out my
trusty map of London. Where to eat? Hmmn. . . ? Oh,
yes! I've got a sack lunch. I almost forgot. I noticed
that Hyde Park was nearby, so I decided to walk there
and brown bag it in style on a park bench. Refueled, I
then took the subway (the "tube," as Londoners call it)

and rode to Oxford Circus, another of London's famous shopping districts.

I spent the afternoon in several department stores (none as impressive as Harrods), in a store that claimed to be the world's largest toy store, and in a store that advertised itself as London's largest record store—four floors of records and tapes! As I left the record store, I glanced at my watch and decided that I needed to find the hotel if I wanted to get fed that night. Heading toward the tube stop, I blended in with hundreds of other Londoners on their way home.

7

As I look back, I think that the day I spent shopping in London helped me to gain an independence that I had never before experienced. I discovered I could actually take care of myself in a totally unfamiliar foreign city. This is why London is still so memorable to me.

8

**41d**

*rev*

Sitting here at college, I recall a special evening in Paris. Patti, another student-ambassador, and I were seated on a park bench, enjoying a deep discussion. Everything was very peaceful in the park, a small one on a corner near our hotel. Suddenly there were intruders: I noticed a group of students approaching us, about to ruin the evening's peacefulness. I can remember a feeling of nervousness came over me as the students sat down next to us on one of the park's three benches. The quiet, the deepening darkness, the approach of these strangers . . . I had a weird feeling that we were about to be mugged. I'm sure that I jumped three feet when finally one of them spoke. I didn't know what he said, because I don't speak any French.

9

"I don't speak French," I replied nervously and

10

slowly so that the strangers could understand me.

11    "You are Americans? No?"

12    I certainly hadn't expected any of them to address me in English. I responded, "You speak English?"

13    "Yes, I try," the student said.

14    In the following conversation we discussed the differences between French and American school systems, rock music, and favorite pastimes. Patti and I were fascinated with the fact that the French student could speak two languages. I asked many questions about his mastery of English. Probably most fascinating—and difficult to comprehend—was that all of these students loved their native language. I really couldn't care less which language I speak, while the French love to hear the sound of their own language.

15    Looking back, I realize that during the entire conversation I was learning about French culture. I found the talking to the students very stimulating for the simple fact that I was learning about their world. Furthermore, I enjoyed the spontaneity of the conversation. Meeting and talking with total strangers in the middle of a foreign city was a unique and exciting experience. For these reasons, I will never forget that evening in Paris.

**41d**

*rev*

16    In Austria, I spent a week living with the Staudlbauer family. Several of these "homestays" were part of our trip. Not until sometime later did I realize the significance of this particular homestay. One evening my homestay mother cooked a typical Austrian meal: Rindsbraten (pork roast), sauerkraut, knudel (dumplings), and a salad. After dinner my homestay father, Peter, and brother, Patrick, and I took a

leisurely bicycle ride on some of the nearby country
roads.

We spoke of politics, business, athletics, farming,    17
and life in general. My father claimed that he didn't
speak any English, but ironically the whole conversation
was in English. As Patrick and I talked, I spoke slowly
and Peter followed along as best he could, nodding where
it was appropriate. Occasionally he would say "Ja"
("yes") in response or agreement. Although he may have
felt he could not "speak" English, I believe he
understood quite a bit. Any language barrier seemed
much less important than his participation in the
conversation. I really liked my homestay father for
that.

When we said goodbye on the last day of the    18
homestay, I saw tears in Peter's eyes. I, too, felt a
pang in my throat as our bus left the small Austrian
town of 5,000. I would miss the Staudlbauers, and I
resolved to go back someday and visit. But next time I
intend to go back knowing how to speak German, so that I
can talk with Peter in his own language.

I feel that the trip has made me more mature. It    19
helped to broaden my views through exposing me to
different viewpoints. It helped to increase my
independence through my exploration of the big cities
that we visited. Most of all, the trip has taught me to
be open to new experiences and, especially, new people.
Again and again, strangers became friends—sometimes in
the course of several days, sometimes in the course of
an hour or two. Because of these things, last summer's
trip is an unforgettable part of my life.

**41d**

*rev*

# 42

## WRITING PARAGRAPHS

When you initially draft a paragraph, your major concern is probably just getting your ideas down before you forget them. The actual contents and shape of the paragraph are the result of your planning decisions about your subject and purpose, attitude toward the subject, the nature of the audience, the voice or role you have assumed, and other goals that are part of the process of writing. You may even write your paper without being especially conscious of where or why you have placed paragraph indentions.

But when we read paragraphs, we have definite expectations about what they should do—based on what we have seen them do in the writing of others. Paragraphs "package" the writer's meaning for the reader. What do readers expect the paragraph packages to provide? They expect **unity** that derives from a **controlling idea** around which the paragraph is organized; **coherence** (from a Latin word meaning "to hang together") that links the thoughts within a paragraph, as well as relating the paragraph to those that precede and follow it; sufficient **development** to explain and illustrate the controlling idea.

You may ask, "Do readers really expect all these things? And how do I provide them if I'm busy working out my plans and trying to get my ideas down?" The answer to the first question is yes: research studies have conclusively shown that unity, coherence, and development are important to readers' ability to perceive and understand meaning. The answer to the second question is you don't try to do everything at once: some effective paragraphing may come on the first try, but more than likely it will result from revision, looking at your rough draft and reworking the paragraphs.

Unity, coherence, and development are abstract terms that may not seem very meaningful to you, but you can recognize the problems that occur in paragraphs lacking any of these three elements.

### PARAGRAPH LACKING UNITY
Club Tropic's beaches are beautiful, and the surrounding countryside is quite scenic. The quality of the food leaves a lot to be desired. Many vacationers enjoy the variety of outdoor activities and the instruction available in such sports as sailing and scuba diving. Unfortunately, security is poor; several vacationers' rooms have been broken into and their valuables stolen. Christmas in the Bahamas can make the thought of New Year's in Chicago bearable.

The paragraph lacking unity jumps from subject to subject with no clear sense of goal or purpose. What have scenery, food, sports, and security to do with each other? Until the author provides a controlling idea to unite the sentences and give them focus, we will never know.

Compare the following revision with the original version. Notice that the writer has supplied a controlling topic sentence at the beginning and eliminated those sentences that do not contribute to the paragraph's main idea. As a result, the paragraph's concluding sentence now makes sense.

UNIFIED PARAGRAPH WITH TOPIC SENTENCE

For vacationers sick and tired of the frozen north, a week at Club Tropic can provide just the midwinter thaw they need. Club Tropic's beaches are beautiful, and the surrounding countryside is quite scenic. Many vacationers also enjoy the variety of outdoor activities and the instruction available in such sports as sailing and scuba diving. Christmas in the Bahamas can make the thought of New Year's in Chicago bearable.

The next example paragraph, showing lack of coherence, contains a topic sentence, and all the other sentences bear some relation to that controlling idea: vacationers' dissatisfaction. However, because the individual sentences are not clearly connected, the ideas in the paragraph don't "stick together."

PARAGRAPH LACKING COHERENCE

Club Tropic's isolation created dissatisfaction among some vacationers. The quality of the food was poor. People want a choice of entertainment in the evening. Most of us spent too much time together day after day. People expect to be able to go out for a meal if they feel like it.

In the following revision, notice how the writer has used transition words and a new organization, among other things, to establish logical relationships among ideas.

COHERENT PARAGRAPH

Club Tropic's isolation created dissatisfaction among some vacationers. Many people expect to be able to go out for a meal if they feel like it, but the club's location far from populated areas made that impossible. To make matters worse, the quality of the food was poor. The isolated location also forced people to spend all their time together—day after day. By evening nearly everyone was ready for a choice of food, entertainment, and company.

The following example paragraph, lacking development, leaves too many questions in the reader's mind.

**42**

¶

PARAGRAPH LACKING DEVELOPMENT
A vacation at Club Tropic has its good points and bad points.
The beaches are nice, but they may not be enough for some vaca-
tioners.

Only one "good point" (nice beaches) is mentioned. Are there others?
No example of a bad point is given, so how is the reader to judge
whether nice beaches are enough to attract vacationers to Club
Tropic? And what, exactly, does "enough" mean? If the reader is to
understand the controlling idea, or even be interested in it, it must be
explained and supported sufficiently. Compare the original with the
following revision.

DEVELOPED PARAGRAPH
A midwinter vacation at Club Tropic has its good points and bad
points. The beaches are clean and uncrowded. The surrounding
countryside is lush and soothing to winter-weary eyes. Furthermore,
being able to take sailing and scuba diving lessons, while friends
back home shovel snow, makes the outdoor activities extra-enjoyable.
On the other hand, several features of Club Tropic are substandard.
The food is poor, and, because the club is isolated, eating elsewhere
is impossible. Security could also be better, as thefts from several
guests' rooms indicated. So, for some vacationers, nice scenery and
fun activities may not be enough to offset the possibility of poor
service and lax security.

By now you should have some idea of the differences between
paragraphs with and without unity, coherence, and development. An
important key, as always, is your reader. You may know perfectly well
what you mean, what point you are trying to make in any given paragraph. You may be able to see it all in your mind's eye. But your
readers cannot. They have not lived your life, do not necessarily share
your perceptions, and should not be asked to "read between the lines."

**42**

**¶**

---

## WRITERS REVISING: PARAGRAPHS

Michelle had drafted an essay on the Social Security system for her American government class. Typing with a
word-processing program on her computer, she could draft
quickly and make corrections easily—with no evidence of the
changes. The printout looked like a clean, finished essay. Ap-
pearances aside, Michelle knew that she had been pouring out
her ideas without much attention to paragraphing. Below is a

portion of her essay. Reparagraph it as you think necessary, looking for topic sentences, units of ideas, and transition markers. Then compare your version to Michelle's revision at the end of this section. Be prepared to explain your choices, which may differ from hers. What differences in emphasis and meaning do the various paragraph changes make?

### Michelle's Draft

D 1      With only 116 million workers paying into the

D 2    Social Security program and a whopping 36 million

D 3    receiving benefits, it is overburdened. After

D 4    fifty years of existence, the world's largest

D 5    social program is on the verge of collapse. To

D 6    understand the shortcomings of the Social Security

D 7    system, we must be aware of the conditions under

D 8    which and the intentions with which the system was

D 9    created. In 1935 President Franklin Roosevelt

D10    signed the Social Security Act.

D11      In those days 35 million workers supported

D12    the program with their payroll taxes, and only 106

D13    thousand beneficiaries drew from the program. In

D14    addition, the average life span was shorter in

D15    1935 than it is today. Because of the relatively

D16    small number of eligible retirees and the short

D17    life span, the average worker paid only a maximum

D18    of $30 per year, while beneficiaries received a

D19    maximum of $492 per year. Today, however, the

D20    maximum payroll tax is $2,792 annually, and only

D21    three workers support each beneficiary who

D22    receives up to $15,000 in benefits. To make

D23    things worse, the number of retirees is on the

D24    rise, and it will continue to rise as the baby

42
¶

D25 boom generation ages. The bottom line is

D26 that the Social Security Administration will

D27 operate at a deficit by the year 2020 despite

D28 corrective legislation passed by Congress in 1983

D29 that was designed to make the program solvent for

D30 years to come.

This *Writers Revising* continues on page 431.

## 42a Paragraph unity: using a controlling idea

A unified paragraph has a single clear focus, and all its sentences relate to that focus. As we noted in the Club Tropic example, any unrelated sentence seems to be off the subject and thus destroys the paragraph's unity. The focus for a paragraph is achieved by means of a **controlling idea** around which the paragraph is organized, just as the focus of a whole essay is achieved by means of a controlling idea. In an essay that idea appears in the thesis, either clearly implied or explicitly stated. Similarly, in a paragraph the controlling idea is clearly implied or, more commonly, explicitly stated in the **topic sentence.**

Like a thesis statement, a topic sentence presents the subject of the paragraph in the subject position of the sentence. The predicate contains the focus words, the assertion being made about the subject. Sometimes this main idea is expressed as a generalization, and the rest of the paragraph provides the supporting evidence, concrete examples, and explanatory detail. The first sample paragraph that follows in this section (p. 398) shows a topic-sentence generalization with supporting details.

**42a**

**¶ un**

**1. Nature of the topic sentence.** The exact nature of a topic sentence will depend on the purpose of the paragraph. For example, some paragraphs are meant merely to deliver information without making a particularly forceful assertion about the information. A paragraph about parent-child bonding might have as its topic sentence *Touching is one of the main ways bonding occurs between a mother and her newborn* and then go on to describe other types of bonding behavior as well, without the reader's feeling the paragraph has become disunified. This topic sentence can be described as having rather loose control over its paragraph. Other topic sentences present stronger assertions, going beyond statements of fact to make arguable propositions.

These types of topic sentences often exert strong control, defining more sharply what ideas are and are not relevant to the paragraph. The topic sentence *Some of the problems of psychologically disturbed children can be traced to a lack of bonding in infancy* allows for no digressions if the paragraph is to fulfill readers' expectations concerning unity. This paragraph will go about the business of showing a cause-and-effect relationship between parent-child bonding and psychological problems. Both types of topic sentences can be appropriate for their contexts; after all, paragraphs perform a variety of functions—from introducing a subject to providing transition between the events in a narrative to summarizing the points of an argument.

   **2. Placement of the topic sentence.** Research has shown that from the reader's standpoint the best place for a topic sentence is the beginning of a paragraph. Understanding will be quicker and more complete if the reader has a general idea of the subject and where the writer is headed with it. Topic sentences provide this information—which explains why your English teachers have often encouraged you to start your paragraphs with a topic sentence.

   But we also know from observation that many excellent writers and many, many quite satisfactory paragraphs do not position the topic sentence first. The explanation is that what readers need is an initial sentence that orients them, provides an appropriate frame of reference for relating new information to what they already know (or have read), an opening sentence that readies readers to understand "what this is going to be about." This orienting sentence need not be the topic sentence.

   The emphatic positions in paragraphs are the same as in sentences—first and last. As readers, we expect to find the key information first. If it's not delivered in the form of a topic sentence, then some other orienting words must be supplied. When they are not, we have to make inferences and build our own meanings—a time-consuming and risky business, since we are apt to create meanings quite different from the writer's intention.

   The following paragraphs illustrate various placements for the topic sentence. When it is not positioned first in a paragraph, note how the writer initially orients the reader.

   **a. *Topic sentence first*.** Such paragraphs state their central idea first and then add details supporting it. This kind of paragraph occurs in expository writing, but it also appears in persuasive and descriptive writing as well.

TOPIC SENTENCE FIRST
   The ENCYCLOPAEDIA BRITANNICA, *although a valuable research tool, is difficult to read and hard to handle—hardly designed for the hasty researcher.* Each article is thorough and detailed, but the tiny print is

extremely hard to read. To be assured of getting every fact and detail, the researcher needs a strong light and, unless his eyes are keen, a magnifying glass. To pick up a volume in the first place, one needs both hands. One doesn't balance a *Britannica* volume in one hand while scribbling furiously with the other. A table or desk to lay the volume open on is absolutely necessary. But even sitting comfortably at a desk with a *Britannica* presents problems. To avoid crushing or tearing the onion-thin pages requires slow, deliberate, careful moves. Haste or carelessness could easily result in obliterating the whole article one wishes to read. Given these disadvantages to using the *Encyclopaedia Britannica*, fly-by-night researchers should consider other general reference books.

*Student paragraph*

**b.** *Transitional topic sentence.* A paragraph's first sentence may combine a transition from the preceding paragraph with the topic statement of the new paragraph. In the following example, the references to Dawson's location and size allude to topics in the paragraph preceding the one reproduced here; the clause in italics states the topic of the example paragraph.

TRANSITIONAL INFORMATION AND TOPIC SENTENCE FIRST
    Although it lay in the shadow of the Arctic Circle, more than four thousand miles from civilization, and although it was the only settlement of any size in a wilderness area that occupied hundreds of thousands of square miles, *Dawson was livelier, richer, and better equipped than many larger Canadian and American communities.* It had a telephone service, running water, steam heat, and electricity. It had dozens of hotels, many of them better appointed than those on the Pacific Coast. It had motion-picture theaters operating at a time when the projected motion picture was just three years old. It had restaurants where string orchestras played *Cavalleria Rusticana* for men in tailcoats who ate pâté de fois gras and drank vintage wines. It had fashions from Paris. It had dramatic societies, church choirs, glee clubs, and vaudeville companies. It had three hospitals, seventy physicians, and uncounted platoons of lawyers. Above all, it had people.

PIERRE BERTON, *The Klondike Fever*

**42a**

**¶** *un*

**c.** *Topic sentence last.* Such paragraphs give details first and lead up to the main point in the final sentence.

TOPIC SENTENCE LAST
    Beginning at breakfast with flying globs of oatmeal, spilled juice, and toast that always lands jelly-side down, a day with small children grows into a nightmare of frantic activity, punctuated with shrieks, cries, and hyena-style laughs. The very art of playing turns the house into a disaster area: blankets and sheets that are thrown over

tables and chairs to form caves, miniature cars and trucks that race endlessly up and down hallways, and a cat that becomes a caged tiger, imprisoned under the laundry basket. After supper, with more spilled milk, uneaten vegetables, and tidbits fed to the cat under the table, it's finally time for bed. But before they fall blissfully asleep, the children still have time to knock over one more bedtime glass of water, jump on the beds until the springs threaten to break, and demand a last ride to the bathroom on mother's back. *Constant confusion is a way of life for parents of small children.*

*Student paragraph*

**d.** *Topic sentence first and last.* In such paragraphs the last sentence repeats the idea of the first, frequently restating it with some amplification or a slightly different emphasis in the light of the intervening details or discussion.

TOPIC SENTENCES FIRST AND LAST

*A metal garbage can lid has many uses.* In the spring it can be used to catch rainwater in which a small boy can create a world of his own, a world of dead leaves and twigs inhabited by salamanders, small frogs, and worms. In the summer it can be turned on its top, the inside lined with aluminum foil, and used to hold charcoal for a barbecue. In the fall it can be used, with a similar lid, to frighten unsuspecting Halloween "trick-or-treaters." In the winter, if the handle is removed or flattened, the lid can be used by children to speed down snow-packed hills. *A garbage can lid covers garbage most of the time, but with a little imagination, one can uncover new uses for it.*

*Student paragraph*

**42a**

**¶ un**

**e.** *Implied topic sentence.* Sometimes a writer may decide not to use an explicitly stated topic sentence. This is frequently the case in narrative and descriptive paragraphs, but it can also be appropriate in other types of writing. However, implied topic sentences carry risks; omit a topic sentence only if you are very sure that your reader can state the controlling idea if asked to do so. In the following paragraph by Joan Didion, for example, the controlling idea might be stated thus: "Though the sources of one's childhood imaginings are long lost, the record of those imaginings perhaps reveals lifelong habits of mind."

NO EXPLICIT TOPIC SENTENCE; IMPLIED CONTROLLING IDEA

My first notebook was a Big Five tablet, given to me by my mother with the sensible suggestion that I stop whining and learn to amuse myself by writing down my thoughts. She returned the tablet to me a few years ago; the first entry is an account of a woman who believed herself to be freezing to death in the Arctic night, only to find, when day broke, that she had stumbled onto the Sahara Desert, where she would die of the heat before lunch. I have no idea what turn of a five-year-old's mind could have prompted so insistently "ironic" and exotic a story, but it does reveal a certain predilection for the extreme which has dogged me into adult life; perhaps if I were analytically inclined I would find it a truer story than any I might have told about Donald Johnson's birthday party or the day my cousin Brenda put Kitty Litter in the aquarium.

JOAN DIDION, "On Keeping a Notebook"

---

EXERCISE 42a(1)
Following are two topic sentences, each accompanied by a set of statements. Some of the statements are relevant to the topic, some are not. Eliminate the irrelevant ones, and organize the rest into a paragraph.

1. What does work mean to you?

Do you think of it as an activity that takes more from you than it gives to you?

Some workers are workaholics.

Do you think of the distinction between play and work as that between pleasure and pain?

Many dislike the work they do because it doesn't pay enough.

Do you live to work?

Do you work to live?

Regardless of your answers one thing is certain: work is here to stay.

Rewarding work discourages clock watchers.

By work, I mean the human expenditure of time and energy (both physical and mental) to complete a task.

This definition is a very broad one.

When you stop and think about it, it means that you spend the overwhelming majority of your waking hours at work.

Work, like death and taxes, is an all-encompassing and inescapable reality of life.

2. We owe some of our notions of radar to scientific observation of bats.

Most people hate bats.

Bats are commonly considered unattractive, ugly creatures.

They really look more like mice with wings than anything else.

Scientists noticed that bats rarely collided with anything in their erratic flight.

Keen eyesight could not be the reason for their flying the way they do, since bats are blind.

It was found that bats keep sending out noises inaudible to people and that they hear the echoes of those noises.

This principle whereby they fly safely was found to be similar to the main principle of radar.

42a

¶ *un*

EXERCISE 42a(2)

What is the topic sentence, expressed or implied, in each of the following paragraphs?

1.   Is it not just an intelligent appraisal of his circumstances that transforms the single man. It is not merely a desire for companionship or "growth." It is a deeper alchemy of change, flowing from a primal source. It seeps slowly into the flesh, the memory, the spirit; it rises through a life, until it can ignite. It is a perilous process, full of chances for misfire and mistake—or for an ever more mildewed middle age. It is not entirely understood. But we have seen it work, and so have we seen love. Love infuses reason and experience with the power to change a man caught in a morbid present into a man passionately engaged with the future.

GEORGE BILDER, "Naked Nomads: Unmarried Men in America"

2.   In a world of ever-accelerating competition and change in the conditions of the workplace, of ever-greater danger, and of ever-larger opportunities for those prepared to meet them, educational reform should focus on the goal of creating a Learning Society. At the heart of such a society is the commitment to a set of values and to a system of education that affords all members the opportunity to stretch their minds to full capacity, from early childhood through adulthood, learning more as the world itself changes. Such a society has as a basic foundation the idea that education is important not only because of what it contributes to one's career goals but also because of the value it adds to the general quality of one's life. Also at the heart of the Learning Society are educational opportunities extending far beyond the traditional institutions of learning, our schools and colleges. They extend into homes and workplaces; into libraries, art galleries, museums, and science centers; indeed, into every place where the individual can develop and mature in work and life. In our view, formal schooling in youth is the essential foundation for learning throughout one's life. But without life-long learning, one's skills will become rapidly dated.

DAVID P. GARDNER, *A Nation at Risk*

¶ *un*

3.   Every writer has his own ways of getting started, from sharpening pencils, to reading the Bible, to pacing the floor. I often rinse out my mind by reading something, and I sometimes manage to put off getting down to the hard struggle for an unconscionable time. Mostly I am helped through the barrier by music. I play records while I am writing and especially at the start of each day one particular record that accompanies the poem or chapter I am working at. During these last weeks it has been a record by Albinoni for strings and organ. I do not always play that key record, but it is there to draw on—the key to a certain piece of work, the key to that mood. The romantic composers, much as I enjoy listening to them at other times, are no help. Bach, Mozart, Vivaldi—they are what I need—clarity and structure.

MAY SARTON, "The Art of Writing"

4.      An atmosphere that is a strange mixture of bleakness, tranquil-
lity, and expectancy pervades the downstairs hall of the old gym
early in the morning. As I walk from the chilly dawn outdoors into
the basement of the old gym, I feel the dry heat on my face; although I assume that I am alone, I am surrounded by the impersonal noises of an antiquated steam-heating system. All the doors,
which stand like sentries along the walls of the hallway, are locked,
so that the deserted nature of that place and that hour are apparent;
pipes hang from above, making the ceiling resemble the ugly, rarely
viewed underside of a bizarre animal. I feel peaceful, however, in
this lonely place, because of the silence. I know, moreover, that the
desertlike heat is a sign that preparation has been made for my arrival and a signal that the day of work is about to begin.

*Student paragraph*

5.      Some mysteries, however, persisted. How to account for the continuing disappearance of fingers, in part or whole? Why was it that
parts of fingers would vanish from one day to the next? Were they
knocked off? There was nothing to indicate that bones of lepers
were any more brittle than the bones of normal people. If a leper
cut off a finger while using a saw, or if a finger were somehow broken off, it should be possible to produce the missing digit. But no
one ever found a finger after it had been lost. Why?

NORMAN COUSINS, *Anatomy of an Illness*

---

# 42b  Paragraph coherence: organizing ideas

A coherent paragraph moves logically from thought to thought,
knitting the thoughts together in an orderly way. The ideas should
flow into one another so that their relation to the paragraph's main
point is clear. Unfortunately, "flow" is difficult to define, although its
absence is easy to detect.

**42b**

**¶ coh**

You can apply several strategies to achieve coherence in your
paragraphs as you write them or to check for it as you revise and edit
them. One strategy is to use organizational structures both familiar to
your reader and appropriate to the development of your paragraph's
controlling idea. These structures are also used to organize whole essays (see Section **41**).

Organization can help readers understand your ideas because it
provides a familiar shape, a built-in structural logic that can aid the
reader. Organizational structure alone can't make a paragraph coherent; Sections **42c** and **42d** explain other types of structure necessary
to coherent paragraphs. The following are organizational options for
coherent paragraphs.

**1. Time.** Narrative paragraphs naturally arrange themselves in
the order in which the events occur, as in this paragraph recounting
the death of an eagle. Such ordering of events is *chronological*.

CHRONOLOGICAL ORDER
On her own, one of the female's bold hunting trips was to prove fatal. The male saw from high above that she was making an attack on a ground squirrel in a dry arroyo. Her path would take her over an embankment at low altitude. Hidden from her view were two hunters walking close to the bluff. The male tensed as he saw his mate approach the men. As her black form swept over the hunters, they whirled and raised their guns. The female saw, but too late. As she banked sharply, two shots sang out and one slug tore through her body, sending her crashing in a crumpled mass. Helpless and distraught, the male watched from above as the hunters stretched out the wings of his mate and examined their prize. With the fear of man reinforced in his mind, he turned away and mounted up to return to the safety of the back country.

KENT DURDEN, *Flight to Freedom*

Specific directions and explanations of processes also arrange themselves naturally in time order. The following directions for mixing powdered clay proceed step by step through the process.

CHRONOLOGICAL ORDER
Clay purchased in powder form is mixed with water to make it a plastic mass. To mix, fill a large dishpan or small tub about one-third full of water, sift clay over [the] water, one handful at a time, until [the] clay settles on top of the water to make a coating about 1 inch thick. Cover [the] pan with paper or cloth and let the unstirred mixture set overnight. On the following day mix and stir it thoroughly. If [the] mass is too thick to knead, add more water. If too thin, add dry clay. Clay is in a state to store when it is soft and pliable but does not stick to the hands. Since clay improves with aging in a damp condition, mix as far ahead of time of use as you can. Wrap [the] clay in damp cloth and store in a covered crock for at least one week before using.

HERBERT H. SANDERS, "How to Make Pottery and Ceramic Sculpture"

**42b**

**¶ coh**

**2. Space.** Many descriptive paragraphs arrange themselves easily according to some spatial order, from east to west, from bottom to top, from near to far, from the center outward, and the like. In the following paragraph, the writer is describing the interior of her church's sanctuary. She carefully orders the details, always keeping the relative position of parts clear with such directional words and phrases as *over, above, on each side,* and with such descriptive verbs as *separated, line, hang, guard, flank,* and *arching.*

SPATIAL ORDER
The sanctuary of the First Presbyterian Church is a study in nineteenth century architecture. *The sections* of contoured, crescent-shaped oak pews *separated* by *two main aisles line the wedge-shaped main*

*floor. Over the main floor in the rear hangs a balcony* supported by two Greek columns whose decorative gilt tops complement similar ornamentation *at the front upper corners of the auditorium. Brass rails guard the balcony seats and separate* the raised *podium from the choir loft behind it. Above and on each side of the podium* are opera-box windows of beveled glass and brass. *Three stained-glass windows flank each side* of the sanctuary and, gleaming in the sunlight, depict such simple religious subjects as lilies, the cross, and Christ in his roles of Shepherd and Comforter. The most distinctive feature, however, is the *huge fifteen-foot rotunda opening up the center* of the ceiling and arching its way to heaven.

*Student paragraph*

**3. General to particular or particular to general.** Many paragraphs begin with a topic sentence that makes a general statement, followed by sentences supporting the general statement with details, examples, and evidence. Other paragraphs reverse this order, presenting a series of details or reasons first and concluding with a general statement that summarizes.

In the following paragraph the author begins with a general statement—that teenage rejection-in-love is tormenting—and then she describes the specific behavior that constitutes the supporting particulars of the paragraph.

GENERAL-TO-PARTICULAR ORDER

Rejection-in-love is one of the most tormenting aspects of teenage life you will ever be forced to witness. Because it's like this: The first time a teenage boy ever gets serious about a girl, he realizes that she is a very highly evolved creature. That unlike his two best friends, Chuck and Ernie, she is actually able to carry on a conversation without bugging her eyes, belching, swearing, or kicking parking meters. So he tells this girl some *very important junk* about his innermost psyche, and if it works, great. If it doesn't—well, it doesn't become the end of the world; but the end of the world will certainly be visible from where he's sitting.

STEPHANIE BRUSH, "Understanding Teenage Boys"

**42b**

**¶ coh**

In the following paragraph, the author begins by asserting that disasters may not be as widespread as records indicate. To support this statement, she contrasts the range of events reported in the news with the relative normalcy of most people's typical day. She then states the "law" she has formulated on the basis of her perception of the true situation. The paragraph thus moves from general to particular back to general.

GENERAL-TO-PARTICULAR ORDER

Disaster is rarely as pervasive as it seems from recorded accounts. The fact of being on the record makes it appear continuous and ubiquitous whereas it is more likely to have been sporadic both in time and place. Besides, persistence of the normal is usually greater than the effect of disturbance, as we know from our own times. After absorbing the news of today, one expects to face a world consisting entirely of strikes, crimes, power failures, broken water mains, stalled trains, school shutdowns, muggers, drug addicts, neo-Nazis, and rapists. The fact is that one can come home in the evening—on a lucky day—without having encountered more than one or two of these phenomena. This has led me to formulate Tuchman's Law, as follows: "The fact of being reported multiplies the apparent extent of any deplorable development by five- to tenfold" (or any figure the reader would care to supply).

BARBARA TUCHMAN, *A Distant Mirror*

In contrast to the two preceding paragraphs, the following paragraph moves from particular to general. The writer, at the time the head of the Environmental Protection Agency, talks about people's particular frustrations with the agency first and then moves to the generalization that solutions to these frustrations do not depend on which political party is in power in Congress or the White House.

PARTICULAR-TO-GENERAL ORDER

When people get frustrated—understandably, to be sure—about why their dump isn't cleaned up or why there is still acid in the rain or asbestos in their schools, it is natural for them to look around for [somebody] to grab [by the lapels] and we are all they've got. I suppose this is bearable as long as we disabuse ourselves of the idea that these problems are susceptible to partisan interpretations. They are not. They are real, and in spite of what you may hear in the next five weeks [of the congressional election campaign], you can't vote them out of office.

WILLIAM RUCKELSHAUS, "Lapel Shaking"

**42b**

**¶ coh**

**4. Climax.** Many paragraphs can be made coherent as well as more effective by arranging details or examples in order of increasing importance. The writer of the following paragraph arranged its examples—kinds of jobs—in order of climax. Drucker's evidence moves from those jobs in which skill at expressing oneself (the paragraph's subject) is least important to those in which it is most important.

CLIMACTIC ORDER

If you work as a soda jerker you will, of course, not need much skill in expressing yourself to be effective. If you work on a machine, your ability to express yourself will be of little importance. But as soon as you move one step up from the bottom, your effectiveness depends on your ability to reach others through the spoken or the written word. And the further away your job is from manual work, the larger the organization of which you are an employee, the more important it will be that you know how to convey your thoughts in writing or speaking. In the very large business organization, whether it is the government, the large corporation, or the Army, this ability to express oneself is perhaps the most important of all the skills a man can possess.

PETER F. DRUCKER, "How to Be an Employee"

---

**EXERCISE 42b(1)**

Some organizational patterns share characteristics that can work nicely together when the patterns are combined in a single paragraph. For example, try writing a paragraph that uses both chronological order and climactic order, or try spatial order and climactic order together.

---

**5. Comparison and contrast.** Some controlling ideas naturally suggest organization by comparison and contrast. Consider these topic sentences:

My brother is a natural student; I am a natural nonstudent.

Women have a long way to go before they have genuinely equal opportunity and recognition, but they have gone some of the distance since my mother finished high school.

Foreign wines may have virtues, but if we compare them carefully to their American counterparts, we'll choose the American.

Such sentences either directly assert or imply a contrast and almost require the writer to fill out the details of that contrast.

The paragraph that follows compares poetry and advertising, developing the assertion that they are alike in many ways by giving three examples of their similarity. The parallel constructions that mark the successive points of comparison and help give the paragraph coherence are in italics.

**42b**

**¶ coh**

COMPARISON

Nevertheless, poetry and advertising have much in common. To begin with, *they both make extensive use* of rhyme and rhythm ("What's the word? Thunderbird!"). *They both use words chosen* for their affective and connotative values rather than for their denotative content ("Take a puff . . . it's springtime! Gray rocks and the fresh green leaves of springtime reflected in a mountain pool. . . . Where else can you find air so refreshing? And where can you find a smoke as refreshing as Salem's?"). William Empson, the English critic, said in his *Seven Types of Ambiguity* that *the best poems are ambiguous;* they are richest when they have two or three or more levels of meaning at once. *Advertising, too,* although on a much more primitive level, *deliberately exploits ambiguities* and plays on words: a vodka is advertised with the slogan "Leaves you breathless"; an automobile is described as "Hot, Handsome, a Honey to Handle."

S. I. HAYAKAWA, *Language in Thought and Action*

In the preceding paragraph, the similarity between two things constitutes the central idea. But in many paragraphs, although the controlling idea does not state a comparison or contrast, it requires one. In the following paragraph, for example, the author contends that because beginning writers do not know how writing differs from speech, they proceed under false assumptions. Her assertion requires her to explain some of the contrasts between writing and speaking.

CONTRAST

Here the problem of unfamiliar forms merges with the second pedagogical problem—that *the beginning writer does not know how writers behave.* Unaware of the ways in which writing is different from speaking, he imposes the conditions of speech upon writing. As an extension of speech, writing does, of course, draw heavily upon a writer's competencies as a speaker—his grammatical intuitions, his vocabulary, his strategies for making and ordering statements, etc., but it also demands new competencies, namely the skills of the encoding process (handwriting, spelling, punctuation) and the skill of objectifying a statement, of looking at it, changing it by additions, subtractions, substitutions, or inversions, taking the time to get as close a fit as possible between what he means and what he says on paper. Writers who are not aware of this tend to think that the point in writing is to get everything right the first time and that the need to change things is a mark of the amateur. (Thus a student who saw a manuscript page of Richard Wright's *Native Son,* with all its original deletions and substitutions, concluded that Wright couldn't have been much of a writer if he made all those "mistakes.")

MINA SHAUGHNESSY, *Errors and Expectations*

**42b**

**¶ coh**

In any comparison or contrast, it is important to arrange the points of similarity or difference clearly. The more extended the comparison, the more crucial clear ordering becomes. Note how careful the writer of the two following paragraphs is to keep the same order within the two paragraphs. In each, he speaks first of Roosevelt, then of Churchill; in each he moves back, at the end of the paragraph, to a telling final point of comparison. The careful point-by-point ordering of the paragraphs helps keep them coherent. (See also Section **41a(5).**

COMPARISON AND CONTRAST

*Roosevelt,* as a public personality, was a spontaneous, optimistic, pleasure-loving ruler who dismayed his assistants by the gay and apparently heedless abandon with which he seemed to delight in pursuing two or more totally incompatible policies, and astonished them even more by the swiftness and ease with which he managed to throw off the cares of office during the darkest and most dangerous moments. *Churchill* too loves pleasure, and he lacks neither gaiety nor a capacity for exuberant self-expression, together with the habit of blithely cutting Gordian knots in a manner which often upsets his experts; but he is not a frivolous man. *His nature possesses a dimension of depth—and a corresponding sense of tragic possibilities, which Roosevelt's lighthearted genius instinctively passed by.* Roosevelt played the game of politics with virtuosity, and both his successes and his failures were carried off in splendid style; his performance seemed to flow with effortless skill. Churchill is acquainted with darkness as well as light. Like all inhabitants and even transient visitors of inner worlds, he gives evidence of seasons of agonized brooding and slow recovery. *Roosevelt might have spoken of sweat and blood, but when Churchill offered his people tears, he spoke a word which might have been uttered by Lincoln or Mazzini or Cromwell but not Roosevelt, greathearted, generous, and perceptive as he was.*

ISAIAH BERLIN, "Mr. Churchill"

A special kind of comparison is **analogy.** An analogy draws a parallel between two things that have some resemblance on the basis of which other resemblances are to be inferred; it compares the unfamiliar with the familiar or points up striking or unusual similarities between familiar things. When a comparison is drawn between a large city and an anthill or between a college and a factory or between the human nervous system and a telephone system, that is analogy. Although they may be quite inexact in many respects, parallels of this sort enable us to visualize ideas or relationships and therefore to understand them better, as the following analogy about a herd of African elephants illustrates.

ANALOGY

A herd of elephant, as seen from a plane, has a quality of an hallucination. The proportions are wrong—they are like those of a child's drawing of a field mouse in which the whole landscape, complete with barns and windmills, is dwarfed beneath the whiskers of the mighty rodent who looks both able and willing to devour everything, including the thumb-tack that holds the work against the schoolroom wall.

BERYL MARKHAM, *West with the Night*

42b

¶ *coh*

In the paragraph that follows, the writer compares the student's job of managing time to that of the juggler's coordinating multiple tennis balls or Indian clubs.

ANALOGY

A college student trying to organize studies and activities is like a juggler trying to manage several tennis balls or Indian clubs at once. Each student takes several courses that have varying types and amounts of required work. He or she must learn to manage time so as to get all work for each course done on schedule. The task of the student in managing the work of four or five different courses alone is similar to that of the juggler coordinating four or five tennis balls at once. But in addition to four or five courses, the student must also fulfill responsibilities to perhaps two or three organizations and manage social activities with friends. If the student cannot learn to distribute time wisely among all these different demands, he or she may begin to feel like the juggler who has lost coordination; work and activities may begin to scatter in disarray, like the juggler's tennis balls which fall to the ground around him. In contrast, the student who learns to manage time effectively keeps studies and varied activities flowing smoothly, just as the juggler who successfully creates a smooth circle of six or eight flying tennis balls or Indian clubs.

*Student paragraph*

**6. Analysis and classification.** Analysis takes things apart. Classification groups things together on the basis of their differences or similarities. You use them both every day. You break your days into morning, noon, and night; in the supermarket you look for pepper among the spices and hamburger in the meat department, because you know that's the way they're classified. Similarly in writing, in both individual paragraphs and entire essays, analysis and classification frequently can serve as guides to organization.

In the next example, the writer humorously analyzes the types of assignments that college students are asked to do during a semester. She classifies each assignment on the basis of the emotional effect it has on the student.

CLASSIFICATION

After the first semester at a university, a student may notice that homework assignments can be categorized according to the various emotional states they produce. For example, "The I'll-Do-It-Later-Tonight" assignment is a relatively easy assignment which takes no more than five or ten minutes and causes the student little inconvenience or worry. Related to this type is "The-I-Thought-I-Could-Do-It-Later-Tonight" assignment, which seems simple but is in reality much more than the student bargained for. This type often causes a sleepless night for the panicking student. "The-Impossible-Dream" assignment also causes the student a certain amount of panic. These assignments, also known as semester projects, are designed to take the majority of the semester to complete, and they seem to hang over the student's head like a dark cloud of doom. Much like this assignment, but perhaps even more traumatic, is "The-I'm-Going-To-Fail-This-Course" assignment. The purpose of this one is to rid the instructor of half the class. This assignment may be seriously pursued with genuine interest and yet remain incomprehensible. The student must face the fear of a low grade-point average if he or she encounters many assignments of this type. Of all the types of assignments, this is the most dreaded.

*Student paragraph*

**7. Definition.** Full and exact paragraphs of definition are frequently important parts of papers, essays, and articles (see Sections

**41a(7)** and **43e**). Definition is necessary to set the limits within which a topic or a term is used, especially in dealing with abstract matters. Note that paragraphs of definition may use details and examples, comparison and contrast, or restatement, to insure clarity.

The following definition first states the two basic elements of the fairy story—"a human hero and a happy ending." The author develops the paragraph by describing the kind of hero and the kind of story pattern that are the special marks of the fairy tale. Italics show the movement of the paragraph, following the progress of the hero from beginning to end of the tale.

DEFINITION

A *fairy story,* as distinct from a merry tale, or an animal story, *is a serious tale with a human hero and a happy ending. The progression of its hero is the reverse of the tragic hero's: at the beginning* he is either socially obscure or despised as being stupid or untalented, lacking in the heroic virtues, *but at the end,* he has surprised everyone by demonstrating his heroism and winning fame, riches, and love. *Though ultimately he succeeds, he does not do so without a struggle* in which his success is in doubt, for opposed to him are not only natural difficulties like glass mountains, or barriers of flame, but also hostile wicked powers, stepmothers, jealous brothers, and witches. *In many cases indeed, he would fail were he not* assisted by friendly powers who give him instructions or perform tasks for him which he cannot do himself; that is, in addition to his own powers, he needs luck, but this luck is not fortuitous but dependent upon his character and his actions. *The tale ends with the establishment of justice;* not only are the good rewarded but also the evil are punished.

W. H. AUDEN, Introduction to *Tales of Grimm and Andersen*

**42b**

**¶ coh**

In the two paragraphs that follow, John Holt defines intelligence. Holt relies upon contrast to develop his definition: intelligence is not, he tells us, what it is often said to be—an ability to score well or do well. Rather, it is a "way of behaving" in certain situations. We might call the development here a not-this-but-that development.

The three-sentence first paragraph sets the general contrast between the two definitions. The second moves initially to the more specific but quickly returns to the basic pattern. The italicized phrases will help you follow the controlling, not-this-but-that flow of the definition. The two paragraphs here could have been combined. By using two paragraphs, however, Holt is better able to draw attention to his description of how a person acts in a new situation—a description that is very important in clarifying his definition.

DEFINITION

*When we talk about intelligence, we do not mean* the ability to get a good score on a certain kind of test, or even the ability to do well in school; these are at best only indicators of something larger, deeper, and far more important. *By intelligence we mean* a style of life, a way of behaving in various situations, and particularly in new, strange, and perplexing situations. *The true test of intelligence is not how* much we know how to do, *but how* we behave when we don't know what to do.

*The intelligent person, young or old, meeting a new situation or problem,* opens himself up to it; he tries to take in with mind and senses everything he can about it; he thinks about *it,* instead of about himself or what it might cause to happen to him; he grapples with it boldly, imaginatively, resourcefully, and if not confidently at least hopefully; if he fails to master it, he looks without shame or fear at his mistakes and learns what he can from them. *This is intelligence.* Clearly its roots lie in a certain feeling about life, and one's self with respect to life. *Just as clearly, unintelligence is not* what most psychologists seem to suppose, the same thing as intelligence only less of it. *It is an entirely different* style of behavior, arising out of an entirely different set of attitudes.

JOHN HOLT, How Children Fail

**8. Causes and effects.** Some kinds of central ideas invite organization by an examination of causes or effects. Pollution and poverty exist. What causes them? What are their effects? What are the effects of television? Of the widespread use of computers? What are the causes behind the movements for equality of women, the popularity of football, the fluctuations in the unemployment rate?

In the paragraph that follows, the writer discusses the causes of a problem faced by his father, a high-school teacher, and other teachers. Note how many examples the writer gives of the causes of the effect, "shell shock" that teachers experience every day. The writer makes good use of parallel grammatical structure to reinforce the impact of the examples on the reader.

**42b**

**¶ coh**

CAUSE AND EFFECT

My father is a public high-school teacher. He and the other teachers face a growing number of problems that seem to have no solutions. Having observed my father's behavior for several years, I have concluded that high-school teachers are suffering from a disorder formerly associated with war veterans—shell shock. Besides teaching five or six classes a day, teachers are also expected to sponsor clubs, coach athletic teams, raise money, head committees, chaperone dances, arrange parades, light bonfires, publish newspapers, and sell pictures. In my father's work, paperwork means more than just grading papers. It also means filling out a never-ending stream of forms that insure racial equality in the classroom, that provide free lunches to the needy, that reassure administrators that everything is in its place, and that even request more forms to be filled out. Discipline has also taken on a new meaning in public schools. Today, discipline means searching for drugs, putting out fires, disarming students, and breaking up gang fights. Faced with these daily problems and demands, it is no wonder that teachers like my father are becoming less like educators and more like soldiers suffering from combat fatigue.

*Student paragraph*

---

## EXERCISE 42b(2)

Assume you are writing an essay on the subject "out of sight, out of mind." Write a paragraph with the topic sentence first. Then revise the paragraph, making the necessary changes so that the topic sentence comes last. Which organizational structure did your first paragraph follow? Which organizational structure resulted from placing the topic sentence last?

---

## EXERCISE 42b(3)

You can see how the order of sentences in a paragraph contributes to its coherence if you examine a paragraph in which the original order has been changed. The following paragraphs were coherent as they were originally written, but the order of sentences has been changed. Rearrange each group of sentences to make a coherent paragraph.

1. (1) In March 1979 Wertheimer and physicist Ed Leeper, Ph.D., published this ominous finding in the *American Journal of Epidemiology*, one of the foremost epidemiological journals in the world. (2) In addition, appliances tend to be used sporadically and therefore do not constitute sources of chronic, or continuous, magnetic-field exposure. (3) They pointed out, however, that unlike the magnetic fields given off by power lines, the fields from most household appliances fall off sharply with distance from the appliance. (4) Their article noted that certain household appliances—hair dryers, toasters, and electric drills—can also produce strong magnetic fields. (5) They wrote that power lines "are taken for granted and generally assumed to be harmless," but that this assumption had "never been adequately tested."

   PAUL BRODEUR, "Radiation Alert"

**42b**

**¶ coh**

2. (1) American Indians think of trees as our elders. (2) That monumental tree is 85 feet high and has a limb spread of 145 feet. (3) Indians once held their powwows under the branches of great live oaks, such as the one at Middleton Place, an 18th century plantation near Charleston, S. C. (4) They were here before we were born; they are likely to be here after we are gone; therefore we ought to respect them. (5) It is about 1,000 years old, and still going strong, even though no more Indians meet in its shade.

   CHARLES FENYVESI, "Why a Tree"

---

## EXERCISE 42b(4)

Name appropriate organizational structures for paragraphs based on the following topic sentences. Explain your choices. Then write a coherent paragraph on one of the topics. Did that paragraph develop according to your original notion?

1. Attending a college football game can be a study in personality types.
2. Shopping in a supermarket has disadvantages as well as advantages.
3. I enjoy only two types of movies.
4. Soap opera heroes tend to fall into three categories.
5. There are several reasons why I will never go to Murphy's Bar and Grill again.
6. Students who cheat on exams, and the teachers who permit cheating, are the products of social conditioning.
7. Slang is a puzzle to the uninitiated.
8. Many people do not know what I mean when I refer to country rock music.
9. A poor diet can result in psychological as well as physical problems.
10. A rolling stone gathers no moss.

## 42c Paragraph coherence: connecting ideas

In addition to the organizational "superstructures" that shape ideas into coherent paragraphs, hierarchical structures can be employed within paragraphs to achieve unity as well as flow. If the topic sentence or controlling idea appears at the top of the hierarchy (level 1) in the first sentence, then all the other sentences in the paragraph should relate to it as parallel or subordinate ideas. For example:

**42c**

**¶ coh**

1. A good vacation means different things to different people.
  2. For some, the best vacation is the one that takes them away from home.
    3. They crave new sights, new sensations.
      4. A trip to the beach or the mountains refreshes the city dweller,
      4. while a trip to the city excites the country dweller.
  2. For others, a chance to stay at home is the best vacation.
    3. These folks want the ease and restfulness of familiar surroundings.
      4. They like lying around the house in old clothes.
      4. They enjoy puttering in the garden and talking to the neighbors.
    3. For them, the "new sight" or "new sensation" of not having to face the world or go to work in the morning is vacation enough.

You'll notice that the indentation technique used to examine the preceding paragraph (known as the Christensen method) looks very much like an outline. Like an outline, it reveals the relationships between main ideas and subordinate ideas. Thus, it reveals their interconnecting logic. The paragraph is well-knit, unified, and coherent, as can be seen from its structure of parallel and subordinate ideas. Each generality is supported by at least one level of specificity. You might want to check the relationships between elements in your own paragraphs by comparing sentence levels in this way.

Another option for visualizing paragraph structures is to construct an idea tree (see Section **40g(5)** and Exercise **40i(1)**). By using a tree diagram to chart the organization of your paragraph, you will be able to see not only its hierarchical arrangement but also the spatial relationship between ideas. For some people, this spatial representation makes it easier to see whether ideas are satisfactorily arranged and connected. Following is a tree diagram of the paragraph previously outlined using the indentation method.

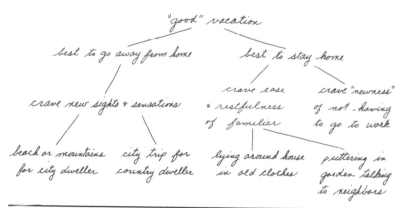

---

EXERCISE 42c(1)

Outline the following paragraphs using the Christensen indentation method or the tree diagram method illustrated in Section 42c. How do the levels of generality and specificity and the relationships between main ideas and subordinate ideas contribute to each paragraph's coherence? Do they help develop the paragraph's topic? Do you see any similarities in the structure of the two paragraphs that increase the coherence of the two taken together?

**42c**

**¶ coh**

There was a time when the deathbed was a kind of proscenium, from which the personage could issue one last dramatic utterance, full of the compacted significance of his life. Last words were to sound as if all of the individual's earthly time had been sharpened to that point: he could now etch the grand summation. "More light!" the great Goethe of the Enlightenment is said to have cried as he expired. There is some opinion, however, that what he actually said was "Little wife, give me your little paw."

In any case, the genre of great last words died quite a few years ago. There are those who think the last genuinely memorable last words were spoken in 1900, when, according to one version, the dying Oscar Wilde said, "Either that wallpaper goes, or I do."

LANCE MORROW, "A Dying Art: The Classy Exit Line"

---

EXERCISE 42c(2)
Using the Christensen method or a tree diagram, outline the paragraph you wrote for Exercise 42b(4). Revise the paragraph, incorporating changes the outline suggests for improving coherence.

---

**42d**   Paragraph coherence: connecting language

Besides positioning the ideas and sentences in a paragraph so that they relate logically to one another, you can use language cues that clarify relationships for readers. The most obvious ones are repeated key words and phrases, parallel grammatical structures, and transitional markers. Less obvious but equally helpful is using old information to introduce new information.

**1. Repeated key words and phrases.** Many well-constructed paragraphs rely on the repetition of key words and phrases, often with slight modification, to emphasize major ideas and carry the thought from sentence to sentence. Pronouns referring to clearly established antecedents in the previous sentence function in the same way. In the following paragraph the words and phrases that are repeated to provide clear links from sentence to sentence and produce a closely integrated whole are in italics.

REPETITION OF KEY WORDS AND PHRASES

In discussing the pre-Civil War South, it *should be remembered* that the large plantation owners constituted only a small part of the *total Southern population*. By far the greater part of *that population* was made up of *small farmers*, and of course the slaves themselves. Some *small farmers* had acquired substantial acreage, owned three or four slaves, and were relatively prosperous. But most of the *small farmers* were terribly poor. They rented their land and worked it themselves, sometimes side by side with the slaves of the great *landowners*. In everything but *social position* they were worse off than the slaves. But it must *also be remembered* that they were as jealous of that superior *social position* as the wealthy *landowner* himself.

*Student paragraph*

**42d**

**¶ coh**

**2. Parallel grammatical structure.** Using parallel grammatical structure in successive sentences is one of the most important ways of connecting them. Just as parallel grammatical form in coordinate parts of a single sentence emphasizes the coordinate relationship of the ideas, so parallel structure from sentence to sentence within a paragraph emphasizes the relationship of these sentences to the single idea of the paragraph. (See also Section **32a.**)

PARALLEL GRAMMATICAL STRUCTURES

Life has often been described as a game, and if one is to play any game successfully, *he must know how to balance his skills* and blend them into the combination most effective for transferring potential into actual performance. *Regardless of how many times* a guard has held his man scoreless, *if he himself has not scored* for his team, his effort is incomplete. *Regardless of how many points* a forward or center averages per game, *if he has not guarded the lane* at every attempt of penetration by the opposition, he is inefficient. The most valuable player trophy is awarded to the player *who scores considerably, who grabs rebounds mechanically* off the backboard, and *who hustles relentlessly* from the initial center jump until the final buzzer sounds. A successful player at his life's game *must also balance his skills. If he always leads, people may tire* of following; *if he always follows, others may consider* him unworthy of a leadership position when he desires it. The secret, then, is to incorporate the two so that a mediocre character is transformed into an exceptional one.

*Student paragraph*

**3. Transitional markers.** A transitional marker is a word or a phrase placed at or near the beginning of a sentence to indicate its relation to the preceding sentence. The coordinating conjunctions *and, but, or, nor, so,* and *yet* are often used this way, particularly in informal writing, for they provide easy bridges from one sentence to another. But English provides a wide variety of transitional markers, as suggested in the lists below. Good modern writing uses the more formal markers sparingly. Be wary of cluttering your writing with unnecessary *however*'s, *moreover*'s, and *consequently*'s. But you should be equally careful to know them and to use them when they create clarity.

Here is a list of many of the common transitional words and phrases:

TO INDICATE ADDITION
again, also, and, and then, besides, equally important, finally, first, further, furthermore, in addition, last, likewise, moreover, next, second, third, too

TO INDICATE CAUSE AND EFFECT
accordingly, as a result, consequently, hence, in short, otherwise, then, therefore, thus, truly

TO INDICATE COMPARISON
in a like manner, likewise, similarly

TO INDICATE CONCESSION
after all, although this may be true, at the same time, even though, I admit, naturally, of course

TO INDICATE CONTRAST
after all, although true, and yet, at the same time, but, for all that, however, in contrast, in spite of, nevertheless, notwithstanding, on the contrary, on the other hand, still, yet

**42d**

**¶ coh**

TO INDICATE SPECIAL FEATURES OR EXAMPLES
for example, for instance, incidentally, indeed, in fact, in other
words, in particular, specifically, that is, to illustrate

TO INDICATE SUMMARY
in brief, in conclusion, in short, on the whole, to conclude, to summarize, to sum up

TO INDICATE TIME RELATIONSHIPS
after a short time, afterwards, as long as, as soon as, at last, at length,
at that time, at the same time, before, earlier, immediately, in the
meantime, lately, later, meanwhile, of late, presently, shortly, since,
soon, temporarily, thereafter, thereupon, until, when, while

Transitional words and phrases are italicized in the following:

TRANSITIONAL WORDS AND PHRASES

*As I have remarked,* the pilots' association was now the compactest
monopoly in the world, perhaps, and seemed simply indestructible.
*And yet* the days of its glory were numbered. *First,* the new railroad
stretching up through Mississippi, Tennessee, and Kentucky, to
Northern railway-centers, began to divert the passenger travel from
the steamboats; *next* the war came and almost entirely annihilated
the steamboating industry during several years, leaving most of the
pilots idle and the cost of living advancing all the time; *then* the trea-
surer of the St. Louis association put his hand into the till and
walked off with every dollar of the ample fund; *and finally,* the railroads intruding everywhere, there was little for steamers to do,
when the war was over, but carry freights; *so straightway* some genius
from the Atlantic coast introduced the plan of towing a dozen
steamer cargoes down to New Orleans at the tail of a vulgar little
tugboat; and behold, in the twinkling of an eye, *as it were,* the association and the noble science of piloting were things of the dead and
pathetic past!

MARK TWAIN, *Life on the Mississippi*

**4. Old information introducing new information.** Like repeated key words or parallel grammatical structures, this technique
builds on readers' expectations by using repetition. People appreciate
receiving new information by way of known information, so sentences
that begin with the known (or previously mentioned) and then tie it to
the unknown (newly mentioned) meet readers' expectations and replicate a familiar mental process. The following paragraph indicates
this process with italic type for old information and boldface type for
new information.

OLD INFORMATION INTRODUCING NEW INFORMATION

Basically a **word processor does** what a *typewriter does,* only better. The **main difference** between *them* is that on a *word processor*

**42d**

**¶ coh**

what you write is **stored as electronic or magnetic impulses,** instead of as *marks on paper.* Word *processors* can do this because **they're computers** that have been programmed to let you type in text, edit it, and have it printed out.

ARTHUR NAIMAN, *Introduction to WordStar*

Not every sentence above begins with old information. Because the writer's purpose is to define *word processor,* the paragraph begins with the term to be defined. But the unfamiliar is immediately explained by comparing it to the familiar *(a typewriter).* Similarly, the second sentence starts with new information *(main difference)* but describes the difference *(electronic impulses)* in terms of the known and familiar *(marks on paper).*

Thinking carefully about readers' needs is important when you are building new information on top of old information. Use repetition and connections where readers need this type of assistance for understanding meaning, not where it merely slows down comprehension and makes them impatient.

---

EXERCISE 42d(1)

Make a coherent paragraph of the following statements. First, use the Christensen method or a tree diagram (Section 42c) to help determine an appropriate order for the sentences. Then link them smoothly with connecting language to achieve coherence.

(1)This attitude shows a naive faith in the competency of secretaries. (2) Practicing engineers and scientists say they spend half their time writing letters and reports. (3) Many students foolishly object to taking courses in writing. (4) College students going into business think their secretaries will do their writing for them. (5) Students going into technical or scientific fields may think that writing is something they will seldom have to do. (6) Young business people seldom have private secretaries. (7) Their notion that only poets, novelists, and newspaper reporters have to know how to write is unrealistic. (8) Other things being equal, people in any field who can express themselves effectively are sure to succeed more rapidly than those whose command of the language is poor.

**42e**

**¶ *dev***

---

EXERCISE 42d(2)

Review the paragraph you wrote for Exercise 42b(4) and revised for Exercise 42c(2), adding any necessary connecting language to improve coherence.

---

**42e**   Paragraph development: filling in the gaps

Readers want details—they *need* details—to be able to understand your thinking. Consider, for example, the following paragraph from a letter written by an Alaskan to a friend in the Midwest whom he had not seen in several years

During the same summer you and Nancy were here, in August Faye and I were severely mauled by a grizzly bear on the Yukon River about 22 miles below Dawson. We spent three weeks in the Whitehorse hospital, and when we got home Faye was in and out of hospitals in Fairbanks and Anchorage all the rest of the winter and spring. It was kind of rough going there for awhile, but we're back in shape and back on the river again this winter.

You can imagine the reader's reaction. Bear! How big? Severely mauled! What do you mean by "severely"? Rough going! That must be the understatement of the year. Details, man, details! The paragraph is logically organized according to chronology, it is fairly unified and coherent, and it certainly has a controlling idea. But without adequate details, it obviously will not satisfy the reader.

The problem here is a misalignment of goals. The writer's goal was to reassure his friend that he and his wife are now all right by deemphasizing the mauling incident. Although this goal is also important to his friend, the friend's goal is to learn the details of the incident. The writer has focused on effects; the reader wants to know about causes.

Not every paragraph is as dramatic as the preceding example, of course, or as frustrating in its lack of development. Still, all writers owe their audiences sufficient details, examples, evidence, and reasons to support the central idea adequately. A paragraph's controlling idea is usually a relatively general statement. To make readers understand what that general statement means and to keep them interested, you must explain and support it.

The following paragraph does not go far beyond its topic sentence:

**42e**

**¶ dev**

It is not always true that a good picture is worth a thousand words. Often writing is much clearer than a picture. It is sometimes difficult to figure out what a picture means, but a careful writer can almost always explain it.

The writer of this paragraph has given us no details that explain why it is not true that pictures are worth more than words, or any reasons for believing his topic sentence. The second sentence merely restates the topic sentence, and the final sentence does very little more.

Compare the following paragraph built on the same topic sentence.

It is not always true that a picture is worth a thousand words. Sometimes, in fact, pictures are pretty useless things. Far from being worth more than words, they can be downright frustrating. If you buy a new typewriter, would you rather have a glossy picture of it, or a 1,000-word booklet explaining how it works? If your carburetor is clogged, do you need a picture of the carburetor, or an explanation of how to unclog it? If you can't swim and you fall in the river and start gulping water, will you be better off to hold up a picture of yourself drowning, or start screaming "Help!"?

In contrast to the first writer, this writer has given us three concrete examples of how words may in fact be worth more than pictures. We may object that pictures of both the typewriter and the clogged carburetor would be helpful along with the words. But we understand what the writer means, and we've been kept interested.

---

**EXERCISE 42e**
Choose two of the following topic sentences and develop each into a meaningful paragraph by supporting it with details, examples, evidence, and reasons.

1. No news is good news.
2. High ACT scores do not necessarily mean a student will do well in college.
3. It is a mistake to try to work 40 hours a week and go to school, too.
4. This season should show everyone we need a new coach.
5. A good man is hard to find.
6. A first impression is not always a reliable basis for judgment.
7. Good news seldom makes the headlines.
8. Keeping a detailed budget is more trouble than it's worth.
9. People tend to fear the new or the unfamiliar.
10. Fashions in clothes (books, slang, hairstyles, music, etc.) change from one year to the next.

---

# 42f  Paragraph development: deciding on length

**42f**

¶ *dev*

A paragraph can *look* long enough and still not be adequately developed. Conversely, a paragraph can be too long, even though on a single topic, for a reader to digest easily. No magic number of sentences will predictably give you just the right paragraph length for every writing task. However, the following guidelines are helpful.

**1. Reader expectations.**   From experience, readers expect that paragraphs in novels or history books will be longer than paragraphs in newspaper articles or business letters. Readers' expectations also grow from their experience with content: a philosophical argument, for example, is likely to require longer paragraphs to accommodate extended explanations of complex ideas; an instruction manual, on the other hand, will use short paragraphs to mark off each step in a process.

**2. Visual appeal.**   The narrowness of a newspaper column makes lengthy paragraphs difficult to read. The undifferentiated letters and wide type blocks of a typescript need the white space of frequent paragraphing to provide a visual and a mental resting place for the reader. In the case of an instruction manual, the reader knows without actually comprehending the words but by simply observing the visual paragraph cues where the steps in the procedure are located. In short, effective paragraphing packages ideas into manageable chunks for readers so they can more easily absorb and understand information.

Remember that where you mark a paragraph has a definite effect on meaning. Because readers expect the first sentence in a paragraph to be an orienting sentence, their specific interpretation of the paragraph will be shaped by that sentence, whatever it is. Thus you should not think of indenting to signal the start of a paragraph as an arbitrary act. Paragraphing defines a unit of coherent thought for your reader.

**3. Dividing paragraphs that are too long.** A useful strategy is to think about paragraphs not only in terms of topics but also in terms of *aspects* of topics. If your development of a topic needs to be fairly lengthy to provide adequate support, divide it into manageable chunks—aspects or subtopics that will be easier for the reader to handle.

For example, Section **42e**'s grizzly bear paragraph would have been much more satisfying if divided in two: the first paragraph developing the details of the mauling, the second paragraph discussing the hospitalization and recuperation and ending with the reassurance that the couple was all right. Similarly, the paragraph developing the good points and bad points of the Club Tropic vacation (p. 000) might have been divided, with one paragraph devoted to good points and the other to bad points.

It is especially important to apply the techniques for achieving coherence when you divide a paragraph. The reader needs connecting language such as that described in Section **42d** to be able to see relationships between as well as within paragraphs.

**4. Revising paragraphs that are too short.** Short, insufficiently developed paragraphs usually show a lack of attention to detail and an imperfect grasp of the full idea of the paragraph. When you want to revise short, choppy paragraphs, look for a controlling idea that might direct them. What is the overall point you want to make? Can several short paragraphs be combined and refocused under a single controlling idea? Or you might outline each paragraph by the Christensen indentation method (**42c**), looking for omissions in the paragraph's levels of supporting detail.

The following sample paragraphs are all insufficiently developed. The arguments are undirected, and the generalizations are inadequately supported. Simply stitching these fragments together would not produce a coherent, unified statement; instead, the material needs to be thought through again and rewritten.

**42f**

**¶ *dev***

I am in favor of tightening the drunk driving laws in this state. Too many people are getting killed on the highway. For one thing, the legal drinking age is too low. For another, the legal blood alcohol limit is too high.

The penalties are not stiff enough either. We ought to throw the book at people arrested for drunk driving. A light sentence or a suspended sentence doesn't save lives.

---

EXERCISE 42f(1)

Revise the preceding sample paragraphs on drunk driving so that they are adequately developed, unified, and coherent and comprise a brief essay on the topic.

---

EXERCISE 42f(2)

Group the following sentences into two paragraphs. Provide transitional markers for the sentences, and, when possible, combine sentences.

Martin Luther King was an ordained minister from Atlanta, Georgia. He gained prominence as a civil-rights leader during the 1950s and 1960s. In 1956 he led a boycott by Montgomery, Alabama, blacks against segregated city bus lines. After his success in Montgomery, he founded the Southern Christian Leadership Conference. This gave him a base to expand the civil-rights movement in the South and throughout the nation. In 1963 he organized a massive civil-rights march on Washington, D.C., which brought together more than 200,000 people. It was there that he delivered his famous "I Have a Dream" speech. In the years that followed, King broadened his political involvement. He continued to work for civil rights, but he also became an outspoken critic of the Vietnam war. His criticism of the war was based on his belief that the war was contributing to poverty in America. He argued that our valuable national resources were being used to finance the war rather than to fight poverty at home. In 1968 he planned another large-scale march to Washington. It was to be called the Poor People's March. He never fulfilled his wish though. In April of 1968 he went to Memphis, Tennessee, to help settle a strike by sanitation workers. While there he was assassinated.

**42f**

¶ *dev*

---

EXERCISE 42f(3)

Read the following paragraphs and explain why you think the writer divided them into two instead of using one long paragraph. How have unity and coherence been maintained between the two paragraphs? State the controlling idea.

Many people find New York an unattractive city to inhabit because of the physical filth, and while, God knows, the city is filthy, I doubt that that element plays an important role in our decision to leave. Naples is far dirtier, and so are Bombay and countless other cities, but a tolerance for dirt seems to grow where some fondness exists. Tangiers is one of the dirtiest cities in the world, yet a friend of mine who possesses flawless taste lives in the casbah there and would live nowhere else. A few days ago in Central Park I saw a man leaning on a litter can drinking a carton of orange juice, and when he finished he tossed the container not in the receptacle but on the ground.

I don't understand this, but there is a lot about New York I don't understand. Mainly, I don't understand why the city has no soul, no detectable heartbeat, why the chief element in the city's emotional economy is indifference. I think that's what sent me on my way. Vienna almost suffocates the Viennese with care, Paris manages to imbue her own with an obsession for their fulfillment, San Francisco exudes a pride that even gathers to her heart total strangers; but the key to New York's character is that it doesn't really care about anything.

CASKIE STINNETT, from "Farewell, My Unlovely"

---

## 42g Paragraph consistency

When you read effective writing, you may be struck by the fact that something more than mere adherence to an organizational principle seems to hold the sentences together. Such writing has an inner consistency that unites everything into an authoritative whole. In part, you are responding to the writer's care in situating both reader and writer, in indicating positions or roles for each. This positioning is largely a matter of point of view and tone.

**1. Consistent point of view.** Readers need to be on solid ground. Unnecessary shifts in person, tense, or number within a paragraph destroy the solid footing, leaving readers to wonder who is speaking and to whom (person), what the time sequence is (tense), and how many are being discussed (number). (See also Section **10**.)

**42g**

¶ *con*

UNNECESSARY SHIFT IN PERSON
A pleasant and quiet place to live is essential for a serious-minded college student. If possible, you should rent a room from a landlady with a reputation for keeping order and discipline among her renters. Moreover, a student ought to pick a roommate with a similar temperament. Then you can agree to and keep a schedule of study hours.

UNNECESSARY SHIFT IN TENSE
Every time I have seen one of Clint Eastwood's Dirty Harry movies, I suffered conflicting reactions. Harry Callahan, Dirty Harry, was a policeman who follows his own code of justice rather than the code of the law. Harry's justice amounts to vigilante action which he carried out by excessively violent means—usually with a handgun as big as a bazooka. These movies' brutal violence repulses me, but I could sympathize with Harry's feelings. Although reason tells us vigilante justice is wrong, especially in a law-enforcement officer, these

films replaced audiences' reason with emotions that make such violence at least momentarily acceptable.

### UNNECESSARY SHIFT IN NUMBER

Of great currency at the moment is the notion that education should prepare students for "life." A college graduate no longer goes out into the world as a cultivated individual. Instead students feel obliged to prepare themselves for places in the business world. Consequently, we are establishing courses on how to get and keep a mate, how to budget an income, and how to win friends and influence people—that is, how to sell yourself and your product. The study of things not obviously practical to a business person is coming to be looked upon as unnecessary.

Unnecessary shifts of this type disorient readers and make it impossible for them to trust the writer's control and understanding of the material.

**2. Consistent tone.** In its usual sense, tone means the quality of a sound—the pitch, the duration. In writing, tone has to do with the "sound" of the text, the attitude about subject and audience that the writer projects. Tone can be variously described as the manner of expression (*she affected a breezy tone in her letter to hide her disappointment*), general atmosphere (*Poe's short story "The Fall of the House of Usher" has the most somber tone, full of darkness and foreboding*), or dominant impression (*didn't you think the retraction printed in today's newspaper sounded patronizing rather than apologetic?*).

Sentence structure and length, word choice, methods of organization and development, the kinds of examples, illustrations, and details, as well as other factors combine to create the "tone of voice" that reveals a writer's stance toward his or her subject and audience. Even punctuation or the use of sentence fragments can influence a reader's perception of a writer's tone. Ranging from impersonal to personal, formal to informal, literal to ironic, sentimental to sarcastic, enthusiastic to indifferent, dogmatic to doubtful, hostile to friendly, flippant to respectful, modest to authoritative, serious to humorous, the tone a writer creates should suit his or her purposes. For example, in some situations a hostile tone will put readers off—not what the writer intended; in other situations, it may rouse them to action—just what the writer intended. The key is to choose an *appropriate* tone.

An **appropriate tone** reflects the writer's understanding of and respect for the needs and feelings of the readers. While generalizations about tone are risky, the following tactics will probably offend your readers: talking down to them by repeating the obvious; talking over your audience's heads, merely to impress them, by using words, allusions, or examples they don't understand; being excessively dogmatic or sarcastic; being excessively or falsely enthusiastic. It is hard

**42g**

**¶ con**

to imagine situations in which such tones would be appropriate. Consider the following opening from a student paper:

**INAPPROPRIATE TONE**
No one can tell me that people who vote for the slimeballs on the Republican ticket aren't putting their own selfish interests ahead of the true good of the country.

Whatever readers may think of this thesis, the writer's dogmatic attitude and inappropriately hostile tone will discourage them from reading further. The offensive manner of expression makes any sort of balanced or reasoned discussion of the topic seem unlikely.

**Consistent tone** requires maintaining a particular tone once you have set it. A jarring shift in tone may ruin the effect of a paragraph, even one that otherwise meets the tests of unity, coherence, and adequate development. The following paragraph from a student essay illustrates the point:

**JARRING SHIFT IN TONE**
Curiosity has developed ideas that have been vastly beneficial to humankind. We have seen humankind emerge from the age of great darkness into the age of great light. Today every hot-rod artist profits from the ideas of past inventors and every home has a kitchen full of push-button gadgets that it couldn't have without ideas. Above all, modern scientific theory leads us to a clearer and deeper comprehension of the universe. So we see curiosity is really a helpful tool.

**42g**

**¶ con**

The first two sentences and the next to last sentence of this paragraph set a serious, somewhat formal tone by such phrases as *vastly beneficial, we have seen humankind emerge*, the parallel phrases *age of great darkness* and *age of great light*, and *clearer and deeper comprehension of the universe*. But the language of both the third and last sentences, and the examples cited in the third sentence, depart completely from this tone of seriousness and formality. Having been prepared for comment about the great concepts of religion, politics, education, or science, readers are offered *hot-rod artists* and *push-button gadgets*. The effect is something like that of a cat meowing in a church service. When used deliberately, to achieve effects such as humor or irony, shifts of tone can be appropriate. However, the paragraph above shows uncontrolled writing rather than planned divergence from the tone initially established.

---

EXERCISE 42g(1)
The following paragraphs and paragraph parts are marred by inconsistent point of view (person, tense, number). Revise them to ensure consistency.

1.    Many children are injured every day because of carelessness in the home. Some of these injuries include electrical shock and ingestion of poisonous chemicals. Most people have stored cleaning solutions, pesticides, and other chemicals under the sink; this is in perfect reach for a small child. Electrical outlets draw a child's attention because it's at their eye level.

2.    "Battle Royal," by Ralph Ellison, tells of an incident in a young black man's life when he comes face to face with the arrogant attitude that "the town's leading white citizens" have toward the blacks. After giving an impressive speech at his graduation, the boy was invited to give the same speech at a gathering of prominent white citizens. At this gathering, where most of the white men were drunk, the boy and group of nine other young black men were put through a series of humiliating circumstances for the entertainment of the white men. After he gave his speech, during which he is ridiculed and taunted by the men, the boy is given a scholarship to a state college for Negroes as a reward.

3.    One of the books I read in high school English was Dickens's *Tale of Two Cities*. In it the author tells of some of the horrors of the French Revolution. He spent several pages telling about how the French aristocrats suffered. The climax part of the book tells how a ne'er-do-well who failed in life sacrifices himself for another. He took his place in a prison and went stoically to the guillotine for him.

---

EXERCISE 42g(2)
Study the following paragraphs. Describe the tone of each and discuss the factors that contribute to it.

1.    Viewed from the distance of the moon, the astonishing thing about the earth, catching the breath, is that it is alive. The photographs show the dry, pounded surface of the moon in the foreground, dead as an old bone. Aloft, floating free beneath the moist, gleaming membrane of bright blue sky, is the rising earth, the only exuberant thing in this part of the cosmos. If you could look long enough, you would see the swirling of the great drifts of white cloud, covering and uncovering the half-hidden masses of land. If you had been looking for a very long, geologic time, you could have seen the continents themselves in motion, drifting apart on their crustal plates, held afloat by the fire beneath. It has the organized, self-contained look of a live creature, full of information, marvelously skilled in handling the sun.

LEWIS THOMAS, *The Lives of a Cell*

2.    Even though large tracts of Europe and many old and famous States have fallen or may fall into the grip of the Gestapo and all the odious apparatus of Nazi rule, we shall not flag or fail. We shall go on to the end. We shall fight in France, we shall fight in the seas and oceans, we shall fight with growing confidence and growing strength in the air; we shall defend our Island, whatever the cost

may be. We shall fight on the beaches, we shall fight on the landing grounds, we shall fight in the field and in the streets, we shall fight in the hills; we shall never surrender; and even if, which I do not for a moment believe, this Island or a large part of it were subjugated and starving, then our Empire beyond the seas, armed and guarded by the British Fleet, would carry on the struggle, until, in God's good time, the New World, with all its power and might, steps forth to the rescue and liberation of the Old.

WINSTON CHURCHILL, *Speech at Dunkerque*

3.     My education and that of my Black associates were quite different from the education of our white schoolmates. In the classroom we all learned past participles, but in the streets and in our homes the Blacks learned to drop *s*'s from plurals and suffixes from past-tense verbs. We were alert to the gap separating the written word from the colloquial. We learned to slide out of one language and into another without being conscious of the effort. At school, in a given situation, we might respond with "That's not unusual." But in the street, meeting the same situation, we easily said, "It be's like that sometimes."

MAYA ANGELOU, *I Know Why the Caged Bird Sings*

4.     This was Raymond talking to the wavy-haired fellow with the stick, the dealer, at the craps table about 3:45 Sunday morning. The stickman had no idea what this big wiseacre was talking about, but he resented the tone. He gave Raymond that patient arch of the eyebrows known as a Red Hook brushoff, which is supposed to convey some such thought as, I am a very tough but cool guy, as you can tell by the way I carry my eyeballs low in the pouches, and if this wasn't such a high-class joint we would take wiseacres like you out back and beat you into jellied madrilene.

TOM WOLFE, *The Kandy-Kolored Tangerine-Flake Streamline Baby*

**42g**

¶ *con*

## PARAGRAPHS FOR STUDY

There is no substitute for writing if you want to learn to do it well. However, reading is an integral part of this learning process. Research shows what many people have suspected for years: those who read widely, attentively, and often are usually better writers than those who do not. The reason is that frequent readers are more comfortable with language and familiar with a wider range of options and techniques for using language. Reading and analyzing what you read to understand how it is written can add to your own writing skills. Test your understanding of the principles of good paragraphs by studying the samples that follow. Analyze each to determine the controlling idea, the topic sentence if one is provided, the transitional markers and other means of achieving coherence, the organizational patterns, the level of development, and the tone. Identify what you believe to be the author's goal in each paragraph: what is it that he or she wants to accomplish?

Then **write a paragraph** explaining how one of the writers tries to accomplish his or her goal. Your paragraph should not be a summary of the paragraph's contents. It should be a discussion of the writing techniques the author has used and how successful these techniques are in accomplishing the goal.

1.   Going to work for the Eclipse [computer] Group could be a rough way to start out in your profession. You set out for your first real [engineering] job with all the loneliness and fear that attend new beginnings, drive east from Purdue or Northwestern or Wisconsin, up from Missouri or west from MIT, and before you've learned to find your way to work without a road map, you're sitting in a tiny cubicle or, even worse, in an office like the one dubbed the Micropit, along with three other new recruits, your knees practically touching theirs; and though lacking all privacy and quiet, though it's a job you've never really done before, you are told that you have almost no time at all in which to master a virtual encyclopedia of technical detail and to start producing crucial pieces of a crucial machine. And you want to make a good impression. So you don't have any time to meet women, to help your wife buy furniture for your apartment, or to explore the unfamiliar countryside. You work. You're told, "Don't even mention the name Eagle outside the group." "Don't talk outside the group," you're told. You're working at a place that looks like something psychologists build for testing the fortitude of small animals, and your boss won't even say hello to you.

TRACY KIDDER, *The Soul of a New Machine*

2.   The whole aim of good teaching is to turn the young learner, by nature a little copycat, into an independent, self-propelling creature, who cannot merely learn but study—that is, work as his own boss to the limit of his powers. This is to turn pupils into students, and it can be done on any rung of the ladder of learning. When I was a child, the multiplication table was taught from a printed sheet which had to be memorized one "square" at a time—the one's and the two's and so on up to nine. It never occurred to the teacher to show us how the answers could be arrived at also by addition, which we already knew. No one said, "Look: if four times four is sixteen, you ought to be able to figure out, without aid from memory, what five times four is, because that amounts to four more one's added to the sixteen." This would at first have been puzzling, *more* complicated and difficult than memory work, but once explained and grasped, it would have been an instrument for learning and checking the whole business of multiplication. We could temporarily have dispensed with the teacher and cut loose from the printed table.

JACQUES BARZUN, *Teacher in America*

**42g**

¶ *con*

3.    The definition of equality varies from woman to woman. For some women, equality means being equal to men politically and socially. They feel that the traditional codes of chivalry are no longer applicable and resent men who open their doors, pull out their chairs, and help them with their coats. On the other hand, for some women, equality means that they should have the same opportunities and benefits as men yet also enjoy the tradition of chivalry. These women, although they may hold prestigious positions in government, education or medicine, don't resent a man who opens the door for them. Still for other women, equality is little more than a public interest story which has no effect upon their lives. They are secure in their lifestyles, whether domestic or not, and tend not to question the issue. Perhaps there is no one definition of equality for women but many, since each woman must decide how important equality is to her own self-esteem before she can determine what equality means.

*Student paragraph*

4.    For years, nuclear-power advocates have claimed that nuclear power is the most economical form of energy available; but in light of a few facts, one begins to doubt this claim. The cost of building the Sequoiah nuclear plant, for example, exceeded a billion dollars. For this astronomical amount of money, one can expect this reactor to be out of operation approximately thirty percent of the time. After thirty or forty years, it will become too "hot" to operate and will be shut down permanently. Even though the reactor will be shut down, it will still be highly radioactive and will have to be totally encased in concrete and lead—all at a cost of another few million dollars and guarded virtually forever. Nuclear power is neither cheap nor economical; it is both expensive and wasteful.

*Student paragraph*

**42g**

**¶ con**

5.    Often at my desk, now, I sit contemplating the fish. Nor does it have to be a fish. It could be the long-horned Alaskan bison on my wall. For the point is, you see, that the fish is extinct and gone, just as those great heavy-headed beasts are gone, just as our massive-faced and shambling forebears of the Ice [Age] have vanished. The chemicals still about me here took a shape that will never be seen again so long as grass grows or the sun shines. Just once out of all time there was a pattern that we call *Bison regius*, a fish called *Diplomystus humilis*, and, at this present moment, a primate who knows, or thinks he knows, the entire score.

LOREN EISELEY, *The Night Country*

6.    The gym detonates, fifteen hundred throats in peril of rupture. The town's best game in years has ended in a tie, Hamilton equalling Hamilton. The crowd owes the night to Robbie Hodge, and no one begrudges him the credit. From the Garfield side comes "Hodge! Hodge! Hodge!" and the Taft side echoes. The sound builds until no words at all can be heard. It is almost like silence, the gym roaring for a performance that on Broadway gets a ten-minute curtain call and in Madrid two ears and a tail.

PETER DAVIS, *Hometown*

# WRITER'S REVISING: PARAGRAPHS
*(continued from page 395)*

Here is How Michelle reparagraphed her essay on Social Security.

## Michelle's Revision

R 1    With only 116 million workers paying into the

R 2    Social Security program and a whopping 36 million

R 3    receiving benefits, it is overburdened. After

R 4    fifty years of existence the world's largest

R 5    social program is on the verge of collapse.

R 6        To understand the shortcomings of the Social

R 7    Security system, we must be aware of the

R 8    conditions under which and the intentions with

R 9    which the system was created. In 1935 President

R10    Franklin Roosevelt signed the Social Security Act.

R11    In those days 35 million workers supported the

R12    program with their payroll taxes, and only 106

R13    thousand beneficiaries drew from the program. In

R14    addition, the average life span was shorter in

R15    1935 than it is today. Because of the relatively

R16    small number of eligible retirees and the short

R17    life span, the average worker paid only a maximum

R18    of $30 per year.

R19        Today, however, the maximum payroll tax is

R20    $2,792 annually, and only three workers support

R21    each beneficiary who receives up to $15,000 in

R22    benefits. To make things worse, the number of

R23    retirees is on the rise, and it will continue to

R24    rise as the baby boom generation ages.

R25        The bottom line is that the Social Security

R26    Administration will operate at a deficit by the

**42g**

**¶ con**

```
R27    year 2020 despite corrective legislation passed by

R28    Congress in 1983 that was designed to make the

R29    program solvent for years to come.
```

**Analysis**

As she begins her revision, Michelle sees that her introductory paragraph has actually ended in line 5. When she begins to discuss the shortcomings of the Social Security system, she has introduced a new aspect of the subject, a new topic. She also sees that this sentence (R6), with the word *shortcomings,* serves as a good transitional bridge from the first paragraph, referring to a possible collapse, to the information about the system's background. Michelle decides to use it as the topic sentence for a paragraph dealing solely with conditions in 1935. The word *today* makes a clear transition to a brief discussion of the current state of the system. Her conclusion is a one-sentence paragraph summarizing why she could say in her introductory paragraph that the system is on the verge of collapse. The new paragraphing has created a much more coherent expression of Michelle's thoughts; her readers will have the full benefit of the "chunking" that paragraphing brings to ideas. Grouping and transitions now provide emphases that aid the readers' understanding.

# 43
## *CRITICAL THINKING AND ARGUMENT*

During your lifetime most of your writing will have a distinctly persuasive character. Your U. S. history exam may require that you write a short essay answering the question "What were the major causes of the Civil War?" Your English professor, explaining possible topics for a research paper, may say, "I don't want to read papers 'all about' a topic. I want you to digest your research and draw your own conclusions about the subject." Your company's regional manager may ask you for a proposal assessing several new sales strategies. The school board may decide to close your child's school, sending him or her to one in another neighborhood, and you and your neighbors may want to write a letter of protest.

All these writing tasks require more than assembling facts and summarizing information. They require critical thinking: analysis and logical evaluation so that the information builds a case that supports a stand on the issues. In short, few of us put words on paper, whether by desire or request, unless we have some point to make (see Sections **40f, 40i(2)**). Making an assertion places us in the realm of argument, because an assertion is a statement that can (or should) be supported with facts, with reasons—in other words, with evidence.

## WRITERS REVISING: SOUND ARGUMENTS

The following student editorial appeared a few years ago in a college newpaper, occasioning a great deal of debate in the "Letters" column of subsequent issues. Exercise your critical thinking skills by analyzing the editorial's success as an argument. Note places in the editorial where you think the author does an especially good or especially poor job of arguing his point of view. Be sure to mark places where you think the reasoning is illogical or the language is unfairly slanted. After you have read through Section **43**, reread the editorial and refer to the instructions at the end of the section to see if you have revised your initial opinion.

### SELECTIVE DEMOCRACY

The President signed into law last week a bill banning radio and TV advertisements of any smokeless tobacco product. The law also called for one of the following three warnings to be placed on the packages of smokeless tobacco products: "This product may cause mouth cancer," "This product may cause gum disease and tooth loss," or "This product is not a safe alternative to cigarettes."

These warning labels, with the possible exception of the latter, are necessary and acceptable. Clear statements, such as those listed above, give people who are unqualified to assess the risks of tobacco themselves—in this case, anyone outside the medical field—information on the consequences of tobacco use.

However, taking from a company the opportunity to advertise its product is not only unfair; it is in direct contrast with the ideals and principles inherent in a democracy.

Once again, we see a company recognized as legally providing a product being refused the chance to use two of the most powerful media—television and radio. The Editorial Board's solution is, as it has been in similar matters in the past, quite simple: (1) make tobacco companies illegal and, on that basis, refuse to accept their advertising, or (2) recognize tobacco companies as legal and entitled to the rights other companies possess, and allow advertising for tobacco products on television and in other media.

**43**

*arg*

In keeping with the second, and decidedly more democratic, approach, other businesses now prohibited from advertising on television and radio would be given the opportunity to use these and other media. Liquor and cigarettes would enjoy the same chance to reach the public as douches, Twinkies, and any other product.

It seems only fair.

This *Writers Revising* continues on page 455.

## 43a   Practicing critical thinking

Although you may have learned critical thinking skills in high school, it is more likely that you are developing these skills as you progress through your college studies. College freshmen are sometimes confused because the methods they used to respond to high school assignments do not net the high grades they hope for in college. These students spend a lot of time trying to figure out "what the professor wants." Most of the time professors want critical thinking—not just a summary of the lectures, not just a review of the assigned reading and a comment containing the student's opinion of it, not just a "pulling together" or synthesis of the ideas in several readings. All of these things are important and useful, but they stop short of the goal. Critical thinking goes a step further to analyze ideas and interpret them. Critical thinking goes beyond asking the question, "What are the main ideas?" It answers the question, "What does it all mean?" Critical thinkers evaluate information and reformulate it, drawing conclusions based on their evaluation of the evidence. Further, critical thinking provides the basis for sound arguments.

Repeating the sequence of events that led up to the Civil War is not critical thinking: it is a summary. Explaining why certain events triggered the war uses critical thinking. Pulling together information from half a dozen sources about senior citizens' social roles is not critical thinking: it is a synthesis. Evaluating those roles as compared to society's needs calls for critical thinking. A report reviewing three new sales strategies is not critical thinking: it is a summary. Weighing the pros and cons of each and recommending the strongest strategy requires critical thinking. A letter stating that you and your neighbors object to the closing of a local school is not critical thinking: it is an unsupported opinion. Presenting workable ways to keep the school open shows critical thinking.

## 43b   Planning for your audience

In each of the situations previously cited, the audience is clear: the professors, the regional manager, the school board. But even when you do not personally know your readers, making educated guesses about them and assessing their probable characteristics can be as important to your argument as thinking about the points you want to present.

In setting your goal for an argumentative paper, you should understand that three outcomes are possible. The first—most nearly ideal but also the most unlikely—is that you will change your reader's point of view from opposition to agreement with your own. The second possibility is that you will be able to modify your reader's point of view, bringing it closer to your own. Although your audience may not agree with you on all points, you will have clarified and added to their understanding, as well as having gained some acceptance for your position. Naturally you hope the strength of your argument will modify the reader's position substantially. The final possibility is that you will not change your audience's mind at all. Even in the face of faultless logic, readers can reject your argument for a variety of reasons that to you may seem thoroughly irrational.

You will therefore want to set your goal in accordance with the relative likelihood of the possible outcomes. Just presenting your view point is not enough. Assessing the audience will help you decide on an effective approach. Do you know the readers' average age and level of education? What other factors such as gender, lifestyle, income, occupation, political or geographic affiliation may make them more or less receptive to your point of view? Most important, is your audience likely to agree with you or disagree with you?

If your audience already agrees with you, clearly you do not need to persuade them further. Rather, your goal is to get them to act. When Thoreau delivered his address "Civil Disobedience," he knew his audience was already opposed to slavery; his task was not to convince them of slavery's evils but to inspire them to act on behalf of the antislavery cause. Thoreau's essay, full of emotionally charged language, passionately calls for action.

How much emotion you can effectively communicate will depend on the subject and the intensity of belief you and your readers share. If your readers think you are making a mountain out of a mole hill, your argument will fail. On the other hand, don't talk about an issue readers believe to be a serious problem as if it were a minor inconvenience. Use a tone appropriate to your audience, subject, and goal. (See Section **42g(2)**.)

If readers are likely to disagree with you, you must take a different approach. No matter how strongly you believe that abortion is wrong or that welfare should be increased or that writing courses should not be required in college, there are nonetheless persuasive arguments for believing the opposite. If you want readers who disagree with your point of view to at least listen to your position, start out by recognizing theirs. If you begin by acknowledging their arguments, even admitting the strength of some of those arguments, you can then move on to suggest their weaknesses, and finally to set your own arguments against them (see Section **43i**). If you go about the task of persuading with respect for readers' convictions, you will be much more likely to get them to listen. Your purpose, after all, is to persuade. If you say (or even suggest) that your readers are ignorant, stupid, or ridiculous to believe as they do, you will only antagonize them. You will never persuade them.

An effective argument is more, then, than an attempt to persuade readers that what you do or believe is right or just—or what others do or believe is wrong or unjust. At its most fundamental level, an effective argument is an outgrowth of critical thinking; it is a statement of judgment or opinion that is supported with logical and persuasive evidence.

## 43c Learning to recognize arguable assertions

The novelist Joseph Conrad wrote, "Every sort of shouting is a transitory thing, after which the grim silence of facts remains." A corollary to Conrad's statement is that some things are simply not debatable, in view of the evidence. Learn to distinguish arguable assertions from those that are not arguable. Trying to argue an assertion that cannot be supported with valid reasons is pointless.

**1. *A priori* is a term of logic meaning, roughly, "before examination." Assertions based on an *a priori* premise cannot be argued because such a premise can be neither proved nor disproved;** people are simply convinced of its truth or untruth. Although they cannot be supported by factual evidence, *a priori* premises have the force of fact because they are so deeply held.



Many deeply held and widely shared assumptions about human nature are *a priori* premises with cultural, racial, social, and moral or religious roots. If you argue from an *a priori* premise with someone who does not share it, you will find yourself arguing in circles or along parallel lines—but never toward resolution—because legitimate proof is not possible. For instance, many arguments about the value of one social system or government versus another are often futile because they are based on different *a priori* premises. Or if one person believes, *a priori,* that human beings are basically good, altruistic, and trustworthy, while another person believes human nature is essentially wicked, selfish, and dishonest, then the two can never reach a conclusion about human nature—no matter how many examples each person cites.

*A priori* premises may change or be replaced over time, as attitudes toward gender roles in American society show. *A priori* assumptions underlying assertions about the "weaker sex," parenting, or inherently masculine and feminine characteristics are not nearly as widely shared today as they once were.

**2. Subjective expressions of taste and nonrational reactions cannot be argued.** The Latin phrase *de gustibus non disputandum est,* "there is no disputing about tastes," is another way of saying subjective reactions do not lend themselves to reasoning. Similarly, no matter how sound your logic that there is plenty of oxygen in a stalled elevator, to a claustrophobic the sense of suffocation is very real.

**3. Matters of fact cannot be argued.** If a fact is verifiable, there is no point in debating it. It can either be true (a *bona fide* fact) or false (not a fact), but in neither case is it a matter for argument because the record can be checked. The earth is round, or nearly so. This fact was verified by fifteenth-century explorers and more recently by means of space flights.

**4. Statements involving unverifiable facts cannot be argued.** While it is interesting to speculate about whether there is life after death, we simply cannot know.

**5. Statements based on insufficient facts cannot be argued conclusively.** For instance, people enjoy arguing that life exists on other planets. Statistically, the odds favor extraterrestrial life forms. But we have no hard evidence at this point to prove the assertions. All we can say is perhaps. Should information pointing one way or the other come to light, a conclusion may eventually be drawn. In the meantime, logical reasoning on the topic won't carry us very far.

Keep in mind that facts are slippery and not necessarily static. What may be accepted as verifiably true this year may be proven false by next. Before sailors circled the globe, the populace accepted as fact that the world was flat. During the Middle Ages the plague that killed millions was attributed to God's wrath; people had no knowledge that fleas could transmit microorganisms from rats to humans and thus infect the population. What was once the "fact" of God's wrath is now regarded as a problem of hygiene. Correspondingly, what serves as fact today may be tomorrow's quaint, ignorant notion. Time and scientific inquiry have taught us that very little is immutably certain. The best we can do is draw conclusions from available data, deciding to formulate an argument when the supporting data warrant it.

**43c**

**arg**

---

EXERCISE 43c

Decide which of the following assertions are arguable and which are not. Be prepared to explain why each assertion does or does not lend itself to argument.

1. All horror movies are basically silly and not worth the viewer's time.
2. Most women can't handle stressful jobs requiring decision-making skills.
3. Cotton handkerchiefs wrinkle more easily than polyester ones.

4. The football team is losing this year because of poor recruiting, disgruntled players, and inexperienced coaches.
5. Whole wheat bread is more nutritious than white bread.
6. One should always tell the truth.
7. Small businesses employ more workers than all of the *Fortune* 500 companies combined.
8. The universe and everything in it was created in six days.
9. Harry Truman was an effective president.
10. People usually deserve what life dishes out to them.

## 43d  Learning the parts of an argument

An **assertion,** which states the stand or point of view on a topic (see Section **40i(2)**), is sometimes called a thesis, claim, or proposition. It must be supported by valid evidence if the reader is going to believe it.

**Evidence** is the part of an argument the reader is willing to accept as true without further proof. Most evidence can be categorized as either fact or opinion: that is, (1) a verifiable occurrence or experience or (2) a trusted judgment believed reliable because the source is knowledgeable, prestigious, and authoritative. We have already noted that facts can be slippery. In a later section **(43g)**, you will see that prestigious opinion also has its pitfalls if the source is not truly knowledgeable. Nevertheless, a plausible argument depends on evidence that is accurate, pertinent to the main assertion, and sufficient to support it.

Evidence often comprises a major portion of an argument, especially if the topic is controversial or complex. How much evidence is enough depends on the nature of your topic and the characteristics of your audience—on how likely the readers are to agree or disagree with your assertion.

You have probably experienced the frustration of reading on your English compositions the comments "not enough support" or "more examples needed." Bear in mind the benchmark of shared experience; that is, the more widely shared or commonly acknowledged an experience, the fewer examples you need to convince readers. The sun rises in the east. No one is going to argue with you. If in a paper on the value of home remedies, however, you offer as fact the statement that mustard-plasters are good for curing colds, you will have to cite a wide and representative sampling of incidents as well as testimony from respected medical authorities to convince your audience. Most readers would view your statement not as fact but as an assertion needing proof.

Evidence is only as good as its accuracy and your audience's willingness to accept it. Consequently, persuading the reader means looking at the evidence from the reader's point of view and then supplying statistics, illustrations, specific examples, personal experience, occurrences reported by authorities to validate the evidence in your reader's eyes.

Arguments also contain a third element, sometimes implied rather than stated, that shows the connection between the truth of the supporting evidence and the truth of the assertion. This third element is often called the **warrant.**

ASSERTION:   We can expect college tuition to increase.

EVIDENCE:    The cost of living keeps going up.

WARRANT:     Since colleges are subject to the same economic pressures as everyone else, tuition increases will be necessary to meet rising costs.

Using an implied warrant, and a different order of presentation, the same argument might be written:

EVIDENCE:    Because the cost of living keeps going up,

ASSERTION:   we can expect college tuition to increase as well.

The words *because* and *as well* serve as the warrant, clearly implying the reason why or connection between the truth of the evidence and the truth of the assertion.

---

EXERCISE 43d
Find the assertion, evidence, and warrant in each of the following passages. If any of the parts is implied, point out the words that indicate the implied part or supply the missing words.

1. Our state should pass a law requiring all motorcyclists to wear helmets.
2. Professor Smith is a bad teacher. Some students fall asleep in class while others look out the window.
3. Marcia should be promoted to district manager because she gets along with many different types of people.
4. Rock music should be labeled so that parents can monitor their children's listening because the lyrics glorify illicit sex, drugs, and violence.
5. If you don't behave yourself, Santa Claus won't bring you any presents.
6. The Surgeon General has determined that cigarette smoking is dangerous to your health.
7. National political conventions are merely ritualistic pageants. Their intended function, selecting the party's presidential candidate, has been taken over by the state primaries.
8. Some acreage in California's San Joaquin Valley is suffering from a build-up of salt deposits, the result of irrigation without adequate drainage. Irrigation can bring life to crop lands, but it can also bring slow death.

**43d**

*arg*

9. No business can survive without some profit. Contrary to what some people believe, profits are not used primarily to line the pockets of company owners but to provide capital needed for investment in plant and equipment, the development of new products or services, the expansion of the work force—all important if a company is to survive in today's competitive marketplace.

10. It's no wonder that our state ranks among the highest in numbers of high school dropouts and among the lowest in SAT scores and numbers of students going on to college. We also rank among the lowest in teacher salaries and in state dollars allocated per student.

---

## 43e   Defining terms in argument

Much senseless argument arises because people fail to agree on meanings. Readers have to understand your terms before they can follow your reasoning. The assertion *If the people of this country had believed the Vietnam war was right, we would have won it* is unsatisfactory on several counts, not the least of which is the slippery term *right*. The reader is bound to ask, "What do you mean by 'right'?"

The word *right* is an abstraction, and abstract terms are among the most difficult to define. However, the assertion itself could have provided some useful clues. Consider the statement *A good first-grade teacher is one who keeps the children quiet and in their seats*. This assertion defines *good* by using a concrete example: a teacher whose class is quiet and in place. Definitions, then, supply words or examples known and familiar to the reader, more easily understood than the term being defined, and show what items should be included or excluded from the category the term covers.

**43e**

*arg*

**1. Definition by word substitution.** Many terms can be satisfactorily defined by merely offering a synonym the reader is likely to know. This is particularly true for technical or other little-known terms. Often an **appositive**—another noun or a group of words used as a noun—placed immediately after the term will be useful for such a definition.

cardiac arrest, stopping of the heart

aerobic (oxygen-requiring) bacteria

aquifer, a natural underground water reservoir

layette, clothing or equipment for a newborn child

**2. Formal definition.** We learn about something new by discovering that it resembles things we already know and then by noting how it differs from them. Constructing a **formal definition**—sometimes called a *technical, Aristotelian, logical,* or *sentence definition*—requires exactly the same steps. First, we explain the class of things—the **genus**—to which a term belongs, and then we determine how it differs from other things in that class—its **differentiation.** Formal definitions characteristically take the form *x is y;* that is why they are termed *sentence definitions.*

      **a.** *The first step in formal definition is to put the term into the class of items to which it belongs.* This process is called **classification.**

| Term | | Genus |
|------|------|-------|
| A carpet | is | a floor covering. |
| A crumpet | is | a light, soft bread similar to a muffin. |

In general the narrower the classification, the clearer the eventual definition.

     **NOT**   A crumpet is a bread.

     BUT   A crumpet is a light, soft bread similar to a muffin.

     **NOT**   A rifle is a weapon.

     BUT   A rifle is a firearm.

Indeed, a crumpet is classified as bread, but so is pumpernickel. Though *weapon* is a legitimate classification for *rifle,* the class includes more than is necessary (knives, spears, clubs, and so on).

      **b.** *Distinguish the term from other members of its class.* This process is called **differentiation.**

| Term | | Genus | Differentiation |
|------|------|-------|-----------------|
| A carpet | is | a floor covering | of woven or felted fabric usually tacked to a floor. |
| A crumpet | is | a light, soft bread similar to a muffin | baked on a griddle, often toasted and served with tea. |

Defining a term by genus and differentiation is analogous to the comparison and contrast methods of paragraph and essay development (see Sections **41a** and **42b**). The term is first classified according to similarity and then differentiated according to dissimilarity.

      **c.** *Use parallel form in stating the term to be defined and its definition.* Do not use the phrases *is when* or *is where* in definitions. (See also Section **14a**.)

     **NOT**   A debate *is when* two people or sides argue a given proposition in a regulated discussion.

     BUT   A debate is a regulated discussion of a given proposition between two matched sides.

      **d.** *Be sure the definition itself does not contain the name of the thing defined or any derivative of it.* John Keats's line "Beauty is truth, truth beauty" is poetic, but not very helpful as a definition. Nothing is achieved when definitions are **circular,** when words are defined in terms of themselves.

**43e**

*arg*

| | |
|---|---|
| **NOT** | A rifle is a firearm with *rifling* inside its barrel to impart rotary motion to its projectile. |
| BUT | A rifle is a firearm with spiral grooves inside its barrel to impart rotary motion to its projectile. |
| **NOT** | Traditionally, masculinity has been defined as the behavioral *characteristics of men.* |
| BUT | Traditionally, masculinity has been defined as the behavioral characteristics of courage, forcefulness, and strength. |

e. *Whenever possible, define a term in words that are familiar to the reader.* It doesn't do much good to describe a truffle as "a fleshy, subterranean fungus, chiefly of the genus *Tuber*, often esteemed as food" if your reader won't know the meaning of *subterranean* or *fungus.* "An edible, lumpy plant that grows underground and is related to the mushroom" may be a much more understandable definition of *truffle*, depending on your audience.

Ordinarily, of course, you will define terms without being aware of giving them a genus and a differentiation. But it is always possible to check your definition against the criteria given above. Consider the following example from a student paper:

> Finally, college is valuable to a person interested in success. By *success* I don't mean what is usually thought of when that word is used. I mean achieving one's goals. Everybody has goals to achieve, all of them very different. But whatever they are, college will give one the know-how and the contacts needed to achieve them successfully.

**43e**

*arg*

The specifications for definition help clarify why and how this unsatisfactory definition breaks down. If the statement that this paragraph makes about *success* is isolated, it comes out like this: *Success is the successful achievement of goals that know-how and contacts gained at college help one achieve.* First, this statement violates one of the principles of definition because it defines the word in terms of itself: *success is the successful achievement.* Next, the writer does not make clear what she means by *goals*, and the qualifying clause *that know-how and contacts gained at college help one achieve* does nothing to help us grasp her intended meaning because we do not know how she defines *know-how* and *contacts.* Hence, both aspects of good definition are violated: the terms are neither put into an understandable class nor really differentiated. What is said is that success means being successful, which is not a definition.

**3. Extended definition.** Many terms, particularly abstract words like *propaganda, democracy, happiness, religion, justice,* and *satisfaction,* require more than a formal definition if their meaning is to be clear.

Extended definitions usually have a formal definition at their core but expand upon it using synonyms, examples, analogies, descriptions of operations and results, and various other explanations to show the reader more precisely what is meant. Extended definitions may be one paragraph long or longer; entire articles or even books can be structured as extended definitions.

The following paragraph illustrates a simple extended definition. Note that the first sentence in this definition gives a kind of dictionary definition of *induction*. *Induction* is put into a class of things— in this case *the art of reasoning*. It differs from other things in that class—in this case by being that kind of reasoning in which we first examine particulars and then draw a conclusion from them. This general definition is then developed in two parts: (1) by explaining the kind of scientific reasoning that is inductive, and (2) by explaining, through a series of specific examples, how our everyday reasoning is inductive.

EXTENDED DEFINITION

> Induction is the kind of reasoning by which we examine a number of particulars or specific instances and on the basis of them arrive at a conclusion. The scientific method is inductive when the scientist observes a recurrent phenomenon and arrives at the conclusion or hypothesis that under certain conditions this phenomenon will always take place; if in the course of time further observation supports his hypothesis and if no exceptions are observed, his conclusion is generally accepted as truth and is sometimes called a law. In everyday living, too, we arrive at conclusions by induction. Every cat we encounter has claws; we conclude that all cats have claws. Every rose we smell is fragrant; we conclude that all roses are fragrant. An acquaintance has, on various occasions, paid back money he has borrowed; we conclude that he is frequently out of funds but that he pays his debts. Every Saturday morning for six weeks the newspaper boy is late in delivering the paper; we conclude that he sleeps on Saturday mornings and we no longer look for the paper before nine o'clock. In each case we have reasoned inductively from a number of instances; we have moved from an observation of some things to a generalization about all things in the same category.
>
> NEWMAN AND GENEVIEVE BIRK, *Understanding and Using English*

**43e**

*arg*

Extended definition can be used to clarify terms in an argument, but frequently it constitutes a whole argument—in and of itself—used not only to inform but also to persuade. In such a case the writer is trying to convince readers to share his or her beliefs in addition to clarifying a term. Thoreau wrote "Civil Disobedience" not only to explain the concept but also to justify it as a course of action. Alvin Toffler's book *Future Shock* provided our language with a new term, and the book is an extended definition of that term. But *Future Shock* does more than identify and describe a phenomenon: in Toffler's words the book's purpose is "to help us cope more effectively with both personal

444 THE WRITING PROCESS

and social change. . . . Toward this end, it puts forward a broad new theory of adaptation." In short, *Future Shock* argues for a set of new attitudes and behavioral patterns.

---

EXERCISE 43e(1)
Examine the following definitions and be prepared to answer the following questions about each. Is the class (genus) to which the term belongs clearly named? Is the class narrow enough to be satisfactory? Does the definition clearly differentiate the term from other things in the class? Does the definition repeat the term it is defining? Is it stated in parallel form? If you think a definition is unsatisfactory, rewrite it.

1. An orange is a fruit.
2. A secretary types, files, and distributes mail.
3. Parched peanuts are when the peanuts have been roasted for about 40 minutes at 350 degrees.
4. Gravy is a brown sauce made with meat drippings and flour.
5. Gravy is what slick politicians call fringe benefits.
6. A coaster is a small piece of wood, plastic, or other material placed under a glass to keep watermarks from marring the tabletop.
7. Chaos is when everything gets out of control.
8. A touchdown pass is when the player throws the ball for a touchdown.
9. Skiing is strapping two boards to your feet, pushing yourself off the top of a mountain with two sticks, and praying you will live to see the bottom.
10. A computer manipulates pieces of electronic information. Each single piece of information, called a "bit," exists in electrical form as a high voltage or a low voltage.

---

**43e**

**arg**

EXERCISE 43e(2)
Without using a dictionary, write formal definitions of two of the following terms. Then compare your definitions with those in the dictionary.

1. fire engine
2. timetable
3. sauté
4. sweater
5. soccer

---

EXERCISE 43e(3)
Select one of the following terms and write a paragraph of extended definition. Use your first sentence to state a formal definition of the term and then clarify it in the rest of the paragraph.

1. worship
2. guilt
3. obscenity
4. carefree
5. recreation

# 43f Avoiding fallacies of oversimplification

A convincing argument presents sufficient evidence to support its assertions and presents it in a manner that is logically error-free. Errors of logic in argument, called **fallacies**, weaken an argument, making it unreliable. Most fallacies fall into two categories: **fallacies of oversimplification** and **fallacies of distortion.** Common fallacies of oversimplification are **hasty generalization, inadequate cause-and-effect relationships, false analogies,** and **either/or fallacies.**

**1. Support and qualify all generalizations.** A **generalization** asserts that what is true of several particulars (objects, experiences, people) of the same class (genus) is true of most or all particulars of that class. For example, *Drinking coffee in the evening always keeps me awake at night* is a generalization based on several particular experiences on separate evenings. Generalization is essential to thinking; without it, we could not evaluate experience—only accumulate isolated facts. Similarly, generalization is essential to argument, since evaluation is part of the critical thinking fundamental to the argumentative process. In fact, generalizations often appear as thesis statements in argumentative essays and as topic sentences in paragraphs (see Sections **40** and **42**).

An argument's main assertion may be presented as a generalization: *Most people are indifferent to local politics.* Moreover, because arguments of any length or complexity are comprised of clusters or chains of smaller, related arguments whose proof supports the main assertion, the writer typically uses a number of generalizations in the course of convincing the reader. Thus, generalization is very important—but it has its dangers, as noted below.

**43f**

***arg***

**a.** *Avoid hasty generalizations.* Do not leap to conclusions on the basis of insufficient evidence. We all tend to generalize from a few striking examples, especially when they agree with what we want to believe. But unless examples are irrefutably typical, they can lead to fallacies, even absurd assertions.

| | |
|---|---|
| PARTICULAR A | Mrs. Jones's son never gets home when his mother tells him to. |
| PARTICULAR B | Sally, the girl down the street, won't go to college though her father wants her to. |
| PARTICULAR C | My brother keeps telling his daughter not to go out with that boy, but she keeps right on doing it. |
| HASTY GENERALIZATION | Young people today don't obey their parents. [Does this generalization include Henry and John and Mike, who are always home on time? Or Katie, who is in college though she doesn't want to be? Or the brother's other daughter, who married the son of her father's best friend?] |

| PARTICULAR A | The newspaper reported that a child was recently mauled by a pit bull dog. |
| PARTICULAR B | My mother's mail carrier was bitten by a pit bull dog last year. |
| PARTICULAR C | The gas meter reader said a pit bull chased him from its yard. |
| HASTY GENERALIZATION | As a breed, pit bull dogs are vicious. |

Hasty generalizations are dangerous because they rely on unfair **stereotypes;** they make assertions about groups containing thousands of individuals on the basis of a small number of examples. And more often than not, the writer knows of examples that don't fit the generalizations but, giving in to the temptation to oversimplify, leaves them out.

To protect an argument's validity, as well as to be fair to your readers, never advance a generalization unless you can support it with sufficient evidence. Sometimes two or three examples may be enough, but sometimes you will need to analyze the evidence in detail. If you can think of exceptions to the generalization, you can be sure your readers will too; you should prepare a counterargument to handle them (see Section **43i**).

**b.** *Avoid broad generalizations.* Be careful about using words such as *always, never, all, none, right, wrong* in generalizations. Broad generalizations, like hasty generalizations, arise from inadequate evidence. Sweeping statements invite readers to start thinking of exceptions, to start picking apart your argument even before you've presented your evidence. Many an otherwise reasonable assertion has foundered for lack of *seldom* instead of *never, usually* instead of *always.*

**43f**

*arg*

| OVERSTATED | Playing football always results in injury. |
| | Playing football results in injury. |
| QUALIFIED | Playing football sometimes results in injury. |
| | Playing football can result in injury. |

Note that an overstated generalization need not specifically state that it applies to *all* people. By not making a qualification it clearly implies *all,* as in the second overstatement above. Similarly, words other than modifiers can act as qualifiers. For example, the verb *can* and *may* prevent overstatements, as in the second qualification above, where *can* implies possibility rather than certainty.

**2. Don't assume that a cause-and-effect relationship exists between two facts simply because one follows the other in time.** This inadequate assessment of cause and effect results in the fallacy of oversimplification known as **post hoc, ergo propter hoc** ("after this, therefore because of this").

The Navy began allowing women to serve on its ships in the 1970s, and its preparedness has decreased steadily since then. [The newspaper columnist who made this statement ignored other important factors such as cuts in defense spending and a shortage of new vessels and equipment, all of which adversely affected the Navy's military strength.]

**3. Don't assume that because two circumstances or ideas are alike in some respects, they are alike in all respects.** This fallacy, **false analogy**, shares some characteristics of broad generalizations. Because one or two points are analogous, it is very tempting to go overboard and claim two situations or concepts are wholly analogous. Political speeches are full of oversimplified, faulty analogies, as are moral diatribes.

I don't believe you can run a major U.S. company from abroad. George III tried to run the United States from Britain, and look what happened to him.                                    SIR GORDON WHITE

[About the only commonality between the eighteenth-century monarch facing the American Revolution and the head of a twentieth-century multinational corporation is the ocean between continents.]

Analogy can be a useful persuasive tool, but keep in mind that while it can clarify, it can never prove a point. Analogy's value increases in direct proportion to the number of parallels you cite and decreases with every difference your reader thinks of.

**4. Don't claim there are only two alternatives if, in fact, there are several. Either/or fallacies** result if you oversimplify choices, proposing only two when several actually exist. Truth sometimes is an either/or sort of thing: either you passed the examination, or you failed it. But most things about which we argue are not as clear-cut. Arguing as if only two possibilities exist when the facts justify a variety of possibilities is also known as the **all-or-nothing fallacy** or **false dilemma.** (These two fallacies are frequently distinguished from each other, but both involve ignoring alternatives.)

Students come to college for one of two reasons: they come either to study or to party. Judging by Mack's attendance at campus mixers, I'd say he didn't come to study. [It's possible Mack studies very little, if at all. It's also possible he studies very efficiently and thus has free time to go to parties. Clearly, many combinations of studying and partying, to say nothing of the endless possibilities that include neither studying nor partying, are available to both the prudent and the not-so-prudent college student.]

A woman can't have it both ways. She has to choose between career and family. [Statistics show that a significant proportion of married women and mothers in this country hold jobs. Somebody ob-

**43f**

**arg**

viously has seen through the false dilemma to at least a third possibility.]

---

EXERCISE 43f
Explain what is wrong with the reasoning in the following statements, and try to identify the fallacies of oversimplification that occur.

1. The best place for a child is with his or her parents.
2. Your repeated failures indicate you lack ambition.
3. My fifteen-year-old niece is pregnant. I knew those sex education classes would cause something like this.
4. Maxine makes playing tennis look almost effortless. She must have a natural gift for the game.
5. All televangelists are crooks.
6. Any member of Congress who goes on a junket is just taking a vacation at the taxpayer's expense.
7. All this emphasis on "career training" has turned the university into an assembly line. Poke the students in at one end, keep piling on the required courses, and out they pop at the other end with a diploma but no individuality or ability to think creatively.
8. If you really loved me, you'd spend our anniversary here at home instead of going on that business trip.
9. World War I started during Wilson's term. World War II started during Roosevelt's term, and the Vietnam War escalated during Johnson's term; if we elect another Democratic president, he'll start another war.
10. Anyone who heads a large corporation got to the top by ruthless maneuvering and looking out for "number one."

---

**43g**

*arg*

## **43g**  Avoiding fallacies of distortion

If you ignore counterarguments, you will weaken your own position. Worse yet, if you try to divert attention from counterarguments by appealing to your readers' prejudices and emotions, your argument will be distorted and unfair. You may be successful in your diversion, but you will have avoided the real issues being discussed and failed the test of logical thinking

**Slanted language** is one of the most common kinds of argumentative distortion. Slanted language "twists out of shape," distorts meaning by using **connotation** to appeal to emotion and prejudice (see Section **38**). For example, today words like *radical, permissive,* and *cover-up* produce negative responses from many people, while words like *freedom, responsibility,* and *efficiency* produce positive responses. Consequently, the calculated—or careless—use of such words in argument tends to evoke emotional rather than reasoned reactions. Ironically, it's not unusual to find diametrically opposed positions described by the same connotative language. "Fiscal responsibility" can mean a tax cut in one politician's campaign and a tax increase in another's. This shows the danger of slanted language: people are persuaded to draw conclusions without learning the facts of the matter

**Fallacies of distortion** can also twist and bend an argument, misrepresenting all or part of its meaning. Among the most common distortion techniques are **transfer, argument to the man, argument to the people, non sequitur, begging the question,** and **red herring.**

**1. Don't associate an idea or term with a famous name in the hope of imbuing the former with characteristics of the latter.** The erroneous technique of **transfer (argumentum ad verecundiam)** uses positive or negative association rather than reason as a basis for conclusion. When used negatively, transfer becomes a form of **name calling.** In either case, the hope is that characteristics will transfer, even when logically there is no connection—which explains the notable incongruity of professional athletes' endorsements of motor oil or coffee makers.

> We are the political party of Franklin D. Roosevelt and John Kennedy. Our campaign platform follows in that great democratic tradition.
>
> If Miss America can get beautiful hair like this using X shampoo, you can too.

Not to be confused with transfer, **argument from authority** is a legitimate form of persuasion. When you argue from authority, you cite the research and learned opinions of those considered to be experts on matters you are discussing. For example, if you are arguing for the value of a liberal arts education, you might cite the opinions of Father Theodore Hesburgh, who was the highly respected president of the University of Notre Dame for thirty-five years. Always remember, however, that argument from authority is persuasive only in so far as your audience acknowledges the authenticity and credibility of the authority you are citing.

**43g**

*arg*

**2. Don't sidestep an argument by trying to discredit the person who proposed it. Argument to the man (argumentum ad hominem)** ignores the point being argued and attacks a person's character instead. This distortion technique is similar to that of red herring [see Section **43g(6)**] because it substitutes a false issue for *bona fide* proof. Furthermore, even though discredited for one thing, a person may be right about others.

> Why should you believe what Hartwell says about the needs of our schools? He is suspected of taking bribes. [Apart from the fact that Hartwell is only "suspected of taking bribes," what he has to say about school needs may be based upon extensive study and analysis.]

**3. Don't sidestep an argument by appealing to the instincts and prejudices of the crowd.** **Argument to the people (argumentum ad populum)** arouses emotions people have about institutions and ideas. When politicians evoke God, country, family, or motherhood, they are making such an appeal—as, for example, when candidates say they will protect the interests of the American family.

A slightly different fallacy that uses similar crowd appeal is the **bandwagon** approach. This fallacy says that what is right for the masses is right for the individual: one must go along with the crowd in belief or action. Obviously this is not true, as many incidents of mob rule have shown. Nevertheless, the bandwagon is a favorite ploy among advertisers (and children) who claim "everyone" is buying or doing something.

> Fifty million people can't be wrong! Drink Slurp-o!
>
> But Mom, all the kids are wearing shorts (*or* roller-skates *or* green wigs) to the prom!
>
> The responsible citizens of this state know that a vote for Jenkins is a vote for open and honest government.

**4. Don't substitute inference for a logically sound conclusion.** A **non sequitur** ("it does not follow") attempts a fallacious leap in logic, omitting proof.

> This is the best play I have seen this year, and it should win the Pulitzer prize. [Unless you have seen all the plays produced this year and are qualified to judge the qualities that make one a Pulitzer prize winner, it doesn't follow that the one you like best should win.]

**5. Don't assume the truth of something you are trying to prove.** **Begging the question** is a fallacy that occurs when a premise requiring proof is put forward as true. A related fallacy is called **circular argument**.

> This insurance policy is a wise purchase. It covers all expenses related to cancer treatment. [While the policy may pay cancer-related expenses, the statement assumes the buyer will get cancer. If he or she does not, the policy will not have been a wise purchase.]
>
> His handwriting is hard to read because it is illegible. [This argument does not move from premise to conclusion but merely moves in a circle. *Illegible* means "difficult or impossible to read," so the author has said only that the handwriting is hard to read because it is hard to read.]

**6. Don't introduce a false issue in the hope of leading your reader away from a real one.** A most graphically termed fallacy, a **red herring** supplies a false scent in an argument, diverting the hounds from their quarry and leading them down an irrelevant trail. Usually the false issue elicits an emotional reaction, side-tracking the reader's attention from the real issue and the proof it needs.

> American cars really are superior to Japanese imports. After all, we should "buy American" and support our own economy rather than sending our dollars overseas. ["Buying American," a disguised appeal to patriotism, diverts attention from real issues such as mileage ratings, repair records, safety, and so on, exhibited generally by American cars as compared with Japanese cars.]

---

EXERCISE 43g

Explain the errors in reasoning in the following statements, and try to identify the fallacies of distortion that occur.

1. My parents taught us that if we did our very best on every job we would never be without one.
2. This dull teacher should be fired.
3. After her divorce, Mrs. Jones went to work as a cocktail waitress. I don't think she should get custody of her children.
4. Since all my friends have a 1:00 a.m. curfew, I shouldn't have to come in at 12:00 p.m.
5. Senator Torres never fails to mention his long-term marriage and his four successful children in his campaign speeches. Since he is such a devoted family man, I am going to vote for him again. Our country needs more men like him in government.
6. He knew how to run a lathe, but I didn't hire him because he spent a year in reform school and once a criminal, always a criminal.
7. How can you support the Equal Rights Amendment? Do you want women and men sharing the same restrooms?
8. In that TV commercial for Uppity Airlines, Herman Hero says their plane is the safest thing in the sky. He used to be an astronaut, so he must know what he's talking about.
9. Obviously a good golf game is the key to success in this company. Most of the rising young executives play golf, so I'd better practice my putting.
10. Senator Graft wouldn't have been charged with accepting bribes if there weren't some truth to it.

---

**43h** **arg**

---

## 43h Generating ideas for your argument

In addition to the planning techniques described in Section **40**, you may want to try some of the following activities as you think about what to include in your argument.

**1. Pinpoint exactly what you want your reader to do after reading your argument.** Writing a sentence describing the actual results you would like to achieve helps you to clarify the purpose of your argument. It also helps you to begin thinking about your audience's needs and point of view. For example, in the case of a letter to the school board to protest a school closing, the author might write *I want* *the board to decide that a moderate decrease in enrollment is an insufficient reason to close our neighborhood school.*

**2. List the things that would motivate your audience toward the results you want.** Preparing such a list will help you think about approaches to take and reasons you will need to offer in your argument. For the anti-school-closing argument, the author might list *find ways to cut costs to keep school open, smaller classes/improved instruction, smaller classes/fewer discipline problems, smaller classes/happier teachers, research showing how children benefit from small classes, more parental involvement, projections of increased numbers of elementary school children in next ten years (baby boomers' kids).*

**3. Draw a flowchart of the things that need to happen in a reader's mind for him or her to accept your point of view.** In this way you can anticipate the audience's thought processes and, consequently, its objections to your viewpoint. This analysis will help you to prepare convincing counterarguments and especially to think about possible organizational structures. The points on the diagram might be turned into subheadings for an outline you can use when you draft the argument. The school closing letter might result from a flowchart such as the following.

43h
arg

*board's point of view:*
*keeping school open with declining*
*enrollment is too costly*

↓

*rebut argument that primary*
*goal is to save money:*
*must have balance between*
*economics and education*

*rebut argument that there are*
*no educational differences*
*between big and small*
*elementary schools*

*rebut argument that most parents*
*are indifferent about where their*
*children go to school*

*rebut argument that enrollment*
*will continue to decline:*
*cite neighborhood growth*
*patterns and baby boom*
*birthrate*

## 43i Answering objections from the opposition

A successful argument takes into account counterarguments that the reader is likely to raise and tries to refute them fairly and reasonably. If counterpoints are indeed valid, the best strategy is to recognize their validity but provide sufficient evidence to substantiate the truth of your assertions overall. In fact, you may want to summarize the opposition's point of view before presenting your own. This strategy, named *Rogerian argument* after the psychologist Carl Rogers, involves describing the opposing position accurately and fairly. If you demonstrate that you understand and respect that point of view, your opponents are less likely to feel threatened or defensive and more likely to give your position a fair hearing.

Another associated strategy is to find a common ground, a shared goal, one or more points on which you and your readers can agree. Establishing some common goals may help persuade your reader of the relevance of your overall point of view. For example, suppose your thesis is that science teachers should be paid higher salaries because they are in short supply and because better salaries will attract more scientists to teaching. While your readers may initially disagree with your assertion, if you can find common ground in the viewpoint that science education needs to be improved, you may be able to persuade your audience that higher salaries are the best means for accomplishing that goal.

---

EXERCISE 43i
Find a newspaper or magazine article, or better yet a person, expressing an opinion with which you disagree. Consider the opinion carefully and then restate it in your own words as accurately as you can. Ask another person to read your version and compare it to the original. Then write a counterargument that rebuts the original and supports your own point of view.

**43i**

*arg*

## 43j Structuring your argument to fit your audience and goal

By definition, the rhetorical purpose of an argument is to persuade. Consequently, your broad goal is to change or modify your reader's point of view or move him or her to action. As we noted in Section 40 on the writing process, a number of organizational patterns lend themselves to persuasive purposes. The ones most commonly found in arguments are cause and effect, detail and example, particular to general, general to particular, and climax.

Order of climax, building from least important to most important, satisfies our natural preference for dramatic effect. In an argumentative paper you might state the opposition's viewpoint first and then provide counterarguments that first dispose of the weakest points and finally tackle the most important, difficult, or memorable issues.

Writers often structure arguments in either the particular-to-general or the general-to-particular order because these patterns parallel two fundamental logical processes: induction and deduction.

**Inductive reasoning** (as you learned from the example of extended definition in Section **43e**) proceeds from the particular to the general. *If* particular facts are shown to be true time after time or *if* a laboratory experiment yields the same result whenever it is run or *if* people in a wide and varied sampling respond the same way to a given question, *then* a general conclusion may be drawn. Repeated experimentation and testing led to the conclusion that the Sabin vaccine would prevent polio. Scientists use induction when they test and retest a hypothesis before stating it as a general truth. The scientific method proceeds by inductive reasoning.

**Deductive reasoning** proceeds from the general to the particular. From a general conclusion other facts are deduced. The validity of the deduction depends on the truth of the initial conclusion. Because you know that penicillin is an effective weapon against infection, seeking a doctor to administer it to you if you have an infection is valid deductive reasoning.

There is also an induction-deduction cycle of reasoning. Sound conclusions reached through induction may in turn serve as the basis for deduction. For example, over many years the National Safety Council has kept careful records of the occurrence and circumstances of highway accidents and has reached the valid conclusion that the proportion of accidents to cars on the road on holiday weekends is the same as the proportion on weekends that are not holidays. From this conclusion, arrived at inductively, you may deduce that you can travel as safely by car to a Memorial Day celebration as you can to church the Sunday before.

**43i**

**arg**

In this way, the arguments you construct may use both induction and deduction. Sometimes you reason from conclusions a reader accepts as true; sometimes you must prove the truth of the conclusions themselves. In either case, the assertions you make in the course of the argument should be adequately supported, and there should be no errors in the logic.

"Abolishing the Penny Makes Good Sense," the sample essay at the end of this section, follows an overall inductive pattern with details and examples to support its thesis. It uses analogy, contrast, and several other subordinate structures along the way, but on the whole the essay moves inductively through a series of illustrations supporting the author's contention that the penny is too expensive to be worth keeping around.

> ≋ **WRITERS REVISING: SOUND ARGUMENTS**
> *(continued from page 433)*
>
> Reread the student editorial "Selective Democracy" that appears in the "Writers Revising" near the beginning of Section 13, and evaluate it using the questions listed in Review Exercise, Part C. Does your current evaluation differ from your initial opinion of the editorial? Next, either (1) write up your analysis as a short persuasive essay with your instructor as the audience, (2) revise the editorial to remedy any weaknesses you find in the argument, or (3) write a rebuttal to the editorial framed as a letter to the student editor.

---

## REVIEW EXERCISE ON ARGUMENT (Section 43)

### PART A

Prepare a counterargument for at least one of the arguments stated below. Be sure your counterargument exposes any fallacious reasoning you find in the statements and does not itself contain fallacies. Also be sure to anticipate and defuse objections likely to be raised by the opposition.

1. We should not allow women to become police officers. They would have to work long hours with men and would create morale problems for the men's wives.
2. There is no excuse for the large number of homeless people. The jobs are out there if they want them.
3. Since 1964 scores on Scholastic Aptitude Tests have been dropping. What's more, students graduating from high school today can neither read nor write nor do arithmetic at their grade level. Clearly, the minimum competency testing program used in Jacksonville, Florida, should be instituted nationwide. A student who can't pass these standardized tests shouldn't graduate.
4. My roommate will make a terrific veterinarian. She just loves animals. She's always bringing home stray dogs and cats. It really upsets her to see an animal suffer.
5. If a coat or suit becomes old, ragged, and out of style, we don't continue to wear it. We replace it with a new one. Similarly, employees who reach age sixty five should be forced to retire to make way for younger people with energy and fresh ideas.

**43i**

*arg*

### PART B

Analyze several automobile advertisements, several cosmetic or drug advertisements, and several cigarette advertisements in current magazines or on television on the basis of the following questions:

1. What specific appeals are made? (For example, automobile advertising makes wide use of the bandwagon approach; cosmetic advertising often uses transfer methods.) How logical are these appeals?
2. Are all terms clearly defined?
3. What kinds of generalizations are used or assumed? Are these generalizations adequately supported?
4. Is evidence honestly and fairly presented?
5. Are cause-and-effect relationships clear and indisputable?
6. Is slanted, loaded language used? What is the advertiser trying to achieve with the connotative language?

PART C

Read "Abolishing the Penny Makes Good Sense," the argumentative essay that follows. Use the questions below to evaluate the essay.

**CRITICAL QUESTIONS**

1. What is the author's apparent purpose? What action do you believe he wants readers to take?
2. In your own words, what is the essay's assertion? Where is the assertion stated in the essay?
3. What generalizations does the author make? Are they supported with adequate evidence?
4. Does the author provide arguments that anticipate and defuse counterarguments likely to be raised by the opposition?
5. Do any parts of the argument rest on shaky assumptions or *a priori* premises?
6. Is the author's reasoning sound? Does the argument contain fallacies? If so, what types?
7. Describe the author's tone. Does it change? Is it appropriate throughout?
8. Is any of the language unfairly slanted?
9. Do you find the essay persuasive? Why or why not?

**43i**

*arg*

### ABOLISHING THE PENNY MAKES GOOD SENSE

An economist rarely has the opportunity to recommend a policy change that benefits 200 million people, imposes costs on virtually no one, and saves the government money to boot. But I have such a suggestion to offer the nation as a holiday gift: Let's abolish the penny.

Yes, the old copperhead has outlived its usefulness and is by now a public nuisance—something akin to the gnat. Pennies get in the way when we make change. They add unwanted weight to our pockets and purses. Few people nowadays even bend down to pick a penny off the sidewalk. Doesn't that prove that mining and minting copper into pennies is wasteful? Today, if it rained pennies from heaven, only a fool would turn his umbrella upside down: The money caught would be worth less than the ruined umbrella.

I have been antipenny for years, but final proof came about two years ago. I used to dump my pennies into a shoe box. Eventually, I accumulated several hundred. Dismayed by the ever-growing collection of useless copper, I offered the box to my son William, then 8, warning him that the bank would take the pennies only if he neatly wrapped them in rolls of 50. William, obviously a keen, intu- itive economist, thought the matter over carefully for about two sec- onds before responding: "Thanks, Dad, but it's not worth it." If it's not worth the time of an 8-year-old to wrap pennies, why does the U.S. government keep producing the things?

More than the time of 8-year-olds is involved. Think how often you have waited in line while customers ahead of you fumbled through their pockets or purses for a few—expletive deleted— pennies. A trivial problem. Yes, until you multiply your wasted sec- onds by the billions of cash transactions that take place in our econ- omy each year. I estimate that all this penny-pinching wastes several hundred million hours annually. Valuating that at, say, $10 an hour adds up to several billion dollars per year. . . .

We also must consider the cost of minting and maintaining the penny supply. There are roughly 91 billion pennies circulating, and every year the U.S. Treasury produces 12 billion to 14 billion more, at a cost of about $90 million. Since this expenditure just produces a nuisance for society, it should be at the top of everyone's list of budget cuts.

There are no coherent objections to abolishing the penny. It has been claimed, apparently with a straight face, that eliminating pen- nies would be inflationary, because all those $39.99 prices would rise to $40. Apart from the fact that such increases would be penny-ante, the claim itself is ludicrous. A price such as $39.99 is designed to keep a four from appearing as the first digit—something the retailer deems psychologically important. In a penny-less society merchants probably would change the number to $39.95, not raise it to $40. Even if only one-fifth of all merchants reacted this way, abolishing the penny would be disinflationary.

Sales tax poses a problem. How would a penny-free economy cope with, for instance, a 7% sales tax on a $31 purchase, which comes to $2.17? The answer leads to the second part of my sugges- tion. Let all states and localities amend their sales taxes to round all tax bills to the next-highest nickel. In the example, the state would collect $2.20 instead of $2.17. The customer would lose 3¢ but—if my previous arguments are correct—would actually be better off without the pennies. What other tax leaves the taxpayer happier for having paid it?

Only tradition explains our stubborn attachment to the penny. But sometimes traditions get ridiculous. Surely the smallest currency unit a country uses should be related to its average income. Yet countries with lower standards of living than the U.S. have mini- mum currency units worth more than 1¢—while we have been mint- ing the penny for two centuries. . . .

Sure, the penny has sentimental value. That motivates the last part of my suggestion. Rather than call in all the pennies and melt them, which would be too expensive and perhaps heartrending, the government should simply announce that it is demonetizing the penny . . . and let collectors take many of the pesky coppers out of

**43i**

**arg**

circulation. After hobbyists and investors accumulated whatever stockpiles they desired, the rest could be redeemed by the government—wrapped neatly in rolls of 50, of course.

Let's get penny-wise and abolish the 1¢ piece. The idea is so logical, so obviously correct, that I am sure the new Congress will enact it during its first days in office.

ALAN S. BLINDER

**43i**

*arg*

# RESEARCHED WRITING

*Research is . . . the attempt to take external events and data and,*
*by passing them through the sensibilities of the writer, to produce a text that*
*reflects both the outer and the writer's inner worlds of meaning.*

> JAMES V. CATANO, "Navigating the Fluid Text"

*Knowledge is of two kinds. We know a subject ourselves, or we know where we*
*can find information upon it.*

> SAMUEL JOHNSON, Boswell's *Life of Johnson*

# 44

## *LOCATING AND WORKING WITH SOURCES*

Researched writing plays an important part in most people's college education. Although conducting research and writing up the results may seem new to you, and although you may be somewhat unsure about how to proceed, you have actually been engaged in research for most of your life. Research is a basic human activity—as fundamental as a child's trial-and-error approach to learning about a hot stove, and as sophisticated as a chemist's hypothesis-testing in the laboratory. Somewhere in between lies the research that students conduct in college. Broadly speaking, everyone engaged in the activity of acquiring knowledge is engaged in research.

Research takes many forms. You conduct research when you observe people and events, perform laboratory experiments, tape-record an interview, write notes in the library, or compare your experiences with those of someone else. But research is more than gathering data; it is also selecting, organizing, analyzing, interpreting, and evaluating data so that valid statements can be made about some aspect of reality.

Research requires critical thinking, not just summarizing and reporting. To conduct research is to apply a systematic approach to obtaining information, drawing and testing conclusions, and sharing these conclusions with others. When you conduct research, you begin with what is known and move into the unknown, with the aim of exploring some aspect of the world and making verifiable statements about it.

Whether they are college students or rocket scientists, researchers frequently present the results of their work in writing so that others can share and evaluate them. These results may appear as an article in a scholarly journal or magazine, a presentation at a business meeting, testimony before a congressional subcommittee, a patent application for a new drug, specifications for an improved automobile ignition system, or a term paper for a college political science course. But whatever form the research "publication" takes, the fundamental research process is similar across disciplines.

Sections **44, 45,** and **46** chart the process of producing researched writing. These sections follow Toni Mitchell, a student writer, as she collects material and writes a research paper for a course called "Social Change." The process Toni uses in planning her search strategy; locating and working with her sources; sorting, evaluating, and organizing her material; and finally writing, documenting, and revising her paper, will show you an effective way to handle a researched writing project.

## 44a   Planning a search strategy

The cornerstone of most research projects is a *preliminary* or *working bibliography,* a list of articles, books, and other sources you plan to consult in researching your subject. It is called a "working" bibliography because as your research progresses you will add to the initial list when you come across useful-looking references, and you will delete items that do not turn out to be helpful.

Unfortunately, when faced with a research assignment, too many students begin by aimlessly thumbing the subject cards in the library's card catalog. They waste time and create frustration for themselves because they turn to the card catalog long before they are ready to benefit from its information. With a good search strategy, you not only can save yourself time but can be reasonably sure you are developing an informed, balanced view of your subject.

**1. Begin by talking to knowledgeable people.** Before looking for books, talk to people. Once you have decided on the general subject area you want to explore, talk to professors, graduate students, or other researchers at your school who are likely to know something about your subject. Business people, social workers, scientists, or other professionals in your research area may also serve as excellent resources. These people are often glad to help you learn about a subject and will probably be able to suggest relevant books and articles to read as well as other individuals you might profitably talk to. They may even know of existing bibliographies you can use to begin your library search. Such people can frequently provide information about prevailing schools of thought on a subject and tell you about the most authoritative scholars and sources. In fact, your professors may be authoritative sources themselves. You may want to interview one or more of these people, taking notes for later use in your research paper.

For her sociology term paper, Toni Mitchell knew that she was interested in researching the general subject of the elderly. She learned from one of her professors that there were several prevalent theories about the future of the aged in the next century. When she began her reading she was therefore able to spot proponents of one theory or another more easily and take their biases into account in her evaluation.

**2. Tune your eyes and ears to your subject.** Campus and community events can provide sources of information: special lectures, workshops, or programs that relate to your topic. Step up your reading of periodicals and newspapers. If your subject is a current one, you will probably discover useful articles in daily metropolitan newspapers or in weekly magazines such as *Time, Newsweek,* or *Business Week.* You may also come across radio or television programs that provide information about your subject, and some documentary and news programs have written transcripts that may be obtained by mail. Toni happened to see a public television program that started her thinking about the role of elderly people throughout history. She was fortunate in that the program series had also been printed as a book, which she was able to check out of the library.

Tell your friends and family about your topic. They may provide helpful leads. For example, conversations with her grandmother helped Toni explore aspects of her subject. Grandmother Mitchell's definite ideas about unfair stereotyping of the elderly inspired Toni to pay particular attention to that topic in her research. In addition, her father remembered reading a recent *Business Week* article about projected trends among senior citizens.

## 44b  Learning about your library's resources

Libraries have three principal kinds of holdings: a general collection of books; a collection of periodicals, bulletins, and pamphlets; and a collection of reference works.

**1. General collection of books.** The general collection includes most of the books in the library—all those that are available for general circulation. Some libraries have open shelves where you can select books yourself. Other libraries keep the general collection in closed stacks; to obtain a book you submit a "call slip" bearing the call number, author, and title of the book and library personnel get the book for you. In either case, you first must obtain information from the card catalog (discussed later) so that your book can be located on the shelves.

**2. Periodicals, bulletins, pamphlets.** A **periodical** is a publication that appears at regular (periodic) intervals. Periodicals (also called *serials*) include popular magazines, specialized magazines, and professional or scholarly journals. General periodicals include both popular and specialized magazines such as *Time, Fortune, National Geographic, Road & Track,* and *Psychology Today.* Professional and scholarly journals include those such as *American Historical Review, PMLA, Journal of Organic Chemistry,* and *International Social Sciences Journal.* Both types of periodicals are good research sources, but remember that professional or scholarly journals will provide more detailed, learned investigations of subjects and are often considered primary sources. (Definitions of primary and secondary sources appear on page 480.)

**Bulletins** and **pamphlets** may or may not be periodicals, depending on whether they are issued as parts of a series or as separate, single publications. They are usually kept in the stacks with the main collection of books. Most libraries keep recent issues of magazines, journals, and newspapers in the open shelves of the reading room. Older issues are bound in volumes and shelved in the stacks. Back issues of major newspapers may be stored on microfiche or microfilm. Libraries usually do not allow periodicals to be checked out.

Periodicals are invaluable research aids because they contain the most recent material on a subject and reflect opinions current at the time of publication. Also, information is likely to appear in periodicals before it is published in books.

**3. Reference materials.** Your library's reference collection contains encyclopedias, dictionaries, indexes, directories, handbooks, atlases, and guides. These are usually located on open shelves in the main reading room, and they should not be removed from the reference area. Some of them, particularly indexes, may be stored on microfiche or in computerized data banks rather than in bound volumes.

You can use the subject, title, and author headings in reference works to find journal, magazine, and newspaper articles and to locate bibliographies. You can obtain statistics and biographical information in the reference collection or scan book reviews that will help you determine if a particular work is worth reading or not. You can also locate abstracts (summaries) of journal articles to help you decide whether you want to find and read a whole article.

**44c**   Using reference works to develop an overview of your subject

To benefit from sources that discuss your subject in detail, you first will need to gain a general view of it. Your library's reference collection—rather than the card catalog—is the best place to start. Reference works such as those listed on the following pages, and others that your reference librarian may suggest, can supply not only a subject overview but also numerous items for your working bibliography. Keeping a research log, a notebook or journal of the steps you take and the works you check during your research, can be very helpful. Then, if you need to find a source that initially looked unimportant, you will be able to relocate it easily. Part of Toni's research log is given below, showing her search procedure in her college library's reference collection.

**44c**

*res*

Tuesday evening
1. Stopped by reference desk and picked up handout "The Federal Government: Sources in the Library." Know that several government agencies deal with aging and senior citizens. Found Administration on Aging, U.S. Department of Health and Human Services, in *Government Agencies* listed on the handout.
2. Checked *Social Sciences Index* under "age," "aging," etc. and found ten pages of bibliographic entries. Lots of these look good. Many articles appear in a handful of journals: *Gerontologist, Journal of Gerontological*

*Social Work, Aging and Society*, etc. Must mean these journals are important in the field. Remember to ask Professor Cesneros which journals are considered "leading."

3. Using subject headings in *Sociological Abstracts*, read its summaries of some journal articles on topic. Discovered it did not abstract many of the articles I'm looking for.

### Wednesday afternoon

4. Checked serials listing (on microfiche) to see if our library has the journals I need. Doesn't have *Journal of Aging Studies* (two interesting-looking articles). Reference librarian sent me to Interlibrary Loan, where I filled out request forms. Should take 2 weeks to get articles. Good thing I started this project early!

5. While looking at serials listing, decided to check under key-word headings to see if anything turned up. Found journal called *Aging* published by U.S. Administration on Aging (Washington, D.C.). Great! Current issues in periodicals room. Thumbed through a few issues. Photocopied some articles. Looks like a really good source. Need to explore further.

6. Used *Essay and General Literature Index* to locate individual essays published in books. *Handbook of the Psychology of Aging* cited frequently. Found out our library has it when I checked the online database. Learned that all serials and books added to the library after June 1976 are listed in database. Older books still listed in the card catalog.

### Wednesday evening

7. Checked *Reader's Guide to Periodical Literature* to locate some *Time* magazine articles remember as having discussed senior citizens issues. Checked *Business Periodicals Index* for *Business Week* issue Dad mentioned. Wonder if that issue is laying around home anywhere?

8. Looked through index of *Newsbank* microfiche for relevant newspaper articles. Most were too general or repeated info better presented in more specialized source

9. Asked reference librarian about best sources for demographic information on elderly population. Didn't look forward to losing my way among shelves of U. S. census data. She said I wouldn't have to—pointed me to _Statistical Abstracts_ volume in reference collection. Has all the population figures I need.

10. Looked up Betty Friedan in _Who's Who_. Wrote one of articles sent for through Interlibrary Loan. Name sounded sort of familiar. Turns out she's a feminist (wrote _The Feminine Mystique_) who has begun to do work on aging. Has quite a reputation (controversial).

Not only can reference books add to your working bibliography but they can also help you decide which sources are worth pursuing. As Toni's research log shows, she began to evaluate potential sources as she used materials in the reference and periodicals collections. Working back and forth between indexes, listings, and other sources, she was able to rule out some things and note others for further investigation. Rather than reading randomly and perhaps missing important material, you too can develop a planned approach for gathering the best available information.

**1. Learning about standard reference works.** Become familiar with the kinds of reference works available in your library and with the most important works of each kind. If you cannot find the book you want or if you do not know what sources will help you most, ask the reference librarian. Librarians are not simply custodians; they are teachers trained to show you effective ways of using the library as part of your search strategy.

The following is a representative list of reference books available in most libraries. Some reference books are revised periodically, appearing in new editions, or have supplements. You will usually want to look for the most recently published version.

**44c**

*res*

GUIDES TO REFERENCE SOURCES

Brownstone, David, and Gorton Carruth. *Where to Find Business Information.* Directory to over 5,000 sources including data bases, information services, government publications, books, and periodicals.

Galin, Saul, and Peter Spielberg. *Reference Books: How to Select and Use Them.*

Gates, Jean Key. *Guide to the Use of Books and Libraries.*

Sheehy, Eugene P. *Guide to Reference Books.* Supplement.

Shove, Raymond H., et al. *The Use of Books and Libraries.*

*Statistical Sources.* A subject guide to locating statistics sources.

CATALOGS

*Books in Print.* Author and title indexes for *Publishers' Trade List Annual Subject Guide to Books in Print.*

*Cumulative Book Index.* Monthly listing of published books in English. Cumulated annually.

*Monthly Catalog of U.S. Government Publications.* 1895 to date.

*National Union Catalog.* Subject and author listings of Library of Congress holdings as well as titles from other libraries, motion pictures, recordings, and film strips.

*Union List of Serials in Libraries of the United States and Canada.* Lists of periodicals and newspapers. Supplemented monthly by *New Serial Titles.*

*Vertical File Index.* 1935—. Supplements to date. (Formerly called *Vertical File Service Catalog.* 1935–54.) Monthly, with annual cumulations. Subject and title index to selected pamphlet material.

GENERAL ENCYCLOPEDIAS

*Chambers Encyclopedia.* 15 vols.

*Collier's Encyclopedia.* 24 vols.

*Encyclopedia Americana.* 30 vols.

*Encyclopaedia Britannica.* 30 vols.

*Encyclopedia International.* 20 vols.

*New Columbia Encyclopedia.* 1 vol.

DICTIONARIES, WORD BOOKS

*Abbreviations Dictionary.* International in scope.

*Acronyms, Initialisms and Abbreviations.*

*American Heritage Dictionary.* Good notes on usage.

*Dictionary of American English on Historical Principles.* 4 vols. 1938–44.

*Dictionary of American Regional English.*

Evans, Bergen, and Cornelia Evans. *A Dictionary of Contemporary American Usage.*

Fowler, Henry W. *Dictionary of Modern English Usage.* 2nd ed. Rev. by Sir Ernest Gowers.

*Funk & Wagnalls New Standard Dictionary.* Unabridged.

*Oxford Dictionary of English Etymology.*

*Oxford English Dictionary.* 2nd ed. 20 vols. Also known as *New English Dictionary.* Unabridged.

Partridge, Eric. *A Dictionary of Slang and Unconventional English.*

*Random House Dictionary of the English Language.* Unabridged.

*Roget's International Thesaurus.* Several editions available.

*Webster's Dictionary of Proper Names.*

*Webster's New Dictionary of Synonyms.*

*Webster's Third New International Dictionary.* Unabridged.

Wentworth, Harold, and Stuart B. Flexner. *Dictionary of American Slang.*

**44c**

*res*

YEARBOOKS

*Americana Annual.* 1924—.

*Britannica Book of the Year.* 1938—.

*Congressional Record.* 1873—. Issued daily while Congress is in session: revised and issued in bound form at end of the session.

*Facts on File.* A weekly digest of world events. 1940—.

*Historical Statistics of the United States: Colonial Times to 1970.* 2 vols. 1975. Supplement to *Statistical Abstract.* Both published by U.S. Bureau of the Census.

*Negro Almanac.* 1967—.

*New International Year Book.* 1907—.

*Official Associated Press Almanac.* 1969—. An almanac with longer articles, strong emphasis on statistical data and biographical information.

*Statistical Abstract of the United States.* 1878—.

*United Nations Statistical Yearbook.* 1945–1968. Monthly supplements.

*World Almanac and Book of Facts.* 1868—.


ATLASES AND GAZETTEERS

*Columbia-Lippincott Gazetteer of the World.*

*Commercial and Library Atlas of the World.* Frequently revised.

*Encyclopaedia Britannica World Atlas.* Frequently revised.

*National Geographic Atlas of the World.*

*New Cosmopolitan World Atlas.* Issued annually.

*The Times Atlas of the World.*

*Webster's New Geographical Dictionary.*


GENERAL BIOGRAPHY

*American Men and Women of Science.*

*Biographical Dictionaries Master Index.* A guide to over 725,000 listings of biographies appearing in current dictionaries and collective biographical sources.

*Biography Index.* 1946—. Quarterly. Cumulated annually, with permanent volumes every three years.

*Current Biography: Who's News and Why.* 1940—. Published monthly with semiannual and annual cumulations.

*Dictionary of American Biography.* 17 vols., supplements.

*International Who's Who.* 1936—.

*Webster's Biographical Dictionary.*

*Who's Who.* (British) 1849—.

*Who's Who in America.* 1899—.

*Who's Who of American Women.* 1958—.

*Who Was Who.* 1897–1960.

*Who Was Who in America.* Historical Volume. 1607–1896.

**44c**

*res*

BOOKS OF QUOTATIONS

Bartlett, John. *Familiar Quotations.*

Evans, Bergen. *Dictionary of Quotations.*

*The Macmillan Book of Proverbs, Maxims, and Famous Phrases.*

*Oxford Dictionary of Quotations.*

MYTHOLOGY AND FOLKLORE

*Brewer's Dictionary of Phrase and Fable.*

Bullfinch, Thomas. *Bullfinch's Mythology.*

*Funk & Wagnalls Standard Dictionary of Folklore, Mythology, and Legend.* 2 vols.

Hammond, N. G., and H. H. Scullord. *The Oxford Classical Dictionary.*

*Larousse World Mythology.*

LITERATURE, DRAMA, FILM, AND TELEVISION

Aaronson, C. S., ed. *International Television Almanac.* 1956—.

Adelman, Irving, and R. Dworkin. *Modern Drama: A Checklist of Critical Literature on Twentieth Century Plays.*

Baugh, Albert C., ed. *A Literary History of England.*

Benét, William Rose. *The Reader's Encyclopedia.*

Bukalski, Peter J. *Film Research: A Critical Bibliography.*

Cassell's *Encyclopedia of World Literature.*

Cawkwell, Tim, and John Milton Smith, eds. *World Encyclopedia of the Film.*

*Columbia Dictionary of Modern European Literature.*

*Contemporary Authors: A Bio-bibliographical Guide to Current Authors and Their Works.* 1962—.

*Dictionary of World Literary Terms.*

Hart, J. D. *Oxford Companion to American Literature.*

Hartnoll, Phyllis. *The Oxford Companion to the Theatre.*

Harvey, Sir Paul, and J. E. Heseltine. *Oxford Companion to Classical Literature.*

_____.*Oxford Companion to English Literature.*

Holman, C. Hugh. *A Handbook to Literature.*

*International Encyclopedia of the Film.*

*Literary History of England.* 4 vols.

*Literary History of the United States.* 2 vols.

*MLA International Bibliography of Books and Articles on the Modern Languages and Literatures.* Published annually since 1922.

*New York Times Film Reviews, 1913–70.*

Spiller, Robert E., et al., eds. *Literary History of the United States.*

Whitlow, Roger. *Black American Literature.*

Woodress, James, ed. *American Fiction 1900–1950: A Guide to Information Sources.*

**44c**

*res*

*Cambridge Ancient History.* 5 vols. Plates.

*Cambridge Medieval History.* 1967—.

*Dictionary of American History.* 8 vols.

Durant, Will, and Ariel Durant. *The Story of Civilization.* 11 vols.

*Encyclopedia of American History.*

*Harvard Guide to American History.* 2 vols.

Johnson, Thomas H. *Oxford Companion to American History.*

Langer, William L. *An Encyclopedia of World History.*

*New Cambridge Modern History.* 14 vols.

*Political Handbook and Atlas of the World.* Published annually.

*Political Science: A Bibliographical Guide to the Literature.*

Schlesinger, Arthur M., and D. R. Fox, eds. *A History of American Life.* 13 vols. 1927–48.

Apel, Willi. *Harvard Dictionary of Music.*

Bryan, Michael. *Bryan's Dictionary of Painters and Engravers.* 5 vols.

Canaday, John C. *The Lives of the Painters.* 4 vols.

Chujoy, Anatole, and P. W. Manchester. *The Dance Encyclopedia.*

*Encyclopedia of Painting.*

*Encyclopedia of World Art.* 15 vols.

Feather, Leonard. *Encyclopedia of Jazz.*

Fletcher, Sir Banister F. *A History of Architecture.*

*Focal Encyclopedia of Photography.* 2 vols.

*Grove's Dictionary of Music and Musicians.*

Myers, Bernard S. *McGraw-Hill Dictionary of Art.* 5 vols.

Osborne, Harold. *Oxford Companion to Art.* 1970.

*Popular Music: An Annotated List of American Popular Songs.* 6 vols.

Scholes, Percy A. *Oxford Companion to Music.*

Stambler, Eric. *Encyclopedia of Pop, Rock, and Soul.*

Thompson, Oscar, and N. Slonimsky. *International Cyclopedia of Music and Musicians.*

**44c**

*res*

Adams, Charles, ed. *A Reader's Guide to the Great Religions.*

*The Concise Encyclopedia of Western Philosophy and Philosophers.*

*Encyclopedia Judaica.* 16 vols.

*Encyclopedia of Philosophy.* 4 vols.

Ferm, Vergilius. *Encyclopedia of Religion.*

Grant, Frederick C., and H. H. Rowley. *Dictionary of the Bible.*

*New Catholic Encyclopedia.* 17 vols.

*New Schaff-Herzog Encyclopedia of Religious Knowledge.* 12 vols. and index.
*Universal Jewish Encyclopedia.* 10 vols.

SCIENCE, TECHNOLOGY
*Chamber's Technical Dictionary.* Revised with supplement.
*Dictionary of Physics.*
*Encyclopedia of Chemistry.*
*Encyclopedia of Physics.*
Gray, Peter, ed. *The Encyclopedia of the Biological Sciences.*
*Handbook of Chemistry and Physics.* 1914—.
*McGraw-Hill Encyclopedia of Science and Technology.* 15 vols.
*Universal Encyclopedia of Mathematics.* 1964.
*Van Nostrand's Scientific Encyclopedia.*

SOCIAL SCIENCES, BUSINESS, AND ECONOMICS
Davis, John P., ed. *The American Negro Reference Book.*
Deidler, Lee J., and Douglas R. Carmichael. *Accountant's Handbook.*
*A Dictionary of Psychology.*
*Encyclopedia of Educational Research.*
*Encyclopedia of Human Behavior: Psychology, Psychiatry, and Mental Health.*
*Encyclopedia of Social Work.* (Formerly *Social Work Yearbook,* 1929–1960.)
Good, Carter V. *Dictionary of Education.*
Greenwald, Douglas. *The McGraw-Hill Dictionary of Modern Economics.*
Heyel, Carl. *The Encyclopedia of Management.*
*International Encyclopedia of the Social Sciences.* 17 vols. Supplement.
Klein, Barry T., ed. *Reference Encyclopedia of the American Indians.*
Mitchell, Geoffrey D. *A Dictionary of Sociology.*
Munn, G. G. *Encyclopedia of Banking and Finance.*
*Thomas Register of American Manufacturers.* 1910—. Multivolume. Updated annually. Includes alphabetical listings of company profiles, also brand names and trademarks.
White, Carl M., et al. *Sources of Information on the Social Sciences.*

**44c**
*res*

**2. Using general and special periodical indexes.** A library's catalog merely shows what periodicals are available. Periodical indexes, which are usually shelved in the reference section of the library, help you to locate the articles you need in those periodicals. Such indexes are usually classed as general or special indexes. **General indexes** list articles on many different kinds of subjects. **Special indexes**

limit themselves to articles in specific areas. Although general indexes
are very helpful for locating articles giving an overview of a subject,
don't limit yourself to looking only in general indexes. To achieve the
depth of research appropriate for most college-level courses, you will
need to consult specialized indexes that can direct you to articles written by experts. Articles listed in general indexes are more likely to be
written by journalists reporting on someone else's research rather than
by the experts themselves, who are more likely to write for publications listed in specialized indexes. College-level research writing
should draw upon the most authoritative and most primary sources
available at the student's level of understanding. Toni used several
popular magazines such as *Time* and *Newsweek* to get a general view of
senior citizens' issues, but she referred mainly to scholarly articles written by gerontologists and other researchers for most of her term paper. She found these research articles in specialized indexes rather
than general indexes. Representative lists of both kinds of indexes
follow.

GENERAL INDEXES

*Readers' Guide to Periodical Literature.* 1900 to date. Published semimonthly; cumulated every three months and annually. The *Readers'
Guide* gives entries under author, title, and subject for articles appearing in about 160 popular periodicals.

This is the most widely known and used of the general indexes.
Because many periodical indexes use systems very similar to that of
the *Readers' Guide,* it is worth examining the sample entries below.
The headings for 1 through 5 are **subject entries;** 6 and 7 are
**author entries.** Entry 8, a subject entry, indicates that an article indexed under the subject heading *Graffiti* was published in the June
1969 issue of *Science Digest,* volume 65, pages 31 through 33. Titled
"Walls Remember," it was illustrated and unsigned. (All abbreviations
and symbols used are explained in the first pages of any issue of the
*Readers' Guide.*)

The second listing under entry 1 refers the user to a series of
articles by D. Wolfle published in *Science* and titled "Are Grades Necessary?" The first article appeared in the issue of November 15, 1968
(volume 162, pages 745–46); the second and third appeared, respectively, in the issues for April 18 and June 6, 1969. Entry 2, under the
subject heading *Graduate Students,* indexes a review by D. Zinberg and
P. Doty in the May 1969 issue of *Scientific American* of a book, *New
Brahmins: Scientific Life in America,* by S. Klaw. The + that follows the
page references is an indication that the review is continued on a page
or pages past 140. Entries 3, 4, and 7 are cross-references to the places
in the *Guide* at which the user can find the subject or author listed.

**44c**

*res*

**1 GRADING and marking (students)**
Answer to Sally; multiple-choice tests. W. R. Link. Ed Digest 34:24–7 My '69
Are grades necessary? D. Wolfle; discussion. Science 162:745–6; 164:245, 1117–18 N 15 '68. Ap 18. Je 6 '69
ROTC: under fire but doing fine. il U S News 66:38 My 19 '69

**2 GRADUATE students**
New Brahmins: scientific life in America, by S. Klaw. Review
    Sci Am 220:139–40 + My '69. D. Zinberg and P. Doty

**3 GRADUATION.** See Commencements

**4 GRADUATION addresses.** See Baccalaureate addresses

**5 GRAEBNER, Clark**
Profiles. J. McPhee. por New Yorker 45:45–8 + Je 7: 44–8 + Je 14 '69

**6 GRAEF, Hilda**
Why I remain a Catholic. Cath World 209:77–80 My '69

**7 GRAF, Rudolf F.** See Whalen, G. J. jt. auth.

**8 GRAFFITI**
Walls remember. il Sci Digest 65:31–3 Je '69

From *Readers' Guide to Periodical Literature,* July 1969, p. 73. Reproduced by permission of The H. W. Wilson Company.

Three other general indexes are valuable supplements to the *Readers' Guide:*

*International Index.* 1907–65. Became *Social Sciences and Humanities Index.* 1965–73. Divided into *Social Sciences Index.* 1974—, and *Humanities Index.* 1974—.

*Poole's Index to Periodical Literature,* 1802–81. Supplements through January 1, 1907. This is a subject index to American and English periodicals.

*Popular Periodicals Index.* 1973—. An author and subject guide to popular articles appearing in about 25 periodicals not indexed by major indexing services.

**44c**

**res**

SPECIAL INDEXES

These indexes list articles published in periodicals devoted to special concerns or fields.

*The Bibliographic Index.* 1938—. Indexes current bibliographies by subject; includes both bibliographies published *as* books and pamphlets and those that appear *in* books, periodical articles, and pamphlets.

*Book Review Digest.* 1905—. Monthly, cumulated annually. Lists books by author and quotes from several reviews for each. Covers 75 journals and newspapers.

*Book Review Index.* 1965—. Covers 230 journals and lists books that have one or more reviews.

*Current Book Review Citations.* 1976—. Indexes over 1,000 periodicals and includes fiction, nonfiction, and children's books.

*Essay and General Literature Index.* 1934—. Indexes collections of essays, articles, and speeches.

*New York Times Index.* 1913—. Semimonthly, with annual cumulation. Since this index provides dates on which important events, speeches, and the like, occurred, it serves indirectly as an index to records of the same events in the other newspapers.

*Ulrich's International Periodicals Directory.* 2 vols. Lists 65,000 periodicals under the subjects they contain, with detailed cross-references and index, thus indicating what periodicals are in a particular field. Also indicates in what other guide or index each periodical is indexed, thus serving indirectly as a master index.

The titles of most of the following special indexes are self-explanatory.

*Agricultural Index.* 1916 to date. A subject index, appearing nine times a year and cumulated annually.

*Applied Science and Technology Index.* 1958 to date. (Formerly *Industrial Arts Index.*)

*The Arts Index.* 1929 to date. An author and subject index.

*Articles on American Literature.* 1900–1950. 1950–1967. 1968–1975.

*Business Periodicals Index.* 1958 to date. Monthly. (Formerly *Industrial Arts Index.*)

*Dramatic Index.* 1909–1949. Continued in *Bulletin of Bibliography,* 1950 to date. Annual index to drama and theater.

*The Education Index.* 1929 to date. An author and subject index.

*Engineering Index.* 1884 to date. An author and subject index.

*General Science Index.* 1978— . Supplements monthly except June and December.

*Granger's Index to Poetry.*

*Index to Legal Periodicals.* 1908 to date. A quarterly author and subject index.

*Industrial Arts Index.* 1913–1957. An author and subject index, monthly, with annual cumulations. (In 1958 this index was split into *Applied Science and Technology Index* and *Business Periodicals Index.*)

*Monthly Catalog of United States Government Publications.* 1905—.

*Physical Education Index.* 1978—. Covers not only physical education but sports in general. Published quarterly.

*Play Index.* 1978.

*Public Affairs Information Service Bulletin.* 1915 to date. Weekly, with bi-monthly and annual cumulations. An index to materials on economics, politics, and sociology.

*Quarterly Cumulative Index Medicus.* 1927 to date. A continuation of the *Index Medicus,* 1899–1926. Indexes books as well as periodicals.

*Short Story Index.* 1953—. Supplements.

*Song Index.* 1926. Supplement.

*United Nations Documents Index.* 1950—.

**44c**

*res*

Two reference books provide descriptions of periodicals found in most libraries. These books give publication information as well as types of subject matter, authors, and readers usually associated with a periodical. Such information can be helpful in evaluating a particular periodical's biases, authority, and credibility.

Farber, Evan I. *Classified List of Periodicals for the College Library.* 5th ed. 1972. Organizes scholarly and professional journals in the liberal arts and sciences by field. Does not cover technology or engineering.
Katz, Bill and Linda S. *Magazines for Libraries.* 4th ed. 1982. Describes most popular and many scholarly periodicals.

**3. Using electronic databases.** Accessing electronic databases of stored information is becoming increasingly widespread and thus increasingly important to library research. Many of these databases are available through information retrieval services to which libraries and individuals may subscribe; that is, the user pays a fee for "dialing up and logging on" to the service via computer, modem, and telephone. CompuServe, DIALOG Information Retrieval Service, Bibliographic Retrieval Service (BRS), and Dow Jones News/Retrieval are but a few of the many database vendors. Check with your librarian to see which ones may be available at your school. Through online computerized searches you can consult indexes, retrieve statistical information, examine law case records, check stock market prices, or look at research citations in education or a number of other fields. If your library has access to electronic databases, the library staff will show you how to use them.

**44d**   Continuing your search at the card catalog

**44d**

*res*

Once you have gained an overview of your subject, tentatively decided on a direction, and begun compiling a preliminary bibliography, you will be able to use the library's card catalog more effectively. This catalog lists alphabetically all the books and periodicals the library contains. Its cards tell you the call number you need to locate books on the shelves. Your library may list periodicals in a separate serials catalog, either on cards, microfiche, or computer printout. In fact, some libraries store their entire catalog listing on microform or in computer files.

**Classification systems.** The classification system on which a card catalog is based is a kind of map of library holdings. Library holdings are divided into categories with numbers or letters assigned to each. Consequently, if you know the numbers or letters for the general category you need, you occasionally might want to bypass the card catalog, go directly to the appropriate shelves, and browse through the books.

The chief purpose of a classification system is to permit easy retrieval of stored materials. To further that objective, every item in the library is given a call number. Be sure to copy the call number fully and exactly as it appears on the catalog card.

American libraries use either the **Dewey decimal system** or the **Library of Congress system** to classify books.

The Dewey system divides books into ten numbered classes:

| | | | |
|---|---|---|---|
| 000–099 | General works | 500–599 | Pure science |
| 100–199 | Philosophy | 600–699 | Useful arts |
| 200–299 | Religion | 700–799 | Fine arts |
| 300–399 | Social sciences | 800–899 | Literature |
| 400–499 | Philology | 900–999 | History |

Each of these divisions is further divided into ten parts, as:

| | | | |
|---|---|---|---|
| 800 | General literature | 850 | Italian literature |
| 810 | American literature | 860 | Spanish literature |
| 820 | English literature | 870 | Latin literature |
| 830 | German literature | 880 | Greek literature |
| 840 | French literature | 890 | Other literatures |

Each of these divisions is further divided as:

| | | | |
|---|---|---|---|
| 821 | English poetry | 826 | English letters |
| 822 | English drama | 827 | English satire |
| 823 | English fiction | 828 | English miscellany |
| 824 | English essays | 829 | Anglo-Saxon |
| 825 | English oratory | | |

**44d**

*res*

Further subdivisions are indicated by decimals. *The Romantic Rebels*, a book about Keats, Byron, and Shelley, is numbered 821.09, indicating a subdivision of the 821 English poetry category.

The Library of Congress classification system, used by large libraries, divides books into lettered classes:

| | |
|---|---|
| A | General works |
| B | Philosophy, Religion |
| C | History, Auxiliary sciences |
| D | Foreign history and topography |
| E–F | American history |
| G | Geography, Anthropology |

| H | Social sciences |
| J | Political science |
| K | Law |
| L | Education |
| M | Music |
| N | Fine arts |
| P | Language and literature |
| Q | Science |
| R | Medicine |
| S | Agriculture |
| T | Technology |
| U | Military science |
| V | Naval science |
| Z | Bibliography, Library science |

Each of these sections is further divided by letters and numbers that show the specific call number of a book. *English Composition in Theory and Practice* by Henry Seidel Canby and others is classified in this system as PE 1408.E5. (In the Dewey decimal system this same volume is numbered 808 C214.)

If your library uses the Library of Congress classification system, you will find near the card catalog several volumes entitled *Library of Congress Subject Headings.* By looking up key words (descriptor terms, subject headings) related to your topic in these volumes, you will learn which headings to check in the subject section of the catalog.

If your library uses the Dewey decimal system, you will have to compare your list of key words directly with the catalog's subject cards to discover which ones are used as subject headings relevant to your topic. A reference book entitled *Sears List of Subject Headings* lists headings applicable to either the Dewey system or the Library of Congress system. Toni Mitchell used the *Sears List* next to her library's card catalog to find the headings pertaining to the elderly in the workforce. Under the main heading "Age and employment," she found subheadings including the following: Aged workers, Employment and age, Middle age and employment, Middle aged workers, Aged—economic conditions, Discrimination in employment. She chose the most likely looking headings with which to begin her key word search at the library's online electronic catalog. The headings would serve equally well for searching an ordinary card catalog.

Besides **subject cards,** library card catalogs also contain **author cards** and **title cards** (no title card is used when the title begins with words as common as "A History of . . ."). Following are author, title, and subject cards for a book Toni Mitchell found by looking under the subject heading "Grandparents." Following the cards is an explanation of some of the information they contain.

**44d**

*res*

AUTHOR
CARD

| 306.87 | Cherlin, Andrew J., 1948– |
| C423n | The new American grandparent : a place in the family, a life apart / Andrew J. Cherlin, Frank F. Furstenberg, Jr. — — New York : Basic Books, c1986. |
| | x, 278 p. ; 22 cm. |
| | Includes index. |
| | ISBN 0—465—04993—1 |

1. Grandparents — — United States.
2. Grandparent and child — — United States. I. Furstenberg, Frank F., 1940—   II. Title

InLP       03 DEC 86       13582957       IPL1ac       86—73884

---

TITLE
CARD

The New American grandparent

2 | 306.87 | Cherlin, Andrew J., 1948–
   | C423n | The new American grandparent : a place in the family, a life apart / Andrew J. Cherlin, Frank F. Furstenberg, Jr. — — New York : Basic Books, c1986.
   | | x, 278 p. ; 22 cm.
   | | Includes index.
   | | ISBN 0—465—04993—1

1. Grandparents — — United States.
2. Grandparent and child — — United States. I. Furstenberg, Frank F., 1940—   II. Title

InLP       03 DEC 86       13582957       IPL1st       86—73884

---

SUBJECT
CARD

1 GRANDPARENTS — — UNITED STATES.

2 | HO759.9 | 3 Cherlin, Andrew J., 1948–
   | .C44 | 4     The new American grandparent : a place in the family, a life apart / Andrew J. Cherlin, Frank F. Furstenberg, Jr. — — New York : Basic Books, c1986.
   | 1986 | 5     x, 278 p. ; 22 cm.
   | | 6     Includes index.
   | | 7     ISBN 0—465—04993—1

8     1. Grandparents — — United States.
2. Grandparent and child — — United States. I. Furstenberg, Frank F., 1940—   II. Title

9 InLP       03 DEC 86       13582957       IPL1st       86—73884

**44d**

*res*

1. "GRANDPARENTS—UNITED STATES" is a **heading** under which the card is filed in the subject section of the catalog.

2. HQ759.9
.C44      ⟩ gives the call number for the book in the Li-
1986      ⟩ brary of Congress system.
306.87    ⟩ gives the call number for this book in the
C423n     ⟩ Dewey decimal system.

Except for the difference in the call number, catalog cards that use the Library of Congress system are identical with those in libraries using the Dewey system.

3. "Cherlin, Andrew J." gives the **name of the author** (surname first). This card also shows the author's birth year after the name, followed by a dash, indicating that the author was living at the time the card was printed.

4. "The new American grandparent: a place in the family, a life apart . . . 1986" gives the **full title,** shows that the book is **coauthored** (by Frank F. Furstenberg, Jr.), and gives the **place of publication,** the **publisher,** and the **date of publication** (copyright date). Note that the library practice of capitalization differs from standard practice.

5. "x, 278 p.; 22 cm." indicates that the book contains 10 introductory **pages numbered in Roman numerals** and 278 **pages numbered in Arabic numerals.** There are no portraits or illustrations in the book; if there were, they would be listed next as "ports" and "ils." The book is 22 centimeters high (an inch equals 2.54 centimeters).

6. The book contains an **index.**

7. The **ISBN** (International Standard Book Numbering) number by which the book is identified for sale purposes is ISBN 0-465-04993-1.

8. "1. Grandparents . . . II. Title" are the **tracings** indicating that the book is listed in the catalog under two subject headings and two author/title headings. Subject headings are marked by Arabic numerals, and author and title headings are marked by Roman numerals.

9. "InLP . . . 85-73884" contains **library identification information** such as the card's order number and the purchase date. The last few lines on some catalog cards also show the call numbers for both types of library classification systems and whether the book is held by the Library of Congress.

44d
res

Two portions of a catalog card can be especially helpful in your search. The **contents note** (6) will tell you if the work contains a bibliography that you might use to find other related books or articles. For instance, one of the books Toni Mitchell located in her library's card catalog listed a 40-page bibliography which she found very helpful. The **tracings** (8) will show other catalog subject headings to check for additional books.

## 44e   Evaluating your selections

Once you have copied the author, title, and call number of the books and bound periodicals you've been adding to your preliminary bibliography, find them on the shelves if your library has open stacks. While you're at it, look at the books adjacent to the ones you've selected. Since books are classified by subject matter, you should expect to find other pertinent volumes nearby.

You'll save yourself some valuable time if you first scan the table of contents and index and then quickly skim portions of the books you've chosen before you check them out of the library. Not every book that looked promising on a catalog card or in *Book Review Digest* will be worth carrying home. Toni decided some of her selections were of only limited value when she examined the following:

1.  **Table of contents.** It indicates which chapters might be useful.
2.  **Preface.** It usually explains the book's purpose and the author's method. The preface may indicate that certain material has been omitted or included and why.
3.  **Introduction.** It often gives a critical overview of the subject, establishing the focus and summarizing the approach taken.
4.  **Glossary.** If included, it lists and defines terminology.
5.  **Index.** It lists specific names, subjects, events, terms, and concepts covered in the book.
6.  **Bibliography** and **footnotes** or **endnotes.** These may list additional important books and articles.

Students frequently carry home a mountain of books and begin reading from the top of the heap. No wonder research sometimes seems so laborious! Develop the habit of skimming your selections before leaving the library. Five minutes spent glancing through its introduction, for instance, can tell you how pertinent a book will be to your research subject. Go back to the reference collection and see what *Book Review Digest* has to say about a book if you need to. Similarly, skim a few magazine and journal articles on your list. Rather than locating all of them in the stacks, check to see if any have been summarized in abstracts in the reference collection.

You'll want to narrow your sources to those that are most relevant and reliable. After all, your research paper will be judged on the merits of the evidence you present as well as on your use of that evidence.

**44e**

*res*

## 44f    Distinguishing between primary and secondary sources

The difference between a primary and a secondary source is that the former is an original, first-hand report, whereas the latter is second-hand information.

**1. Primary sources** include novels, short stories, poems, notes, letters, diaries, manuscripts, and other original documents; autobiographies; surveys, investigations, and interviews reported by the original recorder; original accounts of events by first recorders in newspapers and magazines.

**2. Secondary sources** include histories; biographies; encyclopedias and other reference works; essays, books, and articles that report or interpret the works of others.

When you use primary sources, you can evaluate the original information and draw your own conclusions, rather than depending on someone else's interpretation. Much of the time, however, you will probably have to rely on secondary sources. When you do, try to separate fact from opinion and informed opinion from bias. Using secondary sources written by well-respected authorities improves reliability, but keep in mind that even the most knowledgeable authorities often disagree. Comparing secondary sources with one another and with available primary sources often helps you to arrive at a balanced view of a subject.

---

EXERCISE 44(1)

Draw a diagram of the reference room of your library, indicating on it the position of the following reference books and indexes.

1. *Encyclopaedia Britannica*
2. *Encyclopedia of Religion and Ethics*
3. *Jewish Encyclopedia*
4. *Dictionary of American History* (DAH)
5. *Dictionary of American Biography* (DAB)
6. *American Authors, 1600–1900*
7. *Who's Who*
8. *Facts on File*
9. *World Almanac*
10. *New English Dictionary* (NED), often referred to as *Oxford English Dictionary* (OED)
11. *General Card Catalog* (if not in a separate room)
12. *Readers' Guide to Periodical Literature*
13. *The New York Times Index*
14. *The Art Index*
15. *Business Periodicals Index*

**44f**

*res*

---

## EXERCISE 44(2)
Answer each of the following questions by consulting one of the standard reference guides listed in Exercise 44(1).

1. Where can you find articles published on AIDS in 1989?
2. Where can you find information on Alaska, its government, and the events leading to its statehood?
3. Among which tribe of American Indians is the highest development of shamanism found?
4. What was the first invention of Peter Cooper, American inventor, manufacturer, and philanthropist (d. 1883)?
5. What did the word *gossip* mean in twelfth-century England?

## EXERCISE 44(3)
To find a magazine article in *Readers' Guide* (or any periodical index), you must first know how to convert its information into conventional English. Demonstrate your familiarity with the *Readers' Guide* by examining the following excerpt and filling in the blanks.

**Job applications**
    *See also*
    Employment interviewing
Courtesy and consideration: a plea to employers from a gypsy
    scholar. J. S. Goldberg. *Change* 15:8–10 Ja/F '83
Does your résumé emphasize the right things? il *Glamour*
    81:158 F '83
Four personal ways to get a job. S. S. Fader. *Work Woman*
    8:36+ Ja '83
Résumés: how to write them. How to use them. M. Paul. il
    *Sr Sch* 115:19 F 4 '83
Work resumes at 40 [women] C. Tuhy. il *Money* 12:81–2+
    Ja '83

Articles on employment résumés are collected in the periodical index under the subject heading _____. These articles are arranged alphabetically by the _____ of the article. "Résumés: how to write them" is the title of an article written by _____. "il" means the article includes _____. "Sr Sch" is the _____ of the title of the periodical. The periodical's full title is spelled out in the _____ of the *Readers' Guide*. The article is in _____ 115, on _____ 19. "F 4 '83" stands for _____, the _____ the article was published.

## EXERCISE 44(4)
Select a specific research subject of interest to you. Then use your library's resources to answer the following questions.

1. What are the titles of general or special encyclopedias (or handbooks or other general works such as textbooks) that have articles providing information on your subject?
2. If any of these articles contain relevant bibliographies, write down the full bibliographic information for a few of the most useful items.
3. What three subject headings found in the *Library of Congress Subject*

44f

*res*

*Headings* or *Sears List of Subject Headings* volumes are most closely related to your subject?

4. Examine the tracings on at least two relevant subject cards in the card catalog. Which tracings fit your subject best?

5. Names of people and organizations appear in the subject section of the card catalog. What names related to your subject are listed?

6. Using the subject headings in the catalog, look for the subject division "—Bibliography." If you find any book-length bibliographies, cite a few of those that look most useful.

7. Use the catalog subject headings and list two books that have bibliographies in them. Give the page numbers for the bibliography sections if they are listed on the catalog card.

8. In a book review index, locate reviews for one of the books relevant to your subject. Which book review index did you use? Where and when did the review originally appear?

9. List four periodical indexes (including one newspaper index and one collection of abstracts) showing useful articles on your subject. Write out the title, author (if any), and publication information for three articles. Using Katz's *Magazines for Libraries* and/or Farber's *Classified List of Periodicals for the College Library*, summarize their comments about the periodicals in which the articles are published.

10. Using the *Essay and General Literature Index*, give the following information pertaining to your research subject: (a) subject heading(s) used; (b) author of relevant essay; (c) title of that essay; (d) title of the book in which the essay appears; (e) call number of the book, if the library owns it.

# 45

## DRAFTING AND REVISING THE RESEARCH PAPER

**45**

*res*

### 45a   Understanding the purposes of research papers

The paper that reports "all about" a subject is not research. The aim of a true research paper is not just to summarize information or to show that you can use the library and know correct documentation form. Although these skills contribute to a research paper's success, the purpose of the paper should be to analyze and interpret information, to explore ideas and demonstrate their application, to think critically about the available evidence and draw valid conclusions from it.

Research projects usually start with a need for knowledge, or with an observation about what is known, and then systematically explore the subject with the aim of furthering the reader's understanding or breaking new ground. Consequently, research papers frequently test a theory, follow up on previous research, or explore a problem posed by other research or by events.

The opening section of a research paper typically introduces the broad subject and narrows it to the specific aspect the author intends to discuss. The opening often notes previous research, provides a context for the paper, or alerts the reader to points of view that will be explored later. Sophomore Toni Mitchell's sociology paper, reprinted at the end of Section **46**, begins with a two-paragraph introduction that does all of these things. The author's research method or approach may also be mentioned in the introduction. And finally, the author indicates his or her point of view regarding the subject—the thesis or conclusions that the paper will demonstrate. Although these points may appear in a different order and with varying amounts of detail, they are usually all present in successful research papers.

## 45b   Determining your purpose and approach

Instead of taking notes with the nearly impossible aim of "learning everything," you should direct your reading. Once you have an overview of your subject, you may decide you want to apply an accepted theory to a particular aspect of the subject. Or you may want to disagree with or modify someone else's conclusions, adding to and reinterpreting the evidence. Or perhaps your subject requires careful observation and field or lab work, the recording of data, and then hypothesis formulation and testing. In any case, part of your research strategy should be deciding where you can make a contribution to the body of knowledge about your subject and then reading your sources with that goal in mind.

Toni Mitchell, the student writer we met in Section **44** and whose paper appears at the end of Section **46**, thought carefully about her audience. Since the paper was an assignment for a course, she knew her primary reader was her sociology professor, who would expect her to approach her subject from a sound sociological perspective as a relatively inexperienced but nonetheless serious researcher in the field.

Toni had read several alarming articles in the popular press about the "war between the generations" that was predicted to occur in the not-too-distant future when old people would greatly outnumber young people and become a burden on society. She had also heard a classmate argue that the Social Security system, supported by fewer and fewer workers, would eventually be overwhelmed by huge numbers of retirees drawing pensions. Others disclaimed such alarmist views and cited evidence to the contrary. Closer to home, she noticed that her own alert, active grandmother seemed to be an exception to the portrait of the infirm, elderly widow so often painted in the media. These conflicting viewpoints held more than academic interest for Toni. She herself was a member of a generation demographically

**45b**

*res*

much smaller than her parents' generation. What might their old age—and her own old age—be like? She decided to try to sort the optimists from the pessimists and see what point of view the evidence actually supported.

She also knew she couldn't discuss the entire subject of old age in a ten-page paper, so she began thinking about how to narrow the scope of her research. For a while she collected bibliographic references in two areas: the effects of aging on mental ability and changing social roles for the elderly. Although the first topic fascinated her, the second topic fit her sociology course's focus better. Consequently, Toni disciplined herself to stick to research related to social roles. With this focus she could take notes more purposefully, with a better idea of the types of background material she needed to assemble, the range of views she wanted to present, and the kinds of information needed to formulate her conclusions. She also felt confident that although she would probably "over-research" and collect more evidence than she could include in her paper, nothing she read or took notes on now would be completely useless in writing the paper.

Now she was ready to sketch a rough outline to guide her note-taking, using the points that emerged from conversations with her professor and her family as well as insights gained from her preliminary reading. Toni used an outline composed of questions she hoped her research would help her answer, but her thinking might well have taken the form of a mind map, idea tree, or other notation schemes to help her do initial planning.

```
        I.   What is ''old''?
             A. Historical definitions
             B. Prevalent definitions today
        II.  What have been traditional social roles for elderly?
             A. Role as ''expert'' (cite Burke TV program)
             B. Role as community ''memory''
             C. Other?
        III. Are these roles still valid? Are there others possi-
             ble, more valid?
        IV.  What are the effects of longer life span and in-
             creased numbers of elderly?
               (need demographics: find census figures)
             A. Burden to society? (try to get statistics on ill-
             ness, poverty, etc.)
             B. Resource for society? (look for areas of contribu-
             tion)
        V.   What do the elderly themselves think about their fu-
             ture?
```

**45b**

*res*

This working outline differs from the final one Toni submitted with her research paper, of course. It would undergo several revisions as her research developed, but at this stage it served its purpose well: to help her organize her thinking and plan her note-taking.

## 45c Recording exact bibliographic information for each source

You will need exact bibliographic information for the "Works Cited" pages at the end of your research paper. Therefore, throughout your preliminary search, carefully make an individual bibliography card for each article, book, or other source you think you might use. Follow this procedure consistently, even though it may seem tedious. Failing to get all the necessary bibliographic information when you are consulting a book, article, or reference source such as an index or the card catalog usually delays and inconveniences you later. At best, omitting a particularly useful piece of information may necessitate looking through several books, periodicals, or bibliographies to relocate exact information for a bibliographic citation.

Bibliography cards are the best method of keeping an accurate record. The common card sizes are $3'' \times 5''$, $4'' \times 6''$, and $5'' \times 8''$. Researchers often use larger cards for note-taking and $3'' \times 5''$ cards for bibliographic entries. You will probably find that the smaller cards do not provide enough room for good research notes but are fine for bibliographic citations. *Write out a separate card for each source.* Separate cards will make compiling the final bibliography much easier, because all you will have to do is sort out the cards for the works you actually used in your final draft and then arrange them in alphabetical order for typing as "Works Cited."

Although the exact information for various kinds of sources varies, all entries require three basic kinds of information: author, title, and publication information. After you have checked with your instructor as to the bibliographic (or documentation) form you will be using for your paper, you can write out your bibliography cards in the exact format required by that specific form. Pages 500–509 cover the bibliographic formats required by the Modern Language Association (MLA) for humanities papers, the American Psychological Association (APA) for papers in the social sciences, and the number reference system, used for scientific papers.

## 45d Taking careful notes: summary, paraphrase, and direct quotation

Taking notes on cards is usually more efficient than writing them on full sheets of paper; cards are easier to carry and easier to rearrange when you are deciding on the organization for your paper. Limiting each note card to a single subject or even a single subtopic facilitates such rearrangements.

Some students write all their research notes as direct quotations from their sources. However, this method is tedious, time-consuming, and unnecessary. Furthermore, the act of transcribing prevents you from assimilating and evaluating the material as you read it. Take most of your notes in summary or paraphrase form, reserving direct quotations for material that is especially well stated or for points that might require the clout of a respected authority's exact words.

**1. Summary notes.** A **summary** is a brief note that captures information quickly without regard for style or careful expression. Your purpose is simply to record the facts or important points, to give a rough sketch of the material. (Be aware that summary notes differ in some important respects from the summary writing described in Section **47.**) Whenever you include a summary in your research paper, be sure to cite the source appropriately.

**2. Paraphrase notes.** A **paraphrase** is a restatement of the source material in your own words, syntax, and style but preserving the tone of the original (humor, doubt, etc.) and of approximately the same length. A paraphrase uses the original author's idea and presents it in your own language. Since in paraphrasing you are borrowing someone's thoughts, you must document the source when you use the paraphrase in your paper.

**3. Direct quotation notes.** A **direct quotation** records exactly the words of the original source (as well as the exact punctuation and even any spelling errors; see Section **26b** for the use of *sic* in such instances). Like summaries and paraphrases, direct quotations require citations in your paper crediting the source from which you copied them. Always put quotation marks around all the material you take word for word from any source. In general, use direct quotations only for particularly telling phrases or for information that must be rendered exactly as you found it.

Opposite are summary, paraphrase, and direct quotation notes Toni wrote as she read her resource material. Notice that each note indicates the source (complete bibliographic information is recorded on her bibliography cards) and shows the page numbers where the information appeared. She also has given each card a topic heading for easy sorting later.

Toni's notes reflect her evaluation of the material she read. The paraphrase card contains a comment in brackets where she noted a connection to another article she had read. The direct quotation card contains two sets of ellipses. At these spots Toni decided not to copy original phrases that related detail unnecessary to the focus of her paper.

**45e**   Drafting the paper: do not plagiarize the work of others, either by accident or by design.

Plagiarism consists of passing off the ideas, opinions, conclusions, facts, words—in short, the intellectual work—of another as your own. **Plagiarism is dishonest and carries penalties** not only in academic environments but in all professions, as well as in copyright law.

45e

*res*

**SUMMARY**

Bass, 403 — potential influence of elderly

Increased influence in society--will not result simply from sheer numbers alone. Will occur only if sufficient numbers of elderly
1. become dissatisfied with their role
2. have the will and resources to act for a change

**PARAPHRASE**

Williamson, et al., 229 — old age stereotypes: "deviant" or "devalued"?

According to authors, a deviant role comes from illegal or immoral behavior: deliberately in violation of a social norm. A devalued role is a low-status or otherwise undesirable role. They say that old people are labelled by society as devalued, not deviant--"unfortunate," not "reprehensible"--but the results are the same in terms of stigma and separation. [this may help explain "fear" of elderly/aging. See Wilcox, 106]

**DIRECT QUOTATION**

Friedan, 123 — prevalence of negative norms

"We associate age with disease. Even gerontologists or geriatricians concentrate on the most negative aspects of aging... pathologies of aging, not the norms of aging at all. ... To limit discussion of aging to negative norms... ignores the growth that so often accompanies aging."

45e

*res*

   The most obvious kind of plagiarism occurs when you appropriate whole paragraphs or longer passages from another writer for your own paper. Long word-for-word quotations are rarely appropriate to a paper, but when they are, you must indicate clearly that they *are* quotations and indicate their exact source. No less dishonest is the use of all or most of a single sentence or an apt figure of speech appropriated without acknowledgment from another source.

Suppose, for example, that you are working on a paper about families and have read a book by Jane Howard entitled *Families*. You have a note card on which you have written the partial sentence "Good families have a switchboard operator—someone who cannot help but keep track of what all the others are up to . . ." Your notes indicate that this is a quotation. But when you turn to writing your paper, this and other phrases from the same source seem so apt to your purposes in a slightly different context that you yield to temptation and write, as if in your own words, "All families need at least two things: someone around whom others cluster and someone who cannot help but keep track of what all the others are up to—a kind of switchboard operator." You have plagiarized just as badly as the writer who has appropriated a whole paragraph. The words are not yours, they are Jane Howard's, and honesty requires that you give her credit for them.

You are unlikely to copy directly from another writer without being consciously dishonest as you do so. But even though you acknowledge the source in a citation, you are also plagiarizing when you incorporate in your paper faultily paraphrased or summarized passages from another author in which you follow almost exactly the original's sentence patterns and phrasing. Paraphrasing and summarizing require that you fully digest an author's ideas and interpretations and restate them in your own words. It is not enough simply to modify the original author's sentences slightly, to change a word here and there. Consider the following original together with the sample paraphrases and summary:

ORIGINAL

The craft of hurricane forecasting advanced rapidly in the Sixties and early Seventies, thanks to fast computers and new atmospheric modeling techniques. Now there is a lull in the progress, strangely parallel to the lull in the storm cycle. The Center shoots for a 24-hour warning period, with 12 daylight hours for evacuation. At that remove, it can usually predict landfall within 100 miles either way. Longer lead times mean much larger landfall error and that is counterproductive. He who misses his predictions cries wolf.

WILLIAM H. MACLEISH, "Our Barrier Islands," *Smithsonian* Sept. 1980: 54.

FAULTY PARAPHRASE

Hurricane forecasting made rapid progress in the sixties and seventies due to fast computers and new atmospheric techniques, but there is now a lull in the progress. The Warning Center tries for a 24-hour warning period, including 12 hours of daylight. That close to a storm, it can usually predict landfall within 100 miles either way. If lead times are longer, there will be a much larger error, which will be counterproductive (Macleish 54).

45e
*res*

Even though the writer acknowledges the author (as indicated by the citation at the end of the paragraph), this is a clear example of plagiarism. The author has combined the first two sentences of the original and changed a few words here and there but in no way indicated that most of the paragraph's structure and phrasing is almost exactly that of the original.

IMPROVED PARAPHRASE

New techniques, together with computers, have significantly increased the accuracy of hurricane forecasting. Now it is possible to predict where a hurricane will hit land with an error of not more than 100 miles if a warning of 24 hours is allowed. If more than 24 hours is required, the error will be proportionately greater (Macleish 54).

This paraphrase successfully puts the information in the words of the researcher. Both the sentence structure and the phrasing are clearly the researcher's, not the original author's. But such a full paraphrase of a relatively simple passage is probably much more complete than someone researching hurricane warning problems and developments in a variety of sources would need. In many contexts, a simple, brief summary statement like the following might well be sufficient:

SUMMARY

With computers and new techniques, forecasters can now provide a 24-hour hurricane warning and predict within 100 miles either way where a storm will hit (Macleish 54).

---

EXERCISE 45d–e
For each of the following passages, write a summary note and a paraphrase note. If you think a passage contains subtopics that would best be handled as separate notes, prepare a summary and paraphrase for each subtopic. Be sure that you have avoided plagiarism: restate the original ideas in your own words. If you think that in a few spots there is no adequate substitute for the original language, put those words in quotation marks.

45e

*res*

1. "But rock music has one appeal only, a barbaric appeal, to sexual desire—not love, not eros, but sexual desire undeveloped and untutored. It acknowledges the first emanations of children's emerging sensuality and addresses them seriously, eliciting them and legitimating them, not as little sprouts that must be carefully tended in order to grow into gorgeous flowers, but as the real thing. Rock gives children, on a silver platter, with all the public authority of the entertainment industry, everything their parents always used to tell them they had to wait for until they grew up and would understand later."

ALLAN BLOOM, from *The Closing of the American Mind*

2. "Any education that matters is *liberal*. All the saving truths and healing graces that distinguish a good education from a bad one or a full education from a half-empty one are contained in that word. Whatever ups and downs the term 'liberal' suffers in the political vocabulary, it soars above all controversy in the educational world. In the blackest pits of pedagogy the squirming victim has only to ask, 'What's liberal about this?' to shame his persecutors. In times past a liberal education set off a free man from a slave or a gentleman from laborers and artisans. It now distinguishes whatever nourishes the mind and spirit from the training which is merely practical or professional or from the trivialities which are no training at all. Such an education involves a combination of knowledge, skills, and standards."

ALAN SIMPSON, from *The Marks of an Educated Man*

3. "In almost every college or university, the library is acknowledged by faculty, students, and administrators as the 'heart of the campus.' Yet on many college campuses the potential of the library goes unrealized. The library becomes an underutilized, expensive storehouse. Librarians are seen as, or what is worse, perform as keepers of the books, or, in the words of a Cambridge University faculty member, 'warehouse managers.' Consequently, library materials purchased to support the curriculum lie unused on the shelves. Students who frequent the library often use it as a study hall or as a convenient location for a social gathering. In addition when students have a course assignment or research paper that requires the use of library materials, they often perform poorly and spend more time than necessary. The reason for such poor performance is that most students do not have the necessary skills to effectively identify and use appropriate library materials."

CARLA J. STOFFLE, "The Library's Role in Facilitating Quality Teaching"

## 45f  Learning when and how to use quotations

A research paper loaded with quotations or consisting of long quotations stitched loosely together with brief comments will almost always be an unsatisfactory paper. The point of research is to present in your own words the interpretations and judgments you have come to as a result of your investigation, making clear and accurate references to the sources you have consulted.

The almost irresistible temptation for inexperienced writers is to justify every major point they make in their research paper with a quotation from an authority. First, you are entitled to draw conclusions about your research subject; not everything you say requires backing up with a source. Second, use paraphrases and summaries instead of quotations in most cases where sources are cited. Frequently, the point can be made better in your own words, with proper citation, than in the words of the original.

Of course a research paper does lead to more direct quotation than you would ordinarily use in an essay presenting your own personal views. Learning to use quotations wisely when you have good reason and learning how to fit them easily, naturally, and logically into your paper are signs of effective composition. Your *use* of a quotation, not the quotation itself, is part of your research contribution. When readers come upon a quotation, they should never feel that it has been "chopped" from the original source and "dropped" upon them suddenly. One of your tasks as a researcher and writer is to provide appropriate contexts for the quotations you are using. Consequently, it is often a good idea to mention the source or the importance of a quotation in the text of your paper. By providing an introductory phrase such as "according to a leading authority," or "a recent government study shows that . . . ," you not only supply a frame of reference for the quotation but you establish its authority and credibility in your reader's mind. Thus the quotation becomes an intrinsic part of the whole weave of your paper.

Many contexts can support the use of brief and—less frequently—long quotations. But the contexts in which they are most likely to be preferable to paraphrase or summary are those in which the original phrasing is striking, memorable, or lends concreteness or authenticity; the force of the statement is important and would be lost in paraphrase; the quotation is an example of what is being discussed; or, in writing about a writer or a literary work, the quotations exemplify the writers' style or typify a character, theme, or the like.

In her paper, Toni Mitchell uses two quotations long enough to require setting off by indentation (see Section **25c**). In the first, Ken Dychtwald described the harsh realities of mid-nineteenth-century family life, using late twentieth-century jargon such as "empty nest" to do so. Toni quoted Dychtwald's words, because she felt his juxtaposition of modern terms and century-old events most effectively brought home the differences between nineteenth- and twentieth-century life. In the second long quotation, very near the end of her paper, Toni believed that Betty Friedan's sentiments neatly summarized the main points she was making in her paper (see Section **41b**, "Effective Endings"). She used the Friedan quotation as a backboard off of which to bounce her own concluding sentence. Her inclusion of these long quotations shows two situations in which they are justified: when the ideas are most effectively conveyed in the words of the source.

Toni provides a suitable introduction for the long quotations, making clear the purpose they serve and establishing the context in which they are to be understood (see pages 525 and 553). She has also been selective, using ellipses in the second quotation to indicate omitted material extraneous to her purpose. Such omissions are permissible, even advisable, as long as they do not change the meaning of the original.

**45f**

*res*

Like long quotations, short ones need to be fitted naturally into the flow of your paper. Short quotations should be worked smoothly into the syntax of your sentences; furthermore, they should be introduced in a way that establishes the connection between the source and the point you are making. Notice how the following examples by student writers achieve these goals with phrases such as *John Frederick Nims remarks, reports that, in Mary McCarthy's words, H. L. Mencken recorded . . . and observed that,* or *preaching that . . . those who tell us that.* (The numbers in parentheses are in-text page citations.)

Not all Victorian women were the shy, timid, modest beings they are sometimes imagined to be. Elizabeth Barrett Browning once submitted a poem about women as sex objects which her editor rejected "for indecency." As John Frederick Nims remarks, "Who would have expected such a poem from a Victorian lady with three names?" (187).

Any study of the music of Bela Bartok can well begin by taking note of the commanding presence of the man himself. Yehudi Menuhin, describing his first meeting with the composer, reports that he "felt at once that I was facing someone pared down to the essential core" (16).

The book which is most informative about Mary McCarthy as a person is perhaps her *Memories of a Catholic Girlhood,* which reflects, in part, her early life with her great-aunt, who, in McCarthy's words, "had a gift for turning everything sour and ugly" (49).

Distrust of and distaste for "new fangled inventions" is long. English writers of the nineteenth century denounced the arrival of the railroad in their beloved Lake country. Fifty years ago, H. L. Mencken recorded in characteristically pungent language his dislike for automobiles, phonographs, and movies, and observed that although he saw "potentialities" for the radio, he was convinced they would never be realized "so long as the air is laden and debauched by jazz, idiotic harangues by frauds who do not know what they are talking about, and the horrible garglings of ninth-rate singers" (272).

There is nothing like a time of inflation, declining productivity, burgeoning government expenditures, and increasing taxes to unleash a flood of conflicting economic theory. Our own period is fertile ground for such debate, and we find ourselves choosing sides between those who believe that only a return to the virtues of old-line capitalism can save us, preaching that we must untax the rich so that they may invest, since "the creation of wealth is the only salvation of the poor," (Abelson 21) and those who tell us that only a "fundamental restructuring of American society" (Fitzpatrick 383) will keep us from going down.

**45f**

*res*

Whenever you use direct quotations in your writing, be sure to transcribe them accurately. Make it a rule to check and recheck each quotation, including its punctuation. Make sure that you understand the mechanical conventions of quoting material. Indicate omissions from a quotation by using ellipses (see Section **26c**), and make sure that what you retain is grammatically coherent. If you insert words of your own in the original, indicate your insertion by placing brackets around it (see Section **26a**). If the quotation contains a mistake or peculiarity of spelling or grammar, retain it in your quotation but indicate that it appears in the original by using *sic* ("thus it is") in brackets immediately following it (see Section **26b**).

---

EXERCISE 45f
Choose one of the passages from Exercise 45e–f and write a paragraph or two about the topic the passage discusses. Incorporate at least two direct quotations from the passage into your paragraph. Work them smoothly and naturally into your writing, avoiding "chop-and-drop" quotations. Be sure to use punctuation correctly, including any ellipses and brackets.

---

## 45g  Revising the research paper

Writing a successful research paper requires uniting many parts into a coherent whole. Because of its length and scope, the argumentative nature of its thesis, and the complexity and variety of evidence gathered to uphold that thesis, a research paper presents a very challenging task for the writer. Sometimes writers discover that their paper does not prove the point they set forth in the beginning and does not succeed as a coherent whole, even though they have worked very hard at the research and drafting. Major revisions may be necessary. Several steps will help you manage your research paper and revise it as necessary.

**1. Allow yourself enough time to research the subject and write the paper.** A paper begun Friday night when it is due Monday morning will be an extremely superficial paper, if not a total failure. You will suffer from short-term memory overload, be unable to see crucial connections between ideas, and use only whatever research materials you can quickly lay hands on—rather than those materials that will best aid your work. It is not too soon to start your paper a month before it is due. Some research projects will require even longer, possibly a whole term. Professional researchers may spend years on their projects.

**2. Give the paper a cooling-off period—at least two or three days—after you have completed the first draft.** You will need the objectivity several days can provide if you want to be able to reread your paper critically and revise it effectively.

**3. Check each paragraph before you revise to be sure it has clear and explicit connections to the thesis and adds something new and important to the proof.** Check your paper to be sure all the parts

45g

*res*

relate to the thesis. Compare the paper and its final outline against the rough outline or idea tree you worked from when you began your research. Has your paper wandered from its focus? Or does your draft improve upon your original scheme? Secondly, when you have worked hard to research and compile evidence, it is very tempting to include too much material in the first draft. Make sure that everything in your paper is necessary. Ruthlessly cut the portions that are repetitious or off the main line of your argument.

**4. Be sure you have provided adequate transitions between ideas and sections.** What seems obvious to you because you have been thinking about the subject so intensely may not be obvious to your readers. Provide your audience with clear road signs: spell out the logic of your argument wherever it might not be clear.

**5. Look at every quotation.** Is each one necessary, or would a paraphrase or summary be better? Does the paper provide sufficient and correct documentation (see Section **46**)? Are the quotations integrated into the paper (no "chop-and-drop")? Does the paper supply appropriate contexts for the words or ideas of others?

**6. Have you written a paper that shows you have thought critically about your subject and the work of others on that subject?** Your research paper should be more than a conglomeration of other people's words and ideas. It should show your critical analysis of those ideas, persuasively present your informed conclusions, and express your contribution to an on-going dialogue on the subject.

# 46

## *DOCUMENTING THE RESEARCH PAPER*

One of the purposes of keeping accurate bibliography cards and notes that carefully distinguish between direct quotation and summary or paraphrase is to provide the information you will need for documenting the source material you have used in your research paper. You must acknowledge all the facts, ideas, interpretations, opinions, and conclusions of others that you incorporate into your own paper by documenting the sources—whether they be books, periodicals, interviews, speeches, or lab or field studies.

### **46a** Deciding what to document, and what not to document

**1. What to acknowledge.** Always acknowledge all direct quotations, charts, diagrams, tables, and the like, that you reproduce entirely or partially in your paper. Always acknowledge your paraphrases and summaries of the interpretations, opinions, and

conclusions presented in your sources. Keep in mind that the interpretations and conclusions reached by researchers and scholars are in
many ways more important contributions than the bald facts they may
have gathered and are therefore even more deserving of acknowledgment.

**2. What not to acknowledge.** You do not have to provide documentation for facts that are considered common knowledge. "Common knowledge" consists of standard historical and literary information available in many different reference books—the fact that John F.
Kennedy died in 1963, the fact that Charles Dickens created such
characters as Uriah Heep and Mr. Micawber, or that Darwin's theory
of evolution was the subject of great intellectual debate in the nineteenth century. Such information is considered common knowledge as
far as documentation is concerned, even though you may have learned
it for the first time when you began your research.

In contrast, common sense will tell you that highly specialized
facts—the cost of a six-room house in the 1830s, the number of Polar-
oid cameras sold between 1980 and 1990, the estimated population of
Mongolia in 1960, the highest recorded tide in San Francisco Bay, or
the number of earthquakes in Peru during the twentieth century—are
unlikely to be common knowledge.

In addition to information that is widely available and undis-
puted, facts agreed upon by nearly all authorities discussing a particular subject are considered common knowledge. As soon as you explore any subject to some depth, you will quickly come to see that
certain material is taken as established fact while other material is dis-
puted or has been established by some special investigation. A student
writing on the poet Wordsworth for the first time, for instance, may
not have known initially that the *Preface to the Lyrical Ballads* was first
published in 1800, but it will not take long to discover that everyone
writing on the subject accepts this as an established fact. Such information will not need to be acknowledged. In contrast, the exact date
of a particular poem may be a matter of dispute or may have been
established by a scholar's diligent research. This kind of information
must be acknowledged.

**46b**

*doc*

## 46b   Using appropriate documentation form

Documentation is the means by which you acknowledge material
you have used from outside sources. In professional scholarship, documentation forms are complex and varied. Most forms have evolved
from the demands of professional scholarship, itself a precise and exacting business. Furthermore, the preferred form for citations and
bibliographic entries varies considerably among disciplines. Each of
the natural sciences, the American Medical Association, the American
Bar Association, such fields as linguistics, and many other disciplines

have their own preferred styles, each of which is described in the particular group's style manual. For any discipline in which you write, *always check the professional publications and relevant style manuals to determine the appropriate documentation form.* When you write for a specific assignment, ask your instructor which documentation style he or she prefers.

**1. The MLA name and page system.** The **name and page system** described by the Modern Language Association in its *MLA Handbook for Writers of Research Papers* (1988) is the documentation form used by some 80 professional journals in the languages, humanities, and some social sciences. This system uses **in-text citations** (rather than footnotes or endnotes) to acknowledge the words or ideas of outside sources where they are used in a paper. The only exceptions are **content and bibliographical endnotes.** You will find examples of these exceptions on page 555 of Toni Mitchell's research paper and definitions on the facing page.

**a.** *In-text citations.* All references cited in the text are listed alphabetically in a section called *Works Cited* at the end of the paper. As illustrated on pages 556–57, the "Works Cited" list functions as a bibliography, usually listing references by author's last name, if known, or by title if the author is not known. Sometimes a work will be listed by an editor's, translator's, or other person's name.

Using the MLA name-page documentation form, the work referred to in Toni Mitchell's sentence "Gerontologist Robert Morris speaks of the "transformed family" (424)—a nontraditional family that may be headed by a single parent or composed of biologically unrelated members" is listed under *Morris* in "Works Cited" as follows:

```
Morris, Robert. "Concluding Remarks: Consequences of the

     Demographic Revolution," Gerontologist 27 (1987):423–24.
```

**46b**

*doc*

As the Morris example shows, the name-page documentation system places relevant names (usually authors' names) and pages of the works being cited either directly in the text sentences or in parentheses in the text. What you cite in the text has a direct bearing on what you place in parentheses: that is, when information appears in a text sentence, it is not repeated in parentheses, as the following reference to Lundquist shows. Notice that in the parenthetical material referring to Klinkowitz there is neither an abbreviation for "page" nor any punctuation between the author's name and the page number.

```
Kurt Vonnegut has been described as "a popular artifact

which may be the fairest example of American cultural change"
```

```
(Klinkowitz 16). According to critic James Lundquist, each of

Vonnegut's novels is a warning (15).
```

Notice in the example above that the parenthetical reference is placed as close as possible to the documented material without disrupting the grammar or sense of the material. Usually this location is at the end of the sentence. Contrary to normal quotation/punctuation conventions, the parenthetical information should be placed inside any concluding punctuation but outside any quotation marks, as shown above.

For the sake of readability, look for ways to integrate citations smoothly into your sentences. Your goal should be to keep parenthetical references concise. If you can do so in a convenient and readable fashion, integrate reference information into the text:

```
Hamlet's well-known "To be, or not to be" lines (56-89) in

Act II, scene i are probably the most famous of Shakespeare's

soliloquies and also probably one of the most misinterpreted.
```

rather than:

```
The well-known "To be, or not to be" lines are probably the

most famous of Shakespeare's soliloquies and also probably

one of the most misinterpreted (Hamlet, 2.1.56-89).
```

Besides at the end of a sentence, references may sometimes be placed conveniently at the ends of phrases or clauses, after statistics, and so forth. For example:

```
Norton and Monroe's survey found that 57 percent of America's

drivers do not use their seat-belts (73), but we suspect the

percentage is much higher.
```

The name-page system enables readers to find a source in your bibliography and also the place in the source where the cited material appears. Giving the author's last name and the page number usually fulfills this purpose, but some cases require additional in-text information. For example:

**46b**

*doc*

TWO OR THREE AUTHORS; MORE THAN THREE AUTHORS

```
The question then becomes whether "work produced by the

institutional computer is looked upon as the work of the

organization" (Pendergast, Slade, and Winkless 130); in

contrast, the personal computer is identified with the

individual (Elbring et al. 54).
```

Vonnegut believes large families, whether biological or
artificial, help sustain sanity (Sunday 66), and they nurture
idealism. As the protagonist in Jailbird says, "I still
believe that peace and plenty and happiness can be worked out
some way. I am a fool" (57–58). This idealism endears
Vonnegut to his readers ("Forty–Six" 79).

When a "Works Cited" section lists more than one work by the
same author, in-text citations should contain the title (or a shortened
version, such as *Sunday* for *Palm Sunday*) so readers will know which
of the author's works you are referring to. For references to unsigned
(anonymous) works, cite the title (or shortened form) and page number. The example above refers to an unsigned book review entitled
"Forty-Six and Trusted."

LITERARY WORKS

P.D. James uses lines from a play by John Webster as clues in
her detective novel The Skull Beneath the Skin—for instance
in the note left at the murder scene (145; bk. 3, ch. 4):
"Other sins only speak; murder shrieks out" (Duchess of
Malfi, 4.2.261).

Novels or plays that appear in several editions are best cited not only
by page number (given first in the entry) but also by such information
as chapter (ch.), part (pt.), or book (bk.) number, so that readers can
follow your citations in editions other than the one you refer to. References to verse plays or poems customarily omit page numbers altogether, instead listing more helpful information such as division numbers (act, scene, canto, etc.) followed by line numbers. The numbers
56–89 and 261 in the citations of *Hamlet* and *The Duchess of Malfi* are
line numbers.

**46b**

*doc*

MULTIVOLUME WORK; SEVERAL WORKS IN ONE CITATION

The last half–dozen years of Queen Elizabeth's reign began
with Shakespeare's Love's Labour's Lost and ended with her death
at age 70 (Harrison, vol. 2). As Harrison puts it, on March
24, 1603, the queen died "having reigned 44 years 5 months
and odd days" (2: 383). Historians regard her as a master of
statecraft (Johnson 2; Elton 46; Bindoff 377).

When citing an entire volume as you would a general reference to an entire work, give the author and the volume number preceded by the abbreviation *vol.* When citing specific material in a multivolume work, give first the volume number and then the page number, but omit abbreviations, as in the second reference to Harrison, above. Here, *2* stands for Volume 2 and *383* is the page number. Note the use of a colon and a space to separate volume number from page number. When documenting several works in a single parenthetical reference, cite each as you normally would, separating the citations with semicolons. If multi-work references get too bulky, place them in a bibliographical endnote.

### INDIRECT SOURCES

The failure of his play Guy Domville seems to have had

positive benefits for Henry James's later novels in that he

spoke of transferring to his fiction the lessons he had

learned from the theater, using those "scenic conditions

which are as near an approach to the dramatic as the novel

may permit itself" (qtd. in Edel 434; pt. 6, ch. 1).

It is always best to cite original sources in your work, but sometimes a secondary source may be all that is available. In that case, indicate the secondary nature of the source by using *qtd. in* (quoted in) followed by pertinent reference information. In the reference above, the source is indicated by author's name, page (434), and, since the book is divided formally into parts and chapters, by part and chapter numbers (pt. 6, ch. 1). Note that a semicolon and a space separate the main reference information (author and page) from the rest of the identifying information (part and chapter numbers).

You will find examples of these and other types of in-text citations in the sample research paper at the end of this section. Study them to familiarize yourself with the form and to see how information may be introduced smoothly into the text.

**46b**

*doc*

   **b.** *The "Works Cited" page.* As we discussed in Section **45,** sources are acknowledged both within the paper and in a list of works cited at the end of the research paper. Just as there are specific guidelines for citing sources within the paper, there are also guidelines for preparing entries for the "Works Cited" page. The following bibliographic entries show the types of information and the form required for bibliographies using the conventions established by the MLA.

   Notice that different types of entries require different types of information. For example, if your source is a translation or an edited book, you will need the name of the translator or editor as well as that of the author. If your source is an article in a periodical, you will need to record the inclusive page numbers of the article. Writing the library call number on the bibliography card is also helpful for locating sources on the shelves later. You will also notice that the bibliography entries use shortened forms for publishers, such as Prentice for Prentice Hall or UP for University Press. They also use common abbreviations for months (Apr., Oct.) and for such things as "no date" (n.d.) and "translator" (trans.). A list of common scholarly abbreviations appears at the end of the bibliography samples on pages 513–14.

### FORM FOR BIBLIOGRAPHIC ENTRIES—"WORKS CITED"

*Books*

BOOK WITH ONE AUTHOR

Boorstin, Daniel J. <u>The Discoverers</u>. New York: Random, 1983.

The major parts of an entry—author, title, and publication information (place of publication, publisher, date of publication)—are each separated by a period, followed by two spaces. Give the author's name in its fullest or most usual form, last name first. Obtain the information for bibliographical entries from the title page of the work cited, not from library catalog cards, other bibliographies, or indexes. These other sources may omit capital letters or use different punctuation that is specific to the style conventions of those sources only. You *must* use the information as it is presented on the work itself. If the copyright date is not located on the title page, it usually appears on the copyright page—the back of the title page—with other publication information. In books published outside the United States, publication information may be located in the colophon (publisher's inscription) at the back of the book.

Notice that only the city is given for the place of publication. If the city is outside the United States, also provide an abbreviation of the country name (or Canadian province) if the city name is ambiguous or likely to be unfamiliar to your readers. For example, you would probably need to include the country abbreviation for Bern (Bern, Switz: Bohner, 1983) or for Cambridge (Cambridge, Eng.: Cambridge UP, 1985), because it might be confused with Cambridge, Massachusetts, but not for London, England (London: Longman, 1977). If the publisher lists more than one city on the title page or copyright page, list only the first in your citation.

BOOK WITH TWO OR THREE AUTHORS

Bryan, Margaret B., and Boyd H. Davis. <u>Writing About</u>

<u>Literature and Film</u>. New York: Harcourt, 1975.

Notice that in citations involving multiple authors only the first author's name is inverted. Other authors' names appear in normal

**46b**

*doc*

order. If an entry requires more than one line of type, indent the second and any subsequent lines five spaces from the left margin.

BOOK WITH MORE THAN THREE AUTHORS

```
Brown, Herbert C., et al. Organic Synthesis Via Boranes. New
     York: Wiley, 1975.
```

*Et al.* is an abbreviation indicating that the work has more than three authors. Note that in the entry *et al.* should not be capitalized. If there are no more than three authors, list them as you would for a work with two authors.

BOOK IN EDITION OTHER THAN THE FIRST

```
Weidenaar, Dennis J., and Emanuel T. Weiler. Economics: An
     Introduction to the World Around You. 2nd ed. Reading:
     Addison, 1979.
```

When citing editions other than the first, it is correct to use *2nd, 4th, 17th,* etc. rather than *second, fourth, seventeenth,* and the like. *Edition* is abbreviated *ed.* If a work has a subtitle, as in the example above, be sure to use a colon between the main title and subtitle (even though some indexes and bibliographies may show the punctuation as a comma).

BOOK IN A SERIES

```
Ryf, Robert S. Henry Green. Columbia Essays on Modern
     Writers 29. Ed. William York Tindall. New York:
     Columbia UP, 1967.
```

**46b**

*doc*

WORK IN TWO OR MORE VOLUMES

```
Morrison, S. E., and H. S. Commager. The Growth of the
     American Republic. 3rd ed. 2 vols. New York: Oxford UP,
     1942.
```

TRANSLATION

```
Eco, Umberto. The Name of the Rose. Trans. William Weaver.
     New York: Harcourt, 1983.
```

See also the entries and discussion under the heading "Book with Author and Editor,"

REPUBLISHED BOOK (REPRINT)

Tuchman, Barbara W.  A Distant Mirror: The Calamitous 14th

    Century. 1978. New York: Ballantine, 1979.

The publication date of the original hard cover printing is *1978*. *New York: Ballantine, 1979* is the publication information for the paperback reprint. Such information is important because although the reader needs to know exactly which edition was used in the research, it is also important to know when a work was initially published.

EDITED BOOK

Schorer, Mark, ed.  Modern British Fiction.  New York: Oxford

    UP, 1961.

BOOK WITH AUTHOR AND EDITOR

Melville, Herman.  Billy Budd: Sailor.  Eds. Harrison Hayford

    and Merton M. Sealts, Jr.  Chicago: U of Chicago P, 1962.

Hayford, Harrison, and Merton M. Sealts, Jr., eds.  Billy

    Budd: Sailor.  By Herman Melville.  Chicago: U of Chicago

    P, 1962.

Compare the two entries for *Billy Budd*. These are entries for exactly the same book. The first one is appropriate for a paper about *Billy Budd* and/or Herman Melville. The second one is appropriate for a paper that discusses Hayford's and Sealts's work as editors. When an editor's name is the first (alphabetizing) information unit in an entry, *ed.* (editor) comes after the name and is not capitalized; otherwise, it precedes the name and is capitalized. (If there is more than one editor, make the abbreviation plural by adding an *s*.) The same distinctions apply to translations and *trans.* (translator) and other such works and contributors.

**46b**

*doc*

SELECTION IN ANTHOLOGY OR COLLECTION

Murray, Donald M.  "Writing as Process: How Writing Finds Its

    Own Meaning."  Eight Approaches to Teaching Composition.

    Ed. Timothy R. Donovan and Ben W. McClellend.  Urbana:

    NCTE, 1980. 3–20

The title of the selection appears first after the author's name and is enclosed in quotation marks. The title of the work in which the selection appears is listed next and is underlined or italicized. A period separates the two titles. The inclusive page numbers of the selection appear at the end of the entry.

ARTICLE REPRINTED IN A CASEBOOK, ANTHOLOGY, OR COLLECTION

Spenser, Theodore. "Hamlet and the Nature of Reality."

　　Journal of English Literary History 5 (1938):255–71.

　　Rpt. in Cyrus Hoy, ed. Hamlet. By William Shakespeare.

　　New York: Norton, 1963. 142–57.

Summers, Joseph P. "The Poem as Hieroglyph." George Herbert,

　　His Religion and Art. London: Chatto, 1954. 123–46. Rpt.

　　in Seventeenth Century English Poetry. Ed. William R.

　　Keast. New York: Galaxy–Oxford UP, 1962. 215–37.

The two entries above are for essays reprinted, first in a casebook and second in a collection. Notice that the first essay originally appeared in a scholarly journal (as indicated by the manner of the journal's citation). Also notice that in the citation of the reprint casebook the editor's name (Cyrus Hoy) is listed first and Shakespeare, the author of the play for which the casebook is entitled, is listed later. This manner of listing, with the emphasis on the editor, indicates the casebook format of the text—that it features a major literary work accompanied by essays of literary criticism compiled by the editor and pertaining to the literary work. The manner of the second entry indicates that the article originally appeared as part of a book authored by Summers and has been reprinted in a collection of essays.

Notice also that the second entry cites a publisher's special imprint (Galaxy). When you cite a book that is a publisher's special imprint, list the imprint first, followed by a hyphen and then the publisher.

ANONYMOUS BOOK

Norwegian Folk Tales. Trans. Pat Shaw Iversen and Carl

　　Norman. Oslo: Dreyers Forlag, 1961.

Works without an author, editor, or other acknowledged "authorlike" person are alphabetized in "Works Cited" by the first important word in their title. They are not listed as *anonymous* or *anon.*

PAMPHLET

Latin, Giorgio Lilli. Art in Italy. Rome: Italian State

　　Tourist Dept., 1978.

**46b**

*doc*

Stein, Robert A. "Paradise Regained in the Light of

  Classical and Christian Traditions of Criticism and

  Rhetoric." Diss. Brandeis U, 1968.

Quaker Education As Ministry. Proc. of 4th Annual Conference.

  Haverford: Friends Assn. for Higher Education, 1983.

*Proc.* is the abbreviation for *Proceedings.*

### Articles in Reference Books

Goodwin, George C. "Mammals." Collier's Encyclopedia. 1976 ed.

"Universities." Encyclopaedia Britannica: Macropaedia.

  1974 ed.

Familiar reference books, especially those that are reprinted frequently in new editions, are cited by edition-year only. When the abbreviation *ed.* appears with a year, it stands for *edition,* rather than *editor.* Full publication information is not necessary. However, less familiar reference works, or those that have been printed in only one edition, should be accompanied by full publication information, as in the entry that follows.

"28 July 1868 Reconstruction." The Almanac of American

  History. Ed. Arthur M. Schlesinger, Jr. New York:

  Putnam, 1983.

### Periodicals

Palmer, Glenn E. "Computer Applications in the Freshman

  Laboratory." Journal of Chemical Education

  58 (1981): 995–96.

The title of the journal is followed by the volume number, the year of publication in parentheses, a colon, and the pages on which

**46b**

*doc*

the article appears. Some documentation styles may use *Vol.* for *volume* and roman instead of Arabic numerals. MLA style uses no abbreviation and Arabic numerals only. Notice that the colon is the only separating punctuation used after the journal title and that abbreviations such as *p.* or *pp.* *(page* or *pages)* are not used.

ARTICLE FROM JOURNAL WITH EACH ISSUE PAGINATED
INDEPENDENTLY

Mendelson, Michael. "Business Prose and the Nature of the

Plain Style." Journal of Business Communication 24.2

(1987): 3-11.

Because pagination begins over again with each issue of the journal rather than with each volume, it is necessary to give the issue number. Here the order is journal title, volume number, separating period, issue number, year of publication in parentheses, colon, and page numbers.

ARTICLE FROM WEEKLY OR BIWEEKLY PERIODICAL

Alexander, Charles P. "The Billion-Dollar Boys." Time 9

Jan. 1984: 46-48.

Notice that the date of the periodical's publication is inverted and presented in "military" or "continental" style as well as abbreviated: *9 Jan. 1984.* As in other periodical citations, the abbreviations *p.* or *pp.* are not used. Instead, the meaning of the numbers is indicated by their placement in the entry.

ARTICLE FROM MONTHLY OR BIMONTHLY PERIODICAL

Jordan, Robert Paul. "Ghosts on the Little Bighorn."

National Geographic Dec. 1986: 787+.

**46b**

*doc*

The abbreviation + following the page number *787* indicates that the article continues, but not on consecutive pages.

ARTICLE FROM DAILY NEWSPAPER

Morris, Betsy. "Thwack! Smack! Sounds Thrill Makers of

Hunt's Ketchup." Wall Street Journal 27 Apr. 1984,

midwestern ed., sec. 1:1+.

This newspaper article carried a by-line, so the author's name is known. If the article were unsigned, it would be alphabetized in

"Works Cited" by its title rather than by its author. For newspaper articles, give the date of publication, the edition if the paper is printed in more than one edition (either location or time of day, whichever is relevant), and the section number as well as the page number if the newspaper is divided into sections that are paginated separately. The citation given here refers to pages 1 and following of the midwestern edition of the *Wall Street Journal* for April 27, 1984.

SIGNED BOOK REVIEW

Morris, Jan. "Visions in the Wilderness." Rev. of Sands

River, by Peter Matthiessen. Saturday Review Apr. 1981:

68–69.

UNSIGNED ARTICLE OR REVIEW

"Form and Function in a Post and Beam House." Early American

Life Oct. 1980: 41–43.

*Government and Legal Documents*

GOVERNMENT PUBLICATION

United States. Dept. of Health, Education, and Welfare.

National Center for Educational Statistics. Digest of

Educational Statistics. Washington: GPO, 1968.

This entry shows an example of "corporate authorship." That is, an institution is considered the author, although clearly one or several people wrote the document. Corporate authorship is not uncommon for works from governmental and educational institutions, foundations, agencies, or business firms.

**46b**

*doc*

CONSTITUTION

U.S. Const. Art. 2, sec. 4.

COURT CASES

Bundy v. Jackson. 24 FEP Cases 1155 (1981).

Seto v. Muller. 395 F. Supp. 811 (D. Mass. 1975).

Methods for citing court cases and legal documents vary: the ones shown here are representative, however. The name of the case is given first, followed by identification numbers, references to courts and relevant jurisdictions (for example, "FEP Cases" means "Federal Employment Practices Cases"; "F. Supp." means "Federal Superior Court"), and the year in which the case was decided. The best guide for legal references is the most recent edition of *A Uniform System of Citation* (Cambridge: Harvard Law Rev. Assn.). It should be available in your college or university library.

### Letters and Interviews

PUBLISHED LETTER

Mills, Ralph J. Jr., ed. Selected Letters of Theodore

  Roethke. Seattle: U of Washington P, 1968.


UNPUBLISHED LETTER

McCracken, Virginia. Letter to Colonel Thomas McCracken.

  1 July 1862.


INTERVIEWS

Silber, John R. Personal interview. 5 June 1979.

Kennedy, Senator Edward. Telephone interview. 3 May 1980.

### Information Services, Computer Software

INFORMATION SERVICE

Beam, Paul. COMIT English Module. ERIC ED 167 189.

Labe, P. "Personal Computer Industry." Drexel Burnham

  Lambert, Inc. 23 Apr. 1987: n.pag. Dow Jones News/

  Retrieval Investext file 12, item 32.

**46b**

*doc*

Material from information services and databases is cited the same way as any other printed material, with the addition of a reference to the source—in this case ERIC (Educational Resources Information Center) and Dow Jones News/Retrieval. Notice that the Dow Jones entry is unpaginated (n. pag., meaning "no page"). Be aware that information services, data banks, microform services, and other suppliers sometimes indicate how they should be cited in references. Follow their suggestions but, if necessary, adapt them to the particular documentation style you are using. The NewsBank information service Toni consulted showed two citation forms, one of them developed by the editors of the *MLA Handbook for Writers of Research Papers* for use in papers following MLA style.

SOFTWARE

<u>SuperCalc</u>. Computer software. Sorcim, 1981. CP/M—based

    microcomputer, disk.

For an entry documenting computer software, supply the following information: the author of the software (if known), the title of the program (treated like the title of any work and underlined or italicized), a descriptive label (Computer software), the name of the distributor, and the year of publication. Other information can be included at the end if it will be important to the reader. For example, this entry lists the type of computer on which the program can be used (CP/M-based) and its form (disk).

### Films, Television, Radio, Recordings, Works of Art

FILM

<u>Children of a Lesser God</u>. Dir. Randa Haines. Paramount,

    1986.

Films, television programs, movies, works of art, recordings, and the like are treated similarly to printed works except that the type of medium logically dictates the type of information to be included. The title of the work is always given. If the performer, composer, director, producer, or artist is of primary importance, then the name of that person will head the entry, appearing in the author position. If the work is more important than its creator or performer, then the title will occupy the lead position in the entry—as in the case of the audiotape *Footloose*, listed below. Provide whatever information the reader will need to identify or locate the work, such as dates of performances, broadcasts, or recordings; networks; recording companies; catalog numbers; etc. The following examples are representative.

**46b**

*doc*

TELEVISION AND RADIO

<u>Casey Stengel</u>. Writ. Sidney and David Carroll. Perf. Charles

    Durning. PBS, Boston. 6 May 1981.

Keillor, Garrison. "The News from Lake Wobegon." <u>A Prairie</u>

    <u>Home Companion</u>. Minnesota Public Radio. WBAA, West

    Lafayette. 13 June 1987.

RECORD

Moussorgsky, Modeste. <u>Pictures at an Exhibition</u>. Leonard

    Pennario, piano. Capitol, P—8323, n.d.

AUDIOTAPE; COMPACT DISC; VIDEOTAPE

<u>Footloose</u>. Audiotape. Perf. Kenny Loggins et al. Columbia,

JST 39242, 1984.

Beethoven, Ludwig van. <u>The Five Piano Concertos</u>. Perf.

Rudolf Serkin. Cond. Seiji Ozawa. Compact disc. Boston

Symphony Orchestra. Telarc, CD 80061-5, 1984.

Allen, Woody, dir. <u>Hannah and Her Sisters</u>. Videocassette.

HBO Video, 1985. 1 hr., 43 min.

WORK OF ART (PAINTING)

Picasso, Pablo. <u>A Woman in White</u>. The Metropolitan Museum of

Art, New York.

**2. The APA name and year system.** The **name and year system** is exemplified by the form described in the *Publication Manual of the American Psychological Association* (1983). APA style is widely used in the social sciences. This system cites works in the text by the last name of the author and the year of publication. These citations of "name and year" permit readers to find full bibliographic information about the work in the reference list. If the author's name is mentioned in the text itself, only the year of publication is given in parentheses. If both author and year appear in the text, no parenthetical information is required:

Romonovic (1979) finds no correlation between the growth

of unemployment and urban unrest. However, in 1981 Kemper

reported conclusive evidence to the contrary. One study

(Bordman, 1983) points out that reliable statistics on the

subject are extremely scarce.

46b

*doc*

Page numbers are given for direct quotations and are inserted within the parentheses:

Bellinki questions whether the research methods used to

obtain the data "could ever have been considered valid"

(1986, pp. 34-35).

When this system is used, all references are listed alphabetically by the author's last name at the end of the paper. If two or more studies by the same author are cited, they are listed in chronological sequence by year, the earliest first. If two or more studies by the same author with the same publication date are cited, they are arranged alphabetically and distinguished by lower case letters after the year (Jones 1986a, Jones 1986b, and so on). The information given on each work in the listing is essentially the same as that required by the MLA form—author, title, and publication information—but entries differ in the order in which the information is arranged and in some mechanical details. Only the last name and initials of the author are given. Only the first word of the title is capitalized, if the work is a book.

> Perkins, J. (Ed.). (1986). <u>Neurotic characteristics as indicators of author success</u> (2nd ed.). Englewood Cliffs, NJ: Prentice Hall.
>
> Stretham, C.P. (1978). <u>Achievement and longevity</u>. New York: John Wiley.

If the work being listed is a periodical, only the first word of the article's title is capitalized. The article's title has no quotation marks around it, nor is it underlined. The title of the periodical in which the article appears is given in full upper and lowercase letters and is underlined (for italics). The volume number is also underlined.

> French, J. R. P., Ross, I. C., Kirby, S., Newlson, J. R., & Smyth, P. (1958). Employee participation in a program of industrial change. <u>Personnel</u>, <u>35</u>, 16–29.

Notice that when referring to works with more than one author, all the authors' names are in inverted form and an ampersand (&) is used to indicate *and*. In the in-text citation, however, use the word *and* rather than an ampersand *(Bose and Page discovered that . . . .)* For works with two to five authors, in-text citations should give all the authors' names at the first reference; use the first author's name and *et al.* thereafter. For works with six or more authors, the first and all subsequent in-text references should list only the first author's name and *et al.*, with all names given in correct form in the reference list.

> Wilson et al. (1987) believe that any planning system for the semiconductor industry must be able to schedule for multiple sites.
>
> Wilson, E. L., Sznaider, K. A., Jue, C., Russ, C., Rigodanzo, C. W., & Turner, L. T. (1987). A planning solution for

```
the semiconductor industry. Hewlett-Packard Journal, 38,

21-27.
```

A similar format is followed for magazine and newspaper articles. Use *p.* or *pp.* before page numbers in references to magazines and newspapers, but not in references to journals. If an article has no author, use a short title for the parenthetical citation, and in the references list alphabetize it by the first significant word in the title.

```
Gray, P. B. (1987, February 23). Taste buds atingle, recipe

    hounds keep stars under siege. The Wall Street Journal,

    pp. 1, 13.

Summer air fares gain altitude. (1987, June 22). Business

    Week, p. 54.
```

Pages 560–62 show part of Toni Mitchell's research paper documented in APA style.

**3. The number system.** In the **number system** of documentation, used widely in the natural sciences and mathematics, if the author's name is mentioned in the text itself, the reference is indicated only by a number in parentheses. If the author's name is not mentioned, the reference given parenthetically in the text includes the author's last name followed by the appropriate number. References are numbered in this way sequentially throughout the text. In the list of references at the end of the paper, each item is given a corresponding number and listed in the *order of its occurrence in the text* (not in alphabetical order). In the text the reference will appear as follows:

```
    Oliver (11) finds that only one type of halophyte,

Salicornia europa, or pickleweed, will germinate in water

with a saline content of 36 parts per thousand.
```

or:

```
    Research indicates that only one type of halophyte,

Salicornia europa, or pickleweed, will germinate in water

with a saline content of 36 parts per thousand (Oliver 11).
```

**46b**

*doc*

The list of references would then show this entry:

```
11. Oliver, W. H. Salinity tolerance among halophytes. New

    York: Academic Press, 1978.
```

In a variant of the number system, used in the military and elsewhere, the reference list is made first. The entries are alphabetized and then numbered. A work is then cited in the text by the number already assigned to it in the reference list. Thus, for example, all references to Burton Ringwald's *Tennessee Battles*, entry 19 in the reference list, give only that number throughout the body of the paper.

**4. The footnote (endnote) system.** The **footnote** (or **endnote**) **system** is a traditional documentation method used widely prior to 1984 in language and literature but now employed mainly in the disciplines of fine arts and humanities, such as religion and philosophy. This system documents in-text quotations, paraphrases, summaries, and the like, by means of a raised Arabic numeral immediately following the final word or punctuation mark of the citation. The consecutive numerals refer to corresponding documentation notes placed at the bottom of the page or gathered at the end of the paper.

Notes placed at the bottoms of pages are generally single-spaced, with double-spacing between them. When gathered as endnotes, they are double-spaced both within and between notes. The first line of each note is indented five spaces, the raised numeral appearing in the fifth space with no space between it and the first word of the note. Second and subsequent lines of a note are flush with the left margin.

As with other forms of documentation, the footnote system cites author, title, and publication information, including relevant page numbers. The major divisions of the note are separated by commas, and the entry is closed with a period. A sample of this documentation style follows:

According to A. G. Dickens, Puritanism "gave the cutting

edge to the forces which shaped parliamentary, legal, and

religious liberties" in America as well as in England.[1]

Historian Elbert Russell points out that the relative

tolerance of Oliver Cromwell's Puritan Commonwealth allowed

dissenting religious sects to organize and spread their

doctrines.[2] As a result, one sect--the Quakers--were to have

a profound influence on the United States Constitution,

particularly the First Amendment. Using William Penn's Great

Laws for Pennsylvania as a model, "every one of the colonies

enacted laws recognizing the right of conscience."[3] Later

when the colonies had become states and were asked to ratify

the new federal constitution, all refused until it was

amended to include a Bill of Rights for which Pennsylvania

**46b**

*doc*

and Maryland made the first proposals: "the rights of

conscience should be held inviolable."[4]

---

[1]A. G. Dickens, Reformation and Society in Sixteenth-
Century Europe (New York: Harcourt, 1966), p. 181.

[2]Elbert Russell, The History of Quakerism (Richmond, IN:
Friends United Press, 1979), p. 17.

[3]Harrop A. Freeman, "William Penn, Quakers, and Civil
Liberties," Friends Journal, 56 (October 15, 1982), p. 15.

[4]Ibid.

Footnotes 1 and 2 in the foregoing sample show the form for books.
Footnote 3 illustrates the form for a periodical. Footnote 4 illustrates
that references repeating an immediately preceding source may list
*Ibid.*—without a page number if the references are to the same page.
Subsequent references to a work already cited may be listed by author's last name and page number (for example: Dickens, p. 43.). If
more than one work by a single author appears in the notes, to avoid
confusion the author's last name, a shortened form of the title, and
page number are used in second and subsequent references (for example: Dickens, *Calvinism,* p. 75.). Depending on the discipline, papers using the footnote system may or may not have separate bibliographies.

Toni Mitchell had a choice of several documentation styles for
her sociology paper. For example, she could have followed the style
of the Modern Language Association or that of the American Psychological Association, both documentation forms being acceptable in the
field. Toni chose to use MLA conventions, illustrated in the following
research paper. At the end of this section, the last few paragraphs of
her research paper are also reproduced in APA style, a form frequently used in the social sciences.

## 46c   Common scholarly abbreviations

46c

*doc*

The following list contains many of the scholarly abbreviations
you are likely to need in writing a bibliography or that you are likely
to see while conducting research.

| anon. | anonymous |
|---|---|
| art., arts. | article(s) |
| c., ca. | *circa* (about); used with approximate dates |
| cf. | *confer* (compare) |
| ch., chs., chap., chaps. | chapter(s) |

| | |
|---|---|
| col., cols. | column(s) |
| dir. | director, directed by |
| diss. | dissertation |
| ed., edn. | edition |
| ed., eds. | editor(s) |
| e.g. | *exempli gratia* (for example) |
| et al. | *et alii* (and others) |
| ERIC | Educational Resources Information Service |
| f., ff. | and the following page(s) |
| GPO | Government Printing Office |
| ibid. | *ibidem* (in the same place) |
| i.e. | *id est* (that is) |
| illus. | illustrator, illustrated by, illustration |
| introd. | introduction |
| l., ll. | line(s) |
| loc. cit. | *loca citato* (in the place cited) |
| ms, mss | manuscript(s) |
| n.b. | *nota bene* (take notice) |
| n.d. | no date (of publication) given |
| n.p. | no place (of publication) given |
| n. pag. | no pagination |
| no., nos. | number, numbers |
| NTIS | National Technical Information Service |
| numb. | numbered |
| op. cit. | *opere citato* (in the work cited) |
| p., pp. | page(s) |
| passim | throughout the work, here and there |
| perf. | performed by, performer |
| proc. | proceedings |
| prod. | produced by, producer |
| q.v. | *quod vide* (which see) |
| qtd. | quoted in |
| rev. | review, revised |
| rpt. | reprint, reprinted |
| sec. | section |
| sic | thus it is |
| trans., tr. | translator, translated |
| univ., U, UP | university, university press |
| v. (vs.) | versus (against) |
| vol., vols. | volume(s) |

**46d**

*res*

## 46d  Sample research paper

Toni Mitchell's research paper, presented in this section, is a successful student paper. For this assignment she had to choose a subject, narrow its scope to a manageable focus, gather authoritative information from a number of sources, and then organize the information clearly in a paper of approximately ten pages, excluding notes and bibliography.

Toni's task as a researcher was not only to report information but also to evaluate it in a way that contributed to an understanding of the knowledge in the field. The assignment also required a thesis statement, a sentence outline, a bibliography in proper form, and appropriate documentation of evidence.

The commentary accompanying this paper explains Toni's writing process, as the preceding pages have outlined her research process. It details some of the writing and documentation problems she faced and solved.

**46d**

*res*

*Research Paper Commentary*

**The title page.** MLA format uses **no title page.** Instead, the writer places a double-spaced heading on the first page, one inch from the top and flush with the left margin. The heading states the writer's name, the instructor's name, the course name, and the date. Toni Mitchell's sociology professor, on the other hand, asked her students to use a title page because she found it convenient to write comments and the grade on this cover sheet. Many instructors outside the field of literature prefer papers to include a title page, particularly if they are longer than a few pages. Be sure to ask your instructor what he or she prefers.

Had Toni followed MLA format exactly, her paper's first page would have looked like the sample opposite.

**46d**

*res*

Mitchell 1

Toni Mitchell

Professor S. Willard

Sociology 214

25 April 1991

Social Roles for the Elderly in the 21st Century

Over the last ten years, the college-age U.S. population
of 18–24 year-olds has decreased by 13.9% while the number of
people between the ages of 65 and 74 has increased 17.4% and
the number of people over the age of 75 has increased by

**46d**

*res*

**The format.** The title of each part of Toni's paper (outline, paper, endnotes, "Works Cited") is centered one inch below the top of the page. The text is double-spaced, with well-balanced left and right margins of about one inch. Consecutive Arabic numerals are used to number the pages of the paper itself, including the endnotes and bibliography. Small Roman numerals are used to number the "front matter," the pages containing the outline (or any other material preceding the first text page of the paper). Notice that Toni's last name appears before the page number on every page of the paper except the title page.

Keep in mind that different fields require different formats. Check the style manual or representative publications in the field for which you are preparing your research paper.

**The title, thesis statement, and sentence outline.** The first three sections give a quick summary of this research paper (1) *the title* provides a very general statement; (2) *the thesis statement* briefly explains what the paper attempts to do; and (3) *the outline* supplies a rather full statement.

**46d**

*res*

Social Roles for the Elderly

In the 21st Century


by

~~Toni Mitchell~~

BRIDGET MCGINTY


Professor ~~Sonja Willard~~ JOHN COLLIGAN

~~Sociology 214~~
FRESHMAN COMPOSITION

~~26 April 1991~~
24 MAY 1995

**46d**

*res*

Outline

<u>Thesis</u> <u>statement:</u> Several role options for the elderly to contribute positively to society in the 21st century are emerging: two of these options extend the traditional adult roles of wage earning and parenting, but in social contexts different from today.

   I. The American population is getting older, with older people outnumbering younger ones.
    A. Demographics show a shift from youth to age.
    B. Until relatively recently, few people lived to reach old age.
  II. The role of the elderly has evolved in Western civilization.
    A. Before the invention of the printing press, the elderly were respected as repositories of wisdom and expertise.
    B. After the invention of the printing press, books became the repositories of knowledge; authority shifted, devaluing old age.
 III. The resulting "youth cult" encouraged "ageism," negative stereotypes of old age.
    A. "Infantilization" is one form of ageism.
    B. An emphasis on the pathologies of aging is another form of ageism.
    C. "Lumping" the heterogeneous elderly population into a homogeneous group encourages ageism.
  IV. Prolonging or reinitiating the wage earning role is a viable option for many elderly people.

**46d**

*res*

A. For emotional and economic reasons, older people may reject 65 as retirement age.

B. As the pool of younger workers continues to decrease, businesses may encourage seniors to stay in the work force.

V. Extending the parenting (or grandparenting) role offers another viable option.

   A. Grandparent–grandchild relationships can strengthen traditional family structures.

   B. Surrogate grandparents can offer vital support in nontraditional settings.

      1. Seniors can serve as day care substitutes for working mothers or one-parent families.

      2. Seniors involved in school enrichment programs provide instructional opportunities of all kinds, as well as helping children reject ageism.

VI. The able elderly don't necessarily need new roles; rather, they need increased opportunities and encouragement to extend existing roles into new areas where society has the most to gain from their contributions.

**46d**

*res*

**Paragraphs 1 and 2.** Toni uses her first paragraph to set the scene. She focuses the reader's attention on the "booming" growth of the population of older Americans, knowing that her relatively young audience will find this information startling. She introduces her broad research subject in the second paragraph: changing social roles for the elderly in the 21st century. The last three sentences of paragraph 2 provide the thesis for the paper. Although expressed as more than one sentence here, the thesis corresponds exactly to the single-sentence version that headed the outline at the beginning of her paper. The remainder of the paper will explore and develop the controlling idea that viable future roles for the elderly are extensions of current adult roles, but within new social contexts.

**46d**

*res*

Mitchell 3

Social Roles for the Elderly in the 21st Century

Over the last ten years, the college-age U.S. population of 18-24 year-olds has decreased by 13.9%, while the number of people between the ages of 65 and 74 has increased 17.4%, and the number of people over the age of 75 has increased by 31.2% (U.S. Bureau of the Census 15). This trend toward a growing elderly population is predicted to continue as the baby boomers advance through middle age toward retirement. By 2025, people over the age of 65 are predicted to outnumber teenagers two to one; by 2050, forecasters say, one out of every four Americans will be over 65 (Dychtwald 21), truly a "senior boom."

There is no question that this kind of a population shift will redefine roles in society. It would be impossible for such a large shift in demographics not to have a tremendous impact on American life. So the question is not whether social roles will change but rather how people's roles will change. Human beings have spent millenia trying to survive to an old age. Now that the goal is finally being realized, no one really knows how to handle it. Researchers point out that there is currently "an imbalance between a rapidly growing, vital older population and opportunities available in the social structure." Or, as one scholar puts it, society currently offers "tenuous roles" to its older members (qtd. in Hagestad 418). Clearly, ways must be found to ensure that the nearly 40 million elderly people alive in the early 21st century will contribute positively to society rather than become a drain upon it. Several options are emerging. Two of these options extend the traditional adult roles of wage earning and parenting. The principal difference

**46d**

*res*

**Paragraphs 3, 4, and 5.** These paragraphs compare and contrast views of old age, enabling Toni to show how relative attitudes are about age. In paragraph 4 she uses the block quotation from Dychtwald to drive home to readers the recency of the "empty nest" phenomenon. Notice that the block quotation (required for quotations of more than four lines) is introduced by an attribution to the source (Dychtwald), whose qualification as authority is identified (gerontology). The attribution is followed by a colon (usual in formal introductions to long quotations). Also notice that in this case the page citation follows the end punctuation. For other than block quotations, the parenthetical page citation would appear between the ending quotation mark and the terminal punctuation, as shown at the end of paragraph 5.

is the social context in which older people will carry out
these roles.

3      Old age depresses people. It has been represented as a time
of costly and painful chronic or severe illness, loneliness,
poverty, and deprivation. Actress Lucille Ball's television
portrayal of an elderly bag lady probably comes close to the
image many younger people have of old age--and the fears many
older people have for their future. Mick Jagger of the Rolling
Stones strikes a responsive chord when he sings, "What a drag it
is getting old" ("Mother's Little Helper").

4      But what, exactly, is "old"? "Old" age is a relative thing.
People born in 1776 could expect to live to about age 35. The
median (or average) age was about 16. By America's centennial,
life expectancy had increased only about five years, and the
median age was 21. In contrast, a child born today can expect to
live 75 years, on average. The median age is now 32, and
climbing. Gerontologist Ken Dychtwald says:

> Americans in earlier times didn't give much thought to
> how they were going to handle their old age. Middle-
> aged people didn't worry very much about how to care
> for their aging parents, because most of their parents
> were already gone. And couples didn't wonder how they
> might relate to each other after the kids had grown up
> and left home; in the middle of the last century, the
> average "nest" could expect to be "empty" for no more
> than 18 months before one or both of the parents were
> dead. (4)

5      He points out that during most of human history only one
person in ten lived to the age of 65, what most of us would

**46d**

*res*

**Paragraph 6.** In order to discuss social roles for today's and tomorrow's elderly, Toni must first establish an historical context. In paragraph 6 she refers to veneration traditionally shown the aged in Eastern cultures. She considered this information to be common knowledge obtained from reading and class discussions both in college and in high school. Consequently, she saw no need to document it.

**Paragraphs 7 through 10.** Toni uses information from James Burke's television series and book of the same name *(The Day the Universe Changed)* to show why the "cult of youth" replaced the "cult of age" after reading and writing became widespread in Europe. Predominantly summaries of facts from the television program and paraphrases from the book, these paragraphs cover a lot of history in a relatively few words. Her first versions were substantially longer, but Toni realized that, while the details might be interesting, her readers needed only a broadly brushed history lesson. Paragraphs 6 and 7 illustrate how to handle references to different works by the same author: use the author's name and a shortened title. In this case, the referenced television program had a different title than the program series—which carried the same title as the book—much as a book chapter has a title different from the book in which it appears.

46d

*res*

consider retirement age. Now, in the last decade of the
twentieth century, almost 80% of Americans will live past age
65. One hundred years ago, less than 4% (2.4 million) of the
U.S. population was over 65. Today that number is 12% (30
million), and it is expected to increase by at least six million
people per decade. The statistics are similar for much of the
industrialized world. In the U.S., the number of people over the
age of 65 surpassed the number of teenagers in 1983. Dychtwald
comments, "We are no longer a nation of youths" (6-8).

As "young" as the majority of human beings has been until
recently, it is important to understand the historical social
role that "old" people have played if we wish to think
constructively about the social roles they may have in the
future. Veneration of the elderly in Eastern cultures is well
known: for example, ancestor worship in pre-Communist China.
While perhaps less apparent, veneration for the old has been
present in Western cultures as well--if not veneration, then at
least a high degree of respect.

In his PBS television series The Day the Universe Changed,
historian and journalist James Burke illustrated the crucial
role the elderly played in pre-literate European life during the
Middle Ages. Settling inheritance disputes, for example, did not
depend on written records--because almost no one could write or
read. Instead, the village elders were called as witnesses,
either because they were present at previous events or to serve
as a kind of human calendar. Their memories of natural and
social occurrences such as eclipses, storms, hard winters, wars,
births, and deaths could be used to "date" other occurrences and
thus verify someone's age or claim (Burke, "Matter of Fact").

**46d**

*res*

**Paragraphs 11 and 12.** Toni presents another point of view about the transition to the "youth cult," one that broadens the explanation to include significant movements in Western history. The point is not whether Burke or Rosenmayr is right about the cause of the devaluing of old age; the point is that this devaluing exists and that several scholars have observed it. These observations set up the next section, which explores negative attitudes toward old age.

The old were the principal repositories for and transmitters of whatever collective knowledge the society possessed.

8       "In an age when experience was what counted most, power was in the hands of the elders. They approved local customs and practice, and in matters of legal dispute they were the judges. They resisted change," says Burke (Universe 92). Things were done a certain way because the elders said they had always been done that way. But a technological innovation helped to undermine the authority and thus, according to Burke, some of the respect given to the oldest members of European society. That innovation was the printing press.

9       The printing press caused an explosion in the number of people who learned to read in fifteenth-century Europe. After the Bible and certain Latin and Greek classics, the best-selling books were how-to books. Now, instead of having to rely solely on learning from a master craftsman by word-of-mouth and example, one could obtain accurate and detailed information from a book (116).

10      The basis for authority had shifted. As Burke explains, society became forward-looking rather than backward-looking: "A printed fifteenth-century history expressed the new opinion: 'Why should old men be preferred to their juniors when it is possible, by diligent study, for young men to acquire the same knowledge?' The cult of youth had begun" (123).

11      Although by means of a slightly different path, Austrian sociologist Leopold Rosenmayr arrives at a similar conclusion, noting that in Western civilization old age eventually ceased to be a value in itself (302). He locates the beginnings of the youth cult in classical Greek culture, in which youths were

**46d**

*res*

**Paragraph 13.** This paragraph begins a section of old-age stereotypes. Toni provides an important term, *ageism,* and its definition. She refers to several sources to establish that old people are unfairly stereotyped simply because of their age. This point in her argument becomes especially important later, when she argues that the elderly are a heterogeneous rather than a homogeneous population. Notice again how she smoothly and succinctly provides her authorities' credentials and avoids "chopping-and-dropping" the quotations in the text.

**Paragraphs 14 and 15.** The two-paragraph discussion of "infantilization" links the aged to other minority groups, showing how stereotyping makes people powerless and subjects them to various kinds of abuse.

**46d**

*res*

specially and collectively trained to participate in a society
where change, not stasis, was anticipated.

12    Rosenmayr sees this youth-cult orientation appearing
throughout Western history: in the Renaissance emphasis on
youthful individualism, in the philosophical and political
rejection of traditionalism that characterized the eighteenth-
century Enlightenment and American Revolution, in the
nineteenth-century European wars of liberation, in the early
twentieth-century youth movements, and in the student protest
movement of the 1960s (302). The experience of age gave way to
the vitality of youth. In the United States, it was youth that
won the west and conquered the last frontier, outer space. The
preference for youth over age in our society is visible in
everything from fashions to TV sitcoms and automobile design.

13    Furthermore, negative perceptions about senior citizens are
everywhere, even among seniors themselves. "All too often, the
word aging is associated with the word problem. The dominant
popular image of old age is one of inevitable decline, senility,
and dependency," remarks researcher Gunhild Hagestad (418).
Prejudices and stereotypes applied to older people simply
because of their age are known as "ageism." Robert N. Butler,
former director of The National Institute on Aging, says that
ageism, "like racism and sexism, is a way of pigeonholing people
and not allowing them to be individuals with unique ways of
living their lives" (2).

14    "Infantilization" is a common stereotype that has been
pinned on a number of minority groups besides the aged,
including African-American slaves and women pressed to remain
housewives rather than take jobs outside the home (Arluke and

**46d**

*res*

532    RESEARCHED WRITING

Paragraph 16. By mentioning housewives as a powerless minority in paragraph 14, Toni has provided a natural transition to Betty Friedan, a well-known feminist of the 1960s and 1970s. During the 1980s Friedan became a knowledgeable spokesperson on senior citizens issues. Toni fully identifies Friedan to establish the connection. Notice the use of ellipses in paragraph 16. Here words have been cut from the middle of two sentences, requiring three spaced periods to indicate the omissions.

46d

*res*

Levin 10). This negative image portrays the minority group member as having child-like qualities and as being intellectually, socially, morally, and/or physically immature. The members of the minority group are consequently also portrayed as dependent in various ways upon the dominant group.

15    When applied to the elderly, this stereotype usually takes the form of "second childhood" in which the older person is viewed as unable to cope as an adult. Arluke and Levin note that the second childhood image has a long history of association with the elderly, and they trace it through television and print advertising to illustrate its prevalence today. Older people are shown throwing tantrums, eating like children (small portions, bland food), having the physical problems of children (incontinence or constipation), and being entertained as if they were children (parties with silly hats). "This dim view of the elderly suggests that they are losing, or have lost, the very things a growing child gains. It implies a backward movement to earlier developmental stages," they write (8), and denies the lifetime of experience that separates age from youth. For the elderly, the three principal negative consequences are a lowering of social status, the subsequent potential loss of political power, and the danger of allowing things to be done to them that would not ordinarily be permitted (such as unwarranted institutionalization or declaration of incompetency) (Arluke and Levin 10).

6    Betty Friedan, author of The Feminine Mystique, the book that helped kick off the woman's movement in the 1970s, believes that a discriminatory "mystique of age" must also be overcome. She argues that aging has been unfairly linked with disease.

**46d**

*res*

**Paragraphs 17, 18, and 19.** These three paragraphs explore the issue of homogeneity versus heterogeneity, using ageism as the transitional link. Paragraph 19 relies on some startling statistics to support the conclusion that the elderly are no more homogeneous than younger people. Paragraph 17 shows the in-text documentation style for citing two sources that make the same point. Note that they appear within a single set of parentheses but are separated by a semicolon and a space. Paragraph 17 also contains the number for the first of two notes Toni used in her paper. This one is a bibliographical note referring the reader to several other sources. The note itself appears at the end of the paper. Paragraph 18 illustrates the use of a reference quoted in a second source written by someone else. "Qtd. in" makes clear that the information is second-hand reporting, in this case U.S. Census statistics quoted in *Time* magazine. While it is usually preferable to locate the primary source, if available, Toni felt *Time*'s reporting of the information would be reliable and that hunting for exactly the same statistics in government publications would not be worth her time. Paragraph 19 contains the reference to the second of Toni's endnotes, a content note that explains discrepancies in the categories "young old," "oldest old," and so forth. Since authorities did not always agree on these definitions, she felt she needed to point out the discrepancies but did not want to interrupt the flow of the paragraph to do so.

**46d**

*res*

Mitchell 9

Even gerontologists and geriatricians, whom she implies should

know better, concentrate on "pathologies of aging, not the norms

of aging. . . . To limit discussion to the negative norms

. . . ignores the growth that so often accompanies aging" (123).

17      Ageism of this sort encourages the general public to

continue to view older people as homogeneous rather than

heterogeneous. One of the constant themes in gerontological

research is the heterogeneity of the elderly. Neither the

stereotype of the ill, infirm, and isolated older person

subsisting on a meager pension check nor the stereotype of the

wealthy retiree who spends the "golden years" traveling the

world or playing golf five mornings a week is accurate.

Somewhere in between lies the majority of older Americans who

live adequately in homes that are paid for, whose children call

or visit them with some frequency, and who lead relatively

satisfying lives. For example, fewer than 10% of Americans

between the ages of 65 and 74 have health problems requiring

daily assistance or institutional care (Hagestad 418). Only one

in ten between the ages of 60 and 72 is poor (in contrast, one

in five of America's children is growing up in poverty) ("'Young

Old'" 145; Palmore 66).

18      Senior citizens are as different from one another as any

other segment of the population. However, the problems of

changing public attitudes are compounded by the fact that the

mass media often lump senior citizens into a single huge age

group. For example, Time magazine categorizes United States

Census Bureau population figures into age groups 0–17, 18–24,

25–44, 45–64, and 65+ (qtd. in "You Can Look It Up" 36). The

reasons for choosing these age classifications are no doubt many

**46d**

*res*

**Paragraph 20.** Here Toni begins her argument concerning one of the emerging roles for the elderly: continuing as employees after retirement age. She uses Chen's statistical projections to lay groundwork for the assertion that an "official" retirement age of 65 has negative consequences.

**46d**

*res*

Mitchell 10

and varied, but the fact remains that when a mass-circulation magazine lumps everyone over 65 into one category it helps to perpetuate negative stereotypes about the elderly.

19          The injustice of this "lumping" becomes clear when one considers that there are as many years between 60 and 90 as there are between 20 and 50 (Soulsman B3). No one would think of lumping 20-year-olds with 50-year-olds. Why, then, lump the "young old" (those between 60 and 74) together with the "oldest old" (those 85 and above)?[2] When we consider that in the next 20 years the number of people over the age of 75 will increase from slightly over 13 million to more than 18 million--a 36% increase--but that the number of people between the ages of 64 and 74 will increase by less than 15%--from about 18 million to slightly over 21 million--it is easier to see the importance of differentiating among segments of the elderly population (U.S. Bureau of the Census 15). Their needs and desires vary tremendously; the roles they will want to play and be able to play in society are likely to vary tremendously as well.

20          In considering future roles for the elderly, some researchers have tentatively concluded that improved health and longevity will change the norm of retirement at age 65. In this connection, economics professor Young-Ping Chen discusses the "so-called old age dependency ratio," which is calculated from the number of persons in the work force versus the number of older people no longer working. This ratio has been growing in the United States since the 1940s, and is projected to increase dramatically in the 21st century: "In 1940 there were about 11 elderly persons for every 100 persons of working age; 21 persons estimated in the year 2000; nearly 30 persons in the

**46d**

*res*

**Paragraphs 21 and 22.** The argumentation chain begun in paragraph 20 is extended, ultimately citing the historical but rather arbitrary selection of age 65 as "official." Toni also uses paragraph 22 to highlight the information that "mandatory" retirement is in fact now pegged at age 70 by law.

**Paragraphs 23 through 25.** Toni marshalls demographic and economic evidence supporting the continuance or re-entry of senior citizens in the work force. Paragraph 23 illustrates how to handle the in-text citation of words quoted from a second source rather than from the original, in this case quoted from a book review of Mowsesian's *Golden Goals, Rusted Realities.*

46d

*res*

year 2020, and almost 39 persons in the period 2040–2060"
(Chen 410).

21        These figures worry governmental planners because the
projections suggest that a heavier burden must be shouldered by
working people, who contribute directly or indirectly to the
support of older people. However, Chen points out that the ratio
changes significantly if the retirement age gradually increases
to a maximum of 73.01 by the year 2060: "There is a 62% increase
in the old age dependency ratio from 1985 to 2060. This increase
is still significant, but not nearly as much as the 106%
increase . . . under the invariant retirement age of 65" (411).

22        Why do Americans retire at 65, even though the 1981 Age
Discrimination in Employment Act prohibits mandatory retirement
before age 70? Since the Social Security Act of 1935 was passed,
65 is the age when a person becomes eligible for full Social
Security benefits and, hence, the "official" retirement age for
most people. In fact, the first official retirement age was 70—
the biblical three score and ten—set by Germany's Chancellor
Otto von Bismarck in 1889 when he established the first state
social security system. Later, German bureaucrats changed it to
65 (Dychtwald 32).

23        University of Texas psychologist Richard Mowsesian believes
society should stop using chronological age to determine when
people should retire. At a time when Americans are living longer
and more actively, he finds it "unconscionable" that people
should be removed from the work force, the implication being
that they are no longer capable or competent. They are forced to
suffer "'the ultimate in job discrimination." To be old in a
work-oriented society such as the U.S. is to be relegated to

**46d**

*res*

Paragraph 26. Sometimes a source refers to the research of another but does not identify that source clearly or at all, thus preventing the writer from locating it for further reading. At other times, the original source may be unavailable to the writer. Such is the case of the research study to which Toni refers in paragraph 26. She wanted to use the information to strengthen her argument, but she lacked a reference to the primary source. Her option, then, was to cite the work in which she found the reference to the original research ("cit. in Braddy and Gray 565").

**46d**

*res*

Mitchell 12

being a nonperson," writes Mowsesian. Among other things, he
advocates changes in Social Security regulations that would
allow people to work at least part-time without jeopardizing
their benefits (qtd. in Kennedy 18, 19)

24      Chen notes that a decline in numbers of working-age people
is likely to result in encouragement to older people to stay in
or re-enter the work force. In fact, because of better health
and longer life, people may simply want to work longer.
Furthermore, he thinks voluntarily postponing retirement will
economically and emotionally benefit not only the elderly
themselves but also younger people, who will receive the fruits
of this increased national productivity (414).

25      Some businesses are already taking steps to hire older
workers, as the pool of teenagers, traditionally part-time
workers in such industries as fast-food and retail sales,
diminishes. It is increasingly common to see senior citizens
behind the counter at McDonalds, for example. U.S. Labor
Department statistics show that 45% of men and 60% of women over
65 now hold part-time jobs, as compared to 35% and 50% in 1968
("'Young Old'" 145). In addition, some companies are rehiring
retired workers or paying them as consultants. Some firms also
help find jobs in other companies for those retirees who want
them.

**46d**

*res*

26      Although most current pension systems do not now encourage
working after 65 (DeViney and O'Rand 536) and although opinion
polls show most workers still favor early retirement ("'Young
Old'" 145), financial incentives and social norms may change. Do
people really want as much as 25 adult years outside the
traditional child-rearing and wage-earning mainstream of life?

**Paragraph 27.** This paragraph introduces Toni's second emerging social role, that of the elderly as caregivers. She begins by establishing the extending role of grandparents within their own nuclear families. Later she will argue that this role should be extended beyond the nuclear family.

**Paragraph 28.** Notice that the in-text citation lists two page numbers with commas between them (419, 420) rather than a dash (419–20). The comma indicates that the preceding paraphrase and quotation from Hagestad condense separate ideas appearing on two different pages, not ideas that run from one page to the next.

**46d**

*res*

According to one study, between 25% and 75% of current employees
would like to work at least part-time after they reach
retirement age (cit. in Braddy and Gray 565). As shortages in
the labor supply drive up wages, and as longer life expectancy
adds years of potential productivity, many senior citizens may
decide that some amount of employment is more attractive than
full retirement.

27      The second arena for changing social roles involves the
family. As society ages, families potentially may encompass four
or more generations. Children will be more likely to have
grandparents living during their adulthood; parents and children
may have 50 years or more together. Hagestad outlines four
aspects of family life in which multi-generational relationships
provide benefits. First, longevity will mean more durable
relationships. This, in turn, results in an accumulation of
shared experience that promotes a common conception of reality
and ultimately strengthens family bonds. Third, multi-
generational family members "also help one another deal with a
changing historical context. . . . Older family members help the
young build bridges to the past, and the young can help make a
rapidly changing culture and technology more understandable" to
their elders (Hagestad 419). She cites as an example a middle-
aged woman who spent an evening learning home-canning from her
mother and grandmother and disco-skating from her grandson
(419).

**46d**

*res*

28      Fourth, shortened childrearing years relative to lengthened
"empty nest" years may be resulting in a new role for
grandparents. Traditionally in an important supporting role when
their children become parents, longer-living grandparents may

**Paragraphs 29 and 30.** Toni shifts from grandparents' roles in the nuclear family to a discussion of non-nuclear, even nonfamily situations to which caregiving roles can be extended. Her particular point is that the elderly can serve as surrogates in situations where nurturing parents, particularly women, are unavailable.

also assume a similar role for their adult grandchildren, but
without exerting the pressures parents sometimes bring to bear
on their grown children.

> The emerging picture of today's grandparent,
> especially in the later phases of grandparent-
> grandchild relations, is one of a family member who
> . . . has lived and learned to put things in
> perspective, whose most important function may just be
> being there for younger generations (Hagestad 419,
> 420).

Hagestad mentions particularly the stabilizing influence
grandparents can have for younger generations during times of
family stress such as divorce. Grandparents may provide either
financial, emotional, or childcare support--sometimes all three.

29    Unfortunately, contemporary realities can disrupt such
beneficial intergenerational family relationships. Divorce often
separates children from at least one set of grandparents.
Americans' high mobility puts hundreds or thousands of miles
between family members, sometimes making even holiday visits
difficult. Because the elderly often spend most of their time in
senior centers and housing projects, the older and younger
generations are routinely isolated from each other, notes Fran
Pratt, the director for the Center for Understanding Aging. And
on a national scale, the migration of younger people from
declining farming areas and ethnic urban neighborhoods to the
suburbs has further weakened contact between older people and
younger ones (Pratt 26).

30    Children not only may be without a grandparent's attention
and support but may in fact be without the attention and support

**46d**

*res*

**Paragraph 31.** This paragraph provides a supporting example of the caregiving role senior citizens can fulfill—and the burden that could be lifted from "the sandwich generation" of working females.

**Paragraphs 32 through 34.** Continuing with supporting examples, Toni is interested in showing that not only is the caregiving role possible, it is already succeeding in parts of the country, particularly in educational and day care settings.

**46d**

*res*

Mitchell 15

of parents, given the high incidence of divorce, abandonment, single working parents, and other disruptions of the traditional nuclear family. However, where traditional intergenerational structures and roles are absent, senior citizens can provide beneficial substitutes. In perhaps the most crucial role change that could affect the well-being of the nation's children as well as the older population, the elderly are beginning to assume educational and care-giving functions vacated by younger women.

31        One example of care giving that will absorb increasing amounts of national attention is care for the elderly themselves. Ever larger numbers of oldest old, the group most likely to be ill or infirm, will require care that traditionally has been supplied by middle-aged daughters and daughters-in-law. Now that many of these women are in the work force, they are coming to be known as "the sandwich generation"--caught between the demands of their children, their aging parents, and their jobs. The mass media have focused most of their attention on corporate and government programs to help sandwich-generation women ("Graying of America" 60-61), but the young old can also step in to help the oldest old with home care and management of finances, or simply to offer needed companionship ("'Young Old'" 148).

32        Another area where senior citizens can step into roles increasingly vacated by younger adults is child care and education. Already operating are children's programs that place the elderly in either paid or volunteer positions as teachers' aides and tutors, day care providers, counselors, trained "listeners," business advisors--a long list of positions that

46d

res

**Paragraph 35.** Toni uses this paragraph to initiate a return to the theme of ageism, the Pratt quotation providing support for the claim that placing the elderly in childcare roles also helps combat ageism stereotyping among the young. She is beginning to bundle the threads of her argument, in preparation for the paper's conclusion.

**46d**

*res*

enable the elderly to share their wisdom and life experiences.
Among the more well-known volunteer programs are Foster
Grandparents (18,000 people nationwide) and Retired Senior
Volunteers (384,000 people nationwide) (Elder 19).

33        School systems have been active in recruiting older
volunteers as classroom assistants, guest speakers, crafts
demonstrators, oral history resources, teachers of photography,
art, woodworking, music, or other skills. Boston, Ann Arbor, and
San Diego are just a few of the cities finding that
intergenerational programs fill important, unmet needs.

34        Other programs offer paying positions, most often at
minimum wage, sometimes funded by governmental human services
agencies. For example, in Milwaukee, Wisconsin, Juniors and
Elders Together (JET) provides preschool programs as well as
after-school programs for latchkey children. After six weeks of
training, JET senior aides are prepared to help children develop
social as well as academic skills. The JET project director
reports that the supply of senior aides falls far short of the
demand. The day care centers prefer the mature, trained senior
citizens over younger aides ("Brighter Afternoons" 21).

35        "Educators at all levels are beginning to recognize the
need to prepare young people for long life in an aging society,"
says Pratt, and intergenerational programs "have proved to be
the most powerful means of breaking down stereotypes based on
age" (20, 24). Pratt points out that when they share activities
with older people, school children learn by extension that
"millions of people who are so easily lumped together using
labels like 'the elderly,' 'the aged' or 'Senior Citizens' are
actually individuals of all kinds who cannot be prejudged simply

**46d**

*res*

**Paragraphs 36 and 37.** Here Toni restates and elaborates one of her key claims: that nonfamily social structures and relationships are as valid as traditional nuclear ones, that surrogates can fill very real needs. She argues that we should be willing to broaden the definition of what constitutes a family so that those who need care and those who are able to give care (of whatever kind) may be encompassed—thus making maximum use of the talents the elderly can contribute to society.

46d

*res*

on the basis of age" (20). These children are learning that people of all ages can share common ground and benefit from one another.

36    Through such encounters, the elderly also learn that society needs what they have to contribute. If traditional family structures that keep the generations in close contact are no longer possible, then functional artificial structures must replace them. A foster grandparent is no less real or effective than a biological grandparent in his or her ability to share experiences, supply information and insight, or provide encouragement, support, and affection.

37    When one takes the long view of the senior boom, one discovers that the social roles for the elderly may not need to be changed drastically. Particularly for the young old, or "able elderly," contributing to a society's productivity as a part-time wage earner or as a care giver who makes wage-earning more viable for someone else is simply an extension of roles performed earlier in life. The difference lies in how we define the institutions in which these roles are played out. The traditional nuclear family has been the focus of these adult role activities in American society, as recipient of both income and care giving. Gerontologist Robert Morris speaks of the "transformed family" (424)--a nontraditional family that may be headed by a single parent or composed of biologically unrelated members. Rather than denying the growing older population avenues by which they might contribute to society, we should be encouraging broader attitudes and definitions of social roles and institutions in which the elderly can contribute.

**46d**

*res*

**Paragraph 38.** The final paragraph of the paper draws upon themes previously developed, including the importance of removing the barriers artificially imposed on the elderly. Toni brings her paper to a close with a block quotation from Betty Friedan that pulls together several of the paper's threads: unnecessary barriers, productive versus unproductive members of society, the skills and wisdom the elderly have to offer. Against this summarizing quotation, Toni juxtaposes her final sentence—deliberately intended to be sharp, even stark, in contrast. She ends by personalizing the abstraction of the social roles she has hypothesized for America's elderly. She reminds her audience of the real people who might benefit from these redefined roles: a child, a parent—perhaps the reader's.

**46d**

*res*

38      For that to take place, Betty Friedan points out that

barriers have to be broken: specifically, barriers in

employment, age discrimination, people's expectations for

themselves and others, expectations about disease or dependence,

and environments that restrict rather than challenge human

potential (124). Friedan says:

> Unless we break through the age mystique, we endlessly
>
> ruminate on the problem, How can we deal with this mass
>
> of unproductive older people? . . . We have to
>
> reformulate our thinking. How do we develop and use our
>
> human potential in age as a part of a productive
>
> society? . . . We must do so not just out of compassion
>
> toward the aged: we must do so out of a need to involve
>
> their skills and their wisdom in enriching our whole
>
> society (124).

If that means redefining the family to include someone else's

child or someone else's parent, so be it.

**46d**

*res*

**Notes.** Two types of notes may be used along with MLA-style in-text citations: bibliographical notes and content notes. Such notes are placed either at the end of the research paper (as endnotes) or at the bottoms of pages (as footnotes). Notes are indicated in the text by raised (superscript) Arabic numerals.

**Note 1** in Toni's paper is a **bibliographical note** referring the reader to two sources not quoted but important as background reading. These journal articles are listed in the bibliography. No page numbers are cited in the note because Toni considered the whole of both articles to be important. Bibliographical notes can also be used to document multiple sources that would make reading awkward if they were all cited in the text.

**Note 2** is a **content note.** Some editors and instructors discourage the use of such notes. They believe that if the information is important it should be included in the text; otherwise it should not appear at all. Others think a content note is permissible if the information is relevant but too digressive or complex to place in the text itself. Check with your instructor or refer to the style manual for the field before you use content notes. Certainly avoid content notes that become essays lacking real relevance to the text.

**Bibliography.** The form presented on pages 556–57 follows MLA style and, therefore, is headed "Works Cited" rather than "Bibliography." Compare the entries listed in Toni's bibliography with those listed on pages 500–509 for a thorough explanation of MLA style as it pertains to various types of sources.

**46d**

*res*

Notes

[1]See, for example, Neugarten and Maddox, who discuss the
heterogeneity of the elderly.

[2]The term "oldest old" was coined by the National Institute
on Aging. There is some disagreement about exactly which ages
are included in each category, but the most frequently cited age
groups are as follows: young-old, 60–74; old or old-old, 75–84;
oldest-old, 85+ (Fowles 45). One authority defines young-old as
55–75 (Foner 4).

**46d**

*res*

Mitchell 20

## Works Cited

Arluke, Arnold, and Jack Levin. "Another Stereotype: Old Age as a Second Childhood." Aging 346 (1984): 7-11.

Braddy, Barri A., and Denis O. Gray. "Employment Services for Older Job Seekers: A Comparison of Two Client-Centered Approaches." Gerontologist 27 (1987): 565-68.

"Brighter Afternoons for Latchkey Children." Aging 358 (1989): 20-21.

Burke, James. The Day the Universe Changed. Boston: Little, 1985.

---. "Matter of Fact." The Day the Universe Changed. Writ. and dir. James Burke. PBS. WFYI, Indianapolis. 21 Sept. 1989.

Chen, Young-Ping. "Making Assets Out of Tomorrow's Elderly." Gerontologist 27 (1987): 410-16.

DeViney, Stanley, and Angela M. O'Rand. "Gender-Cohort Succession and Retirement Among Older Men and Women, 1951 to 1984." Sociological Quarterly 29 (1988): 535-40.

Dychtwald, Ken, and Joe Flower. Age Wave: The Challenges and Opportunities of an Aging America. Los Angeles: Tarcher, 1989.

Elder, Jean K. "The 'Youth 2000' Campaign." Aging 356 (1987): 17-19.

Foner, Nancy. Ages in Conflict: A Cross-Cultural Perspective on Inequality Between Old and Young. New York: Columbia UP, 1984.

Fowles, Donald G. "The Numbers Game." Aging 356 (1987): 44-45.

Friedan, Betty. "The Mystique of Age." Journal of Geriatric Psychiatry 20 (1987): 115-124.

"The Graying of America Spawns a New Crisis." Business Week 17 Aug. 1987: 60-61.

46d

res

Mitchell 21

Hagestad, Gunhild. "Able Elderly in the Family Context:

   Changes, Chances, and Challenges." Gerontologist 27 (1987):

   417–22.

Jagger, Mick, and Keith Richards. "Mother's Little Helper." The

   Rolling Stones: Through the Past Darkly (Big Hits Vol. 2)

   Compact disc. ABKCO Music and Records Inc., 80032 NCD3,

   1986.

Kennedy, William E. Rev. of Golden Goals, Rusted Realities, by

   Richard Mowsesian. Business Week 17 Aug. 1987: 18–19.

Maddox, George L. "Aging Differently." Gerontologist 27 (1987):

   557–64.

Morris, Robert. "Concluding Remarks: Consequences of the

   Demographic Revolution." Gerontologist 27 (1987): 423–24.

Neugarten, B. "Age Groups in American Society and the Rise of

   the Young Old." Annals of the American Academy of Political

   and Social Science 415 (1974): 187–98.

Palmore, Erdman B. "The Retired." Handbook on the Aged in the

   United States. Ed. Erdman B. Palmore. Westport: Greenwood,

   1984. 63–76.

Pratt, Fran. "Teaching Today's Kids—Tomorrow's Elders." Aging

   346 (1984): 19–26.

Rosenmayr, Leopold. "On Freedom and Aging: An Interpretation."

   Journal of Aging Studies 1 (1987): 299–316.

Soulsman, Gary. "'Oldest Old' Fast-Growing Population." Journal

   and Courier [Lafayette-West Lafayette, IN] 5 July 1989: B3.

U.S. Bureau of the Census. Statistical Abstract of the United

   States: 1989. Washington, GPO, 1989.

"You Can Look It Up." Time 22 May 1989: 36.

"The 'Young Old': Forget the Rocking Chairs." Business Week 25

   Sept. 1989: 145, 148.

**46d**

*res*

**46e**   Sample excerpt in APA style showing name-date documentation system

The following is a repetition of paragraphs 16 through 19 of Toni's paper and her bibliography prepared according to the *Publication Manual of the American Psychological Association* (APA). Although these pages cannot show you all the documentation requirements of this style, you will be able to see the general name-date format and compare it to name-page MLA style. Notice that only in the case of direct quotation are page numbers cited in the text.

APA style allows for two types of notes: content notes and copyright permission notes. Although these are called footnotes, they appear on a separate sheet after the Bibliography pages. As in MLA style, notes are indicated in the text by consecutively numbered superscript (raised) Arabic numerals. The excerpt below contains one note (the bibliographic note from the MLA version of the research paper would not be included in APA style).

---

Social Roles

5

kick off the woman's movement in the 1970s, believes that a    16

discriminatory "mystique of age" must also be overcome:

> We associate age with disease. Even gerontologists or
>
> geriatricians concentrate on the most negative aspects
>
> of aging . . . pathologies of aging, not the norms of
>
> aging at all. To limit discussion of aging to the
>
> negative norms . . . ignores the growth that so often
>
> accompanies aging" (Friedan, 1987, p. 123).

Ageism of this sort encourages the general public to    17

continue to view older people as homogeneous. One of the

constant themes in gerontological research is the heterogeneity

of the elderly. Neither the stereotype of the ill, infirm, and

isolated older person subsisting on a meager pension check nor

the stereotype of the wealthy retiree who spends the "golden

years" traveling the world or playing golf five mornings a week

---

**46e**

*res*

Social Roles

6

is accurate. Somewhere in between lies the majority of older Americans who live adequately in homes that are paid for, whose children call or visit them with some frequency, and who lead relatively satisfying lives. For example, fewer than 10% of Americans between the ages of 65 and 74 have health problems requiring daily assistance or institutional care (Hagestad, 1987). Only one in ten between the ages of 60 and 72 is poor (in contrast, one in five of America's children is growing up in poverty) ("'Young Old,'" 1989; Palmore, 1984).

Senior citizens are as different from one another as any other segment of the population. However, the problems of changing public attitudes are compounded by the fact that the mass media often lump senior citizens into a single huge age group. For example, _Time_ magazine categorizes United States Census Bureau population figures into age groups 0–17, 18–24, 25–44, 45–64, and 65+ ("You Can," 1989). The reasons for choosing these age classifications are no doubt many and varied, but the fact remains that when a mass-circulation magazine lumps everyone over 65 into one category it helps to perpetuate negative stereotypes about the elderly.

The injustice of this "lumping" becomes clear when one considers that there are as many years between 60 and 90 as there are between 20 and 50 (Soulsman, 1989). No one would think of lumping 20-year-olds with 50-year-olds. Why, then, lump the "young old" (those between 60 and 74) together with the "oldest old" (those 85 and above)? When we consider that in the next 20 years the number of people . . . .

18

19

**46e**

_res_

REFERENCES

Arluke, A., & Levin, J. (1984). Another stereotype: Old age as a
    second childhood. Aging, 346, 7-11.

Braddy, B. A., & Gray, D. O. (1987). Employment services for
    older job seekers: A comparison of two client-centered
    approaches. Gerontologist, 27, 565-568.

Brighter afternoons for latchkey children. Aging, 358, 20-21.

Burke, J. (1985). The day the universe changed. Boston: Little
    Brown.

Burke, J. (Writer and Director). (1989, September 21). Matter of
    fact. The day the universe changed. [Television broadcast].
    PBS. WFYI, Indianapolis.

Chen, Y. P. (1987). Making assets out of tomorrow's elderly.
    Gerontologist, 27, 410-416.

DeViney, S., & O'Rand, A. M. (1988). Gender-cohort succession
    and retirement among older men and women, 1951 to 1984.
    Sociological Quarterly, 29, 535-540.

Dychtwald, K., & Flower, J. (1989). Age wave: The challenges and
    opportunities of an aging America. Los Angeles: Tarcher.

Elder, J. K. (1987). The 'Youth 2000' campaign. Aging, 356,
    17-19.

Foner, N. (1984). Ages in conflict: A cross-cultural perspective
    on inequality between old and young. New York: Columbia
    University Press.

Friedan, B. (1987). The mystique of age. Journal of Geriatric
    Psychiatry, 20, 115-124.

**46e**

*res*

Social Roles

13

The graying of America spawns a new crisis. (1987, August 17).

Business Week, pp. 60–61.

Hagestad, G. (1987). Able elderly in the family context:

Changes, chances, and challenges. Gerontologist, 27,

417-422.

Jagger, M., & Richards, K. (Writers and Performers). (1986).

Mother's little helper. The Rolling Stones: Through the

past darkly (big hits vol. 2) (Compact Disc 80032 NCD3).

ABKCO Music and Records Inc.

Kennedy, W. E. (1987, August 17). [Review of Golden goals,

rusted realities by Mowsesian, R.]. Business Week, pp.

18–19.

Maddox, G. L. (1987). Aging differently. Gerontologist, 27,

557–64.

Morris, R. (1987). Concluding remarks: Consequences of the

demographic revolution. Gerontologist, 27, 423–424.

Neugarten, B. (1974). Age groups in American society and the

rise of the young old. Annals of the American Academy of

Political and Social Science, 415, 187-198.

Palmore, E. B. (1984). The retired. In E. B. Palmore (Ed.),

Handbook on the aged in the United States (pp. 63–76).

Westport: Greenwood.

Pratt, F. (1984). Teaching today's kids—tomorrow's elders.

Aging, 346, 19–26.

Rosenmayr, L. (1987). On freedom and aging: an interpretation.

Journal of Aging Studies, 1, 299–316.

Soulsman, G. (1989, July 5). 'Oldest old' fast-growing

population. Lafayette Journal and Courier, p. B3.

**46e**

*res*

U.S. Bureau of the Census. (1989). Statistical abstracts of the
    United States: 1989. Washington, D.C.: U.S. Government Printing
    Office.

You can look it up. (1989, May 22). Time, p. 36.

The 'young old': Forget the rocking chairs. (1989, September
    25). Business Week, pp. 145, 148.

**46e**

*res*

# SPECIAL
# WRITING
# APPLICATIONS

*The only way some people know you is through your writing. It can be your most frequent point of contact, or your only one, with people important to your career. . . . To those men and women, your writing is you. It reveals how your mind works.*

        KENNETH ROMAN AND JOEL RAPHAELSON, *Writing That Works*

# 47

## *SUMMARIES*

The ability to summarize effectively—to strip a paragraph, a chapter, or an oral presentation down to its central meaning without distorting the author's original thought and approach—is extremely useful. In college, writing a summary of reading or lectures can be a good way to study for a test. And, as Section **45** explained, writing summary notes is important in the preparation of research papers. Summary writing can also help you on the job; for example, you may be asked to review a great deal of information and prepare a **precis** (another term for summary) highlighting the main points. Or at a staff meeting your boss may want you to report on a conference you attended, so you will need to prepare summary notes from which to speak.

To summarize effectively you must read or listen carefully, discriminating between principal and subordinate ideas, noticing groupings and arrangements of thoughts, observing differences between crucial information and embellishing detail. Sharpening your reading and listening skills—and then applying the critical thinking skills of preparing a summary—can also help you improve your writing style and aid you in revising the wordiness that can creep into writing.

---

### WRITERS REVISING: SUMMARIES

Carl wanted to use Roger Rosenblatt's statement of why the U.S. cannot seem to handle street crime in a paper for his persuasive writing class. Here is the original paragraph from Rosenblatt's 1981 *Time* cover story. Applying the principles in this section, try your hand at summarizing it, and then compare your summary with Carl's.

> Anyone who claims it is impossible to get rid of the random violence of today's mean streets may be telling the truth, but is also missing the point. Street crime may be normal in the U. S., but it is not inevitable at such advanced levels, and the fact is that there are specific reasons for the nation's incapacity to keep its street crime down. Almost all these reasons can be traced to the American criminal justice system. It is not that there are no mechanisms in place to deal with American crime, merely that the existing ones are impractical, inefficient, anachronistic, uncooperative, and often lead to as much civic destruction as they are meant to curtail.

**Carl's Summary**

Carl knew he wanted to reduce the passage to its essence, so he would have to pinpoint the main idea and do so in his own words. Read Carl's first draft below and critique it for length, focus, and language; then revise your summary of the paragraph and compare your version with Carl's final draft which appears at the end of this section.

**First Draft**

D1       To claim it is not possible to rid the

D2    streets of crime is to miss the point. The reasons

D3    street crime is so high can be found in the

D4    American criminal justice system. It has

D5    mechanisms of dealing with crime, but they are

D6    impractical, inefficient, anarchronistic, and

D7    uncooperative, frequently leading to as many

D8    problems as they were organized to prevent.

This *Writers Revising* continues on page 568.

## 47a   The summary writing process

**1.** Study the passage you intend to summarize (or review your notes if you are summarizing an oral presentation) to discover the author's purpose and point of view. As you read, pick out the central ideas and notice how they are arranged. Be on the lookout for the author's own compact summaries, either at the beginning or end of a passage or at a point of transition.

**2.** Try to reduce the original material to about one-third its original length. You will often be able to reduce a whole paragraph, or even a group of paragraphs, to a single sentence. However, if the ideas in the material are complex, several sentences may be needed.

**3.** Use a simple or complex sentence rather than a compound sentence to summarize a paragraph—unless the original itself is poorly organized. A compound sentence implies that there are two or more equally dominant ideas in the paragraph. If you have written a compound summarizing sentence, check the original paragraph to make sure you haven't missed some (perhaps implied) subordinating relationship. In determining the author's intent, be alert to such writing techniques as parallel clauses and phrases, which indicate ideas of equal weight, and transitional words and phrases, which show relationships among ideas (see Sections **31** and **32**).

**47a**

*sum*

**4. Summarize ideas in the order in which they appear, but avoid following the wording too closely.** If you try to preserve the flavor of the original too precisely, your summary will be too long. Do pick up the author's key terms and phrases, for they are useful in binding the precis together. Discard any figures of speech, digressions, or discussions that are not essential to the "trunk and main branches" of the paragraph. However, be sure that you have faithfully reflected the author's point of view. Your task is to focus objectively on *someone else's* ideas, to produce an **informative abstract** of those ideas. (There may be times when you need to summarize someone else's ideas from your own viewpoint, including your evaluation of the ideas as part of the summary. This is called a **critical abstract.** You should be sure you know which type of abstract is appropriate to your summarizing task.)

**47b**   An illustration of summary writing

When you are through summarizing, you should have reduced the material to about one-third its original length. Study the following example:

> We very rarely consider, however, the process by which we gained our convictions. If we did so, we could hardly fail to see that there was usually little ground for our confidence in them. Here and there, in this department of knowledge or that, some one of us might make a fair claim to have taken some trouble to get correct ideas of, let us say, the situation in Russia, the sources of our food supply, the origin of the Constitution, the revision of the tariff, the policy of the Holy Roman Apostolic Church, modern business organization, trade unions, birth control, socialism, the League of Nations, the excess-profits tax, preparedness, advertising in its social bearings; but only a very exceptional person would be entitled to opinions on all of even these few matters. And yet most of us have opinions on all these, and on many other questions of equal importance, of which we may know even less. We feel compelled, as self-respecting persons, to take sides when they come up for discussion. We even surprise ourselves by our omniscience. Without taking thought we see in a flash that it is most righteous and expedient to discourage birth control by legislative enactment, or that one who decries intervention in Mexico is clearly wrong, or that big advertising is essential to big business and that big business is the pride of the land. As godlike beings why should we not rejoice in our omniscience?

JAMES HARVEY ROBINSON, *The Mind in the Making*

This paragraph hinges on the sentence beginning *And yet most of us have opinions on all these. . . .* This sentence suggests the pattern that your summarizing sentence should take. The central idea of the paragraph is that we do not ordinarily take pains in forming our convictions on important matters, but we nevertheless express our opinions as a matter of right and even take delight in our apparent omniscience. The main clause of your summarizing sentence will express the second part of the central idea, retaining the author's ironic approach.

> We are godlike beings who delight in our ability to form and express convictions on birth control, on intervention in Mexico, or on the role of big business, without a moment's thought.

To preserve the author's qualification in the first part of the paragraph, however, you must precede the main clause with a subordinate clause.

> Although the few pains we take to understand such things as the situation in Russia, the sources of our food supply, the origin of the Constitution, the revision of the tariff, the policy of the Holy Roman Apostolic Church, modern business organization, trade unions, birth control, socialism, the League of Nations, the excess-profits tax, preparedness, and advertising in its social bearings give us little reason to have confidence in our opinions on these matters, we are godlike beings who delight in our ability to form and express convictions on birth control, on intervention in Mexico or on the role of big business, without a moment's thought.

But this summary is almost half as long as the original. To reduce it further, replace the specific examples with general terms.

> Although the few pains we take to understand such things as social, political, economic, religious, and medical issues give us little reason to have confidence in our convictions on these matters, we are godlike beings who delight in our ability to form and express such convictions without a moment's thought.

This summary, less than one-third the length of the original, would be acceptable for most purposes, but occasionally even a shorter summary is desirable.

> Although we have little reason to trust our convictions on the important issues of life, we delight in forming and expressing such opinions without a moment's thought.

**47h**

*sum*

Clearly this last sentence does not express everything in Robinson's paragraph, but a summary is concerned only with the central thought; and the central thought is preserved in even the shortest statement above.

EXERCISE 47(1)
Write a two-sentence summary of the paragraph by Jacques Barzun on p. 429.

EXERCISE 47(2)
Write a one-sentence summary of the same paragraph.

EXERCISE 47(3)
Try to write a one-sentence summary of the following paragraph. Does the effort tell you anything about the weakness of the paragraph itself?

> The first point brought up by those who want to pay athletes is that college athletes are not serious students. So, since the majority of them don't want a college education and the rest will never use it, why shouldn't we pay them for playing football? This idea of the opposition's is full of fallacies and wishful thinking on their part. If a young man does not want a college education, then he should simply not go to college. He should not waste the precious time of the teachers, counselors, and even the students. For they all will be trying to give him an education that he supposedly does not want. A study done by the American Testing Program revealed the graduation rates within a five-year period ending in 1980 for male athletes to be ten percent higher than that for nonathletes. With this in focus it does seem that several young men do enter college with more hopes than going to the Sugar Bowl. Colleges are formed to educate, not to be breeding grounds for the pros.

EXERCISE 47(4)
Select a magazine article totaling one and a half to two pages of text. Write a summary no longer than one-third the original. Exchange your summary with a classmate. Then, without reading his or her article, write a one-paragraph summary (four or five sentences) of your classmate's precis. Finally, compare your one-paragraph summaries with the two original summaries and with the articles, discussing how successful you each have been in distilling the main points. The comparison and discussion should help both of you sharpen your summary-writing skills.

**47b**

*sum*

WRITERS REVISING: SUMMARIES
*(continued from page 564)*

**Carl's Final Draft**

R1      The failure to keep down crime on U.S.

R2    streets today may be traced almost entirely to the

| R3 | American criminal justice system whose mechanisms |
|---|---|
| R4 | to deal with crime are inefficient and outmoded. |

**Analysis**

The first draft summary is too long, almost half the length of the original, and it does not pinpoint the main idea of the paragraph. The main point is not that some people claim it is impossible to reduce crime or that the mechanisms sometimes create more havoc than they prevent, but that the failure to reduce street crime lies within the justice system. The terms *impractical* and *uncooperative* are implicit in *inefficient,* and so one word can be substituted for two. To reduce dependence on the original wording in the last sentence and cut the number of words in the summary, the final draft keeps the term *efficient* and substitutes *outmoded* for *anachronistic.*

# 48

## *ESSAY EXAMS*

What you have learned from this handbook about effective writing also applies to writing essays for exams. You will be expected to write standard English, to organize material intelligently, and to provide evidence and detail to support generalizations. When you have several days to write a paper or a take-home exam, you spend a good part of the time on planning—thinking about the subject, gathering material, making notes, organizing your ideas, outlining. You also have time to revise your first draft, correcting errors and clarifying your meaning. However, you cannot expect to do all this in the limited time you have for an in-class exam. You are writing under pressure. Therefore, it saves time to go into essay exams knowing how to proceed.

48

*exam*

### WRITERS REVISING: ESSAY EXAMS

When Melissa got her mid-term literature test back, her instructor pointed out that although Melissa had some good detail in one of her answers, she had not provided a cover statement tying her answer together. Read the test question and

Melissa's answer; then try your hand at providing a cover statement and compare it with Melissa's at the end of this section.

Question: Although Ivan Ilych is clearly the main character of ''The Death of Ivan Ilych,'' the minor characters play important roles. Briefly discuss the roles of Peter Ivanovich, Ivan's colleague, and Gerasim, Ivan's servant.

D 1  Peter Ivanovich is a colleague of Ivan's. They've
D 2  known each other since they were young boys
D 3  at school and have remained friends. Peter
D 4  is like Ivan in many ways; in fact, his
D 5  name "Ivanovich," means "son of Ivan." He is
D 6  arrogant and proud and enjoys having a
D 7  good time. He has a wife but doesn't
D 8  seem to be a family man. He doesn't
D 9  want to go to the funeral because it will
D10  cut into his time for playing bridge. He
D11  thinks of the promotions and transfers that
D12  will occur after Ivan dies, something Ivan
D13  himself would have done at Peter's funeral.
D14  Understanding Peter helps to understand Ivan.
D15  Gerasim was a servant of Ivan Ilych's home.
D16  After Ivan became ill it was Gerasim who
D17  took care of him. Ivan liked Gerasim. He
D18  was a happy, cheerful young man and
D19  did not mind caring for Ivan. The main
D20  thing Ivan liked about Gerasim was that
D21  he knew Ivan was dying and didn't
D22  pretend that he wasn't. He was sympathetic
D23  and understanding when no one else was.
D24  He helped make Ivan's miserable illness
D25  a little easier. Gerasim contrasts both
D26  Peter and Ivan. He also ties in with the

**48**
*exam*

D27 *theme of the story—that love and self-*
D28 *sacrifice make life more rewarding than*
D29 *riches and station in life.*

This *Writers Revising* continues on page 575.

## 48a  Preparing for exams

Most of your planning must be done before you go to the exam. How can you do that when you don't know what questions will be asked? You won't have free choice of subject; it will be chosen for you—or, at best, you will be allowed to choose from among two or three. You do know the *general subject* of the exam, however; it is the subject matter of the course or one part of the course. Your goal, then, is *to go to the exam having in mind a rough outline of the course seg ments and the contents of each.*

This process of outlining should begin with the first lecture or reading assignment and continue uninterrupted to the day of the exam. Take notes during lectures, underline key passages and make marginal notations in your textbooks, summarize your reading, look over your gathered material from time to time, evaluate it, and structure it. As you study, write a more formal outline based on an overview of the course material and any guidelines suggested by your instructor. Writing such an outline and studying it can help to fix the general subject in your mind.

Also think about your audience. What expectations will your instructor have concerning the subject matter and its treatment? What is the purpose of the exam? To answer these questions, think about the emphasis your instructor has placed on various topics during the term. As a general rule, the more time spent on a topic, the more important or complex the instructor judges it to be. Although you should review all relevant course material, you may be able to anticipate some exam questions if you think about topics and issues that have been stressed during the term. On the other hand, don't forget about readings that may have been assigned but not discussed. The exam may contain questions on this material, too. If you are not sure, by all means ask your instructor just how much material an exam will cover.

## 48b  Planning your answer

As soon as you see the specific questions in an exam, your subject is limited for you. Say, for example, your general subject was the history of Europe from 1815 to 1848—the segment of the course on

**48a**

*exam*

which you are being examined. Now you are given fifty minutes to answer four questions, the first of which is *What were the four major political and social developments in Europe during the period of 1815–1848?* Or, your general subject was three stories by Nathaniel Hawthorne and two by Herman Melville—the stories you discussed in class. Now you are given fifty minutes to answer two questions, the first of which is this: *Hawthorne has been called a "moralist-psychologist." Define the term and evaluate Hawthorne's effectiveness as moralist-psychologist by making specific reference to two of his tales.*

1. **Read the examination question carefully.** Never start writing without thinking about what you are being asked to do. One of the most common errors students make during examinations is to read too hastily, and they consequently misunderstand the question. Underlining key words in the exam question can be helpful. For example, if the question says "compare and contrast," you are being asked to discuss both similarities *and* differences, not just one or the other. As you read an exam question, identify the task you are being asked to perform. Are you being asked to summarize or to analyze? Are you being asked to comment on a given statement, possibly to disagree with it, or to prove it by providing supporting evidence? Instructors think carefully about their exam questions; the wording will frequently provide you with a structure for your answer. The Hawthorne question, for instance, assigns two distinct tasks: defining and evaluating. If a student's response provides a thorough and well-supported evaluation but does not define "moralist-psychologist" adequately, his or her exam score will suffer despite the sound evaluation.

The European history question directs you to furnish information (what *are* the four major developments?). You have only about ten minutes to answer the question, so you will not be able to go into great detail. Don't try to fill up half a blue book with everything you know about the subject. In the second question, you are asked to define and evaluate; you must make a critical judgment on the basis of specific evidence in Hawthorne's stories. You have approximately twenty-five minutes to organize and write the essay. Make it a rule to take a minute or two to think about the question, and answering it will be easier.

2. **Gather material and prepare a rough outline of the limited topic.** Typical notes for the history question could include the following:

1815—Congress of Vienna
1848—Revolutions
Nationalism—C. of V. denied rights to Poles, Belgians, Greeks, etc.
Conservative-Liberal Conflict—Cons. anti-reform. Lib. underground

Industrial Expansion—Intro. of machines. Transportation—railroads, steam transport, etc.

Class conflict—Lower class vs. middle class

An answer to the question on Hawthorne could develop from the following notes:

How human beings behave (psych.) and how they ought/ought not to (moral)

"Ambitious Guest"—psychological study of human ambitions—moralistic application

"Wakefield"—integration of psych. and moral—people tied to systems

After briefly studying such notes, you have only to number them in the order you wish to present them—and you have an outline.

As in all outlining and other such planning, you should not feel rigidly bound to the material and its structure. As you write, other ideas may come to you and a better structure may suggest itself. The student who answered the Hawthorne question, for example, decided to write on "Egotism" rather than "The Ambitious Guest." With time looking over your shoulder, though, you probably cannot afford to change your plans more than once.

## 48c   Writing a cover statement

On the basis of your notes you should now be able to begin your examination essay by writing a sentence or two that will serve as a thesis statement. The students who answered the above questions began as follows:

Although there were no major conflicts among the European powers between the Congress of Vienna (1814–1815) and the Revolutions of 1848, important developments were taking place that would affect the future history of Europe. Four of these developments were the rise of nationalism, the conflict between the conservatives and the liberals, the conflict between the lower and middle classes, and the expansion of industry.

Hawthorne is a moralist-psychologist who is concerned not only with *how* people behave but also with how they *ought* or *ought not to* behave. He is most successful when he integrates the two approaches, as in "Wakefield," and least successful when his moralizing gets away from him, as in "Egotism; or, The Bosom Serpent."

**48c**

*exam*

Often, of course, the pressure of the exam keeps you from composing such a thorough cover statement. If coming up with a good cover statement is delaying you, limit your opening to what is specifically required by the question (e.g., Define "moralist-psychologist"), then develop your ideas, and then conclude, after looking over what you have written, with the summary or evaluation (e.g., "Hawthorne, then, is most successful when. . . ."). In some examinations you will not be in a position to summarize or evaluate until you have addressed yourself to a number of particulars in the body of your answer.

Whether you begin your answer with a cover statement or not, resist the temptation, so powerful during the first few minutes of an exam, to start writing down everything you know. Don't begin to write until you have planned the direction you want your answer to take. And remember, your instructor is your audience: he or she knows the subject, so don't waste valuable time on writing background information or overexplaining facts.

## 48d   Writing your answer

Provide supporting evidence, reasoning, detail, or example. Nothing weakens a paper so much as vagueness, unsupported generalizations, and wordiness. Don't talk about "how beautiful Hawthorne's images are and what a pleasure it was to read such great stories," etc., etc. If necessary, go back to your jotted notes to add supporting material. If you have written a cover statement, look at it again and then jot down some hard evidence in the space at the top of the page.

Say you have been asked to discuss the proper use of the I.Q. score by a teacher. Your notes read: *Intelligence—capacity for learning. Must interpret carefully. Also child's personality. Score not permanent. Measures verbal ability.* You have formulated this cover statement: *"Intelligence" is a vague term used to describe an individual's capacity for learning. The teacher must remember that I.Q. scores tell only part of the story and that they are subject to change.* Now you must provide the evidence. Think about specific I.Q. tests, specific studies that support your generalizations. Such notes as the following will help you develop your essay:

> 10% of children significant change after 6 to 8 years
> High motivation often more important than high I.Q.
> Stanford-Binet—aptitude rather than intelligence
> Verbal ability—children from non-English-speaking families—culturally divergent—low verbal score
> N.Y. study—remedial courses, etc.—40% improvement in scores

You now have some raw material to work with, material you can organize and clearly relate to your cover statement. Even if you do not fully succeed in integrating your data into a perfectly coherent and unified essay, you will have demonstrated that you read the material and have some understanding of it. Padding, wordiness, and irrelevancies prove only that you can fill up pages.

Must you never toss in a few interesting tidbits not specifically called for by the question? There is nothing wrong with beginning a discussion of the significance of the Jefferson-Adams correspondence with: "In their 'sunset' correspondence of more than 150 letters, Jefferson and Adams exchanged their ideas on world issues, religion, and the nature and future of American democratic society, almost until the day they both died—July 4, 1826." Although only the middle third of this sentence is a direct response to the question, the other information is both relevant and interesting. Such details cannot *substitute* for your answer, but they can enhance it, just as they would an out-of-class essay.

## 48e Taking a last look at your answer

Try to leave time at the end of the exam to read and revise what you've written. Check to see if you have left out words or phrases. See if you can add an additional bit of detail or evidence; you can make insertions in the margins. Correct misspellings and awkward sentences. See if your cover statement can be improved. You are not expected to write a perfectly polished essay in an exam, but make your essay as readable as you can in the time you have left.

---

EXERCISE 48
With a classmate, think of a question that might appear on an essay exam in one of your classes. Create the question as if you were the instructor preparing the test. Separately, outline an answer to the question, supplying the specific information, evaluation, organization, and presentation the question requires. Then compare your outlines and jointly determine where they can be improved with more facts, better analysis, clearer relationships between ideas, sharper focus on the tasks the question specifies.

---

## WRITERS REVISING: ESSAY EXAMS
*(continued from page 569)*

After reading Section **48** on writing essay exams, Melissa reviewed her answer. She saw almost immediately that she did indeed have some good detail, and she had referred to the function of each of the characters. She had not, however, made their functions clear from the beginning.

**48e**

*exam*

**Revision**

R1  Two minor characters - Peter Ivanovich and Gerasium -
R2  play major roles in revealing character and theme in
R3  "The Death of Ivan Ilych."

> **Analysis**
>
> The cover statement is derived from referring to the question itself for the base of the cover statement—two minor characters play minor roles—and to the analysis itself for the function of the minor characters—to reveal character and theme.

# 49

## *BUSINESS CORRESPONDENCE*

Both academic and business writing require attention to the same elements of composition: purpose, audience, tone, style, grammar, mechanics, and organization. Because its fundamental goal is to help get things done, good business writing has efficiency as its hallmark. An efficient letter or memo makes its point quickly, often telling the reader what he or she most needs to know in the opening paragraph. Thus the reader learns the purpose of the correspondence without first having to wade through background information or detail. Besides being efficient, business correspondence should also be effective, the contents and tone persuasive. Readers appreciate correspondence that is straightforward but that also considers their needs and point of view. Tina Rodriguez's memos in Section **41** (pp. 379–80) show how one business writer revised her memo to make it more efficient in its delivery of information and more considerate of her readers' views and needs.

**49**

*bus*

> ### WRITERS REVISING: BUSINESS CORRESPONDENCE
>
> The university debate team has asked Dennis to write a letter which will be sent to all heads of high school speech departments in the county advertising a debate workshop to be held on campus. The team is especially eager to have good attendance to boost a closer relationship with the high schools from which the speech department will be recruiting students and to raise the level of competition at this year's high school debate rally to be held on campus. Read Dennis's first draft and suggest ways for him to improve his letter using the material in this section and that in Sections **40–41** on the writing process. Then compare your suggestions with Dennis's revision, which appears at the end of this section.

4262 July St.
Baton Rouge, LA 70812
February 14, 1990

Mrs. Susie Tanner
Speech Coordinator
Valley High School
243 Yellow St.
Baton Rouge, LA 70809

D 1    Dear Mrs. Tanner,

D 2        A special debate workshop will be offered for
D 3    you and your debate team to orient you with this
D 4    year's topic, Resolved: that the American judicial
D 5    system has overemphasized the freedom of the
D 6    press.

D 7        The six-hour workshop will familiarize your
D 8    debaters with the major court cases regarding
D 9    freedom of the press, major sources of evidence,
D10    including the books of Ben Bagdikian and major
D11    theoretical ideas which will enable your teams to
D12    prepare for this year's rally.

D13        The workshop will be held on Saturday, March
D14    16, 1990, at Coates Hall (Speech Lab) on the State
D15    University campus. We have enclosed a map for your
D16    convenience. We will begin at 9:00 a.m. and work
D17    until 12:00 p.m. You will have a one hour break
D18    for lunch. You might consider eating at the many
D19    fast-food establishments just a block away. The
D20    workshop will resume at 1:00 p.m. and go through
D21    4:00 p.m. During this time Judge Roy Hebert of the
D22    State Supreme Court will answer any questions re-
D23    lated to the judicial system. A formal schedule
D24    with more details is enclosed.

D25        Please call the Speech Department anytime be-
D26    tween 8:00 a.m. and 4:30 p.m. and tell them if you
D27    plan to attend. We need to know this information
D28    to prepare the proper amount of packets for the
D29    seminar. A nominal amount of $5.00 per debater is
D30    also needed when you arrive at the workshop. This
D31    money will be used to provide theory packets,
D32    notebook, glue sticks, and miscellaneous materials
D33    for each participant.

D34        Please consider attending the seminar seri-
D35    ously. It could benefit your teams immensely. It
D36    will give them the edge in the race for this
D37    year's championship. We look forward to seeing you
D38    at 9:00 a.m. on Saturday, March 16.

Sincerely,

*Dennis Jones*

Dennis Jones

**49**

*bus*

This *Writers Revising* continues on page 586.

## 49a   Memos and letters

The most common types of business correspondence are the memorandum (memo) and the letter. The principal difference between the two is really only a matter of audience: a memo is *internal* correspondence written to your fellow employees, a letter is *external* correspondence written to someone outside your company or organization. A memo reflects this difference in its **routing information.** Instead of the return and inside addresses, salutation, complimentary close, and signature found on a letter, a memo provides this "sender-receiver" information in abbreviated form at the upper left of its first page.

```
TO:        Robin Kaufman, Sales Representative
FROM:      Jo Carter, District Manager
DATE:      March 13, 199–            J. C.
SUBJECT:   April Sales Meeting Agenda

As we agreed on the phone yesterday, the April
sales meeting should be used to develop new
strategies for improving the sales of our summer
sportswear line. Historically, the most unprofitable
territory has been New England, even though
```

Remember that most memos, other than personal notes, will frequently have more than one reader. Accurate and complete headings are important for routing, reference, and filing.

You may have noticed that Jo Carter's memo contains signed initials next to the name. Although initialing a memo is not mandatory, to do so indicates that the sender has reread and approved the memo after it was typed.

In most other respects, memos differ little from letters. Both are single-spaced with double-spacing between paragraphs and sections.

## 49b   Visual cues in business correspondence

Use of such things as white space around and between items of information, headings, paragraphing, lists, underlining, enumeration, and so forth is more common in business text than in academic writing. As the sample letters at the end of this section illustrate, paragraphs tend to be shorter than in an essay or research paper. Information may be divided into list-like chunks, and series may include bullets or dashes (see the Rodriguez memos, pp. 379–80, and sample letter 1 in this section) or numbers that would probably be omitted in an essay.

One reason for these visual devices is that business correspondence often serves as a reference document, so readers must be able

49a

bus

to find items quickly and easily. By dividing the text more frequently into subtopics and by providing more visual cues, the writer also aids the reader's understanding. In effect, these visual devices divide the document into manageable chunks of information that are easier for the reader's mind to process than are long, unbroken passages.

## 49c Parts of a business letter

The standard business letter has six parts: (1) the heading, which includes the return address and date; (2) the inside address; (3) the salutation; (4) the body; (5) the complimentary close; (6) the signature. **Sample letter 1** illustrates a widely used format—**full block style**—with the six parts labeled.

Another common format is the **modified block style;** this style places the heading, date, complimentary close, and signature on the right side of the page (instead of flush left, as in the block style). The modified block format may use either indented or flush-left (not indented) paragraphs.

A more unusual business letter format is known as the **simplified format.** Simplified letters use full block style, with all parts flush at the left margin. The salutation and complimentary close are eliminated. A subject line appears where the salutation ordinarily would be placed. Like any block letter, this format is easy to type because no tab stops are needed. Furthermore, the subject is immediately clear, and the lack of salutation resolves problems when the name of the recipient is not known. The simplified format is useful for routine requests or when personalization is unimportant. **Sample letter 2** shows the simplified format.

## 49d Kinds of business letters

**1. Letters of application.** Though letters requesting information, registering complaints, and the like are probably those you will write most often, letters in which you apply for a job are almost certainly among the most important you will write. For application letters, keep the following advice in mind:

**a.** Application letters are usually of two kinds: solicited applications and prospecting applications. You will write a **solicited application** letter when "applications are being solicited"; that is, when you know an opening exists because you have heard about the vacancy or seen it advertised. In addition to specifying the opening for which you are applying, mention the source of your information—newspaper advertisement, placement office posting, referral, or whatever. When you have no direct knowledge that an opening currently exists but you want to be considered if a job is available, your application letter is a **prospecting application** (see **sample letter 1**). In this case you identify

**49c**

*bus*

the type of position you desire and briefly explain why you are interested in working for the company you are addressing.

**b.**   Describe those parts of your education or previous work experience that you believe prepare you for the job you want. If you are short on relevant paid work experience, it is certainly all right to discuss pertinent extracurricular activities or volunteer work that shows skills applicable to the job you are seeking. Be brief, direct, and factual, but at the same time present the information to your advantage; a job application letter and accompanying résumé should be persuasive documents as well as informative ones.

Don't just list your education and experience; *use* it to show the prospective employer how you are qualified to contribute to the company. Remember that the employer is the "buyer" and that you are "marketing" your credentials and skills. Although the tone of your letter should not be egotistical, neither should it be apologetic or pleading. There is no need to close with a line such as "I would be very grateful if you would be so gracious as to review my credentials. Thanking you in advance. . . ." Write a letter that is confident, courteous, and informative.

**c.**   Offer to provide references. In some cases (part-time or summer jobs, for instance), you may want to list your references in the letter or on an accompanying sheet. However, if the purpose of your letter is to secure a job interview, standard practice is to offer to provide references upon request. If the interviewer decides you are a good job candidate, he or she will then request a list of your references. In any case, you should have contacted the people you intend to use as references and obtained their permission before you write an application letter. Remember that references must come from people who actually know your work first hand; a potential employer consulting one of your references will want to know specific things about your ability and your reliability. People for whom you have worked successfully and instructors with whom you have taken relevant courses are often among your best references.

**d.**   An application letter is similar to a request letter: you are asking the reader to do something for you—consider you for a job interview. Consequently, you should use an action ending, as you would in a request letter. Since the next step in the employment process is usually an interview, you can end your letter by asking the reader to let you know when it would be convenient for you to come for an interview. A stronger, but permissible, ending is to say courteously that you will call to arrange an interview—as does the author of **sample letter 1.** Always tell the reader when, where, and how you can be reached if you are not available at your return address during the reader's business hours.

**e.**   For many part-time or temporary jobs, it is sufficient to describe your qualifications in the body of your letter. For full-time po-

**49d**

*bus*

sitions, it is wiser to present the information in clear, quickly readable form on a résumé. This enables you to use your application letter to highlight particularly important information, to supply explanations, and to provide additional persuasive details, while conveniently presenting the necessary facts in the resume. Be sure to mention your résumé in your letter. An accompanying résumé follows **sample letter 1.**

**2. Request letters.** Perhaps the most common kind of business letter is one asking someone to do something: give us information, send us something we have seen advertised, or correct a mistake. Such letters should be direct, businesslike, and courteous, even when you are registering a complaint.

Clarity is extremely important. The letter must directly state what you want the reader to do, and it must give the exact information the reader needs to meet your request. Notice that **sample letter 2** concludes by telling the reader what results the writer expects. Conclusions of this type are called **action endings.**

Request letters can be grouped into two categories: (1) those with reader benefit—fulfilling the writer's request benefits the reader in some way; and (2) those without reader benefit—the reader has little or nothing to gain from fulfilling the request. **Sample letter 2,** although registering a complaint, falls into the reader-benefit category because the company clearly gains when its customers are satisfied and loses when they are unhappy.

What about requests without reader benefit? In such cases you are really relying on your reader's goodwill. Besides writing clearly, you should take up as little of the reader's time as possible, make your request reasonable, and—if you can—encourage the reader's goodwill, perhaps by paying an honest compliment. Requests for information can frequently be handled in this way.

**3. Transmittal letters.** If you are relaying information, answering a question, or sending some item such as a report or a piece of equipment, you may need to write a letter to transmit whatever you are sending. This type of letter has two main purposes: to say "here is the information (or item)" and to generate goodwill. Transmittal letters usually cite the reason for the transmittal, supply any necessary information about whatever is being transmitted, and include courteous remarks that will encourage the reader to view the writer and his or her firm in a positive light.

**49e**

**bus**

## 49e   Employment résumés

Following sample letter 1 is a résumé showing a widely used, traditional format. This format works well when you want to emphasize your education and experience. Another format, which is effective if you want to emphasize capabilities, organizes information according to skills, placing education and a list of employers near the end of the résumé. This format may be advantageous for people whose work experience is varied or not continuous, or whose education or employment history is not obviously applicable to the job they are seeking.

**1. Whatever format you use for your résumé, list items in order of importance within each section.** It is not necessary to list work experience, for instance, in chronological order. Organize the jobs from most important to least important in terms of their relevance to the position you want.

**2. When writing your résumé, remember that work experience applies not only to jobs for which you were paid but also to volunteer work,** community service, leadership roles in campus organizations, and so forth. The only requirement is that the experience be relevant to the job for which you are applying. Similarly, you may want to list education that did not result in a degree. Consider for your résumé and your job application letter evening classes, courses taken at a community center, art museum, or computer store—in short, any training that is relevant to your employment goal.

**3. Use action verbs to describe your experience:** *organized, developed, assisted, sold, built* instead of *duties included.* Talk about what you accomplished, goals you met or exceeded, skills you learned or demonstrated. Indicate any measurable results: *increased sales by $2,000, saved the sorority $700 on heating bills, increased the student newspaper's circulation by 20 percent.* Like your application letter, your résumé should be persuasive.

**4. Do not include information that is not pertinent to the job.** For example, height and weight are not likely to be relevant. Laws forbidding job discrimination based on marital status, age, sex, race, or religion have also changed the personal data appearing on résumés; employers cannot require this type of information from job applicants. For instance, if you are seeking a sales position that involves extended periods on the road or a job with a company that routinely transfers its employees, you might list willingness to travel or relocate under personal data; but you need not indicate whether you are male or female, single or married.

**49e**
*bus*

## SAMPLE LETTER 1: BLOCK STYLE

Single space text; double-space between paragraphs and sections

```
848 Plains Street
Fort Pierre, South Dakota 57067        ⎤⊢ HEADING
April 4, 199-                          ⎦

Judith Stafford                        ⎤
Curator                                │
W. H. Over Western Museum              ⊢ INSIDE ADDRESS
University of South Dakota             │
Vermillion, South Dakota 57069         ⎦

Dear Ms. Stafford:                     ⎤⊢ SALUTATION
```

BODY

I believe I can offer practical ideas, backed by experience
in several museum settings, that will help the W. H. Over
Western Museum attract funding, increase community interest,
and improve quality--constant goals even in well-managed
facilities such as yours. I would like the opportunity to put
my ideas to work for your museum.

As the enclosed résumé shows, my experience includes the
following museum operations:

  * collecting and cataloging specimens

  * researching and mounting exhibits

  * designing special children's programs

  * working with academics, students, funding agencies,
    the media, and the general public

  * writing successful grant proposals

One of the most rewarding aspects of this experience has been
seeing community participation broaden and financial
resources increase as a result of my efforts. I have a talent
for explaining things, as illustrated by the college teaching
award I received and the children's natural history program I
developed. This skill will be an asset for the educational
activities that are an important part of museum work.

My college and summer museum experiences have been a very
good introduction to my chosen career. I would like to talk
with you about employment possibilities at the W. H. Over
Western Museum and will call your office next week to see
about scheduling an interview. I look forward to meeting you.

Sincerely,                        ⊐⊢ COMPLIMENTARY CLOSE

*John Lewkowski*                  ⊐⊢ SIGNATURE

John Lewkowski                    ⊐⊢ TYPED SIGNATURE

**49e**

*bus*

# RÉSUMÉ

Single-space text; double-space between sections

John Lewkowski
848 Plains Street
Fort Pierre, South Dakota  57067
605-555-9745

## Employment Objective

A museum staff position leading eventually to a curatorship.

## Education

B.A., Earlham College, Richmond, Indiana, 1991.
Major: history    Minor: biology    GPA: 3.85/4.00 = A

State University of New York, course in researching, cataloging, and mounting exhibits, summer 1989.

## Experience

Museum volunteer, Joseph Moore Museum, Earlham College, 1989-91. Assisted director of small natural history museum. Developed traveling museum program for four local elementary schools. Identified and cataloged specimens, maintained exhibits.

Summer intern, Tippecanoe County Historical Museum, Lafayette, Indiana, 1990. Wrote grant proposal resulting in $10,000 award for archeological dig at 18th-century French and Indian trading settlement. Worked with state and federal agencies, university faculty, museum staff.

Laboratory assistant, Earlham College, spring term, 1991. Supervised freshman biology lab, prepared lab materials and specimens, answered students' questions, and graded lab reports. Was selected Outstanding Teaching Assistant in the Natural Sciences.

## Honors and Activities

Earlham Alumni Scholarship, 1988-91
Outstanding Teaching Assistant, 1991
Earlham College tennis team, 1989-91

## Personal Data

Speak and write French.  Interests: travel and photography.

References Furnished Upon Request

**49e**

*bus*

584

# SAMPLE LETTER 2: SIMPLIFIED STYLE

Single-space text; double-space between sections.

444 West Wilson Street
Madison, Wisconsin 53715
July 9, 199–

Cambridge Camera Exchange, Inc.
7th Avenue and 13th Street
New York, N.Y. 10011

INCOMPLETE SHIPMENT

The Minolta SRT 201 camera outfit I ordered from you on June 21 arrived today and appears to be in good working order. However, your advertisement in The New York Times for Sunday, June 16, listed six items as being supplied with this outfit, including a film holder and a sun shade. Neither of these items was included in the package I have just received, nor do I find any notice that they will be sent at a later date.

I am sure that this omission is unintentional and that you will correct it. Will you please let me know when I may expect to receive the film holder and sun shade, as advertised. If there is a dealer in the immediate area, I would be happy to get them from him or her if you will authorize me to do so at your expense.

*Marilyn A. Conway*

Marilyn S. Conway

**49e**

*bus*

## WRITERS REVISING: BUSINESS
## CORRESPONDENCE *(continued from page 576)*

Dennis decided he would look carefully at his letter to see if it was an efficient piece of writing. He would want to make his point quickly and tell his reader what she needed to know early. He could then fill in with a discussion aimed at persuading her to take advantage of the debate team's offer. He also knew he needed a strong appeal in the conclusion if the team was going to get the attendance it hoped for.

4262 July St.
Baton Rouge, LA 70812
February 14, 1990

Mrs. Susan Tanner
Speech Coordinator
Valley High School
234 Yellow St.
Baton Rouge, LA 70809

Dear Mrs. Tanner:

The State University debate team is offering you and your de-bate team a special six-hour debate workshop on Saturday, March 16, from 9:00 a.m. to 4:00 p.m., in Coates Hall, Room 210. The workshop program will focus on this year's topic for the high school debate rally—Resolved: that the American ju-dicial system has overemphasized the freedom of the press.

The workshop will familiarize your debators with the major court cases regarding freedom of the press, major sources of evidence, including the books of Ben Bagdikian, and major theoretical ideas which will enable your teams to prepare for this year's rally. Our main speaker will be Judge Roy Hebert of the State Supreme Court, who will also answer any ques-tions your debators might have on this year's topic.

The morning session will begin at 9:00 and go until 12:00. After a lunch break, it will resume at 1:00 and end at 4:00. Several fast-food restaurants are nearby and will be able to accommodate students during their lunch break. A map and a detailed program of the day's activities are enclosed for your convenience.

Please call the Speech Department at 766-3833 any time be-tween 8:00 a.m. and 4:30 p.m. from Monday to Friday to make your reservations. Your call will enable us to make packets for all your students. A nominal fee of $5.00 per debator to cover the cost of theory packets, notebooks, glue sticks, and miscellaneous materials is due upon arrival.

We here at State hope you will bring your debators to the workshop. It could benefit your teams immensely, giving them

49e
*bus*

the edge in the race for this year's championship. We look
forward to seeing you at 9:00 on Saturday, March 16.

Sincerely,

*Dennis Jones*

Dennis Jones
State Debate Team

Enclosures

### Analysis

The revision gets to the point of the letter quickly in the
first paragraph. Next, it follows with crucial information about
the program content and the featured speaker to nail down the
importance of the workshop for Mrs. Tanner's students. Then
comes the schedule to answer questions about lunch, and then a
note about enclosures. A firm request for reservations and an
announcement about the cost of the workshop and what the cost
will cover precedes a friendly, positive appeal for action in the
concluding paragraph. Finally, the format and spelling are corrected, and an enclosure line is added.

# 50
# *WRITING ABOUT LITERATURE*

You may feel confident about tackling many subjects—nuclear
power, pollution, aerobics, and the like—but intimidated by writing
about literature. You'll say "This poem (or play, or short story) is in
the library! It's special! What can I have to say about it?" What you
should realize is that writing about the subject of literature—and the
subject matter of literature—is in most ways exactly like writing about
the subjects of political science or psychology or history. **Literary analysis** means examining a piece of literature, or part of it, to develop a
deeper understanding of it, and to convey that understanding to your
readers. To write a literary analysis, you use the writing process described in Sections **40** and **41**, just as you would in any other paper.

**50**
*lit*

## 50a  What should you know when writing about literature?

Here are some key points to remember when writing about literature.

**1.   The key element to literature is its language.** Every word in
a literary work is carefully chosen. If you pay attention to the words,

you can figure them out. Examining particular examples of language usually will give you plenty of material for your paper.

**2. Everyone has some questions about a particular work of literature,** and these often provide excellent paper topics. Start with the parts of the work that startled, confused, intrigued, or annoyed you. Why did the author decide to talk about these ideas in this form (poem, novel, play, etc.)? Your curiosity is a good guide. If you want to investigate some aspect of a work, it's quite possible that your readers will, too.

**3. You don't have to talk about a whole work in a short paper.** *Moby Dick* is a long book; you can't do it justice in seven pages. But you might be able to write about a small part of the novel, such as the motto ("O Time, Strength, Cash, and Patience!") which ends Chapter 32. If you take too big a bite of the work in a short paper, you'll end up just summarizing the plot or making vague, general statements, rather than conveying a specific message to your readers. As noted in Section **40i**, it's important to set boundaries for your subject and to focus on a few carefully selected ideas—perhaps just one aspect of a literary work.

**4. Your readers will be curious about your interpretation.** Make sure you provide plenty of evidence—especially quotes from the actual work—to show your readers why you interpret the work as you do. Refer to Section **46** for information on incorporating and documenting quotes in your paper and remember that all documentation in literary papers should follow the MLA guidelines presented in that section, unless your instructor tells you otherwise.

**5. No work of literature has only one "right" reading.** Literature by its nature has many interpretations. Some will be more valid than others, because you can provide more evidence for them. But don't worry about finding the "right" answer—instead, work on an interpretation you can support without stretching the evidence.

**50b** What are some approaches for researching and analyzing a piece of literature?

If you are asked to write a longer paper about literature, you may need to do some research in the library to gather information about your topic. The following list gives you an idea of the range of approaches you can take.

**1. How does this work relate to other works by the author?** Becoming familiar with an author's other works may help you better understand the one you are writing about. For instance, Henry James's literary criticism explains many of the techniques he tries to work out in his novels.

**2. How did the author write this work?** Often, an author's letters, diaries, journals, and drafts will show you the writing process at work in detail; you may find it comforting to see that even Shelley wrote "Da dum Da dum Da dum dum" to work out the rhythms of some of his poems!

**3. How does this work relate to its time?** Literary works are important records of the political, social, and artistic developments of their times. Adrienne Rich's poetry, for instance, can be examined in the context of the rise of feminism or the gay rights movement.

**4. How does this work relate to literary theory?** Authors as well as critics read and write literary theory. Often, works are not only artistic statements but attempts to apply new theoretical principles, and you can examine these efforts. *Lyrical Ballads* by Wordsworth and Coleridge for instance, is an attempt to write poetry in the language of the common people; a possible topic to write upon would be how successful it is.

**5. How does this work relate to the author's life?** While you must use caution in speculating about things you don't know about—and authors' private lives aren't always well documented—you can look at works in relation to the events in the authors' lives that they reflect. For instance, do the tortured wives in Virginia Woolf's novels have anything to do with her own marriage or mental illness?

**6. How does this work fit into a literary tradition?** Nearly every work of literature has some literary "ancestors." How is the work you're looking at like other works of its kind that came before? Does it present any advances or innovations in technique? For instance, does Henry Fielding's novel *Tom Jones* owe anything to Cervantes' *Don Quixote*, written some 150 years earlier?

**7. Does this work have a textual history worth discussing?** Not all works remain in the same form throughout their histories. Ezra Pound, for instance, imposed heavy editorial changes on T. S. Eliot's *The Wasteland,* and Dicken's publishers forced him to write a happy ending for the novel form of *Great Expectations* after his unhappy ending disappointed readers of the magazine version.

**8. How have other readers reacted?** Did the critics like the work? Was it banned? Did theoretical schools build up around it? Did the work make the author an overnight success or contribute to the author's downfall?

## 50c   What are some approaches for writing about literature?

You may want to examine one or more of the following approaches when writing a short paper on a work of literature.

**1. Speaker.** Who presents the work of literature? Is it a first person *I?* An all-knowing third person? What role does that speaker have in the work: a detached observer? A major or minor participant? A person looking back at events across time? What effects does the author achieve by having that particular voice recount the work? How would the work be different if another voice told it?

**2.   Character.** How do we learn about the people in the work? Do characters tell us about themselves and their motives? Do their actions give us indications of their natures? Do other characters, or narrators, or other devices let us know what these people are up to? Do they sound and act like "real" people or like stereotypes?

**3.   Form.** What genre is the work in—poetry, fiction, or drama? Does the choice of this form give the writer particular advantages or handicaps that another form wouldn't? Is this work typical of the form, or does it challenge the conventions you associate with the form?

**4.   Setting.** Where and when does the work take place? What is important about the setting? Do the time and location have an effect on the people and actions in the work?

**5.   Pace and structure.** What kind of rhythm or pace does the work have? When do actions speed up and slow down? Are there discernible parts to the work? What parts get the author's most and least attention? Why?

The answers to one or two of these questions, worked out in detail, will usually provide you with enough material for a short literary paper.

## 50d   What special considerations apply to writing about literature?

**1. Develop a clear thesis statement.** Like the other papers you write, the literary paper must have a clear thesis statement—and the more precisely you construct that thesis statement, the more coherently you can organize the paper (see Section **40**). A weak thesis statement might be "Rain is an important element in Hemingway's *A Farewell to Arms.*" This statement doesn't tell readers *why* rain is important. A better thesis statement would be "Hemingway uses rain not only to signal death in *A Farewell to Arms* but to remind readers that death comes as naturally and as inexorably as rainfall in our existence." This statement tells your readers why you think rain is important in the novel, and it helps them make sense out of the arguments you'll produce to support your thesis statement.

**2. Analyze the work.** The most common impulse in writing about literature is to summarize the plot (*what* goes on in a work) rather than to analyze the technique (*how* the author conveys the message to readers). Unless your assignment specifically tells you to summarize a work, assume that your readers—especially your teacher—know what happened in the work, and put your energies into explaining the *hows* and *whys* of the work instead.

**3. Do not look for one "right" analysis.** Another pitfall in writing about literature is trying to find that one "right" solution—and feeling uncomfortable when you don't. If you can't find the evidence in the work to support the interpretation you want to support, find another focus; don't present generalizations without proof. And be proud that you have found a focus; don't apologize by writing "This may not be the right way to read *The Color Purple*, but I think that. . ." Such apologies make your readers lose all confidence in your interpretations.

**4. Become familiar with literary terminology.** Literary study has standard terminology, just like statistics or chemistry or sociology. Be sure to use the proper terms to describe the work. A dramatic monologue is not a play; a nonfiction essay is not a story; a metaphor is not a simile. You can find a complete description of literary terms in reference works such as C. Hugh Holman and William Harmon's *A Handbook to Literature*, 5th edition; B. Bernard Cohen's *Writing about Literature;* or Alex Preminger's *Princeton Encyclopedia of Poetry and Poetics.* Your reference librarian can help you locate these and similar books.

## SAMPLE LITERARY ESSAY

The assignment for the following short literary essay asked students to examine one element in a particular short story they had read. One student writer, Julie, selected James Joyce's story "Araby" and chose to examine how the descriptive imagery helped convey Joyce's message to the readers. The first paragraph identifies the story, the author, and the writer's thesis clearly; the rest of the brief essay supports the thesis with specific examples from the text. There are no citations of secondary sources, because the assignment allowed Julie to use her own instincts and observations as research. The page references for in-text citations of the short story appear in parentheses, following MLA style (see Section **46**). To help you see how Julie structured her analysis, we've underlined her thesis statement and the evidence which supports it.

**50d**

*lit*

The End of the Innocent

Perhaps nothing is certain but death and taxes, but in James Joyce's story "Araby" another distressing predicament is examined——the loss of a child's innocence. In a harrowing manner, Joyce relates the dawning of awareness in a young boy who has a crush on the sister of one of his playmates. Through his descriptive imagery concerning the boy's environment, his infatuation with Mangan's sister, and his subsequent awakening, Joyce makes the theme of "Araby" painfully realistic to his readers.

The boy lives in an extremely dreary setting, one which forces him to seek some form of escape. The setting is established largely through images of darkness, decay, and imprisonment. The boy lives on a "blind" street, and plays near "sombre houses," "dark muddy lanes," "dark dripping gardens," and "dark odorous stables" (348). His house is cluttered with outdated newspapers and faded books, and has a shabby garden with "a few straggling bushes" (348). The air in the house is "musty from having been long enclosed" (348), and his only escape, the school, is described as a prison. These negative characteristics have symbolic as well as literal meanings; his world is morally, spiritually, and intellectually blind, and unable to encourage growth of any sort.

The boy's escape from this world comes when he discovers Mangan's sister. Here, Joyce uses descriptive imagery to show the boy's idealistic point of view. The boy perceives Mangan's sister as a beautiful angel who piously foregoes a visit to the exciting Araby bazaar to attend a religious retreat at her convent school. Like a saint, she becomes the object of his

50d
*lit*

"strange prayers and praises" (349). He idealistically imagines himself a knight of the Holy Grail, out to serve this perfect lady, with his love "a chalice . . . [he bears] through a throng of foes" (349). He determines to find an offering worthy of this angel/saint at the exotic Araby bazaar. The religious images Joyce employs show us how innocent and idealistic the boy is, and thereby set him up for the harrowing disillusionment the bazaar will provide.

The trip to Araby--the one the boy hoped would be the most gratifying of his life--ends his innocence. The darkness, emptiness, and triviality of the bazaar represent the cold realities of the life the boy cannot escape. The greater portion of the hall where the bazaar is held is in a darkness, and "a silence like that which pervades a church after a service" (350) engulfs it. Most of the booths are closed; only a handful of people attend those which are still open. The only noticeable activity is that of two men counting money. As the boy examines the few "treasures" Araby still contains, he overhears a flirtatious conversation:

> "O, I never said such a thing!"
> "O, but you did!"
> "O, but I didn't!"
> "Didn't she say that?"
> "Yes, I heard her."
> "O, there's a . . . fib!" (350)

And in a flash--what Joyce later called an epiphany--the boy realizes that his notions of life, love, and escape, are false. Life is not an exotic, faraway bazaar or a holy church, but a dark, deserted hall containing only moneychangers. Love is not a chivalrous, holy experience, but trivial, lustful infatuation- a

**50d**

*lit*

fib. As he stands in complete darkness, the boy sees himself as a "creature driven and derided by vanity; and [his] eyes [burn] with anguish and anger" (351). And there is no escape; he cannot pretend that he "never said such a thing" or felt such dreams. The innocent is innocent no more.

On a superficial level, "Araby" is a very subdued story; the initiation of the boy into manhood employs little action and few characters—most of them nameless. But Joyce more than compensates for this lack of action with abundant descriptive imagery, which readers must consider carefully if they are to comprehend the full story. Without such consideration, the story appears as insignificant as the conversation the boy overhears at the bazaar.

**50d**

*lit*

# GLOSSARIES

*glos*

*What grammarians say should be has perhaps less influence on what shall be than even the more modest of them realize; usage evolves itself little disturbed by their likes and dislikes. And yet the temptation to show how better use might have been made of the material to hand is sometimes irresistible.*

H. W. FOWLER, *Modern English Usage*

# 51

## GLOSSARY OF GRAMMATICAL TERMS

This glossary provides brief definitions of the grammatical terms used in this text. Cross-references refer you to pertinent sections of the text. For further text references to terms defined, as well as for references to terms not included in the glossary, consult the index.

**absolute phrase**   Absolute constructions modify the sentence in which they stand. They differ from other modifying word groups in that (1) they lack any connective joining them to the rest of the sentence and (2) they do not modify any individual word or word group in the sentence. Compare *Seeing the bears, we stopped the car,* in which the participial phrase modifies *we,* with *The rain having stopped, we saw the bears,* in which the construction *the rain having stopped* is an absolute modifying the rest of the sentence. The basic pattern of the absolute phrase is a noun or pronoun and a participle. (*She having arrived,* we all went to the movies. We left about ten o'clock, *the movie being over.*) Such phrases are sometimes called **nominative absolutes,** since pronouns in them require the nominative case.

Absolute phrases may also be prepositional phrases (*In fact,* we had expected rain) or verbal phrases (It often rains in April, *to tell the truth. Generally speaking,* July is hot.)

For the punctuation of absolute phrases see **20e.**

**abstract noun**   See *noun.*

**acronym**   An abbreviation formed from the initial letters of words, pronounced as a single word. (*MADD* means *M*others *A*gainst *D*runk *D*riving.) See **17a.**

**active voice**   See *voice.*

**adjectival**   Any word or word group used as an adjective to modify a noun. Some modern grammars limit the meaning of **adjective** strictly to words that can be compared by adding *-er* and *-est* (*new, newer, newest; high, higher, highest*). Such grammars apply the term **adjectival** to other words that ordinarily modify nouns, and to any other word or word group when it is used as an adjective. In such grammars the italicized words below may be called **adjectivals.**

| | |
|---|---|
| LIMITING ADJECTIVES | *my* suit, *a* picture, *one* day |
| NOUNS MODIFYING NOUNS | *school* building, *home* plate, *government* policy |
| PHRASES MODIFYING NOUNS | man *of the hour* |
| CLAUSES MODIFYING NOUNS | girl *whom I know* |

**adjective**   A word used to describe or limit the meaning of a noun or its equivalent. According to their position, adjectives may be (1) **attributive,** i.e., placed next to their nouns (*vivid* example; *a* boy, *strong* and *vigorous*), or (2) **predicative,** i.e., placed in the predicate after a linking verb (She was *vigorous*).

According to their meaning, adjectives may be (1) **descriptive,** naming some quality (*white* house, *small* child, *leaking* faucet); (2) **proper,** derived from proper nouns (*Roman* fountain, *French* custom); or (3) **limiting.** Limiting adjectives may indicate possession (*my, his*), may point out (*this, former*), may number (*three, second*), or may be articles (*a, the*).
See **1b(1)** and Section **3.**

**adjectival clause**    A subordinate, or dependent, clause used as an adjective.

> The man *who lives here* is a biologist. [The adjective clause modifies the noun *man.*]

> Dogs *that chase cars* seldom grow old. [The adjective clause modifies the noun *dogs.*]

> See also **1d.**

**adjectival phrase**    See *phrase.*

**adverb**    A word used to describe or limit the meaning of a verb, an adjective, another adverb, or a whole sentence.

According to function, adverbs may (1) modify single words (went *quickly, quite* shy, *nearly* all men); (2) modify whole sentences (*Maybe* he will go); (3) ask questions (*When* did he go? *Where* is the book?); or (4) connect clauses and modify their meaning (see *conjunctive adverb*).

According to meaning, adverbs may indicate (1) manner (*secretly* envious); (2) time (*never* healthy); (3) place (*outside* the house); or (4) degree (*quite* easily angered).
See **1b(1)** and Section **3.**

**adverbial**    A term used to describe any word or word group used as an adverb. Common adverbials are nouns in certain constructions (She went *home*), phrases (She went *in a great hurry*), or clauses (She went *when she wanted to go*). Compare *adjectival.*

**adverbial clause**    A subordinate, or dependent, clause used as an adverb.

> *When you leave,* please close the door. [The adverb clause, indicating time, modifies the verb *close.*]

> The sheep grazed *where the grass was greenest.* [ The adverb clause, indicating place, modifies the verb *grazed.*]

> Adverb clauses also indicate manner, purpose, cause, result, condition, concession, and comparison.
See **1d.**

**adverbial phrase**    See *phrase.*

**adverbial conjunction**    See *conjunctive adverb.*

**adverbial objective**    Sometimes applied to nouns used as adverbials. (They slept *mornings.* He ran a *mile.*)

**agreement**    A correspondence or matching in the form of one word and that of another. Verbs agree with their subjects in number and person (in *She runs,* both *she* and *runs* are singular and third person). Pronouns agree

**51**

*terms*

with their antecedents in person, number, and gender (in *He wanted his way, he* and *his* are both third person singular, and masculine). Demonstrative adjectives match the nouns they modify in number *(this kind, these kinds)*. See Section **8.**

**antecedent**   A word or group of words to which a pronoun refers.

> She is a *woman who* seldom writes letters. [*Woman* is the antecedent of the pronoun *who.*]
>
> *Uncle Henry* came for a brief visit, but *he* stayed all winter. [*Uncle Henry* is the antecedent of the pronoun *he.*]

**appositive**   A word or phrase set beside a noun, a pronoun, or a group of words used as a noun, that identifies or explains it by renaming it.

> John, my *brother*
>
> his hobby, *playing handball*
>
> Albany, that is, *New York's state capital*
>
> modifiers, *words that describe or limit*

The appositives illustrated above are **nonrestrictive:** they explain the nouns they follow but are not necessary to identify them. When appositives restrict the meaning of the nouns they follow to a specific individual or object, they are **restrictive:** *my sister Sue* (that is, *Sue,* not *Carol* or *Lisa*); *Huxley the novelist* (not *Huxley the scientist*). See **20c(2).**

**article**   The words *a, an,* and *the* are articles. *A* and *an* are **indefinite** articles; *the* is a **definite** article. Articles are traditionally classed as limiting adjectives, but since they always signal that a noun will follow, some modern grammars call them **determiners.**

**auxiliary**   A verb form used with a main verb to form a verb phrase; sometimes called a **helping verb.** Auxiliaries are commonly divided into two groups. The first group is used to indicate tense and voice. This group includes *shall, will,* and the forms of *be, have,* and *do (shall* give, *will* give, *has* given, *had* given, *does* give, *is* giving, *was* given).

The second group, called **modal auxiliaries,** includes *can, could, may, might, must, ought, should,* and *would.* These are used to indicate ability, obligation, permission, possibility, etc., and they do not take inflectional endings such as *-s, -ed,* and *-ing.* See Section **4.**

**cardinal numbers**   Numbers such as *one, three, twenty,* used in counting. Compare *ordinal numbers.*

**case**   The inflectional form of pronouns or the possessive form of nouns to indicate their function in a group of words. Pronouns have three cases: (1) **nominative or subjective** *(we, she, they),* used for the subject of a verb, or a subjective complement; (2) the **possessive,** used as an adjective *(their dog, anybody's guess);* and (3) the **objective** *(us, her, them),* used for objects of verbs, verbals, and prepositions. Possessive pronouns may also stand alone (The car is *his*). Nouns have only two cases: (1) a **common** case *(woman, leopard)* and (2) a **possessive** case *(woman's, leopard's).* See Section **2.**

**clause**   A group of words containing a subject and a predicate. Clauses are of two kinds: main, or independent; and subordinate, or dependent.

**Main clauses** make independent assertions and can stand alone as sentences. **Subordinate clauses** depend on some other element within a sentence; they function as nouns, adjectives, or adverbs, and cannot stand alone.

MAIN    *The moon shone,* and *the dog barked.* [Two main clauses, either of which could be a sentence]

SUBORDINATE    *When the moon shone,* the dog barked. [Adverb clause]

    *That he would survive* is doubtful. [Noun clause]

See **1d.**

**collective noun**    A noun naming a collection or aggregate of individuals by a singular form *(assembly, army, jury).* Collective nouns are followed by a singular verb when the group is thought of as a unit and a plural verb when the component individuals are being referred to (the majority *decides;* the majority *were* college graduates). See **8a(3)** and **8b.**

**comma splice**    A sentence error in which two independent clauses are joined only by a comma without a coordinating conjunction. See Section **7.**

**common noun**    See *noun.*

**comparison**    Change in the form of adjectives and adverbs to show degree. English has three degrees: (1) **positive,** the form listed in dictionaries *(loud, bad, slowly);* (2) **comparative** *(louder, worse, more slowly);* and (3) **superlative** *(loudest, worst, most slowly).* See **3e.**

**complement**    In its broadest sense, a term for any word, excluding modifiers, that completes the meaning of a verb (direct and indirect objects), a subject (subject complements), or an object (object complements).

VERB COMPLEMENTS    Give *me* the *money.* [*Money* and *me* are direct and indirect objects, respectively.]

SUBJECT COMPLEMENTS    Helen is a *singer.* She is *excellent.* [The noun *singer* and the adjective *excellent* refer to the subject.]

OBJECT COMPLEMENTS    We elected Jane *secretary.* That made Bill *angry.* [*Secretary* and *angry* refer to the direct objects *Jane* and *Bill.*]

**complete predicate**    See *predicate.*

**complete subject**    See *subject.*

**complex sentence**    See *sentence.*

**compound**    Made up of more than one word but used as a unit, as in compound noun *(redhead, football),* compound adjective *(downcast, matter-of-fact),* or compound subject (Both *patience* and *practice* are necessary). See also *sentence.*

**compound-complex**    See *sentence.*

**compound sentence**    See *sentence.*

**compound subject**    See *subject.*

**concrete noun**    See *noun.*

**51**

*terms*

**conjugation**  A list of inflected forms for a verb, displaying the forms for first, second, and third person singular and plural for each tense, voice, and mood. A synopsis of the third person singular (*he, she, it,* and singular nouns) forms for a regular and an irregular verb is shown in the list that follows.

|  | *SIMPLE FORM* | *PROGRESSIVE FORM* |
|---|---|---|
| *Active Voice* | | |
| PRESENT | *he/she* asks/drives | *he/she* is asking/driving |
| PAST | *he/she* asked/drove | *he/she* was asking/driving |
| FUTURE | *he/she* will ask/drive | *he/she* will be asking/driving |
| PRESENT PERFECT | *he/she* has asked/driven | *he/she* has been asking/driving |
| PAST PERFECT | *he/she* had asked/driven | *he/she* had been asking/driving |
| FUTURE PERFECT | *he/she* will have asked/driven | *he/she* will have been asking/driving |
| *Passive Voice* | | |
| PRESENT | *he/she* is asked/driven | *he/she* is being asked/driven |
| PAST | *he/she* was asked/driven | *he/she* was being asked/driven |
| FUTURE | *he/she* will be asked/driven | *he/she* will be being asked/driven |
| PRESENT PERFECT | *he/she* has been asked/driven | *he/she* has been being asked/driven |
| PAST PERFECT | *he/she* had been asked/driven | *he/she* had been being asked/driven |
| FUTURE PERFECT | *he/she* will have been asked/driven | *he/she* will have been being asked/driven |

51

*terms*

Forms for first and second person singular and all plural forms may be described briefly as follows:

The present tense forms for other persons are *I/you/we/they* ask/drive.

The past and future tense forms for all persons are the same as those shown for the third person.

All perfect tense and passive voice forms that use *has* as an auxiliary in the third person use *have* in all other persons.

All perfect tense and passive voice forms that use *is/was* in the third person use *am/was* for the first person *(I)* and *were* in all other persons.

**conjunction**    A part of speech used to join and relate words, phrases, and clauses. Conjunctions may be either coordinating or subordinating.
**Coordinating conjunctions** connect words, phrases, and clauses of equal grammatical rank: *and, but, or, nor, for.*
**Subordinating conjunctions** join dependent clauses to main clauses: *after, although, as if, because, since, when.*
See **1b(2).**

**conjunctive adverb**    An adverb used to relate and connect main clauses in a sentence. Common conjunctive adverbs are *also, consequently, furthermore, hence, however, indeed, instead, likewise, moreover, nevertheless, otherwise, still, then, therefore, thus.* **Conjunctive adverbs,** unlike **coordinating** and **subordinating conjunctions,** are movable and can thus occupy different positions within the main clause in which they stand. See **21b.**

**connective**    A general term for any word or phrase that links words, phrases, clauses, or sentences. **Connectives** thus include conjunctions, prepositions, and conjunctive adverbs. See **1b(2).**

**construction**    A general term describing any related groups of words such as a phrase, a clause, or a sentence.

**coordinate**    Having equal rank, as two main clauses in a compound sentence. See Section **31a.**

**coordinating conjunction**    See *conjunction.*

**correlatives**    Coordinating conjunctions used in pairs to join sentence elements of equal rank. Common correlatives are *either . . . or; neither . . . nor; not only . . . but also; whether . . . or; both . . . and.* See **1b(2).**

**count noun**    Count nouns name things that can be counted individually. They have plural forms. (Where are the garden *tools?*) See *noun* and **1a.**

**dangling modifier**    A modifying word or phrase that has no grammatically logical word to modify in a sentence. (*While on vacation,*the neighbors fed our cat.) See Section **12.**

**declension**    See *inflection* and *case.*

**degree**    See *comparison.*

**demonstrative pronoun**    *This, that, these,* and *those* are called **demonstrative pronouns** or **demonstratives** when used as pointing words. (Someone must have turned off *that* percolator, because *this* coffee is cold.)

**dependent clause**    See *clause.*

**derivational suffix**    See *suffix.*

**determiner**    A word such as *a, an, the, his, our, your,* that indicates that one of the words following it is a noun.

**direct address**    A noun or pronoun used parenthetically to point out the person addressed, sometimes called **nominative of address** or **vocative.**

**51**

*terms*

(*George,* where are you going? I suppose, *gentlemen,* that you enjoyed the lecture.)

**direct and indirect quotation**    A direct quotation is an exact quotation of a speaker's or writer's words (sometimes called **direct discourse**). In **indirect discourse** the speaker's or writer's thought is summarized without direct quotation. See **25a.**

> DIRECT    He said, "I must leave on the eight o'clock shuttle."
>
> INDIRECT    He said that he had to leave on the eight o'clock shuttle.

**direct object**    See *object* and *complement.*

**double negative**    The use of two negative words within the same construction. In certain forms, two negatives are used in the same statement in English to give a particular emphasis to a positive idea. (He was *not* entirely *un*prejudiced). In most instances, the double negative is nonstandard. (He *didn't* do *no* work. We *didn't* see *no*body.) See **36b.**

**elliptical construction**    An omission of words necessary to the grammatical completeness of an expression but assumed in the context. The omitted words in elliptical expressions are understood *(He is older than I* [am]. *Our house is small, his* [house is] *large).*

**expletive**    The word *it* or *there* used to introduce a sentence in which the subject follows the verb. See **1a, 33c,** and **38a(3).**

> *It* is doubtful that he will arrive today. [The clause *that he will arrive today* is the subject of the verb *is.*]
> *There* are two ways of solving the problem. [The noun *ways* is the subject of *are.*]

**faulty predication**    A grammatical fault that results when a subject and its verb or a subject and its complement in a subject/linking verb/complement construction are mismatched in meaning. See Section **14a.**

**finite verb**    A verb form that makes an assertion about its subject. Verbals (infinitives, participles, gerunds) are not finite forms. All finite verbs can add -*s* in the third person singular of the present tense to show agreement with their subject. Nonfinite verb forms cannot make this inflectional change. See Section **4.**

**function word**    A term used to describe the words, such as articles, auxiliaries, conjunctions, and prepositions, that are more important for their part in the structure of the sentence than for their meaning. They indicate the function of other words in a sentence and the grammatical relations between those words. Compare *lexical word.*

**fused sentence (run-on)**    Two or more grammatically complete thoughts with no separating punctuation. See Section **7c.**

**51**
*terms*

**gender**    The classification of nouns and pronouns as masculine *(man, he),* feminine *(woman, she),* and neuter *(desk, it).* A few English nouns have special forms to indicate gender *(salesman, saleswoman; hero, heroine).*

**genitive case**    The possessive case. See Section **2.**

**gerund** A verbal that ends in *-ing* and is used as a noun. Gerunds may take complements, objects, and modifiers. See **1b(3).**

**helping verb** See *auxiliary.*

**idiom** An expression established by usage and peculiar to a particular language. Many idioms have unusual grammatical constructions and make little sense if taken literally. Examples of English idioms are *by and large, catch a cold, lay hold of, look up an old friend.* See **37e.**

**imperative** See *mood.*

**indefinite pronoun** A pronoun, such as *anybody, anyone, someone,* that does not refer to a specific person or thing.

**independent clause** See *clause.*

**independent element** An expression that has no grammatical relation to other parts of the sentence. See *absolute.*

**indicative** See *mood.*

**indirect object** See *object.*

**indirect quotation** See *direct and indirect quotation.*

**infinitive** A verbal usually consisting of *to* followed by the present form of the verb. With a few verbs *to* may be omitted (heard her *tell;* made it *work*). Infinitives can serve as nouns (*To swim* is to relax), as adjectives (I have nothing *to say*), or as adverbs (We were ready *to begin*). See **1b(3).**

**inflection** Variation in the form of words to indicate case *(he, him),* gender *(he, she, it),* number *(mouse, mice),* tense *(walk, walked),* etc. **Declension** is the inflection of nouns and pronouns; **conjugation** is the inflection of verbs; and **comparison** is the inflection of adjectives and adverbs.

**inflectional suffix** See *suffix.*

**intensifier** A term applied to such modifiers as *much, so, too,* and *very,* which merely add emphasis to the words they modify. Words such as *actually, mighty, pretty,* and *really* often occur as vague intensifiers in colloquial English.

**intensive pronoun** Any compound personal pronoun ending with *-self* used for emphasis. (I did it *myself.* The dean *himself* wrote the letter.)

**interjection** A word or group of words that is grammatically independent and used to show mild, strong, or sudden emotion. (*Ych.* I hate caterpillars. *Say!* Let's go to a movie.)

**intransitive verb** See *verb.*

**inversion** A reversal of normal word order. (*Dejected, he left the witness stand. The verdict he clearly foresaw.*)

**irregular verb** A verb that forms its past tense and past participle by a change in an internal vowel, or by some other individualized change, as opposed to the usual addition of *-d* or *-ed* to the basic form of so-called **regular verbs,** as in *walk, walked, walked (begin, began, begun; do, did, done; fall, fell, fallen).* See Section **1.**

**51**

*terms*

**kernel sentence** A term used in some contemporary grammars to describe one of a limited number of basic sentence patterns from which all grammatical structures can be derived. See **1a.**

**lexical word** Nouns, verbs, adjectives, and adverbs are sometimes termed lexical words, that is, words that carry most of the meaning in English, in contrast to *function words*, which indicate relationships among lexical words. Compare *function word.*

**linking verb** A verb that shows the relation between the subject of a sentence and a complement. *(He seems timid. The cake tastes sweet. She is my sister.)* The chief linking verbs are *be, become, appear, seem,* and the verbs pertaining to the senses *(look, smell, taste, sound, feel).* See Section **4.**

**main clause** See *clause.*

**mass noun** Mass nouns name things not usually counted individually. They do not have plural forms. (Look at the *snow* on my hat.) See *noun* and **1a.**

**misplaced modifier** See *modifier.*

**mixed construction** A grammatical fault that consists of joining as a sentence two or more parts that do not fit in grammar or meaning. See Section **14.**

**modal auxiliary** See *auxiliary.*

**modification** Describing or limiting the meaning of a word or group of words. Adjectives and adjective phrases or clauses modify nouns; adverbs and adverb phrases or clauses modify verbs, adjectives, or adverbs. See Section **3.**

**modifier** A general term given to any word or word group that is used to limit, qualify, or otherwise describe the meaning of another word or word group. Adjectives, adverbs, prepositional and verbal phrases, and subordinate clauses are the usual modifiers in English. See Section **3** for adjectives and adverbs and Section **1** for various word groups as modifiers. For a discussion of misplaced modifiers, see Section **11.**

**mood** The form of a verb used to show how the action is viewed by the speaker. English has three moods: (1) **indicative,** stating a fact or asking a question (The wheat *is* ripe. *Will* he *go?*); (2) **imperative,** expressing a command or a request (*Report* at once. Please *clear* your desk.); and (3) **subjunctive,** expressing doubt, wish, or condition contrary to fact (The grass looks as if it *were* dying. I wish he *were* more friendly.) See Section **5.**

**nominal** A word or word group used as a noun. (The *blue* seems more suitable. *Eating that pie* will not be easy.) Compare *adjectival.* See Section **38a(1).**

**nominative case** See *case.*

**nonfinite verb** Infinitives, participles, and gerunds are nonfinite verbs. They cannot stand alone as main verbs in sentences or clauses, do not indicate person or number, and cannot by themselves make an assertion about a subject. See Section **4(4).**

**nonrestrictive modifier**   A modifying phrase or clause that is not essential to pointing out or identifying the person or thing modified.

Smith, *who was watching the road,* saw the accident.

The latest breakthrough, *reported last week,* has everyone talking.

See Section **20c.**

**noun**   A word, like *man, horse, carrot, trip, theory,* or *capitalism,* that names a person, place, thing, quality, concept, or the like. Nouns usually form plurals by adding *-s,* and possessives by adding *'s,* and most frequently function as subjects and complements, although they also function in other ways. See **1a.**

Nouns are divided into various subclasses according to their meaning. The most common classes are the following:

| Class | Meaning | Examples |
|---|---|---|
| common | general classes | *tiger, house, idea* |
| proper | specific names | *Chicago, Burma, Lee* |
| abstract | ideas, qualities | *liberty, love, emotion* |
| concrete | able to be sensed | *apple, noise, perfume* |
| collective | groups | *herd, bunch, jury* |
| count | able to be counted | *chicken, slice, book* |
| mass | not ordinarily counted (not used with *a, an*) | *salt, gold, equality* |

**noun clause**   A subordinate clause used as a noun. (*What I saw* was humiliating. I shall accept *whatever he offers.*) See **1d.**

**number**   The form of a noun, pronoun, verb, or demonstrative adjective to indicate one (singular) or more than one (plural).

**object**   A general term for any word group or word that is affected by or receives action of a transitive verb or verbal, or of a preposition. A **direct object** receives the action of the verb. (I followed *him.* Keep *whatever you find.*) An **indirect object** indicates to or for whom or what something is done. (Give *me* the money.) The **object of a preposition** follows the preposition and is related to another part of the sentence by the preposition (We rode across the *beach*). See also *complement* and **1a** and **2c.**

**object complement**   See *complement.*

**objective case**   See *case.*

**ordinal numbers**   Numbers such as *first, third, twentieth, sixty-fifth,* used to indicate order. Compare *cardinal numbers.*

**parenthetical expression**   An inserted expression that interrupts the thought of a sentence. (His failure, *I suppose,* was his own fault. I shall arrive—*this will surprise you*—on Monday.)

**participial phrase**   See *participle* and *phrase.*

**participle**   A verbal used as an adjective. As an adjective, a participle can modify a noun or pronoun. The **present participle** ends in *-ing (running, seeing, trying).* The **past participle** ends in *-d, -ed, -t, -n, -en,* or changes

**51**

*terms*

the vowel *(walked, lost, seen, rung)*. Though a participle alone cannot make an assertion, it is derived from a verb and can take an object and be modified by an adverb *(swimming the river, completely beaten)*. When accompanied by a form of the verb *to be* to create a verb phrase, the **present participle** is used to indicate the progressive tense—action continuing at the time indicated. (The dog *was chasing* a frisbee.) When accompanied by a form of the verb *have* to create a verb phrase, the **past participle** is used to indicate the perfect tense—action completed before a given point in time. (The rain *has stopped*, and the sun *has come* out.) When combined with forms of the verb *to be*, the past participle indicates passive voice. (The sun *was covered* by the storm clouds.) See also Sections **1b** and **5.**

**parts of speech**   The classes into which words may be divided on the basis of meaning, form, and function. The traditional parts of speech are noun, pronoun, verb, adjective, adverb, preposition, conjunction, and interjection. See **1a** and **1b** and separate entries in this glossary.

**passive voice**   See *voice.*

**past participle**   See *participle.*

**person**   The form of a pronoun and verb used to indicate the speaker (first person—*I am*); the person spoken to (second person—*you are*); or the person spoken about (third person—*she is*).

**personal pronoun**   See *pronoun.*

**phrase**   A group of related words lacking both subject and predicate and used as a single part of speech (see Section **1c**). Phrases may be classified as follows:

| | |
|---|---|
| PREPOSITIONAL | We walked *across the street.* |
| PARTICIPIAL | The man *entering the room* is my father. |
| GERUND | *Washing windows* is tiresome work. |
| INFINITIVE | *To see the sunset* was a pleasure. |
| VERB | She *has been educated* in Europe. |

**plain form**   A term often used for the infinitive or dictionary form of a verb, as *run, stand, pounce.* See Section **4.**

**positive, positive degree**   See *comparison.*

**possessive**   See *case.*

**predicate**   The part of a sentence or clause that makes a statement about the subject. The *complete predicate* consists of the verb and its complements and modifiers. The *simple predicate* consists of only the verb and its auxiliaries. See **1a.**

**predicate adjective**   An adjective serving as a subject complement (We were *silent*). See *complement.*

**predicate noun**   A noun serving as a subject complement (He was a *hero*). See *complement.*

**prefix**   One or more syllables, such as *a-, mis-, sub-,* or *un-,* that can be added at the beginning of a word or root to change or modify its meaning:

**51**

*terms*

*a* + moral = amoral; *mis* + print = misprint; *sub* + standard = substandard; *un* + zipped = unzipped. See **35c.**

**preposition**  A word used to relate a noun or pronoun to some other word in the sentence. A preposition and its object form a **prepositional phrase.** (The sheep are *in* the meadow. He dodged *through* the traffic.) See **1c.**

**prepositional phrase**  See *phrase* and *preposition.*

**present participle**  See *participle.*

**principal clause**  A main or independent clause. See *clause.*

**principal parts**  The three forms of a verb from which the various tenses are derived; the **present infinitive** *(join, go),* the **past tense** *(joined, went),* and the **past participle** *(joined, gone).* See Section **4.**

**progressive**  The form of the verb used to describe an action occurring, but not completed, at the time referred to (I *am studying.* I *was studying.*). See Section **4.**

**pronoun**  A word used in place of a noun. The noun for which a pronoun stands is called its **antecedent.** (See **1a** and **8b.**) Pronouns are classified as follows:

| | |
|---|---|
| PERSONAL | *I, you, he, she, it,* etc. |
| RELATIVE | *who, which, that* |
| | I am the man *who* lives here. |
| | We saw a barn *that* was burning. |
| INTERROGATIVE | *who, which, what* |
| | *Who* are you? *Which* is your book? |
| DEMONSTRATIVE | *this, that, these, those* |
| INDEFINITE | *one, any, each, anyone, somebody, all,* etc. |
| RECIPROCAL | *each other, one another* |
| INTENSIVE | *myself, yourself, himself,* etc. |
| | I *myself* was afraid. You *yourself* must decide. |
| REFLEXIVE | *myself, yourself, himself,* etc. |
| | I burned *myself.* You are deceiving *yourself.* |

**proper adjective**  See *adjective.*

**proper noun**  See *noun.*

**reciprocal pronoun**  See *pronoun.*

**reflexive pronoun**  See *pronoun.*

**regular verb**  See *irregular verb.*

**relative clause**  A subordinate clause introduced by a relative pronoun. See *pronoun.*

**relative pronoun**  See *pronoun.*

**restrictive modifier**  A modifying phrase or clause that is essential to pointing out or identifying the person or thing modified. (People *who live*

**51**

*terms*

*in glass houses* shouldn't throw stones. The horse *that won the race* is a bay mare.) See **20c.**

**run-on** See *fused sentence.*

**sentence** A complete unit of thought containing a subject and a predicate. Sentences can be classified according to their form as **simple, compound, complex,** and **compound-complex.**

| | |
|---|---|
| SIMPLE | They rested. [One main clause] |
| COMPOUND | They rested and we worked. [Two main clauses] |
| COMPLEX | They rested while we worked. [One main clause, one subordinate clause] |
| COMPOUND-COMPLEX | They rested while we worked, but we could not finish. [Two main clauses, one containing a subordinate clause] |

**sentence fragment** A group of words capitalized and punctuated as a sentence but not containing both a subject and a finite verb. See Section **6.**

**simple predicate** See *predicate.*

**simple sentence** See *sentence.*

**simple subject** See *subject.*

**squinting modifier** A word or phrase that can modify either a preceding word or a following word, thus confusing the reader. See **11d.**

**subject** The person or thing about which the predicate of a sentence or clause makes an assertion or asks a question. The **simple subject** is the word or word group with which the verb of the sentence agrees. The **complete subject** is the simple subject together with all its modifiers. In *The donkey that Jones keeps in the back yard brays all the time, donkey* is the simple subject, and *the donkey that Jones keeps in the back yard* is the complete subject. See Section **1.**

**subject complement** See *complement.*

**subjective** See *case.*

**subjunctive mood** See *mood.*

**subordinate clause, subordination** See *clause.*

**subordinator** See *conjunction.*

**substantive** A word or group of words used as a noun. Substantives include pronouns, infinitives, gerunds, and noun clauses.

**substantive clause** A noun clause. See *clause.*

**suffix** An ending that modifies the meaning of the word to which it is attached. Suffixes may be **inflectional,** such as the *-s* added to nouns to form plurals (*rug, rugs*) or the *-ed* added to verbs to indicate past tense (*call, called*). Or they may be called **derivational,** such as *-ful, -less,* or *-ize* (*hope, hopeful; home, homeless; union, unionize*). Derivational suffixes often, though not always, change the part of speech to which they are added. See *inflection* and **35c.**

**51**
*terms*

**superlative**    See *comparison.*

**syntax**    The part of grammar that describes the structure and function of meaningful word groups such as phrases, clauses, and sentences, as opposed to **morphology,** the part of grammar that describes the formation, function, and classification of words.

**tag question**    A question that implies or confirms the expected answer, attached to the end of a statement. Tag questions typically consist of a pronoun and an auxiliary verb. The pronoun usually refers to the subject or implied subject of the sentence. (It's too early to go stand at the bus stop yet, *isn't it?* Let's order another cup of tea, *shall we?*)

**tense**    Verbs show tense—the time of their action or state—by means of changes in form. Verbs have three basic tenses: **present** (the bus *stops*), **past** (the bus *stopped*), and **future** (the bus *will stop*). Verbs also show time relationships to other actions or events by means of the following forms: **simple** (the bus *stops*), **perfect** (the bus *has stopped*), **progressive** (the bus *is stopping*), and **perfect progressive** (the bus *has been stopping*). See Section **5.**

**tone**    The attitude, stance, or point of view writers express about their subject matter and their audience. Tone is created by means of vocabulary choice, sentence length and structure, verb tense and mood, and so forth. See **40d, 41b, and 42g(2).**

**transitive verb**    See *verb.*

**verb**    A word, like *confide, raise, see,* which indicates action or asserts something. (See **1a.**) Verbs are inflected and combine with auxiliaries to form **verb phrases.** Verbs may be **transitive,** requiring an object (He *made* a report), or **intransitive,** not requiring an object (They *migrated*). Many can function both transitively and intransitively. (The wind *blew.* They *blew* the whistle.) **Linking verbs,** such as *be, become,* and *appear,* are followed by complements that refer to the subject. See Section **4.**

**verb complement**    See *complement.*

**verb phrase**    See *phrase.*

**verbal**    A word derived from a verb and able to take objects, complements, modifiers, and sometimes subjects but unable to stand as the main verb in a sentence. See *gerund, infinitive,* and *participle.* See also **1b(3)** and **1c.**

**verbal phrase**    A phrase containing an infinitive, participle, or gerund. For examples, see *phrase.*

**voice**    The form of the verb that shows whether the subject acts **(active voice)** or is acted upon **(passive voice).** Only transitive verbs can show voice. A transitive verb followed by an object is **active** (They *bought* flowers). In the **passive** the direct object is made into the subject (The flowers *were bought*). See **1a,** and Section **5.**

**word order**    The order of words in a sentence or smaller word group. Word order is one of the principal grammatical devices in English.

**51**

*terms*

# 52

## GLOSSARY OF USAGE

Choosing the right word—or not choosing the wrong one—is one of the most difficult problems for writers. This glossary is intended to help you with some of the most commonly troublesome words and phrases. However, it is necessarily brief; you should keep a good college dictionary at hand and consult it both for words not listed here and for additional information about words that are listed.

For information about labels used in dictionaries, see Section **35**. The following two labels are used in this glossary:

COLLOQUIAL  Commonly used in speech but inappropriate in all but the most informal writing

NONSTANDARD  Generally agreed not to be standard English

In addition to specifically labeled words, some words and phrases are included here because, although widely used, they are wordy or redundant (e.g., *but that, inside of, in the case of*); vague and overused (e.g., *contact, really*); or objected to by many readers (e.g., *center around, hopefully* meaning *it is hoped, -wise* as a suffix). A few word pairs often confused (e.g., *imply, infer*) are included, but Section **37c** has a more extensive list of such pairs.

**a, an**  *A* is used before words beginning with a consonant sound, even when the sound is spelled with a vowel (*a dog, a European, a unicorn, a habit*). *An* is used before words beginning with a vowel sound or a silent *h* (*an apple, an Indian, an hour, an uproar*).

**accept, except**  To *accept* is to receive. To *except* is to exclude. As a preposition *except* means "with the exclusion of." (*He accepted the list from the chairman. The list excepted George from the slate of candidates. He asked why it included all except George.*).

**actually**  Like *really*, frequently overworked as an intensifier.

**adverse, averse**  These adjectives both mean "hostile" or "opposed." *Adverse*, however, means something is opposed to the subject; *averse* means the subject is opposed to something (*Cats are averse to adverse weather such as rain*).

**advice, advise**  *Advice* is a noun; *advise* is a verb (*Don't ask for my advice unless you really want me to advise you*).

**affect, effect**  As verbs, to *affect* is to influence, to *effect* is to bring about. *Effect* is more commonly used as a noun meaning "result." (*Recent tax reforms affect everyone. They are intended to effect a fairer distribution of taxes. The effects have yet to be felt.*)

**aggravate, irritate**  Although the two words tend to be used interchangeably in informal conversation, the primary meaning of *aggravate* is "to make worse," whereas the primary meaning of *irritate* is "to exasperate, vex, or annoy." The distinction is useful and worth preserving. *Scratching your poison ivy rash will only aggravate the itching and further irritate your mother, who told you to stay on the path and out of the underbrush.*

**agree to, agree with**   To *agree to* is to consent; to *agree with* means "to concur" *(I agree with Gail's opinion, and will therefore agree to the contract).*

**ain't**   A contraction of *am not,* extended to *is not, are not, has not, have not.* Though often used in speech, it is strongly disapproved by the majority of speakers and writers.

**a lot, alot**   The correct spelling is *a lot;* often considered to be colloquial.

**all, all of**   Constructions with *all of* followed by a noun can frequently be made more concise by omitting the *of;* usually the *of* is retained before a pronoun or a proper noun; *all of Illinois,* but *all the money, all this confusion.*

**allude, refer**   To *allude to* is to refer to indirectly; to *refer to* is to direct attention to *(When he spoke of family difficulties, we knew he was alluding to his wife's illness even though he did not refer directly to that).*

**allusion, illusion**   An *allusion* is an indirect reference; an *illusion* is a false impression *(He was making an allusion to magicians when he spoke of people who were adept at creating illusions).*

**already, all ready**   *Already* is an adverb meaning "previously" *(We had already left)* or "even now" *(We are already late).* In the phrase *all ready, all* modifies *ready;* the phrase means "completely prepared" *(We were all ready by eight o'clock).*

**alright, all right**   *All right* remains the only established spelling. *Alright* is labeled nonstandard in both the *New World* and *Random House* dictionaries, although *Webster's* lists it without a usage label.

**also, likewise**   Not acceptable substitutes for *and (We packed our clothes, our food, and* [not *also* or *likewise*] *our books).*

**altogether, all together**   *Altogether* means "wholly, completely"; *all together* means "in a group," "everyone assembled" *(She was altogether pleased with her new piano, which she played when we were all together for our reunion).*

**alumnus, alumna**   An *alumnus* (plural *alumni*) is a male graduate. An *alumna* (plural *alumnae*) is a female graduate. *Alumni* is now usually used for groups including both men and women.

**among, between**   *Among* implies more than two persons or things; *between* implies only two. To express a reciprocal relationship, or the relationship of one thing to several other things, however, *between* is commonly used for more than two *(She divided the toys among the three children. Jerry could choose between pie and cake for dessert. An agreement was reached between the four companies. The surveyors drove a stake at a point between three trees.).*

**amount, number**   *Amount* refers to quantity of mass; *number* refers to countable objects *(Large numbers of guests require a great amount of food).*

**an**   See *a, an.*

52

*usage*

**and etc.**  *Etc.* (Latin *et cetera*) means "and so forth." The redundant *and etc.* means literally "and and so forth." See **16a(4).**

**and/or**  A legalism to which some readers object.

**and which, and who**  Use only when *which* or *who* is introducing a clause that coordinates with an earlier clause introduced by *which* or *who* (*John is a man who has opinions and who often expresses them*).

**ante-, anti-**  *Ante-* means "before," as in *antedate. Anti-* means "against," as in *anti-American.* The hyphen is used after *anti* before capital letters, and before *i,* as in *anti-intellectual.*

**any more, anymore**  Either spelling is correct. Meaning *now* or *nowadays,* the expression is used only in negative contexts (*He doesn't live here any more*). Used in affirmative contexts the expression is regional and should be avoided in writing (*What's the matter with you anymore?*).

**anyone, everyone, someone**  Not the same as *any one, every one, some one. Anyone* means "any person" (*He will talk to anyone who visits him*). *Any one* means "any single person or thing" (*He will talk to any one of his neighbors at a time, but not more than one at a time*).

**anyplace**  Colloquial for *any place.*

**anyway, any way, anyways**  *Anyway* means "nevertheless, no matter what else may be true" (*They're going to leave school anyway, no matter what we say*). Do not confuse it with *any way* (*I do not see any way to stop them*). *Anyways* is a colloquial form of *anyway.*

**apt**  See *liable.*

**around**  Colloquial as used in *stay around* meaning "stay nearby" and in *come around to see me.* As a synonym for the preposition *about, around* is informal and objected to by some in writing; write *about one hundred* rather than *around one hundred.*

**as**  In introducing adverbial clauses, *as* may mean either "when" or "because." Thus it is best avoided if there is any possibility of confusion. As a substitute for *that* or *whether* (*He didn't know as he could go*) or for *who* (*Those as want them can have them*), *as* is nonstandard. For confusion between *as* and *like,* see *like, as, as if.*

**as . . . as, so . . . as**  In negative comparisons, some authorities prefer *not so . . . as* to *not as . . . as,* but both are generally considered acceptable.

**as, like**  See *like, as.*

**as to**  A wordy substitute for *about* (*He questioned me about* [not *as to*] *my plans*). At the beginning of sentences, *as to* is standard for emphasizing (*As to writing, the more he worked, the less successful he was*).

**at**  Wordy in such constructions as *"Where are you eating at?"* and *"Where is he at now?"*

**athletics**  Plural in form, but often treated as singular in number. See **8a(10).**

**awful, awfully** In formal English *awful* means "inspiring awe" or "causing fear." Colloquially it is used to mean "very bad" or "unpleasant" *(an awful joke, an awful examination)*. *Awfully* is colloquial as an intensifier *(awfully hard, awfully pretty)*.

**awhile, a while** *Awhile* is an adverb and must modify a verb, an adjective, or another adverb. *A while* is an article with a noun. *(She said awhile ago that she would be gone for a while this afternoon)*.

**bad, badly** Often confused. *Bad* is an adjective and should be used only to modify nouns and as a predicate adjective after linking verbs *(She had a bad cold and felt bad* [not *badly*]*)*. *Badly* is an adverb *(She hurt her leg badly* [not *bad*]*)*. See **3c.**

**basically** An overworked intensifier meaning "actually" or "really."

**being that, being as (how)** Nonstandard substitutions for the appropriate subordinating conjunctions *as, because, since.*

**beside, besides** *Beside* is a preposition meaning "by the side of." *Besides* is an adverb or a preposition meaning "moreover" or "in addition to" *(He sat beside her. Besides, he had to wait for John.)*.

**better** See *had better.*

**between, among** See *among, between.*

**bring, take** *Bring* should be used only for movement from a farther to a nearer location. *Take* is used for any other movement *(You may take my raincoat, but don't forget to bring it back with the other things you have borrowed)*.

**bunch** Colloquial when used to mean a group of people or things *(a bunch of dishes, a bunch of money)*. Used in writing to refer only to things growing or fastened together *(a bunch of bananas, a bunch of celery)*.

**bursted, bust, busted** The principal parts of the verb are *burst, burst, burst. Bursted* is an old form of the past and past participle, which is no longer considered good usage. *Bust* and *busted* are nonstandard.

**but, hardly, scarcely** All are negative and should not be used with other negatives. *(He had only* [not *didn't have but*] *one hour. He had scarcely* [not *hadn't scarcely*] *finished. He could hardly* [not *couldn't hardly*] *see.)*

**but however, but yet** Redundant. Use *but, however,* or *yet* but not two together *(I was ill, but* [not *but yet*] *I attended)*.

**but that, but what** Wordy equivalents of *that* as a conjunction or relative pronoun *(I don't doubt that* [not *but that* or *but what*] *you are right)*.

**can, may** Informally *can* is used to indicate both ability *(I can drive a car)* and permission *(Can I use the car?)*. In formal English, *may* is reserved by some for permission *(May I use the car?)*. *May* is also used to indicate possibility *(I can go to the movies, but I may not)*.

**can't help but** This expression is redundant. Use either *I can't help (wondering if she saw us)* or the more formal expression *I cannot but help (wondering if she saw us)*.

**52**

*usage*

**case, in the case of**  Wordy and usually unnecessary. See Section **38.**

**censor, censure**  To *censor* means "to examine in order to delete or suppress objectionable material." *Censure* means "to reprimand or condemn."

**center around, center about**  Common expressions, but objected to by many as illogical. Prefer *center on (The debate centered on* [not *centered around* or *centered about] the rights of students).*

**character**  Wordy. *He had an illness of a serious character* means *He had a serious illness.*

**cite, site**  *Cite* is a verb meaning "to quote or mention"; *site* is a noun meaning "a particular place" *(I can cite the passage that refers to the site of the battle).*

**complected**  A colloquial or dialect equivalent of *complexioned* as in *light-complected.* Prefer *light-* or *dark-complexioned* in writing.

**complement, compliment**  *Complement* comes from "complete" and means "to add to"; to *compliment* means "to flatter" *(Let me compliment you on that tie. It certainly complements your suit.).*

**complete**  See *unique.*

**conscious, conscience**  *Conscious* is an adjective meaning "aware"; *conscience,* a noun, refers to one's sense of right and wrong. *(He was not conscious of his conscience).*

**consensus of opinion**  Redundant; omit *of opinion. Consensus* means "a general harmony of opinion."

**considerable**  Standard as an adjective *(considerable success, a considerable crowd).* Colloquial as a noun *(They lost considerable in the flood).* Nonstandard as an adverb *(They were considerable hurt in the accident).*

**contact**  Overused as a vague verb meaning "to meet, to talk with, to write," etc. Prefer a more specific word such as *interview, consult, write to, telephone.*

**continual, continuous**  *Continual* means "frequently repeated" *(He was distracted by continual telephone calls). Continuous* means "without interruption" *(We heard the continuous sound of the waves).*

**continue on**  Redundant; omit *on.*

**convince, persuade**  Widely used interchangeably, but many careful writers *convince* people that something is so, but *persuade* them to do something. The distinction seems worth preserving.

**could of**  Nonstandard for *could have.*

**couple**  Colloquial when used to mean "a few" or "several." When used before a plural noun, it is nonstandard unless followed by *of (We had a couple of* [not *couple] minutes).*

**credible, creditable, credulous**  Sometimes confused. *Credible* means "believable" *(Their story seemed credible to the jury). Creditable* means "praiseworthy" *(You gave a creditable violin recital). Credulous* means "inclined to believe on slight evidence" *(The credulous child really believed the moon was made of cheese).*

**criteria**    See *data.*

**data, criteria, phenomena**    Historically *data* is a plural form, but the singular *datum* is now rare. *Data* is often treated as singular, but careful writing still often treats it as plural *(These data* [not *this] are* [not *is] the most recent).* *Criteria* and *phenomena* are plurals of the same kind for the singular forms *criterion* and *phenomenon.*

**deal**    Colloquial in the sense of *bargain* or *transaction (the best deal in town);* of *secret arrangement (I made a deal with the gangsters);* and of *treatment (I had a rough deal from the dean).* Currently overworked as a slang term referring to any kind of arrangement or situation.

**definite, definitely**    Colloquial as vague intensifiers *(That suit is a definite bargain; it is definitely handsome).* Prefer a more specific word.

**differ from, differ with**    To *differ from* means "to be unlike." To *differ with* means "to disagree."

**different from, different than**    *From* is idiomatic when a preposition is required; *than* introduces a clause. See **37e.**

**discreet, discrete**    *Discreet* means "tactful" and comes from "discretion"; *discrete* means "separate and distinct" *(Her criticism of their behavior was discreet, but she observed that the police report showed four discrete instances of public disturbance).*

**disinterested, uninterested**    Now frequently used interchangeably to mean "having no interest." The distinction between the two, however, is real and valuable. *Uninterested* means "without interest"; *disinterested* means "impartial" *(Good judges are disinterested but not uninterested).*

**don't**    A contraction for *do not,* but not for *does not (She doesn't* [not *don't]* want a new dress).*

**doubt but what**    See *but that.*

**due to**    Some writers object to *due to* as a preposition meaning "because of" or "owing to" *(The fair was postponed because of* [or *owing to,* not *due to]* rain).* Acceptable when used as an adjective *(My failure was due to laziness).*

**due to the fact that**    Wordy for *because.*

**each and every**    Unnecessarily wordy.

**effect**    see *affect, effect*

**elicit, illicit**    *Elicit* is a verb meaning "to bring out or draw forth"; *illicit,* an adjective, means "illegal" *(The detective elicited a confession concerning an illicit drug sale).*

**elude, allude**    To *elude* means "to avoid or escape from"; to *allude* means "to refer to" *(I alluded to his elusive nature; he never seemed to be at home when we called).*

**emigrate, immigrate**    *Emigrate* means "to leave one's country or region"

**52**

**usage**

for the purpose of settling in another. *Immigrate* means "to settle in a foreign country," usually permanently. It may help you to remember the difference if you can recall that *emigrate* comes from a Latin word meaning "move *away from*," and *immigrate* comes from a Latin word meaning "to move *into*."

**eminent, imminent**    *Eminent* means "distinguished"; *imminent* means "impending or about to occur" *(The arrival of the eminent guest was imminent).*

**ensure, insure, assure**    *Ensure* and *insure* both mean "to make certain." However, *insure* usually carries the connotation of protection from financial loss, as in an *insurance policy (To ensure that we would always have transportation to work, we asked the agent to include replacement auto rental in the coverage when we insured our car.)* The primary meaning of *assure* is "to inform confidently," connoting a promise *(The agent assured us that this extra coverage would not be expensive.)*

**enthused, enthusiastic**    *Enthused* is a colloquial verb form used to mean "enthusiastic about." It should be avoided in formal writing.

**equally as good**    The *as* is unnecessary. *Equally good* is more precise.

**etc.**    See *and etc.* and **16a(4).**

**everyday, every day**    *Every day* is an adjective *(every)* modifying a noun *(day)* to explain which day. *Everyday* is an adjective meaning "ordinary, commonplace, usual" *(Every day that he wore his comfortable everyday shoes to the office someone was sure to comment that he looked "down at the heel.")*

**everyone, every one**    See *anyone.*

**everywheres**    Nonstandard for *everywhere.*

**except**    See *accept, except.*

**expect**    Colloquial when used to mean "suppose" or "believe" *(I suppose* [not *expect*] *I should do the dishes now).*

**explicit, implicit**    *Explicit* means "fully expressed"; *implicit* means "unexpressed," although capable of being understood. *(Although he never explicitly said no, his disapproval was implicit in his tone of voice).*

**farther, further**    Some writers perfer to use *farther* to refer to distance and restrict *further* to mean "in addition" *(It was two miles farther to go the way you wished, but I wanted no further trouble).* Dictionaries recognize the forms as interchangeable.

**fewer, less**    *Fewer* refers to numbers, *less* to amounts, degree, or value *(We sold fewer tickets than last year, but our expenses were less).*

**field**    Wordy and overworked. Say, for example, *in atomic energy* not *in the field of atomic energy.* See Section **38.**

**fine**    As an adjective to express approval *(a fine person) fine* is vague and overused. As an adverb meaning "well" *(works fine) fine* is colloquial.

**flunk**    Colloquial; a conversational substitute for *fail.*

**former, latter**    *Former* refers to the first-named of two; *latter* refers to

**52**

*usage*

the last-named of two. *First* and *last* are used to refer to one of a group of more than two.

**function**   As a noun meaning "event" or "occasion," *function* is appropriate only when the event is formal *(a presidential function)*. As a verb meaning "work," "operate," *function* is currently overused and jargonish *(I work* [not *function*] *best after I've had a cup of coffee)*.

**further**   See *farther, further.*

**get**   A standard verb, but used colloquially in many idioms inappropriate in most writing. *(Get wise to yourself. That whistling gets me. You can't get away with it.).*

**good and**   Colloquial as a synonym for *very (good and hot, good and angry).*

**good, well**   *Good* is colloquial as an adverb *(The motor runs well* [not *good*]). *You look good* means "You look attractive, well dressed," or the like. *You look well* means "You look healthy."

**graduate**   Either I *graduated from* college or I *was graduated from* college is acceptable, but I *graduated college* is nonstandard.

**had better, had best**   Standard idioms for *ought* and *should*, which are more formal *(You had better* [or *had best*] *plan carefully.)* More formally: *You ought to* [or *should*] *plan carefully. Better* alone *(You better plan carefully)* is colloquial.

**had ought, hadn't ought**   Nonstandard for *ought* and *ought not.*

**hang, hung**   The principal parts of the verb are *hang, hung, hung,* but when referring to death by hanging, formal English uses *hang, hanged, hanged (We hung the pictures. The prisoners hanged themselves.).*

**hardly**   See *but.*

**have, of**   See *of, have*

**he or she**   See **8b(1)** and **8c.**

**himself**   See *myself.*

**hisself**   Nonstandard for *himself.*

**hopefully**   *Hopefully* means "in a hopeful manner" *(They waited hopefully for money).* It is now widely used in the sense of "it is hoped" *(Hopefully, you can send me money).* Many readers object to this use.

**hung**   See *hang, hung.*

**idea**   Often used vaguely for *intention, plan, purpose,* and other more exact words. Prefer a more exact choice. *(My intention* [not *idea*] *is to become an engineer. The theme* [not *idea*] *of the movie is that justice is colorblind.).*

**ignorant, stupid**   The distinction is important. An *ignorant* child is one who has been taught very little; a *stupid* child is one who is unable to learn.

**illusion**   See *allusion, illusion.*

**immigrate**   See *emigrate, immigrate.*

**52**

*usage*

**implicit, explicit**   See *explicit, implicit.*

**imply, infer**   To *imply* means "to suggest without stating"; to *infer* means "to draw a conclusion." Speakers *imply;* listeners *infer (They implied that I was ungrateful; I inferred that they didn't like me).*

**in, into**   *In* indicates "inside, enclosed, within." *Into* is more exact when the meaning is "toward, from the outside in," although *in* is common in both meanings. *(I left the book in the room and went back into the room to get it.)*

**in back of, in behind, in between**   Wordy for *back of, behind, between.*

**incredible, incredulous**   Something that is *incredible* is "unbelievable"; someone who is *incredulous* is "unbelieving" *(I was incredulous—surely I could not have won such an incredible amount of money).*

**infer**   See *imply, infer.*

**ingenious, ingenuous**   *Ingenious* means "clever"; *ingenuous* means "naive" *(Inventors are usually ingenious, but some are too ingenuous to know when they have been cheated).*

**in regards to**   Nonstandard for *as regards* or *in regard to.*

**inside of, outside of**   The *of* is unnecessary *(He stayed inside* [not *inside of*] *the house).*

**in the case of, in the line of**   See *case.*

**irregardless**   Nonstandard for *regardless.*

**is when, is where, is because**   Faulty predications in such sentences as: *A first down is when the football is advanced ten yards in four plays or fewer. A garage is where . . . . The reason is because . . . .* See **14a.**

**its, it's**   The possessive pronoun has no apostrophe. *It's* is a contraction of *it is.*

**-ize**   The suffix *-ize* is one of several used to form verbs from nouns and adjectives *(hospitalize, criticize, sterilize).* Writers in government, business, and other institutions have often used it excessively and unnecessarily in such coinages as *finalize, concretize, permanize.* Such coinages are widely objected to; it is best to limit your use of *-ize* words to those that are well established, and resist the temptation to coin new ones. See Section **38a(1).**

**judicial, judicious**   A *judicial* decision is one reached by the court or a judge, but a *judicious* decision is one showing sound judgment.

**kind, sort**   These are frequently treated as plural in such constructions as *these kind of books* and *those sort of dogs.* Preferred usage in both speech and writing requires singular or plural throughout the construction, as in *this kind of book* or *these kinds of books.*

**kind of, sort of**   Colloquial when used to mean *somewhat, rather (I was rather* [not *kind of*] *pleased).*

**kind of a, sort of a**   Omit the *a.*

**later, latter**   *Later* refers to time, but *latter* refers to the second of two *(Of the twins, Meg was born first. Peg, the latter, was born three minutes later.).*

**52**

*usage*

**latter**   See *former, later.*

**lay, lie**   To *lay* means "to place, put down" *(Lay the book on the table).* To *lie* means "to recline" *(The dog lies on the floor).* See **4c.**

**learn, teach**   To *learn* means "to gain knowledge"; to *teach* means "to give knowledge" *(We learn from experience; experience teaches us much).*

**leave, let**   To *leave* is to depart; to *let* is to permit or allow *(I must leave now. Will you let me go?).*

**less**   See *fewer, less.*

**let**   See *leave, let.*

**liable, apt, likely**   Often used interchangeably. But careful writing reserves *liable* for "legally responsible," or "subject to," *likely* for "probably," and *apt* for "having an aptitude for" *(I am likely to drive carefully, for I am not an apt driver, and I know I am liable for any damages).*

**lie, lay**   See *lay, lie,* and see **4c.**

**like, as, as if**   *Like* is a preposition; *as* and *as if* are conjunctions. Though *like* is often used as a conjunction in speech, writing preserves the distinction *(He looks as if* [not *like*] *he were tired).* Note that *as if* is followed by the subjunctive *were.*

**likely**   See *liable.*

**loose, lose**   *Loose* means "to free." *Lose* means "to be deprived of." *(He will lose the dog if he looses him from his leash).*

**lots, lots of, a lot of**   Colloquial for *much, many,* or *a great deal (I had a great deal of* [not *lots of*] *money and bought many* [not *lots of* or *a lot of*] *cars).* Note spelling: *alot* is incorrect.

**mad**   Dictionaries recognize *mad* as a synonym for *angry,* or *very enthusiastic,* but some readers object to its use in these meanings.

**manner**   Often unnecessary in phrases like *in a precise manner* where a single adverb *(precisely)* or a "with" phrase *(with precision)* would do.

**may**   See *can, may.*

**may of**   Nonstandard for *may have.*

**maybe, may be**   *Maybe* means "perhaps"; *may be* is a verb form. Be careful to distinguish between the two.

**media**   A plural form (singular *medium*) requiring a plural verb *(The mass media are* [not *is*] *sometimes guilty of distorting the news).*

**might of**   Nonstandard for *might have.*

**moral, morale**   *Moral* is usually used as an adjective meaning "concerned with what is good or evil" or "acting according to the norms of good behavior." Occasionally, the word is used as a noun, as in "the moral of the story." *Morale* is always a noun and means "state of mind with respect to confidence, cheerfulness, and so forth" *(The scouts began their hike with high morale, whistling and singing as they walked).*

**52**

*usage*

**most**   Colloquial as a substitute for *almost* or *nearly*.

**must of**   Nonstandard for *must have*.

**myself, yourself, himself**   *Myself* is often used in speech as a substitute for *I* or *me* but is not standard in written English. Reserve *myself* for emphatic *(I myself will do the work)* or reflexive use *(I hurt myself)*. The same applies to the forms *yourself, himself, herself*, etc.

**nohow**   Nonstandard for *not at all, in no way*.

**none**   The indefinite pronoun *none* may take either a singular or a plural verb, depending on its context *(None of the gold was stolen; None of the men were absent)*. See **8a(2)**.

**nothing like, nowhere near**   Colloquial for *not nearly (I was not nearly* [not *nowhere near*] *as sick as you)*.

**nowheres**   Nonstandard for *nowhere*.

**number**   See *amount, number*.

**of, have**   In speech the auxiliary *have* in such combinations as *could have, might have*, etc., sounds very much like *of*, leading some people to write *could of, might of*, etc. All such combinations with *of* are nonstandard. In writing be careful to use *have*.

**off of, off from**   Wordy and colloquial *(The paper slid off* [not *off of*] *the table)*.

**OK, O.K., okay**   All are standard forms, but formal writing prefers a more exact word.

**on account of**   Wordy for *because of*. Regional for *because (She bought the car because* [not *on account of*] *she needed it)*.

**outside of**   Colloquial for *except (Nobody was there except* [not *outside of*] *Henry)*. See also *inside of*.

**over with**   Colloquial for *ended, finished, completed*.

**per**   Appropriate in business and technical writing *(per diem, per capita, feet per second, pounds per square inch)*. *As per your request* is inappropriate. In ordinary writing prefer *a* or *an (ninety cents a dozen, twice a day)*.

**percent, percentage**   Both mean "rate per hundred." *Percent* (sometimes written *per cent*) is used with numbers *(fifty percent, 23 percent)*. *Percentage* is used without numbers *(a small percentage)*. Avoid using either as a synonym for *part (A small part* [not *percentage*] *of the money was lost)*.

**perfect**   See *unique*.

**persuade**   See *convince, persuade*.

**phenomena**   See *data*.

**52**

*usage*

**plan on**   Colloquial in such phrases as *plan on going, plan on seeing*, for *plan to go, plan to see*.

**plenty**   Colloquial as an adverb meaning "very, amply" *(I was very* [not *plenty*] *angry)*. Note that as a noun meaning "enough, a large number," *plenty* must be followed by *of (I've had plenty of money)*.

**plus** *Plus* is a preposition and, thus, part of a prepositional phrase containing its object. It means "with the addition of" or "increased by" and is most appropriately used in contexts referring to quantity *(My scalloped potatoes plus your baked beans ought to be enough to serve everybody)*. Avoid the temptation to use *plus* as a substitute for the conjunction *and* or as a substitute for the adverb *besides*. Not *Mom plus my sisters met my plane* but *Mom and my sisters met my plane*. Not *I'm not going to get this paper finished by Friday. Plus I have a calculus test on Thursday afternoon* but *I'm not going to get this paper finished by Friday. Besides, I have a calculus test on Thursday afternoon.*

**practical, practicable** *Practical* means "useful, not theoretical." *Practicable* means "capable of being put into practice" *(Franklin was a practical statesman; his schemes were practicable)*.

**precede, proceed** *Precede* is a verb and means "to come before." *Proceed* is also a verb but means "to move on, to advance" *(You must precede me in the line-up for graduation or the sergeant-at-arms will not let us proceed onto the stage)*.

**principal, principle** As an adjective *principal* means "chief, main"; as a noun it means "leader, chief officer," or, in finance, "a capital sum, as distinguished from interest or profit." The noun *principle* means "fundamental truth" or "basic law or doctrine." *(What is my principal reason for being here? I am the principal of the local elementary school. That bank pays 5 percent interest on your principal. The textbook explained the underlying principle.)*.

**provided, providing** Both are acceptable as subordinating conjunctions meaning "on the condition" *(I will move to Washington, providing [or provided] the salary is adequate)*.

**raise, rise** *Raise, raised, raised* is a transitive verb *(They raised potatoes)*. *Rise, rose, risen* is intransitive *(They rose at daybreak)*.

**real** Colloquial for *really* or *very (real cloudy, real economical)*.

**reason is because** See *is when* and **14a(3).**

**reason why** Usually redundant *(The reason [not reason why] we failed is clear)*.

**refer** See *allude, refer.*

**regarding, in regard to, with regard to** Overused and wordy for *on, about,* or *concerning (We have not decided on [not with regard to] your admission)*.

**respectively, respectfully** *Respectively* means "separately" or "individually"; *respectfully* means "full of respect" *(The participants in the debate were St. Lawrence High School and Delphi High School, respectively. The students respectfully stated their arguments.)*.

**right** Colloquial or dialectal when used to mean "very" *(right fresh, right happy)*. *Right along* and *right away* are colloquial for *continuously, immediately*.

**52**

*usage*

**rise, raise**   See *raise, rise.*

**round**   See *unique.*

**said**   *Said* in such phrases as *the said paragraph, the said person* occurs frequently in legal writing. Avoid the use in ordinary writing.

**scarcely**   See *but, hardly, scarcely.*

**set, sit**   Often confused. See **4c.**

**shall, will, should, would**   *Will* is now commonly used for all persons *(I, you, he, she, it)* except in the first person for questions *(Shall I go?)* and in formal contexts *(We shall consider each of your reasons)*. *Should* is used for all persons when condition or obligation is being expressed *(If he should stay . . . . We should go)*. *Would* is used for all persons to express a wish or customary action *(Would that I had listened! I would ride the same bus every day.)*.

**should**   See *shall.*

**should of**   Nonstandard for *should have.*

**since, because**   The subordinating conjunction *because* always indicates cause. *Since* may indicate either cause or time *(It has rained since yesterday. Since you need money, I'll lend you some)*. Be careful to avoid using *since* in sentences where it could indicate either cause or time and thus be ambiguous. In *since we moved, we have been working longer hours,* it is unclear whether *because we moved* or *from the time we moved* is meant.

**sit, set**   See *set, sit.*

**so**   *So* is a loose and often imprecise conjunction. Avoid using it excessively to join independent clauses. For clauses of purpose, *so that* is preferable *(They left so that* [not *so*] *I could study)*. *Because* is preferable when cause is clearly intended *(Because it began to rain, we left* [not *It began to rain, so we left*]).

**some**   Colloquial and vague when used to mean "unusual, remarkable, exciting" *(That was some party. This is some car.)*. In writing use a more specific word.

**someone, some one**   See *anyone.*

**sometime, some time**   Use one word in the sense of a time not specified; use two words in the sense of a period of time *(Sometime we shall spend some time together)*.

**somewheres**   Nonstandard for *somewhere.*

**sort, sort of, sort of a**   See *kind, sort, kind of, sort of, kind of a.*

**stationary, stationery**   *Stationary* means "not moving"; *stationery* is writing supplies.

**straight**   See *unique.*

**stupid**   See *ignorant, stupid.*

**such**   Colloquial and overused as a vague intensifier *(It was a very* [not *such a*] *hot day)*.

**52**

*usage*

**supposed to**    Be careful to preserve the *d* in writing *(He was supposed to* [not *suppose to] take out the trash).*

**sure**    Colloquial for *surely, certainly (I was surely* [not *sure] sick).*

**sure and, try and**    Colloquial for *sure to, try to.*

**take and**    Nonstandard in most uses *(Lou slammed* [not *took and slammed]* *the book down).*

**teach, learn**    See *learn, teach.*

**than, then**    Don't confuse these. *Than* is a conjunction *(younger than John). Then* is an adverb indicating time *(then, not now).*

**that**    Colloquial when used as an adverb *(She's that poor she can't buy food. I didn't like the book that much).*

**that, which, who**    *That* always introduces restrictive clauses: *which* and *who* may introduce either restrictive or nonrestrictive clauses. See **20c.** Some writers and editors prefer to limit *which* entirely to nonrestrictive clauses *(This is the car that I bought yesterday. This car, which I bought yesterday, is very economical).* Use *which* when referring to things or ideas *(Liberty, which is cherished by all people, does not come without responsibility).* Use *who* when referring to people. *(The veterinarian who treated my dog* [not *The veterinarian which treated my dog]* *stays open until six o'clock.*

**theirselves**    Nonstandard for *themselves.*

**then, than**    See *than, then.*

**there, their, they're**    Don't confuse these. *There* is an adverb or an expletive *(He walks there. There are six.). Their* is a pronoun *(their rooms). They're* is a contraction for *they are (They're too eager).*

**these kind, these sort**    See *kind, sort.*

**this here, that there, these here, them there**    Nonstandard for *this, that, these, those.*

**thusly**    Nonstandard for *thus.*

**till, 'til, until**    *Till* and *until* are interchangeable spellings, both acceptable in formal English. However, note that *till* is not a shortened form or contraction of *until* and should never be spelled with an apostrophe. The shortened form, *'til,* is not commonly used in contemporary prose.

**to, too, two**    Carefully check your spelling of these three homophones (words that have the same sound but different spellings and different word origins). *To* is a preposition. *Too* is an adverb meaning "also" *(She laughed too)* or "more than enough" *(You worked too hard).* In the sense of *indeed,* it is colloquial *(She did too laugh). Two* is an adjective *(Two geese flew overhead).*

**toward, towards**    Both are correct, though *toward* is more common in the United States, *towards* in Britain.

**try and**    See *sure and.*

**type**    Colloquial for *type of (This type of* [not *type] research is expensive).* Often used, but usually in hyphenated compounds *(colonial-type architecture, tile-type floors, scholarly-type text)*. Omit *type* for such expressions wherever possible.

**uninterested**   See *disinterested, uninterested.*

**unique**   Several adjectives such as *unique, perfect, round, straight,* and *complete* name qualities that do not vary in degree. Logically, therefore, they cannot be compared. Formal use requires *more nearly round, more nearly perfect* and the like. The comparative and superlative forms, however, are widely used colloquially in such phrases as *the most unique house, most complete examination, most perfect day.* Their occurrence even in formal English is exemplified by the phrase *more perfect union* in the Constitution.

**used to**   In writing be careful to preserve the *d (We used to* [not *use to]* get *up at six every morning).*

**used to could**   Nonstandard for *used to be able.*

**wait on**   Colloquial when used to mean "wait for"; *wait on* means "to serve, attend" *(We waited for* [not *waited on] the clerk to wait on us).*

**well, good**   *Well* may function as an adjective (for example when modifying the subject after a linking verb: *The baby doesn't feel well)* or as an adverb (when modifying a verb, adjective, or another adverb: *The baby slept well after she was well fed by her mother). Good* always functions as an adjective, modifying a noun or noun substitute *(She allowed her mother to get a good night's sleep).* See Section **3.**

**which, that**   See *that, which, who.*

**who's, whose**   *Who's* is the contraction for *who is. Whose* is the possessive form of the pronoun *who (Who's the person whose books are spread across the kitchen table?).*

**-wise**   A suffix often needlessly attached to root words to mean "with regard to" or "concerning." Particularly in writing, standard usage strongly resists this form. Other more economical substitutes are preferable. Not *Careerwise, I think electronics is a good choice for me* but *I think electronics is a good career choice for me.* Not *Things are at a standstill, trafficwise* but *Traffic is at a standstill.* Standard usage does accept *-wise* to indicate direction in such words as *clockwise, crosswise, lengthwise.*

**would of, should of**   Nonstandard forms of *would have* and *should have.* Not *We should of taken an umbrella* but *We should have taken an umbrella.*

**you're, your**   *You're* is a contraction for *you are. Your* is the second-person possessive pronoun. *(You're not going to eat your other doughnut, are you?)*

**you was**   Nonstandard for *you were.*

**52**

*usage*

# INDEX

**Note:** Numbers in **boldface** refer to section designations; other numbers refer to pages. Thus, for example, the entry **40f**:324 refers to Section 40f on page 324.

# CORRECTION SYMBOLS

| Symbol | Section Number | Meaning | Symbol | Section Number | Meaning |
|--------|----------------|---------|--------|----------------|---------|
| *ab* | 16 | Improper abbreviation | *p* | 19–30 | Error in punctuation |
| *ad* | 3 | Improper use of adjective or adverb | ¶ *coh* | 42b–d | Paragraph lacks coherence |
| *agr* | 8 | Error in agreement | ¶ *con* | 42g | Paragraph lacks consistent tone |
| *appr* | 36 | Inappropriate level of diction | ¶ *dev* | 42c–f | Paragraph is poorly or inadequately developed |
| *awk* | 14 | Awkward construction | | | |
| *ca* | 2 | Faulty pronoun case | ¶ *un* | 42a | Paragraph lacks unity |
| *comp* | 13 | Faulty or incomplete comparison | ‖ | 32 | Faulty parallelism |
| | | | *plan* | 40 | Paper is poorly planned |
| *cs* | 7 | Comma splice | | | |
| *dgl* | 12 | Dangling modifier | *q* | 25–26 | Faulty punctuation of quoted material |
| *dir* | 38 | Indirectness, redundancy, weakening repetition | | | |
| | | | *ref* | 9 | Faulty pronoun reference |
| *ef* | 31–34 | Sentence effectiveness | *rev* | 41 c–d | Paper needs revision |
| *emp* | 33 | Lack of needed emphasis | *sen flt* | 6–14 | Sentence fault |
| | | | *sp* | 39 | Error in spelling |
| *end p* | 19 | Faulty end punctuation | *ss* | 1 | Sentence sense |
| | | | *sub* | 31 | Poor subordination |
| *ex* | 37 | Inexact word | *syl* | 18 | Improper division of word |
| *frag* | 6 | Unacceptable sentence fragment | | | |
| | | | *t* | 5 | Wrong tense of verb |
| *fs* | 7 | Fused (run together) sentence | *var* | 34 | Sentence structure lacks variety |
| *glos* | 50–51 | Check glossary | *vb* | 4 | Error in verb form |
| *gr* | 1–5 | Faulty grammar | *wds* | 35–39 | Error in word use |
| *int p* | 20–24 | Faulty internal punctuation | *word p* | 27–30 | Faulty word punctuation |
| *log* | 43 | Faulty logic | *x* | | Obvious error |
| *mis pt* | 11 | Misplaced part | *?* | | Is this right? Do you mean this? |
| *nos* | 15 | Error in use of numbers | | | |
| *om* | 13 | Careless omission, incomplete construction | | | |

# PROOFREADERS' MARKS

| | | | |
|---|---|---|---|
| ℒ | Delete / | ⌃ | Caret (indicates the point at which a marginal addition to be inserted) |
| ℒ | Delete and close up | ⊙ | Period |
| ◡ | Close up | ⌃ | Comma |
| # | Insert space | :/ | Colon |
| stet | Let it stand (i.e., the crossed out material above the dots) | ;/ | Semicolon |
| ¶ | Begin a new paragraph | '/ | Apostrophe or single quotation mark |
| no ¶ | Run two paragraphs together | ''/'' | Quotation marks |
| sp | Spell out (e.g., 20 ft. ) | ?/ | Question mark |
| tr | Transpose | !/ | Exclamation point |
| lc | Lowercase a Capital letter | = | Hyphen |
| cap | capitalize a lowercase letter | ⊥M | Dash |
| o/ | Correct an error | (/) | Parentheses |
| ? | Superior number | [/] | Brackets |
| ? | Inferior number | | |

# ORGANIZATION CHART